APA Style

Writing
from Sources

Writing
from Sources

SIXTH EDITION

Brenda Spatt

The City University of New York

BEDFORD/ST. MARTIN'S   Boston ◆ New York

For Bedford/St. Martin's

Developmental Editor: John Elliott

Editorial Assistant: Elizabeth Alsop

Editorial Assistant, Publishing Services: Maria Teresa Burwell

Production Supervisor: Tina Cameron

Marketing Manager: Brian Wheel

Project Management: Books By Design, Inc.

Cover Design: Lucy Krikorian

Cover Art: Rythme coleur by Sonia Delaunay, oil on canvas, 1939, Musée des Beaux-Arts, Lille. © L & M Services B. V. Amsterdam 20020314. Photo: Réunion des Musées Nationaux/Art Resources, NY.

Composition: Books By Design, Inc.

Printing and Binding: Haddon Craftsmen, an RR Donnelley & Sons Company

President: Joan E. Feinberg

Director of Marketing: Karen R. Melton

Editor in Chief: Nancy Perry

Director of Editing, Design, and Production: Marcia Cohen

Manager, Publishing Services: Emily Berleth

Library of Congress Control Number: 2002101241

Manufactured in the United States of America.

8 7 6 5 4 3
f e d c b

For information, write: Bedford/St. Martin's, 75 Arlington Street, Boston, MA 02116 (617-399-4000)

ISBN: 0-312-39098-X

Acknowledgments

Acknowledgments and copyrights are continued at the back of the book on pages 545–547, which constitute an extension of the copyright page.

To the Instructor

The big news about the sixth edition of *Writing from Sources* is its intensive focus on the Internet. For many students, the Web now serves as more than just an effective means of gaining and distributing information—it has become a way of life, a source of instant knowledge, a shortcut to research. Unfortunately, the Web is at once the friend and the enemy of serious research. As instructors increasingly realize, in comparison with print sources Web material remains unreliable, its quality often abysmal. Whether or not you use a trustworthy search engine or consult a respected database, you are likely to encounter far more dross than gold. And too often our students, seduced by the abundance of online sources and the speed of surfing, lack the knowledge to make the crucial distinctions between a good Web site, a bad one, and one that falls somewhere in between.

More than ever, college students need to be shown how to engage in worthwhile research. Given the plethora of databases, directories, and search engines for print and Web sources, they need clear explanations of how to find the best sources and how to judge which ones are worth reading and citing. They need opportunities to simulate the experience of carrying out research, to slow down the process of locating and evaluating sources while working together, with an instructor's guidance, to understand what makes one source useful and another a waste of time.

To this end, Chapters 5 ("Finding Sources") and 6 ("Evaluating Sources") have been extensively rewritten. To demonstrate the initial stages of research, Chapter 5 undertakes a search for information about Lawrence of Arabia, the man and the movie, using a variety of databases, from the Library of Congress to Google and Copernic, with portions of the search results presented so that students can see for themselves how informed choices should be made. In Chapter 6, the process of selection is scrutinized in even greater detail as students learn about the criteria for choosing sources while following a search for information—emphasizing Web material—about animal rights. For this edition, the former Chapters 7 ("Taking Notes") and 8 ("Organizing and Writing the Research Essay") have been combined into a single expanded chapter that deals with the transformation of raw material into finished text. Throughout, there is an emphasis on the technical skills needed to make the best use of computers for research and writing. For example, the new Chapter 7 (now titled simply "Writing the Research Essay") demonstrates the most effective ways to organize an essay by cutting-and-pasting on the screen while maintaining a record of attributions for later documentation. To provide the necessary practice with Web sources, I have added new exercises and included fresh material in some of the old ones.

This emphasis on technology and new ways of carrying out research does not mean that the basic thrust of *Writing from Sources* has been altered or even modified. The skills and techniques needed to produce an accurate and reliable research essay still loom as large as issues of content. The book remains what it has been for over twenty years: a comprehensive, step-by-step guide to the research process, beginning with strategies for the analysis, synthesis, and presentation of sources. The first two chapters are still devoted to the skills of reading for understanding, summarizing, quoting, and paraphrasing. Next, in the sequential approach that makes this book unique, these skills are used in preparing first a single-source essay and then a multiple-source essay that teaches organization through synthesis. By breaking down the writing process and the use of sources into manageable segments of progressive difficulty, the text enables students to gain confidence through practice so that the transition to writing an extended research essay becomes natural.

Writing a successful research essay, as much as any other form of expression, depends on finding meaning and pleasure in the task. The title of this book is *Writing from Sources*, not *Writing about Sources:* Sources are to be used as springboards for new ideas, for personal approaches to understanding issues and solving problems, for different ways of seeing our world. Throughout the sixth edition, I have tried to select topics and readings that will interest both students and instructors and that will inspire interesting work. The readings are drawn from a variety of disciplines ranging from astrophysics to film studies, sociology to law. Authors include Edwidge Danticat, Sissela Bok, Leon Botstein, Ian Frazier, and Stephen Carter. Some of the topics are perennials: the deficiencies of high school, the rights of animals, the worship of celebrities, the cult of violence, the decline of civility. Some are contemporary phenomena: fast food is the topic for the sequence of passages used to evaluate sources, and a number of distinguished scientists debate the latest arguments for and against genetic engineering in the casebook provided in Appendix E. My own favorite is a stimulating diatribe against employing housecleaners, by Barbara Ehrenreich, that may well polarize classroom opinion as it did those readers of the article who wrote vehement responses.

Here is a summary of the changes in and additions to the sixth edition of *Writing from Sources* that enhance its usefulness as a text, a reader, an exercise book, and a research-essay guide:

- An entirely new guide to locating print and Web sources using databases, directories, and search engines
- A revised and expanded guide to evaluating print and Web sources, explaining—with copious illustrations—how to avoid the pitfalls inherent in Web research

- A realistic methodology for using computers to take notes from sources and organize them on the screen

- A new sample research essay using endnotes in Chapter 9, incorporating a fairly sophisticated level of documentation in exploring the topic of cannibalism from a historical and anthropological perspective

- A revised selection of reference sources, emphasizing electronic databases across the disciplines, contained in Appendix A

- Expanded and updated guidelines for documenting sources in MLA and APA styles, contained in Appendix B

- An entirely new casebook of readings on "Genetic Engineering and Cloning," contained in Appendix E, that can provide the basis for a complete research essay or, alternatively, can be supplemented by student research

- A new model for synthesizing sources, in Chapter 4, built around the topic of promotion in elementary school

Finally, in preparing the new material, I have tried to make the style and tone as straightforward and practical as possible. *Writing from Sources* will be an effective textbook only if it is accessible to students. Throughout, I have made every effort to emphasize the how as much as the why, and to illustrate both with the clearest of examples. I hope that you and your students will enjoy using the book and will learn as much from reading it as I have from writing it.

For this sixth edition of *Writing from Sources*, I want to acknowledge once again the students—mine and yours—who inspired me first to write the book and then to try to improve it with each new edition. The following instructors who reviewed this text deserve my special thanks: Sandra Clark, Anderson University; Patricia Coward, Frostburg State University; Leslie A. Crabtree, North Central University; Stephen Knapp, Arkansas State University–Beebe; David Miller, Mississippi College; Suzanne Patterson, Arkansas State University–Beebe; Thom Satterlee, University of Miami; Sylvia Stacey, Oakton Community College; Mary Steible, Southern Illinois University–Edwardsville; and Kathleen Welsch, Clarion University of Pennsylvania. John Elliott has been a thoughtful and painstaking editor; Nancy Perry has provided invaluable support now as she did for the first edition twenty-five years ago. In addition, I remain obliged to Marianne Ahokas, who provided portions of the section on deductive and inductive logic for the fourth edition, and Eve Zarin, who prepared the basis for Appendix C for the fourth edition. From Derek Brooks in London and Syva Meyers in New York, I have received the unflappable technical support which has kept me from hurling my computer out of a window to the detriment of innocent passersby below.

Brenda Spatt

To the Student

Every day, as you talk, write, and work, you use sources. Most of the knowledge and many of the ideas that you express to others originate outside yourself. You have learned from your formal schooling and from observing the world around you, from reading, from watching television and movies, from the Internet, and from a multitude of other experiences. Most of the time, you do not consciously think about where you got the information; you simply go about your activities, communicating with others and making decisions based on your acquired knowledge.

In college, however, using sources becomes more concentrated and deliberate. Each course bombards you with new facts and ideas. Your academic success depends on how well you can understand what you read and hear in your courses, distinguish the more important from the less important, relate new facts or ideas to what you already have learned, and, especially, communicate your findings to others.

Most college writing is both informative and interpretive; that is, it contains material that you take from sources and ideas that are your own. Depending on the individual course and assignment, a college paper may emphasize your own conclusions supported by knowledge you have gathered, or it may emphasize that knowledge, showing that you have mastered a certain body of information. In any case it will contain something of others and something of you. If twenty students in your class are all assigned the same topic, the other nineteen papers will all be somewhat different from yours.

The main purpose of college writing assignments is to help you consolidate what you have learned and to expand your capacity for constructive thinking and clear communication. These are not merely academic skills; there are few careers in which success does not depend on these abilities. You will listen to the opinions of your boss, your colleagues, and your customers; or read the case histories of your clients or patients; or study the marketing reports of your salespeople or the product specifications of your suppliers; or perhaps even analyze the papers of your students! Whatever your job, the decisions that you make and the actions that you take will depend on your ability to understand and evaluate what your sources are saying (whether orally or in writing), to recognize any important pattern or theme, and to form conclusions. As you build on other people's ideas, you certainly will be expected to remember which facts and opinions came from which source and to give appropriate credit. Chances are that you will also be expected to draft a memo, a letter, a report, or a case history that will summarize your information and present and support your conclusions.

To help you see the connection between college and professional writing, here are some typical essay topics for various college courses, each followed by a parallel writing assignment that you might have to do on the job. Notice that all of the pairs of assignments call for much the same skills: The writer must consult a variety of sources, present what he or she has learned from those sources, and interpret that knowledge in the light of experience.

ACADEMIC ASSIGNMENT	PROFESSIONAL ASSIGNMENT	SOURCES
For a *political science* course, you choose a law now being debated in Congress or the state legislature and argue for its passage.	As a *lobbyist, consumer advocate,* or *public relations expert,* you prepare a pamphlet to arouse public interest in your agency's program.	debates Congressional Record editorials periodical articles your opinions
For a *health sciences* course, you summarize present knowledge about the appropriate circumstances for prescribing tranquilizers and suggest some safeguards for their use.	As a *member of a medical research team,* you draft a report summarizing present knowledge about a specific medication and suggesting likely directions for your team's research.	books journals government and pharmaceutical industry reports online abstracts
For a *psychology* course, you analyze the positive and negative effects of peer-group pressure.	As a *social worker* attached to a halfway house for adolescents, you write a case history of three boys, determining whether they are to be sent to separate homes or kept in the same facility.	textbooks journals case studies interviews Web sites personal experience
For a *business management* course, you decide which department or service of your college should be eliminated if the budget were cut by 3 percent next year; you defend your choice.	As an *assistant to a management consultant,* you draft a memo recommending measures to save a manufacturing company that is in severe financial trouble.	ledgers interviews newspapers journals financial reports Dow Jones news Dialog
For a *sociology* or *history* course, you compare reactions to unemployment in the 1990s with reactions in the 1930s.	As a *staff member in the social services agency* of a small city, you prepare a report on the social consequences that would result from closing a major factory.	newspapers magazines books interviews statistics

ACADEMIC ASSIGNMENT	PROFESSIONAL ASSIGNMENT	SOURCES
For a *physical education* course, you classify the ways in which a team can react to a losing streak and recommend some ways in which coaches can maintain team morale.	As a *member of a special committee of physical-education teachers,* you help plan an action paper that will improve your district's performance in interscholastic sports.	textbooks articles observation and personal experience
For an *anthropology* course, you contrast the system of punishment used by a tribe that you have studied with the penal code used in your home or college town.	As *assistant to the head of the local correction agency,* you prepare a report comparing the success of eight minimum-security prisons around the country.	textbooks lectures articles observation and personal experience
For a *physics* course, you write a definition of "black holes" and explain why theories about them were fully developed in the second half of the twentieth century—not earlier, not later.	As a *physicist* working for a university research team, you write a grant application based on an imminent breakthrough in your field.	books journals online abstracts e-mail
For a *nutrition* course, you explain why adolescents prefer junk food.	As a *dietician* at the cafeteria of a local high school, you write a memo that accounts for the increasing waste of food and recommends changes in the lunch menu.	textbooks articles interviews observation
For an *engineering* course, you describe changes and improvements in techniques of American coal mining over the last hundred years.	As a *mining engineer,* you write a report determining whether it is cost-effective for your company to take over the derelict mine that you were sent to survey.	books articles observation and experience e-mail

Writing from Sources will help you learn the basic procedures that are common to all kinds of academic and professional writing and will provide enough practice in these skills to enable you to write from sources confidently and successfully. Here are the basic skills.

1. *Choosing a topic:* deciding what you are actually writing about; interpreting the requests of your instructor, boss, or client, and determining the scope and limits of the assignment; making the project manageable.

2. *Finding sources and acquiring information:* deciding how much supporting information you are going to need (if any) and locating it; evaluating

sources and determining which are most suitable and trustworthy for your purpose; taking notes on your sources and on your own reactions; judging when you have sufficient information.

3. *Determining your main idea:* determining the purpose of what you are writing and your probable conclusions; redefining the scope and objective in the light of what you have learned from your sources.

4. *Taking notes:* presenting your sources through summary, paraphrase, and quotation; learning when each skill is most appropriate.

5. *Organizing your material:* determining what must be included and what may be eliminated; arranging your evidence in the most efficient and convincing way, so that your reader will reach the same conclusions as you; calling attention to common patterns and ideas that will reinforce your thesis; making sure that your presentation has a beginning, middle, and end, and that the stages are in logical order.

6. *Writing your assignment:* breaking down the mass of information into easily understood units or paragraphs; constructing each paragraph so that the reader will receive a general idea that will advance your main idea, as well as providing supporting examples and details that will make it convincing.

7. *Giving credit to your sources:* ensuring that your reader knows who is responsible for which idea; distinguishing between the evidence of your sources and your own interpretation and evaluation; assessing the relative reliability and usefulness of each source so that the reader can appreciate your basis for judgment.

This list of skills may seem overwhelming right now. But remember: You will be learning these procedures *gradually.* In Part I, you will learn how to get the most out of what you read and how to use the skills of summary, quotation, and paraphrase to provide accurate accounts of your sources. In Part II, you will begin to apply these skills as you prepare an essay based on a single reading and then a synthesis essay drawing on a group of sources. Finally, in Part III, you will begin the complex process of research. The gradual increase in the number of sources will make each stage of the process more complex and demanding, but not essentially different.

The best way to gain confidence and facility in writing from sources is to master each skill so thoroughly that it becomes automatic, like riding a bicycle or driving a car. To help you break the task down into workable units, each procedure will first be illustrated with a variety of models and then followed by exercises to give you as much practice as you need before going on to the next step. As you go on to write essays for other courses, you can concentrate more and more on *what* you are writing and forget about *how* to write from sources, for these methods will have become natural and automatic.

Contents

PART II
WRITING FROM SOURCES   117

PART III
WRITING THE RESEARCH ESSAY   227

5   *Finding Sources*   231

Writing
from Sources

Part I

MAKING YOUR SOURCES YOUR OWN

Academic writers continually study and use the ideas of others. However good and original their own ideas may be, academic writers must explore the work of authorities in their field, to estimate its value and its relevance to their own work, and then to place the ideas and the words of others side by side with their own. We call this process *research*.

To make use of another person's ideas in developing your own work, you need to appreciate (and even temporarily share) that person's point of view. Naturally, you need to read extensively and learn to understand what you read. In Chapter 1, you will learn to distinguish the main ideas of an essay and to grasp its strategy and development. You can measure your comprehension by your ability to sum up a group of related ideas briefly, yet completely. Chapter 1 ends with some practice in presenting a source through *summary.*

In order to use what you have learned from your reading and to write about your sources in essays, you must learn two other basic methods of presenting sources. Chapter 2 will show you how to use *quotation* and *paraphrase* to represent your sources fairly. You must make it clear to your reader whether a specific idea, sentence, or group of sentences is the product of your work or that of another.

- *Quotation* shows that someone else is responsible for the precise phrasing, as well as the ideas, in the quoted sentences.
- Through *paraphrase,* you express the ideas of others in your own words and so demonstrate your understanding of the source and your ability to integrate these ideas into your own work.

Using quotation or paraphrase and including the source's name helps you to avoid the dishonest "borrowings," called *plagiarism,* that occur when the reader cannot tell who wrote what and so gives you credit for work that you did not do. Finally, whether you paraphrase or quote, you must always acknowledge your source with a clear citation of the writer's name.

▪1▪

Reading for Understanding

Before class began, I happened to walk around the room and I glanced at some of the books lying open on the desks. Not one book had a mark in it! Not one underlining! Every page was absolutely clean! These twenty-five students all owned the book, and they'd all read it. They all knew that there'd be an exam at the end of the week; and yet not one of them had had the sense to make a marginal note!

Teacher of an English honors class

Why was this teacher so horrified? The students had fulfilled their part of the college contract by reading the book and coming to class. Why write anything down, they might argue, when the ideas are already printed on the page. All you have to do is read the assignment and, later on, review by skimming it again. Sometimes it pays to underline an important point, but only in very long chapters, so that you don't have to read every word all over again. Taking notes wastes a lot of time, and anyway, there's never enough space in the margins.

Effective reading requires concentration. *Reading is hard work.* Responding to what you are reading and participating in a mental dialogue between yourself and an author can be challenging but difficult. But only this kind of involvement can prevent your eyes from glazing over and your thoughts from wandering off to next weekend or next summer.

As with any job, active reading seems more rewarding if you have a product to show for your labors. In active reading, this product is *notes:* the result of contact (even friction) between your mind and the author's.

UNDERLINING

Underlining is used for selection and emphasis. When you underline, you are distinguishing between what is important (and worth rereading) and what

3

Guidelines for Effective Reading

- As you read and reread, notice which ideas make you react.

- Pause frequently—not to take a break but to think about and respond to what you have read. If the reading has been difficult, these pauses will provide time for you to figure out questions to ask yourself to gain full understanding.

- As you read, have a pencil in your hand so that you can make lines, checks, and comments in and around what you are reading. You may even want to use several colored pens to help you distinguish between different ideas or themes as they recur. Of course, if you don't own the book, always take notes on separate paper. If you underline or write in a library book, you are committing an act of vandalism, like writing graffiti on a wall. If the material comes from a computer screen, you will often benefit from printing it out and working with a "hard" copy. Or if the material is downloaded into a file, type comments into the text [using brackets to indicate your own work].

---

you can skip on later readings. Underlining text on a first reading is usually hard, since you don't yet know what is crucial to the work's main ideas.

Underlining can be a sophisticated analytical skill, the active sign of passive reading. You can underline while you are half asleep; the brain doesn't need to work in order to make the pencil move across the page. Too often, underlining merely represents so many minutes spent on an assignment: the pencil running over the page indicates that the eyes have run over the same lines. Many pages are underlined or colored with "hi-liter" so completely that there is hardly anything left over. Everything has been chosen for emphasis.

Underlining means selection. Some points are worth reviewing, and some are not. Try *underlining* and also *circling* and *bracketing* words and phrases that seem worth rereading and remembering. You probably would want to underline:

- important generalizations and topic sentences
- examples that have helped you understand a difficult idea
- transitional points, where the argument changes

Or try "underlining" by using *checks in the margin*. Either way, deciding what to mark is the important step.

ANNOTATING

Annotation refers to the comments you write in the margins when you interpret, evaluate, or question the author's meaning, define a word or phrase, or clarify a point.

You are annotating when you jot down short explanations, summaries, or definitions in the margin. You are also annotating when you note down an idea of your own: a question or counterargument, perhaps, or a point for comparison. Annotation is different from taking notes on a separate page (a procedure that will be discussed in Chapter 7). Not every reading deserves to be annotated. Since the process takes time and concentration, save your marginal notes for material that is especially difficult or stimulating.

Here is an example of a passage that has been annotated on the second reading. Difficult words have been defined; a few ideas have been summarized; and some problems and questions have been raised.

from LAND OF DESIRE
William Leach

[margin note: why quotes?]

To make customers feel welcome, merchants trained workers to treat them as "special people" and as "guests." The numbers of <u>service workers</u>, including those

[margin note: entrust: customers are precious possessions]

(entrusted) with the care of customers, rose fivefold between 1870 and 1910, at two and a half times the rate of increase of <u>industrial workers</u>. Among them were the restaurant and hotel employees hired to wait on tables in exchange for wages and

[margin note: all European]

"tips," nearly all recent immigrants, mostly poor <u>Germans</u> and <u>Austrians</u>, but also Italians, Greeks, and Swiss, who suffered nerve-wracking seven-day weeks, eleven-hour days, low wages, and the sometimes terrible heat of the kitchens. <u>Neglected</u>

[margin note: True of all service workers?]

by major unions until just before World War I, they endured (sweated) conditions equal in their misery only to those of the garment and textile workers of the day.

[margin note: depends on luck, not good service]

Tipping was supposed to encourage waiters and waitresses to (tolerate) these conditions in exchange for <u>possible windfalls</u> from customers. Tipping was an un-

[margin note: tastes and manners of the upper classes]

usual practice in the United States before 1890 (although common in the luxurious and (aristocratic) European hotels), when the prevailing "American Plan" entailed serving meals at fixed times, no frills, no tipping, and little or no follow-up service.

[margin note: meals at any time; more choice in return for higher prices]

After 1900 the <u>European system</u> of culinary service expanded very quickly in the United States, introduced first to the (fancy) establishments and then, year by year, to the more popularly priced places. By 1913 some European tourists were even expressing "outrage" at the extent of tipping in the United States. Its effect on

[margin note: why extremely?]

workers was (extremely) mixed. On the one hand, it helped keep wages low, increased the frenzy and tension of waiting, and <u>lengthened the hours.</u> "The tipping business is a great evil," wrote an old, retired waiter in the 1940s. "It gives the

[margin note: Waiter portrayed as victim]

waiter an inferiority complex—makes him feel he is <u>at the mercy of the customers</u> all the time." On the other hand, some waiters were stirred by the "speculative excitement" of tipping, the risk and (chance). *chance = luck, not opportunity*

[margin note: cliché statement of theme expressed in parag. 2]

For customers, however, tipping was intended to have only one effect—to make them feel at home and in the (lap of luxury.) On the backs of an ever-growing sweated workforce, it aristocratized consumption, integrating upper-class patterns of comfort into the middle-class lifestyle. Tips rewarded waiters and waitresses for making

[right margin notes:]
1
service grew faster than industry (same in 1980s & 90s)
Did they speak English? Who trained them?
sweatshop = long hours / low wages
2
barely endure
"American Plan"—based on middle-class culture
luxurious? expensive?
middle class attracted by upper class style
Hours were longer because of tipping or because of greater service?
3
tipping as a marketing device

all these
quotation
marks are
distracting

all an
illusion

the customer "feel like 'somebody,'" as one restaurant owner put it. Such a "feeling," he wrote, "depends" on the "service of the waiter," who ushers us to "our table" and "anticipates our every want or whim." "Courteous service is a valuable asset to the restaurateur. There is a curious little twist to most of us: We enjoy the luxurious feeling of affluence, of being 'somebody,' of having our wishes catered to."

it's the
customer
who has the
inferiority
complex

As this annotated passage demonstrates, annotation works best as an aid to memory, reminding you of ideas that you have thought about and understood. Some of these notes provide no more than a shorter version of the major ideas of the passage. However, marginal notes can also remind you of places where you disagreed with the author, looked at the ideas in a new way, or thought of fresh evidence. Your marginal notes can even suggest the topic for an essay of your own.

Finally, when you write marginal notes, *try always to use your own words* instead of copying or abbreviating a phrase from the text. You will remember the point more easily if you have made the effort to express it yourself.

EXERCISE 1: ANNOTATING A PASSAGE

Read the following passage carefully. Then reread it, underlining and circling key ideas and inserting annotations in the margins.

from THE SMOKING BOOK
Lesley Stern

For the smoker, smoking becomes second nature—like breathing and talking and eating and touching. There was a time when it would almost go unnoticed. Certainly in our society, smoking as a practice is part of quotidian existence: it isn't ritualized, mediated by and confined to the realm of the shamans. Nevertheless, every act of smoking is potentially ceremonial, a staged performance of the everyday, a way of enabling so many daily pleasures and struggles, repetitious moments of work and leisure.

Take the first cigarette after quitting, the lapsing cigarette, the breaking of the fast, the sundering of continuity. This cigarette is unlike any other, and yet the smoking of it enacts a commemoration of other acts and is thus a ritualized reenactment: it is like a substitution of the first time, a reentry into the continuity of life, relationships, a social fabric that holds together. It banishes absence, death, denial, starvation. . . .

There is a forgetfulness to passion and a tenacity to sensate memory, and smoke can weave a spell of empathy where least expected. In life-crisis situations, or even in the midst of celebration or unexpected intimacy, you might reach for a cigarette, and blow smoke out, smoke like life-giving mist that purifies and reinvigorates the weak and wards off evil spirits.

ASKING QUESTIONS

As you read actively and try to understand what you read, you will find your-self asking questions about your source. Sometimes you will want to write your answers down; sometimes answering your questions in your head is enough.

As the questions in the box below suggest, to understand what you read, your mind has to sweep back and forth between each sentence on the page and the larger context of the whole paragraph or essay. You can misunderstand the author's meaning if you interpret ideas out of context, ignoring the way in which they fit into the work as a whole.

Being a fast reader is not necessarily an advantage. Thorough comprehension takes time and careful reading. In fact, it is usually on the second reading, when you begin to understand the overall meaning and structure of the work, that questions begin to pop into your head and you begin to read more carefully.

Questions to Aid Understanding

- What is the meaning of this word?
- How should I understand that phrase?
- Where do I have difficulty understanding the text? Why? Which passages are easy for me? Why?
- What does this passage remind me of?
- What is the topic sentence of the paragraph?
- What is the connection between these two points?
- What is the transitional word telling me?
- This concept is difficult: how would I express it in my own words?
- Is this point a digression from the main idea, or does it fit in with what I've already read?
- Can the whole page be summarized briefly?
- Does the essay have a main idea—a thesis? Is the writer trying to make a particular point?

Annotating and Asking Questions: "A Question of Degree"

Read "A Question of Degree" once, and then go over it more slowly a second time. During your second reading, as you read each paragraph:

A. *Underline and annotate* the text, while asking yourself *comprehension questions* based on the list of questions above.

B. *Compare your annotations* with the annotated version of the first two paragraphs on p. 11.

C. *Compare your comprehension questions* with the list of sample questions starting on p. 12. (The paragraphs in the essay are numbered so that you can go back and forth from essay to list.) Think of your own response to each question, and then compare your answers with the ones that are provided in the right-hand column.

Some of the sample questions may seem very subtle to you, and you may wonder whether you would have thought of all of them yourself. But they are model questions, to show you what you *could* ask if you wanted to gain an especially thorough understanding of the essay.

A QUESTION OF DEGREE
Blanche D. Blank

Perhaps we should rethink an idea fast becoming an undisputed premise of American life: that a college degree is a necessary (and perhaps even a sufficient) precondition for success. I do not wish to quarrel with the assumptions made about the benefits of orthodox education. I want only to expose its false god: the four-year, all-purpose, degree-granting college, aimed at the so-called college-age population and by now almost universally accepted as the stepping-stone to "meaningful" and "better" jobs.   1

What is wrong with the current college/work cycle can be seen in the following anomalies: we are selling college to the youth of America as a take-off pad for the material good life. College is literally advertised and packaged as a means for getting more money through "better" jobs at the same time that Harvard graduates are taking jobs as taxi drivers. This situation is a perversion of the true spirit of a university, a perversion of a humane social ethic and, at bottom, a patent fraud. To take the last point first, the economy simply is not geared to guaranteeing these presumptive "better" jobs; the colleges are not geared to training for such jobs; and the ethical propriety of the entire enterprise is very questionable. We are by definition (rather than by analysis) establishing two kinds of work: work labeled "better" because it has a degree requirement tagged to it and nondegree work, which, through this logic, becomes automatically "low level."   2

This process is also destroying our universities. The "practical curriculum" must become paramount; the students must become prisoners; the colleges must become servants of big business and big government. Under these conditions the university can no longer be an independent source of scientific and philosophic truth-seeking and moral criticism.   3

Finally, and most important, we are destroying the spirit of youth by making college compulsory at adolescence, when it may be least congruent with emotional and physical needs; and we are denying college as an optional and continuing experi-   4 ence later in life, when it might be most congruent with intellectual and recreational needs.

Let me propose an important step to reverse these trends and thus help restore freedom and dignity to both our colleges and our work-places. We should outlaw employment discrimination based on college degrees. This would simply be another facet of our "equal opportunity" policy and would add college degrees to sex, age, race, religion and ethnic group as inherently unfair bases for employment selection.

People would, wherever possible, demonstrate their capacities on the job. Where that proved impractical, outside tests could still serve. The medical boards, bar exams, mechanical, mathematical and verbal aptitude tests might still be used by various enterprises. The burden of proof of their legitimacy, however, would remain with the using agencies. So too would the costs. Where the colleges were best equipped to impart a necessary skill they would do so, but only where it would be natural to the main thrust of a university endeavor.

The need for this rethinking and for this type of legislation may best be illustrated by a case study. Joe V. is a typical liberal-arts graduate, fired by imaginative art and literature. He took a job with a large New York City bank, where he had the opportunity to enter the "assistant manager training program." The trainees rotated among different bank departments to gain technical know-how and experience and also received classroom instruction, including some sessions on "how to write a business letter." The program was virtually restricted to college graduates. At the end of the line, the trainees became assistant bank managers: a position consisting largely of giving simple advice to bank customers and a modest amount of supervision of employees. Joe searched for some connection between his job and the training program, on the one hand, and his college-whetted appetites and skills on the other. He found none.

In giving Joe preference for the training program, the bank had bypassed a few enthusiastic aspirants already dedicated to a banking career and daily demonstrating their competence in closely related jobs. After questioning his superiors about the system, Joe could only conclude that the "top brass" had some very diffuse and not-too-well-researched or even well-thought-out conceptions about college men. The executives admitted that a college degree did not of itself ensure the motivation or the verbal or social skills needed. Nor were they clear about what skills were most desirable for their increasingly diverse branches. Yet, they clung to the college prerequisite.

Business allows the colleges to act as recruiting, screening and training agencies for them because it saves money and time. Why colleges allow themselves to act as servicing agents may not be as apparent. One reason may be that colleges are increasingly becoming conventional bureaucracies. It is inevitable, therefore, that they should respond to the first and unchallenged law of bureaucracy: Expand! The more that colleges can persuade outside institutions to restrict employment in fa- vor of their clientele, the stronger is the college's hold and attraction. This ration- ale becomes even clearer when we understand that the budgets of public universities hang on the number of students "serviced." Seen from this perspec- tive, then, it is perhaps easier to understand why such matters as "university inde- pendence," or "the propriety" of using the public bankroll to support enterprises that are expected to make private profits, can be dismissed. Conflict of interest is difficult to discern when the interests involved are your own. . . .

What is equally questionable is whether a college degree, as such, is proper evi- dence that those new skills that are truly needed will be delivered. A friend who works for the Manpower Training Program feels that there is a clear divide be- tween actual job needs and college-degree requirements. One of her chief frus- trations is the knowledge that many persons with the ability to do paraprofessional mental-health work are lost to jobs they could hold with pleasure and profit because the training program also requires a two-year associate arts degree.   10

Obviously, society can and does manipulate job status. I hope that we can ma- nipulate it in favor of the greatest number of people. More energy should be spent in trying to upgrade the dignity of all socially useful work and to eliminate the use of human beings for any work that proves to be truly destructive of the human spirit. Outlawing the use of degrees as prerequisites for virtually every job that our media portray as "better" should carry us a long step toward a healthier soci- ety. Among other things, there is far more evidence that work can make college meaningful than that college can make work meaningful.   11

My concern about this degree/work cycle might be far less acute, however, if everyone caught up in the system were having a good time. But we seem to be generating a college population that oscillates between apathy and hostility. One of the major reasons for this joylessness in our university life is that the students see themselves as prisoners of economic necessity. They have bought the media messages about better jobs, and so they do their time. But the promised land of "better" jobs is, on the one hand, not materializing; and on the other hand the student is by now socialized to find such "better" jobs distasteful even if they were to materialize.   12

One of the major improvements that could result from the proposed legislation against degree requirements for employment would be a new stocktaking on the part of all our educational agencies. Compulsory schools, for example, would un- derstand that the basic skills for work and family life in our society would have to be compressed into those years of schooling.   13

Colleges and universities, on the other hand, might be encouraged to be as un- restricted, as continuous and as open as possible. They would be released from the pressures of ensuring economic survival through a practical curriculum. They might best be modeled after museums. Hours would be extensive, fees minimal, and services available to anyone ready to comply with course-by-course demands.   14

Colleges under these circumstances would have a clearly understood focus, which might well be the traditional one of serving as a gathering place for those persons who want to search for philosophic and scientific "truths."

This proposal should help our universities rid themselves of some strange and gratuitous practices. For example, the university would no longer have to organize itself into hierarchical levels: B.A., M.A., Ph.D. There would simply be courses of greater and lesser complexity in each of the disciplines. In this way graduate education might be more rationally understood and accepted for what it is—more education. 15

The new freedom might also relieve colleges of the growing practice of instituting extensive "work programs," "internships" and "independent study" programs. The very names of these enterprises are tacit admissions that the campus itself is not necessary for many genuinely educational experiences. But, along with "external degree" programs, they seem to pronounce that whatever one has learned in life by whatever diverse and interesting routes cannot be recognized as increasing one's dignity, worth, usefulness or self-enjoyment until it is converted into degree credits. 16

The legislation I propose would offer a more rational order of priorities. It would help recapture the genuine and variegated dignity of the workplace along with the genuine and more specialized dignity of the university. It should help restore to people of all ages and inclinations a sense of their own basic worth and offer them as many roads as possible to reach Rome. 17

"A Question of Degree": Example of Annotations

everyone believes it

Perhaps we should rethink an idea fast becoming an undisputed premise of American life: that a college degree is a (necessary) (and perhaps even a (sufficient)) precondition for success. I do not wish to quarrel with the assumptions made about the benefits of (orthodox) education. I want only to expose its (false god) the four-year, all-purpose, degree-granting college, aimed at the so-called college-age population and by now almost universally accepted as the stepping-stone to "meaningful" and "better" jobs. 1

everyone thinks is a good education

necessary vs. sufficient?

=false idol

S.B. doesn't agree

college leads to work

What is wrong with the current (college/work cycle) can be seen in the following (anomalies): we are selling college to the youth of America as a take-off pad for the (material) good life. College is literally (advertised and packaged) as a means for getting more money through "better" jobs at the same time that Harvard graduates are taking jobs as taxi drivers. This situation is a (perversion) of the true spirit of a university, a perversion of a humane social ethic and, at bottom, a (patent) fraud. To take the last point first, the economy simply is not geared to guaranteeing these presumptive "better" jobs; the colleges are not geared to training for such jobs; and the (ethical propriety) of the entire enterprise is very questionable. We are by (definition) (rather than by (analysis)) establishing two kinds of work: work labeled "better" because it has a degree requirement tagged to it and nondegree work, which, through this logic, becomes automatically "low level." 2

inconsistencies

high salary + expensive possessions

therefore, the premise is false

to reward good work

presented to the public

=corruption

=obvious

colleges can't deliver what they promise

morality

definition= by saying so

analysis = by observing what's right and true

2 levels exist because of the convenience of these institutions. [But surely the "better" vs. "low level" work existed long before colleges saw profit in the difference!]

"A Question of Degree": Questions and Answers

Paragraph One

A. What does "false god" mean?

A. A false god is an idol that does not deserve to be worshiped.

B. In what context can a college degree be a false god?

B. Colleges are worshiped by students who believe that the degree will magically ensure a good career and a better life. Blank suggests that college degrees no longer have magic powers.

C. Why does Blank put "meaningful" and "better" in quotation marks?

C. Blank uses quotation marks around "meaningful" and "better" because she doesn't believe the adjectives are applicable; she is showing disagreement, disassociating herself through the quotation marks.

Paragraph Two

D. What is an anomaly?

D. An anomaly is anything that is inconsistent with ordinary rules and standards.

E. What conclusion can be drawn from the "Harvard graduates" sentence? (Note that the obvious conclusion is not stated.)

E. If Harvard graduates are driving taxis, a degree does not ensure a high-level job.

F. What does "perversion" mean? How many perversions does Blank mention? Can you distinguish between them?

F. Perversion means distortion or corruption of what is naturally good or normally done. If degrees are regarded as vocational qualifications, the university's proper purpose will be perverted, society's conception of proper qualifications for promotion and advancement will be perverted, and, by implication, young people's belief in the reliability of rewards promised by society will be perverted.

G. In the last two sentences, what are the two types of "fraud" that are described?

G. One kind of fraud is the deception practiced on young college students who won't get the good jobs that they expect. A second type of fraud is practiced on workers without degrees whose efforts and successes are undervalued because of the division into "better" and "worse" jobs.

Paragraph Three

H. What is the "practical curriculum"?

H. "Practical curriculum" refers to courses that will train college students for specific jobs; the term is probably being contrasted with "liberal arts."

I. What is the danger to the universities? (Use your own words.)

I. The emphasis on vocational training perverts the university's traditional pursuit of knowledge for its own sake, as it makes financing and curriculum very closely connected with the economic needs of the businesses and professions for which students will be trained.

J. What groups have suffered so far as a result of "compulsory" college?

J. Blank has so far referred to three groups: students in college; workers who have never been to college; and members of universities, both staff and students, interested in a liberal-arts curriculum.

Paragraph Four

K. What new group, not mentioned before, does Blank introduce in this paragraph?

K. Blank introduces the needs of older people who might want to return to college after a working career.

Paragraph Five

L. Can you explain "'equal opportunity' policy" in your own words?

L. Equal-opportunity policy for employment means that the only prerequisite for hiring should be the applicant's ability to perform the job.

M. What is Blank's contribution to "our 'equal opportunity' policy"?

M. Blank suggests that a college degree does not indicate suitability for employment and therefore should be classed as discriminatory, along with sex, age, etc.

Paragraph Six

N. What does "legitimacy" mean in this context?

N. If certain professions choose to test the qualifications of aspirants, professional organizations should prove that examinations are necessary and that the results will measure the applicant's suitability for the job. These organizations should be responsible for the arrangements and the financing; at present, colleges serve as a "free" testing service.

Paragraphs Seven and Eight

O. What point(s) does the example of Joe help to prove?

O. Joe V.'s experience supports Blank's argument that college training is not often needed in order to perform most kinds of work. Joe V.'s expectations were also pitched too high, as Blank has suggested, while the experience of other bank employees whose place was taken by Joe exemplifies the plight of those workers without college degrees whose experience is not sufficiently valued.

Paragraph Nine

P. What are the colleges' reasons for cooperating with business? (Explain in your own words.)

P. Colleges are competing for students in order to increase their enrollment; they therefore want to be able to assure applicants that many companies prefer to hire their graduates. Having become overorganized, with many levels of authority, the bureaucratic universities regard enrollment as an end in itself.

Q. What is the conflict of interest mentioned in the last sentence, and why is it hard to discern?

Q. The interests of an institution funded by the public might be said to be in conflict with the interests of a private, profit-making company; but the conflict is not apparent now that colleges choose to strengthen their connections with business.

Paragraph Eleven

R. Can you restate the third sentence in your own words?

R. Instead of discriminating between kinds of workers and kinds of work, we should distinguish between work that benefits everyone and should therefore be considered admirable, and work that is degrading and should, if possible, not be performed by people.

S. Is Blank recommending that everyone go to work before attending college (last sentence)?

S. Although Blank is not insisting that working is preferable to or should have priority over a college education, she implies that most people gain more significant knowledge from the work experience than from college.

Paragraph Twelve

T. Can you explain the meaning of "prisoners of economic necessity"?

T. Young people who believe that a degree will get them better jobs have no choice but to spend a four-year term in college, whether or not they are intellectually and temperamentally suited to the experience.

Paragraph Thirteen

U. What are the "compulsory schools" and how would their role change if Blank's proposal were adopted?

U. Compulsory schools are grade and high schools, which students must attend up to a set age. If students were not automatically expected to go on to college, the lower schools would have to offer a more comprehensive and complete education than they do now.

Paragraph Fourteen

V. What role does Blank envisage for the university in a healthier society? (Try not to use "museum" in your answer.)

V. Blank sees the colleges in a role quite apart from the mainstream of life. Colleges would be storehouses of tradition, to which people could go for cultural refreshment in their spare time, rather than training centers.

Paragraph Fifteen

W. What are the "strange and gratuitous" practices of the universities? What purpose do they serve?

W. The universities divide the process of education into a series of clearly defined levels of attainment. Blank finds these divisions "gratuitous" or unnecessary, perhaps because they are "hierarchical" and distinguish between those of greater or lesser achievements and status.

Paragraph Seventeen

X. What, according to Blank, would be a "rational order of priorities"? Does she see any connection at all between the work experience and the educational experience?

X. Blank's first priority is the self-respect of the average member of society who presently may be disappointed and frustrated at not being rewarded for his or her work, whether at the job or at college. Another priority is restoration of the university to its more purely intellectual role.

EXERCISE 2: UNDERSTANDING WHAT YOU READ

Read either "A Savage Life" or "Westbury Court" twice, and then answer the comprehension questions that follow the essay. You will notice that some of the "questions" resemble instructions, very much like examination questions, directing you to explain, define, or in other ways annotate the reading. *Answer in complete sentences*, and use your own words as much as you can.

A SAVAGE LIFE

Suzanne Winckler

Every few years I butcher chickens with a friend named Chuck who lives near the farm my husband and I own in northern Minnesota. Chuck buys chicks and takes care of them for the 10 weeks it takes them to mature. I share in the feed costs, but my main contribution—for which I get an equal share of birds—is to help slaughter them.

One day last fall, Chuck, two other friends and I butchered 28 chickens. We worked without stopping from 10 A.M. to 6 P.M. By the time it was over we had decapitated, gutted, plucked, cleaned and swaddled each bird in plastic wrap for the freezer. We were exhausted and speckled with blood. For dinner that night we ate vegetables. 2

Butchering chickens is no fun, which is one reason I do it. It is the price I pay for being an omnivore and for eating other meat, like beef and pork, for which I have not yet determined a workable way to kill. 3

The first time I caught a chicken to chop its head off, I noticed, as I cradled it in my arms, that it had the heft and pliability of a newborn baby. This was alarming enough, but when I beheaded it, I was not prepared to be misted in blood or to watch it bounce on the ground. Headless chickens don't run around. They thrash with such force and seeming coordination that they sometimes turn back flips. When I first saw this, three things became clear to me. 4

I realized why cultures, ancient and contemporary, develop elaborate rituals for coping with the grisly experience of killing any sentient creature. I understood why so many people in my largely bloodless nation are alarmed at the thought of killing anything (except insects) even though they eat with relish meat other people process for them. I saw why a small subset of my contemporaries are so horrified by the thought of inflicting pain and causing death that they maintain people should never kill anything. 5

One risk I run in this self-imposed food-gathering exercise is leaving the impression, or perhaps even furtively feeling, that I am superior to the omnivores who leave the killing of their meat to someone else. I don't think I am. Slaughtering my own chickens is one of two opportunities (gardening is the other) where I can dispense with the layers of anonymous people between me and my food. I have no quarrel with them. I just don't know who they are. They are not part of my story. 6

Killing chickens provides narratives for gathering, cooking and sharing food in a way that buying a Styrofoam package of chicken breasts does not. I remember the weather on the days we have butchered our chickens, and the friends over the years who've come to help, who have included a surgical nurse, a cell biologist, a painter of faux interiors, a Minnesota state representative who is also a logger, a zoologist, a nurse with Head Start and a former Army medic who now runs the physical plant at a large hospital. I can measure the coming of age of my partner's two kids, who were tykes the first time we butchered chickens 10 years ago, and who this go-round were well into puberty with an array of pierced body parts. 7

My mother, who was born in 1907, belonged to the last generation for whom killing one's food was both a necessity and an ordinary event. Her family raised chickens for the purpose of eating them, and her father taught all his children to 8 hunt. My survival does not depend on killing chickens, but in doing so I have found that it fortifies my connection to her. It also allows me to cast a tenuous filament back to my feral past. In 1914, Melvin Gilmore, an ethnobotanist, wrote, "In savage and barbarous life the occupation of first importance is the quest of food." Having butchered my own chickens, I now feel acquainted with the savage life.

As exhilarating as this may be, I do not thrill at the prospect of beheading chick-   9
ens. Several days before the transaction, I circle around the idea of what my friends and I will be doing. On the assigned morning, we are slow to get going. There are knives and cleavers to sharpen, vats of water to be boiled in the sauna house, tables and chairs to set up, aprons and buckets to gather, an order of assembly to establish. In their own ritual progression, these preparations are a way to gear ourselves up. I feel my shoulders hunch and my focus narrow. It is like putting on an invisible veil of resolve to do penance for a misdeed. I am too far gone in my rational Western head to appropriate the ritual of cultures for whom the bloody business of hunting was a matter of survival. But butchering chickens has permitted me to stand in the black night just outside the edge of their campfire, and from that prospect I have inherited the most important lesson of all in the task of killing meat: I have learned to say thank you and I'm sorry.

Paragraph One

A. The first paragraph establishes two time frames. What are they? What does the first time frame tell us about the author?

B. Winckler refers to her "contribution." To what is she contributing?

Paragraph Two

C. The subject of each sentence in this paragraph is "we" (or the equivalent). What effect does that create? Is there a reason why each sentence has a short, simple structure?

D. This paragraph contains a series of specific details, some involving numbers: the number of people involved; the number of chickens killed; the exact time that they began and ended. Why is Winckler being so numerically exact?

E. Why does Winckler use "swaddled" instead of "wrapped"?

F. Why do they eat vegetables for dinner?

Paragraph Three

G. Winckler uses the verb "butchering" as opposed to "killing" or "slaughtering," repeating it in each of the first three paragraphs. Why?

H. Explain how and why butchering chickens "is the price I pay for being an omnivore."

Paragraph Four

   I. How does the description in this paragraph continue the themes established in Paragraph Two?

Paragraph Five

   J. How do "elaborate rituals" help people to cope with the act of slaughter?

   K. What does "largely bloodless nation" mean?

   L. What language links together Winckler's three observations?

Paragraph Six

   M. Compare "exercise" with "ritual" and "slaughtering" with "gardening."

   N. Why would killing her own food make Winckler superior to those who don't? Do you agree that she doesn't feel or present herself as superior?

Paragraph Seven

   O. Why is it desirable to create "narratives" based on the slaughter of animals? Is a "narrative" like a "ritual"? Could Winckler and her friends build an equally sustaining narrative around a less lethal activity?

   P. Why does Winckler include the descriptive list of her friends?

   Q. How does the language of the last sentence continue the previously established themes?

Paragraph Eight

   R. How does the inclusion of Winckler's mother parallel the inclusion of the list of friends in the previous paragraph?

   S. Explain the phrase "feral past."

   T. In the last sentence, how does "feel acquainted" undercut the phrase "savage past." (Consider also the word "exhilarating" at the beginning of the next paragraph.)

Paragraph Nine

   U. In what sense is this essay "circling around" an anticipated action?

   V. Despite her disclaimers, is Winckler, in this essay, "appropriat[ing] the ritual" of certain earlier societies (including, perhaps, her mother's)?

   W. For whose "misdeed" might Winckler "resolve to do penance"?

   X. Which do you think is the climactic sentence of the essay: "It is like putting on an invisible veil of resolve to do penance for a misdeed" or "But butchering chickens has permitted me to stand in the black night just outside the edge of their campfire"? How does each sentence suggest a different interpretation of the essay?

WESTBURY COURT
Edwidge Danticat

When I was fourteen years old, we lived in a six-story brick building in a cul-de-sac off of Flatbush Avenue, in Brooklyn, called Westbury Court. Beneath the building ran a subway station through which rattled the D, M, and Q trains every fifteen minutes or so. Though there was graffiti on most of the walls of Westbury Court, and hills of trash piled up outside, and though the elevator wasn't always there when we opened the door to step inside and the heat and hot water weren't always on, I never dreamed of leaving Westbury Court until the year of the fire.   1

I was watching television one afternoon when the fire began. I loved television then, especially the afternoon soap operas, my favorite of which was *General Hospital*. I would bolt out of my last high school class every day, pick up my youngest brother, Karl, from day care, and watch *General Hospital* with him on my lap while doing my homework during the commercials. My other two brothers, André and Kelly, would later join us in the apartment, but they preferred to watch cartoons in the back bedroom.   2

One afternoon while *General Hospital* and afternoon cartoons were on, a fire started in apartment 6E, across the hall. There in that apartment lived our new neighbors, an African-American mother and her two boys. We didn't know the name of the mother, or the names and ages of her boys, but I venture to guess that they were around five and ten years old.   3

I didn't know a fire had started until two masked, burly firemen came knocking on our door. My brothers and I rushed out into the hallway filled with smoke and were quickly escorted down to the first floor by some other firemen already on our floor. While we ran by, the door to apartment 6E had already been knocked over by the fire squad and inside was filled with bright flames and murky smoke.   4

All of the tenants of the building who were home at that time were crowded on the sidewalk outside. My brothers and I, it seemed, were the last to be evacuated. Clutching my brothers' hands, I wondered if I had remembered to lock our apartment door. Was there anything valuable we could have taken?   5

An ambulance screeched to a stop in front of the building, and the two firemen who had knocked on our door came out carrying the pliant and lifeless bodies of the two children from across the hall. Their mother jumped out of the crowd and ran toward them, screaming, "My babies—not my babies," as the children were lowered into the back of the ambulance and transferred into the arms of the emergency medical personnel. The fire was started by the two boys, after their mother had stepped out to pick up some groceries at the supermarket down the street. They had been playing with matches.   6

(Later my mother would tell us, "See, this is what happens to children who play with matches. Sometimes it is too late to say, 'I shouldn't have.'" My brother Kelly, who was fascinated with fire and liked to hold up a match to the middle of his palm until the light fizzled out, gave up this party trick after the fire.)   7

We were quiet that afternoon when both our parents came home. We were the closest to the fire in the building, and the most religious of our parents' friends saw it as a miracle that we had escaped safe and sound. When my mother asked how come I, the oldest one, hadn't heard the children scream or hadn't smelled the smoke coming from across the hall, I confessed that I had been watching *General Hospital* and was too consumed in the intricate plot.

(After the fire, my mother had us stay with a family on the second floor for a few months, after school. I felt better not having to be wholly responsible for myself and my brothers, in case something like that fire should ever happen again.)

The apartment across the hall stayed empty for a long time, and whenever I walked past it, a piece of its inner skeleton would squeak, and occasionally burnt wood that might have been hanging by a fragile singed thread would crash down and cause a domino effect of further ruptures, unleashed like those children's last cries, which I had not heard because I had been so wrapped up in the made-up drama of a world where, even though the adults' lives were often in turmoil, the children came home to the welcoming arms of waiting mommies and nannies who served them freshly baked cookies on porcelain plates and helped them to remove their mud-soaked boots, if it was raining, lest they soil the lily-white carpets. But should their boots accidentally sully the carpet, or should their bright yellow raincoats inadvertently drip on the sparkling linoleum, there would be a remedy for that as well. And if their house should ever catch fire, a smart dog or a good neighbor would rescue them just in time, and the fire trucks would come right quick because some attentive neighbor would call them.

Through the trail of voices that came up to comfort us, I heard that the children's mother would be prosecuted for negligence and child abandonment. I couldn't help but wonder, would our parents have suffered the same fate had it been my brothers and me who were killed in the fire?

When they began to repair the apartment across the hall, I would occasionally sneak out to watch the workmen. They were shelling the inside of the apartment and replacing everything from the bedroom closets to the kitchen floors. I never saw the mother of the dead boys again and never heard anything of her fate.

A year later, after the apartment was well polished and painted, two blind Haitian brothers and their sister moved in. They were all musicians and were part of a group called les Frères Parent, the Parent Brothers. Once my parents allowed my brothers and me to come home from school to our apartment, I would always listen carefully for our new tenants, so I'd be the first to know if anything went awry.

What I heard coming from the apartment soon after they moved in was music, "engagé" music, which the brothers were composing to protest against the dictatorship in Haiti, from which they had fled. The Parent Brothers and their sister, Lydie, did nothing but rehearse a cappella most days when they were not receiving religious and political leaders from Haiti and from the Haitian community in New York.

The same year after the fire, a cabdriver who lived down the hall in 6J was killed on a night shift in Manhattan; a good friend of my father's, a man who gave great

Sunday afternoon parties in 6F, died of cirrhosis of the liver. One day while my brothers and I were at school and my parents were at work, someone came into our apartment through our fire escape and stole my father's expensive camera. That same year a Nigerian immigrant was shot and killed in front of the building across the street. To appease us, my mother said, "Nothing like that ever happens out of the blue. He was in a fight with someone." It was too troublesome for her to acknowledge that people could die randomly, senselessly, at Westbury Court or anywhere else.

Every day on my way back from school, I hurried past the flowers and candles piled in front of the spot where the Nigerian, whose name I didn't know, had been murdered. Still I never thought I was living in a violent place. It was an elevated castle above a clattering train tunnel, a blind alley where children from our building and the building across the street had erected a common basketball court for hot summer afternoon games, an urban yellow brick road where hopscotch squares dotted the sidewalk next to burned-out, abandoned cars. It was home.   16

My family and I moved out of Westbury Court three years after the fire. Every once in a while, though, the place came up in conversation, linked to either a joyous or a painful memory. One of the girls who had scalded her legs while boiling a pot of water for her bath during one of those no-heat days got married last year. After the burglar had broken into the house and taken my father's camera, my father— an amateur photography buff—never took another picture.   17

My family and I often reminisce about the Parent Brothers when we see them in Haitian newspapers or on television; we brag that we knew them when, before one of the brothers became a senator in Haiti and the sister, Lydie, became mayor of one of the better-off Haitian suburbs, Pétion-Ville. We never talk about the lost children.   18

Even now, I question what I remember about the children. Did they really die? Or did their mother simply move away with them after the fire? Maybe they were not even boys at all. Maybe they were two girls. Or one boy and one girl. Or maybe I am struggling to phase them out of my memory altogether. Not just them, but the fear that their destiny could have so easily been mine and my brothers'.   19

A few months ago, I asked my mother, "Do you remember the children and the fire at Westbury Court?"   20

Without missing a flutter of my breath, my mother replied, "Oh those children, those poor children, their poor mother. Sometimes it is too late to say, 'I shouldn't have.'"   21

Paragraph One

A. What is a cul-de-sac?

B. "Westbury Court" is named three times in the first paragraph; it is also the title of the essay. Given its negative description, why is Danticat emphasizing the building? Is there any significance in its name?

Paragraphs Two and Three

C. What does her daily routine tell us about Edwidge?

Paragraphs Three through Six

D. Consider Edwidge's reaction to the fire and evacuation. How do you account for her initial indifference to the danger from the fire?

Paragraphs Seven and Eight

E. Why does Danticat flash forward—using parentheses—to her mother's later comments? "Sometimes it is too late to say, 'I shouldn't have'" is repeated at the end of the story. What effect does it have at *this* point?

F. Kelly is fascinated with fire. What fascinates Edwidge?

G. Consider the phrase "consumed in the intricate plot." How does it summarize the content of the essay so far?

Paragraph Ten

H. The first sentence—unusually long—is arguably the key to the themes of the essay. Explain some of its elements. Why do you think Danticat changes her style and uses a longer sentence structure at this point?

I. Consider the language used in Edwidge's description of soap-opera life: "freshly baked cookies," "lily-white carpets," "bright yellow raincoats," "sparkling linoleum," "good" or "attentive" neighbors. How do they contribute to our understanding of her fantasy?

Paragraph Eleven

J. Does the "trail of voices" belong to the real fire or the fantasy fire? How many parallel worlds has Danticat established in the essay?

Paragraphs Twelve through Fourteen

K. How does the text show that Danticat is terminating one story/world and beginning another?

Paragraph Fifteen

L. Does the catalog of misfortunes at the beginning of the paragraph support Edwidge's mother's belief in causality? Or Edwidge's belief in random disorder?

M. Why does Danticat include a reference to Westbury Court, this time followed by "or anywhere else."

Paragraph Sixteen

N. Explain the references to "castle," "blind alley," and "yellow brick road."

O. What does "home" now mean to Danticat? Has her experience with the fire changed her feelings about Westbury Court?

Paragraphs Seventeen and Eighteen

P. Edwidge's memories include pain (the lost children), joy (the successful Parent Brothers), and pain turning into joy (the girl who scalded her legs). How would you describe her father's experience?

Paragraph Nineteen

Q. How does Edwidge account for her shifting memories of the "fire" neighbors? Are there any other explanations?

Paragraphs Twenty and Twenty-One

R. Edwidge's mother repeats the same sentence that's quoted in Paragraph Seven. Does it have the same effect? How does it tie up the themes of the essay?

LOGIC AND ARGUMENTATION

Drawing Inferences

When you actively read and annotate a text, you may sometimes find yourself projecting your own thoughts and assumptions into what you are reading. While you may intend to make a statement supported by information found in your source, your generalization may not accurately reflect the factual evidence. After a while, it becomes difficult to differentiate between your own ideas, inspired by what you have read, and the evidence found in the source. Should such confusion occur, you can easily attribute to your source ideas that are not there at all. When you generalize from specific facts—statistics, for example—you have to be especially careful to make sure that your statement is based on a correct interpretation of the information.

There are several different ways to describe how your source uses evidence and how you form conclusions from that evidence: *proving, stating, implying,* and *inferring.* These terms will be explained and illustrated with excerpts from an article about patterns of marriage in America during the early 1980s.

Quoting a Census Bureau report, this 1984 *New York Times* article begins by *stating* that:

More and more young Americans are putting off marriage, possibly to begin careers. . . .

At this point in the article, the *Times* is offering no specific evidence to support this conclusion. You probably accept the statement as true because you know that the *Times* is a newspaper of record, and you assume that the Census Bureau has provided statistics that justify the claim. And, in fact, several paragraphs later, we find evidence to *prove* the statement:

The trend toward postponed marriage has been growing steadily in recent years. The study found that 74.8 percent of men aged 20 to 24 had never married, compared with 68.8 percent in 1980 and 54.7 percent in 1970. Among women aged 20 to 24, 56.9 percent were single in this year's survey, as against 50.2 percent in 1980 and 35.8 percent in 1970.

Here is an example of a statement (in italics) that is immediately followed by proof:

Traditional married couples continue to make up the majority of family households in the United States, but the report documents the steady erosion of this group's dominance. The 50.1 million traditional families constitute 58.6 percent of American households, compared with 60.8 percent in 1980 and 70.5 percent in 1970.

Since the article is about postponing marriage and also refers to the increasing number of unmarried couples living together, you might jump to the conclusion that most households in the United States consist of unmarried couples or single-parent families. As the previous paragraph clearly indicates, that would be a *false conclusion*.

So far, we have been examining only what the article *explicitly states* or what it *proves*. But, in addition, most sources inform you indirectly, by *implying* obvious conclusions that are not stated in so many words. The implications of a statement can be easily found within the statement itself; they just are not directly expressed. For example, according to the Census Bureau report:

Three-quarters of American men and more than half of American women under 25 are still single.

Although it does not say so, it *implies*—and it would be perfectly safe to conclude—that *more men than women are waiting until they are over 25 to marry.* The following paragraph also contains implication as well as statement:

"Many of these young adults may have postponed their entry into marriage in order to further their formal education, establish careers or pursue other goals that might conflict with assuming family responsibilities," said the bureau's study of households, families, marital status and living arrangements. The report also found that Americans are once again forming new households at high rates after a decline, apparently recession-induced, last year.

In addition to several *statements* about likely reasons for postponing marriage, the paragraph also provides you with an important *implication: economic conditions seem to be a factor in predicting how many new households are formed in the United States.*

Finally, it is perfectly acceptable to draw a conclusion that is not implicit in the source, as long as you reach that conclusion through reasoning based on sound evidence. Unlike implication, *inference* requires the analysis of information—putting 2 and 2 together—for the hidden idea to be observed. The article implies; the reader infers.

In the following brief and factual statement from the article, little of interest is *implied,* but important conclusions can be *inferred:*

> A slight increase was noted in the number of unmarried couples living together; they totaled almost two million as of March and represent about 4 percent of the couples.

From this information, as well as previous evidence provided about postponement of marriage, it would be safe to *infer* that *one reason why people are marrying later may be that they are living together as unmarried couples first.*

It is perfectly correct to draw your own inferences from the sources that you are writing about, as long as you fulfill two conditions:

1. There must be a reasonable basis within the source for your inference.
2. The inferences should be clearly identified as yours, not the source's.

When in an essay you cite a specific work as the basis of an inference, your reader should be able to go to the source, locate the evidence there, and draw a similar inference.

What inferences can you draw from the following paragraph, when you put this information together with everything else that you have read in the article?

> Though the report said that most young people are expected to marry eventually, it noted that the longer marriage was delayed the greater the chance that it would not occur. "Consequently, the percentage of today's young adults that do not ever marry may turn out to be higher than the corresponding percentage of their predecessors," the report speculated.

First, notice that the connection between delaying marriage and never marrying at all is *stated,* not *proved.* Assuming that the statement is correct, and realizing that the years of fertility are limited, it would be reasonable to *infer* that *the trend to marry later in life may be a factor in the declining birth rate.*

Because inferences are not totally rooted in the information provided by your source, they tend to be expressed in tentative terms. Both inferences cited above, for example, use "may be" to convey an appropriate degree of uncertainty. The following inference hedges in a different way: *if the trend toward later marriages continues at a steady rate, eventually there will be no more married couples in this country.* Here, the sweeping and improbable generalization—no more married couples—is put into some perspective through the conditional: "*if this trend continues at a steady rate. . . .*" However, given the variety of unpredictable influences affecting the decision to marry, the negative trend is unlikely to continue at a steady rate. In fact, this inference is absurd.

EXERCISE 3: DRAWING INFERENCES

Read "Study Finds Families Bypassing Marriage." Then decide which of the sentences that follow are *stated;* which are *implied* (or suggested by the essay); which can be *inferred* from the essay; and which are *unproven,* according to the information in the article.

STUDY FINDS FAMILIES BYPASSING MARRIAGE
Eric Nagourney

The number of couples who live together out of wedlock, often with children, is increasing rapidly, a new study reports. 1

The study, by a sociologist at the Institute for Social Research at the University of Michigan, reports that about two in five children will spend at least some time living with their mother and her unmarried partner. Less often, children will live with their father and his partner. 2

"I think that the public will be surprised that almost half of all children will be likely to experience this type of household," said Pamela J. Smock, the sociologist who prepared the study. 3

The report also suggested that the number of children believed to be living in single-parent homes may be significantly exaggerated. About 40 percent of children born outside of marriage are actually living in homes with two adults, the report said. 4

"A large share of children born to supposedly 'single' mothers today are born into two-parent households," Dr. Smock wrote. "Moreover, the widely cited increase in recent years in nonmarital childbearing is largely due to cohabitation, and not to births to women living without a partner." 5

The study was an effort to bring focus to dozens of reports on the subject that have been done scattershot over the last decade or so. Drawing a broad portrait of the American family as it has been redefined since the 1960's, the study found that cohabitation—both before and in lieu of marriage—had become so commonplace that it is practically the norm, and that it crosses most boundaries of age, income and race. 6

The study is to be published this summer in the 2000 volume of the *Annual Review of Sociology.* Among its findings: 7

- Fifty-six percent of all marriages between 1990 and 1994 were preceded by cohabitation. From 1965 to 1974, that figure was about 10 percent.

- From 1987 to 1995, the number of women in their late 30's who reported having cohabited rose to 48 percent from 30 percent.

- Fifty-five percent of people who live together end up marrying, but 40 percent later divorce.

- Cohabitation does not mean childlessness. About half of the divorced people who live together have children in the household, as do 35 percent of those who have never married.

Experts generally agree about the main reasons for the rise in cohabitation. Some are obvious, like the cultural revolution that began in the 1960's, removing the stigma from sex out of wedlock. But others go further back, including a divorce rate that, while now level, climbed over the last century. Children of divorce are less likely to marry and divorced adults are more likely to live together than marry. The marriage rate in America was 8.3 per 1,000 people in 1998, the lowest since 1958.   8

Some sociologists, including Dr. Smock, said the fact that many children are, despite earlier assumptions, living with both parents did not mean they were living in stable households. They pointed to the generally short-lived nature of cohabitation, as well as to studies suggesting a greater level of discontent among people who live together than among married couples.   9

It is not at all clear how the increase in cohabitation may affect society and the traditional role of marriage.   10

Indeed, there is disagreement among sociologists over whether cohabitation is replacing marriage or simply serving as a new stage of engagement. A third view, less widely held, suggests that it may be a phenomenon affecting primarily single people who may never marry.   11

The main effect, many sociologists agree, may well be on the growing number of children being raised in such households. Although only about 11 percent of children are born to cohabiting parents, the number seems likely to increase.   12

Complicating the ability to explain the social change, experts say, is that it comes against a backdrop of marriage itself being redefined. As women play a bigger role as income providers and more men assume child care duties, the traditional notion of a typical household has altered.   13

"The underlying issue is whether we can gauge what cohabitation means if we are using a standard that is also changing," the report said.   14

1. At least half the children in the United States experience traditional, two-parent family life.

2. Many children of single mothers live in a household that includes their biological father.

3. Sociologists disagree about whether cohabitation has replaced marriage.

4. Fewer people question the morality of cohabitation now than they did in 1960.

5. Older women are more likely than younger women to cohabit.

6. In the early 1990s, the majority of newlywed couples had lived together before marriage.

7. The majority of children are born to married couples.

8. The increased incidence of divorce has greatly contributed to the increased incidence of cohabitation.

9. If they eventually marry, cohabitors have a greater chance of divorcing than people who marry without cohabiting first.

10. Family ties are looser now than they were 50 years ago.

Logical Reasoning

When making an inference, you generalize or draw a specific conclusion from the available information, drawing on personal knowledge and experience to predict a likely conclusion or next step. For instance, if you look out a window and observe that the street and sidewalk are wet and the sky is overcast, you would most likely conclude that it had rained recently. You didn't directly observe the rain, but you can generalize from past experiences with the same evidence. Although this may seem like a simpleminded illustration, it is typical of the logical reasoning we all engage in every day.

There are two types of reasoning in formal logic—*deductive* reasoning and *inductive* reasoning, each a distinct process for arriving at defensible conclusions based on available evidence.

Deductive Reasoning

The classic format for deductive reasoning is the *syllogism*, which consists of a series of carefully limited statements, or premises, pursued to a circumscribed conclusion:

All reptiles are cold-blooded.	[premise]
Iguanas are reptiles.	[premise]
Therefore, iguanas are cold-blooded.	[conclusion]

This is a line of reasoning based on classification, that is, the creation of a generalized category based on shared traits. Members of the group we call "reptiles" have cold-bloodedness in common—in fact, cold-bloodedness is a defining trait of reptiles. Iguanas are members of the group reptiles, which means that they must also have that shared trait. Notice that the opening premise of a syllogism is a statement that the reader will be willing to grant as true without explicit proof. Deductive reasoning always begins with beliefs or knowledge that the writer and reader share, and the syllogism builds from that undisputed statement.

Deductive reasoning follows an almost mathematical rigor; provided the premises are true and the line of reasoning valid, the conclusion must necessarily be true.

Inductive Reasoning

In inductive reasoning, a conclusion or common principle is reached by generalizing from a body of evidence, as in the example of the wet street and overcast sky. The conclusions reached through inductive reasoning are always conditional to some extent—that is, there's always the possibility that some additional evidence may be introduced to suggest a different conclusion. Given the available evidence, you were perfectly justified in concluding that it had rained when you observed a wet street and overcast sky; but suppose you then turned on the radio and learned that a water main in the area had broken overnight. That overcast sky may be coincidental, and you should be prepared to revise your original conclusion based on the new information.

Inductive reasoning uses the available evidence to construct the most likely conclusion.

Logic in Argumentation

Most arguments contain elements of both inductive and deductive reasoning. In argumentation, the writer attempts to prove a claim by presenting evidence and reasoning so that the reader can recreate the writer's logic. The core of the argument is usually *deductive,* but rarely based on a classical syllogism; rather, it consists of a series of *premises* or *assumptions* that the reader shares—or can be persuaded to share—with the writer. These premises often depend on *common cultural values.* That is why arguments can lose their force over time as values change. One hundred years ago, writers could safely base arguments on the premise that heroism is defined by slaying the enemy in battle, or that engaging in sex before marriage warrants a girl's expulsion from polite society, or that whipping young children is an effective and acceptable punishment. Today, those arguments would not have wide credibility.

The point of argument is to convince your reader to view an issue as you do, to share your belief that a certain result is worth achieving, and to agree that the method you propose is the best way of achieving it. To do that, you must establish common ground between you and your reader. Don't assume that your underlying assumptions will automatically be shared. Spell them out; make them seem desirable, even inevitable.

For instance, few people would challenge you if you simply claimed that cruelty to animals is bad, but there is a wide range of opinion regarding exactly what constitutes cruelty, or whether certain specific activities (the use of animals in scientific research, for instance) are or are not cruel. Is inflicting pain, or even discomfort, "cruel" by definition? If inflicting pain serves some larger purpose, is it still cruel, or does "cruelty" refer only to *unnecessary* or *unjustifiable* pain? Before contesting the ethics of medical research practices, a persuasive argument about this issue would have to begin by establishing a premise—in this case, a definition of "cruelty"—that both the reader and the writer will find acceptable.

To be fully convincing, the argument that emerges from your premises must be *inductive* as well: it must be supported by a range of *evidence,* which you present, analyze, and interpret for your reader. Evidence usually consists of *facts,* which you verify and document by specifying the sources. If your evidence depends on *data* and *statistics,* the sources must be reliable, and the results based on an adequate and representative sample and an appropriate population. How many people took part in the survey? If percentages are cited, what was the base population? If you say that 60 percent of those surveyed want to raise the tax on cigarettes, do you mean fifty or five hundred or five thousand people? Were they smokers or nonsmokers? What was their age? Their income? These and other factors have some bearing on the validity of such data as evidence.

- *Generalizing from a representative sample*
  Public opinion polls use limited evidence (the opinions of, say, 1,000 respondents) to predict the opinions of a much larger group—possibly the entire nation—by assuming that the opinions of the smaller group reflect proportionately the opinions of the larger. Here, for instance, is part of a survey on attitudes toward health care taken in 1989:

  The Harvard University School of Public Health and Louis Harris and Associates surveyed nearly 4,000 American, Canadian and British adults about their country's health care. . . . A full 89 percent of U.S. citizens feel our health-care system is fundamentally flawed. . . .

  You can readily see how the writer uses the responses of the 4,000 people surveyed to make larger claims about whole national groups ("A full 89 percent of U.S. citizens feel . . .").

- *Citing authority*
  Another source of evidence is *authority:* the testimony of experts whose reputation makes them credible. You need to cite the evidence of such authorities in reasonable detail and, if possible, convey the strength of their credentials. Your argument should not depend on nameless sources such as "1,000 doctors" or "authorities in the field."

- *Reasoning through analogies*
  One other basis for argument, loosely related to deduction, is *reasoning through analogies.* A writer may compare a disputed idea or situation to some other, less controversial idea in order to reveal an inconsistency or to advocate a particular course of action. For instance, some might claim that the wide availability of foreign-made consumer products is analogous to an infection that threatens to destroy the health of the nation's economy. What similarities in the two situations is this writer exploiting? What parallels can be drawn between them?

nation	=	person
foreign-made consumer product • produced outside the nation • invades national economy	=	**infection** • originates outside the person • invades body of individual
harmful: threatens economic health of nation • workers laid off when American-made products aren't bought	=	**harmful:** threatens physical health of person • virus or infection destroys healthy cells, or otherwise weakens person
remedy: discourage imports	=	**remedy:** prevent invasive virus or infection; destroy existing virus or infection

In both cases, some entity (in the first case a nation, and in the second a human being) is "invaded" by something potentially harmful (such as a Japanese-made VCR or German-built car in the case of the nation, and a virus or bacterial infection in the case of the person). Having suggested these similarities, the writer can extend the analogy: The undisputed remedy in the case of sickness—destroying or preventing the cause of the sickness—suggests the remedy for the economy's illness—discouraging the importation of foreign-made consumer products.

Analogies can provide vivid and persuasive images, but they are also easily distorted when pushed too far, and an alternative analogy may suggest itself to the reader. Foreign-made consumer products may have "invaded" the United States, but considering their popularity with U.S. consumers, they have also in some sense been "invited." To U.S. auto manufacturers or workers, foreign imports probably do seem very like opportunistic microbes, but consumers preparing to buy a new car are less likely to "destroy" them than to regard them as inexpensive generic medicines designed to heal ailing pocketbooks. Careful writers recognize the limits of their analogies.

Ineffective Arguments and Logical Fallacies

Not every argument convinces us to accept the writer's conclusion. What undermines the credibility or persuasiveness of an inductive or deductive argument?

- An argument may be based on an initial premise that is unconvincing.

- The line of reasoning that connects premise to premise may be flawed.

- The evidence itself may be misrepresented in some way.

It's easy to accept *initial premises* uncritically because they're generally expressed with confidence in the reader's agreement—remember, the writer assumes that the reader will grant the argument's opening premises without explicit proof. As you read, you should be careful to identify the assumptions a writer uses in constructing an argument. For example, look at the following opening premise, from the second paragraph of an unsigned editorial attacking the logic of a proposed ban on tobacco products. The editorial appeared in the magazine *National Review* in 1994.

> Even though nine-tenths of smokers don't die of lung cancer, there are clearly health dangers in cigarettes, dangers so constantly warned about that smokers are clearly aware that these dangers are the price they pay for the enjoyment and relaxation they get from smoking.

The writer claims here that because the health risks connected with smoking have been widely publicized, the decision to smoke is rational—that is, based on smokers' weighing their desire for "enjoyment and relaxation" against the potential health risks. You might grant the dangers of smoking have been well documented and publicized, but does it necessarily follow that knowing the risks involved ensures a rational decision? If, as has also been widely demonstrated, cigarettes are addictive, then the decision to smoke may *not* be entirely rational—that is, the decision to smoke may *not* be freely made after a careful consideration of the available data and the possible consequences.

The writer here is committing a common logical lapse known as *begging the question*. The assumption here is false; it assumes that a crucial point is self-evident and requires no further argument. The key word here is "clearly"— "smokers are clearly aware"—which may persuade the careless reader that the point has already been proven. When a writer is begging the question, you often find language that preempts the issue and discourages scrutiny: "obviously," "everyone knows," or "it goes without saying."

Sometimes, the process of begging the question is more subtle. Here, a writer arguing against euthanasia begins with a strong statement:

> Every human being has a natural inclination to continue living. Our reflexes and responses fit us to fight attackers, flee wild animals, and dodge out of the way of trucks. In our daily lives we exercise the caution and care necessary to protect ourselves. Our bodies are similarly structured for survival right down to the molecular level. . . . Euthanasia does violence to this natural goal of survival. It is literally acting against nature because all the processes of nature are bent towards the end of bodily survival.

By limiting his view of existence to purely bodily functions, J. Gay-Williams simplifies the complex issue of euthanasia. What he omits are the key functions of the mind, will, and emotions, which, some would say, can override the force of the instinct toward "bodily survival" and make the choice to die. The key here is the first sentence: "Every human being has a natural inclination to continue living." This broad assumption allows for no exceptions. It begs the question by telling only part of the story.

Even if the premises of an argument are valid, there may be *fallacies* in the reasoning that holds the premises together. Logical fallacies are breakdowns in the reasoning that connects the premises of an argument; they occur when the writer makes *unjustifiable* generalizations like the one above or draws *unjustifiable* conclusions from the available evidence. Cause-and-effect reasoning, for example, can slide into before-and-after fallacies (known as *post hoc ergo propter hoc*—after this, therefore, before this). This fallacy assumes that any event that precedes another must somehow cause the second event. It is often true that one event causes a second, later event, as in the case of rain causing the wet street you observe the next morning. But if you make that reasoning a universal rule, you might, for instance, conclude that because swimsuits habitually appear in your local clothing stores in May, and summer follows in June, swimsuits somehow cause summer. It may be perfectly true that swimsuits appear in stores in May and that summer usually begins in June, but this argument fails to consider alternative explanations—in this case, that the approach of summer actually causes manufacturers to ship and retailers to display swimsuits in May, rather than the other way around; the swimsuits *anticipate*, rather than cause, summer.

Most fallacies result from a tendency to oversimplify issues, to take shortcuts in dealing with complex and diverse ideas. An easy fallacy to slip into is the *false dilemma*. In effect, you limit the ground for argument by proceeding as if there were only two alternatives; everything else is ignored. Here is part of the argument presented by a writer who supports euthanasia:

> Reality dictates the necessity of such laws because, for some dying patients experiencing extreme suffering, a lethal prescription is the only way to end an extended and agonizing death. Consider the terrible dilemma created when so-called passive measures fail to bring about the hoped-for death. Are we to stand helplessly by while a patient whose suicide we legally agreed to assist continues to suffer and deteriorate—perhaps even more so than before? Or do we have a moral imperative, perhaps even a legal responsibility, to not only alleviate the further suffering we have brought about but to take action to fulfill our original agreement [to withdraw life support]?

Barbara Dority has reduced the situation to a simple choice: passive doctor and patient in agony versus active doctor who brings an end to suffering, who abides by morality, and who keeps her promise. There are many possibilities for intervention between these two extremes, but, at this point in her argument, the writer does not acknowledge them. Through her language, she also loads the dice: does one identify with the doctor "stand[ing] helplessly" by or with the doctor with a "moral imperative" who knows how to "take action" to "alleviate . . . suffering"?

The tendency to oversimplify, to base our claims on insufficient evidence, can result in the *hasty generalization*. A convincing generalization will be supported by strong evidence. Avoid generalizing on the basis of one or two examples. And when you do cite examples, make sure that they are typical ones and that they clearly support your argument. Gertrude Himmelfarb, for example, builds her argument about the decline of morality in our society by criticizing an increasing tendency to be nonjudgmental. She offers the following generalization:

> Most of us are uncomfortable with the idea of making moral judgments even in our private lives, let alone with the "intrusion," as we say, of moral judgments into public affairs.

To support her generalization, she observes that public officials, such as the president's cabinet and the Surgeon General, tend to avoid using the word "immoral." In one of her two examples, the Secretary of Health and Human Services is quoted as saying:

> I don't like to put this in moral terms, but I do believe that having children out of wedlock is just wrong.

This last quotation, in itself, hardly strengthens Professor Himmelfarb's initial point since many would consider "wrong" a judgment equivalent to "immoral." Then, on the basis of these limited examples, she reiterates her original claim:

> It is not only our political and cultural leaders who are prone to this failure of moral nerve. Everyone has been infected by it, to one degree or another.

The argument has moved around in a circle, from one hasty generalization to another.

One unpleasant kind of logical fallacy is the *ad hominem* [about the man] argument. Here, the basis for argument is a personal attack: first you point out all the bad qualities of a prominent person who opposes your views; then, without considering whether those flaws are relevant to the issue, you conclude that they must taint that person's beliefs. As you have realized, the ad hominem argument is often used in political campaigns and in other well-publicized controversies. A discussion of euthanasia, for example, will sometimes get stuck in a consideration of Dr. Jack Kevorkian's conduct and motives.

Paul McHugh, for example, spends the first half of his argument against euthanasia demonstrating why he regards Dr. Kevorkian as "'certifiably' insane," comparing him with other zealots who would do anything to advance their cause, and finally citing "the potential for horror in an overvalued idea held by a person in high authority" such as Adolf Hitler. Certainly, the comparison is strained—Dr. Kevorkian is not "in high authority." Yet, even though Professor McHugh now moves to a completely different basis for argument, the opprobrium generated by the association between Kevorkian and Hitler reverberates throughout the rest of the essay.

Yet another logical fallacy derives from reasoning through analogies: in a *false analogy,* the two ideas or circumstances being compared are not actually comparable. Here is an example of a false analogy based on statistics that is being used in an argument against euthanasia:

> Gomez calculates that euthanasia accounts for about 7 percent of all deaths in the Netherlands. If the United States had a similar rate, there would be about 140,000 cases annually. If Fumento's 9 percent figure is correct, the United States number would be 180,000. And if it is correct that half of the Dutch euthanasias are unconsented, applying that proportion here would mean that the number of physician-inflicted unconsented deaths in this country would be between 70,000 and 90,000 annually.

Even though Robert Bork is not sure which of his sources is correct, he uses their statistics to develop an analogy between what has probably happened in the Netherlands (give or take a few percentage points) and what might happen in the United States. Are the two nations comparable in this regard? Professor Bork does not explore the national character, the nature of doctor-patient relationships, the availability of palliatives like medication or hospices. The only point of distinction that he raises is the higher cost of health care in the United States, which supports the conclusion encouraged by his analogy: if it were legalized in the United States, the incentive to bring down medical costs would turn euthanasia into "a license to kill."

For another example of false analogy, let's return to the editorial on the proposed tobacco ban from the *National Review*. Here's the entire paragraph:

> Even though nine-tenths of smokers don't die of lung cancer, there are clearly health dangers in cigarettes, dangers so constantly warned about that smokers are clearly aware that these dangers are the price they pay for the enjoyment and relaxation they get from smoking. As mortals we make all kinds of trade-offs between health and living. We drive automobiles knowing that forty thousand people die in them in the U.S. each year; we cross busy streets, tolerate potentially explosive gas in our homes, swim in fast-moving rivers, use electricity though it kills thousands, and eat meat and other foods that may clog our arteries and give us heart attacks and strokes. All the . . . demagoguery about the tobacco industry killing people could be applied with similar validity to the automobile industry, the electric utilities, aircraft manufacturers, the meat business, and more.

Here, the reader is asked to compare the health risks associated with smoking with those of parallel but comparatively uncontroversial activities, such as crossing a busy street. According to the writer, the situations are comparable because both involve voluntarily engaging in activities known to be health risks, and that similarity is used to suggest that laws *prohibiting* smoking would be logically inconsistent because we don't prohibit other risky activities. If potential health risks justify regulation or even prohibition, then any number of modern activities should, by analogy, be regulated. Yet, in spite of the risks in crossing busy streets, no one ever suggests preventing people from doing so for their own good; smoking, however, is singled out for regulation and possible prohibition. The reader can further *infer* from this line of reasoning that, since we daily engage in all kinds of risky activities, individuals in all cases should be allowed to decide without government interference which risks to take.

In arguments based on false analogies, the reasoning can be attacked merely by demonstrating that the differences in the two situations are more significant than the similarities. In this case, we need to consider:

- if the decision to smoke and the decision to cross a busy street are *genuinely* comparable; and
- if there may be sound reasons for regulating smoking, and equally sound reasons for *not* regulating crossing the street.

Most people could not live a normal life without crossing a busy street, but the same cannot be said of smoking. In addition, if a minimal amount of caution is exercised in crossing busy streets, most people will not be injured; when injuries do occur, they're the result of accidents or some other unexpected or unusual set of events. The same is true of the other "hazards" described in the editorial (driving automobiles, using gas appliances, and so on): injuries result from their *misuse*. By contrast, cigarettes pose a serious health threat when used exactly as intended by their manufacturers; no amount of caution will protect you from the risks associated with cigarettes.

You might also object to this argument on grounds that go beyond the logic of the reasoning to the ways the evidence is presented. The writer mentions, for instance, only that 9 in 10 smokers don't die of lung cancer, implying not only that a 10 percent death rate is insignificant but that death or lung cancer is the only potential health risk connected to smoking worth mentioning. The writer also states that "forty thousand people die" in automobiles each year in the United States, but because that number isn't presented as a percentage of all drivers on the road over the course of the year, it doesn't really address the *comparable* level of risk—those 40,000 may represent fewer than 1 percent of all drivers, which would make driving considerably less risky than smoking. Misrepresenting the evidence in this way prods the careful reader to question the writer's trustworthiness and credibility. (For another discussion of distortion in argumentation, see Chapter 7, pp. 353–357.)

Guidelines for Assessing Arguments

1. Examine the writer's initial premises. Are you willing to grant those statements without explicit proof?
2. How is the writer assembling the evidence? How is the reasoning structured, and is it sound? Can you see acceptable alternatives to the conclusion the writer has drawn?
3. Is the writer manipulating the facts and their presentation to suit the purposes of the argument?

WRITING A SUMMARY

When you underline and annotate a text, when you ask yourself questions about its contents, you are helping yourself to understand what you are reading. When you write a summary, you are *recording* your understanding for your own information; when you include the summary in an essay of your own, you are *reporting* your understanding to your reader.

A summary of a source is usually *a condensation of ideas or information*. It is neither necessary nor desirable to include every repetition and detail. Rather, you are to extract only those points that seem important—the main ideas, which in the original passage may have been interwoven with less important material. Thus, a summary of several pages can sometimes be as brief as one sentence.

In a brief summary, you should add nothing new to the material in the source, nor should you change the emphasis or provide any new interpretation or evaluation. For the sake of clarity and coherence, you may rearrange the order of the ideas; however, you should strive to remain in the background.

The brief summary is often used as part of a larger essay. You have probably summarized your own ideas in the topic sentence of a paragraph or in the conclusion of an essay. When you discuss another piece of writing, you generally summarize the contents briefly to establish for your reader the ideas that you intend to analyze. The writer of a research essay is especially dependent on the summary as a means of referring to source materials. Through summary, you can condense a broad range of information, and you can present and explain the relevance of a number of sources all dealing with the same subject.

Summarizing a Paragraph

Before you can begin to summarize a short reading—a paragraph, for example—you must, of course, read the passage carefully and understand the significance of each idea and the way it is linked to the other ideas. The summary should above all be comprehensive, conveying as much as possible the totality of thought within the passage. Sometimes, you will find a single comprehensive sentence in the text itself, to be taken out verbatim and used as a summary.

The following paragraph can be summarized adequately by one of its own sentences. Which one?

It is often remarked that science has increasingly removed man from a position at the center of the universe. Once upon a time the earth was thought to be the center and the gods were thought to be in close touch with the daily actions of humans. It was not stupid to imagine the earth was at the center, because, one might think, if the earth were moving around the sun, and if you threw a ball vertically upward, it would seem the ball should come down a few feet away from you. Nevertheless, slowly, over many centuries, through the work of Copernicus, Galileo, and many others, we have mostly come to believe that we live on a typical planet orbiting a typical star in a typical galaxy, and indeed that no place in the universe is special.

GORDON KANE, from "Are We the Center of the Universe?"

Both the first and last sentences are possibilities, but the first is a broader generalization and a more comprehensive summary.

Usually, even when you find a strong sentence that suggests the main idea of the paragraph, you will still need to tinker with that sentence, expanding its meaning by giving the language a more general focus. Here, for example, is a paragraph in which no one sentence is broad enough to sum up the main idea, but which contains a scattering of useful phrases:

In a discussion [with] a class of teachers, I once said that I liked some of the kids in my class much more than others and that, without saying which ones I liked best, I had told them so. After all, this is something that children know, whatever we tell them; it is futile to lie about it. Naturally, these teachers were horrified. "What a terrible thing to say!" one said. "I love all the children in my class exactly the same." Nonsense; a teacher who says this is lying, to herself or to others, and probably doesn't like any of the children very much. Not that there is anything wrong with that; plenty of adults don't like children, and there is no reason why they should. But the trouble is that they feel they should, which makes them feel guilty, which makes them feel resentful, which in turn makes them try to work off their guilt with indulgence and their resentment with subtle cruelties—cruelties of a kind that can be seen in many classrooms. Above all, it makes them put on the phony, syrupy, sickening voice and manner, and the fake smiles and forced, bright laughter that children see so much of in school, and rightly resent and hate.

JOHN HOLT, from *How Children Fail*

Here, you might begin by combining key phrases: "a teacher who says" that she "loves all the children" "is lying to herself, or to others," and makes herself (and probably the children) "feel guilty" and "resentful." However, this kind of summarizing sentence resembles a patchwork, with the words and phrasing pulled straight out of the original. Even if you acknowledged the borrowings, by using quotation marks, as above, you would still be left with a weak sentence that is neither yours nor the author's. It is far better to construct an entirely new sentence of your own, such as this one:

In Holt's view, although it is only natural for teachers to prefer some students to others, many teachers cannot accept their failure to like all equally well and express their inadequacy and dissatisfaction in ways that are harmful to the children.

Finally, some diffuse paragraphs give you no starting point at all for the summary and force you to write an entirely new generalization. How would you summarize this paragraph?

To parents who wish to lead a quiet life, I would say: Tell your children that they are very naughty—much naughtier than most children. Point to the young people of some acquaintances as models of perfection and impress your own children with a deep sense of their own inferiority. You carry so many more guns than they do that they cannot fight you. This is called moral influence, and it will enable you to bounce them as much as you please. They think you know and they will not have yet caught you lying often enough to suspect that you are not the unworldly and scrupulously truthful person which you represent yourself to be; nor yet will they know how great a coward you are, nor how soon you will run away, if they fight you with persistency and judgment. You keep the dice and throw them both for your children and yourself. Load them then, for you can easily manage to stop your children from examining them. Tell them how singularly indulgent you are; insist on the incalculable benefit you conferred on them, firstly in bringing them into the world at all, but more particularly in bringing them into it as your children rather than anyone else's. Say that you have their highest interests at stake whenever you are out of temper and wish to make yourself unpleasant by way of balm to your soul. Harp much upon these highest interests. Feed them spiritually upon such brimstone and treacle as the late Bishop of Winchester's Sunday stories. You hold all the trump cards, or if you do not you can filch them; if you play them with anything like judgment you will find yourselves heads of happy, united God-fearing families, even as did my old friend Mr. Pontifex. True, your children will probably find out all about it some day, but not until too late to be of much service to them or inconvenience to yourself.

SAMUEL BUTLER, from *The Way of All Flesh*

A summary of this paragraph would recommend that parents intimidate their children and thus put them in their place. However, although such a generalization sums up the series of examples contained in the paragraph, it does not convey the fact that, in his caricature of family life, Butler is exaggerating outrageously. A comprehensive summary, then, would have to include not only the essence of Butler's recommendations, but also his implied point: that he does not expect anyone to follow his advice. *Irony* is the term used to describe the conflict between Butler's real meaning—parents should not be monsters, but sometimes are—and the meaning apparently expressed by his words as he urges them to treat their children tyrannically. Here is one way to summarize the paragraph:

When he ironically suggests that parents can gain tranquillity and domestic happiness by tyrannizing over their children and making them feel morally inferior, Butler seems to be urging parents to treat their children with respect and justice.

Notice that this summarizing sentence includes Butler's name. Mentioning the author's name effectively emphasizes that what you are summarizing is not your own work. By making it clear who is responsible for what, you are avoiding any possibility of *plagiarizing*—borrowing from your source without acknowledgment.

Guidelines for Summarizing a Brief Passage

1. Find a summarizing sentence within the passage (and, if you are using it in your own essay, put it in quotation marks); *or*
2. Combine elements within the passage into a new summarizing sentence; *or*
3. Write your own summarizing sentence.

EXERCISE 4: SUMMARIZING A PARAGRAPH

Summarize each of the following paragraphs by doing *one* of three things:

A. Underline a sentence that will serve as a comprehensive summary; or
B. Combine existing phrases; then rewrite the sentence, based on these phrases, to create a comprehensive summary; or
C. Invent a new generalization to provide a comprehensive summary.

Be prepared to explain your summary in class discussion.

1. The neurotic individual may have had some special vulnerability as an infant. Perhaps he was ill a great deal and was given care that singled him out from other children. Perhaps he walked or talked much later—or earlier—than children were expected to, and this evoked unusual treatment. The child whose misshapen feet must be put in casts or the sickly little boy who never can play ball may get out of step with his age mates and with the expectations parents and other adults have about children. Or a child may be very unusually placed in his family. He may be the only boy with six sisters, or a tiny child born between two lusty sets of twins. Or the source of the child's difficulties may be a series of events that deeply affected his relations to people—the death of his mother at the birth of the next child or the prolonged illness or absence of his father. Or a series of coincidences—an accident to a parent, moving to a new town and a severe fright—taken together may alter the child's relationship to the world.

   MARGARET MEAD, from *Some Personal Views*

2. Not all untruths are malicious. Telling the truth can complicate or destroy social relationships. It can undermine precious collective myths. Honesty can be

cruel. Sometimes deception is not a vice but a social virtue, and systematic deception is an essential part of the order of the (social) world. In many countries—Japan and Western Samoa, for example—social harmony is valued far more than truthfulness as such. To tell another person what he or she wants to hear, rather than what one might actually feel or believe, is not permitted but expected.

ROBERT C. SOLOMON, from "Is It Ever Right to Lie?"

3. Perhaps the most disturbing revelation of student evaluations, however, is the extent to which every class has become a show and every instructor a personality. The liveliness of the lectures, the use of videos and the professor's ability to draw frequent laughs count more than content. "The professor knows how to teach in an entertaining way (almost like TV)," concluded one admiring student. "The lectures were informative and, most importantly, entertaining," wrote another. I think the students who suggested a laser light show and a warm-up dance before the lesson were kidding, but these days one can never be sure.

GLENN C. ALTSCHULER, from "Let Me Edutain You"

4. Most observers with a historical orientation seem to agree that the commercialization of culture accelerated rapidly after World War II. As the sense of national and international crisis caused by fascism waned, commitment to altruistic goals diminished accordingly. The media gradually lowered their standards and traditional criteria of cultural stratification were relaxed as a consequence. Mass leisure and mass communication, which are essential for the intensive commodification of popular culture, became increasingly normative and pervasive for large numbers of Americans beginning in the 1950s. Warren Susman observed that for many families the culmination of a visit to Disneyland after 1955 was a special exhibit called "American Journeys," a selective, nostalgic reprise of the American past. "Immobilized and passive," Susman remarked, "having visited a world in which one can consume to the presumed satisfaction of all desires," visitors confirmed the sense of well-being that accompanied constant reminders that they enjoyed the world's highest standard of living.

MICHAEL KAMMEN, from American Culture, American Tastes

5. The great traditional arena for male shopping behavior has always been the supermarket. It's here, with thousands of products all within easy reach, that you can witness the carefree abandon and restless lack of discipline for which the gender is known. In one supermarket study, we counted how many shoppers came armed with lists. Almost all of the women had them. Less than a quarter of the men did. Any wife who's watching the family budget knows better than to send her husband to the supermarket unchaperoned. Giving him a vehicle

to commandeer, even if it is just a shopping cart, only emphasizes the potential for guyness in the experience. Throw a couple of kids in with Dad and you've got a lethal combination; he's notoriously bad at saying no when there's grocery acquisitioning to be done. Part of being Daddy is being the provider, after all. It goes to the heart of a man's self-image.

PACO UNDERHILL, from *Why We Buy*

6. Many native-born Americans believed that the Latin habit of taking leisurely meals, accompanied by wine, was symptomatic of their sloth and inability to contribute to the culture of a nation whose inhabitants demonstrated their dynamism and commitment to work and to bettering themselves by taking as little time as possible over their meals. It was also widely believed by those in authority that the immigrants would not be able to free themselves of their old-country attitudes toward work, society, and politics until they abandoned their old-country ways of living and eating. Hence the attack on drinking wine with food. "The American does not think it is necessary to drink with his meals," explained the English expatriate Maurice Low at the beginning of the twentieth century. "It is a foreign and extravagant fashion that he does not encourage."

ANDREW BARR, from *Drink: A Social History of America*

Summarizing an Article

When you want to summarize an essay in a few sentences, how do you judge which points are significant and which are not? Some essays, especially newspaper articles, have rambling structures and short paragraphs, so you don't even have fully developed paragraphs in which to search for summarizing topic sentences. Are there any standard procedures to help you decide which points to summarize?

Guidelines for Summarizing an Article

1. Read the entire article more than once.
2. Ask yourself why the article was written and published.
3. Look for repetitions of and variations on the same idea.

Read "Holdup Man Tells Detectives How to Do It" from the *New York Times*, and, on the second reading, observe your own method of pinpointing the key ideas.

HOLDUP MAN TELLS DETECTIVES HOW TO DO IT
Selwyn Raab

His face hidden by a shabby tan coat, the career holdup man peeked out at his audience of detectives and then proceeded to lecture them on how easy it was to succeed at his trade in New York.   1

"I don't think there's much any individual police officer can do," the guest lecturer told 50 detectives yesterday at an unusual crime seminar sponsored by the Police Department. "Once I knew what the police officer on the beat was up to I wasn't much concerned about the cops."   2

The holdup man, who identified himself only as "Nick," is serving a prison term of 6 to 13 years. He said his most serious arrest occurred after he was shot three times by a supermarket manager—not in any encounter with the police.   3

When asked by a detective taking a course in robbery investigations what the best deterrent would be against gunmen like himself, Nick replied crisply: "Stiffer sentences."   4

After being seriously wounded in his last robbery attempt, Nick said he decided it was time to retire.   5

"I'm close to 40 and not getting any younger," he explained. "I just don't want to spend any more time in jail."   6

Nick also offered the detectives some tips on how robbers pick their targets and make their getaways in the city.   7

Except for wearing a hat, Nick said he affected no disguise. "I usually picked a store in a different neighborhood or in another borough where I was unknown."   8

Leads on places to hold up usually came from other criminals or from employees. There were no elaborate plannings or "casings," he said, adding: 9

"I liked supermarkets because there's always a lot of cash around. Uniformed guards didn't deter me because they're not armed, they usually just have sticks. It's better to pick a busy area rather than the suburbs. The chances of someone noticing you are greater in residential or suburban areas."   10

The detectives, sitting at desks with notepaper in front of them, were rookies as well as veterans. Besides city detectives, the audience included policemen from the Transit Authority, the Housing Authority, the Yonkers Police Department and from Seattle.   11

They listened carefully as Nick outlined how he or a confederate would inspect the area for signs of uniformed or plainclothes police officers.   12

The retired robber said he had preferred supermarkets or stores with large window advertisements or displays because these materials prevented him from being seen by passers-by on the street.   13

"I was always a little nervous or apprehensive before a job," he continued. "But once you're inside and aware of the reaction of the people and you know the possibilities then your confidence comes back."   14

Nick said he always made his escape in a car and he preferred heavily trafficked roads because it made the getaway vehicle less conspicuous than on little used side streets. 15

In New York, cheap handguns were selling from $15 to $70, he told the detectives. Such weapons as shotguns or automatic rifles, Nick said, could be rented for about $100 an hour. 16

Nick said he had been a holdup man since the age of 20 and had committed about 30 "jobs," but was uncertain of the exact number. The biggest robbery he had participated in netted a total of $8,000, and overall he got about $30,000 in his criminal activities. 17

Asked why he went back to robbing after his first arrest, Nick said: "I wanted whisky, women and big autos. Like most who rob I was not socially accepted. Big money elevates you above the people you think are looking down on you." 18

Short prison sentences, for first arrests, Nick asserted, probably do little to discourage holdup men. "I see them laying up in jail and it doesn't make any difference," he said. "They just go ahead planning the next one in a different way." 19

During his "on-and-off" criminal career, Nick said he had never fired any of the guns he carried. 20

After his one-hour appearance as guest lecturer, Nick, his face still covered by his coat, was escorted out of the classroom back to his cell at an undisclosed prison. 21

1. Read the entire article more than once.

This direction is not as simple as it sounds. Because you want to identify main ideas, you may underline what you regard as the key sentences on first reading, and, from then on, look only at the "boiled-down" parts. But *don't eliminate minor facts and interesting details too soon.* They do have a function in the article, supporting and illuminating the central ideas. For example, the fact that Nick chose to hide his face during and after his "lecture" hardly seems worth underlining and, in fact, would never by itself be regarded as crucial. But taken together with some of Nick's remarks, that minor fact helps you to recognize a key point of the article: The robber's reliance on *anonymity* enables him to commit a successful crime; Nick may at some point wish to resume his profession despite his "retirement." Although you should always underline your key points, remember to reread and consider every part of the article as you prepare your summary.

2. Ask yourself why the article was written and published.

What does the newspaper want its readers to learn? A news article's purpose is frequently twofold—to describe an event and to suggest the event's significance—and so it is easy for you to confuse the *facts* being recorded with the underlying *reasons* for recording them. Here are two one-sentence summaries of the article that are both off the mark because they concentrate too heavily on the event:

Nick, a convicted retired criminal, was guest speaker at a police seminar and told detectives how robbers pick their targets and make their getaways in New York.

Nick, after committing thirty robberies, suggested to detectives some possible methods of thwarting future robberies.

Both writers seem too concerned with Nick's colorful history and the peculiarity of his helping the police at all. They ignore the significance of what Nick was actually saying. The second summary—by emphasizing the phrase "thwarting future robberies"—is misleading and almost contradicts the point of the article; in fact, Nick is really suggesting that the police will continue to be ineffectual.

A news article can also mislead you into thinking that a headline is a summary: the headline "Holdup Man Tells Detectives How to Do It" does not summarize the material in the article, but, because it is broad and vague, it "sounds" good. What, for example, is meant by the "it" of the headline—robbery or detection? What does Nick tell the detectives?

3. Look for repetitions of and variations on the same idea.

There is one concrete point that Selwyn Raab and his readers and the police and Nick himself are all interested in: *ways of preventing criminals from committing crimes.* Not only are we told again and again about Nick's contempt for the police, but we are also given his flat statement that only fear of imprisonment ("stiffer sentences") will discourage a hardened criminal.

A brief summary of this article, then, would mention *tougher sentencing as a way of preventing crime.* But, in addition, the theme of *the criminal's need for anonymity* ought, if possible, to be incorporated into a complete summary. In Nick's opinion, his career has been relatively successful because he has managed to appear normal and blend into the crowd. The primary and secondary ideas can be joined in a summary like this one:

Observing with contempt that the police have rarely been able to penetrate his "anonymous" disguise, Nick, the successful robber, argues that the presence of police will not deter most experienced criminals and that only "stiffer sentences" will prevent crime.

EXERCISE 5: SUMMARIZING AN ARTICLE

Carefully read "Summertime Dues" from the *New York Times Magazine.* Determine the article's purpose and pick out the arguments that the author emphasizes; then write a comprehensive summary in two or three sentences.

SUMMERTIME DUES
Walter Kirn

On my first summer job I learned to cheat. I was working in one of those cute, old-timey ice cream shops where the sundaes are decorated with toothpick flags and the staff sings "Happy Birthday" to the customers. The day I clocked in, the owner showed me how to scoop up a generous-looking ball of ice cream that was perfectly hollow in the center. The trick was in the wrist, and it took practice, but eventually I mastered the subterfuge and was serving up great gobs of rocky road that weighed, according to a hidden kitchen scale, exactly 1.5 ounces. I felt rotten. Kids would come in holding flimsy dollar bills—all the money they'd ever had, it seemed—and in return I would give them globes of air that collapsed inward the moment they were licked. I complained to the owner, who threatened to let me go and accused me of being a secret "heavy scooper" who didn't understand the ways of business.

Like millions of other American teenagers, I was doing what was expected of me that summer: preparing myself for the world of work by holding down a minimum-wage job that conveyed no special skills or knowledge but did breed a certain early cynicism. Like prom night and graduation, a summer job was a rite of passage in my town. Whether or not we needed the money or felt we had better uses for our time than topping off radiators at the minilube or repainting the foul lines on the city tennis courts, we teenagers labored straight through to Labor Day, emerging strengthened and toughened at summer's end.

That was two decades ago, another time. These days, according to several recent reports, the summer-job tradition is in decline. Fewer and fewer kids, the experts tell us, are showing an interest in whiling away their holidays folding boxes and weed-whipping cracked sidewalks.

What's more, the once-popular government programs that subsidized such jobs are drying up, the victims of a prosperous economy and a shrinking pool of applicants. A troubling development? Perhaps. Then again, if my own experience means anything, maybe not.

Summer jobs are supposed to build character in teenagers—the question is, What sort of character? A lot of the jobs, let's face it, are pure make-work: clearing dead-end trails through national forests, planting violets around school flagpoles. They're the sort of duties assigned to prison inmates and pensioners in the Soviet Union, and what they mainly teach is the necessity of appearing busy for the boss while doing something that no one really needs done. At the end of the week there's a paycheck, small but helpful, which you promptly pump into the gas tank of your car or blow on Christina Aguilera tickets. The jobs are entitlement programs, basically, or political schemes to keep rambunctious kids out of the way of adults and off the streets.

Not that learning to look busy isn't valuable. One of my own summer jobs was moving books between two floors of a college library. My supervisor was barely

1

2

3

4

5

6

in his 20's, a member of one of those upbeat New Age movements that preach prosperity through optimism. He called me and my coworkers his "team" and referred to our simple duties as "the mission." What he failed to notice, though, in his zeal to convert us to his beliefs, was that, after only four weeks on the job, we'd finished moving every single book. There was no more to do, and two more months to do it. The team made a decision then: say nothing. The job was so easy and the pay so generous that we agreed to keep a good thing going. We emptied half of the shelves that we'd just filled, carried the books downstairs, and started over.

Better training for corporate life would be hard to find. In that sense, the library job fulfilled its promise. I not only learned to work, I also learned when not to work. I learned to protect my friends and even my boss, who might have been laid off had someone realized that he'd fulfilled his objective prematurely. These lessons have come in handy ever since. In office after office, I've seen the price paid by those who complete assignments early, only to be handed yet more work in a continual, exhausting spiral that ends in hospitalization or unemployment. Such eager beavers tend to burn out early, perhaps because they never had summer jobs that taught them how to conserve their vital energy.   7

The kids who are eschewing summer work in favor of more broadening pursuits like travel, athletics and daily moviegoing may find themselves at a disadvantage someday. There's so much they won't know. Like when to steal. I learned to steal while working at a gas station. I resisted at first, but my manager pushed hard, and since he was the nephew of the proprietor, I found him persuasive. The guy stole everything, from cans of Dr. Pepper to tanks of gas, explaining that they belonged not to the station but to a multinational oil company. What's more, he said, if I tattled to his uncle he'd blame me for the thefts. I'd lose my job.   8

Summer work is important. Hop to it, kids. There are some things you just can't learn in school.   9

Summarizing a Complex Essay

When you are asked to summarize a reading containing a number of complex and abstract ideas, a reading that may be disorganized and therefore difficult to comprehend and condense, the best way to prepare for your summary is to isolate each important point and note it down in a list.

Here are some guidelines for summarizing a complex essay:

1. The summary must be comprehensive.
2. The summary must be concise.
3. The summary must be coherent.
4. The summary must be independent.

Here is an essay by Bertrand Russell, followed by a preliminary list of notes, a statement of Russell's thesis, and the final summary. (The numbers in the margin are keyed to the preliminary list of notes on pp. 51–52.) Russell's essay is difficult, so be sure to read it slowly, and more than once. If you get confused at any point, try referring to the list of notes that follows; but be sure to *go back to the essay* after you have identified and understood each numbered point.

THE SOCIAL RESPONSIBILITY OF SCIENTISTS
Bertrand Russell

Science, ever since it first existed, has had important effects in matters that lie outside the purview of pure science. Men of science have differed as to their responsibility for such effects. Some have said that the function of the scientist in society is to supply knowledge, and that he need not concern himself with the use to which this knowledge is put. I do not think that this view is tenable, especially in our age. The scientist is also a citizen; and citizens who have any special skill have a public duty to see, as far as they can, that their skill is utilized in accordance with the public interest. Historically, the functions of the scientist in public life have generally been recognized. The Royal Society was founded by Charles II as an antidote to "fanaticism" which had plunged England into a long period of civil strife. The scientists of that time did not hesitate to speak out on public issues, such as religious toleration and the folly of prosecutions for witchcraft. But although science has, in various ways at various times, favored what may be called a humanitarian outlook, it has from the first had an intimate and sinister connection with war. Archimedes sold his skill to the Tyrant of Syracuse for use against the Romans; Leonardo secured a salary from the Duke of Milan for his skill in the art of fortification; and Galileo got employment under the Grand Duke of Tuscany because he could calculate the trajectories of projectiles. In the French Revolution the scientists who were not guillotined were set to making new explosives, but Lavoisier was not spared, because he was only discovering hydrogen which, in those days, was not a weapon of war. There have been some honorable exceptions to the subservience of scientists to warmongers. During the Crimean War the British government consulted Faraday as to the feasibility of attack by poisonous gases. Faraday replied that it was entirely feasible, but that it was inhuman and he would have nothing to do with it.

Modern democracy and modern methods of publicity have made the problem of affecting public opinion quite different from what it used to be. The knowledge that the public possesses on any important issue is derived from vast and powerful organizations: the press, radio, and, above all, television. The knowledge that governments possess is more limited. They are too busy to search out the facts for themselves, and consequently they know only what their underlings think good for them unless there is such a powerful movement in a different sense that politicians cannot ignore it. Facts which ought to guide the decisions of statesmen—for instance, as to the possible lethal qualities of fallout—do not acquire their due importance if they remain buried in scientific journals. They acquire their due importance only when they become known to so many voters that they affect the course of the elections. In general, there is an opposition to widespread publicity for such facts. This opposition springs from various sources, some sinister, some comparatively respectable. At the bottom of the moral scale there is the financial interest of the various industries connected with armaments. Then there are various effects of a somewhat thoughtless patriotism, which believes in secrecy and in what is called "toughness." But perhaps more important than either of these is the unpleasantness of the facts, which makes the general public turn aside to pleasanter topics such as divorces and murders. The consequence is that what ought to be known widely throughout the general public will not be known unless great efforts are made by disinterested persons to see that the information reaches the minds and hearts of vast numbers of people. I do not think this work can be successfully accomplished except by the help of men of science. They, alone, can speak with the authority that is necessary to combat the misleading statements of those scientists who have permitted themselves to become merchants of death. If disinterested scientists do not speak out, the others will succeed in conveying a distorted impression, not only to the public but also to the politicians.

7

8

9

It must be admitted that there are obstacles to individual action in our age which did not exist at earlier times. Galileo could make his own telescope. But once when I was talking with a very famous astronomer he explained that the telescope upon which his work depended owed its existence to the benefaction of enormously rich men, and, if he had not stood well with them, his astronomical discoveries would have been impossible. More frequently, a scientist only acquires access to enormously expensive equipment if he stands well with the government of his country. He knows that if he adopts a rebellious attitude he and his family are likely to perish along with the rest of civilized mankind. It is a tragic dilemma, and I do not think that one should censure a man whatever his decision; but I do think—and I think men of science should realize—that unless something rather drastic is done under the leadership or through the inspiration of some part of the scientific world, the human race, like the Gadarene swine, will rush down a steep place to destruction in blind ignorance of the fate that scientific skill has prepared for it.

10

It is impossible in the modern world for a man of science to say with any honesty, "My business is to provide knowledge, and what use is made of the knowledge is not my responsibility." The knowledge that a man of science provides may fall into the hands of men or institutions devoted to utterly unworthy objects. I do not suggest that a man of science, or even a large body of men of science, can altogether prevent this, but they can diminish the magnitude of the evil.

There is another direction in which men of science can attempt to provide leadership. They can suggest and urge in many ways the value of those branches of science of which the important and practical uses are beneficial and not harmful. Consider what might be done if the money at present spent on armaments were

11

spent on increasing and distributing the food supply of the world and diminishing the population pressure. In a few decades, poverty and malnutrition, which now afflict more than half the population of the globe, could be ended. But at present almost all the governments of great states consider that it is better to spend money on killing foreigners than on keeping their own subjects alive. Possibilities of a hopeful sort in whatever field can best be worked out and stated authoritatively by men of science; and, since they can do this work better than others, it is part of their duty to do it.

As the world becomes more technically unified, life in an ivory tower becomes increasingly impossible. Not only so; the man who stands out against the powerful organizations which control most of human activity is apt to find himself no longer in the ivory tower, with a wide outlook over a sunny landscape, but in the dark and subterranean dungeon upon which the ivory tower was erected. To risk such a habitation demands courage. It will not be necessary to inhabit the dungeon if there are many who are willing to risk it, for everybody knows that the modern world depends upon scientists, and, if they are insistent, they must be listened to. We have it in our power to make a good world; and, therefore, with whatever labor and risk, we must make it. 12

First Stage: List of Notes and Establishing a Thesis

1. Should scientists try to influence the way their discoveries are used?

2. One point of view: the scientist's role is to make the discovery; what happens afterward is not his concern.

3. Russell's point of view: scientists are like any other knowledgeable and public-spirited people; they must make sure that the products of their knowledge work for, not against, society.

4. In the past, some scientists have made public their views on controversial issues like freedom of religion; others have been servants of the war machine.

5. The power to inform and influence the public is now controlled by the news media.

6. Government officials are too busy to be well informed; subordinates feed them only enough information to get them reelected.

7. It is in the interests of various groups, ranging from weapons makers to patriots, to limit the amount of scientific information that the public receives.

8. The public is reluctant to listen to distasteful news.

9. Since the public deserves to hear the truth, scientists, who are respected for their knowledge and who belong to no party or faction, ought to do more to provide the public with information about the potentially lethal consequences of their discoveries. By doing so, they will correct the distortions of those scientists who have allied themselves with warmongers.

10. It is very difficult for scientists to speak out since they depend on government and business interests to finance their work.

11. While scientists cannot entirely stop others from using some of their discoveries for antisocial purposes, they can support other, more constructive kinds of research.

12. Speaking out is worth the risk of incurring the displeasure of powerful people; since the work of scientists is so vital, the risk isn't too great, especially if they act together.

<u>Russell's Thesis</u>: Contrary to the self-interested arguments of many scientists and other groups, scientists have a social responsibility to make sure that their work is used for, not against, the benefit of humanity.

Second Stage: Summary

Some scientists, as well as other groups, consider that they need not influence the way in which their discoveries are used. However, Bertrand Russell, in "The Social Responsibility of Scientists," believes that scientists have a responsibility to make sure that their work is used for, not against, the benefit of humanity. In modern times, he argues, it has been especially difficult for concerned scientists to speak out because many powerful groups prefer to limit and distort what the public is told, because government officials are too busy to be thoroughly informed, because scientists depend on the financial support of business and government, and because the public itself is reluctant to hear distasteful news. Nevertheless, Russell maintains that scientists have the knowledge and the prestige to command public attention, and their work is too vital for their voices to be suppressed. If they act together, they can warn us if their work is likely to be used for an antisocial purpose and, at least, they can propose less destructive alternatives.

Guidelines for Summarizing a Complex Essay

1. *The summary must be comprehensive.* You should review all the notes on your list, and include in your summary all those ideas that are essential to the author's development of the thesis.

2. *The summary must be concise.* Eliminate repetitions in your list, even if the author restates the same points. Your summary should be considerably shorter than the source.

3. *The summary must be coherent.* It should make sense as a paragraph in its own right; it should not be taken directly from your list of notes and sound like a list of sentences that happen to be strung together in a paragraph format.

4. *The summary must be independent.* You are not being asked to imitate or identify yourself with the author about whom you are writing. On the contrary, you are expected to maintain your own voice throughout the summary. Even as you are jotting down your list of notes, you should try to use your own words. Nevertheless, while you want to make it clear that *you* are writing the summary, you should be careful not to create any misrepresentation or distortion by introducing comments or criticisms of your own. (Such distortion is most likely to occur when you strongly disagree with the material that you are summarizing.) You must make it clear to your reader when you are summarizing directly from the text and when you are commenting on, inferring from, or explaining what is being summarized.

This summary of Russell's essay is not a simple compilation of phrases taken from the text, nor a collection of topic sentences, one from each paragraph. Rather, it is a clear, coherent, and unified summary of Russell's ideas, expressed in the writer's own voice and words.

A *framework* is immediately established in the first two sentences of the summary, which present the two alternative views of the scientist's responsibility. The next sentence, which describes the four obstacles to scientific freedom of speech, illustrates the rearrangement of ideas that is characteristic of summary. While reviewing the list of notes, the summarizer has noticed that points 6, 7, 8, and 10 each refers to a different way in which scientific truth is often suppressed; she has therefore brought them together and lined them up in a parallel construction based on the repeated word "because." Finally, the last two sentences contain a restatement of Russell's thesis and point out that the obstacles to action are not as formidable as they seem.

Notice that the Russell summary excludes points 1, 4, and 5 on the list of notes: point 1 is included in the presentation of points 2 and 3; point 4 is an example, one that is not essential to an understanding of the essay; and point 5 is not directly related to Russell's argument.

In summarizing Russell's essay, it would not be acceptable to include extraneous points, such as the dangers of making scientific secrets public, for that would be arguing with Russell. Such ideas should be reserved for a full-length essay whose purpose is to develop an argument of your own, not just to summarize Russell's. Within limits, however, it is acceptable to go beyond point-by-point summary, to suggest the author's implied intention, and, in a sense, to interpret the work's meaning for your reader. You might state, for example, that ours is an age that encourages interdependence and discourages independent action. Such an interpretation would have to be supported by evidence from the reading. While Russell does not say so specifically, in so many words, the assertion about interdependence is certainly substantiated by the material in the last two paragraphs.

ASSIGNMENT 1: SUMMARIZING AN ESSAY

Summarize one of the following three essays. Before you begin your summary (on your second reading), underline and annotate key ideas and arguments, and make a preliminary list of points.

INTERSTELLAR SPACEFLIGHT: CAN WE TRAVEL TO OTHER STARS?
Timothy Ferris

Living as we do in technologically triumphant times, we are inclined to view interstellar spaceflight as a technical challenge, like breaking the sound barrier or climbing Mount Everest—something that will no doubt be difficult but feasible, given the right resources and resourcefulness.   1

This view has much to recommend it. Unmanned interstellar travel has, in a sense, already been achieved, by the Pioneer 10 and 11 and Voyager 1 and 2 probes, which were accelerated by their close encounters with Jupiter to speeds in excess of the sun's escape velocity and are outward-bound forever. By interstellar standards, these spacecraft are slow: Voyager 1, the speediest of the four at 62,000 kilometers per hour (39,000 miles per hour), will wander for several tens of thousands of years before it encounters another star. But the Wright brothers' first airplane wasn't particularly speedy either. A manned interstellar spacecraft that improved on Voyager's velocity by the same 1,000-fold increment by which Voyager improved on the Kitty Hawk flights could reach nearby stars in a matter of decades, if a way could be found to pay its exorbitant fuel bill.   2

But that's a big "if," and there is another way of looking at the question: Rather than scaling a mountain, one can always scout a pass. In other words, the technical problems involved in traveling to the stars need not be regarded solely as obstacles to overcome but can instead be viewed as clues, or signposts, that point toward other ways to explore the universe.   3

Three such clues loom large. First, interstellar space travel appears to be extremely, if not prohibitively, expensive. All the propulsion systems proposed so far for interstellar voyages—fusion rockets, antimatter engines, laser-light sails and so on—would require huge amounts of energy, either in the manufacturing of fusion or antimatter fuel or in the powering of a laser beam for light sails. Second, there is no compelling evidence that alien spacefarers have ever visited Earth. Third, radio waves offer a fast and inexpensive mode of *communication* that could compete effectively with interstellar *travel*. What might these clues imply?

The high cost of interstellar spaceflight suggests that the payloads carried between stars—whether dispatched by humans in the future or by alien spacefarers in the past—are most likely, as a rule, to be small. It is much more affordable to send a grapefruit-size probe than the starship *Enterprise*. Consider spacecraft equipped with laser-light sails, which could be pushed through interstellar space by the beams of powerful lasers based in our solar system. To propel a manned spacecraft to Proxima Centauri, the nearest star, in 40 years, the laser system would need thousands of gigawatts of power, more than the output of all the electricity-generating plants on Earth. But sending a 10-kilogram unmanned payload on the same voyage would require only about 50 gigawatts—still a tremendous amount of power but less than 15 percent of the total U.S. output.

What can be accomplished by a grapefruit-size probe? Quite a lot, actually, especially if such probes have the capacity to replicate themselves, using materials garnered at their landing sites. The concept of self-replicating systems was first studied by mathematician John von Neumann in the 1940s, and now scientists in the field of nanotechnology are investigating how to build them. If the goal is exploring other planetary systems, one could manufacture a few small self-replicating probes and send them to nearby stars at an affordable cost. Once each probe arrived at its destination, it would set up long-term housekeeping on a metallic asteroid. The probe would mine the asteroid and use the ore to construct a base of operations, including a radio transmitter to relay its data back to Earth. The probe could also fashion other probes, which would in turn be sent to other stars. Such a strategy can eventually yield an enormous payoff from a relatively modest investment by providing eyes and ears on an ever increasing number of outposts.

If colonization is the goal, the probes could carry the biological materials required to seed hospitable but lifeless plants. This effort seems feasible whether our aim is simply to promote the spread of life itself or to prepare the way for future human habitation. Of course, there are serious ethical concerns about the legitimacy of homesteading planets that are already endowed with indigenous life. But such worlds may be outnumbered by "near-miss" planets that lack life but could bloom with a bit of tinkering.

One of the intriguing things about small interstellar probes is that they are inconspicuous. A tiny probe built by an alien civilization could be orbiting the sun right now, faithfully phoning home, and we might never learn of its existence. This would be especially true if the probe were engineered to keep a low profile—for instance, if its radio antenna were aimed well away from the ecliptic, or if it were programmed to turn off its transmitters whenever the beam came near a planet. And that is just how such probes would presumably be designed, to discourage emerging species like ours from hunting them down, dismantling them and putting them on display in the Smithsonian National Air and Space Museum. Similarly, a biological probe could have seeded Earth with life in the first place. The fact that life appeared quite early in Earth's history argues against the hypothesis that it was artificially implanted (unless somebody out there was keeping a close eye out for newborn planets), but such an origin for terrestrial life is consistent with the evidence currently in hand.

From the second clue—that aliens have not yet landed on the White House lawn—we can posit that our immediate celestial neighborhood is probably not home to a multitude of technologically advanced civilizations that spend their time boldly venturing to other star systems on board big, imposing spacecraft. If that were the case, they would have shown up here already, as they evidently have not. (I am, of course, discounting reports of UFO sightings and alien abductions, the evidence for which is unpersuasive.) By similar reasoning we can reach the tentative conclusion that wormholes, stargates and other faster-than-light transit systems favored by science-fiction writers are not widely in use, at least out here in the galactic suburbs. 9

Admittedly, one can poke holes in this argument. Perhaps the aliens know we exist but are courteous enough not to bother us. Maybe they visited Earth during the more than three billion years when terrestrial life was all bugs and bacteria and quietly departed after taking a few snapshots and carefully bagging their trash. In any event, it seems reasonable to conclude that if interstellar interstates exist, we are not living near an exit ramp. 10

The third clue—that radio can convey information much faster and more cheaply than starships can carry cargo—has become well known thanks to SETI, the search for extraterrestrial intelligence. SETI researchers use radio telescopes to listen for signals broadcast by alien civilizations. The SETI literature is therefore concerned mostly with how we can detect such signals and has little to say about how electromagnetic communications might be employed among advanced civilizations as an alternative to interstellar travel. Yet just such a path of speculation can help explain how intelligent life could have emerged in our galaxy without interstellar travel becoming commonplace. 11

When SETI was first proposed, in a paper published in *Nature* by Giuseppe Cocconi and Philip Morrison in 1959, the main method of electronic communication on Earth was the telephone, and the objection most frequently raised to the idea of interstellar conversation was that it would take too long. A single exchange—"How are you?" "Fine"—would consume 2,000 years if conducted between plants 1,000 light-years apart. But, as Morrison himself has noted, conversation is not essential to communication; one can also learn from a monologue. Eighteenth-century 12

England, for instance, was deeply influenced by the ancient Greeks, although no English subject ever had a conversation with an ancient Greek. We learn from Socrates and Herodotus, although we cannot speak with them. So interstellar communication makes sense even if using it as a telephone does not.

In 1975, when I first proposed that long-term interstellar communications traffic among advanced civilizations would best be handled by an automated network, there was no model of such a system that was familiar to the public. But today the Internet provides a good example of what a monologue-dominated interstellar network might be like and helps us appreciate why extraterrestrials might prefer it to the arduous and expensive business of actually traveling to other stars. 13

Experientially, the Internet tends to collapse space and time. One looks for things on the Net and makes use of them as one pleases. It does not necessarily matter whether the information came from next door or from the other side of the planet, or whether the items were placed on-line last night or last year. E-mail aside, the Internet is mostly monologue. 14

Suppose the Internet had been invented several thousand years ago, so that we had access not only to the books of Aristotle and Archimedes but also to their sites on the World Wide Web. What a boon it would be to surf such a web, downloading the lost plays of Sophocles and gazing at the vivid mosaics of Pompeii in colors undimmed by time. Few, I think, would trade that experience for a halting phone conversation with someone from the past. 15

The same may also be true of communications between alien worlds. The most profound gulf separating intelligent species on various star systems is not space but time, and the best way to bridge that gulf is not with starships but with networked interstellar communications. 16

The gulf of time is of two kinds. The first is the amount of time it takes signals to travel between contemporaneous civilizations. If, as some of the more optimistic SETI scientists estimate, there are 10,000 communicative worlds in the Milky Way galaxy today, the average time required to send a one-way message to one's nearest neighbor—across the back fence, so to speak—is on the order of 1,000 years. Therefore, it makes sense to send long, fact-filled messages rather than "How are you?" 17

The other gulf arises if, as it seems reasonable to assume, communicative civilizations generally have lifetimes that are brief by comparison with the age of the universe. Obviously, we do not even know whether alien societies exist, much less how long they normally stay on the air before succumbing to decay, disaster or waning interest. But they would have to last a very long time indeed to approach the age of the Milky Way galaxy, which is more than 10 billion years old. Here on Earth, species survive for a couple of million years on average. The Neanderthals lasted about 200,000 years, *Homo erectus* about 1.4 million years. Our species, *H. sapiens,* is about 200,000 years old, so if we are typical, we may expect to endure for another million or so years. The crucial point about any such tenure is 18 that it is cosmologically insignificant. Even if we manage to survive for a robust 10 million years to come, that is still less than a tenth of 1 percent of the age of our galaxy.

Any other intelligent species that learns how to determine the ages of stars and galaxies will come to the same sobering conclusion—that even if communicative civilizations typically stay on the air for fully 10 million years, *only one in 1,000 of all that have inhabited our galaxy is still in existence.* The vast majority belong to the past. Is theirs a silent majority, or have they found a way to leave a record of themselves, their thoughts and their achievements?   19

That is where an interstellar Internet comes into play. Such a network could be deployed by small robotic probes like the ones described earlier, each of which would set up antennae that connect it to the civilizations of nearby stars and to other network nodes. The network would handle the interstellar radio traffic of all the worlds that know about it. That would be the immediate payoff: one could get in touch with many civilizations, without the need to establish contact with each individually. More important, each node would keep and distribute a record of the data it handled. Those records would vastly enrich the network's value to every civilization that uses it. With so many data constantly circulated and archived among its nodes, the interstellar Internet would give each inhabited planet relatively easy access to a wealth of information about the civilizations that currently exist and the many more worlds that were in touch with the network in the past.   20

Intelligence brings knowledge of one's own mortality—and at the same time, provides a means to transcend it—so the desire for some kind of immortality is, I suspect, widespread among intelligent beings. Although some species may have limited themselves to physical monuments, such as the one erected by Percy Bysshe Shelley's Ozymandias, these must eventually weather away and would in any event require long journeys to be seen and appreciated. Surely most species would elect to contribute to the interstellar Internet, where their thoughts and stories could career around the galaxy forever.   21

If there were any truth in this fancy, what would our galaxy look like? Well, we would find that interstellar voyages by starships of the *Enterprise* class would be rare, because most intelligent beings would prefer to explore the galaxy and to plumb its long history through the more efficient method of cruising the Net. When interstellar travel did occur, it would usually take the form of small, inconspicuous probes, designed to expand the network, quietly conduct research and seed infertile planets. Radio traffic on the Net would be difficult for technologically emerging worlds to intercept, because nearly all of it would be locked into high-bandwidth, pencil-thin beams linking established planets with automated nodes. Our hopes for SETI would rest principally on the extent to which the Net bothers to maintain omnidirectional broadcast antennae, which are economically draining but could from time to time bring in a fresh, naive species—perhaps even one way out here beyond the Milky Way's Sagittarius Arm. The galaxy would look quiet and serene, although in fact it would be alive with thought.   22

In short, it would look just as it does.   23

MOLDING OUR LIVES IN THE IMAGES OF THE MOVIES
Neal Gabler

Nearly 160 years ago, Alexis De Tocqueville observed that Americans lacked an appreciation for what he called the "pleasures of mind." Instead, he wrote, they "prefer books which may be easily procured, quickly read, and which require no learned researches to be understood. They ask for beauties self-proffered and easily enjoyed. . . . They require strong and rapid emotions, startling passages, truths or errors brilliant enough to rouse them up and to plunge them at once, as if by violence, into the midst of the subject."

Those words remain, in fact, a pretty good description of the impulses that drive American popular culture, what one might call a constant quest for ever greater sensationalism. But the characteristics Tocqueville ascribed to our books, poetry and theater are now no longer confined to amusements; they have leached into almost every aspect of American life. Any putative Tocqueville looking at America today would see a whole Republic of Entertainment in which strong and rapid emotions, startling passages and rousing truths pervade journalism, politics, education, religion, art and even crime. Indeed, ours seems to be a world molded in the image of the movies and intended for our viewing pleasure.

To most of us, this has been obvious for some time in the country's public life. However serious their subtexts may be, news events like the O. J. Simpson trials and Lewinskygate are vastly entertaining spectacles that are promoted, packaged and presented very much like the latest Hollywood blockbusters, only these stories happen to be written in the medium of life.

What has been less evident than the transformation of public events into entertainment, however, is something arguably much more important: the extent to which entertainment has gradually infested our own personal lives, converting them into "movies" too. It is not just that audiences may find daily life as entertaining as fictionalized stories, as *The Truman Show* and . . . "edTV" have it. It is that over the years our moviegoing and television watching has been impregnating the American consciousness with the conventions and esthetics of entertainment, until we have become performers ourselves, performing our own lives out of the shards of movies. One might even think of American life, including quotidian American life, as a vast production in which virtually every object is a prop, every space is a set, every person is an actor and every experience is a scene in a continuing narrative.

It has been a long process that has brought us to this point—a process that may have been set in motion by the country's very active sense of democracy. In Europe, where the class hierarchy was rigid and class distinctions obvious, any sort of personal theatricality, aside from that of self-conscious, rebellious Bohemians, was limited to the upperclasses, which could afford flamboyant display. But in America, where class boundaries were more porous and distinctions less apparent, citizens quickly learned that how one looked and behaved largely determined how one was perceived, prompting Walt Whitman to lament the "terrible doubt of appearances."

This emphasis on class by style infused nineteenth-century American life with a kind of subtle theatricality as the middle class and later the working class imitated the affectations of the gentry in hopes of being regarded as gentry themselves. By the early twentieth century, though, these old models of gentility had yielded to new models in the mass media, especially the movies, and the change ushered in a marked difference in aspiration. What had begun in the nineteenth century as a way of appropriating class became in the twentieth a way of making one's life more closely approximate the glamorous visions one read about in novels and picture magazines or saw on the screen.

Today, with the burgeoning of mass culture, this everyday performance art may be America's most ubiquitous art. Though obviously not everyone is willing to concede that he or she is becoming a performer, there are telltale signs everywhere that ordinary life is cinematic. Take fashion. There was a time when fashion was, as Tom Wolfe once put it, the "code language of status," a way to express where one stood in the social order. Nowadays, when nearly everyone has access to designer clothes, even if it is only a pair of jeans, fashion is less expressive than imaginative. What one wears doesn't necessarily convey who one is; it projects who one wants to be—which makes clothing into costume.

It is certainly no coincidence that America's most popular and influential designer, Ralph Lauren, has demonstrated the greatest appreciation for the costume functions of fashion. What Mr. Lauren, born Ralph Lifshitz, understood from his own love of the movies as a boy growing up in the Bronx was that people would pay to transform their lives into their cinematic fantasies: safari outfits to make one a colonialist from *Out of Africa*; denim jackets and jeans to make one a cowboy from a Hollywood western; finely tailored English suits to make one an aristocrat from any number of crisp drawing room melodramas.

At the same time, he realized that these transformations were more than a matter of costuming. With his home furnishings and accessories as well as his ad campaigns, Mr. Lauren sells an image of life, a kind of collage of movie fantasies that, in his own words, "represent living, not fashion" and that, more specifically, provide the "whole atmosphere of the good life" that movies had always purveyed. One writer called him the first image manager, which is exactly what he is. He gave the middle class what the upper classes and celebrities had always had: a conscious esthetic.

What Ralph Lauren is to the materials of image, Martha Stewart is to their deployment. Like Mr. Lauren's, Ms. Stewart's origins were humble, but like Mr. Lauren, she has an instinct for transporting her followers from their daily grind. Identifying with the bedraggled, unfulfilled, unappreciated middle-class housewife, Ms. Stewart, as a life style consultant, offers a vision of domestic perfection that owes more to movies and television sitcoms than to reality. "We have come to realize that the creation of a fine family, a lovely life style and a comfortable home is kind of a national art form in itself," she told her readers of her syndicated column

6

7

8

9

10

with a nod to the theatricality of it. So devout an esthete is Ms. Stewart that she has even issued instructions on how to shovel the snow from your sidewalk: "Always leave an inch of snow so it looks nice and white. Esthetics are very important in snow removal."

While designers like Mr. Lauren and life style counselors like Ms. Stewart are in the business of image management, more and more architects are in the business of creating the sets on which the life movie could unfold. Stores like Niketown and malls like the Mall of America outside Minneapolis or Horton Plaza in San Diego, theme restaurants like the Hard Rock Cafe, Planet Hollywood or Jekyll and Hyde, and hotels, museums, churches and schools were now furnishing stages for the performance of shopping, eating, sleeping, watching, worshiping or learning. As Andy Warhol once said of New York restaurants, "They caught on that what people really care about is changing their atmosphere for a couple of hours"—that is, escaping into their own life movies. 11

Nor was the set restricted to individual spaces. Whole areas had become back lots, to use the Hollywood term for the studios' old tracts where outdoor scenes were shot—areas like West 57th Street and the South Street Seaport in New York or Peachtree Center in Atlanta or Navy Pier in Chicago. The intellectual historian Thomas Bender, looking at the way America's inner cities were being colonized and commercialized by chain stores, theme restaurants and other tourist attractions, summoned a new urban vision in which the city was an "entertainment zone—a place to visit, a place to shop; it is no more than a live-in theme park," which he believed was designed to hide a grittier, dirtier, more problematic city from us. 12

Even so, if many of us now live on stages, dress in costumes and follow esthetic guidance, these things are only symptomatic of a larger reconceptualization of life itself. Nearly 50 years ago, the sociologist David Riesman identified the emergence of a new type of social character in America that he called "other-directed," by which he meant, essentially, that one's goals were directed toward satisfying the expectations of others—an audience. By definition, other-directed Americans were conscious of performance and of the effects of affect, a self-consciousness that led another sociologist, Erving Goffman, to conclude that in the twentieth century "life itself is a dramatically enacted thing." 13

In Goffman's analysis, every American was engaged in a series of plays and a series of roles, an "exchange of dramatically inflated actions, counteractions, and terminating replies"—in short, an enactment of the scenes of daily life. What Goffman didn't seem to foresee when he was writing in the late 1950's was how much more complex the performance would become, how many more scenes and roles there would be to play on a daily basis and how much farther the front stage would extend into the backstage until the show never seemed to end. 14

In effect, the demands of daily performance at work, at school, at social engagements, even at home, would become so onerous that one could no longer be compared to a classical actor digging into his kit bag to find a character the way a 15

Laurence Olivier had. Rather, Americans were on stage so often that they were forced to become Method actors mastering the art of playing themselves by, as Elizabeth Taylor once described the technique, "making their fiction reality." Daily life had become a show. "A whole day of life is like a whole day of television," Andy Warhol observed, anticipating *The Truman Show*. "TV never goes off the air once it starts for the day, and I don't either. At the end of the day the whole day will be a movie."

But if one lived a movie, as Warhol said, it wasn't just the day that qualified as a   16
performance; it was the entire life. It was *life* now that had a beginning, a middle and an end like conventional movies. It was *life* now that was increasingly being plotted to let the "actor" live out his or her fantasies, albeit within the restraints of physical appearance, financial resources, talent, cooperation and a myriad of other impediments. One now chose a genre to which one aspired and then eased into the role. If you wanted to be a young professional or a Bohemian artist or a man of leisure or an outdoorsman, you conformed your life to the conventions of each. You dressed the way they dressed, acted the way they acted, associated with the kinds of people with whom they associated.

Though in practice this was all somewhat amorphous, what really seemed to il-   17
lustrate how rapidly personal life was advancing toward theater was the advent of a new profession: self-styled "life coaches," reportedly 1,500 of them as of last year, who advise clients on how to reorient their lives to reach what one coach calls fulfillment but what someone else might call a happy ending. What the coaches do, along with routine ego boosting, is replot the client's life. They tell him how he should organize his time, how he should deal with business matters, whether or not he should host a party or take a trip. "It's like painting a canvas for a 'life assignment,'" said one coach.

Few people are as overtly self-conscious about their life movies as these clients,   18
but a good many Americans are still embarked on a campaign to live out their life vision as it has been shaped by mass culture. "At one point in cultural history we asked whether movies furnished an adequate likeness of real life," the psychologist Kenneth Gergen once observed. "The good movies were the more realistic. Now we ask of reality that it accommodate itself to film. The good person, like the good party, should be more 'movieistic.'" Or to put it another way, where we had once measured the movies by life, we are learning to measure life itself by how well it satisfies the narrative expectations created by the movies.

In doing so, we have been changing not only the contours of our lives but the very   19
justification for our existence. Traditionally, realizing one's dreams was only one part of the life experience. It was understood that a full life necessarily entailed both our failures and our triumphs, our agonies and our ecstasies. This was why Aldous Huxley's brave new world seemed so terrifying even though its inhabitants were in a perpetual state of bliss. In Huxley's view, they had sacrificed their humanness to their happiness.

Clearly we have not yet arrived at the point where we can shape our lives to   20
our specifications as writers shape movies, but we are probably closer to living in

Pleasantville, . . . the title of the . . . film about a 1950's television universe of un-ruffled joy, than any previous generation. In the movie, the town of Pleasantville is disturbed by the arrival of "real" humans who bring with them a pungent taste of "real" life. In our own Pleasantville, though, the issue is not how much more excit-ing reality is than our movie and television glosses; it is how little reality seems to count when life itself is a gloss. After all, when life is a movie, who needs reality?

Huxley notwithstanding, that may just turn out to be the central question of the   21 next millennium.

THE DOWNSIDE OF THE UPSIDE OF THE DOWNSIDE
Louis Menand

Kozmo.com is the company that takes orders for movies, magazines and several   1 kinds of saturated fat over the Internet and then delivers the stuff to your house in less than an hour. You've probably seen the television commercials. Kozmo.com currently has operations in four cities; the average order is $10. Venture capital-ists have put $28 million into the business, and the company is planning to go pub-lic and raise possibly hundreds of millions more. It is unclear when, or even how, it will make a profit.

This is not, it turns out, a major concern. "The bottom line for me," one of the   2 company's founders told a reporter from *Vanity Fair,* "is I fail, like, let's say, six months after I launch the company. I just absolutely fail. So what's going to happen? I'm go-ing to apply to business school and have an incredible application." Failure is, like, part of the business plan.

This is evidently an Internet industry mantra. "Failure," a partner in one of the   3 venture-capital firms that pumps money into start-ups like Kozmo.com said recently on CNN's *Moneyline,* "is a badge of success on a lot of résumés today. It means you have experienced the downside." He may have been understating the upside. The founder of Amazon.com, the online retailer that has never made a dollar and is estimated to have lost 350 million of them in 1999, was named *Time* magazine's Person of the Year. . . .

Failure is plainly a many-sided concept. Like a lot of other things in America, its   4 cultural valence is partly a function of its size. Americans generally don't mind fail-ure so long as it's spectacular. If your Honda Civic is repossessed, you are a dead-beat; if you blow $28 million, you have bought a ticket to the big time. You are, after all, a person who managed to get his or her hands on $28 million (whereas get-ting one's hands on a Civic is widely thought to be no big trick). And it shows a decent respect for scale. If you are going to fall, try at least to fall off a mountain.

In this context, a low third-grade reading score does not qualify as a major résumé   5 builder. On the other hand, what is the motivational value of test scores and grades in a society where failure is defined as "a badge of success"? There has always been, in America, a disjunction between the culture of the school, where failure is a stigma, and the culture of the marketplace, where it is frequently regarded as a necessary consequence of risk-taking, a sign that you have the entrepreneurial right stuff. Status in the business world is even understood to be somehow incompatible with achievement in the academic world.

Still, as it is in the world of Jeff Bezos, so it is, to some degree, in the land of Rudy   6 Crew. Students are often excellent rationalizers of failure. One of the continually surprising things about teaching is how often, if the class is reasonably large, the very low grades balance out the very high ones, no matter what methods of evaluation you use, and even if you are not grading "on a curve." There is no doubt a statistical explanation, but experience suggests that there are less impersonal factors at work.

For students are not passive participants in the process of evaluation. Grading   7 is a two-way street—a fact that tends to be a little underappreciated in the rhetoric and philosophy of education. There are, of course, students who wish to fail no matter what, on the theory that academic success is a mark of uncoolness. There is nothing very complicated about these students. They will grow up to be failures.

But many students simply prioritize. Given limited amounts of time and apti-   8 tude, they distribute their expectations accordingly. They have made a calculation of what it takes to pass, and whether a mere pass is good enough or something superior is required. If the something superior is, say, a B, and they receive an A on the first assignment, they will be likely to hand in C work for the next. The teacher may be frustrated, since an effort to reward seems to be having an effect opposite from the one intended; but it is just a case of the student's academic budget being met. The teacher judges the value of the student, but the student has already judged the value of the class.

There appears to be no rationale, it's true, for outright failure. But (except in   9 courses where a curve requires it) there are probably not that many earned F's. The stigma for an earned F lies with the teacher (one reason some New York City schoolteachers were apparently caught changing the answers on their students' reading tests). Most F's are probably a result of a calculated bailing out. For an F is, in some respects, more desirable than a C. An F says you didn't care enough to do the work. A C suggests that you might actually be kind of dumb. There is also, in the culture of the school, a pervasive and basically destructive presumption that if you can't ace it, it isn't worth trying very hard.

This logic that prefers an F to any grade except an A plus is the logic behind an   10 enterprise like Kozmo.com. Its founders will be happy if they become billionaires; they will be happy (less happy, maybe, but still happy) if they are failures. What will not make them happy, it seems, is if they turn out to have created a respectable business that satisfies its customers, pays its bills on time and returns a modest income to its owners, enough for them to meet the mortgage payments and take their spouses out to dinner once in a while. This is America! What kind of success is that?

▪ 2 ▪

Presenting Sources to Others

I hate quotations. Tell me what you know.

Ralph Waldo Emerson (1849)

By necessity, by proclivity, and by delight, we all quote.

Ralph Waldo Emerson (1876)

Like Emerson in 1849, most writers hope to rely entirely on what they know and to express their knowledge in their own words. But, as Emerson realized later, one rarely writes about ideas that no one has ever explored. Someone has usually gone part of the way before, so it makes sense to build on that person's discoveries.

Because most of your writing in college will be based directly or indirectly on what you have read, you will need a working knowledge of two more methods of presenting other people's ideas to your readers: *quotation* and *paraphrase*.

REASONS FOR QUOTING

In academic writing, presenting the words of another writer through quotation is the most basic way to support your own ideas. Writers who know how to quote understand the need to give credit to their sources for both borrowed ideas and borrowed words.

- *Correct quotation* tells your reader that you respect your sources, that you know how to distinguish between your own work and theirs, and that you will not *plagiarize*—make unacknowledged use of another writer's words and ideas.

- *Appropriate quotation* tells your reader that you know when to quote and that you are not allowing your sources' words to dominate your writing.

Experienced writers hold quotation marks in reserve for those times when they think it essential to present the source's exact words.

Reasons to Use Quotation

1. For support
2. To preserve vivid or technical language
3. To comment on the quotation
4. To distance yourself from the quotation

---

1. Quoting for Support

You will most often refer to another writer's work as evidence in support of one of your own points. To ensure that the evidence retains its full meaning and impact, you retain the author's original language, instead of putting the sentences in your own words. Very often, quoted material appears in an essay as an *appeal to authority*; the source being quoted is important enough or familiar enough with the subject (as in an eyewitness account) to make the original words worth quoting. For example, the only quotation in a *New York Times* article describing political and economic chaos in Bolivia presents the opinion of a government official:

> Even the Government acknowledges its shaky position. "The polity is unstable, capricious and chaotic," Adolfo Linares Arraya, Minister of Planning and Coordination, said. "The predominance of crisis situations has made the future unforeseeable."

The minister's words in themselves seem vague and glib, and therefore not especially quotable. (Indeed, they may not even be true.) But his position as representative of the government makes the minister's exact words necessary evidence for the reporter's presentation of the Bolivian crisis.

2. Quoting Vivid or Technical Language

The wording of the source material may be so ingenious that the point will be lost if you express it in your own words. *You will want to quote a sentence that is very compact or that relies on a striking image to make its point.* For example, here is a paragraph from a review of a book about Vietnamese history:

> Not many nations have had such a history of scrapping: against Mongols and Chinese seeking to dominate them from the north, and to the south against weaker and more innocent peoples who stood in the way of the Vietnamese march to the rich Mekong Delta and the underpopulated land of Cambodia. Mr. Hodgkin [the

author] quotes from a poem by a medieval Vietnamese hero: "By its tradition of defending the country / the army is so powerful it can swallow the evening star."

The quotation adds authentic evidence to the reviewer's discussion and provides a memorable image for the reader.

It is also important to retain the precise terminology of a *technical or legal document*. Changing one word of the text can significantly change its meaning. Here is a sentence from the final paragraph of a Supreme Court decision upholding the civil rights of three tenth-graders who had been suspended by school officials for "spiking" the punch at a meeting of an extracurricular club:

> We hold that a school board member is not immune from liability for damages if he knew or reasonably should have known that the action he took within his sphere of official responsibility would violate the constitutional rights of the student affected, or if he took the action with the malicious intention to cause a deprivation of constitutional rights or other injury to the student.

Virtually every word of the sentence has potential impact on the way this decision will be interpreted in subsequent legal suits. Note, for example, the distinction between "knew" and "reasonably should have known" and the way in which "intention" is qualified by "malicious."

3. Quoting Another Writer to Comment on the Quotation

In your essay, you may want to analyze or comment on a statement made by another writer. Your readers should have that writer's exact words in front of them if they are to get the full benefit of your commentary; *you have to quote it in order to talk about it.* Thus, when a writer reviewing Philip Norman's biography of the Beatles wants to criticize the biographer's style, he must supply a sample quotation so that his readers can make up their own minds.

> Worst of all is the overwritten prologue, about John Lennon's death and its impact in Liverpool: "The ruined imperial city, its abandoned river, its tormented suburban plain, knew an anguish greater than the recession and unemployment which have laid Merseyside waste under bombardments more deadly than Hitler's blitz." A moment's thought should have made Norman and his publishers realize that this sort of thing, dashed off in the heat of the moment, would quickly come to seem very embarrassing indeed.

4. Gaining Distance through Quotation

Writers generally use quotation to distinguish between the writer of the essay and the writer being cited in the essay. Sometimes, however, you want to distance yourself from your own choice of language. For example, you may use quotation marks to indicate that a word or phrase is not in common or standard use. A phrase may be *obsolete*, no longer in current usage:

Many "flower children" gathered at the rock festivals of the late 1960s.

Or a phrase may be *slang,* not yet having been absorbed into standard English:

She tried to "cop out" of doing her share of the work.

In effect, you want to use the phrase and at the same time "cover" yourself by signaling your awareness that the phrase is not quite right: you are distancing yourself from your own vocabulary. It is usually better to take full responsibility for your choice of words and to avoid using slang or obsolete vocabulary, with or without quotation marks. But if the context requires such phrasing, you may use quotation marks to gain the necessary distance.

You can achieve a different kind of distance when you use quotation marks to suggest *irony:*

The actor was joined by his "constant companion."

The quoted phrase is a familiar *euphemism,* a bland expression substituted for a more blunt term. Again, by placing it in quotation marks, the author is both calling attention to and distancing him- or herself from the euphemism.

Quotation marks also serve as a means of *disassociation* for journalists who wish to avoid taking sides on an issue or making editorial comments.

A fire that roared through a 120-year-old hotel and took at least 11 lives was the work of a "sick arsonist," the county coroner said today. Robert Jennings, the Wayne County coroner, said that he had told county officials that the building was a "fire trap."

The author of this article did not want the responsibility of attributing the fire to a "sick arsonist" or labeling the building a "fire trap"—at any rate, not until the findings of an investigation or a trial make the terminology unquestionably true. Thus, he is careful not only to use quotation marks around certain phrases, but also to cite the precise source of the statement.

USING QUOTATIONS

Quoting requires two actions:

1. By *inserting quotation marks,* you indicate that you are borrowing certain words, as well as certain ideas, that appear in your writing.

2. By *inserting a citation* containing the source's name, you give credit for both ideas and words to the author.

Citation   *Quotation*

Theodore Roosevelt said,   "Speak softly and carry a big stick;
                                               you will go far."

Direct Quotation: Separating Quotations from Your Own Writing

The simplest way to quote is to combine the citation (written by you) with the words you are quoting (exactly as they were said or written by your source). This method of quotation joins together two separate statements, with punctuation—comma or colon—bridging the gap and a capital letter beginning the quoted phrase.

St. Paul declared, "It is better to marry than to burn."

In his first epistle to the Corinthians, St. Paul commented on lust: "It is better to marry than to burn."

In both these forms of direct quotation, the quoted words are not fully integrated into the grammatical structure of your sentence. The *comma or colon* and the *capital letter* at the beginning of the quoted sentence separate the two parts, making it clear that two voices appear in the sentence: yours and your source's. In general, you should choose this kind of direct quotation when you want to differentiate between yourself and the quoted words. There are many reasons for wanting to emphasize this difference; an obvious example would be your own disagreement with the quotation.

The *colon* is used less frequently than the comma. It usually follows a clause that can stand alone as a complete sentence. As such, the colon separates a complete idea of your own from a complementary or supporting idea taken from your source.

Direct Quotation: Integrating Quotations into Your Sentences

In an alternative kind of direct quotation, *only the quotation marks indicate that you are using someone else's words.*

St. Paul declared that "it is better to marry than to burn."

Alvin Toffler defined future shock as "the shattering stress and disorientation that we induce in individuals by subjecting them to too much change in too short a time."

There is no signal for the reader that separates citation from quotation—no comma or colon, no capital letter. The first word of the quoted material, in this second type of direct quotation, is *not* capitalized, even if it was capitalized in the source.

Original

Beware of all enterprises that require new clothes.

HENRY DAVID THOREAU

Quotation

Thoreau warned his readers to "beware of all enterprises that require new clothes."

The effect is very smooth, and the reader's attention is not distracted from the flow of sentences.

The Two Kinds of Direct Quotation

Separated	*Integrated*
■ Comma or colon and quotation marks separate citation and quotation.	■ No punctuation (but quotation marks) separates citation and quotation.
■ The first letter of the quotation is capitalized.	■ The first letter of the quotation is not capitalized.
■ You are distinguishing between your ideas and those of your source.	■ You are integrating your ideas with those of your source.

Because integrating the quotation tends to blur the distinction between writer and source, you must be careful to avoid confusion. Look, for example, at the various ways of quoting this first-person sentence, which was originally spoken by a motorist: "I hate all pedestrians."

Separated Quotation

The motorist said, "I hate all pedestrians."

Integrated Quotation

The motorist said that "I hate all pedestrians."

The first method, quoting with separation by punctuation, requires no alteration in the original sentence. But in the second version, quoting with integration, the original wording does not quite fit.

- The first-person "I" conflicts with the third-person "motorist" (the reader may wonder who "I" is—the motorist or the writer!).
- The present-tense "hate" conflicts with the past-tense "said," so "hate" must be turned into "hated."

But once the person [I] and the tense [hate] of the original statement have been altered for clarity and consistency, only two words—"I all pedestrians"—are actually being quoted:

Direct Quotation

The motorist said that she hated "all pedestrians."

You may even prefer not to put quotations around the remaining two words taken from the original source. If so, you are not quoting anything directly; you are using *indirect quotation*. In indirect quotation, you report rather than quote what has been said.

Indirect Quotation

The motorist said that she hated all pedestrians.

However, the absence of quotation marks in the indirect quotation could be confusing. If you were collecting evidence for a legal suit, quotation marks would indicate that the motorist was responsible for the precise wording. Therefore, direct quotation, separated by punctuation, is probably the most appropriate method of presenting the motorist's opinion of pedestrians.

As a rule, the writer has the obligation to insert quotation marks when using a source's exact words, whether written or oral.

Direct Quotation

Robert Ingersoll condemned those who deny others their civil liberties: "I am the inferior of any man whose rights I trample underfoot."

Indirect Quotation

Robert Ingersoll proclaimed that he was the inferior of any man whose rights he trampled underfoot.

The indirect quotation does not indicate exactly who wrote this sentence. Even if you changed "I" to "he" and the present to the past tense, you are still not using your own words; the basic phrasing of the sentence remains Ingersoll's. *To imply, as this indirect quotation could, that the wording is yours, not Ingersoll's, would be plagiarism.*

For this reason, writers should use indirect quotation with great care. If one of the two forms of direct quotation does not seem appropriate, you should invent your own wording—called *paraphrase*—to express the source's original statement.

The Historical Present Tense

Certain ideas and statements remain true long after their creators have died. By convention, or general agreement, writers often refer to these statements in the present tense.

Shakespeare states, "This above all: to thine own self be true."

When you are devoting part of your own essay to a "discussion" with another writer, you may prefer to conduct the discussion on a common ground of time and use the present tense, called the *historical present*. The historical present is also useful to place a variety of different sources on equal terms, especially when they are from different eras. In the following example, the introductory verbs, all in the present tense, are underlined:

While Shelley acknowledges that poets are creators of language and music and art, he also asserts that they have a civic role: "They are the institutors of laws, and the founders of civil society, and the inventors of the arts of life." Writing one hundred years later, Benedetto Croce affirms Shelley's insistence upon the social and spiritual responsibilities of the poet. According to Croce, Shelley sees poetry "as the eternal source of all intellectual, moral, and civil vitality."

Finally, the historical present is almost always used when you refer to important documents (often written by a group of people, rather than a single author) that remain in force long after they were created. Obvious examples include the Constitution, the Declaration of Independence, the laws of Congress, Supreme Court decisions, the charter of your state government, and the bylaws governing your college or university.

The Constitution guarantees that women—and, indeed, all citizens—shall have the vote in elections; Amendment XIX states that the right to vote "shall not be denied or abridged by the United States or by any State on account of sex."

Punctuating Direct Quotations

You have already learned about punctuating *the beginning of the quotation:*

1. In a separated direct quotation, the citation is followed by a comma or a colon.

2. In an integrated direct quotation, the citation is followed by no punctuation at all.

Some writers tend to forget this second point and include an unnecessary comma:

Incorrect Quotation

Ernest Hemingway believed that, "what is moral is what you feel good after and
what is immoral is what you feel bad after."

Remember that *an integrated quotation should have no barriers between citation and
quotation:*

Correct Quotation

Ernest Hemingway believed that "what is moral is what you feel good after and
what is immoral is what you feel bad after."

In the integrated direct quotation, note that the first letter of the quotation is not
capitalized.

There is no easy way of remembering the proper sequence of punctuation for
closing a quotation. The procedure has been determined by conventional and arbitrary agreement, originally for the convenience of printers. Although other
countries abide by different conventions, in the United States the following
rules apply—and *there are no exceptions.*

1. *All periods and commas are placed inside the terminal quotation marks.*

It does not matter whether the period belongs to your sentence or to the
quoted sentence: it goes *inside* the marks. This is the most important rule and
the one most often ignored. Don't resort to ambiguous devices such as placing
the quotes directly over the period (".).

P. T. Barnum is reputed to have said that "there's a sucker born every minute."

P. T. Barnum is reputed to have said that "there's a sucker born every minute,"
and Barnum's circuses undertook to entertain each and every one.

Notice that, in the second example, the comma at the end of the quotation
really belongs to the framework sentence, not to the quotation itself; nevertheless, it goes *inside* the marks.

2. *All semicolons, colons, and dashes are placed outside the terminal quotation marks.*

They should be regarded as the punctuation for *your* sentence, and not for the
quotation.

George Santayana wrote that "those who cannot remember the past are
condemned to repeat it"; today, we are in danger of forgetting the lessons of
history.

Occasionally, when a semicolon, colon, or (most likely) a dash appears at the end of the material to be quoted, you will decide to include the punctuation in the quotation; in that case, the punctuation should be placed inside the marks. In the following example, the dash appears in Lucretia Mott's original statement, so it is placed inside the quotation marks.

Lucretia Mott argued urgently for women's rights: "Let woman then go on—not asking favors, but claiming as a right the removal of all hindrances to her elevation in the scale of being—" so that, as a result, she might "enter profitably into the active business of man."

3. *Question marks and exclamation points are sometimes placed inside the quotation marks and sometimes placed outside.*

- If the quotation is itself a question or an exclamation, the mark or point goes *inside* the quotation marks.
- If your own sentence is a question or an exclamation, the mark or point goes *outside* a quotation placed at the very end of your sentence.

In 1864, General Sherman signaled the arrival of his reinforcements: "Hold the fort! I am coming!"

The exclamation is General Sherman's; the exclamation point goes inside the quotation.

Can anyone in the 1980s agree with Dumas that "woman inspires us to great things and prevents us from achieving them"?

Dumas was *not* asking a question; the question mark goes at the very end of the sentence, after the quotation marks.

Sigmund Freud's writings occasionally reveal a remarkable lack of insight: "The great question that has never been answered, and which I have not yet been able to answer despite my thirty years of research into the feminine soul, is: What does a woman want?"

Freud himself asked this famous question; the question mark goes inside the quotation.

Freud was demonstrating remarkably little insight when he wrote, "What does a woman want?" citing his "thirty years of research into the feminine soul"!

The exclamation is the writer's, not Freud's; the exclamation point goes outside the quotation marks.

It is possible to construct a sentence that ends logically in two question marks (or exclamation points): one for the quotation and one for your own sentence. In such cases, you need include only one—and, by convention, it should be placed *inside* the quotation marks:

> What did Freud mean when he asked, "What does a woman want?"

These rules apply only to the quotation of complete sentences or reasonably long phrases. Whether it is a quotation or an obsolete, slang, or ironic reference, a single word or a brief phrase should be fully integrated into your sentence, without being preceded or followed by commas.

> Winston Churchill's reference to "blood, sweat and tears" rallied the English to prepare for war.

Be careful not to quote words or phrases excessively. Even though the quotation marks make it clear that you are borrowing the words, using more than one quotation, however brief, in a sentence or quoting sentence after sentence creates the impression that you cannot express your thoughts in your own words.

Interrupting Quotations

Sometimes it is desirable to break up a long quotation or to vary the way you quote your sources by interrupting a quotation and placing the citation in the middle.

> "I do not mind lying," wrote Samuel Butler, "but I hate inaccuracy."

Butler's statement is divided into two separate parts, and therefore you need to use *four* sets of quotation marks: two introductory and two terminal. The citation is joined to the quotation by a comma on either side. There are two danger points:

- If you forget to use the marks at the beginning of the second half of the quotation, you are failing to distinguish your words from Butler's.
- You must also put the first comma *inside* the terminal quotation marks (because terminal commas *always* go inside the quotation marks) and put the comma that concludes the citation *before* the quotation marks (because it is *your* comma, not Butler's).

Quoting inside a Quotation

Sometimes a statement that you want to quote already contains a quotation. In that case, you must use two sets of quotation marks, double and single, to help your reader to distinguish between the two separate sources.

- *Single quotation* marks are used for the words already quoted by your source (and this is the *only* time when it is appropriate to use single quotation marks).
- *Double quotation* marks are used around the words that you are quoting.

Goethe at times expressed a notable lack of self-confidence: "'Know thyself?' If I knew myself, I'd run away."

At the beginning of World War I, Winston Churchill observed that "the maxim of the British people is 'Business as usual.'"

The same single/double procedure is used even when there is no author's name to be cited.

A Yiddish proverb states that "'for example' is not proof."

Very occasionally, you may need to use triple quotation marks, usually to quote a source who is quoting another source who is using a quoted word or phrase. An article about the author Muriel Spark included the following statement by that novelist:

I draw the line at "forever."

Victoria Glendinning, the author of the article, quoted Spark's statement using single and double quotation marks.

Eternally inquiring and curious about places and people, "I draw the line at 'forever.'"

To quote that sentence in your essay, you would need to distinguish yourself from Victoria Glendinning and Muriel Spark.

In her recent profile, Victoria Glendinning emphasizes Muriel Spark's search for variety: "Eternally inquiring and curious about places and people, 'I draw the line at "forever."'"

Notice that you would deliberately plan the quotation marks so that the double marks are used for the framework quotation.

EXERCISE 6: QUOTING CORRECTLY

A. Correct the errors in the following sentences:

1. Accounting for his winning the Indianapolis 500, Bill Vucovich explained that, "There's no secret. He continued, "you just press the accelerator to the floor and steer left."

2. Do you agree with Cornelia Otis Skinner that: "Woman's virtue is man's greatest invention?"

3. Three may keep a secret" Benjamin Franklin cynically remarked, "if two of them are dead".

4. Thoreau warned his readers to, "Beware of all enterprises that require new clothes.

5. Robert F. Wagner, former mayor of New York, believed in keeping a low profile and offered this advice—"When in danger, ponder; when in trouble, delegate" when in doubt, mumble"

6. Margaret Thatcher, the first female prime minister of Great Britain, had a poor opinion of both sexes—"in the sex-war, thoughtlessness is the weapon of the male, vindictiveness of the female."

7. Have you anything to declare," said the customs official? No, replied Oscar Wilde. "I have nothing to declare', he paused, 'except my genius."

8. Before the Revolutionary War, Patrick Henry made a passionate speech, "is life so dear or peace so sweet, as to be purchased at the price of chains and slavery"? "Forbid it, Almighty God"! I know not what course others may take, but as for me, give me liberty or give me death."!

B. Use quotations from the following group as directed:

- Choose one quotation and write a sentence that introduces a direct quotation with separation.

- Choose a second quotation and write a sentence that introduces a direct quotation with integration.

- Choose a third quotation and write a sentence that interrupts a quotation with a citation in the middle.

  1. War is too important to be left to the generals. (Georges Clemenceau)

  2. Food is an important part of a balanced diet. (Fran Lebowitz)

  3. The optimist proclaims we live in the best of all possible worlds; and the pessimist fears this is true. (James Cabell)

  4. The reason so many people showed up at his funeral was because they wanted to make sure he was dead. (Samuel Goldwyn on L. B. Mayer)

  5. Conscience is the inner voice that warns us somebody may be looking. (Benjamin Franklin)

  6. Whoever named it necking was a poor judge of anatomy. (attributed to Groucho Marx)

  7. I have now come to the conclusion never again to think of marrying, and for this reason: I can never be satisfied with anyone who would be blockhead enough to have me. (Abraham Lincoln)

  8. An expert is one who knows more and more about less and less. (Nicholas Murray Butler)

QUOTING ACCURATELY

Quoting is not a collaboration in which you try to improve on your source's writing. If you value a writer's words enough to want to quote them, you should respect the integrity of the sentence. Don't make minor changes or carelessly leave words out, but faithfully transcribe the exact words, the exact spelling, and the exact punctuation that you find in the original.

Original

Those who corrupt the public mind are just as evil as those who steal from the public purse.

ADLAI STEVENSON

Inexact Quotation

Adlai Stevenson believed that "those who act against the public interest are just as evil as those who steal from the public purse."

Exact Quotation

Adlai Stevenson believed that "those who corrupt the public mind are just as evil as those who steal from the public purse."

Even if you notice an error (or what you regard as an error), you still must copy the original wording. For example, old-fashioned spelling should be retained, as well as regional or national dialect and spelling conventions:

One of Heywood's <u>Proverbes</u> tells us that "a new brome swepeth clean."

In one of his humorous stories, Colonel Davy Crockett predicted the reactions to his own death: "It war a great loss to the country and the world, and to ole Kaintuck in particklar. Thar were never known such a member of Congress as Crockett, and never will be agin. The painters and bears will miss him, for he never missed them."

You do not have to assume the blame if the material that you are quoting contains errors of syntax, punctuation, or spelling. You can use a conventional way to point out such errors and inform the reader that the mistake was made, not by you, but by the author whom you are quoting. The Latin word *sic* (meaning "thus") is placed in square brackets and inserted immediately after the error. The [sic] signals that the quotation was "thus" and that you, the writer, were aware of the error, which was not the result of your own carelessness in transcribing the quotation.

In the following example, [sic] calls attention to an error in subject-verb agreement:

Richard Farson points out that "increased understanding and concern has [sic] not been coupled with increased rights."

You may also want to use [sic] to indicate that the source used archaic spelling:

> In describing Elizabeth Billington, an early nineteenth-century singer, W. Clark Russell observed that "her voice was powerful, and resembled the tone of a clarionet [sic]."

It would be tedious, however, to use [sic] to indicate each misspelling in the Davy Crockett quotation; in your essay about Crockett, you could, instead, explain his use of dialect as you discuss his life and writing.

TAILORING QUOTATIONS TO FIT YOUR WRITING

There are several ways to change quotations to fit the quoted material naturally into your own sentences. Like [sic], these devices are conventions, established by generally accepted agreement: *you cannot improvise; you must follow these rules.* Usually, the conventional rules require you to inform your reader that a change is being made; in other words, they make clear the distinction between your wording and the author's.

Changing Capital and Small Letters

The first way of altering quotations depends entirely on how and where the quotation fits into your sentence.

- When a quotation is *integrated* completely into your sentence (usually when your citation ends in "that"), the first letter of the quotation will be small, whether or not it is a capital in the original. (Two exceptions are the pronoun "I" and proper nouns, which are always capitalized.)
- When a quotation is *separated* from your sentence, and your citation ends in a comma or a colon, the first letter of the quotation will be a capital, whether or not it is a capital in the original.

Integrated Quotation

The poet Frost wrote that "good fences make good neighbors."

Separated Quotation

The poet Frost wrote, "Good fences make good neighbors."

As a rule, it is not necessary to indicate to your readers that you have altered the first letter of your quotation from small to capital or from capital to small.

Using Ellipses to Delete Words

It is permissible to delete words from a quotation, provided that you indicate to the reader that something has been omitted. Your condensed version is as accurate as the original; it is just shorter. But you must remember to insert the conventional symbol for deletion, *three spaced dots,* called an *ellipsis.* Once made aware by the three dots that your version omits part of the original, any reader who wants to see the omitted portion can consult the original source.

Original

It is not true that suffering ennobles the character; happiness does that sometimes, but suffering, for the most part, makes men petty and vindictive.

W. SOMERSET MAUGHAM

Quotation with Ellipsis

Maugham does not believe that "suffering ennobles the character; . . . suffering, for the most part, makes men petty and vindictive."

Notice that:

- The three dots are spaced equally.
- The dots *must* be three—not two or a dozen.
- The semicolon is retained, to provide terminal punctuation for the first part of the quotation.

If you wish to delete the end of a quotation, and the ellipsis coincides with the end of your sentence, you must use the three dots, plus a fourth to signify the sentence's end.

Quotation with Terminal Ellipsis

Maugham does not believe that "suffering ennobles the character; happiness does that sometimes. . . ."

Here, you'll note:

- There are four dots, three to indicate a deletion and a fourth to indicate the period at the end of the sentence.
- The first dot is placed immediately after the last letter.
- The sentence ends with quotation marks, as usual, with the marks placed *after* the dots, not before.

For most systems of documentation, ellipsis as described above remains the appropriate way to indicate omissions from quotations. But there is now one notable exception: MLA style. Since the documentation endorsed by the Modern Language Association is the one most commonly used for preparing general research essays, you should become familiar with this variation on standard ellipsis.

If you are using MLA style, you omit words from a quotation by (1) substituting three spaced dots (as demonstrated above) and (2) surrounding the dots with brackets. Here is the same quotation from Maugham using dots and brackets:

Quotation with Ellipsis/Brackets (MLA)

Maugham does not believe that "suffering ennobles the character; [. . .] suffering, for the most part, makes men petty and vindictive."

In MLA ellipsis, the placement and spacing of the dots remain the same; the only difference is the insertion of the brackets. There is a space *before* the opening bracket and a space *after* the closing bracket. Notice that there is *no space* between the brackets and the dots, but that there are the usual spaces *between* the dots.

Here's what MLA ellipsis looks like at the *end* of a quotation:

Quotation with Terminal Ellipsis (MLA)

Maugham does not believe that "suffering ennobles the character; happiness does that sometimes [. . .] ."

MLA made this change to avoid confusion. Three spaced dots could signify that *the author* whom you're quoting had deleted some material; the same three spaced dots could also indicate that *you* have chosen to delete some material. There's no way for a reader to tell who inserted the ellipsis.

Moreover, if your source material already includes an ellipsis *and* if you then decide to use a second ellipsis to delete some words, your sentence will contain *two* sets of spaced dots. But your reader—confronted with two different sets of dots in one sentence—can't know for sure who's responsible for which omission. With MLA ellipsis, three spaced dots will always signify the *original source's* omission; three spaced dots with brackets will always signify *your* omission.

Whether or not you're using MLA style, three dots can also link two separate quotations from the same paragraph in your source; the ellipsis will indicate the deletion of one or more sentences, but only if the two sentences that you are quoting are fairly near each other in the original. *An ellipsis cannot cover a gap of more than a few sentences.* When you use an ellipsis to bridge one or more sentences, use only *one* set of quotation marks. Your full quotation, with an ellipsis in the middle, is still continuous—a single quotation—even though there is a gap.

When an ellipsis is used following a quoted complete sentence, the period of the quoted sentence is retained so that a total of four dots is used, as in the following example.

Original

In one sense there is no death. The life of a soul on earth lasts beyond his departure. You will always feel that life touching yours, that voice speaking to you, that spirit looking out of other eyes, talking to you in the familiar things he touched, worked with, loved as familiar friends. He lives on in your life and in the lives of all others that knew him.

ANGELO PATRI

Quotation with Ellipsis

Patri states that "in one sense there is no death. The life of a soul on earth lasts beyond his departure. . . . He lives on in your life and in the lives of all others that knew him."

Quotation with Ellipsis (MLA)

Patri states that "in one sense there is no death. The life of a soul on earth lasts beyond his departure. [. . .] He lives on in your life and in the lives of all others that knew him."

An ellipsis should be used to make a quotation fit more smoothly into your own sentence. It is especially convenient when you are working with a long passage that contains several separate points that you wish to quote. But ellipses should *not* be used to condense long, tedious quotations or to replace summary and paraphrase. If you only want to quote a brief extract from a lengthy passage, then simply quote that portion and ignore the surrounding material. An ellipsis is poorly used when it is used too often.

The meaning of the original quotation must always be exactly preserved, despite the deletion represented by the ellipsis.

Original

As long as there are sovereign nations possessing great power, war is inevitable.

ALBERT EINSTEIN

Inexact Quotation

Einstein believes that ". . . war is inevitable."

It would not be accurate to suggest that Einstein believed in the inevitability of war, under all circumstances, without qualifications. To extract only a portion of this statement with ellipsis is to oversimplify and thus to falsify the evidence.

Using Brackets to Insert Words

Brackets have an opposite function: ellipsis signifies deletion; *brackets signify addition or alteration.* Brackets are not the same as parentheses. Parentheses would be confusing for this purpose, for the quotation might itself include a

> ### *Reasons to Use Brackets*
>
> - To explain a vague word
> - To replace a confusing phrase
> - To suggest an antecedent
> - To correct an error in a quotation
> - To adjust a quotation to fit your own writing

parenthetical statement, and the reader could not be sure whether the parentheses contained the author's insertion or yours. Instead, brackets, a relatively unusual form of punctuation, are used as a conventional way of informing the reader that material has been inserted. (You have already seen how to use brackets with [sic], which enables you to comment on the material that you are quoting.) You simply insert the information *inside* the quotation, placing it in square brackets.

The most common reason for using brackets is to clarify a vague word. You may, for example, choose to quote only the last portion of a passage, omitting an important antecedent:

Original

Man lives *by* habits, indeed, but what he lives *for* is thrills and excitement.

WILLIAM JAMES

Quotation with Brackets

William James argues that "what he [man] lives <u>for</u> is thrills and excitement."

William James argues that "what [man] lives <u>for</u> is thrills and excitement."

In the second example, the vague word "he" has been deleted entirely; the brackets themselves indicate that there has been a substitution, but the reader doesn't know what was originally there. For that reason, unless the presentation of both wordings seems very awkward, *it is better to follow the first example: quote the original and also provide the clarification in brackets.* This way, you will leave your reader in no doubt about your source's words.

Brackets can also be used to complete a thought that has been obscured by the omission (often through ellipsis) of an earlier sentence:

Original

A well-trained sensible family doctor is one of the most valuable assets in a community. . . . Few men live lives of more devoted self-sacrifice.

SIR WILLIAM OSLER

Quotation with Brackets

The great surgeon Sir William Osler had enormous respect for his less famous colleagues: "Few men live lives of more devoted self-sacrifice [than good family doctors]."

Here, the quotation marks are placed *after* the brackets, even though the quoted material ends after the word "self-sacrifice." The explanatory material inside the brackets is considered part of the quotation, even though it is not in the source's own words.

Your own explanatory comments in brackets should be very brief and to the point. You might, for example, want to include an important *date* or *name* as essential background information. But whatever is inside the brackets should fit smoothly into the syntax of the quotation and should not distract the reader. For example, do not use brackets to argue with the author you are quoting. The following running dialogue with the entertainer Sophie Tucker is poorly conveyed through the use of brackets.

Confusing Use of Brackets

Sophie Tucker suggests that up to the age of eighteen "a girl needs good parents. [This is true for men, too.] From eighteen to thirty-five, she needs good looks. [Good looks aren't that essential anymore.] From thirty-five to fifty-five, she needs a good personality. [I disagree because personality is important at any age.] From fifty-five on, she needs good cash."

EXERCISE 7: USING ELLIPSES AND BRACKETS IN QUOTATIONS

A. Choose one of the following quotations. By using *ellipses*, incorporate a portion of the quotation into a sentence of your own; remember to include the author's name in the citation.

B. Choose a second quotation. Incorporate a portion of the quotation into another sentence of your own; insert words in *brackets* to clarify one or more of the quoted words.

1. A teacher affects eternity; he can never tell where his influence stops. (Henry Adams)

2. I have never taken any exercise, except sleeping and resting, and I never intend to take any. Exercise is loathsome. And it cannot be any benefit when you are tired, and I am always tired. (Mark Twain)

3. Death cancels everything but truth and strips a man of everything but genius and virtue. It is a sort of natural canonization. (William Hazlitt)

4. Any law which violates the inalienable rights of man is essentially unjust and tyrannical. (Maximilien de Robespierre)

5. I hold this to be the highest task for a bond between two people: that each protects the solitude of the other. (Rainer Maria Rilke)

6. Serious sport has nothing to do with fair play. It is bound up with hatred, jealousy, boastfulness, disregard of all rules and sadistic pleasure in witnessing violence; in other words, it is war minus shooting. (George Orwell)

WRITING CITATIONS

Citing the Author's Name

The first time that you refer to a source, use the author's full name—without Mr. or Miss, Mrs., or Ms.

First Reference

John Stuart Mill writes, "The opinion which it is attempted to suppress by authority may possibly be true."

After that, should you need to cite the author again, use the *last name only.* Conventional usage discourages casual and distracting references such as "John thinks," "JSM thinks," or "Mr. Mill thinks."

Second Reference

Mill continues to point out that "all silencing of discussion is an assumption of infallibility."

When you cite the author's name:

- At first reference, you may (and usually should) include the *title* of the work from which the quotation is taken:

  In *On Liberty,* John Stuart Mill writes . . .

- If there is a long break between references to the same author, or if the names of several other authors intervene, you may wish to repeat the full name and remind your reader of the earlier citation.

  In addition to his warnings about the dangers of majority rule, which were cited earlier in the discussion of public opinion, John Stuart Mill also expresses concern about "the functions of police; how far liberty may legitimately be invaded for the prevention of crime, or of accident."

- Avoid referring to the author twice in the same citation, once by name and once by pronoun. In the following citation, we really can't be sure who "he" is:

  In John Stuart Mill's *On Liberty,* he writes . . .

- Finally, unless you genuinely do not know the author's name, use it! There is no point in being coy, even for the sake of variety:

> A famous man once made an ironic observation about child-rearing: "If you strike a child, take care that you strike it in anger. . . . A blow in cold blood neither can nor should be forgiven."

Your guessing game will only irritate readers who are not aware that this famous man was George Bernard Shaw.

Choosing the Introductory Verb

The citation provides an important link between your thoughts and those of your source. The introductory verb can tell your reader something about your reasons for presenting the quotation and its context in the work that you are quoting. Will you choose "J. S. Mill says," or "J. S. Mill writes," or "J. S. Mill thinks," or "J. S. Mill feels"? Those are the most common introductory verbs— so common that they have become boring! Whenever appropriate, select less stereotyped verbs. As the senses are not directly involved in writing, avoid "feels" entirely. And, unless you are quoting someone's spoken words, substitute a more accurate verb for "says."

Here are some introductory verbs:

argues	adds	concludes
establishes	explains	agrees
emphasizes	believes	insists
finds	continues	maintains
points out	declares	disagrees
notes	observes	states
suggests	proposes	compares

Of course, once you stop using the all-purpose "says" or "writes," you have to remember that verbs are not interchangeable and that you should choose the verb that best suits your purpose.

The citation should suggest the relationship between your own ideas (in the previous sentence) and the statement that you are about to quote.

You should examine the quotation before writing the citation to define the way in which the author makes a point:

- Is it being asserted forcefully?
  Use "argues" or "declares" or "insists."

- Is the statement being offered only as a possibility?
  Use "suggests" or "proposes" or "finds."

- Does the statement immediately follow a previous reference?
  Use "continues" or "adds."

For clarity, the introductory verb may be expanded:

X is aware that . . .
X stresses the opposite view
X provides one answer to the question
X makes the same point as Y
X erroneously assumes . . .

But make sure that the antecedent for the "view" or the "question" or the "point" can be found in the previous sentences of your essay. Finally, all the examples of introductory verbs are given in the *present tense*, which is the conventional way of introducing most quotations.

Varying Your Sentence Patterns

Even if you choose a different verb for each quotation, the combination of the author's name, introductory verb, and quotation can become repetitious and tiresome. One way to vary the citations is occasionally to place the name of the source in a less prominent position, tucked into the quotation instead of calling attention to itself at the beginning.

1. You can interrupt the quotation by placing the citation in the middle.

"I made my mistakes," acknowledged Richard Nixon, "but in all my years of public service, I have never profited from public service. I have earned every cent."

The verb and the name may be placed in reverse order (instead of "Richard Nixon acknowledged") when the citation appears in the middle of the quotation. Remember to include two commas: one at the end of the first portion of the quotation (*inside* the quotation marks), one at the end of the citation.

One citation is quite enough. There is no need to inform your reader back to back, as in this repetitive example:

"The only prize much cared for by the powerful is power," states Oliver Wendell Holmes. He concludes, "The prize of the general . . . is command."

2. You can avoid the monotonous "X says that . . ." pattern by phrasing the citation as a subordinate clause or phrase.

In Henry Kissinger's opinion, "Power is 'the great aphrodisiac.'"

As John F. Kennedy declares, "Mankind must put an end to war or war will put an end to mankind."

3. In your quest for variety, avoid placing the citation after the quotation.

The author's name at the end may weaken the statement, especially if the citation is pretentiously or awkwardly phrased:

Awkward Citation

"I am the inferior of any man whose rights I trample underfoot," as quoted from the writings of Robert Ingersoll.

Clear Citation

A champion of civil liberties, Robert Ingersoll insisted, "I am the inferior of any man whose rights I trample underfoot."

Two rules should govern your choice of citation:

1. Don't be too fancy.
2. Be both precise and varied in your phrasing.

Presenting an Extended Quotation

Occasionally, you may have reason to present an extended quotation, a single extract from the same source that runs *more than four printed or typewritten lines.* For extended quotations, you must, by conventional rule, set off the quoted passage by *indenting the entire quotation on the left.*

- Introduce an extended quotation with a colon.
- Start each line of the quotation 10 spaces from the left-hand margin; stop each line at your normal right-hand margin.
- Some instructors prefer single-spacing within extended quotations; some prefer double-spacing. If possible, consult your instructor about the style appropriate for your course or discipline. If you are given no guidelines, use double-spacing.
- Omit quotation marks at the beginning and end of the quoted passage; the indented margin (and the introductory citation) will tell your readers that you are quoting.

Here is an example of an extended quotation:

Although he worked "hard as hell" all winter, Fitzgerald had difficulty finishing The Great Gatsby. On April 10, 1924, he wrote to Maxwell Perkins, his editor at Scribner's:

> While I have every hope & plan of finishing my novel in June . . . even
> [if] it takes me 10 times that long I cannot let it go unless it has the very

best I'm capable of in it or even as I feel sometimes better than I'm capable of. It is only in the last four months that I've realized how much I've—well, almost <u>deteriorated</u>. . . . What I'm trying to say is just that . . . at last, or at least for the first time in years, I'm doing the best I can.

INTEGRATING QUOTATIONS INTO YOUR PARAGRAPHS

You have learned how to present the words of others with accuracy and appropriate acknowledgment; now, you must learn to make the quotation serve the larger purpose of your paragraph or essay. Here are some suggestions for integrating quotations into your writing.

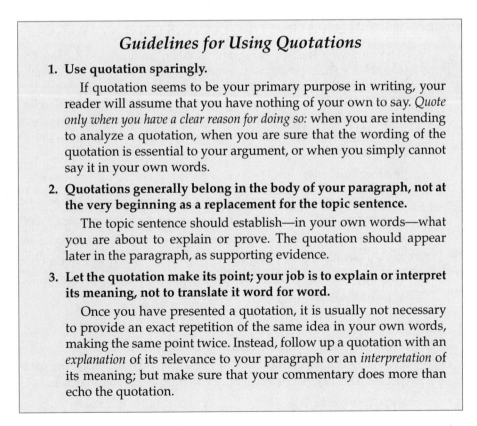

Guidelines for Using Quotations

1. **Use quotation sparingly.**

   If quotation seems to be your primary purpose in writing, your reader will assume that you have nothing of your own to say. *Quote only when you have a clear reason for doing so:* when you are intending to analyze a quotation, when you are sure that the wording of the quotation is essential to your argument, or when you simply cannot say it in your own words.

2. **Quotations generally belong in the body of your paragraph, not at the very beginning as a replacement for the topic sentence.**

   The topic sentence should establish—in your own words—what you are about to explain or prove. The quotation should appear later in the paragraph, as supporting evidence.

3. **Let the quotation make its point; your job is to explain or interpret its meaning, not to translate it word for word.**

   Once you have presented a quotation, it is usually not necessary to provide an exact repetition of the same idea in your own words, making the same point twice. Instead, follow up a quotation with an *explanation* of its relevance to your paragraph or an *interpretation* of its meaning; but make sure that your commentary does more than echo the quotation.

In the following student example, the quotation used in the development of the paragraph is no more or less important than any of the other supporting sentences. The quotation adds interest to the paragraph because of the shift in tone and the shift to a sharper, narrower focus.

Some parents insist on allowing their children to learn through experience. Once a child has actually performed a dangerous action and realized its consequences, he will always remember the circumstances and the possible ill effects. Yvonne Realle illustrates the adage that experience is the best teacher by describing a boy who was slapped just as he reached for a hot iron. The child, not realizing that he might have been burned, had no idea why he had been slapped. An observer noted that "if he had learned by experience, if he'd suffered some discomfort in the process, then he'd know enough to avoid the iron next time." In the view of parents like Yvonne Realle, letting a child experiment with his environment will result in a stronger lesson than slapping or scolding the child for trying to explore his surroundings.

EXERCISE 8: INTEGRATING QUOTATIONS INTO A PARAGRAPH

The following student paragraph is taken from an essay, "The Compulsive Gambler." The second passage comes from *The Psychology of Gambling* by Edmund Bergler.

Choose one appropriate supporting quotation from the Bergler passage, decide where to place it in the student paragraph, and insert the quotation correctly and smoothly into the paragraph. Remember to lead into the quotation by citing the source.

Student Paragraph

One obvious reason for gambling is to make money. Because some gamblers are lucky when they play, they never want to stop. Even when quite a lot of money has been lost, they go on, assuming that they can get rich through gambling. Once a fortune is made, they will feel really powerful, free of all dependency and responsibilities. Instead, in most cases, gambling becomes a daily routine. There is no freedom, no escape.

Source

Every gambler gives the impression of a man who has signed a contract with Fate, stipulating that persistence must be rewarded. With that imaginary contract in his pocket, he is beyond the reach of all logical objection and argument.

The result of this pathologic optimism is that the true gambler never stops when he is winning, for he is convinced that he must win more and more. Inevitably, he loses. He does not consider his winnings the result of chance; to him they are a down payment on that contract he has with Fate which guarantees that he will be a permanent winner. This inability to stop while fortune is still smiling is one of the strongest arguments against the earnest assumption, common to all gamblers, that one can get rich through gambling.

ASSIGNMENT 2: WRITING A PARAGRAPH THAT INCLUDES A QUOTATION

1. Choose one of the following topics. Each is a specific question that can be answered adequately in a single paragraph.

    A. Question: Should children be spanked?

    B. Question: Do teenagers benefit from single-sex high schools?

    C. Question: What is the best way to deal with sibling rivalry?

2. Ask someone you know to comment briefly on the question you have chosen, offering a suggestion or an example. Write down any part of the comment that you think might be worth quoting, transcribe the words accurately, and show the statement to your source to confirm its accuracy. Make sure that you have the name properly spelled. If the first person you ask does not provide you with a suitable quotation, try someone else.

3. Answer your own question in a single paragraph of four to eight sentences, limiting the paragraph to ideas that can be clearly developed in such a brief space. The paragraph as a whole should express *your* views, not those of your source. Choose a *single* quotation from your source and integrate it into the development of your paragraph, using proper punctuation, citation, and (if necessary) ellipses and brackets. If your source agrees with you, use the quotation as support. If your source disagrees, answer the objection in your own way. Try not to quote in the first or second sentence of your paragraph. Hand in both your paragraph and the sheet on which you originally wrote down the quotation.

AVOIDING PLAGIARISM

Quoting without quotation marks is called *plagiarism.* Even if you cite the source's name somewhere on your page, a word-for-word quotation without marks would still be considered a plagiarism.

Plagiarism is the unacknowledged use of another writer's words or ideas. The only way to acknowledge that you are using someone else's actual words is through citation and quotation marks.

Chapter 8 discusses plagiarism in detail. At this point, you should understand that:

- If you plagiarize, you will never learn to write.
- Literate people consider plagiarism to be equivalent to theft.
- Plagiarists eventually get caught!

It is easy for an experienced reader to detect plagiarism. Every writer, professional or amateur, has a characteristic style or voice that readers quickly learn to recognize. In a few paragraphs or pages, the writer's voice becomes familiar enough for the reader to notice that the style has changed and that, suddenly, there is a new, unfamiliar voice. When there are frequent acknowledged quotations, the reader simply adjusts to a series of new voices. When there are unacknowledged quotations, the absence of quotation marks and the change of voices usually suggest to an experienced reader that the work is poorly integrated and probably plagiarized. Plagiarized essays are often identified in this way.

Instructors are well aware of style and are trained to recognize inconsistencies and awkward transitions. A revealing clue is the patched-together, mosaic effect. The next exercise will improve your own perception of shifting voices and encourage you to rely on your own characteristic style as the dominant voice in everything that you write.

EXERCISE 9: IDENTIFYING PLAGIARISM

The following paragraphs contain several plagiarized sentences. Examine the language and tone of each sentence, as well as the continuity of the entire paragraph. Then underline the plagiarized sentences.

A.   The Beatles' music in the early years was just plain melodic. It had a nice beat to it. The Beatles were simple lads, writing simple songs simply to play to screaming fans on one-night stands. There was no deep, inner meaning to the lyrics. Their songs included many words like I, and me, and you. As the years went by, the Beatles' music became more poetic. Sergeant Pepper is a stupefying collage of music, words, background noises, cryptic utterances, orchestral effects, hallucinogenic bells, farmyard sounds, dream sequences, social observations, and apocalyptic vision, all masterfully blended together on a four-track tape machine over nine agonizing and expensive months. Their music was beginning to be more philosophical, with a deep, inner, more secret meaning. After it was known that they took drugs, references to drugs were seen in many songs. The "help" in Ringo's "A Little Help from My Friends" was said to have meant pot. The songs were poetic, mystical; they emerged from a self-contained world of bizarre carnival colors; they spoke in a language and a musical idiom all their own.

B.   Before the Civil War, minstrelsy spread quickly across America. Americans all over the country enjoyed minstrelsy because it reflected something of their own point of view. For instance, Negro plantation hands, played usually by white actors in blackface, were portrayed as devil-may-care outcasts and minstrelmen played them with an air of comic triumph, irreverent wisdom, and an underlying note of rebellion, which had a special appeal to citizens of a young country. Minstrelsy was ironically the beginning of black involvement in the American theater. The American people learned to identify with certain aspects of the black people. The Negro became a sympathetic symbol for a pioneer people who required resilience as a prime trait.

PARAPHRASING

Some passages are worth quoting for the sake of their precise or elegant style or their distinguished author. But many sources that you will use in your college essays are written in more ordinary language. You will gain nothing by quoting undistinguished material; rather, you have a positive duty to help your readers by providing them with a clear paraphrase.

Paraphrase is the point-by-point recapitulation of another person's ideas, expressed in your own words.

Through paraphrase, you are both informing your reader and proving that you understand what you are writing about. When you paraphrase, you retain everything about the original writing but the words.

Using Paraphrase in Your Essays

Paraphrasing helps your readers to gain a detailed understanding of sources that they may never have read and, indirectly, to accept your own thesis as valid. There are two major reasons for using paraphrase in your essays.

1. Use paraphrase to present ideas or evidence whenever there is no special reason for using a direct quotation.

Many of your sources will not have sufficient authority or a distinctive enough style to justify your quoting their words. The following illustration, taken from a *New York Times* article, paraphrases a report written by an anonymous group of "municipal auditors" whose writing merits only paraphrase, not quotation:

A city warehouse in Middle Village, Queens, stocked with such things as snow shovels, light bulbs, sponges, waxed paper, laundry soap and tinned herring, has been found to be vastly overstocked with some items and lacking in others. Municipal auditors, in a report issued yesterday, said that security was fine and that the warehouse was quicker in delivering goods to city agencies than it was when the auditors made their last check, in August, 1976. But in one corner of the warehouse, they said, nearly 59,000 paper binders, the 8½-by-11 size, are gathering dust, enough to meet the city's needs for nearly seven years. Nearby, there is a 10½-year supply of cotton coveralls.

Both the overstock and shortages cost the city money, the auditors said. They estimated that by reducing warehouse inventories, the city could save $1.4 million, plus $112,000 in interest. . . .

2. *Use paraphrase to give your readers an accurate and comprehensive account of ideas taken from a source—ideas that you intend to explain, interpret, or disagree with in your essay.*

The first illustration comes from a *Times* article about the data and photographs provided by *Voyager 2* as it explored the farthest reaches of the solar system. In summarizing a press conference, the article paraphrases various scientists' descriptions of what *Voyager* had achieved during its journey near Triton, one of the moons of the planet Neptune. Note the limited use of carefully selected quotations within the paraphrase.

Out of the fissures [on Triton], roughly analogous to faults in the Earth's crust, flowed mushy ice. There was no eruption in the sense of the usual terrestrial volcanism or the geyser-like activity discovered on Io, one of Jupiter's moons. It was more of an extrusion through cracks in the surface ice.

Although scientists classify such a process as volcanism, Dr. Miner said it could better be described as a "slow-flow volcanic activity." A somewhat comparable process, he said, seemed to have shaped some of the surface features of Ariel, one of the moons of Uranus.

Dr. Soderblom said Triton's surface appeared to be geologically young or "millions to hundreds of millions of years old." The absence of many impact craters was the main evidence for the relatively recent resurfacing of the terrain with new ice.

The next example shows how paraphrase can be used more briefly, to present another writer's point of view as the basis for discussion. Again, the writer of this description of a conference on nuclear deterrence has reserved quotation to express the precise point of potential dispute:

Scientists engaged in research on the effects of nuclear war may be "wasting their time" studying a phenomenon that is far less dangerous than the natural explosions that have periodically produced widespread extinctions of plant and animal life in the past, a University of Chicago scientist said last week. Joseph V. Smith, a professor of geophysical sciences, told a conference on nuclear deterrence here that such natural catastrophes as exploding volcanoes, violent earthquakes, and collisions with comets or asteroids could produce more immediate and destructive explosions than any nuclear war.

Using Paraphrase as Preparation for Reading and Writing Essays

Paraphrase is sometimes undertaken as an end in itself. Paraphrasing difficult passages can help you to improve your understanding of a complex essay or chapter. When you grasp an essay at first reading, when its ideas are clearly stated in familiar terms, then you can be satisfied with annotating it or writing a brief summary. But when you find an essay hard to understand, writing down each sentence in your own words forces you to stop and make sense of what you have read, so that you can succeed in working out ideas that at first seem beyond your comprehension.

Paraphrase can also be *a means to an end*, a preparation for writing an essay of your own. When you take notes for an essay based on one or more sources, you should paraphrase. Quote only when recording phrases or sentences that, in your opinion, merit quotation. All quotable phrases and sentences should be transcribed accurately in your notes, with quotation marks clearly separating the paraphrase from the quotation.

Writing a Good Paraphrase

In a good paraphrase, the sentences and the vocabulary do not duplicate those of the original. *You cannot merely substitute synonyms for key words and leave the sentences otherwise unchanged; that is plagiarism in spirit, if not in fact;* nor does word-for-word substitution really demonstrate that you have understood the ideas.

The level of abstraction within your paraphrase should resemble that of the original: it should be neither more general nor more specific. If you do not understand a sentence, do not try to guess or cover it up with a vague phrase that slides over the idea. Instead:

- Look up difficult words.
- Think of what they mean and how they are used together.
- Consider how the sentences are formed and how they fit into the context of the entire paragraph.
- Then, to test your understanding, write it all out.

Remember that a good paraphrase makes sense by itself; it is coherent and readable, without requiring reference to the original essay.

> ## *Guidelines for a Successful Paraphrase*
>
> - A paraphrase must be accurate.
> - A paraphrase must be complete.
> - A paraphrase must be written in your own voice.
> - A paraphrase must make sense by itself.

When a paraphrase moves completely away from the words and sentence structure of the original text and presents ideas in the paraphraser's own style and idiom, then it is said to be "free." A free paraphrase is not only challenging to write but can be as interesting to read as the original—provided that the substance of the source has not been altered, disguised, or substantially condensed. Because a free paraphrase can condense repetitious parts of the original text, it may be somewhat briefer than the original, but it will present ideas in much the same order.

Here, side by side with the original, is a free paraphrase of an excerpt from Machiavelli's *The Prince*. This passage exemplifies the kind of text—very famous, very difficult—that really benefits from a comprehensive paraphrase. *The Prince* was written in 1513. Even though the translation from the Italian used here was revised in this century, the paraphraser has to bridge a tremendous gap in time and in style to present Machiavelli in an idiom suitable for modern readers.

Original Version

It is not, therefore, necessary for a prince to have [good faith and integrity], but it is very necessary to seem to have them. I would even be bold to say that to possess them and always to observe them is dangerous, but to appear to possess them is useful. Thus it is well to seem merciful, faithful, humane, sincere, religious, and also to be so; but you must have the mind so disposed that when it is needful to be otherwise you may be able to change to the opposite qualities. And it must be understood that a prince, and especially a new prince, cannot observe all those things which are considered good in men, being often obliged, in order to maintain the

Paraphrase

It is more important for a ruler to give the impression of goodness than to be good. In fact, real goodness can be a liability, but the pretense is always very effective. It is all very well to be virtuous, but it is vital to be able to shift in the other direction whenever circumstances require it. After all, rulers, especially recently elevated ones, have a duty to perform which may absolutely require them to act against the dictates of faith and compassion and kindness. One must act as circumstances require and, while it's good to be virtuous if you can, it's better to be bad if you must.

In public, however, the ruler

state, to act against faith, against charity, against charity, and against humanity, and against religion. And therefore, he must have a mind disposed to adapt itself according to the wind, and as the variations of fortune dictate, and . . . not deviate from what is good, if possible, but be able to do evil if constrained.

A prince must take great care that nothing goes out of his mouth which is not full of the above-mentioned five qualities, and to see and hear him, he should seem to be all mercy, faith, integrity, humanity, and religion. . . . Everyone sees what you appear to be, few feel what you are, and those few will not dare to oppose themselves to the many, who have the majesty of the state to defend them; and in the actions of men, and especially of princes, from which there is no appeal, the end justifies the means. Let a prince therefore aim at conquering and maintaining the state, and the means will always be judged honorable and praised by every one, for the vulgar are always taken by appearances and the issue of the event; and the world consists only of the vulgar, and the few who are not vulgar are isolated when the many have a rallying point in the prince.

should appear to be entirely virtuous, and if his pretense is successful with the majority of people, then those who do see through the act will be outnumbered and impotent, especially since the ruler has the authority of government on his side. In the case of rulers, even more than for most men, "the end justifies the means." If the ruler is able to assume power and administer it successfully, his methods will always be judged proper and satisfactory; for the common people will accept the pretense of virtue and the reality of success, and the astute will find no one is listening to their warnings.

Paraphrase and Summary

To clarify the difference between paraphrase and summary, here is a paragraph that *summarizes* the excerpt from *The Prince.*

According to Machiavelli, perpetuating power is a more important goal for a ruler than achieving personal goodness or integrity. Although he should act virtuously if he can, and always appear to do so, it is more important for him to adapt quickly to changing circumstances. The masses will be so swayed by his pretended virtue and by his success that any opposition will be ineffective. The wise ruler's maxim is that "the end justifies the means."

To make the distinction between summary and paraphrase entirely clear, here is a recapitulation of the guidelines for writing a brief summary:

1. *A summary is comprehensive.* Like the paraphrase, the summary of *The Prince* says more than "the end justifies the means." While that is probably the most important idea in the passage, it does not by itself convey Machiavelli's full meaning. For one thing, it contains no reference at all to princes and how they should rule—and that, after all, is Machiavelli's subject.

2. *A summary is concise.* It should say exactly as much as you need—and no more. The summary of *The Prince* is considerably shorter than the paraphrase.

3. *A summary is coherent.* The ideas are not presented in the same sequence as that of the original passage, as they are in the paraphrase; nor are the language and tone at all reminiscent of the original. Rather, the summary includes only the passage's most important points, linking them together in a unified paragraph.

4. *A summary is independent.* What is most striking about the summary, compared with the paraphrase, is the writer's attitude toward the original text. While the paraphraser has to follow closely Machiavelli's ideas and point of view, the summarizer does not. Characteristically, Machiavelli's name is cited in the summary, calling attention to the fact that it is based on another person's ideas.

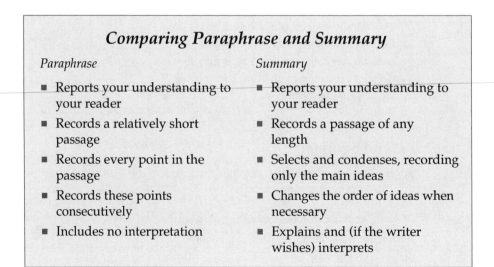

Comparing Paraphrase and Summary

Paraphrase	*Summary*
■ Reports your understanding to your reader	■ Reports your understanding to your reader
■ Records a relatively short passage	■ Records a passage of any length
■ Records every point in the passage	■ Selects and condenses, recording only the main ideas
■ Records these points consecutively	■ Changes the order of ideas when necessary
■ Includes no interpretation	■ Explains and (if the writer wishes) interprets

Either summary or paraphrase should enable you to refer to this passage quite easily in an essay. Which you would choose to use depends on your topic, on the way you are developing your essay, and on the extent to which you wish to discuss Machiavelli.

- In an essay citing Machiavelli as only one among many political theorists, you might use the brief four-sentence summary; then you might briefly comment on Machiavelli's ideas before going on to summarize (and perhaps compare them with) another writer's theories.

- In an essay about a contemporary politician, you might analyze the way in which your subject does or does not carry out Machiavelli's strategies; then you probably would want to familiarize your readers with *The Prince* in some detail through paraphrase. You might include the full paraphrase, interspersed, perhaps, with an analysis of your present-day "prince."

Writing an Accurate Paraphrase

The basic purpose of paraphrase is to present the main ideas contained in the original text. When paraphrase fails to convey the substance of the source, there are three possible explanations:

1. *Misreading:* The writer genuinely misunderstood the text.
2. *Projecting:* The writer insisted on reading his or her own ideas into the text.
3. *Guessing:* The writer had a spark of understanding and constructed a paraphrase centered around that spark, but ignored too much of the original text.

Read Christopher Lasch's analysis of the changing role of the child in family life. Then examine each of the three paraphrases that follow, deciding whether it conveys Lasch's principal ideas and, if not, why it has gone astray. Compare your reactions with the analysis that follows each paraphrase.

Original

The family by its very nature is a means of raising children, but this fact should not blind us to the important change that occurred when child-rearing ceased to be simply one of many activities and became the central concern—one is tempted to say the central obsession—of family life. This development had to wait for the recognition of the child as a distinctive kind of person, more impressionable and hence more vulnerable than adults, to be treated in a special manner befitting his peculiar requirements. Again, we take these things for granted and find it hard to imagine anything else. Earlier, children had been clothed, fed, spoken to, and educated as little adults; more specifically, as servants, the difference between childhood and servitude having been remarkably obscure throughout much of Western history. . . . It was only in the seventeenth century in certain classes that childhood came to be seen as a special category of experience. When that happened, people recognized the enormous formative influence of family life, and the family became above all an agency for building character, for consciously and deliberately forming the child from birth to adulthood.

"Divorce and the Family in America," *Atlantic Monthly*

Paraphrase A

The average family wants to raise children with a good education and to encourage, for example, the ability to read and write well. They must be taught to practice and learn on their own. Children can be treated well without being pampered. They must be treated as adults as they get older and experience more of life. A parent must build character and the feeling of independence in a child. No longer should children be treated as kids or servants, for that can cause conflict in a family relationship.

This paraphrase has very little in common with the original passage. True, it is about child-rearing, but the writer chooses to give advice to parents, rather than present the contrast between early and modern attitudes toward children, as Lasch does. Since the only clear connection between Lasch and this paragraph is the reference to servants, the writer was probably confused by the passage, and (instead of slowing down the process and paraphrasing it sentence by sentence) guessed—mistakenly—at its meaning. There is also some projection of the writer's ideas about family life. Notice how assertive the tone is; the writer seems to be admonishing parents rather than presenting Lasch's detached analysis.

Paraphrase B

When two people get married, they usually produce a child. They get married because they want a family. Raising a family is now different from the way it used to be. The child is looked upon as a human being, with feelings and thoughts of his own. Centuries ago, children were treated like robots, little more than hired help. Now, children are seen as people who need a strong, dependable family background to grow into persons of good character. Parents are needed to get children ready to be the adults of tomorrow.

This paragraph also seems to combine guessing (beginning) and projection (end). The middle sentences do present Lasch's basic point, but the beginning and the end move so far away from the main ideas that the paraphrase as a whole does not bear much resemblance to the original text. It also includes an exaggeration: are servants "robots"?

Paraphrase C

Though the family has always been an important institution, its child-rearing function has only in recent centuries become its most important activity. This change has resulted from the relatively new idea that children have a special, unique personality. In the past, there was little difference seen between childhood and adulthood. But today people realize the importance of family life, especially the family unit as a means of molding the personalities of children from childhood to adulthood.

Although this paraphrase is certainly the most accurate of the three, it is too brief to be a complete paraphrase. In fact, the writer seems to be summarizing, not paraphrasing. Lasch's main idea is there, but the following points are missing:

1. There is a tremendous difference between pre-seventeenth-century and twentieth-century perceptions of childhood.
2. Before the seventeenth century, it was difficult to distinguish between the status and treatment of children and that of servants.
3. Child-rearing has now become of overriding ("obsessive") importance to the family.
4. Children are different from adults in that they are less hardened and less experienced.

The author of Paraphrase C has done a thorough job of the beginning and the end of Lasch's passage, and evidently left the middle to take care of itself. But a paraphrase cannot be considered a reliable "translation" of the original text unless all the supporting ideas are given appropriate emphasis. The omission of Point 2 is particularly important.

Here is a more comprehensive paraphrase of the passage:

Though the family has always been the institution responsible for bringing up children, only in recent times has its child-raising function become the family's overriding purpose and its reason for being. This striking shift to the child-centered family has resulted from the gradual realization that children have a special, unique personality, easy to influence and easy to hurt, and that they must be treated accordingly. Special treatment for children is the norm in our time; but hundreds of years ago, people saw little or no difference between childhood and adulthood, and, in fact, the child's role in the family resembled that of a servant. It was not until the seventeenth century that people began to regard childhood as a distinctive stage of growth. That recognition led them to understand what a powerful influence the family environment must have on the child and to define "family" as the chief instrument for molding the child's personality and moral attitudes.

EXERCISE 10: IDENTIFYING A GOOD PARAPHRASE

The next passage is followed by a group of paraphrases. Examine each one and decide whether it conforms to the guidelines for paraphrasing. Ask yourself whether the paraphrase contains any point that is not in the original passage and whether the key points of the original are *all* clearly presented in the paraphrase.

For machines, calculating is much easier than reasoning, and reasoning much easier than perceiving and acting. Why is this order of difficulty opposite that for humans? For a billion years every one of our ancestors achieved that status by winning a competition for the essentials of life in a hostile world, often by a lifetime of sensing and moving more effectively than the competition. That escalating Darwinian elimination tournament bequeathed us brains spectacularly organized for perception and action—an excellence often overlooked because it is now so commonplace. On the other hand, deep rational thought, as in chess, is a newly acquired ability, perhaps less than one hundred thousand years old. The parts of our brain devoted to it are not so well organized, and, in an absolute sense, we're not very good at it—but, until computers arrived, we had no competition to show us up. Arithmetical calculation lies even further down the spectrum of human proficiency; it became a needed skill—for specialists—only in recent millennia, as civilizations accumulated large populations and pools of property. It is a tribute to our general-purpose perceptual, manipulative, and language skills, and our luck in finding compatible representations of numbers, that we can do arithmetic at all.

HANS MORAVEC, from *Robot*

1. Machines have more problems thinking than working with numbers. People don't have that problem. Through history, human beings have worked hard to beat their enemies, and that fight has made us smart. But we're not so good at games like chess. Our minds are too disorganized, so computers make us look bad. We're even worse at arithmetic, which isn't such a problem since there are technical people to crunch numbers. It's amazing that anyone can do arithmetic.

2. Machines are different from humans. Machines excel at cold, orderly processes like logic and working with numbers. Human beings have had to struggle for their achievements; their ability to outsmart the opposition has changed and grown over time and they have evolved into superb men of action, yet their abilities are often unappreciated. Some say that humans are

deficient in the ability to think deeply, as machines do, but we haven't had that much practice. Arithmetic isn't really important, but we manage to do it anyway.

3. In contrast to machines, which are good at logical thinking and even better at the manipulation of numbers, the strength of human beings lies in their ability to observe and interpret the world around them and act accordingly. If you wanted to win in the evolutionary survival of the fittest, you had to learn to outguess and outsmart the predators. Today, we take for granted our unmatched ability to analyze and take control of real-life problems. Logical skills weren't so important to us until relatively late in the evolutionary process. Our deficiencies only started to bother us when computers—built by us—demonstrated the value of pure reasoning skills. Similarly, until our world became complex, with millions of people and possessions to organize, it wasn't necessary to develop numerical skills. But, as usual, we're clever enough and have the verbal and conceptual skills to master arithmetic if we need to.

Paraphrasing a Difficult Text

Since translating another writer's idiom into your own can be difficult, a paraphrase is often written in two stages.

- In your first version, you work out a *word-for-word substitution,* staying close to the sentence structure of the original, as if, indeed, you are writing a translation. This is the *literal paraphrase.*
- In your second version, you work from your own literal paraphrase, turning it into a *free paraphrase* by reconstructing and rephrasing the sentences to make them more natural and more characteristic of your own writing style.

Writing a Literal Paraphrase

To write a paraphrase that is faithful to the original text is impossible if you are uncertain of the meaning of any of the words. To write a literal paraphrase of a difficult passage:

- Use a dictionary, especially if the passage contains obsolete or archaic language.
- Write down a few possible synonyms for each difficult word, making sure that you understand the connotations of each synonym.
- Choose the substitute that best fits the context of your literal paraphrase.

Too often, the writer of a paraphrase forgets that there *is* a choice and quickly substitutes the first synonym in the dictionary. Even when appropriate synonyms have been carefully chosen, the literal paraphrase can look peculiar and sound dreadful. While the old sentence structure has been retained, the key words have been yanked out and new ones plugged in.

To illustrate the pitfalls of this process, here is a short excerpt from Francis Bacon's essay "Of Marriage and Single Life," written around 1600. Some of the phrasing and word combinations are archaic and may sound unnatural, but nothing in the passage is too difficult for modern understanding *if* the sentences are read slowly and carefully.

> He that hath wife and children hath given hostages to fortune; for they are impediments to great enterprises, either of virtue or mischief. Certainly, the best works and of greatest merit for the public have proceeded from the unmarried or childless men: which both in affection and means have endowed the public.

The passage's main idea is not too difficult to establish: *Unmarried men, without the burden of a family, can afford to contribute to the public good.* But by now you must realize that such a brief summary is not the same as a paraphrase, for it does not fully present Bacon's reasoning.

Paraphrase A

He who has a wife and children has <u>bestowed</u> <u>prisoners</u> to <u>riches</u>; for they are <u>defects</u> in huge <u>business</u> <u>organizations</u> either for <u>morality</u> or <u>damage</u>.

Paraphrase B

He who has a wife and children has <u>given</u> a <u>pledge</u> to <u>destiny</u>; for they are <u>hindrances</u> to large <u>endeavor</u>, either for <u>good</u> or for <u>ill</u>.

Neither sentence sounds very normal or very clear; but the second has potential, while the first makes no sense. Yet, in *both* cases, the inserted words are synonyms for the original vocabulary. In Paraphrase A the words do not fit Bacon's context; in Paraphrase B they do. For example, it is misleading to choose "business organizations" as a synonym for "enterprises," since the passage doesn't actually concern business, but refers to any sort of undertaking requiring freedom from responsibility. "Impediment" can mean either "defect" (as in speech impediment) or "hindrance" (as in impediment to learning); but—again, given the context—it is the latter meaning that Bacon has in mind. You will choose the correct connotation or nuance only if you think carefully about the synonyms and use your judgment: the process cannot be hurried.

A phrase like "hostage to fortune" offers special difficulty, since it is a powerful image expressing a highly abstract idea. No paraphraser can improve on the original wording or even find an equivalent phrase. However, expressing the idea is useful: a bargain made with life—the renunciation of future independent action in exchange for a family. Wife and children become a kind of bond ("hostage") to ensure one's future social conformity. The aptness and singularity of Bacon's original phrase are measured by the difficulty of paraphrasing three words in less than two sentences!

Writing a Free Version of the Literal Paraphrase

Correct though the synonyms may be, the passage from Bacon cannot be left as it is in Paraphrase B, for no reader could readily understand this stilted, artificial sentence. It is necessary to rephrase the paraphrase, ensuring that the meaning of the words is retained, but making the sentence sound more natural. The first attempt at "freeing up" the paraphrase stays as close as possible to the literal version, leaving everything in the same sequence, but using a more modern idiom:

Paraphrase C

Married men with children are hindered from embarking on any important undertaking, good or bad. Indeed, unmarried and childless men are the ones who have done the most for society and have dedicated their love and their money to the public good.

The second sentence (which is simpler to paraphrase than the first) has been inverted here, but the paraphrase is still a point-by-point recapitulation of Bacon. Paraphrase C is acceptable, but can be improved, both to clarify Bacon's meaning and to introduce a more personal voice. What exactly *are* these unmarried men dedicating to the public good? "Affection and means." And what is the modern equivalent of means? Money? Effort? Time? Energy?

Paraphrase D

A man with a family has obligations that prevent him from devoting himself to any activity that pleases him. On the other hand, a single man or a man without children has a greater opportunity to be a philanthropist. That's why most great contributions of energy and resources to the good of society are made by single men.

The writer of Paraphrase D has not supplied a synonym for "affection," assuming perhaps that the expenditure of energy and resources result from interest and concern; affection is almost too weak a motivation for the philanthropist as he is described here.

Paraphrase E

The responsibility of a wife and children prevents a man from taking risks with his money, time, and energy. The greatest social benefactors have been men who have adopted the public as their family.

The second sentence here is the only one of the five versions that approaches Bacon's economy of style. "Adopted the public" is not quite the same as "endowed the public" with one's "affection and means"; but nevertheless, this paraphrase is successful because it speaks for itself. It has a life and an importance of its own, independent of Bacon's original passage, yet it makes the same point that Bacon does.

Guidelines for Paraphrasing a Difficult Passage

1. Look up in a dictionary the meanings of all the words of which you are uncertain. Pay special attention to the difficult words, considering the context of the whole passage.

2. Write a literal paraphrase of each passage by substituting appropriate synonyms within the original sentence structure.

3. Revise your literal paraphrase, keeping roughly to the same length and number of sentences as the original, but using your own sentence style and phrasing throughout. You may prefer to put the original passage aside at this point, and work entirely from your own version.

4. Read your free paraphrase aloud to make sure that it makes sense.

ASSIGNMENT 3: PARAPHRASING A DIFFICULT PASSAGE

Paraphrase one of the following passages, using the guidelines in the box above. (Your instructor may assign a specific paragraph for the entire class to paraphrase; you may be asked to work together with one or more of your classmates.)

1. Viewers who become accustomed to seeing violence as an acceptable, common, and attractive way of dealing with problems find it easier to identify with aggressors and to suppress any sense of pity or respect for victims of violence. Media violence has been found to have stronger effects of this kind when carried out by heroic, impressive, or otherwise exciting figures, especially when they are shown as invulnerable and are rewarded or not punished for what they do. The same is true when the violence is shown as justifiable, when viewers identify with the aggressors rather than their victims, when violence is routinely resorted to, and when the programs have links to how viewers perceive their own entertainment.

SISSELA BOK, from *Mayhem*

2. Can you draw elaborate distinctions on television? No. Can you say everything there is to be said, even everything you have to say, about a given topic? No.

Can you back your way into the subject the way you might write the opening pages of a journal article? Also no. Those are irritants to people trained in academic discourse, but they are not, in themselves, barriers to thought. On the contrary, I think it is the very sharpness of television discourse that dismays many intellectuals. It forces them to be direct. There is no time to gratify your ego by holding the floor, no opportunity to set the terms of the debate in your own favor, no license for exclusive and proprietary language.

MARK KINGWELL, from "The Intellectual
Possibilities of Television"

3. It is somewhat ironic to note that grading *systems* evolved in part because of [problems in evaluating performance]. In situations where reward and recognition often depended more on who you knew than on what you knew, and lineage was more important than ability, the cause of justice seemed to demand a method whereby the individual could demonstrate specific abilities on the basis of objective criteria. This led to the establishment of specific standards and public criteria as ways of reducing prejudicial treatment and, in cases where appropriate standards could not be specified in advance, to the normal curve system of establishing levels on the basis of group performance. The imperfect achievement of the goals of such systems in no way negates the importance of the underlying purposes.

WAYNE MOELLENBERG, from "To Grade or
Not to Grade—Is That the Question?"

4. The distinction of race has always been used in American life to sanction each race's pursuit of power in relation to the other. The allure of race as a human delineation is the very shallowness of the delineation it makes. Onto this shallowness—mere skin and hair—men can project a false depth, a system of dismal attributions, a series of malevolent or ignoble stereotypes that skin and hair lack the substance to contradict. These dark projections then rationalize the pursuit of power. Your difference from me makes you bad, and your badness justifies, even demands, my pursuit of power over you—the oldest formula for aggression known to man. Whenever much importance is given to race, power is the primary motive.

SHELBY STEELE, from "I'm Black, You're White,
Who's Innocent?"

INCORPORATING PARAPHRASE INTO YOUR ESSAY

The paraphrased ideas of other writers should never take control of your essay, but should always be subordinate to *your* ideas. When you insert a paraphrased sentence or a brief paraphrased passage (rather than a quotation) into one of your paragraphs, you minimize the risk that the source material will dominate your writing. *Most academic writers rely on a combination of quotation, paraphrase, and summary to present their sources.*

To illustrate the way in which these three techniques of presentation can be successfully combined, here is an extract from an article by Conor Cruise O'Brien that depends on a careful mixture of paraphrase, summary, and quotation. In "Violence—And Two Schools of Thought," O'Brien gives an account of a medical conference concerned with the origins of violence. Specifically, he undertakes to present and (at the end) comment on the ideas of two speakers at the conference.

VIOLENCE—AND TWO SCHOOLS OF THOUGHT*
Conor Cruise O'Brien

Summary   The opening speakers were fairly representative of the main   1
schools of thought which almost always declare themselves when violence is discussed. The first school sees a propensity to aggression as biological but capable of being socially conditioned into patterns of acceptable behavior. The second sees it as essentially created by social conditions and therefore capable of being removed by benign social change.

Quotation   The first speaker held that violence was "a bio-social phenome-   2
non." He rejected the notion that human beings were blank paper "on which the environment can write whatever it likes." He de-
Paraphrase   scribed how a puppy could be conditioned to choose a dog food it did not like and to reject one it did like. This was the creation of conscience in the puppy. It was done by mild punishment. If human beings were acting more aggressively and anti-socially, despite the advent of better social conditions and better housing, this might be because permissiveness, in school and home, had checked the process of social conditioning, and therefore of conscience-building. He favored the reinstatement of conscience-building, through the use of
Quotation   mild punishment and token rewards. "We cannot eliminate violence," he said, "but we can do a great deal to reduce it."

Summary   The second speaker thought that violence was the result of stress;   3
in almost all the examples he cited it was stress from overcrowding. The behavior of apes and monkeys in zoos was "totally different" from

---

*In its original format in *The Observer,* the article's paragraphing, in accordance with usual journalistic practice, occurs with distracting frequency; the number of paragraphs has been reduced here, without any alteration of the text.

Paraphrase/
Quotation

Paraphrase/
Quotation

Summary

Author's
Comment

Summary/
Paraphrase

Author's
Comment

the way they behaved in "the completely relaxed conditions in the wild." In crowded zoos the most aggressive males became leaders and a general reign of terror set in; in the relaxed wild, on the other hand, the least aggressive males ruled benevolently. Space was all: "If we could eliminate population pressures, violence would vanish."

The student [reacting to the argument of the two speakers] preferred the second speaker. He [the second speaker] spoke with ebullient confidence, fast but clear, and at one point ran across the vast platform, in a lively imitation of the behavior of a charging ape. Also, his message was simple and hopeful. Speaker one, in contrast, looked sad, and his message sounded faintly sinister. Such impressions, rather than the weight of argument, determine the reception of papers read in such circumstances.

Nonetheless, a student queried speaker two's "relaxed wild." He seemed to recall a case in which a troop of chimpanzees had completely wiped out another troop. The speaker was glad the student had raised that question because it proved the point. You see, where that had occurred, there had been an overcrowding in the jungle, just as happens in zoos, and this was a response to overcrowding. Conditions in the wild, it seems, are not always "completely relaxed." And when they attain that attributed condition—through the absence of overcrowding—this surely has to be due to the "natural controls," including the predators, whose attentions can hardly be all that relaxing, or, indeed, all that demonstrative of the validity of the proposition that violence is not a part of nature. Speaker two did not allude to predators. Nonetheless, they are still around, on two legs as well as on four.

4

5

Although we do not have the texts of the original papers given at the conference to compare with O'Brien's description, this article seems to present a clear and comprehensive account of a complex discussion. In the first paragraph, O'Brien uses brief summaries to help us distinguish between the two speakers; next, he provides us with two separate, noncommittal descriptions of the two main points of view.

The ratio of quotation to paraphrase to summary works very effectively. O'Brien quotes for two reasons: *aptness of expression* and *the desire to distance himself from the statement*. For example, he chooses to quote the vivid image of the blank paper "on which the environment can write whatever it likes." And he also selects points for quotation that he regards as open to dispute—"totally different"; "completely relaxed"; "violence would vanish." Such strong or sweeping statements are often quoted so that writers can disassociate themselves from the implications of their source material; this way, they cannot be accused of either toning down or exaggerating the meaning in their paraphrases.

Reasons to Use Quotation

■ You can find no words to convey the economy and aptness of phrasing of the original text.

■ A paraphrase might alter the statement's meaning.

■ A paraphrase would not clearly distinguish between your views and the author's.

Citing Your Paraphrased Sources

The one possible source of confusion in O'Brien's article occurs when he begins his own commentary. In the last two paragraphs, it is not always easy to determine where O'Brien's paraphrase of the speakers' ideas ends and his own opinions begin. In Paragraph 4, his description of the student's reactions to the two speakers appears objective. At the end of the paragraph, however, we learn that O'Brien is scornful of the criteria that the student is using to evaluate these ideas. But at first we cannot be sure whether O'Brien is describing the *student's observation* or giving *his own account* of the speaker's platform maneuvers. It would be clearer to us if the sentence began: "According to the responding student, the second speaker spoke with ebullient confidence. . . ." Similarly, the last sentence of Paragraph 4 is undoubtedly O'Brien's opinion, yet there is nothing to indicate the transition from the student to O'Brien as the source of commentary.

This confusion of point of view is especially deceptive in Paragraph 5 as O'Brien moves from his paraphrased and neutral account of the dialogue between student and speaker to his own opinion that certain predators influence behavior in civilization as well as in the wild. It takes two readings to notice the point at which O'Brien is no longer paraphrasing but beginning to speak in his own voice. Such confusions could have been clarified by inserting citations—the name of the source or an appropriate pronoun—in the appropriate places.

In academic writing the clear acknowledgment of the source is not merely a matter of courtesy or clarity; it is an assurance of the writer's honesty.

> *When you paraphrase another person's ideas, you must cite the author's name, as you do when you quote, or else risk being charged with plagiarism. Borrowing ideas is just as much theft as borrowing words.*

You omit the quotation marks when you paraphrase, but you must not omit the citation. Of course, the citation of the name should be smoothly integrated into your sentence, following the guidelines used for citation of quotations. The source's name need not appear at the beginning of the sentence, but it should signal the beginning of the paraphrase:

> Not everyone enjoys working, but most people would agree with Jones's belief
> that work is an essential experience of life.

The writer of the essay is responsible for the declaration that "not everyone enjoys working" and that most people would agree with Jones's views; but the belief that "work is an essential experience of life" is attributed to Jones. Here, the citation is well and unobtrusively placed; there are no quotation marks, so presumably Jones used a different wording.

Here are additional guidelines for the proper citation of sources:

- When you *quote,* there can never be any doubt about where the borrowed material begins and where it ends: the quotation marks provide a clear indication of the boundaries.
- When you *paraphrase,* although the citation may signal the *beginning* of the source material, your reader may not be sure exactly where the paraphrase *ends.*

There is no easy method of indicating the termination of paraphrased material. (As you will see in Chapter 8, the author's name in parentheses works well if you are using that method of documentation.) It is possible to signal the end of a paraphrase simply by starting a new paragraph. However, you may need to incorporate more than one person's ideas into a single paragraph. When you present several points of view in succession, be careful to acknowledge the change of source by citing names.

In some kinds of essays, it may be appropriate to signal the shift from paraphrased material to your own opinions by using the first person. Instructors' attitudes toward the first person vary, but some find it acceptable to use "I" in certain kinds of writing as long as it is not inserted excessively or monotonously. A carefully placed "I" can leave your reader in no doubt as to whose voice is being heard. Make sure, however, that using "I" is consistent with the tone and point of view of your essay. If you are presenting sources through a narrative in which you otherwise remain in the background, the sudden appearance of "I" would mean a sharp break in the overall tone and would therefore be inappropriate.

EXERCISE 11: DISTINGUISHING BETWEEN QUOTATION, PARAPHRASE, SUMMARY, AND COMMENTARY

1. Read "In Wake of the Scandal over Joseph Ellis, Scholars Ask 'Why?' and 'What Now?,'" by Ana Marie Cox.

2. In the margin, indicate where the author uses description or narration (D/N), quotation (Q), paraphrase (P), summary (S), and commentary (C).

3. In class discussion, be prepared to evaluate the use of quotation, paraphrase, and summary, and to indicate those places in the article where, in your opinion, one of the techniques is inappropriately or unnecessarily used, or where the transition from one technique to the other is not clearly identified.

IN WAKE OF THE SCANDAL OVER JOSEPH ELLIS, SCHOLARS ASK "WHY?" AND "WHAT NOW?"

Ana Marie Cox

The line to get Joseph Ellis to sign copies of his Pulitzer Prize–winning *Founding Brothers* stretches out of the ornate lecture room at the National Archives and into its gray corridors. It is the Friday after the Monday on which the *Boston Globe* dropped a cluster bomb on the bucolic campus of Mount Holyoke College, where Mr. Ellis is a history professor, by reporting that he had for years been lying to colleagues, reporters, and students about his own role in history.   1

The *Globe* reported, and Mr. Ellis later confirmed, that he had fabricated a past in which he was present at some of the most crucial episodes in postwar America: He had said that he was a paratrooper for the 101st Airborne in Vietnam; that he was on General William C. Westmoreland's staff; that back in the United States, he was an antiwar protester and had participated in the civil-rights movement. He had also claimed to have scored the winning touchdown for his high-school football team in the last game of the season. . . .   2

But the discussions about Mr. Ellis and what he did linger on. News coverage and faculty-lounge gossip fixate on motivations: "Why did he do it?"   3

Others are asking, "What now?" That professors shouldn't lie to students is an article of truth that not even Mr. Ellis's supporters deny.   4

So what should Mount Holyoke do about it? Some critics say the college made a mockery of their supposed devotion to teaching by initially defending Mr. Ellis. But what if many of his students say he should be spared? And what if many historians point out that his work on the colonial era remains untainted?   5

What's more, in the past week, *Founding Brothers* moved from No. 10 to No. 8 on the *New York Times*'s best-seller list. Academe may be searching for the right way to discipline Joseph Ellis, but the public is still rewarding him.   6

Many of Mr. Ellis's friends say that at first, they simply refused to believe what the *Globe* had reported. He had taught a popular course on Vietnam and American culture that he enlivened with details based, he said, on what he saw there. He had told colleagues that he considered writing a memoir about Vietnam, that magazines had wanted to interview him about his experiences. Asked one colleague, "If he was lying, why would he even consider doing that?"   7

Some friends said his stories were so compelling and realistic that if it hadn't been for his admission of guilt, they would have assumed that it was the government that was lying. Maybe, the theory went, Mr. Ellis's military records weren't found *for a reason*.   8

Mount Holyoke took a similarly defiant stance; the *Globe* reported last week that the college even attempted to dissuade the newspaper from publishing the original article, calling into question the legal basis of investigating statements made in the classroom.   9

When the newspaper went ahead, Mount Holyoke's president, Joanne V. Creighton, issued a statement: "We at the college wonder what public interest the *Globe* is trying to serve through a story of this nature."

Mr. Ellis at first refused to comment at all. But after the article appeared, in a statement whose passive voice recalls some of the vaguest official pronouncements about Vietnam, he admitted that the *Globe*'s piece was essentially correct. "Even in the best of lives," he said, "mistakes are made."

Patrick Hagopian, a historian at the University of Lancaster, in Britain, has studied the false Vietnam War stories of the men he calls "wannabes." For one thing, he says, referring to Mr. Ellis's Westmoreland tale, "a lot of people don't have credible access to those sorts of centers of power." And most wannabes use a Vietnam nightmare as a kind of get-out-of-expectations-free card: " 'I haven't made much of my life, but here's this terrible thing that's happened to me in Vietnam.' " However, Mr. Hagopian notes, "This is not a plausible motive for a Pulitzer Prize–winning historian."

Glenna Whitley, co-author with B. G. Burkett of *Stolen Valor: How the Vietnam Generation Was Robbed of Its Heroes and Its History,* says Mr. Ellis's stories are different from those of most faux veterans for another reason as well: He didn't stop at lying about going, but lied about protesting the war as well. "I guess he figured that wasn't enough—that the real valor was to turn against the war," Ms. Whitley says. She gives such a turnabout some thought and suggests, "perhaps that's particular to academe."

Of course, one way that Mr. Ellis's statements were "particular to academe" is that they weren't mere boasting, but that he had told at least some of his lies in the course of lectures to students who felt lucky to be learning from the college's most famous professor.

"He lied *in class,*" says David J. Garrow, a professor at the Emory University School of Law. "If he were telling stories in a local bar, who cares?"

The Mount Holyoke president's first, defensive response to the *Globe* article was roundly criticized, chiefly by Mr. Garrow in a blistering opinion piece that ran only a day after the story broke. "It appeared that she didn't particularly care about what he said in class," he says. Within a few days, the college had changed its posture. Alumnae wrote in, calling for Mr. Ellis's dismissal or just asking for a fuller inquiry into exactly what lies Mr. Ellis had told, and how often, and to whom. As of this writing, the professor remains "under investigation," though one may wonder what there is to look into. Didn't he acknowledge that he had lied?

The investigation may, however, be as much about what Mount Holyoke should do as about what Mr. Ellis has done. There is little question among the college's faculty, or in the larger world of academe, that what the professor did was wrong. But how wrong? Mount Holyoke has traditionally put a premium on teaching, which would seem to cast Mr. Ellis's fabrications in the harshest light imaginable, yet some alumnae have defended Mr. Ellis on the very grounds that he is a great teacher.

Karyn Coughlin, a 1995 graduate, had Mr. Ellis as an adviser for her senior thesis. It was on "ideas of truth, specifically postmodern ideas of how there is no truth, and how to incorporate that into history," she says, noting the retrospective irony.

She credits Mr. Ellis's dynamic lectures and obvious love of his subject for prompt-   19
ing her to major in history. She says she never heard him talk about Vietnam in class, only in private conversation, and even then not often. She repeats an argument made by other Holyoke alumnae in letters to the editors in *The Washington Post* and *The New York Times:* "I would hope that when Mount Holyoke investigates him, they take into account how good and popular a professor he is." Besides, she says, "I expect this isn't so unusual." Not that lying to students should be excused—but among charismatic lecturers, spur-of-the-moment exaggerations must be pretty common, she argues. How can colleges expect to keep their best instructors per-fectly in line all of the time?

Even the fiery Mr. Garrow takes a measured step back when pressed on how,   20
exactly, one might hold professors' lectures to the same standards as scholarly writing. "It's a matter of scale and repetition—that's the question for Holyoke," he says. "Right now, it looks like he did it not just occasionally for the last three se-mesters, but the last 10 years. And the lies came in weird and self-contradictory ways." In his opinion piece, Mr. Garrow said Mr. Ellis should be barred from the classroom and from "ever teaching history again." But at the same time, the law pro-fessor noted that the full story has not been told. He ventured no suggestions as to what further punishment Mr. Ellis may deserve. . . .

For all the close scrutiny that scholars are now giving Mr. Ellis's books and in-   21
terviews, no one—not even his harshest critics—has accused him of extending his fabrications back beyond the twentieth century.

"It's not as if he plagiarized. Joe is a good historian. He is a fair-minded and gen-   22
erous man. It would be different if he made up something about Jefferson, but he's true to his material," says Andrew Burstein, a historian of the early Republic at the University of Tulsa. "Lying to students is a very serious error, but we should still sep-arate it from the way he treats archival material."

One historian, who had commented on Mr. Ellis's work before the scandal broke   23
and was contacted by many journalists afterward, has had enough of the matter: "I'm kind of sick of even talking about Joe Ellis. It's psychologists and not historians who should be looking into why he did this." . . .

Mr. Ellis's ability to dramatize the emotional lives of the founders is the aspect   24
of his work that readers—and award judges—respond to. In his talk at the Na-tional Archives, in his books, and in his interviews, Mr. Ellis underscores the notion that the first leaders of the Republic were forged by fire and succeeded against great odds.

"The talent that is latent in this class is pulled out of it in a time of crisis," Mr.   25
Ellis tells the crowd at the National Archives. "Fairly early in the game, most of these men recognized that if they succeeded, they would make history."

Seen against Mr. Ellis's depiction of colonial leaders as heroes, his lies don't look   26
quite so much like evidence of ambition or malice. Rather, they seem like an attempt

to make himself "present at the creation" of a new era—much in the way that the subjects of his books were front and center at the dawning of theirs.

"Joe Ellis is the Vanilla Ice of the historical profession," says N.Y.U.'s [Robin D. G.] Kelley. "I was watching the VH1 special on Vanilla Ice just after I read about Ellis. It's really the Joe Ellis story." Mr. Kelley then recounts the story of the white rap singer, a one-hit wonder who once claimed to have been a street thug, to have been from the ghetto, and to have been beaten up by black youths regularly as a kid. These were, at best, exaggerations—fabricated, Vanilla Ice says, by his managers, in an effort to gain him credibility among people fascinated by gangs.   27

Joe Ellis, Mr. Kelley says, was trying to gain credibility with audiences—both in the classroom and beyond—fascinated by heroes. And today, says Mr. Kelley, people believe that personal experience is the ultimate form of credibility.   28

In today's classroom, he says, "students believe their source of knowledge is themselves. Professors have to trump that. Fifteen years ago you couldn't sit in a classroom and replace the text with your own experience."   29

"Scholars feel pressure to be authentic—more than authentic," says Mr. Kelley. Personal history "carries more weight than having 20 years of research experience. If you write about music, you have to be a musician; if you write about the ghetto, you have to be from the 'hood.'"   30

Even if Mr. Ellis can no longer claim to be an authentic American hero, the fame that rests on his credibility as a historian of American heroes is unchallenged.   31

At the National Archives, the people in line to get their newly purchased books signed say it doesn't matter to them that Mr. Ellis fudged his military record. "He's a good novelist—a good writer," says one woman of Mr. Ellis, who has never written a novel.   32

"People lie all the time," says a man with a Department of Defense ID card dangling from his neck.   33

And hey, Mr. Kelley points out, even Vanilla Ice is trying to make a comeback.   34

PRESENTING SOURCES: A SUMMARY OF PRELIMINARY WRITING SKILLS

1. **Annotation: underlining the text and inserting marginal comments on the page.**

   The notes can explain points that are unclear, define difficult words, emphasize key ideas, point out connections to previous or subsequent paragraphs, or suggest the reader's own reactions to what is being discussed.

2. **Paraphrasing: recapitulating, point by point, using your own words.**

   A paraphrase is a faithful and complete rendition of the original, following much the same order of ideas. Although full-length paraphrase is practical only with relatively brief passages, it is the most reliable way to make sense out of a difficult text. Paraphrasing a sentence or two, together with a citation of the author's name, is the best method of presenting another person's ideas within your own essay.

3. **Quotation: including another person's exact words within your own writing.**

Although quotation requires the least amount of invention, it is the most technical of all these skills, demanding an understanding of conventional and complex punctuation. In your notes and in your essays, quotation should be a last resort. If the phrasing is unique, if the presentation is subtle, if the point at issue is easily misunderstood or hotly debated, quotation may be appropriate. When in doubt, paraphrase.

4. **Summary: condensing the text into a relatively brief presentation of the main ideas.**

Unlike annotation, a summary should make sense as an independent, coherent piece of writing. Unlike paraphrase, a summary includes only main ideas. However, the summary should be complete in the sense that it provides a fair representation of the work and its parts. Summary is the all-purpose skill; it is neither crude nor overly detailed.

Part II

WRITING FROM SOURCES

The previous two chapters have described some basic ways to understand another writer's ideas and present them accurately and naturally, as part of your own writing. Until now, however, you have been working with forms of writing that are brief and limited—the sentence and the paragraph. Now you can use the skills that you practiced in Part I to develop your own ideas in a full-length essay based on sources.

When you write at length from sources, you must work with *two points of view*—your own and those of the authors you're writing about. You therefore have a dual responsibility: you must do justice to yourself by developing your own ideas, and you must do justice to each source by fairly representing its author's ideas. But blending the ideas of two or more people within the same essay can create confusion. Who should dominate? How much of yourself should you include? How much of your source? Moreover, in academic and professional writing you may have to consider a third voice—that of your teacher or supervisor, who may assign a topic or otherwise set limits and goals for your work.

Chapter 3 discusses two approaches to writing based on a single source. Each demonstrates a way to reconcile the competing influences on your writing and blend the voices that your reader ought to hear:

- You can distinguish between your source and yourself by writing about the two separately, first the source and then yourself, and, in the process, developing an argument that supports or refutes your source's thesis.
- You can use your source as the basis for the development of your own ideas by writing an essay on a similar or related topic.

In the end, *your voice should dominate.* It is you who will choose the thesis and control the essay's structure and direction; it is your understanding and judgment that will interpret the source materials for your reader. When you and your classmates are asked to write about the same reading, your teacher hopes to receive, not an identical set of essays, but rather a series of individual interpretations with a common starting point in the same source.

Combining your own ideas with those of others inevitably becomes more difficult when you begin to work with *a group of sources* and must represent several authors. This is the subject of Chapter 4. It is more than ever vital that your own voice dominate your essay and that you do not simply summarize first one source and then the next, without any perspective of your own.

Blending together a variety of sources is usually called *synthesis*. You try to look beyond each separate assertion and, instead, develop a broad generalization that will encompass your source material. Your own generalized conclusions become the basis for your essay's thesis and organization, while the ideas of your sources serve as the evidence that supports those conclusions.

Chapter 4 emphasizes the standard methods of presenting multiple sources:

- The analysis of each source in a search for common themes.
- The establishment of common denominators or categories that cut across the separate sources and provide the structure for your essay.
- The evaluation of each source's relative significance as you decide which to emphasize.
- The citation of references from several different sources in support of a single point.

These skills are closely related to two of the most common and useful strategies for constructing an essay: *definition* and *comparison*.

▪3▪

The Single-Source Essay

When you write from a source, you must understand another writer's ideas as thoroughly as you understand your own. The first step in carrying out the strategies described in this chapter is to read carefully through the source essay, using the skills for comprehension that you learned about in Chapters 1 and 2: annotation, paraphrase, and summary. Once you are able to explain to your reader what the source is all about, you can begin to plan your analysis and rebuttal of the author's ideas; or you can write your own essay on a similar topic.

STRATEGY ONE: ARGUING AGAINST YOUR SOURCE

The simplest way to argue against someone else's ideas is *complete separation between your source and yourself*. The structure of your essay breaks into two parts, with the source's views presented first, and your own reactions given equal (or greater) space immediately afterward. Instead of treating the reading as evidence in support of your point of view and blending it with your own ideas, you write an essay that first analyzes and then refutes your source's basic themes. Look, for example, at Roger Sipher's "So That Nobody Has to Go to School If They Don't Want To."

SO THAT NOBODY HAS TO GO TO SCHOOL
IF THEY DON'T WANT TO

Roger Sipher

A decline in standardized test scores is but the most recent indicator that American education is in trouble.   1

One reason for the crisis is that present mandatory-attendance laws force many to attend school who have no wish to be there. Such children have little desire to learn and are so antagonistic to school that neither they nor more highly motivated students receive the quality education that is the birthright of every American.   2

The solution to this problem is simple: Abolish compulsory-attendance laws and allow only those who are committed to getting an education to attend.   3

This will not end public education. Contrary to conventional belief, legislators enacted compulsory-attendance laws to legalize what already existed. William Landes and Lewis Solomon, economists, found little evidence that mandatory-attendance laws increased the number of children in school. They found, too, that school systems have never effectively enforced such laws, usually because of the expense involved.   4

There is no contradiction between the assertion that compulsory attendance has had little effect on the number of children attending school and the argument that repeal would be a positive step toward improving education. Most parents want a high school education for their children. Unfortunately, compulsory attendance hampers the ability of public school officials to enforce legitimate educational and disciplinary policies and thereby make the education a good one.   5

Private schools have no such problem. They can fail or dismiss students, knowing such students can attend public school. Without compulsory attendance, public schools would be freer to oust students whose academic or personal behavior undermines the educational mission of the institution.   6

Has not the noble experiment of a formal education for everyone failed? While we pay homage to the homily, "You can lead a horse to water but you can't make him drink," we have pretended it is not true in education.   7

Ask high school teachers if recalcitrant students learn anything of value. Ask teachers if these students do any homework. Quite the contrary, these students know they will be passed from grade to grade until they are old enough to quit or until, as is more likely, they receive a high school diploma. At the point when students could legally quit, most choose to remain since they know they are likely to be allowed to graduate whether they do acceptable work or not.   8

Abolition of archaic attendance laws would produce enormous dividends.   9

First, it would alert everyone that school is a serious place where one goes to learn. Schools are neither day-care centers nor indoor street corners. Young peo-   10 ple who resist learning should stay away; indeed, an end to compulsory schooling would require them to stay away.

Second, students opposed to learning would not be able to pollute the educational atmosphere for those who want to learn. Teachers could stop policing recalcitrant students and start educating.   11

Third, grades would show what they are supposed to: how well a student is learning. Parents could again read report cards and know if their children were making progress.   12

Fourth, public esteem for schools would increase. People would stop regarding them as way stations for adolescents and start thinking of them as institutions for educating America's youth.   13

Fifth, elementary schools would change because students would find out early that they had better learn something or risk flunking out later. Elementary teachers would no longer have to pass their failures on to junior high and high school.   14

Sixth, the cost of enforcing compulsory education would be eliminated. Despite enforcement efforts, nearly 15 percent of the school-age children in our largest cities are almost permanently absent from school.   15

Communities could use these savings to support institutions to deal with young people not in school. If, in the long run, these institutions prove more costly, at least we would not confuse their mission with that of schools.   16

Schools should be for education. At present, they are only tangentially so. They have attempted to serve an all-encompassing social function, trying to be all things to all people. In the process they have failed miserably at what they were originally formed to accomplish.   17

Presenting Your Source's Point of View

Sipher opposes compulsory attendance laws. On the other hand, suppose that you can see advantages in imposing a very strict rule for attendance. In order to challenge Sipher convincingly, you incorporate both his point of view and yours within a single essay.

Since your objective is to respond to Sipher, you begin by *acknowledging his ideas and presenting them to your readers*. State them as fairly as you can, without pausing to argue with him or to offer your own point of view about mandatory attendance.

At first it may seem easiest to follow Sipher's sequence of ideas (especially since his points are so clearly numbered). But Sipher is more likely to dominate if you follow the structure of his essay, presenting and answering each of his points one by one; for you will be arguing on *his* terms, according to *his* conception of the issue rather than yours. Instead, make sure that your reader understands what Sipher is actually saying, see if you can find any common ground between your points of view, and then begin your rebuttal.

1. *Briefly summarize the issue and the reasons that prompted the author to write the essay.*

You do this by writing a brief summary, as explained in Chapter 1. Here is a summary of Sipher's article:

> Roger Sipher argues that the presence in the classroom of unwilling students who are indifferent to learning can explain why public school students as a whole are learning less and less. Sipher therefore recommends that public schools discontinue the policy of mandatory attendance. Instead, students would be allowed to drop out if they wished, and faculty would be able to expel students whose behavior made it difficult for serious students to do their work. Once unwilling students were no longer forced to attend, schools would once again be able to maintain high standards of achievement; they could devote money and energy to education, rather than custodial care.

You can make such a summary more detailed by paraphrasing some of the author's arguments and, if you wish, quoting once or twice.

2. *Analyze and present some of the basic principles that underlie the author's position on this issue.*

In debating the issue with the author, you will need to do more than just contradict his main ideas: Sipher says mandatory attendance is bad, and you say it is good; Sipher says difficult students don't learn anything, and you say all students learn something useful; and so on. This point-by-point rebuttal shows that you disagree, but it provides no common context so that readers can decide who is right and who is wrong. You have no starting point for your counterarguments and no choice but to sound arbitrary.

Instead, ask yourself why the author has taken this position, one that you find so easy to reject.

- What are the foundations of his arguments?
- What larger principles do they suggest?
- What policies is he objecting to? Why?
- What values is he determined to defend?
- Can these values or principles be applied to issues other than attendance?

You are now examining Sipher's specific responses to the practical problem of attendance in order to *analyze his premises* and *infer some broad generalizations* about his philosophy of education.

Although Sipher does not specifically state such generalizations in this article, you would be safe in concluding that Sipher's views on attendance derive from a *conflict of two principles:*

1. The belief that education is a right that may not be denied under any circumstances, and

2. The belief that education is a privilege to be earned.

Sipher advocates the second position. Thus, after your summary of the article, you should analyze Sipher's implicit position in a separate paragraph.

> Sipher's argument implies that there is no such thing as the right to an education. A successful education can only depend on the student's willing presence and active participation. Passive or rebellious students cannot be educated and should not be forced to stay in school. Although everyone has the right to an opportunity for education, its acquisition is actually the privilege of those who choose to work for it.

Through this analysis of Sipher's position, you have not only found out more about the issue being argued, but you have also established a common context—*eligibility for education*—within which you and he disagree. Nor is there much room for compromise here; it is hard to reconcile the belief that education should be a privilege with the concept of education as an entitlement. Provided with a clear understanding of the differences between you, your reader now has a real basis for choosing between your opposing views. At the same time, your reader is being assured that this point and no other is the essential point for debate; thus, you will be fighting on ground that *you* have chosen.

You might also note that Sipher's argument is largely *deductive:* a series of premises that derive their power from an appeal to parents' concerns that their children (who faithfully attend) will have their education compromised by the recalcitrant students (who don't). His *supporting evidence* consists of one allusion to the testimony of two economists and one statistic. Both pieces of evidence confirm the subsidiary idea that attendance laws haven't succeeded in improving attendance. His third source of support—the adage about leading a horse to water—does deal more directly with the problem of learning; but can it be regarded as serious evidence?

Presenting Your Point of View

3. *Present your reasons for disagreeing with your source.*

Once you have established your opponent's position, you may then plan your own counterarguments by writing down your reactions and pinpointing the exact reasons for your disagreement. (All the statements analyzed in this section are taken from such preliminary responses; they are *not* excerpts from finished essays.) Your reasons for disagreeing with Sipher might fit into one of three categories:

- You believe that his basic principle is not valid (Student B).
- You decide that his principle, although valid, cannot be strictly applied to the practical situation under discussion (Student C).
- You accept Sipher's principle, but you are aware of other, stronger influences that diminish its importance (Student E).

Whichever line of argument you follow, it is impossible to present your case successfully if you wholly ignore Sipher's basic principle, as Student A does:

Student A

Sipher's isn't a constructive solution. Without strict attendance laws, many students wouldn't come to school at all.

Nonattendance is exactly what Sipher wants: he argues that indifferent students should be permitted to stay away, that their absence would benefit everyone. Student A makes no effort to refute Sipher's point; he is, in effect, saying to his source, "You're wrong!" without explaining why.

Student B, however, tries to establish a basis for disagreement:

Student B

If mandatory attendance were to be abolished, how would children acquire the skills to survive in an educated society such as ours?

According to Student B, the practical uses of education have become so important that a student's very survival may one day depend on having been well educated. Implied here is the principle, in opposition to Sipher's, that receiving an education cannot be a matter of choice or a privilege to be earned. What children learn in school is so important to their future lives that they should be forced to attend classes, even against their will, for their own good.

But this response is still superficial. Student B is confusing the desired object—*getting an education*—with one of the means of achieving that object—*being present in the classroom*; attendance, the means, has become an end in itself. Since students who attend but do not participate will not learn, mandatory attendance cannot by itself create an educated population.

On the other hand, although attendance may not be the *only* condition for getting an education, the student's physical presence in the classroom is certainly important. In that case, should the decision about attendance, a decision likely to affect much of their future lives, be placed in the hands of those too young to understand the consequences?

Student C

The absence of attendance laws would be too tempting for students and might create a generation of semi-illiterates. Consider the marginal student who, despite general indifference and occasional bad behavior, shows some promise and capacity for learning. Without a policy of mandatory attendance, he might

choose the easy way out instead of trying to develop his abilities. As a society, we

owe these students, at whatever cost, a chance at a good and sound education.

Notice that Student C specifies a "chance" at education. Here is a basic accommodation between Student C's views and Sipher's. *Both agree in principle that society can provide the opportunity, but not the certainty, of being educated.* The distinction here lies in the way in which the principle is applied. With his argument based on a sweeping generalization, Sipher makes no allowances or exceptions: there are limits to the opportunities that society is obliged to provide. Student C, however, believes that society must act in the best interests of those too young to make such decisions; for their sake, the principle of education as a privilege should be less rigorously applied. Students should be exposed to the conditions for (if not the fact of) education, whether they like it or not, until they become adults, capable of choice.

Student D goes even further, suggesting that not only is society obliged to provide the student with educational opportunities, but schools are responsible for making the experience as attractive as possible.

Student D

Maybe the reason for a decrease in attendance and an unwillingness to learn is

not that students do not want an education, but that the whole system of disci-

pline and learning is ineffective. If schools concentrated on making classes more

appealing, the result would be better attendance, and students would learn more.

In Student D's analysis, passive students are like consumers who need to be encouraged to take advantage of an excellent product that is not selling well. To encourage good attendance, the schools ought to consider using more attractive marketing methods. Implicit in this view is *a transferral of blame from the student to the school*. Other arguments of this sort might blame the parents, rather than the schools, for not teaching their children to understand that it is in their own best interests to get an education.

Finally, Student E accepts the validity of Sipher's view of education, but finds that the whole issue has become subordinate to a more important problem.

Student E

We already have a problem with youths roaming the street, getting into serious

trouble. Just multiply the current number of unruly kids by five or ten, and

you will come up with the number of potential delinquents that will be hanging

around the streets if we do away with the attendance laws that keep them in

school. Sipher may be right when he argues that the quality of education would

improve if unwilling students were permitted to drop out, but he would be wise to remember that those remaining inside school will have to deal with those on the outside sooner or later.

In this perspective, *security becomes more important than education.* Student E implicitly accepts and gives some social value to the image (rejected by Sipher) of school as a prison, with students sentenced to mandatory confinement.

Student E also ignores Sipher's tentative suggestion (in paragraph 16) that society provide these students with their own "institution," which he describes only in terms of its potential costs. What would its curriculum be? Would they be "special schools" or junior prisons? And when these students "graduate," how will they take their place in society?

A reasonably full response, like those of Students C and E, can provide the material for a series of paragraphs that argue against Sipher's position. Here, for example, is Student E's statement analyzed into the basic topics for a four-paragraph rebuttal within the essay. (The topics are on the left.)

Student E

danger from dropouts if Sipher's plan is adopted (3) custodial function of school (2) concession that Sipher is right about education (1) interests of law and order outweigh interests of education (4)	We already have a problem with youths roaming the street, getting into serious trouble. Just multiply the current number of unruly kids by five or ten, and you will come up with the number of potential delinquents that will be hanging around the streets if we do away with the attendance laws that keep them in school. Sipher may be right when he argues that the quality of education would improve if unwilling students were permitted to drop out, but he would be wise to remember that those remaining inside school will have to deal with those on the outside sooner or later.

Here are Student E's four topics, with the sequence reordered, in outline format. The student's basic agreement with Sipher has become the starting point.

I. Sipher is right about education.
   A. It is possible that the quality of education would improve if unwilling students were allowed to drop out.
II. School, however, has taken on a custodial function.
   A. It is attendance laws that keep students in school.
III. If Sipher's plan is adopted, dropouts might be a problem.
   A. Youths are already roaming the streets getting into trouble.
   B. An increase in the number of unruly kids hanging out in the streets means even greater possibility of disorder.

IV. The interests of law and order outweigh the interests of education.

    A. Educators will not be able to remain aloof from the problems that will develop outside the schools if students are permitted to drop out at will.

Student E can now write a brief essay, with a summary and analysis of Sipher's argument, followed by four full-length paragraphs explaining each point. If a longer essay is assigned, Student E should go to the library to find supporting evidence—statistics and authoritative testimony—to develop these paragraphs. A starting point might be the issue that Sipher omits: how do these nonattenders fare later on when they look for work? What methods have been successful in persuading such students to stay in school?

Guidelines for Writing a One-Source Argument

- Present your source's point of view.
  1. Briefly summarize the issue and the reasons that prompted the author to write the essay.
  2. Analyze and present some of the basic principles that underlie the author's position on this issue.
- Present your point of view.
  3. Present your reasons for disagreeing with (or, if you prefer, supporting) your source.

ASSIGNMENT 4: WRITING AN ARGUMENT BASED ON A SINGLE SOURCE

Read "What Our Education System Needs Is More F's," "Why Animals Deserve Legal Rights," "Let Teenagers Try Adulthood," and "For the Same Reasons That Students Can Be Expelled, Degrees Ought to Be Revocable." As the starting point for an essay, select one source with which you disagree. (Or, with your instructor's permission, bring in an essay that you are certain that you disagree with, and have your instructor approve your choice.)

1. Write a two-part summary of the essay, the first part describing the author's position and explicitly stated arguments, the second analyzing the principles underlying that position.
2. Then present your own rebuttal of the author's point of view.

The length of your essay will depend on the number and complexity of the ideas that you find in the source and the number of counterarguments that you can assemble. The minimum acceptable length for the entire assignment is two printed pages (approximately 500–600 words).

WHAT OUR EDUCATION SYSTEM NEEDS IS MORE F'S
Carl Singleton

I suggest that instituting merit raises, getting back to basics, marrying the university to industry, and . . . other recommendations will not achieve measurable success [in restoring quality to American education] until something even more basic is returned to practice. The immediate need for our educational system from pre-kindergarten through post-Ph.D. is not more money or better teaching but simply a widespread giving of F's.   1

Before hastily dismissing the idea as banal and simplistic, think for a moment about the implications of a massive dispensing of failing grades. It would dramatically, emphatically, and immediately force into the open every major issue related to the inadequacies of American education.   2

Let me make it clear that I recommend giving those F's—by the dozens, hundreds, thousands, even millions—only to students who haven't learned the required material. The basic problem of our educational system is the common practice of giving credit where none has been earned, a practice that has resulted in the sundry faults delineated by all the reports and studies over recent years. Illiteracy among high-school graduates is growing because those students have been passed rather than flunked; we have low-quality teaching because of low-quality teachers who never should have been certified in the first place; college students have to take basic reading, writing, and mathematics courses because they never learned those skills in classrooms from which they never should have been granted egress.   3

School systems have contributed to massive ignorance by issuing unearned passing grades over a period of some 20 years. At first there was a tolerance of students who did not fully measure up (giving D's to students who should have received firm F's); then our grading system continued to deteriorate (D's became C's, and B became the average grade); finally we arrived at total accommodation (come to class and get your C's, laugh at my jokes and take home B's).   4

Higher salaries, more stringent certification procedures, getting back to basics will have little or no effect on the problem of quality education unless and until we insist, as a profession, on giving F's whenever students fail to master the material.   5

Sending students home with final grades of F would force most parents to deal with the realities of their children's failure while it is happening and when it is yet possible to do something about it (less time on TV, and more time on homework, perhaps?). As long as it is the practice of teachers to pass students who should not be passed, the responsibility will not go home to the parents, where, I hope, it belongs. (I am tempted to make an analogy to then Gov. Lester Maddox's statement some years ago about prison conditions in Georgia—"We'll get a better grade of prisons when we get a better grade of prisoners"—but I shall refrain.)   6

Giving an F where it is deserved would force concerned parents to get themselves away from the TV set, too, and take an active part in their children's education.   7

I realize, of course, that some parents would not help; some cannot help. However, Johnny does not deserve to pass just because Daddy doesn't care or is ignorant. Johnny should pass only when and if he knows the required material.

Giving an F whenever and wherever it is the only appropriate grade would force   8
principals, school boards, and voters to come to terms with cost as a factor in improving our educational system. As the numbers of students at various levels were increased by those not being passed, more money would have to be spent to accommodate them. We could not be accommodating them in the old sense of passing them on, but by keeping them at one level until they did in time, one way or another, learn the material.

Insisting on respecting the line between passing and failing would also require   9
us to demand as much of ourselves as of our students. As every teacher knows, a failed student can be the product of a failed teacher.

Teaching methods, classroom presentations, and testing procedures would have to   10
be of a very high standard—we could not, after all, conscionably give F's if we have to go home at night thinking it might somehow be our own fault.

The results of giving an F where it is deserved would be immediately evident.   11
There would be no illiterate college graduates next spring—none. The same would be true of high-school graduates, and consequently next year's college freshmen—all of them—would be able to read.

I don't claim that giving F's will solve all of the problems, but I do argue that unless   12
and until we start failing those students who should be failed, other suggested solutions will make little progress toward improving education. Students in our schools and colleges should be permitted to pass only after they have fully met established standards; borderline cases should be retained.

The single most important requirement for solving the problems of education   13
in America today is the big fat F, written decisively in red ink millions of times in schools and colleges across the country.

WHY ANIMALS DESERVE LEGAL RIGHTS
Steven M. Wise

For centuries, the right to have everything that makes existence worthwhile—like   1
freedom, safety from torture, and even life itself—has turned on whether the law classifies one as a person or a thing. Although some Jews once belonged to Pharaoh, Syrians to Nero, and African-Americans to George Washington, now every human is a person in the eyes of the law.

All nonhuman animals, on the other hand, are things with no rights. The law ig-   2
nores them unless a person decides to do something to them, and then, in most cases, nothing can be done to help them. According to statistics collected annually by the Department of Agriculture, in the United States this year, tens of millions of

animals are likely to be killed, sometimes painfully, during biomedical research; 10 billion more will be raised in factories so crowded that they're unable to turn around, and then killed for food. The U.S. Fish and Wildlife Service and allied state agencies report that hundreds of millions will be shot by hunters or exploited in rodeos, circuses, and roadside zoos. And all of that is perfectly legal.

What accounts for the legal personhood of all of us and the legal thinghood of all of them? Judeo-Christian theologians sometimes argue that humans are made in the image of God. But that argument has been leaking since Gratian, the 12th-century Benedictine monk who is considered the father of canon law, made the same claim just for men in his *Decretum*. Few, if any, philosophers or judges today would argue that being human, all by itself, is sufficient for legal rights. There must be something about us that entitles us to rights.   3

Philosophers have proffered many criteria as sufficient, including sentience, a sense of justice, the possession of language or morality, and having a rational plan for one's life. Among legal thinkers, the most important is autonomy, also known as self-determination or volition. Things don't act autonomously. Persons do.   4

Notice that I said that autonomy is "sufficient" for basic legal rights; it obviously isn't necessary. We don't eat or vivisect human babies born without brains, who are so lacking in sentience that they are operated on without anesthesia.   5

But autonomy is tough to define. Kant thought that autonomous beings always act rationally. Anyone who can't do that can justly be treated as a thing. Kant must have had extraordinary friends and relatives. Not being a full-time academic, I don't know anyone who always acts rationally.   6

Most philosophers, and just about every judge, reject Kant's rigorous conception of autonomy, for they can easily imagine a human who lacks it, but can still walk about making decisions. Instead, some of them think that a being can be autonomous—at least to some degree—if she has preferences and the ability to act to satisfy them. Others would say she is autonomous if she can cope with changed circumstances. Still others, if she can make choices, even if she can't evaluate their merits very well. Or if she has desires and beliefs and can make at least some sound and appropriate inferences from them.   7

As things, nonhuman animals have been invisible to civil law since its inception. "All law," said the Roman jurist Hermogenianus, "was established for men's sake." And why not? Everything else was.   8

Unfortunately for animals, many people have believed that they were put on earth for human use and lack autonomy. Aristotle granted them a few mental abilities: They could perceive and act on impulse. Many Stoics, however, denied them the capacities to perceive, conceive, reason, remember, believe, even experience. Animals knew nothing of the past and could not imagine a future. Nor could they desire, know good, or learn from experience.   9

For decades, though, evidence has been accumulating that at least some nonhuman animals have extraordinary minds. Twelve years ago, 7-year-old Kanzi—a bonobo who works with Sue Savage-Rumbaugh, a biologist at Georgia State University—   10 drubbed a human 2-year-old, named Alia, in a series of language-comprehension tests. In the tests, both human and bonobo had to struggle, as we all do, with trying to make sense of the mind of a speaker. When Kanzi was asked to "put some water on the vacuum cleaner," he gulped water from a glass, marched to the vacuum cleaner, and dribbled the water over it. Told to "feed your ball some tomato," he could see no ball before him. So he picked up a spongy toy Halloween pumpkin and pretended to shove a tomato into its mouth. When asked to go to the refrigerator and get an orange, Kanzi immediately complied; Alia didn't have a clue what to do.

In the 40 years since Jane Goodall arrived at Gombe, she and others have shown that apes have most, if not all, of the emotions that we do. They are probably self-conscious; many of them can recognize themselves in a mirror. They use insight, not just trial and error, to solve problems. They form complex mental representations, including mental maps of the area where they live. They understand cause and effect. They act intentionally. They compare objects, and relationships between objects. They count. Use tools—they even make tools. Given the appropriate opportunity and motivation, they have been known to teach, deceive, and empathize with others. They can figure out what others see and know, abilities that human children don't develop until the ages of 3 to 5. They create cultural traditions that they pass on to their descendants. They flourish in rough-and-tumble societies so intensely political that they have been dubbed Machiavellian, and in which they form coalitions to limit the power of alpha males.   11

Twenty-first-century law should be based on twenty-first-century knowledge. Once the law assumed that witches existed and that mute people lacked intelligence. Now it is illegal to burn someone for witchcraft, and the mute have the same rights as anyone else.   12

Today we know that apes, and perhaps other nonhuman animals, are not what we thought they were in the prescientific age when the law declared them things. Now we know that they have what it takes for basic legal rights. The next step is obvious.   13

LET TEENAGERS TRY ADULTHOOD
Leon Botstein

The national outpouring after the Littleton shootings has forced us to confront something we have suspected for a long time: the American high school is obsolete and should be abolished. In the last month, high school students present and past have come forward with stories about cliques and the artificial intensity of a world defined by insiders and outsiders, in which the insiders hold sway because of superficial definitions of good looks and attractiveness, popularity and sports prowess.   1

The team sports of high school dominate more than student culture. A community's loyalty to the high school system is often based on the extent to which   2 varsity teams succeed. High school administrators and faculty members are often former coaches, and the coaches themselves are placed in a separate, untouchable category. The result is that the culture of the inside elite is not contested by the adults in the school. Individuality and dissent are discouraged.

But the rules of high school turn out not to be the rules of life. Often the high school outsider becomes the more successful and admired adult. The definitions of masculinity and femininity go through sufficient transformation to make the game of popularity in high school an embarrassment. No other group of adults young or old is confined to an age-segregated environment, much like a gang in which individuals of the same age group define each other's world. In no workplace, not even in colleges or universities, is there such a narrow segmentation by chronology.   3

Given the poor quality of recruitment and training for high school teachers, it is no wonder that the curriculum and the enterprise of learning hold so little sway over young people. When puberty meets education and learning in modern America, the victory of puberty masquerading as popular culture and the tyranny of peer groups based on ludicrous values meet little resistance.   4

By the time those who graduate from high school go on to college and realize what really is at stake in becoming an adult, too many opportunities have been lost and too much time has been wasted. Most thoughtful young people suffer the high school environment in silence and in their junior and senior years mark time waiting for college to begin. The Littleton killers, above and beyond the psychological demons that drove them to violence, felt trapped in the artificiality of the high school world and believed it to be real. They engineered their moment of undivided attention and importance in the absence of any confidence that life after high school could have a different meaning.   5

Adults should face the fact that they don't like adolescents and that they have used high school to isolate the pubescent and hormonally active adolescent away from both the picture-book idealized innocence of childhood and the more accountable world of adulthood. But the primary reason high school doesn't work anymore, if it ever did, is that young people mature substantially earlier in the late twentieth century than they did when the high school was invented. For example, the age of first menstruation has dropped at least two years since the beginning of this century, and not surprisingly, the onset of sexual activity has dropped in proportion. An institution intended for children in transition now holds young adults back well beyond the developmental point for which high school was originally designed.   6

Furthermore, whatever constraints to the presumption of adulthood among young people may have existed decades ago have now fallen away. Information and images, as well as the real and virtual freedom of movement we associate with adulthood, are now accessible to every 15- and 16-year-old.   7

Secondary education must be rethought. Elementary school should begin at age 4 or 5 and end with the sixth grade. We should entirely abandon the concept of   8 the middle school and junior high school. Beginning with the seventh grade, there should be four years of secondary education that we may call high school. Young people should graduate at 16 rather than 18.

They could then enter the real world, the world of work or national service, in which they would take a place of responsibility alongside older adults in mixed company. They could stay at home and attend junior college, or they could go away to college. For all the faults of college, at least the adults who dominate the world of colleges, the faculty, were selected precisely because they were exceptional and different, not because they were popular. Despite the often cavalier attitude toward teaching in college, at least physicists know their physics, mathematicians know and love their mathematics, and music is taught by musicians, not by graduates of education schools, where the disciplines are subordinated to the study of classroom management.

For those 16-year-olds who do not want to do any of the above, we might construct new kinds of institutions, each dedicated to one activity, from science to dance, to which adolescents could devote their energies while working together with professionals in those fields.

At 16, young Americans are prepared to be taken seriously and to develop the motivations and interests that will serve them well in adult life. They need to enter a world where they are not in a lunchroom with only their peers, estranged from other age groups and cut off from the game of life as it is really played. There is nothing utopian about this idea; it is immensely practical and efficient, and its implementation is long overdue. We need to face biological and cultural facts and not prolong the life of a flawed institution that is out of date.

FOR THE SAME REASONS THAT STUDENTS CAN BE EXPELLED, DEGREES OUGHT TO BE REVOCABLE

Gary Pavela

The Massachusetts Institute of Technology's decision last summer to revoke, for five years, the degree of a 1998 graduate involved in a hazing incident raises a long-standing question: May a college revoke a degree for a student's violation of institutional rules, if the violation occurred during the student's enrollment but was discovered after the student graduated?

Courts and a number of colleges and universities respond Yes, if the violation entails fraud or deceit in obtaining the degree, and the institution offers the student a fair hearing before revoking the degree.

But what if, as in the case at M.I.T., the violation pertains to misbehavior unrelated to academic evaluation? Is rescinding a degree reasonable, and legally permissible, in that circumstance?

The answer is less clear.

M.I.T.'s action has ignited controversy among administrators, faculty members, students, and others. Some observers have expressed concern that M.I.T. unfairly singled out one student for a kind of misconduct that is widespread on campuses. The harshest criticism has focused on whether the decision raised the specter of a perilous new form of "conduct police" on campus. Critics fear that colleges may begin revoking diplomas arbitrarily, for political, social, and ideological reasons.

The controversy points to a fundamental issue: What does a college or university degree represent? The topic is especially timely, because it highlights a recent and growing philosophical shift at many colleges around the United States, a shift that takes higher education back to an old concept. That concept, widely recognized until the past few decades, holds that the affirmation of good conduct and the development of character are part of the informal curriculum—and, therefore, proper considerations when deciding whether to award a degree.

In 1986, the Ohio Supreme Court considered many of the legal issues involved in whether an institution could revoke a degree—specifically for fraud or error—in *Waliga* v. *Board of Trustees of Kent State University*. In that case, Kent State University revoked the B.A. degrees of two former students after discovering discrepancies in their transcripts—including grades for courses they had never taken. The students challenged Kent State's action but eventually lost. The court wrote in its decision:

"We consider it self-evident that a college or university acting through its board of trustees does have the inherent authority to revoke an improperly awarded degree where (1) good cause such as fraud, deceit, or error is shown, and (2) the degree holder is afforded a fair hearing at which he can present evidence and protect his interest.

"Academic degrees are a university's certification to the world at large of the recipient's educational achievement and fulfillment of the institution's standards," the court continued. "To hold that a university may never withdraw a degree effectively requires the university to continue making a false certification to the public at large of the accomplishment of persons who in fact lack the very qualifications that are certified. Such a holding would undermine public confidence in the integrity of degrees, call academic standards into question, and harm those who rely on the certification which the degree represents."

The *Waliga* decision did not resolve the issue of whether an institution could rescind a degree for reasons other than fraud or error in obtaining that degree. Still, the Ohio Supreme Court gave college administrators ample discretion when it stated that "courts also have traditionally refused to interfere with fundamental university functions, such as the granting and withdrawing of degrees, except to require that good cause be shown and that a fair hearing procedure be made available." A federal appeals court reached a similar conclusion in another case a year later.

But the courts have not offered much guidance about the question: What good cause, other than fraud or error, can institutions show for revoking a degree? That is what most troubles people about the M.I.T. case. What criteria will colleges and universities use to make such an important decision? Would they take away the diplomas of students on the grounds of, for instance, simple non-conformity to traditional mores and practices—say, for publicly denouncing religion at a church-affiliated institution? Would doing so undermine the principles of freedom of expression upon which our system of higher education is based?

One answer is that when a student enters college, he or she and the institution 12 assume reciprocal commitments. The college agrees to provide specified services and instruction, and the student pledges to abide by the institution's established standards for student conduct. Many colleges already specify the point at which a student's breach of regulations warrants suspension or expulsion. Why shouldn't the institution make it clear that a similar breach may also be cause for revoking a student's degree, if the violation occurred while the student was enrolled, but is discovered after the student graduates?

The public appropriately considers a college degree to be more than a certifi- 13 cate of academic proficiency or technical accomplishment. By awarding a degree, an institution assures potential employers, and others, that the recipient had developed some basic degree of "emotional intelligence" and social responsibility, grounded in the ability to abide by reasonable standards of conduct. At the very least, the student should not have committed such a serious breach of those standards as to justify expulsion.

Of course, some critics of the M.I.T. decision have also questioned why the uni- 14 versity revoked a degree for a violation of institutional behavioral standards so belatedly—after the accused student had graduated and left the campus. My response is: If a serious violation remains undiscovered until after a student graduates, the only way to alert others that the student has not abided by fundamental institutional standards is by revoking—after a fair hearing—his or her diploma.

In short, society depends upon some minimal level of integrity in our graduates, 15 not just upon their academic knowledge or skills. If courts and higher-education institutions support the revocation of degrees received through fraud or error, they should also support revoking degrees for serious, proven misconduct in violation of established institutional rules.

The notion that receipt of a degree represents fulfillment of minimal standards 16 of conduct and character isn't new. The "Report of the Commission on the Proposed University of Virginia," signed by, among others, Thomas Jefferson, stated in 1818 that a university education, properly understood, "generates habits of application, of order and the love of virtue; and contours, by the force of habit, any innate obliquities in our moral organization."

One doesn't have to agree with every aspect of Jefferson's optimistic view to 17 share the educational objectives that he endorsed. Those objectives are again becoming explicit, perhaps because personal qualities like honesty and civility assume greater importance as new management styles give individuals and teams in the work force greater autonomy. Freed from layers of management, employees need— and the larger society depends upon—habits of character that inspire trust.

In 1997, the National Association of State Universities and Land-Grant Colleges published a report, "Returning to Our Roots: The Student Experience," promulgating what is fast becoming a national expectation in this regard: "Character, conscience, citizenship, tolerance, civility, and individual and social responsibility . . . should be part of the standard equipment of our graduates, not options." The report's executive summary emphasizes: "State and land-grant universities were established to put students first. In responding to change, we begin by returning to our roots, because too many of us have lost touch with much that was best in the past."   18

I grant that those who oppose degree revocation for violations of campus-conduct rules have reason to worry about potential abuses by college officials. A recent history of social and political intolerance on campuses—using speech codes, for instance, to ban "offensive skits" or to punish "insensitive expression"—is sobering. I can understand why some people are concerned that degree revocation might become a new form of political correctness on our campuses.   19

Still, it's possible to take a minimalist approach to degree revocation, reserving the process for those who have clearly violated long-established behavioral standards— such as prohibition of acts of serious violence.   20

I recommend the following guidelines, influenced by the *Waliga* decision and comparable court opinions: 21

• Institutions should develop and publish, after review by legal counsel, a concise statement affirming the institution's authority to revoke a degree, the reasons for exercising that authority, and the pertinent procedures to be followed. The statement should clearly specify the possible grounds—both academic and non-academic—for the revocation. Besides fraud or error in obtaining the degree, those grounds should include any violation of student-conduct regulations while the student was enrolled that would have been sufficient to justify a student's suspension or expulsion.   22

• When misconduct other than academic fraud is involved, administrators should be very careful in invoking the authority that they affirm. Therefore, college officials should also establish internal guidelines that spell out in advance when it is appropriate to begin proceedings to revoke a degree—and then apply those guidelines consistently. They should not undertake degree-revocation proceedings unless the alleged violation is a fundamental breach of institutional standards—such as serious threats or acts of violence, or sabotaging the work of others—usually indicating that the student poses a continuing danger to the larger community.   23

• Each institution should place a reasonable time limit on its power to revoke a student's degree. A degree should not be some sort of overall, lifetime certification of good character, justifying intrusive control by institutional officials. Ad-   24 ministrators should consult with legal counsel in setting such a time limit, perhaps consistent with their states' statutes of limitation on breach of contract.

- In any case of possible revocation, a designated person or committee—perhaps appointed by the top academic or student-affairs administrators—should conduct a preliminary review of the allegations, in accordance with internal guidelines. The person or committee should have the authority to decline to proceed if the allegations don't fall within the institution's guidelines, or if too much time has elapsed since the alleged violation of institutional rules occurred. In any case, the person or committee should provide written reasons for whatever decisions are made.   25

- College administrators should offer the person subject to degree-revocation proceedings a hearing, with the procedures clearly spelled out. Administrators should give the accused graduate adequate advance notice of the specific charges, the name of the person or persons making the charges, and full access to the case file before and during a hearing. The graduate also should have the right to a legal adviser, and a chance to submit relevant written evidence to the case file. In addition, administrators should allow the graduate to present evidence, and to hear, confront, and call witnesses.   26

    At the same time, traditional adversarial proceedings, with active participation by legal counsel for either side, are neither required nor desirable. In a college setting, courts have consistently ruled that traditional, courtroom-style, adversarial representation before a panel of laypersons is likelier to produce confusion than justice.   27

- Finally, institutional officials should insure a clear and convincing standard of proof—with the burden of proof on the complainant—and give the graduate a written statement of the reasons supporting the final decision.   28

In general, if the authority to award degrees is vested in a governing body, such as a board of trustees, only that body should make the final decision to revoke a degree. Although it may not be necessary for the governing body to read the transcript of a hearing, it should consider written findings and any objections to those findings. The body might agree to hear oral statements by the individual or group making the preliminary investigation, and by the accused graduate.   29

Adopting a minimalist perspective on degree revocation would deal with the concerns of those who fear inappropriate incursions into campus life by the so-called conduct police. At the same time, it would insure that the receipt and retention of a degree continues to mean that a student graduated in good standing, and has not been found to have violated the institution's fundamental standards of conduct. Anyone placing continuing reliance upon the accuracy and integrity of college transcripts would be surprised if colleges and universities wanted anything less.   30

STRATEGY TWO:
DEVELOPING AN ESSAY BASED ON A SOURCE

This strategy gives you the freedom to develop your own ideas and present your own point of view in an essay that is only loosely linked to the source. Reading an assigned essay helps you to generate ideas and topics and provides you with evidence or information to cite in your own essay; but the thesis, scope, and organization of your essay are entirely your own.

1. Finding and Narrowing a Topic

As always, you begin by studying the assigned essay carefully, establishing its thesis and main ideas. As you read, start brainstorming: noting ideas of your own that might be worth developing. You need not cover exactly the same material as the source essay. What you want is a *spin-off* from the original reading, not a summary.

Here is one student's preliminary list of topics for an essay based on Blanche Blank's "A Question of Degree." (Blank's essay can be found on pp. 8–11.) Notice that, initially, this student's ideas are mostly personal.

- "selling college": how do colleges recruit students? how did I choose this college? has my college experience met my expectations?

- "practical curriculum": what are my courses preparing me for? what is the connection between my courses and my future career? why am I here?

- "college compulsory at adolescence": what were my parental expectations? teachers' expectations? did we have any choices?

- "employment discrimination based on college degrees": what kinds of jobs now require a B.A.? was it always like that? what other kinds of training are possible—for clerks? for civil servants? for teacher's aides?

- financing college: how much is tuition? are we getting what we pay for? is education something to be purchased, like a winter coat?

- "dignity of work": job experience/work environment

- "joylessness in university life": describe students' attitudes—is the experience mechanical? is the environment bureaucratic?

- "hierarchical levels": what do the different college degrees mean? should they take as long as they do? should a B.A. take four years?

If you read the essay a few times without thinking of a topic or if you can't see how your ideas can be developed into an essay, test some standard strategies, applying them to the source essay in ways that might not have occurred to the original author. Here, for example, are some strategies that generate topics for an essay based on "A Question of Degree."

Process

You might examine in detail one of the processes that Blank describes only generally. For example, you could write about your own experience to explain the ways in which teenagers are encouraged to believe that a college degree is essential, citing high school counseling and college catalogues and analyzing the unrealistic expectations that young students are encouraged to have. Or, if you have sufficient knowledge, you might describe the unjust manipulation of hiring procedures that favor college graduates or the process by which a college's liberal arts curriculum gradually becomes "practical."

Illustration

If you focused on a single discouraged employee, showing in what ways ambition for increased status and salary have been frustrated, or a single disillusioned college graduate, showing how career prospects have failed to measure up to training and expectations, your strategy would be an illustration proving one of Blank's themes.

Definition

Definition often emerges from a discussion of the background of an issue. What should the work experience be like? What is the function of a university? What is a good education? By attempting to define one of the components of Blank's theme in terms of the ideal, you are helping your reader to understand her arguments and evaluate her conclusions more rationally.

Cause and Effect

You can examine one or more of the reasons why a college degree has become a necessary credential for employment. You can also suggest a wider context for discussing Blank's views by describing the kind of society that encourages this set of values. In either case, you will be accounting for, but not necessarily justifying, the nation's obsession with degrees. Or you can predict the consequences, good or bad, that might result if Blank's suggested legislation were passed. Or you might explore some hypothetical possibilities and focus on the circumstances and causes of a situation different from the one that Blank describes. What if everyone in the United States earned a college degree? What if education after the eighth grade were abolished? B
proach, you are radically changing the circumstances that B
still sharing her concerns and exploring the principles discusse

Problem and Solution

If Cause and Effect asks "why," then Problem and Solution of Blank raises several problems that, in her view, have harmfu quences. What are some solutions? What changes are possible effect them? How, for example, can we change students' expectations of education and make them both more realistic and more idealistic? Note that exploring such solutions means that you are basically in agreement with Blank's thesis.

Comparison

You can alter the reader's perspective by moving the theme of Blank's essay to another time or place. Did our present obsession with education exist a hundred years ago? Is it a problem outside the United States at this moment? Will it probably continue throughout the twenty-first century? Or, focusing on millennial America, how do contemporary trends in education and employment compare with trends in other areas of life—housing, finance, recreation, child-rearing, or communications? With all these approaches, you begin with a description of Blank's issue and contrast it with another set of circumstances, past or present, real or hypothetical.

Before choosing any of these speculative topics, you must first decide:

- What is practical in a brief essay
- Whether the topic requires research
- Whether, when fully developed, the topic will retain some connection with the source essay

For example, there may be some value in comparing the current emphasis on higher education with monastic education in the Middle Ages. Can you write such an essay? How much research will it require? Will a discussion of monastic education help your reader better to understand Blank's ideas? Or will you immediately move away from your starting point—and find no opportunity to return to it? Do you have a serious objective, or are you simply making the comparison "because it's there"?

2. Taking Notes and Writing a Thesis

Consider how you might develop an essay based on one of the topics suggested in the previous section. Notice that the chosen topic is expressed as a question.

Topic: What is the function of a university today?

- After thinking about your topic, start your list of notes *before* you reread the essay, to make sure that you are not overly influenced by the author's point of view and to enable you to include some ideas of your own in your notes.
- Next, review the essay and add any relevant ideas to your list, *remembering to indicate when an idea originated with the source and not with you.*

Here is a complete list of notes for an essay defining the function of a university for our time. The paragraph references, added later, indicate which points were made by Blank and where in her essay they can be found. The thesis, which follows the notes, was written after the list was complete.

WHAT THE UNIVERSITY SHOULD DO

1. to increase students' understanding of the world around them

    e.g., to become more observant and aware of natural phenomena (weather, for example) and social systems (like family relationships)

2. to help students to live more fulfilling lives

    to enable them to test their powers and know more and become more versatile; to speak with authority on topics that they didn't understand before

3. to help students live more productive lives

    to increase their working credentials and qualify for more interesting and well-paying jobs (B.B., Paragraphs 3–9)

4. to serve society by creating better informed, more rational citizens not only through college courses (like political science) but through the increased ability to observe and analyze and argue (B.B., Paragraphs 3, 14)

5. to contribute to research that will help to solve scientific and social problems

    (not a teaching function) (B.B., Paragraphs 3, 14)

6. to serve as a center for debate to clarify the issues of the day

    people should regard the university as a source of unbiased information and counsel; notable people should come to lecture (B.B., Paragraphs 3, 14)

7. to serve as a gathering place for great teachers

    students should be able to regard their teachers as worth emulating

8. to allow students to examine the opportunities for personal change and growth

    this includes vocational goals, e.g., career changes (B.B., Paragraph 4)

WHAT THE UNIVERSITY SHOULD NOT DO

9. it should not divide the haves from the have-nots

   college should not be considered essential; it should be possible to be successful without a college degree (B.B., Paragraphs 8, 10)

10. it should not use marketing techniques to appeal to the greatest number

    what the university teaches should be determined primarily by the faculty
    and to a lesser extent by the students; standards of achievement should
    not be determined by students who haven't learned anything yet

11. it should not ignore the needs of its students and its community by clinging
    to outdated courses and programs

12. it should not cooperate with business and government to the extent that it
    loses its autonomy (B.B., Paragraphs 6, 9)

13. it should not be an employment agency and vocational center to the exclu-
    sion of its more important functions (B.B., Paragraphs 6, 9, 16)

Thesis: As Blanche Blank points out, a university education is not a commodity
    to be marketed and sold; a university should be a resource center for those
    who want the opportunity to develop their intellectual powers and lead more
    productive, useful, and fulfilling lives.

3. Deciding on a Strategy

As a rule, you would consider strategies for your essay as soon as you
have established your thesis. In this case, however, the choice of strategy—definition—was made earlier when you chose your topic and considered several
possible strategies. The notes, divided into what a university should and
should not do, already follow a definition strategy, with its emphasis on
differentiation.

4. Structuring Your Essay

Having made all the preliminary decisions, you are ready to plan the structure of your essay. You organize your notes by arranging them in a lyrical sequence, which is usually called an *outline*. Some outlines use numbers and
letters; some don't. But all outlines represent the relationship of ideas by their
arrangement on the page: major points at the margin, supporting points and
evidence underneath and slightly to the right.

- Mark those portions of the reading that you will need to use in support of your thesis. Your essay will be based on both your own ideas and the ideas of your source.
- Check whether your notes accurately paraphrase the source, and decide how many source references you intend to make so that you can write a balanced outline.
- Double-check to make sure that you are giving the source credit for all paraphrased ideas.
- If appropriate, include some examples from your own experience.
- Organize your notes in groups or categories, each of which will be developed as a separate paragraph or sequence of related paragraphs.
- Decide the order of your categories (or paragraphs).
- Incorporate in your outline some of the points from Blanche Blank's essay that you intend to include. Cite the paragraph number of the relevant material with your outline entry. If the source paragraph contains several references that you expect to place in different parts of your outline, use a sentence number or a set of symbols or a brief quotation for differentiation.

Here is one section of the completed outline for an essay on "Defining a University for the New Millennium." This outline incorporates notes 3, 13, 9, and 8 from the list on pp. 143–144.

I. The university should help students to live more productive lives, to increase their working credentials, and to qualify for more interesting and well-paying jobs. (Paragraph 6—last sentence)

    A. But it should not be an employment agency and vocational center to the exclusion of its more important functions. (Paragraph 9—"servicing agents"; Paragraph 12—"joylessness in our university life"; Paragraph 16)

    B. It should not divide the haves from the have-nots; success without a college degree should be possible. (Paragraph 2—"two kinds of work"; Paragraph 17)

II. The university should allow students to examine the opportunities for personal growth and change; this includes vocational goals, e.g., career changes. (Paragraph 4—"an optional and continuing experience later in life")

5. Writing the Essay

When you write from sources, you are engaged in a kind of partnership. You strive for an appropriate balance between your own ideas and those of your source. By reading your source carefully and using annotation and paraphrase, you familiarize yourself with the source's main ideas and reasoning and prepare to put those ideas in your essay. But *it is your voice that should dominate the essay.* You, after all, are writing it; you are responsible for its contents and its effect on the reader. For this reason, all the important "positions" in the structure of your essay should be filled by you. The topic sentences, as well as the introduction, should be written in your own words and should stress your views, not those of your author. On the other hand, your reader should not be allowed to lose sight of the source essay; it should be treated as a form of evidence and cited whenever it is relevant, but always as a context in which to develop your own strategy and assert your own thesis.

Here is the completed paragraph based on Points I and IA in the outline:

> To achieve certain goals, all of us have agreed to take four years out of our lives, at great expense, for higher education. What I learn here will, I hope, give me the communication skills, the range of knowledge, and the discipline to succeed in a career as a journalist. But, as Blanche Blank points out, a college education may not be the best way to prepare for every kind of job. Is it necessary to spend four years at this college to become a supermarket manager? a computer programmer? a clerk in the social security office? If colleges become no more than high-level job training or employment centers, or, in Blank's words, "servicing agents" to screen workers for business, then they lose their original purpose as centers of a higher form of learning. Blank is rightly concerned that, if a college degree becomes a mandatory credential, I and my contemporaries will regard ourselves "as prisoners of economic necessity," alienated from the rich possibilities of education by the "joylessness in our university life."

6. Revising the Essay

Your work isn't finished until you have reviewed your essay carefully to ensure that the organization is logical, the paragraphs coherent, and the sentences complete. To gain some distance and objectivity, most people put their work aside for a while before starting to revise it. You can also ask someone else to read and comment on your essay, but make sure that you have reason to trust that person's judgment and commitment to the task. It isn't helpful to be told only that "paragraph three doesn't work" or "I don't get that sentence"; your reader should be willing to spend some time and trouble to pinpoint what's wrong so that you can go back to your manuscript and make revisions. Problems usually arise in these three areas.

Overall Structure

If you follow your outline or your revised list of notes, your paragraphs should follow each other fairly well. But extraneous ideas—some of them good

Guidelines for Writing a Single-Source Essay

1. Identify the source essay's thesis; analyze its underlying themes, if any, and its strategy; and construct a rough list or outline of its main ideas.

2. Decide on two or three possible essay topics based on your work in Step 1, and narrow down one of them. (Be prepared to submit your topics for your teacher's approval and, in conference, to choose the most suitable one.)

3. Write down a list of notes about your own ideas on the topic, being careful to distinguish between points that are yours and points that are derived from the source.

4. Write a thesis of your own that fairly represents your list of ideas. Mention the source in your thesis if appropriate.

5. If you have not done so already, choose a strategy that will best carry out your thesis; it need not be the same strategy as that of the source essay.

6. Mark (by brackets or underlining) those paragraphs or sentences in the source that will help to develop your topic.

7. Draw up an outline for your essay. Combine repetitious points; bring together similar and related points. Decide on the best sequence for your paragraphs.

8. Decide which parts of the reading should be cited as evidence or refuted; place paragraph or page references to the source in the appropriate sections of your outline. Then decide which sentences of the reading to quote and which to paraphrase.

9. Write the rough draft, making sure that, whenever possible, your topic sentences express your views, introduce the material that you intend to present in that paragraph, and are written in your voice. Later in the paragraph, incorporate references to the source, and link your paragraphs together with transitions. Do not be concerned about a bibliography for this single-source essay. Cite the author's full name and the exact title of the work early in your essay. (See pp. 85–89 for a review of citations.)

10. Write an introduction that contains a clear statement of your thesis, as well as a reference to the source essay and its role in the development of your ideas. You may also decide to draft a conclusion.

11. Review your first draft to note problems with organization, transitions, or language. Proofread your first draft very carefully to correct errors of grammar, style, reference, and spelling.

12. Prepare the final draft. Even if you use a computer spellcheck, proofread once again.

ones—tend to creep in as you write, and sometimes you need to make adjustments to accommodate them. As you look carefully at the sequence of paragraphs, make sure that they lead into each other. Are parallel points presented in a series or are they scattered throughout the essay? Sometimes, two paragraphs need to be reversed, or two paragraphs belong together and need to be merged. In addition, your reader should be guided through the sequence of paragraphs by the "traffic signals" provided by transitional phrases, such as "in addition" or "nevertheless" or "in fact." The transitions need not be elaborate: words like "also," "so," and "too" keep the reader on track.

Paragraph Development

The paragraphs should be of roughly comparable length, each containing a topic sentence (not necessarily placed at the beginning), explanatory sentences, details or examples provided by your source or yourself, and (possibly) quotations from your source. It's important to have this mix of general material and detail to keep your essay from being too abstract or too specific. Make sure that every sentence contributes to the point of the paragraph. Look for sentences without content, or sentences that make the same point over again. If, after such deletions, a paragraph seems overly brief or stark, consider what illustrations or details might be added to support and add interest to the topic. Check back to the source to see if there are still some points worth paraphrasing or quoting.

Sentence Style

Your writing should meet a basic acceptable standard. Are the sentences complete? Eliminate fragments or run-ons. Is the sentence style monotonous, with the same pattern repeated again and again? Look for repetitions, and consider ways to vary the style, such as starting some sentences with a phrase or subordinate clause. Are you using the same vocabulary again and again? Are too many of your sentences built around "is" or "are"? Search for stronger verbs, and vary your choice of words, perhaps consulting the thesaurus. (But think twice about using words that are totally new to you, or you'll risk sounding awkward. Use the thesaurus to remind yourself of possible choices, not to increase your vocabulary.) Finally, consider basic grammar. Check for apostrophes, for subject-verb agreement, for quotation marks. Don't let careless errors detract from your hard work in preparing and writing this essay.

ASSIGNMENT 5: WRITING AN ESSAY BASED ON A SINGLE SOURCE

A. Read "Feasts of Violence," "Why Are We Entranced by Trashy Thrillers?" "The Sales Call . . . and Other Horrors," and "Politics and the Reasonable Man." One of these four essays will serve as the starting point for an essay of your own. Assume that the essay you are planning will be approximately three pages long, or 600–900 words. Using steps 1 and 2, think of *three* possible topics for an essay of that length, and submit the most promising (or, if your teacher suggests it, all three) for approval.

B. Plan your essay by working from notes to an outline. Be prepared to submit your thesis and outline of paragraphs (with indications of relevant references to the source) to your teacher for approval.

C. Write a rough draft after deciding which parts of the essay should be cited as evidence, distributing references to the source among appropriate sections of your outline, and determining which parts of the reading should be quoted and which should be paraphrased.

D. Write a final draft of your essay.

FEASTS OF VIOLENCE
Sissela Bok

No people before or since have so reveled in displays of mortal combat as did the Romans during the last two centuries B.C. and the first three centuries thereafter, nor derived such pleasure from spectacles in which slaves and convicts were exposed to wild beasts and killed in front of cheering spectators. According to Nicolaus of Damascus, writing in the first decade A.D., Romans even regaled themselves with lethal violence at private banquets; he describes dinner guests relishing the spectacle of gladiators fighting to the death:

> Hosts would invite their friends to dinner not merely for other entertainment, but that they might witness two or three pairs of contestants in a gladiatorial combat; on these occasions, when sated with dining and drink, they called in the gladiators. No sooner did one have his throat cut than the masters applauded with delight at this feat.

Perhaps the delectation and thrill of viewing a fight to the death at such close hand while reclining after a meal with friends provided even greater pleasure than the vast gladiatorial shows in the amphitheater, in which thousands of combatants confronted death each year. Devotees versed in the aesthetics of violence and the "science of pleasure" could study at close hand the subtleties of the moves in each encounter and celebrate the nobility and beauty with which defeated gladiators who had been denied a reprieve bared their necks for decapitation.

The satiric poet Juvenal's phrase "bread and circuses"—*panem et circenses*—that has come down, through the centuries, to stand for public offerings of nourishment and spectacles on a grand scale, would have meant nothing to the earliest Romans. There is no evidence from their period of vast wild beast hunts in circuses or spectacular forms of capital punishment or gladiatorial combats to the death in the arena. The first gladiatorial fight we know of took place in 264 B.C., when the ex-consul Iunius Brutus Pera and his brother, in a ceremony to honor their dead father, presented three pairs of gladiators in the ox market. More such encounters were offered in the ensuing decades by private citizens as a way to honor dead relatives. But gladiatorial combat was increasingly seen, too, as entertainment and as evidence of generosity, even lavishness on the part of public officials.

Barely two centuries after the first gladiatorial fights, they had become the centerpiece of the Roman "games," alongside wild animal hunts with live game brought from every corner of the known world to be slaughtered, and countless slaves, prisoners, and other-victims "thrown to the beasts." Those who died thus were seen either as expendable nonhumans, such as slaves or wild beasts, as criminals or prisoners of war who justly deserved their fate, or as volunteers who had chosen to take part freely or sold themselves into service as gladiators.

Violent spectacles kept the citizenry distracted, engaged, and entertained and, along with reenactments and celebrations of conquests and sacrifices abroad, provided the continued acculturation to violence needed by a warrior state. And the association with bread was constant. Not only were shows in the amphitheater or the circus meant for feasting the eye as well as the emotions: many sponsors also gave out bread, meat, drink, and favorite dishes to the crowds gathered for the games. Elements of entertainment and feasting were combined with ritual and sacrifice. Ancient Rome seems a particularly striking illustration of the claim by literary scholar René Girard that all communal violence can be described in terms of sacrifice, using surrogate victims as means to protect the entire community against its own internal violence. No program could begin without a sacrifice to a deity, often Diana, who presided over the raucous hunting scenes, or Mars, patron of the gladiatorial combats; and after the bloodshed was over, "a figure, representing the powers of the under-world, gave the finishing stroke to the wretches who were still lingering."

Throughout, such violence was regarded as legitimate, fully authorized, even commanded at the highest level of Roman society. The festive atmosphere, the rousing music of the bands, the chanting by the crowds, the betting on who would triumph or lose, the colorful costumes, and the adulation of star gladiators all contributed to the glamour attached to the games. But as historian Kathleen Coleman points out, while "the 'contagion of the throng' may aptly describe the thrill that the Roman spectators experienced in the Colosseum, [it] does not explain why their communal reaction was pleasure instead of revulsion or horror." Part of the reason, she suggests, is that the Roman world "was permeated by violence that had to be absorbed."

Just as Roman spectacles remain the prototype for violent entertainment at its most extreme, so Rome's own history illustrates the development of a prototypical "culture of violence." It was one in which violence was widely sanctioned and hallowed by tradition, in foreign conquest as in domestic culture; in which courage and manhood were exalted and weapons easily available; and in which the climate of brutality and callousness extended from the treatment of newborns and slaves in many homes to the crucifixions and other brutal punishments so common for noncitizens. Entertainment violence officially sponsored on a mass basis served to enhance every one of these aspects of Rome's martial culture.

Among Romans, spectacles of violence had many celebrants and few outspoken challengers. The poet Martial, in his *De Spectaculis,* written in A.D. 80 for the inauguration of the Colosseum, conveyed the magnificence of the fights and wild beast hunts in evocative tones. Speaking of a condemned criminal who, "hanging on no unreal cross gave up his vitals to a Caledonian bear," Martial described his mangled limbs as still living, "though the parts dripped gore, and in all his body was nowhere a body's shape. A punishment deserved at length he won." This death was staged as a performance of the story of Laureolus, a famous bandit leader who had been captured and crucified. This was a favorite subject for dramatic enactment, but as Martial pointed out, the victim in this instance was "hanging on no unreal cross," and his agony was compounded by exposure to the bear.   8

Why did such spectacles have so few outspoken critics among Romans? We can only wonder at the silence of those, like Marcus Aurelius and Epictetus, who proclaimed Stoic and other ideals of goodness and justice, not to mention the many other philosophers, poets, and legal scholars who were openly admiring of the practice. Like most Romans, they may have been too thoroughly acculturated to violence to see any need for criticism. The historian Tacitus recounts that "there are the peculiar and characteristic vices of this metropolis of ours, taken on, it seems to me, almost in the mother's womb—the passion for play actors and the mania for gladiatorial shows and horse-racing." At home as in the lecture halls, the gossip is all about such spectacles; even the teachers dwell largely on such material in their classes.   9

Along with such acculturation, fear was the great silencer of outrage and free debate among the Romans and the peoples they conquered. It was dangerous to speak freely, above all to criticize acts of the emperor and practices linked to his worship. At his whim, critics could be jailed, exiled, or thrown to the lions. But more than acculturation and fear was involved. Opportunistic self-censorship was rampant. Many among the intelligentsia and the aristocracy derived great prestige from sponsoring displays of gladiators. They had a vested interest in seeing the games continue and in deriding criticism.   10

One who did note a moral paradox in the gladiatorial games presenting violence as public entertainment was the philosopher Seneca. He pointed to Pompey, reputedly conspicuous among leaders of the state for the kindness of his heart, who had been the first   11

> to exhibit the slaughter of eighteen elephants in the circus, pitting criminals against them in a mimic battle [and] thought it a notable kind of spectacle to kill human beings after a new fashion. Do they fight to the death? That is not enough! Are they torn to pieces? That is not enough! Let them be crushed by animals of monstrous bulk!

That human beings should kill and maim their fellows was hardly paradoxical in its own right; rather, the oddity was that the pleasure in seeing it carried out could   12 be so relished as to override all sense of respect for life: "Man, an object of reverence in the eyes of men, is now slaughtered for jest and sport . . . and it is a satisfying spectacle to see a man made a corpse." For Seneca, sharing the enjoyment of that spectacle brutalized and desensitized viewers and fostered their appetite for still more cruelty. It undercut the central task of seeking to grow in humanity, in nobility of spirit, in understanding, and in freedom from greed, cruelty, and other desires; and thereby to progress toward self-mastery. Seneca saw *any* diversion as deflecting from this task; but taking pleasure in brutality—in "seeing a man made a corpse"—actually reversed the development, destroyed *humanitas:* the respectful kindness that characterizes persons who have learned how to be fully human among humans. Violent entertainments rendered spectators *crudelior et inhumanior*—"more cruel and more inhumane"—acculturating them to pitilessness and to lack of respect for their fellow humans and other creatures.

The same forces that numbed most Romans' shame or sense of moral paradox inherent in relishing such cruelty—acculturation, fear, and profiteering—also helped to dampen criticism in the provinces. Many Roman military encampments had their own amphitheaters, and hundreds of others were built for the public around the Empire in the first centuries A.D. But though Roman authorities and commercial sponsors encouraged attendance at the games in conquered territories as a form of homage to the emperor-deities, such spectacles could not compete in extravagance with those offered by the emperors in Rome and rarely met with the special exultation elsewhere that they evoked there. A few spoke out against them openly: when King Herod wished to offer spectacles in an amphitheater he had constructed near Jerusalem, "the Jews found such a cruel pleasure to be impious and an abandonment of their ancestral customs."   13

Among the severest critics were Christians, from whose ranks so many were tortured and killed at the games. Late in the second century, Bishop Tertullian thundered, in his *De Spectaculis,* against violent spectacles rooted in pagan religion, with their brutalizing effects on victims, sponsors, combatants, and spectators alike. He lambasted the Christians who took pleasure in such shows and cautioned against the degradation that came, not just from viewing cruelty but from delighting in it, finding it entertaining, developing a "passion for murderous pleasure." With puritanical zeal, he insisted that people should avoid not only violent shows but all spectacles: 14

> There is no public spectacle without violence to the spirit. For where there is pleasure, there is eagerness, which gives pleasure its flavor. Where there is eagerness, there is rivalry, which gives its flavor to eagerness. Yes, and then, where there is rivalry, there also are madness, bile, anger, pain, and all the things that follow from them and (like them) are incompatible with moral discipline.

Tertullian ended on a shrill note that clashed with all that he had said about the evils of taking pleasure in violent spectacles. He appears to have promised his fellow Christians, in spite of all, the reward of "murderous pleasure" in the next life   15 if they would only abjure it in this one. Reveling in the horrors that would befall those who now took any part in spectacles, he predicted that, come the Day of Judgment, Christians could look forward to the thrill, the exultation at being able to watch, as if they were at the games, the infliction on nonbelievers, such as actors, kings, athletes, poets, and philosophers, of suffering, torture, and burning, horrors far worse than at the earthly games and everlasting to boot:

> How vast the spectacle that day, and how wide! What sight shall wake my wonder, what my laughter, my joy, and exultation? As I see all those kings . . . groaning in the depths of darkness! And the magistrates who persecuted the name of Jesus, liquefying in fiercer flames than they kindled in their rage against the Christians! Those sages, too, the philosophers blushing before their disciples as they blaze together. . . and then, the poets trembling before the judgment-seat. . . . And then there will be the tragic actors to be heard, more vocal in their own tragedy; and the players to be seen, lither of limb by far in the fire; . . . Such sights, such exultation—what praetor, consul, quaestor, priest, will ever give you his bounty? And yet all these, in some sort, are ours, pictured through faith in the imagination of the spirit. But what are those things which eye hath not seen nor ear heard, nor ever entered into the heart of man? I believe, things of greater joy than circus, theatre, amphitheatre, or any stadium.

WHY ARE WE ENTRANCED BY TRASHY THRILLERS?
Bruce Fleming

I like trashy films. Not all trashy films, just those slick, pulsing thrillers that have become such popular summer offerings from Hollywood in recent years. I mean the one-man-saves-the-world (or ship, or skyscraper, or bus)-from-a-madman films. The genre is defined by the *Die Hard* movies and their Steven Seagal spinoffs, by that almost-perfect movie *Speed*, by practically anything with Harrison Ford, and by virtually all movies with musclemen, such as Arnold Schwarzenegger and Jean-Claude Van Damme. The James Bond films, including the most recent one, *Tomorrow Never Dies*, are probably the ur-form of trashy movies.

These movies are, of course, exciting. They offer a dazzle of technological gimmicks, hailstorms of bullets, bad-guy bodies flying in all directions, and the constant thud of metal crashing into metal. At the same time, they're touching, at a profound, almost philosophical level. Permeated with the state of dislocation from the world that precedes a leap of religious faith, these films suggest that material objects, including our own bodies, are chaff, and those things we do to acquire or preserve them only vanity. Moreover, though apparently a celebration of the utterly competent male—whom the viewer is meant either to desire or to identify with—these movies ultimately suggest that the dream of men is not to conquer the world, but to be perpetually threatened by it.

The disregard for elementary rules of safety that characterizes the hero in these   3
films is taken to such lengths that it begins to blank out the warp and woof of
normal life, the way a searchlight renders invisible any slighter light source. Why
should we imbibe as children the collective societal wisdom of the actions we
take to insure our continued longevity and good health—from putting iodine on
cuts to looking both ways before we cross the street—only to throw it all away
as adults? By rights, such carelessness should be a horrifying spectacle. Why, instead, are we entranced?

The answer (which pulls us up short when we realize its ramifications) has to   4
be: It's exhilarating to see so much waste. The hero's utter disregard for his own
safety is made possible only by his being at the peak of physical perfection, prepared by years of care and attention to every tiny threat and twinge. These movies
are like one big bash where the laboriously collected pennies of decades are blown
in a single fling. For his foolhardiness, the hero is rewarded with success and, inevitably, the babe. These movies are our revenge on the careful.

Our pleasure in such movies, moreover, shows just how hollow are our preten-   5
sions to having learned to play with other children in the kindergarten sandbox.
These films betray our desire to act exactly as we wish, with no concern for the consequences or for the needs of others—on the condition, of course, that we can
get away with it. Sublime in their return to an infantile solipsism, these movies portray a world in which everyone but the hero is either at his sexual behest or (the
more usual state) dead. These movies suggest that, *pace* Spinoza, man is not a social creature at all. Our childhood illusions of being the center of the universe
haven't been given up; they've been swallowed whole for their own protection, waiting for the proper moment to come roaring back.

In the foreground of these films is the utter unflappability and control of the   6
hero—particularly over the material objects that, in the end, are deemed completely
disposable. Whether the President or a mere policeman, the hero can fly or drive
any vehicle, is at home with all forms of sophisticated warfare, and can get computers to do anything he wants. (*Mission: Impossible* is particularly extreme in this last
regard; ultimately it seems a movie about hacking.) The hero also instantly puts quotidian objects to clever new uses. In *Speed,* he saves an elevator full of hostages
using a hook he has conjured out of his pocket and a construction crane, holds on
under a moving bus by skewering the gas tank with a screwdriver, and gets out
from under the bus alive by coasting off on a piece of the flooring tied to the steer-
ing wheel with a piece of cord that unwinds as the bus moves.

Yet such competence with objects, paradoxically, is only possible because the   7
heroes are not bound by the way the world is supposed to function. Indeed, the
ingenuity these heroes show presupposes an almost Zen-like detachment from the
world, whose objects neither hamper nor anchor them. A fork is not something
for eating peas; it's a brute shape of metal that can be used for a thousand things,
from a weapon to a lever on a bomb. Constantly disproving Heidegger's insistence

that objects are by nature defined by their use in the world, these movies evoke a world of brute material to which the hero alone can give shape and form: Schwarzenegger as Demiurge.

All these heroes are conversant with technology, deft with their fingers while manipulating tiny things, and careful with their preparations. Yet the end of all this precise control is always a great "boom" as something blows up, or a puddle as one more bad guy is eliminated. Enormously complicated machines—and the countless human beings around or on top of them—are destroyed in an instant as a result of careful, technical work.

The attention to detail and care for objects that seem to characterize the heroes constitute the flip side of utter contempt for, or perhaps frustration with, the objects of industrial civilization that make our lives so much easier—and so much more complex. These movies express our very hatred of the material world they seem to showcase so glowingly: Objects have become the enemy to be conquered; human villains are only secondary.

In *True Lies,* Marine Corps airplanes take out sections of what is supposed to be the highway threading through the Florida Keys: The destruction feels good. In *Speed,* the threatened city bus finally not only blows up itself, but takes an airplane with it in an orgasmic ball of fire: That feels good, too. In *Die Hard,* the multimillion-dollar buildings seem the most expendable objects on the set. *Air Force One* is almost an intellectual movie by contrast; we must wait until the end to have much destruction: The huge airliner, now empty save for the traitor, crash-lands and breaks up in the ocean. We even get to feel self-righteous about all this mayhem: The scripts are always careful to justify it as pre-emptive or reactive; the bad guys are evil incarnate; and frequently the hero is doing it all to save a woman.

Such a combination of opposites with respect to objects (fine-tuned control or devil-may-care cavalierness) is ingrained in the male-dominated military, whose ethos seems to be the guiding principle of such movies. Military recruits are neater than the average person: Their heads are shorn clean of the distraction of hair; their racks (beds) are made so tight that a quarter can be bounced on them; rifles are kept clean of even fingerprints. Yet these are the people who are being taught to go out and crawl in the mud under barbed wire, or who may well have their heads turned into a bloody mess by bullets. Most of us live our lives in the middle: Our shirts may be wrinkled and our beds unmade, but neither are we likely to have an arm blown off. One extreme implies the other.

On the surface, these movies celebrate competence and control, suggesting that masculinity (which of course they model) is something we can work for and attain. Yet a world at our behest is not a very exciting one; the fruit of victory, as we see in Tennyson's "Ulysses," is almost always boredom. The volume on the excitement is turned up so high that the ostensible equation of masculinity with control becomes garbled, and abruptly transmutes into its opposite, which is the utter lack of control. Real masculinity, these movies seem to say, goes way beyond competence

8

9

10

11

12

into recklessness. If the hero ultimately isn't conquered by the universe, it's not because he doesn't give it enough opportunity.

It didn't take *Star Wars* to show that such heroes feel an attraction to the dark side they so relentlessly battle. Otherwise, why would they throw themselves against it so unrelentingly? And it didn't take Hemingway to tell us that there's no point in victory unless the bull (elephant, buffalo) can actually kill you, and to point out that you have to love your adversary. The heroes of trashy movies are, to use the choreographer Martha Graham's phrase, "doom-eager." They like being in harm's way. But of course the Marine Corps has known this all along.   13

In the end, victory always comes completely by chance, independent of anything the hero does or does not do. A cable miraculously holds, or the hero is an inch on the right side of the chasm, or the bad guy is distracted and his bullet just misses. In *Mission: Impossible,* success or failure for Tom Cruise hangs on whether a bead of his sweat will drop onto the sensitized floor of a room where he is suspended from the ceiling, involved in a highly technical computer stunt. In *Air Force One,* victory hinges on Harrison Ford's finding a cellular phone among the baggage in the hijacked airplane. Though at first glance celebrations of human ingenuity and strength, these films ultimately are hymns to chance, paeans to luck.   14

Many critics have pointed out that these films are odd mixtures of the realistic and the silly: The dialogue must fit the speakers' social standing, and the clothing and the characterizations, if not deep, must at least correspond to our preconceptions about the contemporary world. But once over those hurdles, the plot can be as outlandish as it wants. Most fundamentally, the hero must survive. That is the most absurd thing of all.   15

Yet it is also the most profound thing about these movies. That the hero is alive after five minutes is already a miracle; that he is so after 15 minutes is ludicrous; that he is so after an hour and a half is only sad. Sad, that is, because of what it shows about our needs and wants.   16

The fact is, we don't want to die; we'd rather be Superman than the fragile creatures of flesh and blood that we are. Trashy movies throw into relief, by contrast, the quieter death of a thousand cuts that is our lot in the real world, the slow aging and erosion by the passage of time, reminding us how much we wish things just weren't this way.   17

It's always interesting watching the audience exit from one of these spectaculars in which a man in the pink of physical condition has outwitted and outgunned an army of malefactors: Only occasionally is there anyone in the audience who could do even a creditable screen test for such a role. Sometimes these movies make me feel mournful. What are they but lifeless spools of celluloid playing over and over again in darkened, cave-like rooms amid the fluorescent glows of a thousand suburban malls, so that a million out-of-shape people of both sexes can identify with someone they have no hope of ever being?   18

So we go to a show that promises a good time, to gain release for an hour and   19
a half from our servitude to the mundane. But when the credits come on, we must
still walk out into the strange light of the parking lot, where we look both ways
before we cross, and check behind us before we back out the car.

THE SALES CALL ... AND OTHER HORRORS
Stephen L. Carter

Let us begin with a common and irritating occurrence. As you sit down to din-   1
ner with your family, the telephone rings. When you answer, you find that you are
being offered a subscription to the local paper or invited to donate to the volunteer fire department. And although you may enjoy reading your local paper and
admire the volunteers who keep the city from burning to the ground, if you are
like me, a wave of frustration passes through you, and you face the serious temptation to say something rude. Although the direct marketing industry insists that
they exist, I have yet to meet any people who are actually pleased when somebody
calls at mealtime, hoping to sell something.

Like many people, my family has adopted a firm rule to deal with these intru-   2
sions: No matter how desirable the product or service being sold, no matter how
noble the cause, we politely inform callers that we never respond to telephone so-
licitations. We invite them to send us any literature in the mail. (They never do.) If
they persist, we warn them once, then hang up.

Now, query: Who is being uncivil? My wife and I for refusing to listen to the sales   3
pitch? Or the salesperson for calling at the dinner hour? To answer that question,
we must consider not simply the dynamics of the conversation—the general problem
of how the student of civility, trying to see God in all people, confronts a sales pitch—
but the technology around which the tale revolves. That technology is the telephone.

The telephone, which came into widespread use fairly early in the twentieth cen-   4
tury, is a marvelous invention—so marvelous that when Alexander Graham Bell
applied for his patent, a worshipful Supreme Court allowed him to skip the legally
required step of building a working model of the device before it could be patented.
Nowadays few devices are more ubiquitous in America. Our nation boasts nearly
two hundred million telephone *numbers*. The instruments themselves are evidently
uncountable, but, certainly, America has more telephones than people.* We tend
to think of our phones as labor-saving devices, increasing the efficiency of both our
business and our personal lives. What we tend to leave out, if we even notice, is that
our love affair with the telephone almost certainly has made us less civil.

*We also have, as of 1998, approximately one portable telephone for every ten people—a much
greater ratio than the ratio of ordinary phones to people in much of the world.

How can this be? Consider something as basic as keeping in touch with our   5
friends. The telephone makes it easier and cheaper to do so—but also changes
dramatically the nature of the interaction. Before the widespread use of the
telephone, we had two means of keeping in touch with friends: stopping in for a
visit or writing a letter. Each involved a significant investment of time and perhaps resources; in other words, maintaining friendships automatically called us to
sacrifice. And, by making those sacrifices, we showed our friends repeatedly how
greatly we valued their friendship. Correspondence, in particular, not only preserved and nurtured a relationship but provided a record of it, a testament to
its enduring character.

We invest far less in our friendships when we decide to call rather than write   6
or meet in person. There is no permanence, nothing enduring, and no significant
investment. At the same time, we demand much more of the friends we call. The
telephone carries an air of immediacy: callers seem to think it our duty to drop
whatever may be going on at the moment, whether it involves family, prayer, work,
or a favorite hobby—or to offer an adequate excuse for not dropping everything—
all because they have chosen that instant rather than some other to indulge the
urge to punch a handful of digits on the control pad of a lightweight construction
of silicon, copper, and plastic. The telephone caller intrudes unasked into the privacy
of the home, and yet it is the one who is called who, if refusing to talk just then, is
considered rude.

Consider the connection of telephones to the business world. Suddenly, every-   7
body is essential to every decision. It grows increasingly hard to find peace and
quiet on a train or a street corner or even in a restaurant because of the number of indispensable people who must carry on loud conversations on cellular
phones lest the office discover it can get along without them. (One wishes that
Isaac Peebles was around to write the rules.) The cherished wall between the
space of commerce and the space of social life is further battered when the telephone allows work to intrude into the most private moments of our lives.

This is not to say that the telephone is not, on the whole, a boon to business.   8
The ability to keep in touch with coworkers can be a great convenience. The
ability to call a store or an airline can be enormously helpful (depending on how
long we must endure "music on hold"). The ability to close deals without leaving one's desk can increase profit. But in the wrong circumstances, the telephone
can lead to trouble.

A number of years ago, I came across a study by two industrial psychologists   9
who insisted that the widespread use of the telephone in business was making us
less, not more, efficient. According to their research (as I now recall it), the telephone creates two separate pressures that can actually slow business activity. First,
employees are more willing than in the past to pass a decision on to the boss, simply because it is now always possible to reach the boss. Second, the boss wants to

be involved in every decision, simply because it is now always possible to reach the employee. As a result, less authority is delegated, discretion vanishes, and businesses spend more and more time in conversation (aided by the telephone) and less and less time on making and implementing decisions. The telephone, in short, has created the possibility (which some professions, like law, seem to exemplify) of reducing all work to a single, endless meeting. According to the two psychologists, the added cost of this eternal conversation is sometimes more than the savings generated by the efficiency of communication.

Inefficiency is not, of course, evidence of incivility; on the contrary, as we have seen, inefficiency is often one of the virtues of civility, for the sacrifices we make for others are what define the depth of our commitment to the principle. And yet the same features of the telephone that may make it, in some circumstances, an inefficient technology, also make it an uncivil technology. [10]

Let us return to the sales call. In the era before telephone solicitation, if I wanted you to buy my product and could not get you into my shop, I probably would have to come to your house. And at once, an entire panoply of considerations of civility would be activated. In the first place, I would have to invest time and resources: going door to door is quite a bit more expensive than going phone number to phone number. Already, by deciding that you are worth that investment, I am practicing a form of civility, for I am according you greater respect if I prepare to meet you in person than if I simply meet you by phone. [11]

Second, if I meet you in person, I must be better groomed and on better behavior than if we meet by phone. I must work harder to make the good impression on which my sale depends. I must watch not only my words but my nonverbal cues: how I stand or sit, what I do with my hands. I must make eye contact. I dare not let my attention wander. This extra work is the extra measure of devotion to the other that civility requires. [12]

Third, by meeting you in person, I prevent either of us from being anonymous to the other. As psychologists like Richard Sennett and sociologists like Lyn H. Lofland have pointed out (and as practical experience confirms), it is far easier to be polite to people we know than to people we do not. When I take the trouble to sit or stand face-to-face with you, I am taking the risk that I will see God in you—a happy circumstance that will force me to be civil. [13]

Of course, telephone solicitation is much less expensive than door-to-door sales, and the products or services we may buy are that much cheaper. But the convenience comes at great cost to the project of reconstructing civility. That is not the fault of the telephone; nor is it really the fault of the companies that train salespeople to call at the dinner hour. It is the fault, rather, of all of us, for letting the technology transform us. The telephone has made it possible to dispense with many precepts of civility; rather than considering whether to keep them, we have simply let them die. . . . [14]

POLITICS AND THE REASONABLE MAN
Susan Estrich

. . . Choice is at the core of criminal liability. The person who *chooses* to kill is more blameworthy than the one who acts out of foolishness or inattention, as Justice Holmes recognized. Even a dog knows the difference between being tripped over and being stepped on. Capacity to choose sets the threshold for criminal liability. Small children are treated differently from adults. The insanity defense recognizes that a defendant must have the mental capacity to appreciate and control his conduct before he can be held criminally responsible for it.

The deliberateness of the choice is in turn measured by *mens rea,* or criminal intent. Criminal intent is divided into four basic categories: purpose (acting with a conscious object—the worst); knowledge (doing something with a virtual certainty of the bad result, which is essentially the same as doing it on purpose); recklessness (knowing a risk is an unreasonable risk, and taking it anyway); and negligence (taking an unreasonable risk, whether you know it or not). Murders are graded according to the intent of the killer: The hit man, who acts on purpose, is worse than the drunk driver, who acts recklessly; the reckless driver who deliberately runs a stop sign is worse than the careless one who doesn't even see the stop sign.

Some crimes are defined on terms that require a conscious purpose: attempted murder, for instance, requires that you act with the purpose of actually killing. And being negligent is generally not a crime at all, unless it results in death; even then, mere negligence—the civil standard that would give rise to a duty to compensate the victim's family—is generally not enough to warrant criminal punishment.

Indeed, in 1962, in *Robinson v. California,* the Supreme Court came close to holding that punishing an individual in the absence of some sort of a choice violated the United States Constitution. In throwing out as cruel and unusual punishment a California statute that made it an offense to "be addicted to the use of narcotics," the Court emphasized that narcotic addiction is an illness, "which may be contracted innocently or involuntarily." The implication was that it might be unconstitutional to punish someone for something he couldn't help, couldn't control.

The four established purposes of punishment—deterrence, incapacitation, rehabilitation, and retribution—are all served by the focus on the will of the defendant. Those who do bad things on purpose are, depending on one's perspective, dangerous and deserving of being locked up (incapacitation) and/or unsocialized and in need of rehabilitation. The prospect of punishment is supposed to deter this person (specific deterrence) and others in the community (general deterrence) from making this wrong choice in the future. To punish in the absence of choice, it is argued by many, cannot deter: how can you deter someone from doing something he didn't choose to do? And as for retribution, aren't we all angrier at the person who intentionally runs down a child than at the person who does it by accident?

To punish in the absence of choice, scholars and judges have argued, is morally un- 6
just: punishment requires fault, and fault requires the ability to do otherwise. If a person was doing the best he could, even if he failed to meet society's standards, the
prospect of punishment would not deter him, and its imposition would be unfair.
The House of Lords, England's highest court, adopted a variant of this position in the
controversial 1976 case of *Regina v. Morgan,* where the Justices concluded that
three drunken sailors could not be convicted of rape if they believed, honestly but
unreasonably, that the woman they were raping was screaming and fighting because
it made sex more exciting for her, as their buddy—the husband of the victim—had
allegedly told them.

Requiring choice works just fine, except when it doesn't—when, as in *Morgan,* the 7
result of requiring choice seems to violate common sense. Even the most enthusiastic proponents of choice, even those who would excuse an individual who makes
an unreasonable mistake, have their limits. It may be impossible to deter someone
who is out of control, but no one wants to license a hothead to kill—even if he is
congenitally short-tempered. Do we really care that he wasn't "choosing" fully? In
their retrial, the *Morgan* defendants were again convicted; the jury either didn't believe them, or didn't care.

The law in many jurisdictions distinguishes between first- and second-degree mur- 8
der based on premeditation and deliberation—a measure of the intensity of the
choice. But taken literally in every case, such a distinction produces unjustifiable
results. The man who kills his spouse after years of mental and physical abuse of
himself and their children ends up guilty of a more serious crime (premeditated
murder) than the murderer who stabs his girlfriend's 10-year-old daughter 60 times
in a sudden act of senseless rage. The resolution adopted by most jurisdictions is
to require premeditation but to hold that it can be done in a matter of seconds.
So much for measuring the intensity of choice.

Of course, it also doesn't work to punish everyone who produces a bad result, 9
regardless of their state of mind. That may be acceptable at least in some circumstances in tort law, where what is involved is monetary compensation for the injured
party; but even in tort law, strict liability remains controversial. Certainly it would be
unjust, as well as a huge waste of resources, to impose strict liability broadly in the
criminal law, to deprive people of life and liberty for every mistake, to turn every car
accident into an assault, much less a murder. It would be hard to find anyone, even
in politics, who wanted to hold everyone criminally accountable for the harms they
cause, to tolerate no excuses at all, not even partial ones. There are differences
among those who produce the same result, even if all the people they kill are equally
dead.

So how do we decide? What is the law? The law is what the "reasonable per- 10
son" would do—in the old days, the "reasonable man." His actions and reactions
provide the guide to when an intentional killing is murder and when it isn't, when

conduct is criminally reckless and when it isn't, when self-defense is legitimate and when it isn't, when provocation is sufficient and when it isn't.

Consider the problem of mistaken self-defense. You kill someone because you   11
honestly believe that if you don't, he really will shoot that gun and kill you. You turn out to be wrong. He wasn't armed. The gun wasn't loaded. The intruder was just a neighborhood kid. Are you guilty of murder? Manslaughter? No crime at all?

The answer, of course, is that it depends. "Detached reflection is not required   12
in the presence of an uplifted knife," as Justice Oliver Wendell Holmes put it. Or a gun. Were you mistaken because you were attacked in the dark, or because you are physically blind, or because you were too drunk to see straight? Did you believe the kid was going to kill you because he reached into his pocket and uttered threatening words, or because you flashed back to your experiences in Vietnam, or because he was black?

Drawing lines turns out to be a far messier process than choosing among a hi-   13
erarchy of intents. All lives have equal value in the eyes of the law—except that, of course, they don't. No one should take the law into their own hands, but only a law student afraid of being stuck on a slippery slope would be reluctant to distinguish between the child abuser who kills an innocent child and the angry parent who kills the child abuser. Both kill on purpose; killing is still wrong; but killing for a reason all of us can relate to is not quite so wrong as killing a child.

Self-defense justifies murder, provided the reasonable man would have also re-   14
sponded with deadly force. Provocation is a partial excuse, provided that the defendant's loss of control was reasonable. Unintentional wrongdoing or negligence will not be punished, unless the risk you took was unreasonable. The reasonable man allows society to set standards for itself, as it should.

But who is this reasonable man? Who does he look like? How much does he look   15
like the defendant? The more the reasonable man resembles the defendant, the more reasonable the defendant's actions will appear to be.

A classic and much-cited statement of self-defense law can be found in the 1849   16
New York case of *Shorter v. People*. The defendant in *Shorter* was a young black man, fifteen at the time of the killing, who was aroused by a racial slur and attacked his victim, initially with his fists and later with a knife. The trial judge, over defense counsel's objection, had instructed the jury that an actual danger to the defendant was required in order to allow his use of self-defense; the defense lawyer had requested an instruction that a reasonable fear was enough. The appeals court reversed; the trial judge was clearly wrong; a requirement of actual danger "would lay too heavy a burden upon poor humanity."

But the court went on to make clear that it was not enough that the defendant   17
believed himself to be in danger; the jury must also find reasonable grounds for that belief. While some scholars have argued that *Shorter* was wrongly decided—a mis-reading of English law, it is argued, leading to the imposition of unjust punishment upon those who cannot or did not choose to murder—its language has be-

come legal boilerplate. Self-defense requires not only that the defendant think he or another was in imminent danger but also that his belief be reasonable.

The law of provocation works much the same way. Provocation is what distinguishes intentional killings that are murder from those treated as the much less serious crime of manslaughter. The doctrine of provocation emerged in sixteenth-century England as a means to spare those who killed in sudden, and sometimes drunken, quarrels, or for breaches of honor, from the automatic penalty of death that followed a conviction of murder. In 1628 Coke defined manslaughter as being "upon a sudden occasion; and therefore is called a chance-medley." In a killing by chance-medley, according to Coke, "all that followed was but a continuance of the first sudden occasion, and the heat of blood kindled by ire was never cooled, till blow was given." By the eighteenth century, chance-medley had disappeared as its own category, incorporated into a more general doctrine that partially excused killings committed in the heat of passion. 18

In order to reduce an intentional killing from murder to voluntary manslaughter, though, it's not enough that the defendant lost control. The loss of control must be reasonable; there must be a "reasonable explanation or excuse" for it. Of course, reasonable people don't kill when provoked; they don't lose control and kill in an angry rage; that's why such conduct is prohibited by law. The only time it is reasonable to kill is in self-defense. In this context, reasonableness is less a normative standard than an empathic one. A woman tells a man she no longer wants to date him. In a rage, he kills her. Should he be treated the same, as a matter of law, as the parent who kills the child abuser? Certainly not. 19

In *Hill v. State* (1918), a murder conviction was reversed after a judge instructed the jury that the defendant could not have killed in self-defense since his attacker was threatening him only with his fists. "It is doubtless true that one may not, ordinarily, repel the attack of an unarmed man by killing him. There may be many cases in which the disparity between the combatants is so overwhelming that the one of superior power may inflict great bodily harm." The rule was soon widely accepted that the reasonable person was the same size and strength of the defendant. 20

Physical disabilities came next. Bad health, bad eyesight, a bandage on the hand, and missing fingers were all accepted by American courts as characteristics of the defendant which could be shared with the reasonable man, and which qualified the objectivity of the standard. 21

The reasonable person also was given the defendant's knowledge of his victim's history of violence. If the defendant knew that his victim was usually armed, or had a reputation for violence, this would be admissible; indeed, in some jurisdictions, it would be admissible even if the defendant didn't know about it. 22

But where do you draw the line? In the famous English case of *Bedder v. Director of Public Prosecutions* (1954), a young man killed a prostitute who taunted him for his impotence and kicked him "in the privates." He was convicted of murder after the trial judge instructed the jury that it should apply the standard of "the 23 reasonable person, the ordinary person" in evaluating the defendant's claim of provocation, and that his sexual impotence did not entitle him "to rely on provocation which would not have led an ordinary person to have acted" as he did. The House of Lords affirmed the conviction, refusing to recognize in sexual impotence the sort of physical disability that would justify an adjustment to the reasonable-man standard.

In a later case in which a fifteen-year-old killed the man who sexually assaulted   24
and laughed at him, the court explicitly declined to follow *Bedder,* ruling that the jury should be allowed to "take into consideration all those factors which in their opinion would affect the gravity of taunts or insults when applied to the person to whom they are addressed."

"Better or worse?" I ask my students, like the doctor trying on different lenses   25
to diagnose nearsightedness. Except that we are comparing killers, not the clarity of images. We ask questions; out of the answers come patterns; out of the patterns, rules. It feels like an objective process, not like choosing your candidate. Hands fly. People "know" the answer. Sometimes we all agree, and it doesn't feel like politics at all—more like Sunday school. There can still be right and wrong on a slippery slope. But we don't spend much time on easy cases; you teach common law by teaching hard cases.

Like the case of Mrs. Burke, the long-suffering (and maybe abused) isolated farm   26
wife in the classic novella and film *Jury of Her Peers,* who strangles her sleeping husband after he strangles her beloved bird. The sheriff's wife and a woman neighbor find the dead bird among her sewing things, while the men are off searching for some evidence of a motive that will tie her to the killing. The women hide the evidence. A jury of her peers, or obstruction of justice? Is she a murderer? Half the class say yes: premeditated and deliberate. Manslaughter? Almost as many hands. Excused as self-defense? Always a few, sometimes more. What is reasonableness? What does the reasonable person/woman do?

In the old days, by the third week of class, my students would start glaring, con-   27
vinced that I somehow knew the answer and was just unwilling to tell them, that once I tired of toying with them, once I'd played the Kingsfield/*Paper Chase* routine through, I would say the magic words—or the guy next to them would figure it out. These days, I tell them the first day. I don't have an answer. There's just the reasonable man.

My students think of the reasonable man as a cop-out, and an untidy one at that.   28
I think of him as a bit of genius, both inevitable and necessary. The reasonable man is the civic standard of responsibility, what we demand and expect of one another. We insist on a defendant's having a choice only to a point; beyond that point, we impose accountability. Where it is reasonable to set that point is a political question; the common law of the reasonable man gives form to an inherently political exercise. Lines do emerge, even if rules can be broken.

The common law rules that have emerged over the last two centuries have much   29
to commend them. They incorporate great respect for the value of human life, along with expectations of restraint. Words alone are not enough to provoke. Outside

of the home, one is required to retreat, if it can be done safely, before using deadly force. The threat of harm, if it is to justify deadly force in self-defense, must be imminent. If you're claiming provocation, there can be no cooling off period between the provocation and the use of force; if you have time to cool off, you're expected to do so.

But the rules, and the patterns of their application, also incorporate the bias of those who framed them. They are the product of the process that produced them, a process almost exclusively conducted by white men. Shorter received no special consideration because he was the black victim of racist taunts, any more than did Bedder, the impotent victim of the prostitute's taunts. The reasonable man is not black and not impotent. If the 1950s were a time of greater clarity in the law, it is not because politics was missing but because the homogeneity of the system made consensus look and feel like something other than a political decision. The areas of disagreement were narrower; the areas of commonality were broader; the decision makers, most of them anyway, saw the world through the same set of experiences. 30

The first recognized exception to the rule that a battery—a touching—was required to constitute adequate provocation was marital infidelity. Adultery was considered an interference with property, while an unfaithful fiancée did not even partially excuse a killing. Doctrinally, the wife's unfaithfulness reduced the crime from murder to manslaughter; in practice, it usually excused it entirely. Indeed, four states explicitly recognized "the honor defense," and most others did in practice. In 1868 a defense attorney who was representing a husband who had killed his wife's lover with an axe was able to argue that "no jury had ever convicted a husband of any offense, under such a state of facts, either in England or in this country." 31

In many places the jealous-husband defense continues to be the most routine way of getting away with murder. If O. J. Simpson hadn't been famous, and if his victims had been the same race as he is, then he might well have been able to portray himself as the classic jealous husband, happening upon his wife with another man, a good guy who lost it for a moment and who should be charged only with manslaughter. Of course, he and his wife were divorced, but their relationship was hardly over, and she would have been portrayed as no angel. One of Robert Shapiro's former clients won his fifteen minutes of fame early in the case by recounting the great deal Shapiro had negotiated on his behalf in similar circumstances. He killed his wife, and he was out in five. 32

What's striking is that O. J. Simpson could not be offered that deal because, in 1996, a manslaughter bargain would have been politically untenable. The problem is that this politically untenable result has continued to be rather routine in the system when people who are not famous are involved, and it has added ammunition to the assault on the reasonable man among critical legal theorists. 33

Compare the treatment of Kenneth Peacock, a Maryland man whose sentencing in the same summer of 1994 attracted attention only because of its parallels to the Simpson case. The noncelebrity defendant was a long-distance truck driver who 34 drank heavily, as did his wife. The two had been married six years, with frequent separations, when he returned unexpectedly one night at midnight and found her in bed with another man. He forced the other man to leave, and then he and his wife began arguing, and drinking. Some hours later, he shot and killed his wife; in a call to the 911 operator after 4 A.M., he said he killed his wife "because she was sleeping around on him." Mr. Peacock did not have a record of criminal convictions although, it emerged later, he had threatened his wife in the past because of her infidelity, and on one occasion he had beaten her so badly that she took refuge in a guarded hotel room. Two of his brothers are Baltimore police officers. The victim was an eighth-grade dropout, married four times.

The prosecutor's office agreed not to charge Peacock with murder (even though   35
he had time to cool down) in exchange for his plea of guilty to the crime of manslaughter (*State v. Peacock*). In Maryland, the maximum sentence for voluntary manslaughter is ten years. In Peacock's case, the prosecution recommended a sentence of three to eight years—which means that Mr. Peacock, with good behavior, would only have to serve two. The sentencing judge decided even that was too harsh, substituting an eighteen-month sentence, with work release, so he could keep his job.

"I cannot think of a circumstance whereby personal rage is more uncontrolla-   36
ble . . . than this for someone who is happily married. I shudder to think what I would do . . . I seriously wonder how many married men, married five years or four years, would have the strength to walk away . . . without inflicting some corporal punishment," said Judge Robert E. Cahill Sr. of the Baltimore County Circuit Court. A few weeks later, a woman was given a longer sentence in the same circuit court for killing her abusive husband. The judge in that case apparently did not relate so easily to her plight.

The vulnerability of the common law to political attack is not limited to its com-   37
parative treatment of angry husbands and abused wives. The common law also accepts, indeed celebrates, a certain brand of machismo whose anthem is "Make my day." Its roots in chance-medley are still apparent, and cases of this sort tend to enjoy a profile that makes them count for more in our understanding and acceptance of the laws than their actual numbers might merit.

The most famous such case involved Bernhard Goetz, who shot four young black   38
men on a New York City subway on December 22, 1984. Goetz was a hero in New York, even though his own version of events failed the traditional requirements of self-defense: he continued shooting after the danger to him, even if he had been "reasonable" about that, had disappeared. The first grand jury refused to indict him, and the jury that ultimately heard the criminal case refused to convict him of anything more than a weapons offense (*People v. Goetz*). Ten years later, a second jury, this one composed only of minorities, imposed damages of $43 million on a bankrupt Goetz in a civil suit brought by the most seriously injured victim.

The question of who the reasonable man is, and what he does on the subway,   39
was the central legal issue in Goetz's criminal trial. After Goetz was finally indicted

for attempted murder, his attorneys convinced first the trial court and then the appellate court to throw out the indictment on the ground that the prosecutor had improperly instructed the grand jury to apply an "objective" standard to the self-defense determination. Goetz, they managed to argue successfully, should be judged based on the way he saw things, not the way a reasonable man who didn't share all his traits would. The New York Court of Appeals finally reversed. One hundred years after *Shorter,* the same court reaffirmed its rejection of a subjective test, emphasizing that New York had not adopted the approach urged by the drafters of the Model Penal Code that would allow even unreasonable mistakes of fact to serve as a partial excuse for murder if the individual honestly believed deadly force was necessary. In New York, the court held, the reasonable person is the only guide to justifiable self-defense.

But who is this reasonable man? How much like Goetz is he? A determination   40
of reasonableness, the court emphasized, must be based on the "circumstances" facing a defendant or his "situation." "Such terms encompass more than the physical movement of the potential assailant . . . These terms include any relevant knowledge the defendant had about that person. They also necessarily bring in the physical attributes of the persons involved, including the defendant. Furthermore, the defendant's circumstances encompass any prior experiences he had which could provide a reasonable basis for a belief that another person's intentions were to injure or rob him or that the use of deadly force was necessary under the circumstances." During the trial, Goetz's lawyer succeeded at drawing a vivid picture of the scariness of the subways.

Every year, it seems, there is another Goetz case—another case that commands   41
public attention, in which a man, usually white, is celebrated for shooting and killing thugs, often minorities. In Los Angeles, 1995's Goetz was William Masters, who confronted two graffiti taggers in his neighborhood, started writing down their license number, and then shot and killed one of them, claiming self-defense. The taggers were Hispanics; Masters was white. After a much publicized review, the District Attorney's office decided to charge him with only a weapons violation. Many in the Hispanic community claimed that Masters had gotten away with murder, particularly after he was quoted as describing his victims as "wetbacks." Many others believed that he should not have been charged with any crime, and celebrated him as a hero.

If you excuse Goetz and Masters because you can identify with them, because   42
you're afraid on the subway, because you hate taggers, they why shouldn't lawyers for battered wives and abused sons be able to prove that their clients are no worse, and that the men they kill are no better than the thugs or the taggers—household rather than street criminals? If Goetz's life experiences are valid, why not Shorter's or Bedder's? The modern political attack on the criminal law is an attack on the reasonable man as being racist and sexist, Western and white. If white men get away with murder, why not everyone?

▪4▪

The Multiple-Source Essay

Until now, most of your writing assignments have been based on information derived from a *single* source. You have learned to paraphrase, summarize, re-arrange, and unify your evidence without sacrificing accuracy or completeness.

Now, as you begin to work with *many* different sources, you will need to understand and organize a wider range of materials. You will want to present the ideas of your sources in all their variety while at the same time maintaining your own perspective.

- How can you describe each author's ideas without taking up too much space for each one?

- How can you fit all your sources smoothly into your essay without allowing one to dominate?

- How can you transform a group of disparate sources into an essay that is yours?

Some of the informal sources that you will work with in this chapter have their equivalents in professional writing. Lawyers, doctors, engineers, social workers, and other professionals often work from notes taken at interviews to prepare case notes, case studies, legal testimony, reports, and market research.

SELECTING INFORMATION
FOR A MULTIPLE-SOURCE ESSAY

In academic writing, you do not usually find the materials for an essay in a neatly assembled package. On the contrary, before beginning an essay, you must find and select your materials. The first stage of a research project is traditionally working in the library or on the computer with a topic to explore and questions to ask, a search for information that will later be interpreted, sifted, and synthesized into a finished essay.

To demonstrate this process, assume that you have been assigned the following project, which calls for a narrow range of research:

> Read an entire newspaper or news magazine published on a day of your choice during the past century (such as your birthday), and write a summary describing what life was like on that day. Your sources are the articles and advertisements in that day's paper.

Given the amount and variety of information contained in the average newspaper, you must first narrow the topic by deciding what and how much to include. You would look for two kinds of evidence—major events that might have altered the fabric of most people's lives, and more ordinary happenings that might suggest how people typically spent their days. While these events may have taken place before your birth, your not having been there may give you the advantage of perspective: as an outsider, you can more easily distinguish between stories of lasting historic importance and those that simply reflect their era.

To begin this project, follow these steps:

1. Read rapidly through the entire newspaper. Then read the same issue again more slowly, jotting down your impressions of important *kinds* of events or *characteristics* of daily life. Search for a pattern, a thesis that sums up what you have read.

2. Review your notes, and isolate a few main ideas that seem worth developing. Then read the issue a third time, making sure that there really is sufficient evidence for the points that you wish to make. Note any additional information that you expect to use, and write down the page number next to each reference in your notes. Remember that you are not trying to use up all the available information.

3. Plan a series of paragraphs, each focusing on a different theme that is either significant in itself or typical of the day that you are describing. Spend some time choosing a strategy for a sequence of paragraphs that will not only introduce your reader to the world that you are describing, but also make apparent the pattern of events—the thesis—that seems to characterize that day.

Drawing Conclusions from Your Information

Through your essay, you should help your readers to form conclusions about the significance of the information it contains. The evidence should not be expected to speak for itself. Consider the following paragraph:

> Some popular books in the first week of 1945 were Brave Men by Ernie Pyle, Forever Amber by Kathleen Winsor, and The Time for Decision by Sumner Welles. The average price of these new, hardcover books was about three dollars each. The price of the daily Times was three cents, and Life magazine was ten cents.

What is probably most interesting to your reader is how little the reading material cost. This evidence would be very informative in a paragraph devoted to the cost of living or the accessibility of information through the media. Here, however, the emphasis is on the books. Can you tell why they were popular? Do they seem typical of 1945's bestseller list? If you don't have sufficient knowledge to answer questions like these, you will do better to focus on some other aspect of daily life that the paper describes in greater detail. Unexplained information is of no value to your reader, who cannot be assumed to know more than—or even as much as—you do.

In contrast, another student, writing about a day shortly after the end of World War II, built a paragraph around a casualty list in the *New York Times*. What seemed significant about the list was the fact that, by the end of the war, casualties had become so routine that they assumed a relatively minor place in daily life. Notice that the paragraph begins with a topic sentence that establishes the context and draws its conclusion at the end.

> For much of the civilian population, the worst part of the war had been the separation from their loved ones, who had gone off to fight in Europe, Africa, and the Pacific. Even after the end of the war, they still had to wait for the safe arrival home of the troops. In order to inform the public, the New York Times ran a daily list of troop arrivals. However, not everyone was destined to return, and the Times also ran a list of casualties. On September 4, that list appeared at the very bottom of page 2, a place where it would be easily overlooked except by those interested in finding a particular name.

Another paragraph about May 6, 1946, informs the reader that the postwar mid-forties were a transitional period.

> The process of switching over from a wartime to a peacetime economy was not without its pains. Then, as now, there was a high rate of unemployment.

> The Times featured a story about the million women production workers who had recently lost their jobs in war industries. Returning male and female veterans were also flooding the job market. Some working wives were waiting to see how their husbands readjusted to postwar jobs. If their ex-GI husbands could bring home enough money to support the family, they could return to their roles as housewives. If their husbands chose to continue their education or vocational training under the GI Bill, they would expect to stay on the job as long as they could.

This paragraph appears to be a straightforward account of the transition from a wartime economy, as expressed in the topic sentence; but the writer is, in fact, summarizing information taken from *several* articles in that day's newspaper. (Notice that, while the source of the information—the *Times*—is cited, the names of the reporters are not considered significant in this very general summary.) The suggestion of a personal comment—unemployment, one gathers, is a recurring problem—adds immediacy and significance to a topic that might otherwise be remote to today's readers.

Finally, it is not always necessary to present your conclusion in a topic sentence at the *beginning* of your paragraph. Here is one in which the evidence is presented first:

> The July 30, 1945, issue of Newsweek lists three bills that were going before Congress. The first, the Burton-Ball-Hatch Bill, proposed that all industries institute a labor management mediation system. The second, the Kilgore Bill, proposed providing $25 a week in unemployment for a period of 26 weeks. And the third, the Mead Bill, proposed raising the minimum wage from 40 cents to 65 cents. It is obvious from these three bills that a great deal of attention was being focused on employment, or the lack of it. Here we have another clue about the lifestyle of 1945. The majority of the working class must have been greatly dissatisfied with economic conditions for their congressmen to have proposed these improvements. These bills were also in keeping with the late President Roosevelt's New Deal policy, which was primarily directed toward the improvement of economic conditions. From these bills, it is safe to assume that the cost of living may have been rising, that unemployment was still something of a problem, and that strikes by workers were becoming so prevalent that a mediation system seemed necessary.

This paragraph explicitly links together three related points, suggests their possible significance, and provides a historical context (the New Deal) in which to understand them.

EXERCISE 12: SELECTING AND PRESENTING INFORMATION

Read the following student essay, a description of life taken from the *New York Times* of September 21, 1967. Analyze each paragraph and be prepared to discuss the following questions:

1. What are the writer's reasons for building a paragraph around that piece of information? (Use your own knowledge of the contents of the average newspaper today to estimate the range of choices that the writer might have had.)
2. How clear is the presentation of the information?
3. Do the topic sentences interpret the information and suggest its significance for the reader?
4. How is the essay organized: the relationship between paragraphs; the sequence of paragraphs; the unity within each paragraph; the transitions between paragraphs?
5. What is the thesis and how well does the author characterize September 21, 1967, as typical of its era and as a contrast to her own era?

  According to the New York Times, on September 21, 1967, there was   1
considerable violence and unrest in the United States, much of it in response to
the United States' involvement in the Vietnam War. The United States had
increased its bombing of Vietnam in an attempt to cut off the port of Haiphong
from contact with the rest of the world. As a result, a group opposed to President
Johnson's Vietnam policy began an "anti-Johnson" campaign. They were a coalition of Democrats who hoped to block his reelection. Meanwhile, seventy female
antiwar demonstrators were arrested outside the White House. Later, to protest
their arrest, 500 members of Women Strike for Peace marched to the White
House and clashed with police.

  There was not only civil unrest on this day, but also a conflict between   2
President Johnson and the House Ways and Means Committee over the president's proposed tax increase. The committee would not approve the increase
without a 5 billion dollar cut in spending. The Senate proposed the following
cuts: a 2 billion dollar decrease in defense spending; a 1 billion dollar decrease
in "long-range research"; and a 2 billion dollar decrease in other civilian services.
However, aid to the poor and to cities was not to be cut. In defense of the president's request, Secretary of Commerce Trowbridge said that a tax increase would
be necessary because of inflation.

  Throughout the rest of the country, there was much racial tension and   3
violence. There had been days of fighting in Dayton, Ohio's West Side, which had

a large black population. A rally took place there to protest the killing of a black Social Security Administration field-worker. There was also a supermarket fire in Dayton, which resulted in $20,000 of damage. In the end, twenty teenagers were arrested. In the Casa Central Outpost, a Puerto Rican neighborhood in Chicago, Governor Romney of Michigan, a would-be presidential candidate, was given a hostile welcome. His visit to the Outpost was blocked by its director, Luis Cuza, who handed him a two-page press release claiming that the Governor was only touring these poor neighborhoods for political gain. Governor Romney expressed outrage at the accusation and the fact that the Outpost had not informed him earlier that he would not be welcome. In the meantime, the streets of Hartford, Connecticut's North End were quiet after three days of racial violence. Civil rights demonstrators were marching against housing discrimination in the South End, a predominantly middle-class Italian neighborhood. There were 66 arrests, mainly of young blacks. To control the violence, five to ten policemen were posted at every intersection, and the mayor asked for a voluntary curfew.

On the local level, a protest against traffic conditions took place in the Bronx, at 149th Street and Courtlandt Avenue. The protesters, four clergymen and dozens of neighbors, wanted Courtlandt Avenue to be one way. Two men refused to leave after police tried to disperse the crowd.   4

There was not only racial unrest in the country on this day, but also many labor disputes and strikes. Seventeen thousand Prudential Insurance Company of America agents threatened to strike if no contract was agreed on in four days. They could not accept any of the proposals previously given to them. Also, the steelhaulers' strike in Chicago was spreading east, and had already resulted in a violent confrontation in Pittsburgh. Finally, on strike were the 59,500 New York public school teachers, whose refusal to enter the classrooms had kept more than a million students out of school for eight days. The teachers' slogan was "no contract, no work."   5

Even the weather was in turmoil. Hurricane Beulah, in Texas, had winds estimated at 80 miles per hour at the center of the storm and 120–150 miles per hour at its peak. Eighty-five percent of Port Isabel, a town at the southern tip of Texas, was destroyed, and four people were killed by the record number of twenty-seven tornadoes spawned by Beulah. All the Gulf states experienced heavy rain in Beulah's aftermath. Meanwhile, rain and thunderstorms also battered the east coast.   6

ASSIGNMENT 6: WRITING AN ESSAY FROM FACTUAL INFORMATION

Choose one of the following:

1. At the library or on the Internet, examine the issue of the *New York Times* that was published on the day that your mother or father was born. (Most libraries keep complete microfilms of the *New York Times*. Ask your librarian how to locate and use these microfilms. Alternatively, locate an issue of a news magazine that covers that week.) Select the articles that seem most interesting and typical of the period, and use them as evidence for an account of what it was like to live on that day. This essay should not merely be a collection of facts; you should suggest the overall significance of the information that you include. Remember that your reader was almost certainly not born on that date, and that your job is to arouse that reader's interest. If you like, draw some parallels with the present time, but don't strain the comparison. The essay should not run much more than 1,000 words: select carefully and refer briefly to the evidence.

2. Use a newspaper or magazine published this week and try to construct a partial portrait of what it is like to live in America (or in your city or town) right now. Don't rely entirely on news stories, but, instead, draw your evidence as much as possible from advertisements and features (like TV listings, classifieds, announcements of all sorts). Try, if you can, to disregard personal knowledge; pretend you are a Martian if that will enable you to become detached from your familiar environment. Don't offer conclusions that the evidence does not substantiate, and don't try to say *everything* that could possibly be said. The essay should not run much more than 1,000 words: select carefully and refer briefly to the evidence.

GENERALIZING FROM EXAMPLES

Summarizing the contents of a newspaper can be difficult because newspaper stories often have little in common except that they all happened on the same day. By contrast, in academic writing a common theme often links apparently dissimilar ideas or facts. The writer has to find that common theme and make it clear to the reader through generalizations that cover several items in the sources.

Assume that you have been asked to consider and react to seven different but related situations, and then formulate *two* generalizations.

A. In a sentence or two, write down your probable reaction if you found yourself in each of the following situations.* Write quickly; this exercise calls for immediate, instinctive responses.

*Adapted from "Strategy 24" in Sidney B. Simon et al., *Values Clarification* (New York: Hart, 1972).

1. You are walking behind someone. You see him take out a cigarette pack, pull out the last cigarette, put the cigarette in his mouth, crumple the package, and nonchalantly toss it over his shoulder onto the sidewalk. What would you do?

2. You are sitting on a train and you notice a person (same age, sex, and type as yourself) lighting up a cigarette, despite the no smoking sign. No one in authority is around. What would you do?

3. You are pushing a shopping cart in a supermarket and you hear the thunderous crash of cans. As you round the corner, you see a two-year-old child being beaten, quite severely, by his mother, apparently for pulling out the bottom can of the pile. What would you do?

4. You see a teenager that you recognize shoplifting at the local discount store. You're concerned that she'll get into serious trouble if the store detective catches her. What would you do?

5. You're driving on a two-lane road behind another car. You notice that one of its wheels is wobbling more and more. It looks as if the lugs are coming off one by one. There's no way to pass, because cars are coming from the other direction in a steady stream. What would you do?

6. You've been waiting in line (at a supermarket or gas station) for longer than you expected and you're irritated at the delay. Suddenly, you notice that someone very much like yourself has sneaked in ahead of you in the line. There are a couple of people before you. What would you do?

7. You've raised your son not to play with guns. Your rich uncle comes for a long-awaited visit and he brings your son a .22 rifle with lots of ammunition. What would you do?

B. Read over your responses to the seven situations and try to form two general statements (in one or two sentences each), one about *the circumstances in which you would take action* and a second about *the circumstances in which you would choose to do nothing*. Do not simply list the incidents, one after the other, divided in two groups.

   You form your generalizations by examining the group of situations in which you *do* choose to take action and determining what they have in common. (It is also important to examine the "leftovers," and to understand why these incidents did not warrant your interference.) As a first step, you might try looking at each situation in terms of either its *causes* or its *consequences*. For example, in each case there is someone to blame, someone who is responsible for creating the problem—except for number five, where fate (or poor auto maintenance) threatens to cause an accident.

   As for consequences, in some of the situations (littering, for example), there is *little potential danger*, either to you or to the public. Do these circumstances discourage action? In others, however, the possible victim is oneself or a member of one's family. Does self-interest alone drive one to act? Do adults tend to intervene in defense of children—even someone else's child—since they cannot stand up for themselves? Or, instead of calculating the consequences of not intervening, perhaps you should imagine *the possible consequences of interference.* In which situations can you expect to receive abuse for failing to mind your own business? Would this prevent you from intervening? As always, only by examining the evidence can you discover the basis for a generalization.

The list of examples has two characteristics worth noting:

1. Each item is intended to illustrate a specific and very different situation. Thus, although it does not include every possible example, the list as a whole constitutes a *set* of public occasions for interfering with a stranger's conduct.

2. Since you probably would not choose to act in every situation, you cannot use the entire list as the basis for your generalization. Rather, you must establish *a boundary line,* dividing those occasions when you would intervene from those times when you would decide not to act. The exact boundary between intervention and nonintervention will probably differ from person to person, as will the exact composition of the list of occasions justifying intervention. Thus, there is no one correct generalization.

This exercise results in a set of guidelines for justifiably minding other people's business. You formulate the guidelines by applying your own standards to a sampling of possible examples.

Broad concepts offer a great deal of room for disagreement and ambiguity and therefore allow a great many interpretations. You can clarify your ideas and opinions about any important abstract issue by inventing a set of illustrations, marking off a subgroup, and then constructing a generalization that describes what is *inside* the boundary: the common characteristics of the contents of the subgroup. Thus, in the previous problem, one person might consider the set of seven examples and then decide to intervene only in Situations 3 (the child beaten in a supermarket), 5 (the wobbly wheel), and 7 (the gift of a gun). What makes these three cases different from the others? They and they alone involve protecting some person from physical harm.

This process of *differentiation,* followed by *generalized description,* is usually called "definition"; it can serve as an essay strategy in its own right or form the basis for a comparison, classification, argumentation, or evaluation essay.

ANALYZING MULTIPLE SOURCES

When you write from sources, your object is not to establish a single "right" conclusion but rather to present a thesis statement of your own that is based on your examination of a variety of views. Some of these views may conflict with your own and with each other. Because of this diversity, organizing multiple sources is more difficult than working with a series of examples, with the contents of a newspaper, or with even a highly complex single essay.

The writing process for multiple sources begins with the analysis of ideas.

Analysis is first breaking down a mass of information into individual pieces and then examining the pieces.

As you underline and annotate your sources, you look for similarities and distinctions in meaning, as well as the basic principles underlying what you read. Only when you have taken apart the evidence of each source to see how it works can you begin to find ways of putting everything back together again in your own essay.

To illustrate the analysis of sources, assume that you have asked five people what the word *foreign* means. You want to provide a reasonably complete definition of the word by exploring all the shades of meaning (or connotations) that the five sources suggest. If each one of the five gives you a completely different answer, then you will not have much choice in the organization of your definition. In that case, you would probably present each separate definition of *foreign* in a separate paragraph, citing a different person as the source for each one. But responses from multiple sources almost always overlap, as these do. Notice the common meanings in this condensed list of the five sources' responses:

John Brown: "Foreign" means unfamiliar and exotic.

Lynne Williams: "Foreign" means strange and unusual.

Bill White: "Foreign" means strange and alien (as in "foreign body").

Mary Green: "Foreign" means exciting and exotic.

Bob Friedman: "Foreign" means difficult and incomprehensible (as in "foreign language").

Planning your essay depends on finding common meanings, not writing down the names of the five sources. That is why the one-source-per-paragraph method should hardly ever be used (except on those rare occasions when all the sources completely disagree).

When you organize ideas taken from multiple sources, you should reject the idea of devoting one paragraph to each page of your notes, simply because all the ideas on that page happen to have come from the same source.

If you did so, each paragraph would have a topic sentence that might read, "Then I asked John Brown for his definition," as if John Brown were the topic for discussion, instead of his views on "foreign." And if John Brown and Mary Green each get a separate paragraph, there will be some repetition because both think that one of the meanings of "foreign" is "exotic." "Exotic" should be the topic of one of your paragraphs, not the person (or people) who suggested that meaning.

Analyzing Shades of Meaning

Here is a set of notes, summarizing the ideas of four different people about the meaning of the word *individualist*. How would you analyze these notes?

Richard Becker: an "individualist" is a person who is unique and does not "fall into the common mode of doing things"; would not follow a pattern set by society. "A youngster who is not involved in the drug scene just because his friends are." A good word; it would be insulting only if it referred to a troublemaker.

Simon Jackson: doing things on your own, by yourself. "She's such an individualist that she insisted on answering the question in her own way." Sometimes the word is good, but mostly it has a bad connotation: someone who rebels against society or authority.

Lois Asher: one who doesn't "follow the flock." The word refers to someone who is very independent. "I respect Jane because she is an individualist and her own person." Usually very complimentary.

Vera Lewis: an extremely independent person. "An individualist is a person who does not want to contribute to society." Bad meaning: usually antisocial. She first heard the word in psych class, describing the characteristics of the individualist and "how he reacts to society."

At first glance, all the sources seem to say much the same thing: the individualist is different and "independent." However, it is worthwhile to examine the context in which the four sources are defining this word. First, *all the responses define the individualist in terms of other people,* either the "group," or the "flock," or "society." Oddly enough, it is not easy to describe the individualist as an individual, even though it is that person's isolation that each source is emphasizing. Whatever is "unique" about the individualist—what is described as "independent"—is defined by *the gap between that person and everyone else.* (Notice that both "unique" and "independent" are words that also suggest a larger group in the background; after all, one has to be independent of something!)

Having found a meaning that is common to all four sources ("independence") and, just as important, having established the context for a definition ("from the group"), you must now look for differences. Obviously, Lois Asher thinks that to be an individualist is a good thing; Vera Lewis believes that individualism is bad; and the other two suggest that both connotations are possible. But simply describing the reactions of the four sources stops short of defining the word according to those reactions.

Richard Becker and Lois Asher, two people who suggest a favorable meaning, describe the group from which the individual is set apart in similar and somewhat disapproving terms: "common"; "pattern set by society"; "follow the flock." Becker and Asher both seem to suggest *a degree of conformity or sameness that the individualist is right to reject,* as Becker's youngster rejects his friends' drugs. But Vera Lewis, who thinks that the word's connotation is bad, sees the individualist in a more benign society, with which the individual ought to identify himself and to which he ought to contribute. To be antisocial is to be an undesirable person—from the point of view of Lewis and society. Simon Jackson (who is ambivalent about the word) uses the phrases "by yourself" and "on your own," which suggest the isolation and the lack of support, as well as the admirable independence, of the individualist. In Jackson's view, the individualist's self-assertion becomes threatening to all of us in society ("antisocial") only when the person begins to rebel against authority. Probably for Jackson, and certainly for Vera Lewis, the ultimate authority should rest with society as a whole, not with the individualist. Even Richard Becker, who admires independence, draws the line at allowing the individualist complete autonomy: when reliance on one's own authority leads to "troublemaking," the term becomes an insult.

EXERCISE 13: ANALYZING SHADES OF MEANING IN MULTIPLE SOURCES

Analyze the following set of notes for a definition of the word *gossip*. Then explore some ways to organize these notes by following these steps:

A. Find the important terms or concepts that can lead to a context for defining *gossip*.
B. Write two generalizations that might serve as topic sentences for a two-paragraph essay. (Do not use "favorable" and "unfavorable" as your two topics.)

Miranda Michaels: pointless, trivial conversation; news gets passed, creates some kind of social tie between people; usually associated with women.

Carl Curtis: to criticize and say unpleasant things about other people. "My sister likes to gossip and pass along the latest news about everybody's private life."

Terry Trollman: talking too much; can't trust someone to keep a secret; bad word because it means untrustworthy. "She gossips so much that I can't tell her anything."

Jackie Gonzalez: talking about someone behind her back; harmful chatter; not to be believed, not facts. "Gossip columnists smear celebrities with their exaggerated stories."

George Goodwin: passing the time of day; taking an interest in other people; usually doesn't mean much. "The ladies gossiped all afternoon and exchanged some interesting stories." The worst that you can say about gossip is that it wastes time.

ASSIGNMENT 7: WRITING A DEFINITION ESSAY FROM MULTIPLE SOURCES

All the words in the following list are in common use and have either more than one usual meaning or a meaning that can be interpreted both favorably and unfavorably. Choose one word from the list as the topic for a definition essay. (Or, if your instructor asks you to do so, select a word from the dictionary or the thesaurus.)

shrewd	justice	self-interest
curiosity	ordinary	respectable
capitalism	power	conservative
bias	flamboyant	polite
progress	eccentric	obedience
habit	politician	ambition
credit	genius	duty
ladylike	failure	poverty
royalty	competition	sophisticated
masculine	peace	humility
cautious	welfare	solitude
bias	immature	spiritual
dominance	culture	sentimental
revolution	aggression	glamorous
passive	failure	self-confidence
influential	feminine	passionate
criticism	imagination	impetuous
jealousy	romantic	successful
small	workman	smooth
cheap	privilege	intrigue
fashion	enthusiast	smart
pompous	mercenary	criticize
obligation	shame	freedom
control	idealistic	artificial
ambition	ethical	perfection

1. Clarify your own definition of the word by writing down your ideas about its meaning.

2. Interview five or six people, or as many as you need, to get a variety of reactions. Your purpose is to become aware of several ways of using your word. Take careful and complete notes of each reaction that you receive.

3. Each person should be asked the following questions:

   ■ What do you think X means? Has it any other meanings that you know of?

   ■ How would you use this word in a sentence? (Pay special attention to the way in which the word is used, and note down the differences. Two people might say that a word means the same thing and yet use it differently.)

- Is this a positive word or a negative word? In what situation could it possibly have a favorable or unfavorable connotation?

In listening to the answers to these questions, do not hesitate to ask, "What do you mean?" It may be necessary to make people think hard about a word that they use casually.

4. As you note reactions, consider how the meaning of the word changes and try to identify the different circumstances and usages that cause these variations. Be alert, for example, for a difference between the *ideal* meaning of the word and its *practical* application in daily life.

5. If one person's reaction is merely an echo of something that you already have in your notes, you may summarize the second response more briefly, but keep an accurate record of who (and how many) said what.

6. Although your notes for each source may run only a few sentences, plan to use a separate sheet for each person.

7. Your notes should include not only a summary of each reaction, but also, if possible, a few quotations. If someone suggests a good definition or uses the word in an interesting way, try to record the exact words; read the quotation back to the speaker to make sure that what you have quoted is accurate; put quotation marks around the direct quotation.

8. Make sure that the names of all your sources are accurately spelled.

9. Analyze your notes and make an outline of possible meanings and contexts.

10. Write a series of paragraphs, first explaining *the most common meaning attributed to the word,* according to your sources. Be sure to cite different examples of this common usage. Then, in successive paragraphs, review the other connotations, favorable and unfavorable, always trying to trace the relationships and common contexts among the different meanings. With your overview of all the variations of meaning, you are in an excellent position to observe and explain what the worst and the best connotations of the word have in common.

There is no set length for this essay. Contents and organization are governed entirely by the kind and extent of the material in your notes. *Your notes should be handed in with your completed essay.*

SYNTHESIZING MULTIPLE SOURCES

Once you have analyzed each of your sources and discovered their similarities and differences, you then reassemble these parts into a more coherent whole. This process is called *synthesis.* Although at first you may regard analysis and synthesis as contradictory operations, they are actually overlapping stages of a single, larger process.

To illustrate the way in which analysis and synthesis work together, let us examine a set of answers to the questions: "Would you buy a lottery ticket? Why?" First, read through these summaries of all seven responses.

Mary Smith: She thinks that lottery tickets were made for people to enjoy and win. It's fun to try your luck. She looks forward to buying her ticket, because she feels that, for one dollar, you have a chance to win a lot more. It's also fun scratching off the numbers to see what you've won. Some people don't buy tickets because they think the lottery is a big rip-off; but "a dollar can't buy that much today, so why not spend it and have a good time?"

John Jones: He would buy a lottery ticket for three reasons. The first reason is that he would love to win. The odds are like a challenge, and he likes to take a chance. The second reason is just for fun. When he has two matching tickets, he really feels happy, especially when he thinks that dollars can be multiplied into hundreds or thousands. "It's like Russian roulette." The third reason is that part of the money from the lottery goes toward his education. The only problem, he says, is that they are always sold out!

Michael Green: He has never bought a lottery ticket in his life because he doesn't want to lose money. He wants to be sure of winning. Also, he says that he isn't patient enough. The buyer of a lottery ticket has to be very patient to wait for his chance to win. He thinks that people who buy tickets all the time must enjoy "living dangerously."

Anne White: Buying a lottery ticket gives her a sense of excitement. She regards herself as a gambler. "When you win two dollars or five dollars you get a thrill of victory, and when you see that you haven't, you feel the agony of defeat." She thinks that people who don't buy tickets must be very cautious and noncompetitive, since the lottery brings "a sense of competition with you against millions of other people." She also knows that the money she spends on tickets goes toward education.

Margaret Brown: She feels that people who buy tickets are wasting their money. The dollars spent on the lottery could be in the bank, getting interest. Those people who buy tickets should expect to have thrown out their money, and should take their losses philosophically, instead of jumping up and down and screaming about their disappointment. Finally, even if she could afford the risk, the laws of her religion forbid her to participate in "any sort of game that is a form of gambling."

William Black: He would buy a lottery ticket, because he thinks it can be fun, but he wouldn't buy too many, because he thinks it's easy for people to get carried away and obsessed by the lottery. He enjoys the anticipation of wanting to win and maybe winning. "I think that you should participate, but in proportion to your budget; after all, one day you might just be a winner."

Elizabeth Watson: She wouldn't buy a lottery ticket because she considers them a rip-off. The odds are too much against you, 240,000 to 1. Also, it is much too expensive, "and I don't have the money to be throwing away on such foolishness." She thinks that people who indulge themselves with lottery tickets become gamblers, and she's against all kinds of gambling. Such people have no sense or self-control. Finally, "I'm a sore loser, so buying lottery tickets just isn't for me."

Making a Chart of Common Ideas

Since you are working with seven sources with varying opinions, you need a way to record the process of analysis. One effective way is to make a *chart of commonly held views*. To do so, follow these two steps, which should be carried out *simultaneously*:

1. Read each statement carefully, and identify each separate reason that is being cited for and against playing the lottery by writing a number above or next to the relevant comment. When a similar comment is made by another person, use *the same number* to provide a key to the final list of common reasons. In this step, you are analyzing your sources. Here is what the first two sets of notes might look like once the topic numbers have been inserted:

Mary Smith: She thinks that lottery tickets were made for people to enjoy and win. It's fun to try your luck. She looks forward to buying her ticket, because she feels that, for one dollar, you have a chance to win a lot more. It's also fun scratching off the numbers to see what you've won. Some people don't buy tickets because they think the lottery is a big rip-off; but "a dollar can't buy that much today, so why not spend it and have a good time?"

John Jones: He would buy a lottery ticket for three reasons. The first reason is that he would love to win. The odds are like a challenge, and he likes to take a chance. The second reason is just for fun. When he has two matching tickets, he really feels happy, especially when he thinks that dollars can be multiplied into hundreds or thousands. "It's like Russian roulette." The third reason is that part of the money from the lottery goes toward his education. The only problem, he says, is that they are always sold out!

2. At the same time as you number each of your reasons, also write a list or chart of reasons on a separate sheet of paper. Each reason should be assigned *the same number* you wrote next to it in the original statement. Don't make a new entry when the same reason is repeated by a second source. Next to each entry on your chart, put the names of the people who have mentioned that reason. You are now beginning to synthesize your sources. (This process is also known as cross-referencing.)

Here's what your completed list of reasons might look like:

Reason	Sources
1. People play the lottery because it's fun.	Smith; Jones
2. People play the lottery because they like the excitement of taking a chance and winning.	Smith; Jones; Green; White; Black
3. People don't play the lottery because they think it's a rip-off.	Smith; Watson
4. People play the lottery because they are contributing to education.	Jones; White
5. People don't play the lottery because they have better things to do with their money.	Green; Brown; Watson
6. People play the lottery because they like to gamble.	White; Brown; Watson
7. People who play the lottery and those who refuse to play worry about the emotional reactions of the players.	Green; White; Brown; Black; Watson

The process of synthesis starts as soon as you start to make your list. The list of common reasons represents the reworking of seven separate sources into a single new pattern that can serve as the basis for a new essay.

Distinguishing between Reasons

One of the biggest problems in synthesis is deciding, in cases of overlapping, whether you actually have one reason or two. Since overlapping reasons were deliberately not combined, the preceding list may be unnecessarily long.

For example, Reasons 1 and 2 reflect the difference between the experiences of *having fun* and *feeling the thrill of excitement*—a difference in sensation that most people would understand. You might ask yourself, "Would someone play the lottery just for fun without the anticipation of winning? Or would someone experience a thrill of excitement without any sense of fun at all?" If one sensation can exist without the other, you have sufficient reason for putting both items on your chart. Later on, the similarities, not the differences, might make you want to combine the two; but, at the beginning, it is important to note down exactly what ideas and information are available to you.

The distinction between the thrill of excitement (2) and the pleasure of gambling (6) is more difficult to perceive. The former is, perhaps, more innocent than the latter and does not carry with it any of the obsessive overtones of gambling.

Resenting the lottery because it is a rip-off (3) and resenting the lottery because the players are wasting their money (5) appear at first glance to be similar reactions. However, references to the rip-off tend to emphasize the "injured victim" whose money is being whisked away by a public agency. In other words, Reason 3 emphasizes *self-protection from robbery*; Reason 5 emphasizes *the personal virtue of thrift*.

Reason 7 is not really a reason at all. Some comments in the notes do not fit into a tidy list of reasons for playing, yet they provide a valuable insight into human motivation and behavior as expressed in lottery playing. An exploration of the emotions that characterize the player and the nonplayer (always allowing for the lottery preference of the source) might be an interesting way to conclude an essay.

Deciding on a Sequence of Topics

The topics in your chart appear in the same random order as your notes. Once the chart is completed, you should decide on a more logical sequence of topics by ordering the entries in the list. You can make an indirect impact on your reader by choosing a logical sequence that supports the pattern that you discovered in analyzing your sources.

Here are two possible ways to arrange the "lottery" reasons. Which sequence do you prefer? Why?

1. fun	1. fun
2. excitement	2. rip-off
3. gambling	3. excitement and gambling
4. education	4. misuse of money
5. rip-off	5. education
6. misuse of money	6. personality of the gambler
7. personality of the gambler	

The right-hand sequence *contrasts the advantages and disadvantages* of playing the lottery. Moving back and forth between paired reasons calls attention to the relation between opposites and, through constant contrast, makes the material interesting for the reader. The left-hand sequence places all the advantages and disadvantages together, providing an opportunity to *explore positive and negative reactions to the lottery separately* without interruption, therefore encouraging more complex development. Both sequences are acceptable.

EXERCISE 14: IDENTIFYING COMMON IDEAS

This exercise is based on a set of interview notes, answering the question "Would you give money to a beggar?"

A. Read through the notes. (1) Identify distinct and different reasons by placing numbers next to the relevant sentences. (2) As you number each new reason, add an entry to the chart. (The first reason is already filled in.)

Reason	Sources
1. I can afford to give to beggars.	
2.	
3.	
4.	
5.	
6.	
7.	
8.	
9.	
10.	

B. Arrange the numbered reasons in a logical sequence. If it makes sense to you, combine those reasons that belong together. Be prepared to explain the logic behind your sequence of points. If you can find two possible sequences, include both, explaining the advantages of each.

Would You Give Money to a Beggar?

Jonathan Cohen: When asked for money on the street, I often apply a maxim of a friend of mine. He takes the question, "Have you got any spare change?" literally: if he has any loose change, he hands it over, without regard for his impression of what the money's for, since he doesn't think ulterior motives are any of his business. Since I can always afford the kind of contribution that's usually asked for—fifty cents or a dollar—or am at least less likely to miss it than the person asking me for it, I usually take the request as the only qualification of "need." I'm more likely to give out money if I don't have to go into my billfold for it, however, and would rather give out transit tokens or food, if I have them. But I want to be sympathetic; I often think, "There but for the grace of God go I."

Jennifer Sharone: I hate to think about what people who beg have to undergo; it makes me feel so fortunate to be well dressed and to have good food to eat and a home and a job. Begging seems kind of horrifying to me—that in this country there are people actually relying on the moods of strangers just to stay alive. I give to people who seem to have fallen on hard times, who aren't too brazen, who seem embarrassed to be asking me for money. I guess I do identify with them a lot.

Michael Aldrich: If a person meets my eye and asks plainly and forthrightly (and isn't falling-down drunk), I try to empty my pocket, or at least come up with a quarter or two. If the person has an unusually witty spiel—even if it's outlandish—I give more freely. I don't mind giving small change; it's quick and easy. I try not to think about whether or not the person really "needs" the money—how could you ever know? On some level, I think that if someone's begging, they need the money. Period. There's an old guy who stands on my corner—he's been there for years. I always give him money, if I have the change. If I don't have it, he says a smile will do. I would hate to think of him going without a meal for a long time or having to sleep out in the rain. He reminds me of my father and my uncle.

Marianne Lauro: I used to give people money, but frankly, I'm too embarrassed by the whole process. It seems to me that folks who really couldn't be all that grateful for somebody's pocket change still make an effort to appear grateful, and then I'm supposed to get to feel magnanimous when I really feel ridiculous telling them they're welcome to a couple of coins that don't even amount to carfare. So the whole transaction seems vaguely humiliating for everyone concerned. Really, the city or the state or the federal government should be doing something about this—not expecting ordinary people, going home from work, or whatever, to support people who have mental or physical impairments or addictions, especially when you're never sure what their money will be used for. But maybe I'm just rationalizing now—maybe the most "humane" thing about these kinds of transactions is the mutual embarrassment.

Donald Garder: I try, when possible, to respond to the person approaching me, by looking at them, perhaps even making eye contact, which frequently lends some dignity to the moment. But then I don't always reach into my pocket. I often give to people with visible physical handicaps, but rarely to someone who's "young and able-bodied." Sometimes I feel guilty, but I'm never sure if the person is for real or not—I've known people who swindled people out of money by pretending to be homeless, so I have a nagging doubt about whether or not a beggar is legitimate.

Darrin Johnson: I never give on the subway—I hate the feeling of entrapment, of being held hostage. The "O.K., so I have you until the next stop so I'm going to wear you down with guilt until I get the money out of you." I really resent that. I flatly refuse to give under those circumstances because it just pisses me off. I might give to somebody just sitting on the street, with a sign and a cup or something—someone who isn't making a big scene, who leaves it up to me whether I give or not. But I hate feeling coerced.

Jenny Nagel: I never give to people on the streets anymore—there are places where people who are really in need can go if they're really starving or need drug treatment or something. Someone once told me, after I'd given money to some derelict looking guy, that he'd probably buy rubbing alcohol or boot polish and melt it down for the alcohol content—that my money was just helping him kill himself. After that I never gave to anyone on the street. I'd rather make a contribution to a social agency.

Paul O'Rourke: I used to give money or if asked I'd give a cigarette. But one day a beggar let loose with a stream of obscenities after I gave him some money. A lot of these people are really messed up—the government should be looking after them, doing more to help them; if they keep getting money from people off the street, they'll just keep on begging. So now I volunteer once a month at a food shelf, and give to charitable organizations, rather than hand out money on the street.

ASSIGNMENT 8: WRITING ABOUT AN ISSUE
FROM MULTIPLE SOURCES

Choose a topic from the following list; or think of a question that might stimulate a wide range of responses, and submit the question for your teacher's approval. Try to avoid political issues and very controversial subjects that may make it difficult for you to control the interview and prevent you from getting a well-balanced set of notes. You want a topic in which everyone you interview can take an interest, without becoming intensely partisan.

Suggestions for Topics

Should wives get paid for housework?

Is jealousy a healthy sign in a relationship, or is it always destructive?

Should boys play with dolls?

Is "traditional" dating still desirable today?

Does it matter whether an elementary-school child has a male or female teacher?

Is there a right age to get married?

What are the ingredients for a lasting marriage?

Should children be given the same first names as their parents?

Is it better to keep a friend by not speaking your mind or risk losing a friend by honesty?

Should community service become a compulsory part of the high school curriculum?

Should English be made the official language of the United States?

Are laws requiring the wearing of seat belts an infringement of individual rights?

Is graffiti vandalism?

Should animals be used in laboratory research?

Should colleges ban drinking alcohol on campus and in fraternity houses?

How should ethics be taught in the schools?

How should the commandment "honor thy parents" be put into practice today?

What, if anything, is wrong with the nuclear family?

Are students forced to specialize too soon in their college experience?

Should schools stay in session all year round?

Should citizens have to pay a fine for not voting?

Should movies have a rating system?

Should children's TV time be rationed?

Should parents be held legally or financially responsible for damage done by their children?

At what age is it acceptable for children to work (outside the family)?

Should high school students be tested for drug use?

Should hosts who serve alcohol be held responsible if their guests later are involved in auto accidents?

Should students have to maintain passing grades in order to participate in school athletics?

How should society deal with homeless people?

When should parents cease to be financially responsible for their children?

1. Once your topic is decided (and, if necessary, approved), interview at least six people, or as many as you need to get a variety of reactions. (Some of your sources should be students in your class.) Your purpose is to learn about several ways of looking at the topic, not to argue, but to exchange views. If you wish, use the following format for conducting each interview:

Name: (first and last: check the spelling!)

Do you think . . . . ?

Why do you think so? What are some of your reasons? (later) Are there any other reasons?

Why do you think people who take the opposite view would do so?

Do any examples come to your mind to illustrate your point?

Quotation:

2. Take careful and complete notes of the comments that you receive. (*You will be expected to hand in all your notes, in their original form, with your completed essay.*) Keep a separate sheet for each person. If one of your sources says something worth quoting, write down the exact words; read them back to make sure that what you have quoted is what the speaker meant to say; then put quotation marks around the direct quotation. Otherwise, use summary or paraphrase. Do not hesitate to ask, "What do you mean?" or "Is this what I heard you say?" or "How does that fit in with what you said just before?"

3. List the ideas from your notes and arrange the points in a sequence of your choice.

4. Write an essay that presents the full range of opinion, paraphrasing and (occasionally) quoting from representative sources. After analyzing the arguments of your sources, conclude your essay with one or two paragraphs explaining which point of view, in your opinion, has the most validity, and why.

ORGANIZING MULTIPLE SOURCES

Playing the lottery is not a subject that lends itself to lengthy or abstract discussion; therefore, charting reasons for and against playing the lottery is not difficult. The article that follows defines an educational and social problem without taking sides or suggesting any solutions. The reporter's sources simply cite aspects of the problem and express baffled concern.

Twenty students were asked to read the article and to offer their opinions; these are presented following the article. As you read the article and the student opinions, assume that you plan to address the issue and synthesize the opinions in an essay of your own.

from RULE TYING PUPIL PROMOTION
TO READING SKILL STIRS WORRY
Gene I. Maeroff

A strict new promotion policy requires the public schools to hold back seventh-grade pupils until they pass the reading test. The difficulty will be compounded this year by a requirement that new seventh graders also pass a mathematics test. 1

"I am frightened that we may end up losing some of these kids, creating a whole new group of dropouts who leave school at junior high," said Herbert Rahinsky, principal of Intermediate School 293, on the edge of the Carroll Gardens section of Brooklyn. 2

Students like Larry, who is 16 years old and in the seventh grade at I.S. 293, are repeating the grade because they scored too low on the reading tests last June to be promoted. If Larry does not do well enough on the test this spring, he will remain in the seventh grade in the fall. 3

An analysis by the Board of Education has shown that about 1,000 of the 8,871 students repeating the seventh grade are already 16 years of age or older. At least one 18-year-old is repeating the seventh grade. 4

Normally, a seventh grader is 12 years old. 5

When the promotion policy, which threatened to hold back students with low reading scores in the fourth and seventh grades, was implemented in 1980, it was hailed by many observers as a welcome effort to tighten standards. 6

But as the program has continued, certain students have failed to show adequate progress. These youngsters are in jeopardy of becoming "double holdovers" in the seventh grade. Some were also held back at least once in elementary school. . . . 7

Authorities theorize that these youngsters form a hard core of poor readers for whom improvement is slow and difficult. Such students often were not held back in prior years because it was easier to move them along than to help them. 8

Educators now wonder whether repeated failure will simply lessen the likelihood of students persisting in school long enough to get a regular diploma. 9

Student Opinions

Diane Basi: If these students are pushed through the system and receive a diploma, not being able to read beyond a seventh-grade level, we will be doing them and society a grave injustice. What good will it do to have a diploma if you cannot read or write? In the end, the students will be hurt more if they are just promoted through the system.

Jason Berg: A student should not be repeatedly held back on the basis of one test. A student's overall performance should be taken into consideration, such as classwork, participation, and attitude. If a student is not up to par for some reason on the day of the test, all the work and effort that was put into school during the year goes down the drain.

Rafael Del Rey: This strict rule has unfortunate consequences. The students who are being forced out don't comprehend what is being taught to them. Exasperated and feeling like social outcasts and inferior beings, it is no wonder that many drop out without skills or goals. Low reading scores mean that students have been neglected by the school system. Educators should be interested in more than just test scores.

Anita Felice: It is extremely embarrassing to be a sixteen-year-old in a class of twelve-year-olds. Such poor students should be promoted to a special program with other students who have the same problems. In time, there should be some improvement in their reading scores. Being held back will only cause frustration and eventually cause them to drop out. Test scores should be a lot less important than they are now.

Joe Gordon: By enforcing a rigid standard, the schools are actually promoting an increased dropout rate and, by doing so, are harming the student and society. What about the teachers? Sometimes students fail a teacher, and for that reason fail the class.

Margaret Jenkins: After two tries, a student should be able to pass a test. It's to the child's advantage to learn and keep learning while moving upward in school. Holding them back is for their own good.

Rachel Limburg: It isn't fair to those students who can do the work just to push these students along. It also isn't fair to the kids who can't pass the test because eventually they are going to have to earn a living. We should look for new ways to help them find their talents and prepare them to face the future.

Barbara Martin: It's a hard question, but I think you have to look at the cost in terms of money, as well as frustration and embarrassment. I'm sorry for kids who are left back, but it's only going to be a problem for everyone later when they can't get a job. Work today is increasingly technical, and everyone needs basic skills. This policy is tough love, and it's necessary.

Len McGee: This policy isn't good enough because it doesn't deal with the individual student; it deals with seventh-graders as a whole. The individual's problems and motivation are not taken into consideration. Sometimes exam pressure defeats intelligence. If left back, the student is trapped in a revolving door and is likely to lose interest in school.

Tina Pearson: It's a mistake to pass students solely on the basis of the reading score. It may show they have learned to read well. But it doesn't mean they learned well in their other classes. Perhaps they worked especially hard on reading and English but just coasted along in their other subjects.

Julius Pena: Automatic promotion is a guarantee that the weak student will face future problems. Making the student repeat is for his own good. Imagine how frustrating it would be for someone who can't fill out a job application. Of course, you shouldn't just throw the student back into the class, but give as much encouragement as possible.

Mark Pullman: We must have certain standards in our educational system. This is a challenge for these students, and repeating the course may encourage them to try harder, making them smarter and better prepared to face life's challenges.

Anthony Raviggio: Strict standards are best for the student. In the long run, individuals who really want the college degree will be glad to remember the ordeal they went through in junior high. It's better to make them keep trying and succeed than to let them think it's okay to fail.

Vivian Ray: If a child has been held back in elementary school and held back again in junior high, it should become quite apparent to teachers and parents that the child has a problem. Being slow to learn is not sufficient reason to hold back a child. The child should be promoted and put in a slower class with more students like himself.

Bernice Roberts: I think there's too much concern for the feelings of the "poor" student and too little concern for the needs of society. Eighteen-year-olds who can't read are likely candidates for welfare. I don't want to have the responsibility of carrying some illiterate kid who couldn't be bothered to learn when he was in school.

Althea Simms: The tough standards are good for these students because they will be motivated to become more serious about doing well. There are kids who don't care whether or not they study for their exams since they know they're going to be promoted to the next grade anyway. Knowing that you may be held back is a strong motivator to study harder.

Patricia Sokolov: Not all students are intellectually gifted, nor is the progress of the nation solely dependent on the effort of intellectuals. Laborers and blue-collar workers have been credited throughout our history for their great contribution to the wealth and progress of our country. Educators should be more concerned with nurturing students' individual potential and less concerned with passing tests.

Matthew Warren: What's the point of promoting a student who won't be able to keep up in his new classes, much less perform his job properly when he's out in the working world? Standards should be enforced regardless of age. What's age? It's just a number.

Michael Willoughby: Educators should recognize that some students don't have the capacity, for whatever social, genetic, or psychological reasons, to fulfill the educa-

3. **Labeling your set of opinions and establishing categories.** In this step, the student moves away from the article to examine the opinions of others who have read the article, determining first the position of each respondent and then the reasoning behind the position. Here, the statements of the twenty respondents are repeated, with a summarizing label following each statement.

Student Opinions

Diane Basi: If these students are pushed through the system and receive a diploma, not being able to read beyond a seventh-grade level, we will be doing them and society a grave injustice. What good will it do to have a diploma if you cannot read or write? In the end, the students will be hurt more if they are just promoted through the system.

Basi: literacy necessary for employment; otherwise, individual and society both suffer

Jason Berg: A student should not be repeatedly held back on the basis of one test. A student's overall performance should be taken into consideration, such as class-work, participation, and attitude. If a student is not up to par for some reason on the day of the test, all the work and effort that was put into school during the year goes down the drain.

Berg: test scores less important than individual potential

Rafael Del Rey: This strict rule has unfortunate consequences. The students who are being forced out don't comprehend what is being taught to them. Exasperated and feeling like social outcasts and inferior beings, it is no wonder that many drop out without skills or goals. Low reading scores mean that students have been negl~s. by the school system. Educators should be interested in more than just ~

Del Rey: test scores less important than individual self-este~ss of twelve-
~am with other
~ome improvement
Anita Felice: It is extremely embarrassing to be a sixt~ ~ration and eventually
year-olds. Such poor students should be prom~ ~important than they are
students who have the same problems. I~ ~ self-esteem
in their reading scores. Being hel~ ~schools are actually promotin~
cause them to drop out. Te~~ harming the student and soc~
now. ~s fail a teacher, and for that reason

Felice: test sc~

Joe Gordon: ~r; bu~
creased dr~
about the ~

Gordon: society suffers if high standards lead to dropping out

Margaret Jenkins: After two tries, a student should be able to pass a test. It's to the child's advantage to learn and keep learning while moving upward in school. Holding them back is for their own good.

Jenkins: enforcing tough standards builds character

Rachel Limburg: It isn't fair to those students who can do the work just to push these students along. It also isn't fair to the kids who can't pass the test because eventually they are going to have to earn a living. We should look for new ways to help them find their talents and prepare them to face the future.

Limburg: fairness requires that both good and bad students get an education

Barbara Martin: It's a hard question, but I think you have to look at the cost in terms of money, as well as frustration and embarrassment. I'm sorry for kids who are left back, but it's only going to be a problem for everyone later when they can't get a job. Work today is increasingly technical, and everyone needs basic skills. This policy is tough love, and it's necessary.

Martin: literacy necessary for employment; otherwise, individual and society both suffer

Len McGee: This policy isn't good enough because it doesn't deal with the individual student; it deals with seventh-graders as a whole. The individual's problems and motivation are not taken into consideration. Sometimes exam pressure defeats intelligence. If left back, the student is trapped in a revolving door and is likely to lose interest in school.

McGee: society suffers if high standards lead to dropping out

Tina Pearson: It's a mistake to pass students solely on the basis of the reading score. It may show they have learned to read well. But it doesn't mean they learned well their other classes. Perhaps they worked especially hard on reading and English ... asted along in their other subjects.

Juliu...
future ...on should be based on a variety of skills
trating it ...
shouldn't ju... promotion is a guarantee that the weak student will face
ment as possi... student repeat is for his own good. Imagine how frus-
Pena: enforcing s... who can't fill out a job application. Of course, you
... k into the class, but give as much encourage-

... offer more help

Mark Pullman: We must have certain standards in our educational system. This is a challenge for these students, and repeating the course may encourage them to try harder, making them smarter and better prepared to face life's challenges.

Pullman: enforcing tough standards builds character

Anthony Raviggio: Strict standards are best for the student. In the long run, individuals who really want the college degree will be glad to remember the ordeal they went through in junior high. It's better to make them keep trying and succeed than to let them think it's okay to fail.

Raviggio: enforcing tough standards builds character

Vivian Ray: If a child has been held back in elementary school and held back again in junior high, it should become quite apparent to teachers and parents that the child has a problem. Being slow to learn is not sufficient reason to hold back a child. The child should be promoted and put in a slower class with more students like himself.

Ray: provide alternate track

Bernice Roberts: I think there's too much concern for the feelings of the "poor" student and too little concern for the needs of society. Eighteen-year-olds who can't read are likely candidates for welfare. I don't want to have the responsibility of carrying some illiterate kid who couldn't be bothered to learn when he was in school.

Roberts: the problem is lack of effort, not lack of ability; it's not society's problem

Althea Simms: The tough standards are good for these students because they will be motivated to become more serious about doing well. There are kids who don't care whether or not they study for their exams since they know they're going to be promoted to the next grade anyway. Knowing that you may be held back is a strong motivator to study harder.

Simms: the problem is lack of effort, not lack of ability

Patricia Sokolov: Not all students are intellectually gifted, nor is the progress of the nation solely dependent on the effort of intellectuals. Laborers and blue-collar workers have been credited throughout our history for their great contribution to the wealth and progress of our country. Educators should be more concerned with nurturing students' individual potential and less concerned with passing tests.

Sokolov: test scores less important than individual potential

Matthew Warren: What's the point of promoting a student who won't keep up in his new classes, much less perform his job properly when the working world? Standards should be enforced regardless of age. What's age? It's just a number.

Warren: literacy necessary for employment

Michael Willoughby: Educators should recognize that some students don't have the capacity, for whatever social, genetic, or psychological reasons, to fulfill the educators' traditional expectations. An alternative effort must be made, emphasizing vocational skills and also basic reading and math, that will permit students to progress at their own pace.

Willoughby: provide alternate track

Betty Yando: I am concerned about the large number of dropouts and their dismal prospects. Why should a student, despite obvious learning disabilities, be forced to continue in an exasperating educational process in which he is making little or no progress? The standards by which we determine whether an individual will make a good worker and a good citizen are too high.

Yando: individual suffers if high standards lead to dropping out

From this list, the student can establish eight *categories* that cover the range of topics. Here is the list of categories:

Category	Source	Notes
Literacy necessary for employment	Warren	
	Basi Martin	Otherwise, individual and society both suffer
The problem is lack of effort, not lack of ability	Simms	
	Roberts	If students can't meet standards, it's not society's fault.
Society suffers if high standards lead to dropping out	Gordon McGee Yando	
Enforcing tough standards builds character	Jenkins Pullman Raviggio	
	Pena	Society should also offer more help to the individual student.

Category	Source	Notes
Test scores less important than individual potential	Sokolov	
	Berg Pearson	Promotion should be based on a variety of skills.
Test scores less important than individual self-esteem	Del Rey Felice	
Society owes an education to bad students as well as good ones	Limburg	
Society should offer an alternative track for failing students	Ray Willoughby	

EVALUATING SOURCES

Although you are obliged to give each of your sources serious and objective consideration and a fair presentation, synthesis also requires a certain amount of selection. Certainly, no one's statement should be immediately dismissed as trivial or crazy; include them all in your chart. But do not assume that all opinions are equally convincing and deserve equal representation in your essay.

The weight of a group of similar opinions can add authority to an idea. If most of your sources hold a similar view, you will probably give that idea appropriate prominence in your essay. However, majority rule should not govern the structure of your essay. Your own perspective determines the thesis of your essay, and you must use your understanding of the topic to evaluate your materials, analyze the range of arguments provided by your sources, and determine for your reader which have the greatest validity.

- Review the hypothesis that you formulated before you begin to analyze the sources. *Decide whether that hypothesis is still valid* or whether, as a result of your full exploration of the subject, you wish to change it or abandon it for another.

- Sift through all the statements and decide which ones seem thoughtful and well-balanced, supported by convincing reasons and examples, and which seem to be thoughtless assertions that rely on stereotypes, catch phrases, and unsupported references. Your evaluation of the sources may differ from someone else's, but you must assert your own point of view and assess each source in the context of your background, knowledge, and experience.

You owe it to your reader to evaluate the evidence that you are presenting, partly through what you choose to emphasize and partly through your explicit comments about flawed and unconvincing statements.

In synthesis, your basic task is to present the range of opinion on a complex subject. You need not draw final conclusions in your essay or provide definitive answers to the questions that have been raised. But you must have a valid thesis, an overall view of the competing arguments to present to your reader. Your original hypothesis, either confirmed or altered in the light of your increased understanding, becomes the *thesis* of your essay.

WRITING A SYNTHESIS ESSAY

Spend some time planning your sequence of ideas and considering possible arrangements and strategies. Do your topic and materials lend themselves to a cause-and-effect structure, or definition, or problem and solution, or comparison, or argument? In writing about the issue of school promotion, you might want to use an overall *problem-solution* strategy, at the same time *arguing* for your preferred solution.

Next, before starting to write each paragraph, review your sources' statements. By now, you should be fully aware of the reasoning underlying each point of view and the pattern connecting them all. But because your reader does not know as much as you do, you need to explain your main ideas in enough detail to make all the complex points clear. Remember that your reader has neither made a list nor even read the original sources. It is therefore important to include some explanation in your own voice, in addition to quoting and paraphrasing specific statements.

If possible, you should present your sources by using all three methods of reference: *summary, paraphrase,* and *quotation.* (See the paragraph in Exercise 15 as an appropriate model.) Remember that, as a rule, paraphrase is far more effective than quotation. When you paraphrase someone's reaction in your own voice, you are underlining the fact that you are in charge, that the opinion you are citing is only one of a larger group, and that a full exploration of the topic will emerge from your presentation of *all* the evidence, not from any one source's quoted opinion. The first sentence presenting any new idea (whether the topic sentence of a new paragraph or a shift of thought within a paragraph) should be written entirely in your own voice, as a generalization, without any reference to your sources.

To summarize, your essay should include the following elements:

- *Topic sentence:* Introduce the category or theme of the paragraph, and state the idea that is the common element tying this group of opinions together.

- *Explanation:* Support or explain the topic sentence. Later in the paragraph, if you are dealing with a complex group of statements, you may need a connecting sentence or two, showing your reader how one reason is connected to the next. For example, an explanation might be needed in the middle of the "enforcing tough standards builds character" paragraph as the writer moves from the need for "tough love" to the obligation of society to offer more help.

- *Paraphrase or summary:* Present specific ideas from your sources in your own words. In these cases, you must of course *acknowledge your sources* by citing names in your sentence.

- *Quotation:* Quote from your sources when the content or phrasing of the original statement justifies word-for-word inclusion. In some groups of statements, there may be several possible candidates for quotation; in others, there may be only one; often you may find no source worth quoting. For example, read the statements made by Sokolov, Berg, and Pearson once again. Could you reasonably quote any of them? Although Berg and Pearson both take strong positions well worth presenting, there is no reason to quote them and every reason to use paraphrase. You might want to quote Sokolov's first sentence, which is apt and well-balanced.

As you analyze the opinions of your sources in the body of your essay, you should remain neutral, giving a fair presentation of each point of view. It is also your responsibility to use the final paragraphs of your essay to present your own conclusions, in your own voice, about this issue—to argue for maintaining society's standards or nurturing the individual student, or to recommend ways to accommodate both sides.

Guidelines for Citing Sources for Synthesis

- *Cite the source's full name,* whether you are quoting or not.

- *Try not to begin every sentence with a name,* nor should you introduce every paraphrase or quotation with "says."

- *Each sentence should do more than name a person;* don't include sentences without content: "Mary Smith agrees with this point."

- If possible, *support your general points with references from several different sources,* so that you will have more than one person's opinion or authority to cite.

- When you have several relevant comments to include within a single paragraph, *consider carefully which one should get cited first—and why.*

- You need not name every person who has mentioned a point (especially if you have several almost identical statements); however, *you may find it useful to sum up two people's views at the same time,* citing two sources for a single paraphrased statement:

  Mary Smith and John Jones agree that playing the lottery can be very enjoyable. She finds a particular pleasure in scratching off the numbers to see if she has won.

- *Cite only one source for a quotation,* unless both have used exactly the same wording. In the example above, the first sentence would not make sense if you *quoted* "very enjoyable."

(continued)

(continued)

- If an idea under discussion is frequently mentioned in your sources, *convey the relative weight of support* by citing "five people" or "several commentators." Then, after summarizing the common response, cite one or two specific opinions, with names. But try not to *begin* a paragraph with "several people"; remember that, whenever possible, the topic sentence should be a generalization of your own, without reference to the supporting evidence.

- *Discuss opposing views within a single paragraph as long as the two points of view have something in common.* Radically different ideas should, of course, be explained separately. Use transitions like "similarly" or "in contrast" to indicate the relationship between contrasting opinions.

EXERCISE 15: ANALYZING A PARAGRAPH BASED ON SYNTHESIS OF SOURCES

Read the following paragraph and decide which sentences (or parts of sentences) belong to each of the categories in the preceding list. Insert the appropriate category name in the left margin, and bracket the sentence or phrase illustrating the term. Be prepared to explain the components of the paragraph in class discussion.

Several people believe that reading test scores are not a valid basis for deciding whether students should be promoted or made to repeat seventh grade. According to Jason Berg, Tina Pearson, and Patricia Sokolov, proficiency in reading is just one factor among many that should count toward promotion. Pearson points out that students with high scores in reading don't necessarily excel in other subjects. In her view, it is unfair to base the decision on just one area of learning. Berg finds it equally unfair that one test should be valued more highly than a year's achievements. But the issue here is not limited to academic competence. Both Berg and Sokolov attach more importance to a student's character and potential than to intellectual attainments. Berg's definition of "overall performance" includes general contributions to the class that demonstrate a positive attitude. For Berg, the context is the classroom; for Sokolov, it is the nation. In her view, intellect alone won't make the nation thrive: "Laborers and blue-collar workers have been credited throughout our history for their great contribution to the wealth and progress of our country." Our primary concern should be to educate good citizens rather than good readers.

ASSIGNMENT 9: WRITING AN ESSAY SYNTHESIZING MULTIPLE SOURCES

Read the following essay by Todd Gitlin.

1. Write a summary of the point at issue, and then write a brief explanation of your opinion of this issue.
2. Use the statements that follow as a basis for a synthesis essay. These statements were written in response to the question: Should college instructors distribute their lecture notes to students? Analyze each statement, label each kind of reason, and organize all the categories in a chart. Then write an essay that presents the full range of opinion, paraphrasing and, if desirable, quoting from representative sources.

DISAPPEARING INK
Todd Gitlin

Hearing that a new Internet company is now posting free notes for core courses at 62 universities threw me back to a time in the 1980's when I was teaching a large class in a lecture hall at the University of California at Berkeley. The student government had approved a note-taking service called, for some arcane reason, Black Lightning. With the professor's approval, a graduate student would attend lectures, take notes and type them up, whereupon Black Lightning would duplicate the notes and offer them to students for a nominal fee (and to the professor for free). 1

With some trepidation, I agreed. Students wanted the service. I read the first few sets of notes and was reasonably impressed. The graduate student in question evidently knew what he was doing. My thinking looked tidier in his transcription than in my own notes. In fact, a professor who wanted to regurgitate the same notes year after year could use those nicely printed notes the next time and the next. 2

But I soon saw that class attendance was down. Not drastically down, but down. I also became aware that questions in class were slacking off. I have long encouraged students to interrupt lectures with questions, partly to raise the plane of comprehension, partly to keep them thinking, partly to generate arguments. Enough students normally did pipe up, during an 80-minute period, to enliven the class. But now that the notes were available in cold black type, the students were less available in spirit. 3

So when that semester was over, I stopped giving permission to Black Lightning. Some students weren't pleased. But I didn't and don't think that the University of California had hired me to please. Needless to say, in an age when the Bill of Rights seems to begin with the right to nonstop entertainment, this is a controversial belief. 4

Now it may well be argued that universities are already shortchanging their students by stuffing them into huge lecture halls where, unlike at rock concerts or basketball games, the lecturer can't even be seen on a giant screen in real time. If 5 they're already shortchanged with impersonal instruction, what's the harm in offering canned lecture notes?

The amphitheater lecture is indeed, for all but the most engaging professors, a 6 lesser form of instruction, and scarcely to be idealized. Still, Education by Download misses one of the keys to learning. Education is a meeting of minds, a process through which the student educes, draws from within, a response to what a teacher teaches.

The very act of taking notes—not reading somebody else's notes, no matter 7 how stellar—is a way of engaging the material, wrestling with it, struggling to comprehend or to take issue, but in any case entering into the work. The point is to decide, while you're listening, what matters in the presentation. And while I don't believe that most of life consists of showing up, education does begin with that—with immersing yourself in the activity at hand, listening, thinking, judging, offering active responses. A download is a poor substitute.

I can't comment on the quality of the notes posted at StudentU.com, the new, 8 advertising-supported Internet venture. When I tried to register yesterday a message came back that my ZIP code in lower Manhattan was unrecognizable to the machine in charge.

Perhaps the server is located on Mars, or is suffering the death of a thousand 9 hackers. No matter. The quality of the notes isn't the point. Glitches will be deglitched, and similar sites will follow as surely as advertisers follow a market. No doubt someone is about to register the Internet addresses Notes!.com and CollegeforDummies.com.

I.P.O.'s won't be far behind. And higher education may be as virtual as black 10 lightning.

Agnes Adams: The professor may want and expect students to take an interest in his lecture and ask questions. But if the lecture is deadly dull, everyone will be asleep. In that case, you might as well distribute notes so people will know what they slept through.

Ronald Blitzstein: The object of going to college is to learn. It doesn't matter how you learn—through lectures, through taking notes, through reading notes. I would support the most effective way of mastering the material. Reading canned notes isn't necessarily the way I'd prefer to learn, but it might be preferable to sitting in a huge lecture hall, where it's too crowded to learn much anyway.

Brook Borne: If we can buy notes, why do we need lectures? I personally don't mind lectures if the professor makes the material interesting. But it would certainly be tempting to get the core material summarized so I could pay more attention to the presentation and not have to sit there scribbling. If you can buy *Cliffs Notes* for great works of literature, why can't you buy lecture notes? Faculty are ostriches if they don't realize that students will get help from wherever they can.

Cathy Cadiz: Neither lectures nor canned notes are what I came to college for. Learning is more than receiving knowledge from on high. College courses should be small discussion sections or seminars, where material can be discussed and the students can develop their ideas. But for those courses that are purely information based, you might as well receive the information in written form.

Wendy Chin: If some graduate student writes up the lectures for the professor, they will end up being carved in stone. The professor will end up working from the notes and delivering the same lecture year after year. That's not what I'm paying tuition for. I came to college to receive the best possible education, and I expect the faculty to stimulate my mind by making the material interesting, even entertaining. I don't expect singing and dancing, but I am entitled to an original and unique delivery of the material.

Don DiCarlo: I think lectures are okay. It's good to be face to face with the professors. We don't have that many opportunities to see them; so many courses are taught by graduate students. College can be a very isolating experience, and lectures add to the sense that you're anonymous, so it would be helpful if the professor in a large lecture hall devised some way to get to know some of the students.

Elihu Eisenberg: We're paying our money to get the professor's point of view, not the opinions of some graduate students. I admit it would be easier to use canned notes, but I'd rather not get my information at second hand. If students want to skip lectures and learn from notes, why didn't they choose distance learning so they could stay in their pajamas all the time?

Noriko Hashimoto: I don't see why you can't have lectures and notes. The notes would serve as a supplement, a reminder of what the professor said. During the lecture, I could concentrate more on the material if I didn't have to write things down.

Philip Jenkins: I'm sure that, if notes were provided, some students would stop coming to lectures. But there are ways around that. The college could always make attendance mandatory. Or, after the first time around, the professor could start putting extra material in his lectures that wasn't in the notes to penalize those who didn't bother to come and reward those who did.

Lauren Marks: I actually don't mind taking notes. It helps me to absorb what's being said; it helps me to concentrate. Laptops make it much easier to take notes—you don't have to read your own handwriting. I don't see what the problem is. Lectures mean learning directly from someone who's an authority. That's what college is about.

Eduardo Martinez: My college is famous for its distinguished faculty. It's their knowledge and expertise that made me come here; it's what I'm paying tuition for. I'd rather listen and take notes during a lecture than rely on what some half-baked graduate student has to say.

Blake Morrison: A good professor will personalize the lecture. You can get a lot out of the way it's presented, the words and the images he uses, even the body language. The material seems more real. I think that experience is an important part of college, and it's preferable to a stack of impersonal notes written by someone who's not an authority on the subject.

Jason McGiver: Canned notes are one step away from research papers bought on the Internet. I suppose that if everyone agreed that it was okay to use canned notes (or even to use canned papers), that would be okay with me. But the college would have to approve. And it would have to be across the board—you shouldn't be given canned notes for one course and be expected to attend and take your own notes for another. That's not fair.

Jamal Peters: I learn best when I'm involved in the process. Discussion courses are best, but lecture courses are okay if the professor is reasonably lively. It can be a nuisance to take notes when I want to concentrate on the subject, but I find it useful to have my own take on the material.

Suzie Quintana: The solution to this problem would be to do away with large lecture courses. Personal contact enhances learning. I don't want to be an anonymous person among a hundred or more students in a large hall. I want to know the professor and have him or her know me. Lectures are not what college is about. Lectures are really no different from taking college courses on the Internet—which is a good deal cheaper!

Michael Rollafson: Canned notes are essentially a shortcut, a quick fix. They're great for students who don't want to make an effort to learn. It's the lazy person's kind of education. I'm earning part of the money for my tuition, and I want to get the most out of college. So I go to lectures and I take notes, and I don't think it's fair if the person down the hall is allowed to use canned notes. Also, if the notes cost students money over and above tuition, that becomes an economic issue.

Bernie Singer: The point about taking notes is what you put in and leave out. You're not supposed to write down every word of the lecture. You're supposed to make decisions about what's important. That's part of the learning experience. In a way, it's an ungraded test of your ability; it teaches you to focus and to summarize, which is important when you take exams.

Rose Szybrowski: Lecture classes are too big. If the college doesn't have respect for students and treat them like individuals, then the students won't respect the faculty. There's no point in going to a lecture when I can find out exactly the same information—and more quickly—from notes. I've got better things to do with my time.

Ralph Tedesco: In some courses, the professors make you buy their textbooks. What's the difference between that and buying canned notes? Is it okay only if the professor makes a profit? There's no particular advantage to having material read to you. Lectures are a waste of time.

Helen Young: I think that it's useful to have the professor's own view of the material. It helps to clarify difficult points. If it's possible to ask questions, so much the better. It would be best if a substantial part of the class were devoted to questions and discussion. That way, new ideas might get introduced. Students who didn't bother coming to class would be the losers—especially if that material appeared on the exam.

ASSIGNMENT 10: WRITING AN ARGUMENT FROM MULTIPLE SOURCES

Read "Maid to Order," and the Letters to the Editor that follow.

1. Write a brief summary of the issue raised by Barbara Ehrenreich, and list her arguments as well as the counterarguments in the Letters to the Editor.
2. Write an essay that explores the arguments on both sides of the issue and finally supports either Ehrenreich's position or that of her opponents. Make sure that you use summary, paraphrase, and quotation to represent the opinions of your sources.

MAID TO ORDER

Barbara Ehrenreich

In line with growing class polarization, the classic posture of submission is making a stealthy comeback. "We scrub your floors the old-fashioned way," boasts the brochure from Merry Maids, the largest of the residential-cleaning services that have sprung up in the last two decades, "on our hands and knees." This is not a posture that independent "cleaning ladies" willingly assume—preferring, like most people who clean their own homes, the sponge mop wielded from a standing position. In her comprehensive 1999 guide to homemaking, *Home Comforts,* Cheryl Mendelson warns: "Never ask hired housecleaners to clean your floors on their hands and knees; the request is likely to be regarded as degrading." But in a society in which 40 percent of the wealth is owned by 1 percent of households while the bottom 20 percent reports negative assets, the degradation of others is readily purchased. Kneepads entered American political discourse as a tool of the sexually subservient, but employees of Merry Maids, The Maids International, and other corporate cleaning services spend hours every day on these kinky devices, wiping up the drippings of the affluent.

I spent three weeks in September 1999 as an employee of The Maids International in Portland, Maine, cleaning, along with my fellow team members, approximately sixty houses containing a total of about 250 scrubbable floors—bathrooms, kitchens, and entryways requiring the hand-and-knees treatment. It's a different world down there below knee level, one that few adults voluntarily enter. Here

1

2

you find elaborate dust structures held together by a scaffolding of dog hair; dried bits of pasta glued to the floor by their sauce; the congealed remains of gravies, jellies, contraceptive creams, vomit, and urine. Sometimes, too, you encounter some fragment of a human being: a child's legs, stamping by in disgust because the maids are still present when he gets home from school; more commonly, the Joan & David–clad feet and electrolyzed calves of the female homeowner. Look up and you may find this person staring at you, arms folded, in anticipation of an overlooked stain. In rare instances she may try to help in some vague, symbolic way, by moving the cockatoo's cage, for example, or apologizing for the leaves shed by a miniature indoor tree. Mostly, though, she will not see you at all and may even sit down with her mail at a table in the very room you are cleaning, where she would remain completely unaware of your existence unless you were to crawl under the table and start gnawing away at her ankles.

Housework, as you may recall from the feminist theories of the Sixties and Seventies, was supposed to be the great equalizer of women. Whatever else women did—jobs, school, child care—we also did housework, and if there were some women who hired others to do it for them, they seemed too privileged and rare to include in the theoretical calculus. All women were workers, and the home was their workplace—unpaid and unsupervised, to be sure, but a workplace no less than the offices and factories men repaired to every morning. If men thought of the home as a site of leisure and recreation—a "haven in a heartless world"—this was to ignore the invisible female proletariat that kept it cozy and humming. We were on the march now, or so we imagined, united against a society that devalued our labor even as it waxed mawkish over "the family" and "the home." Shoulder to shoulder and arm in arm, women were finally getting up off the floor. . . .

The radical new idea was that housework was not only a relationship between a woman and a dust bunny or an unmade bed; it also defined a relationship between human beings, typically husbands and wives. This represented a marked departure from the more conservative Betty Friedan, who, in *The Feminine Mystique*, had never thought to enter the male sex into the equation, as either part of the housework problem or part of an eventual solution. She raged against a society that consigned its educated women to what she saw as essentially janitorial chores, beneath "the abilities of a woman of average or normal human intelligence," and, according to unidentified studies she cited, "peculiarly suited to the capacities of feeble-minded girls." But men are virtually exempt from housework in *The Feminine Mystique*—why drag them down too? At one point she even disparages a "Mrs. G.," who "somehow couldn't get her housework done before her husband came home at night and was so tired then that he had to do it." Educated women would just have to become more efficient so that housework could no longer "expand to fill the time available."

Or they could hire other women to do it—an option approved by Friedan in *The Feminine Mystique* as well as by the National Organization for Women, which she had helped launch. At the 1973 congressional hearings on whether to extend the

3

4

5

Fair Labor Standards Act to household workers, NOW testified on the affirmative side, arguing that improved wages and working conditions would attract more women to the field, and offering the seemingly self-contradictory prediction that "the demand for household help inside the home will continue to increase as more women seek occupations outside the home." One NOW member added, on a personal note: "Like many young women today, I am in school in order to develop a rewarding career for myself. I also have a home to run and can fully conceive of the need for household help as my free time at home becomes more and more restricted. Women know [that] housework is dirty, tedious work, and they are willing to pay to have it done. . . ." On the aspirations of the women paid to do it, assuming that at least some of them were bright enough to entertain a few, neither Friedan nor these members of NOW had, at the time, a word to say. . . .

6   A couple of decades later, . . . women do less housework than they did before the feminist revolution and the rise of the two-income family: down from an average of 30 hours per week in 1965 to 17.5 hours in 1995, according to a July 1999 study by the University of Maryland. Some of that decline reflects a relaxation of standards rather than a redistribution of chores; women still do two thirds of whatever housework—including bill paying, pet care, tidying, and lawn care—gets done. The inequity is sharpest for the most despised of household chores, cleaning: in the thirty years between 1965 and 1995, men increased the time they spent scrubbing, vacuuming, and sweeping by 240 percent—all the way up to 1.7 hours per week—while women decreased their cleaning time by only 7 percent, to 6.7 hours per week. The averages conceal a variety of arrangements, of course, from minutely negotiated sharing to the most clichéd division of labor, as described by one woman to the *Washington Post:* "I take care of the inside, he takes care of the outside." But perhaps the most disturbing finding is that almost the entire increase in male participation took place between the 1970s and the mid-1980s. Fifteen years after the apparent cessation of hostilities, it is probably not too soon to announce the score: in the "chore wars" of the Seventies and Eighties, women gained a little ground, but overall, and after a few strategic concessions, men won.

7   Enter then, the cleaning lady as *dea ex machina,* restoring tranquillity as well as order to the home. Marriage counselors recommend her as an alternative to squabbling, as do many within the cleaning industry itself. A Chicago cleaning woman quotes one of her clients as saying that if she gives up the service, "my husband and I will be divorced in six months." When the trend toward hiring out was just beginning to take off, in 1988, the owner of a Merry Maids franchise in Arlington, Massachusetts, told the *Christian Science Monitor,* "I kid some women. I say, 'We even save marriages. In this new eighties period you expect more from the male partner, but very often you don't get the cooperation you would like to have. The alternative is to pay somebody to come in. . . .'" Another Merry Maids franchise owner has learned to capitalize more directly on housework-related spats; he closes between 30 and 35 percent of his sales by making follow-up calls Saturday mornings, which is "prime time for arguing over the fact that the house is a mess."

The micro-defeat of feminism in the household opened a new door for women, only this time it was the servants' entrance.

In 1999, somewhere between 14 and 18 percent of households employed an outsider to do the cleaning, and the numbers have been rising dramatically. Media-mark Research reports a 53 percent increase, between 1995 and 1999, in the number of households using a hired cleaner or service once a month or more, and Maritz Marketing finds that 30 percent of the people who hired help in 1999 did so for the first time that year. Among my middle-class, professional women friends and acquaintances, including some who made important contributions to the early feminist analysis of housework, the employment of a maid is now nearly universal. This sudden emergence of a servant class is consistent with what some economists have called the "Brazilianization" of the American economy: We are dividing along the lines of traditional Latin American societies—into a tiny overclass and a huge underclass, with the latter available to perform intimate household services for the former. Or, to put it another way, the home, or at least the affluent home, is finally becoming what radical feminists in the Seventies only imagined it was—a true "workplace" for women and a tiny, though increasingly visible, part of the capitalist economy. And the question is, as the home becomes a workplace for someone else, is it still a place where you would want to live? . . .

8

One thing you can say with certainty about the population of household workers is that they are disproportionately women of color: "lower" kinds of people for a "lower" kind of work. Of the "private household cleaners and servants" it managed to locate in 1998, the Bureau of Labor statistics reports that 36.8 percent were Hispanic, 15.8 percent black, and 2.7 percent "other." Certainly the association between housecleaning and minority status is well established in the psyches of the white employing class. When my daughter, Rosa, was introduced to the wealthy father of a Harvard classmate, he ventured that she must have been named for a favorite maid. And Audre Lorde can perhaps be forgiven for her intemperate accusation . . . at the feminist conference [when she suggested that employing black nannies enabled white women to attend] when we consider an experience she had in 1967: "I wheel my two-year-old daughter in a shopping cart through a supermarket . . . and a little white girl riding past in her mother's cart calls out excitedly, 'Oh look, Mommy, a baby maid.' " But the composition of the household workforce is hardly fixed and has changed with the life chances of the different ethnic groups. In the late nineteenth century, Irish and German immigrants served the northern upper and middle classes, then left for the factories as soon as they could. Black women replaced them, accounting for 60 percent of all domestics in the 1940s, and dominated the field until other occupations began to open up to them. Similarly, West Coast maids were disproportionately Japanese American until that group, too, found more congenial options. Today, the color of the hand that pushes the sponge varies from region to region: Chicanas in the Southwest, Caribbeans in New York, native Hawaiians in Hawaii, whites, many of recent rural extraction, in Maine.

9

The great majority—though again, no one knows exact numbers—of paid house-   10
keepers are freelancers, or "independents," who find their clients through agencies or networks of already employed friends and relatives. To my acquaintances
in the employing class, the freelance housekeeper seems to be a fairly privileged
and prosperous type of worker, a veritable aristocrat of labor—sometimes paid
$15 an hour or more and usually said to be viewed as a friend or even treated as
"one of the family." But the shifting ethnic composition of the workforce tells another story: this is a kind of work that many have been trapped in—by racism, imperfect English skills, immigration status, or lack of education—but few have happily
chosen. Interviews with independent maids collected by [sociologist Mary] Romero
and by sociologist Judith Rollins, who herself worked as a maid in the Boston area
in the early Eighties, confirm that the work is undesirable to those who perform
it. Even when the pay is deemed acceptable, the hours may be long and unpredictable; there are usually no health benefits, no job security, and, if the employer has
failed to pay Social Security taxes (in some cases because the maid herself prefers to
be paid off the books), no retirement benefits. And the pay is often far from acceptable. The BLS found full-time "private household cleaners and servants" earning a median annual income of $12,220 in 1998, which is $1,092 below the poverty
level for a family of three. Recall that in 1993 Zoe Baird paid her undocumented
household workers about $5 an hour out of her earnings of $507,000 a year.

At the most lurid extreme there is slavery. A few cases of forced labor pop up   11
in the press every year, most recently—in some nightmare version of globalization—
of undocumented women held in servitude by high-ranking staff members of the
United Nations, the World Bank, and the International Monetary Fund. Consider
the suit brought by Elizabeth Senghor, a Senegalese woman who alleged that she was
forced to work fourteen-hour days for her employers in Manhattan, without any
regular pay, and was given no accommodations beyond a pull-out bed in her employers' living room. Hers is not a particularly startling instance of domestic slavery; no beatings or sexual assaults were charged, and Ms. Senghor was apparently
fed. What gives this case a certain rueful poignancy is that her employer, former
U.N. employee Marie Angelique Savane, is one of Senegal's leading women's rights
advocates and had told *The Christian Science Monitor* in 1986 about her efforts to
get the Senegalese to "realize that being a woman can mean other things than simply having children, taking care of the house."

Mostly, though, independent maids—and sometimes the women who employ   12
them—complain about the peculiar intimacy of the employer-employee relationship.
Domestic service is an occupation that predates the refreshing impersonality of
capitalism by several thousand years, conditions of work being still largely defined
by the idiosyncrasies of the employers. Some of them seek friendship and even what
their maids describe as "therapy," though they are usually quick to redraw the lines
once the maid is perceived as overstepping. Others demand deference bordering
on servility, while a growing fraction of the nouveau riche is simply out of control.
In August 1999, the *New York Times* reported on the growing problem of dinner

parties being disrupted by hostesses screaming at their help. To the verbal abuse add published reports of sexual and physical assaults—a young teenage boy, for example, kicking a live-in nanny for refusing to make sandwiches for him and his friends after school.

But for better or worse, capitalist rationality is finally making some headway into   13
this weird preindustrial backwater. Corporate cleaning services now control 25 to 30 percent of the $1.4 billion housecleaning business, and perhaps their greatest innovation has been to abolish the mistress-maid relationship, with all its quirks and dependencies. The customer hires the service, not the maid, who has been replaced anyway by a team of two to four uniformed people, only one of whom—the team leader—is usually authorized to speak to the customer about the work at hand. The maids' wages, their Social Security taxes, their green cards, backaches, and child-care problems—all these are the sole concern of the company, meaning the local franchise owner. If there are complaints on either side, they are addressed to the franchise owner; the customer and the actual workers need never interact. Since the franchise owner is usually a middle-class white person, cleaning services are the ideal solution for anyone still sensitive enough to find the traditional employer-maid relationship morally vexing. . . .

There are inevitable losses for the workers as any industry moves from the en-   14
trepreneurial to the industrial phase, probably most strikingly, in this case, in the matter of pay. At Merry Maids, I was promised $200 for a forty-hour week, the manager hastening to add that "you can't calculate it in dollars per hour" since the forty hours include all the time spent traveling from house to house—up to five houses a day—which is unpaid. The Maids International, with its straightforward starting rate of $6.63 an hour, seemed preferable, though this rate was conditional on perfect attendance. Miss one day and your wage dropped to $6 an hour for two weeks, a rule that weighed particularly heavily on those who had young children. In addition, I soon learned that management had ways of shaving off nearly an hour's worth of wages a day. We were told to arrive at 7:30 in the morning, but our billable hours began only after we had teamed up, given our list of houses for the day, and packed off in the company car at about 8:00 A.M. At the end of the day, we were no longer paid from the moment we left the car, though as much as fifteen minutes of work—refilling cleaning-fluid bottles, etc.—remained to be done. So for a standard nine-hour day, the actual pay amounted to about $6.10 an hour, unless you were still being punished for an absence, in which case it came out to $5.50 an hour.

Nor are cleaning-service employees likely to receive any of the perks or tips fa-   15
miliar to independents—free lunches and coffee, cast-off clothing, or a Christmas gift of cash. When I asked, only one of my coworkers could recall ever receiving a tip, and that was a voucher for a free meal at a downtown restaurant owned by a customer. The customers of cleaning services are probably no stingier than the employers of independents; they just don't know their cleaning people and probably wouldn't even recognize them on the street. Plus, customers probably assume that

the fee they pay the service—$25 per person-hour in the case of The Maids franchise I worked for—goes largely to the workers who do the actual cleaning.

But the most interesting feature of the cleaning-service chains, at least from an abstract, historical perspective, is that they are finally transforming the home into a fully capitalist-style workplace, and in ways that the old wages-for-housework advocates could never have imagined. A house is an innately difficult workplace to control, especially a house with ten or more rooms like so many of those we cleaned; workers may remain out of one another's sight for as much as an hour at a time. For independents, the ungovernable nature of the home-as-workplace means a certain amount of autonomy. They can take breaks (though this is probably ill-advised if the homeowner is on the premises); they can ease the monotony by listening to the radio or TV while they work. But cleaning services lay down rules meant to enforce a factorylike—or even conventlike—discipline on their far-flung employees. At The Maids, there were no breaks except for a daily ten-minute stop at a convenience store for coffee or "lunch"—meaning something like a slice of pizza. Otherwise, the time spent driving between houses was considered our "break" and the only chance to eat, drink, or (although this was also officially forbidden) smoke a cigarette. When the houses were spaced well apart, I could eat my sandwich in one sitting; otherwise it would have to be divided into as many as three separate, hasty snacks.

Within a customer's house, nothing was to touch our lips at all, not even water—a rule that, on hot days, I sometimes broke by drinking from a bathroom faucet. TVs and radios were off-limits, and we were never, ever, to curse out loud, even in an ostensibly deserted house. There might be a homeowner secreted in some locked room, we were told, ear pressed to the door, or, more likely, a tape recorder or video camera running. At the time, I dismissed this as a scare story, but I have since come across ads for devices like the Tech-7 "incredible coin-sized camera" designed to "get a visual record of your babysitter's actions" and "watch employees to prevent theft." It was the threat or rumor of hidden recording devices that provided the final capitalist-industrial touch—supervision.

What makes the work most factorylike, though, is the intense Taylorization imposed by the companies. An independent, or a person cleaning his or her own home, chooses where she will start and, within each room, probably tackles the most egregious dirt first. Or she may plan her work more or less ergonomically, first doing whatever can be done from a standing position and then squatting or crouching to reach the lower levels. But with the special "systems" devised by the cleaning services and imparted to employees via training videos, there are no such decisions to make. In The Maids' "healthy touch" system, which is similar to what I saw of the Merry Maid's system on the training tape I was shown during my interview, all cleaning is divided into four task areas—dusting, vacuuming, kitchens, and bathrooms—which are in turn divided among the team members. For each task area other than vacuuming, there is a bucket containing rags and the appropriate cleaning fluids, so the biggest decision an employee had to make is which fluid and

16

17

18

scrubbing instrument to deploy on which kind of surface; almost everything else has been choreographed in advance. When vacuuming, you begin with the master bedroom; when dusting, with the first room off of the kitchen; then you move through the rooms going left to right. When entering each room, you proceed from left to right and top to bottom, and the same with each surface—top to bottom, left to right. Deviations are subject to rebuke, as I discovered when a team leader caught me moving my arm from right to left, then left to right, while wiping Windex over a French door.

It's not easy for anyone with extensive cleaning experience—and I include myself in this category—to accept this loss of autonomy. But I came to love the system: First, because if you hadn't always been traveling rigorously from left to right it would have been easy to lose your way in some of the larger houses and omit or redo a room. Second, some of the houses were already clean when we started, at least by any normal standards, thanks probably to a housekeeper who kept things up between our visits; but the absence of visible dirt did not mean there was less work to do, for no surface could ever be neglected, so it was important to have "the system" to remind you of where you had been and what you had already "cleaned." No doubt the biggest advantage of the system, though, is that it helps you achieve the speed demanded by the company, which allots only so many minutes per house. After a week or two on the job, I found myself moving robotlike from surface to surface, grateful to have been relieved of the thinking process.   19

The irony, which I was often exhausted enough to derive a certain malicious satisfaction from, is that "the system" is not very sanitary. When I saw the training videos on "Kitchens" and "Bathrooms," I was at first baffled, and it took me several minutes to realize why: There is no water, or almost no water, involved. I had been taught to clean by my mother, a compulsive housekeeper who employed water so hot you needed rubber gloves to get into it and in such Niagaralike quantities that most microbes were probably crushed by the force of it before the soap suds had a chance to rupture their cell walls. But germs are never mentioned in the videos provided by The Maids. Our antagonists existed entirely in the visible world—soap scum, dust, counter crud, dog hair, stains, and smears—and were attacked by damp rag or, in hardcore cases, by a scouring pad. We scrubbed only to remove impurities that might be detectable to a customer by hand or by eye; otherwise our only job was to wipe. Nothing was ever said, in the videos or in person, about the possibility of transporting bacteria, by rag or by hand, from bathroom to kitchen or even from one house to the next. Instead, it is the "cosmetic touches" that the videos emphasize and to which my trainer continually directed my eye. Fluff out all throw pillows and arrange them symmetrically. Brighten up stainless steel sinks with baby oil. Leave all spice jars, shampoos, etc., with their labels facing outward. Comb out the fringes of Persian carpets with a pick. Use the vacuum to create a special, fernlike pattern in the carpets. The loose ends of toilet paper and paper towel rolls have to be given a special fold. Finally, the house is sprayed with the service's signature   20 air freshener—a cloying floral scent in our case, "baby fresh" in the case of the Mini Maids. . . .

The point at The Maids, apparently, is not to clean so much as it is to create the appearance of having been cleaned, not to sanitize but to create a kind of stage setting for family life. And the stage setting Americans seem to prefer is sterile only in the metaphorical sense, like a motel room or the fake interiors in which soap operas and sitcoms take place.   21

But even ritual work takes its toll on those assigned to perform it. Turnover is dizzyingly high in the cleaning-service industry, and not only because of the usual challenges that confront the working poor—child-care problems, unreliable transportation, evictions, and prior health problems. As my long-winded interviewer at Merry Maids warned me, and my coworkers at The Maids confirmed, this is a physically punishing occupation, something to tide you over for a few months, not year after year. The hands-and-knees posture damages knees, with or without pads; vacuuming strains the back; constant wiping and scrubbing invite repetitive stress injuries even in the very young. In my three weeks as a maid, I suffered nothing more than a persistent muscle spasm in the right forearm, but the damage would have been far worse if I'd had to go home every day to my own housework and children, as most of my coworkers did, instead of returning to my motel and indulging in a daily after-work regimen of ice packs and stretches. Chores that seem effortless at home, even almost recreational when undertaken at will for twenty minutes or so at a time, quickly turn nasty when performed hour after hour, with few or no breaks and under relentless time pressure. . . .   22

The trend toward outsourcing the work of the home seems, at the moment, unstoppable. Two hundred years ago women often manufactured soap, candles, cloth, and clothing in their own homes, and the complaints of some women at the turn of the twentieth century that they had been "robbed by the removal of creative work" from the home sound pointlessly reactionary today. Not only have the skilled crafts, like sewing and cooking from scratch, left the home but many of the "white collar" tasks are on their way out, too. For a fee, new firms such as the San Francisco–based Les Concierges and Cross It Off Your List in Manhattan will pick up dry cleaning, baby-sit pets, buy groceries, deliver dinner, even do the Christmas shopping. With other firms and individuals offering to buy your clothes, organize your financial files, straighten out your closets, and wait around in your home for the plumber to show up, why would anyone want to hold on to the toilet cleaning?   23

Absent a major souring of the economy, there is every reason to think that Americans will become increasingly reliant on paid housekeepers and that this reliance will extend even further down into the middle class. For one thing, the "time bind" on working parents shows no sign of loosening; people are willing to work longer hours at the office to pay for the people—housecleaners and baby-sitters—who are filling in for them at home. Children, once a handy source of household help, are now off at soccer practice or SAT prep classes; grandmother has relocated to a   24 warmer climate or taken up a second career. Furthermore, despite the fact that people spend less time at home than ever, the square footage of new homes swelled by 33 percent between 1975 and 1998, to include "family rooms," home entertainment rooms, home offices, bedrooms, and often bathrooms for each family member. By the third quarter of 1999, 17 percent of new homes were larger than 3,000 square feet, which is usually considered the size threshold for household help, or the point at which a house becomes unmanageable to the people who live in it.

One more trend impels people to hire outside help, according to cleaning experts   25 such as Don Aslett and Cheryl Mendelson: fewer Americans know how to clean or even to "straighten up." I hear this from professional women defending their decision to hire a maid: "I'm just not very good at it myself" or "I wouldn't really know where to begin." Since most of us learn to clean from our parents (usually our mothers), any diminution of cleaning skills is transmitted from one generation to another, like a gene that can, in the appropriate environment, turn out to be disabling or lethal. Upper-middle-class children raised in the servant economy of the Nineties are bound to grow up as domestically incompetent as their parents and no less dependent on people to clean up after them. Mendelson sees this as a metaphysical loss, a "matter of no longer being physically centered in your environment." Having cleaned the rooms of many overly privileged teenagers in my stint with The Maids, I think the problem is a little more urgent than that. The American overclass is raising a generation of young people who will, without constant assistance, suffocate in their own detritus.

If there are moral losses, too, as Americans increasingly rely on paid household   26 help, no one has been tactless enough to raise them. Almost everything we buy, after all, is the product of some other person's suffering and miserably underpaid labor. I clean my own house (though—full disclosure—I recently hired someone else to ready it for a short-term tenant), but I can hardly claim purity in any other area of consumption. I buy my jeans at The Gap, which is reputed to subcontract to sweatshops. I tend to favor decorative objects no doubt ripped off, by their purveyors, from scantily paid Third World craftspersons. Like everyone else, I eat salad greens just picked by migrant farm workers, some of them possibly children. And so on. We can try to minimize the pain that goes into feeding, clothing, and otherwise provisioning ourselves—by observing boycotts, checking for a union label, etc.— but there is no way to avoid it altogether without living in the wilderness on berries. Why should housework, among all the goods and services we consume, arouse any special angst?

And it does, as I have found in conversations with liberal-minded employers of   27 maids, perhaps because we all sense that there are ways in which housework is different from other products and services. First, in its inevitable proximity to the activities that compose "private" life. The home that becomes a workplace for other people remains a home, even when that workplace has been minutely regulated by the corporate cleaning chains. Someone who has no qualms about purchasing rugs woven by child slaves in India or coffee picked by impoverished peasants in Guatemala might still hesitate to tell dinner guests that, surprisingly enough, his or her lovely home doubles as a sweatshop during the day. You can eschew the chain cleaning services of course, hire an independent cleaner at a generous hourly wage, and even encourage, at least in spirit, the unionization of the housecleaning industry. But this does not change the fact that someone is working in your home at a job she would almost certainly never have chosen for herself—if she'd had a college education, for example, or a little better luck along the way—and the place where she works, however enthusiastically or resentfully, is the same as the place where you sleep.

It is also the place where your children are raised, and what they learn pretty quickly is that some people are less worthy than others. Even better wages and working conditions won't erase the hierarchy between an employer and his or her domestic help, because the help is usually there only because the employer has "something better" to do with her time, as one report on the growth of cleaning services puts it, not noticing the obvious implication that the cleaning person herself has nothing better to do with her time. In a merely middle-class home, the message may be reinforced by the warning to the children that that's what they'll end up doing if they don't try harder in school. Housework, as radical feminists once proposed, defines a human relationship and, when unequally divided among social groups, reinforces preexisting inequalities. Dirt, in other words, tends to attach to the people who remove it—"garbagemen" and "cleaning ladies." Or, as cleaning entrepreneur Don Aslett told me with some bitterness—and this is a successful man, chairman of the board of an industrial cleaning service and frequent television guest—"The whole mentality out there is that if you clean, you're a scumball." 28

One of the "better" things employers of maids often want to do with their time is, of course, spend it with their children. But an underlying problem with post-nineteenth-century child-raising, as Deirdre English and I argued in our book *For Her Own Good* years ago, is precisely that it is unmoored in any kind of purposeful pursuit. Once "parenting" meant instructing the children in necessary chores; today it's more likely to center on one-sided conversations beginning with "So how was school today?" No one wants to put the kids to work again weeding and stitching; but in the void that is the modern home, relationships with children are often strained. A little "low-quality time" spent washing dishes or folding clothes together can provide a comfortable space for confidences—and give a child the dignity of knowing that he or she is a participant in, and not just the product of, the work of the home. 29

There is another lesson the servant economy teaches its beneficiaries and, most troublingly, the children among them. To be cleaned up after is to achieve a certain magical weightlessness and immateriality. Almost everyone complains about violent video games, but paid housecleaning has the same consequence-abolishing effect: you blast the villain into a mist of blood droplets and move right along; you drop the socks knowing they will eventually levitate, laundered and folded, back to their normal dwelling place. The result is a kind of virtual existence, in which the trail 30 of litter that follows you seems to evaporate all by itself. Spill syrup on the floor and the cleaning person will scrub it off when she comes on Wednesday. Leave *The Wall Street Journal* scattered around your airplane seat and the flight attendants will deal with it after you've deplaned. Spray toxins into the atmosphere from your factory's smokestacks and they will be filtered out eventually by the lungs of the breathing public. A servant economy breeds callousness and solipsism in the served, and it does so all the more effectively when the service is performed close up and routinely in the place where they live and reproduce.

Individual situations vary, of course, in ways that elude blanket judgment. Some   31
people—the elderly and disabled, parents of new babies, asthmatics who require an allergen-free environment—may well need help performing what nursing-home staff call the "ADLs," or activities of daily living, and no shame should be attached to their dependency. In a more generous social order, housekeeping services would be subsidized for those who have health-related reasons to need them—a measure that would generate a surfeit of new jobs for the low-skilled people who now clean the homes of the affluent. And in a less gender-divided social order, husbands and boyfriends would more readily do their share of the chores.

However we resolve the issue in our individual homes, the moral challenge is,   32
put simply, to make work visible again: not only the scrubbing and vacuuming but all the hoeing, stacking, hammering, drilling, bending, and lifting that goes into creating and maintaining a livable habitat. In an ever more economically unequal culture, where so many of the affluent devote their lives to such ghostly pursuits as stock-trading, image-making, and opinion-polling, real work—in the old-fashioned sense of labor that engages hand as well as eye, that tires the body and directly alters the physical world—tends to vanish from sight. The feminists of my generation tried to bring some of it into the light of day, but, like busy professional women fleeing the house in the morning, they left the project unfinished, the debate broken off in midsentence, the noble intentions unfulfilled. Sooner or later, someone else will have to finish the job.

LETTERS TO THE EDITOR: CALLING A MAID A MAID

Barbara Ehrenreich's article, a tirade against the practice of hiring housekeepers, was elitist and insulting. Obviously, houseworkers should be paid a living wage and have health and pension benefits (preferably, in my opinion, through a union). Obviously, they should be treated with respect by their employers. But Ehrenreich's assertion that the "peculiar intimacy" of housecleaning is demeaning demeans the very people who do it. Her attitude reminds me of the Hindu caste system, in which people who tan leather and make shoes are considered to be lowly, since their trade deals with dead animals and feet. It is precisely this attitude that must be done away with (and yes, you may note my last name).

I remember myself, in my hippie days, sitting poolside with my older, affluent sister-in-law and announcing prissily, "I would never have a maid—it's so patronizing to women and minorities!" To which she replied, "Well, then, what should I do—fire Janice? She's forty-two, she has two kids, and she can't even read or write" (all of which were true). I didn't have an answer then, and I still don't.

By the way, I have never hired a housecleaner but will not hesitate to do so as soon as I can afford it.

PAMELA HUNT SHOEMAKER
New York City

Regarding your article "Maid to Order," am I to understand the author's position is that a woman who has the brains and capacity to find the cure for cancer should *not* devote every waking hour to research but should take the time to clean her own house, thereby reducing research time, in order to not oppress a "cleaning lady"? How ironic it would be if this "cleaning lady" had an out-of-work husband who was sick with a cancer that could be cured by the findings of someone who spends her time on research, not housecleaning.

I find your rhetoric unsustainable.

JENNIFER T. GRAINGER
Stockton, Calif.

No, I don't think scrubbing my own toilet would make me a better person. I have a job I love that pays me well. It makes sense for me to work long hours at a high rate and pay someone else a lower rate to do my housework. I prefer to spend my precious free time relaxing and playing with my children (as opposed to, say, waxing floors or vacuuming under beds). And yes, my maid is a foreign-born woman of color; that seems to be the kind of person who does cleaning work in these parts.

Barbara Ehrenreich's essay ended on a politically correct, self-righteous note that I was frankly disappointed to read in *Harper's:* "the moral challenge is . . . to make work visible again." Give me a break! Work is already a major part of my life and personal makeup. But scrubbing, vacuuming, bending, and lifting aren't the work I choose to do. This was a long story about nothing.

BROOKE STAUFFER
Bethesda, Md.

With the encouragement of feminism, millions of women have pushed aside a whole range of misgivings about paying strangers to take care of their children. Good luck to Barbara Ehrenreich if she thinks she can now get their consciences to twinge over hiring other women to clean their houses.

ELIZABETH BERNSTEIN
Bisbee, Ariz.

We were interested to read Barbara Ehrenreich's article, not least (though not only) because of her claim that the "demand for 'wages for housework' has sunk to the status of a curio, along with the consciousness-raising groups in which women once rallied support in their struggles with messy men." Those of us in the

International Wages for Housework Campaign (now based in England, Spain, the United States, and the Caribbean, and with a number of autonomous organizations in the network, including International Black Women for Wages for Housework), exhausted but exhilarated from just having organized a sixty-country Global Women's Strike on International Women's Day (March 8), are amazed by this.

Clearly, many feminists are only now catching up with this grassroots movement, which is demanding wages for caring work and pay equity in the global market.

SELMA JAMES and PHOEBE JONES SCHELLENBERG
International Wages for Housework Campaign
London and Philadelphia

The Maids International, our franchise owners, and franchise employees are offended by a number of statements made in Barbara Ehrenreich's article. In particular, we are greatly disturbed by the statement, "Household workers . . . are disproportionately women of color: 'Lower' kinds of people for a 'lower' kind of work." At The Maids International, we value the women and men who work in our system. We don't believe that the color of a person's skin has any bearing on the content of his or her character. They are good people who work hard to support their families. We provide a safe and professional working environment with opportunities for advancement. Cleaning homes is not demeaning. It's honest and honorable work that benefits our employees and is appreciated by our customers.

DANIEL J. BISHOP
President, The Maids International, Inc.
Omaha

The ethical dilemma posed by domestic service is much like the problem of slavery as it was experienced in the eighteenth century. Slavery was always considered an undesirable station in life and mistreatment of slaves was always unethical, but no one, not even slaves, considered slavery to be wrong until the moral implications of Thomas Jefferson's Declaration clarified the unsavoriness of slavery in human relations. Freed slaves thought nothing of owning slaves themselves (given the opportunity), just as domestic workers dream of a day when they might hire maids of their own. As for the labor of the children who produce our children's toys—it can best be described as "out of sight, out of mind."

As good people once held slaves, good people will continue to exploit domestic help and sweatshop labor until two things happen: (1) we reach a threshold of moral awareness, and (2) domestic service and other exploited labor are replaced by some less compromised means of accomplishing the same tasks.

K. J. WALTERS
Monroe, N.Y.

As in her essay "Nickel-and-Dimed" [January 1999], Barbara Ehrenreich enters the working class for two weeks but retains her privilege to leave. Predictably, she finds it unacceptable. Of course she does: she has other options. Her position is one envied by many people of even her own socioeconomic class: she is paid for work she loves and has gained national recognition for it. Only at the end of her article, when Ehrenreich parallels the disregard for one's personal detritus with a disregard for industrial waste, does her article graduate from whining to serious criticism. One wishes that she'd spent more time building her argument for environmental awareness and less time moralizing on the evils of employing workers in the home.

KARIN PAYSON
San Francisco

Barbara Ehrenreich's essay was strident, rhetorical, and predictable. Every society is composed of two groups: the rich and powerful who are few, and the poor and oppressed who are many. It was ever thus, and readers of *Harper's Magazine* had better be grateful for it.

ERIC BOURLAND
Arlington, Va.

Barbara Ehrenreich trots out her predictable litany of feminist complaints against men, capitalism, affluent people, and other feminists who don't share her sensibilities. She sees husbands as exploiters of women and chides them for not doing their fair share of housework. There is no apparent effort on her part to acknowledge the fact that men work more hours outside the home, are expected to be the primary providers for the family, and are usually the ones who do the dirtiest, most dangerous, and most life-depleting jobs. Next time, Ehrenreich should write an investigative report that looks sympathetically at the sacrifices made by male firefighters, miners, construction workers, and other men in the "death professions." She dismisses men's contributions to household maintenance and ignores the fact that the husband's full-time job makes it possible for his wife not to have to work outside the home.

CHRISTOPHER C. HEARD
Nashville

Barbara Ehrenreich's otherwise informative essay is marred by a common misconception. She decries the less-than-sanitary results of cosmetic cleaning practices. . . . The maid-for-hire routine is to "create the appearance" of a good cleaning, she complains, rather than to actually clean. This is exactly right. Cleaning, for the most part, *is* a cosmetic practice. Except for ridding dust from the environment of an asthmatic, making sure actual food isn't lying around to attract pests, and scouring cutting surfaces on which food will sit, cleaning simply doesn't matter—despite what our mothers taught us. Humans, like other animals, evolved quite nicely in dirty environs. If people prefer nicely folded toilet tissue and a signature smell rather than sanitized counter scrubs, fine. No one has died of diseases caused by dirty floors. It is refrigeration that saves lives, not clean refrigerators.

KRISTEN HAAS
Grand Rapids, Mich.

Scenes from my life as a maid:

Climbing a ladder to change the kitty litter in an attic twice a week.

Bending over a stairway under the maid-service owner's supervision, sweeping the stairs with dustpan and broom, collapsing with asthma afterwards.

On my hands and knees polishing a tiled kitchen floor under the housewife's supervision. Polishing her bathroom floors likewise. Finding my jacket, which this woman had taken downstairs "to put away" for me, balled up in the bottom corner of the closet. The folds with a hollow where she'd punched it into place. (Her husband had one just like it, she'd said.)

Scrubbing a windowless bathroom, seven years' worth of mold off the shower doors, and reeling out past the glass afterwards, dizzy with unventilated ammonia fumes.

The weight and size of Kirby vacuum cleaners. The sheer weight of them. Lighter ones are universally said, by clients and supervisors alike, "not to clean."

Car in an underground car park, coffee from a thermos: lunch.

I was a maid in the early Eighties in the South Bay area of Los Angeles.

Barbara Ehrenreich gets a lot of it right, but she is wrong when she says that the posture of submission is making a stealthy comeback.

The posture of submission is currently making a blatant comeback. It was stealthy in the early Eighties when Reagan and yuppiedom were just feeling their way.

It was absolutely clear back then that what the client was buying was submission, and, if possible, the right to humiliate.

If the client was home I cleaned kitchen and bathroom floors on my hands and knees; the client insisted. I cleaned stairs the same way.

If the client was not home I was simply alone in the client's landscape of secretion: soap-scummed bathrooms, filthy ovens and broilers and black glass-fronted appliances; refrigerators to be cleaned out, loads of washing (often to be taken to the basement from a third-floor apartment—please dry and fold); acres of shag pile to be separated from the plastic toys unbiodegradably skeined into it, then vacuumed with the impossible monster vacuum; more acres of clear glass door, by the sea, to bear no hint of salt or smear—an impossible schedule, sometimes fitting in unscheduled things ("and if you could . . .") to keep the client from switching services.

I worked for a company, not independently. All the clients were white.

The company charged $15 an hour; I got $5. By the time I got home I was often too tired to eat.

One of my supervisors was white, the other Latina. The owner of the business was Filipina. Inflicting the punishment of poverty on the poor is a game anyone can play. All it takes is money.

I will never hire someone to do my housework. I'll choke to death first.

MOIRA MCAULIFFE
Portland, Ore.

SYNTHESIS AND COMPARISON

Synthesis is a method; it is not an end in itself. Some works do not lend themselves to synthesis, which tends to emphasize similarities at the expense of interesting differences between sources.

The academic writer should be able to distinguish between material that is appropriate for synthesis and material whose individuality should be recognized and preserved. One example of the latter is fiction; another is autobiography. Assume that three writers are reminiscing about their first jobs: one was a clerk in a drugstore, the second a telephone operator, and the third plowed his father's fields. In their recollections, the reader can find several similar themes: accepting increased responsibility; sticking to the job; learning appropriate behavior; living up to the boss's or customers' or father's expectations. But, just as important, the three autobiographical accounts *differ* sharply in their context and circumstances, in their point of view and style. You cannot lump them together in the same way that you might categorize statements about the lottery or opinions about school uniforms, for they cannot be reduced to a single common experience. The three are not *interchangeable*; rather, they are *comparable*.

Since *synthesis* does not always do justice to individual works, *comparison* can be a more effective strategy for writing about several full-length essays with a common theme. In many ways, comparison resembles synthesis. Both involve analyzing the ideas of several sources and searching for a single vantage point from which to view these separate sources. However, there is an important difference. *The writer of a synthesis constructs a new work out of the materials of the old; the writer of a comparison tries to leave the sources intact throughout the organizational process, so that each retains its individuality.*

When you are assigned an essay topic, and when you assemble several sources, you are not likely to want to *compare* the information that you have recorded in your notes; rather, you will *synthesize* that material into a complete presentation of the topic. One of your sources may be an encyclopedia; another a massive survey of the entire subject; a third may devote several chapters to a scrutiny of that one small topic. In fact, these three sources are really not comparable, nor is your primary purpose to distinguish between them or to understand how they approach the subject differently. You are only interested in the results that you can achieve by using and building on this information. In contrast, the appropriate conditions for comparison are more specific and rare. *For comparison, you must have two or more works of similar length and complexity that deal with the same subject and that merit individual examination.*

Point-to-Point Comparison

Point-to-point comparison resembles synthesis. You select certain major ideas that are discussed in all the works being compared and then, to support conclusions about these ideas, describe the full range of opinion concerning *each* point, one at a time.

Because point-to-point comparison cuts across the source essays, as synthesis does, you must work hard to avoid oversimplification. If you are focusing on one idea, trying to relate it to a comparable reaction in another essay, don't forget that the two works are separate and whole interpretations of the topic. Otherwise, you may end up emphasizing similarities just to make your point.

Here is a paragraph taken from a *point-to-point comparison* of three movie reviews:

> None of the three reviewers regards Lady and the Tramp as a first-rate product of the Walt Disney studio. Their chief object of criticism is the sugary sentimentality, so characteristic of Disney cartoons, which has been injected into Lady in excessive quantities. Both John McCarten in the New Yorker and the Time reviewer point out that, for the first time, the anthropomorphic presentation of animals does not succeed because the "human" situations are far too broadly presented. Lady and the Tramp are a "painfully arch pair," says McCarten. He finds the dialogue given to the movie's human characters even more embarrassing than the clichés exchanged by the animals. Even Bosley Crowther of the Times, who seems less dismissive of feature cartoons, finds that Lady and the Tramp lacks Disney's usual "literate originality." Crowther suggests that its oppressive sentimentality is probably made more obvious by the film's use of the wide screen. McCarten also comments on the collision between the winsome characters and the magnified production: "Obviously determined to tug all heartstrings," Disney presents the birth of Lady's puppy "while all the stereophonic loudspeakers let loose with overwhelming barrages of cooings and gurglings." All the reviewers agree that the audience for this film will be restricted to dog lovers, and lapdog lovers at that.

Whole-to-Whole Comparison

In whole-to-whole comparison, you discuss each work, one at a time. This method is more likely to give the reader a sense of each source's individual qualities. But unless your sources are fairly short and simple, this method can be far more unwieldy than point-to-point. If you compare a series of long and complex works, and if you complete your entire analysis of one before you move on to the next, the reader may get no sense of a comparison and forget that you are relating several sources to each other. Without careful structuring, whole-to-whole comparison becomes a series of loosely related summaries, in which readers must discover for themselves all the connections, parallels, and contrasts.

There are two ways to make the structure of whole-to-whole comparison clear to the reader:

1. **Although each work is discussed separately and presented as a whole, you should nevertheless try to present common ideas *in the same order*, an order that will carry out the development of your thesis about the works being compared.**

   Thus, whichever topic you choose as the starting point for your discussion of the first work should also be used as the starting point for your treatment of each of the others. The reader should be able to find the same general idea discussed in (roughly) the same place in each section of a whole-to-whole comparison.

2. **Remind the reader that this is a comparison by frequent *cross-cutting* to works already discussed; you should make frequent use of standard transitional phrases to establish such cross-references.**

   Initially, you have to decide which work to begin with. The best choice is usually a relatively simple work that nonetheless touches on all the major points of comparison and that enables you to begin establishing your own point of view. Beginning with the second work, you should refer back to what you have said about the first writer's ideas, showing how they differ from those of the second. This process can become extremely complex when you are analyzing a large number of essays, which is one reason that whole-to-whole comparison is rarely used to compare more than three works.

Here is the second major paragraph of a *whole-to-whole comparison* that deals with critical reaction to the film *West Side Story:*

> Like the author of the Time review, Pauline Kael criticizes West Side Story for its lack of realism and its unconvincing portrayal of social tensions. She points out that the distinction between the ethnic groups is achieved through cosmetics and hair dye, not dialogue and actions. In her view, the characters are like Munchkins, stock figures without individual identities and recognizable motives. Natalie Wood as the heroine, Maria, is unfavorably compared to a mechanical robot and to the Princess telephone. Just as the Time reviewer accuses the film of oversentimentalizing its teenage characters at society's expense, so Kael condemns the movie's division of its characters into stereotypical good guys and bad guys. In fact, Kael finds it hard to account for the popularity of West Side Story's "frenzied hokum." She concludes that many may have been overwhelmed by the film's sheer size and technical achievements. The audience is persuaded to believe that bigger, louder, and faster has to be better. Her disapproval extends even to the widely praised dancing; like the rest of the movie, the choreography tries too hard to be impressive. In short, Pauline Kael agrees with the Time reviewer: West Side Story never rises above its "hyped-up, slam-bang production."

Whether you choose point-to-point or whole-to-whole comparison depends on your sources. Whichever you choose, begin planning your comparison (as you would begin synthesis) by listing the important ideas discussed by several of your sources.

- If you eventually choose to write a *point-to-point* essay, then your list can become the basis for your paragraph outline.
- If you decide to compare each of your essays *whole to whole,* your list can suggest what to emphasize and can help you to decide the order of topics within the discussion of each work.

These lists can never be more than primitive guidelines; but unless you establish the primary points of similarity or difference among your sources, your essay will end up as a series of unrelated comments, not a comparison.

ASSIGNMENT 11: WRITING A COMPARISON ESSAY

Write a comparison of three reviews of a film. Your first concern should be the reactions of the critics, not your own opinion of the work; you are not expected to write a review yourself, but to analyze and contrast each critic's view of the film. Try to describe the distinctive way in which each reacts to the film; each will have seen a somewhat different film and will have a different understanding of what it signifies.

Don't commit yourself to a specific film until you have seen a sampling of reviews; if they are all very similar in their criticisms or all very short, choose a different film. If you have doubts about the reviews' suitability, let your teacher see a set of copies. *Be prepared to hand in a full set of the reviews with your completed essay.*

Part III

WRITING THE RESEARCH ESSAY

Most long essays and term papers in college courses are based on library research. Sometimes, an instructor will expect you to develop and present a topic entirely through synthesizing preassigned sources; but for many other assignments, you will be asked to formulate your own opinion and then to validate and support that opinion by citing authorities. Whether your essay is to be wholly or partly substantiated through research, you will still have to start your essay by choosing sources.

Your research essay (or extended multiple-source essay) will present you with several new problems, contradictions, and decisions. On the one hand, you will probably be starting out with no sources, no thesis, and only a broad topic to work with. Yet as soon as you go to the library and start your research, you will probably find yourself with too many sources—books and articles in the library and on the Internet from which you will have to make your own selection of readings. Locating and evaluating sources are complex skills, calling for quick comprehension and rapid decision-making.

- At the *electronic databases* and *online computer catalogs,* you have to judge which books are worth locating.
- At the *shelves,* and on the *computer screen,* you have to skim a variety of materials rapidly to choose the ones that may be worth reading at length.
- At the *library table* and *on the Internet,* you have to decide which facts and information should go into your notes and which pages should be duplicated in their entirety.

In Chapters 5, 6, and 7, you will be given explicit guidelines for using the library, choosing sources, and taking notes.

As you have learned, in order to write a multiple-source essay, you have to establish a coherent structure that builds on your reading and blends together your ideas and those of your sources. In Chapter 7, you will find a stage-by-stage description of the best ways to organize and write an essay based on complex sources. But here, again, is a contradiction.

Even as you gather your materials and synthesize them into a unified essay, you should also keep in mind the greatest responsibility of the researcher—accountability. *From your first efforts to find sources at the library and at your computer, you must carefully keep track of the precise source of each of the ideas and facts that you may use in your essay.* You already know how to distinguish between your ideas and those of your sources and to make that distinction clear to your readers.

Now, you also have to make clear which source is responsible for which idea and on which page of which book that information can be found—without losing the shape and coherence of your own paragraphs.

To resolve this contradiction between writing a coherent essay and accounting for your sources, you will use a system that includes the familiar skills of *quotation, paraphrase,* and *citation of authors,* as well as the skills of *documentation* and *compiling a bibliography.* This system is explained in Chapter 8.

Finally, in Chapter 9, you will be able to examine the product of all these research, writing, and documenting techniques: three essays that demonstrate, respectively, how to write a persuasive, narrative, or analytical research essay.

▪5▪

Finding Sources

Chapter 5 shows you how to develop a topic for a research essay as you search for information about that topic in the library and on the Internet. You will learn how to use databases and search engines effectively to identify and locate a range of books, periodical articles, and Web sites that are appropriate for academic research. At the same time, you'll begin the process of transforming these sources into a formal bibliography.

TOPIC NARROWING

When you start your research, sometimes you will know exactly what you want to write about, and sometimes you won't. Your instructor may assign a precise topic. Or you may start with a broad subject and then narrow the focus. Or you may choose your own topic, perhaps developing an idea that you wrote about in your single- or multiple-source essay.

Choosing a good topic requires some understanding of the subject and the available resources. Ask yourself these practical questions before you begin collecting material for your essay:

- How much time do I have?
- What information is available to me?

- How long an essay am I being asked to write?
- How complex a project am I ready to undertake?

The box below contains some approaches to topic narrowing that work well for students starting their first research project.

Guidelines for Narrowing Your Topic

1. Whether your instructor assigns a broad topic for your research paper or you are permitted to choose your own topic, do some preliminary searching for sources to get background information.
2. As you see what's available, begin to break down the broad topic into its components. Try thinking about a specific point in time or the influence of a particular event or person if your topic is *historical* or *biographical*. Try applying the standard strategies for planning an essay if you're going to write about a *contemporary* issue. Try formulating the reasons for and against if you're going to write an *argument*.
3. Once you have some sense of the available material, consider the *scope* of your essay. If the scope is too broad, you run the risk of presenting a superficial overview. If the scope is too narrow, you may run out of material.
4. As you read, consider *your own perspective* and what interests you about the person, event, or issue. If you want to know more about the topic, your research will go smoothly and you're more likely to get your essay in on time.
5. Formulate a few *questions* that might help you to structure your reading and research. As you read, you'll increasingly want to stay within that framework, concentrating on materials that add to your understanding of the topic, skimming lightly over those that don't.
6. As answers to these questions emerge, think about a potential *thesis* for your essay.

Topic Narrowing: Biographical and Historical Subjects

Biographical and historical topics have an immediate advantage: they can be defined and limited by space and time. Events and lives have clear beginnings, middles, and ends, as well as many identifiable intermediate stages. You are probably not ready to undertake the full span of a biography or a complete historical event, but you could select a specific point in time as the focus for your essay.

Assume, for example, that by choice or assignment your broad subject is *Franklin Delano Roosevelt*, who was president of the United States for fourteen years—an unparalleled term of office—between 1932 and 1945. You begin by reading *a brief overview of FDR's life.* An encyclopedia article of several pages might be a starting point. This should give you enough basic information to decide which events in FDR's life interest you enough to sustain you through the long process of research. You might also read a few articles about the major events that formed the background to FDR's career: the Great Depression, the New Deal, the changing role of the president.

Now, instead of tracing *all* the incidents and related events in which he participated during his sixty-three years, you might decide to describe FDR at the point when his political career was apparently ruined by polio. Your focus would be the man in 1921, and your essay might develop a thesis drawing on any or all of the following topics—his personality, his style of life, his physical handicap, his experiences, his idea of government—at *that* point in time. Everything that happened to FDR after 1921 would be relatively unimportant to your chosen perspective. Another student might choose a different point in time and describe the new president in 1933 against the background of the Depression. Yet another might focus on an intermediate point in FDR's presidency and construct a profile of the man as he was in 1940, at the brink of America's entry into World War II, when he decided to run for an unprecedented third term in office.

The topic might be made even more specific by focusing on *a single event and its causes.* For example, the atomic bomb was developed during FDR's presidency and was used in Japan shortly after his death:

- What was FDR's attitude toward atomic research?
- Did he advocate using the bomb?
- Did he anticipate its consequences?
- How has sixty years changed our view of the atomic bomb and FDR's role in its development?

Or you might want to study Roosevelt in the context of an important political tradition:

- How did he influence the Democratic party?
- How did the party's policies influence his personal and political decisions?
- What role did Roosevelt play in the establishment of the United States as a "welfare state"?
- How has the Democratic party changed since his time?

This kind of profile attempts to describe a historical figure, explore his or her motives and experiences, and, possibly, apply them to an understanding of current issues. In effect, your overriding impression of character or intention becomes the basis for the thesis, the controlling idea of your essay. You undertake to demonstrate to your reader that the available evidence supports your thesis.

You can also view a *historical event* from a similar specific vantage point. Your broad topic might be the Civil War, which lasted more than four years, or the Berlin Olympics of 1936, which lasted a few weeks, or the Los Angeles riots of 1991, which lasted a few days. Rather than cover a long span of time, you might focus on an intermediate point or stage, which can serve to illuminate and characterize the entire event. The Battle of Gettysburg, for example, is a broad topic often chosen by those interested in the even broader topic of the Civil War. Since the three-day battle, with its complex maneuvers, can hardly be described in a brief narrative, you would want to narrow the focus even more. You might describe the battlefield and the disposition of the troops, as a journalist would, at a single moment in the course of the battle. In this case, your thesis might demonstrate that the disposition of the troops at this point was typical (or atypical) of tactics used throughout the battle, or that this moment did (or did not) foreshadow the battle's conclusion. In fact, always assuming that sufficient material is available, it makes sense to narrow your focus as much as you can.

In writing about history, you also have to consider your own point of view. If, for example, you set out to recount an episode from the Civil War, you first need to establish your perspective: Are you describing the Union's point of view? the Confederacy's? the point of view of the politicians of either side? the generals? the civilians? industrialists? hospital workers? slaves in the South? black freedmen in the North? If you tried to deal with *all* these reactions to a chosen event, you might have difficulty in settling on a thesis and, in the long run, would only confuse and misinform your reader.

The "day in the life" approach can also be applied to *events that had no specific date.*

- When and under what circumstances were primitive guns first used in battle?
- What was the psychological effect of gunfire on the opposing troops?
- What was the reaction when the first automobile drove down a village street? When television was first introduced into American homes?

Or, rather than describe the effects of a new invention, you might focus on *a social institution that has changed radically.*

- What was it like to shop for food in Paris in 1810?
- In Chicago in 1870?
- In any large American city in 1945?

Instead of attempting to write a complete history of the circus from Rome to Ringling, try portraying *the particular experience of a single person.*

- What was it like to be an equestrian performer in Astley's Circus in London in 1805?
- A chariot racer in Pompeii's Circus Maximus in 61 B.C.?

Setting a tentative target date helps you to focus your research, giving you a practical way to judge the relevance and the usefulness of each of your sources.

As you narrow your topic and begin your reading, watch for your emerging thesis—a clear impression of the person or event that you wish your reader to receive. Whether you are writing about a sequence of events, like a battle or a flood, or a single event or issue in the life of a well-known person, you will still need both a *thesis* and a *strategy* to shape the direction of your essay. A common strategy for biographical and historical topics is the *cause-and-effect sequence*—reasons why a certain decision was made or an event turned out one way and not another.

- Why did the United States develop the atomic bomb before Germany did?
- Why did President Truman decide to use the atomic bomb against Japan as the war was ending?

Remember, too, that you are approaching the topic from a distance and that your insights and conclusions will benefit from the perspective and objectivity of time. Your thesis may contain your own view of the person or event that you're writing about: "FDR had no choice but to support the development of the atomic bomb" or "The development of the supermarket resulted in major changes to American family life" or "The imposition of term limits for the presidency after FDR's fourth term in office was [or was not] good for the United States [or for democracy in the United States or for political parties in the United States or for politicians in the United States]." Notice how simple it can be to enlarge or narrow the scope of a thesis.

Finally, do not allow your historical or biographical portrait to become an exercise in creative writing. Your evidence must be derived from and supported by well-documented sources, not just your imagination. The "Napoleon might have said" or "Stalin must have thought" in some biographies and historical novels is often a theory or an educated guess that is firmly rooted in research—and the author should provide documentation and a bibliography to substantiate it.

Topic Narrowing: Contemporary Subjects

If you chose to write about the early history of the circus, you would find a limited assortment of books describing many traditional kinds of circus activity, from the Roman arena to the Barnum and Bailey big top. But these days an enormous amount of information is available. Reviews and features are printed—and preserved for the researcher—every time Ringling Brothers opens in a new city. Your research for an essay about the circus today might be endless and the results unmanageable unless, quite early, you focus your approach.

The usual way is to analyze a topic's component parts and select *a single aspect* as the tentative focus of your essay. Do you want to write about circus acts? Do you want to focus on animal acts or, possibly, the animal rights movement's opposition to the use of animals for circus entertainment? Or the dangers of trapeze and high wire acts? What does the trend to small, one-ring circuses tell us about people's taste today? Or the advent of the "new-age" Cirque de Soleil? Or you could write about the logistics of circus management—transport, for example—or marketing. Or consider larger issues: Why are circuses still so popular in an age of instant electronic entertainment? How has modern entertainment (e.g., TV) altered the business of circuses?

One practical way to begin narrowing a topic is to do a computer search. Many of the guides, indexes, and online databases not only contain lists of sources but also a useful breakdown of subtopics. As you'll see later in this chapter, "Descriptors" and "Keywords" can suggest possibilities for the direction of your essay.

Yet another way to narrow your perspective is to ask questions about and apply different strategies to possible topics. Suppose that *food* is your broad topic. Your approach might be *descriptive,* analyzing *causes and effects:* you could write about some aspect of nutrition, discussing what we ought to eat and the way in which our nutritional needs are best satisfied. Or you could deal with the production and distribution of food—or, more likely, a specific kind of food—and use *process description* as your approach. Or you could analyze a different set of *causes:* Why don't we eat what we ought to? Why do so many people have to diet, and why aren't diets effective? Or you could plan a *problem-solution* essay: What would be the best way to educate the public in proper nutrition? Within the narrower focus of food additives, there are numerous ways to develop the topic:

- To what degree are additives dangerous?
- What was the original purpose of the Food and Drug Act of 1906?
- What policies does the Food and Drug Administration carry out today?
- Would individual rights be threatened if additives like Nutrasweet were banned?
- Can the dangers of food additives be compared with the dangers of alcohol?

On the other hand, your starting point could be *a concrete object,* rather than an abstract idea: you might decide to write about the Big Mac. You could describe its contents and nutritional value; or recount its origins and first appearance on the food scene; or compare it to best-selling foods of past eras; or evaluate its relative popularity in different parts of the world. All of these topics require research.

It is desirable to have a few approaches in mind before you begin intensive reading. Then, as you start to compile your preliminary bibliography, you can begin to distinguish between sources that are potentially useful and sources that will probably be irrelevant. What you *cannot* do at this stage is formulate a definite thesis. Your thesis will probably answer the question that you asked at the beginning of your research. Although, from the first, you may have your own theories about the answer, you cannot be sure that your research will confirm your hypotheses. Your thesis should remain tentative until your reading has given your essay content and direction.

Topic Narrowing: Issues for Argument

Finding a topic can be easier when you set out to write an argument. Although it is possible to do well with a topic that is new, most people gravitate toward issues that have some significance for them. If nothing immediately occurs to you, try *brainstorming*—jotting down possible ideas in a list. Recall conversations, news broadcasts, class discussions that have made you feel interested, even argumentative. Prepare a list of possible topics over a few days, and keep reviewing the list, looking for one that satisfies the following criteria:

- *Your topic should allow you to be objective.* Your reader expects you to present a well-balanced account of both sides of the argument. Too much emotional involvement with a highly charged issue can be a handicap. If, for example, someone close to you was killed in an incident involving a handgun, you are likely to lose your objectivity in an essay on gun control.

- *Your topic should have appropriate depth.* Don't choose an issue that is too trivial: "Disney World is better than Disneyland." For a general audience, don't choose an issue that is too specialized: "The Rolling Stones were a more influential band than the Beatles," or "*2001: A Space Odyssey* is the most technically proficient science-fiction film ever made." And don't choose an issue that is too broad or too abstract: "Technology has been the bane of the twentieth century" or "A life without God is not worth living." Your topic should be definable in terms that your reader can understand and, perhaps, share. Finally, your topic should lend itself to a clear, manageable path of research. Using the keywords "god" and "life" in a database search will produce a seemingly unending list of books and articles. Where will you begin?

- *Your topic should have appropriate scope.* Consider the terms of your instructor's assignment. Some topics can be explored in ten pages; others require more lengthy development. Some require extensive research; others can be written using only a few selected sources. Stay within the assigned guidelines.

- *Your topic should have two sides.* Some topics are nonissues: it would be hard to get anyone to disagree about them. "Everyone should have the experience of work" or "Good health is important" are topics that aren't worth arguing. (Notice that they are also far too abstract.) Whatever the issue, the opposition must have a credible case.

- *Your topic can be historical.* There are many issues rooted in the past that are still arguable. Should President Truman have authorized dropping the atomic bomb on Japan? Were there better alternatives to ending slavery than the Civil War? Should Timothy McVeigh have been executed?

- *Your topic should be practical.* It may be tempting to argue that tuition should be free for all college students, but, in the process, you would have to recommend an alternative way to pay for the cost of education—something that state and federal governments have yet to figure out.

- *Your topic should have sufficient evidence available to support it.* You may not know for sure whether you can adequately defend your argument until you have done some research. A local issue—should a new airport be built near our town?—might not have attracted a substantial enough body of evidence.

- *Your topic should be within your range of understanding.* Don't plan an argument on "the consequences of global warming" unless you are prepared to present scientific evidence, much of which is written in highly technical language. Evidence for topics in the social sciences can be equally difficult to comprehend, for many depend on surveys that are hard for a nonprofessional to evaluate. Research on literacy and teaching methods, for example, often includes data (such as reading scores on standardized tests) that require training in statistics.

Many of these criteria also apply to choosing a historical narrative or a contemporary subject. What's important in writing any essay—especially one involving a commitment to research—is that the topic interest you. If you are bored while writing your essay, your reader will probably be just as bored while reading it.

EXERCISE 16: PROPOSING A TOPIC

The following topic proposals were submitted by students who had been given a week to choose and narrow their topics for an eight- to ten-page research essay. Consider the scope and focus of each proposal, and decide which ones suggest *practical* topics for an essay of this length. If the proposal is too broad, be prepared to offer suggestions for narrowing the focus.

Student A

Much of the interest in World War II has been focused on the battlefield, but the war years were also a trying period for the public at home. I intend to write about civilian morale during the war, emphasizing press campaigns to increase the war effort. I will also include a description of the way people coped with brown-outs, shortages, and rationing, with a section on the victory garden.

Student B

I intend to deal with the role of women in feudal life, especially the legal rights of medieval women. I would also like to discuss the theory of chivalry and its effects on women, as well as the influence of medieval literature on society. My specific focus will be the ideal image of the medieval lady.

Student C

I have chosen the Lindbergh kidnapping case as the subject of my essay. I intend to concentrate on the kidnapping itself, rather than going into details about the lives of the Lindberghs. What interests me is the planning of the crime, including the way in which the house was designed and how the kidnapping was carried out. I also hope to include an account of the investigation and courtroom scenes. Depending on what I find, I may argue that Hauptmann was wrongly convicted.

Student D

I would like to explore methods of travel one hundred and fifty years ago, and compare the difficulties of traveling then with the conveniences of traveling now. I intend to stress the economic and social background of the average traveler. My focus will be the Grand Tour that young men used to take.

Student E

I'd like to explore quality in television programs. Specifically, I'd like to argue that popular and critically acclaimed TV shows of today are just as good as comparable programs ten and twenty years ago and that there really hasn't been a decline in popular taste. It may be necessary to restrict my topic to one kind of television show—situation comedies, for example, or coverage of sports events.

Student F

I would like to do research on several aspects of adolescent peer groups, trying to determine whether the overall effects of peer groups on adolescents are beneficial or destructive. I intend to include the following topics: the need for peer acceptance; conformity; personal and social adjustment; and peer competition. I'm not sure that I can form a conclusive argument, since most of the information available on this subject is purely descriptive; but I'll try to present an informed opinion.

EXERCISE 17: NARROWING A TOPIC

A. Here are ten different ways of approaching the broad topic of *poverty in America*. Decide which questions would make good starting points for an eight- to ten-page research essay. Consider the practicality and the clarity of each question, the probable availability of research materials, and the likelihood of being able to answer the question in approximately nine pages. Try rewriting two of the questions that seem too broad, narrowing the focus.

1. How should the nation deal with poverty in its communities?
2. What problems does your city or town encounter in its efforts to make sure that its citizens live above the poverty level?
3. What are the primary causes of poverty today?

4. Whose responsibility is it to help the poor?

5. What effects does a life of poverty have on a family?

6. What can be done to protect children and the aged, groups that make up the largest proportion of the poor?

7. Does everyone have the right to freedom from fear of poverty?

8. Which programs for alleviating poverty have been particularly successful, and why?

9. Should all those receiving welfare funds be required to work?

10. What nations have effectively solved the problem of poverty, and how?

B. Make up several questions that would help you to develop the broad topic of *restricting immigration to America* for an eight- to ten-page research essay.

LOCATING SOURCES

Preliminary research takes place in three overlapping stages:

- Identifying and locating possible sources.
- Recording or saving basic facts about each source.
- Noting each source's potential usefulness—or lack of usefulness—to your topic (and, when possible, downloading the useful online ones).

It's rare that you'll be able to locate all your sources first, and then record all your basic information, and after that choose those that are worth including in your essay. The process isn't that tidy. At a later stage of your work, you may come across a useful database and find new materials that must be reviewed, analyzed, and included in your essay even after you've written a draft. Solid research requires perseverance and flexibility.

The three most common kinds of sources are: *books, periodicals* (including magazines, newspapers, and scholarly journals), and *Web sites.* Most books and periodicals are published in print form; you can hold them in your hands (or read articles by inserting microfilm or microfiche into reading machines). Web sites and some periodicals are located in cyberspace on the Internet and appear only on your computer screen. And, increasingly, some periodical articles can be found both in print and on the Web (although sometimes the print and Web versions are not exactly the same).

Databases

Searching for sources is usually done through *electronic databases* that enable you to sit at a computer terminal at home or in the library and, using a menu that appears on the screen, retrieve information about your topic. Increasingly, databases for books and periodical articles are *online,* accessible through the Internet; sometimes the information is stored on *CD-ROMs* (compact disk, read-only memory), which you obtain in the library and insert in a computer. Since databases generally list books or periodical articles, but not both, you'll have to engage in at least two separate searches to find a full range of materials. And searching for information on the Web requires using yet another kind of database, known as a *search engine*. All databases are periodically updated to include the most current listings.

Are Libraries Obsolete?

If you have a personal computer connected to the Internet (and, preferably, to your college's information system), you can do a good deal of research without ever entering the library. Certainly, you can obtain information about potential sources for your topic; you can download Web material for later use; you can find the complete texts of many periodical articles and even some books—all on your computer screen. But you'll still need to use the library:

- To obtain most books
- To read periodical articles that aren't available on the Internet
- To look for older articles in print indexes
- To use microfilm and microfiche machines
- To obtain and use CD-ROMs
- To get assistance from reference librarians

The last reason is probably the most important one. Librarians can provide you with all the information you need to carry out your research successfully. They'll show you how the library is organized, how to navigate the stacks of books, how the online catalogs and databases work, and even how to do a computerized search. Much of this information will be available on the home page of your library's Web site; but it's hard to improve on having your questions answered by a real person in real time.

Computer Searches

Databases and search engines have to manage huge amounts of information. If they added a new subject to their indexes every time a book, article, or Web site appeared, they would soon have overflowing lists and unmanageable systems. Instead, each new work is scanned and then listed only under those subject headings (or "descriptors") that are relevant to its content. This key organizing principle is called *cross-referencing:* a method of obtaining a standardized, comprehensive list of subject headings that can be used to index information. (One example of such a list, used by many libraries as an index for books, is *Library of Congress Subject Headings*, or LCSH.)

One way to start a computer search is to check the database's own list of descriptors (or "thesaurus") for one or more that correspond to your topic. Some search engines (like Google) provide such lists, organized into categories, which you can search. Or you can begin to narrow down your topic by considering just what it is that you want to find and then expressing it briefly, in a word or phrase. Following a series of commands from a menu on the screen, you type the words—known as "keywords"— in the designated slot. Using two or more keywords, along with words like "and" and "not," will further break down and limit your topic. (Every database and search engine has its own techniques for formulating keywords; for an efficient search, it's worth taking the time to check the "Help" page or the "About . . . " page attached to the database that you're using.) This do-it-yourself process, usually called *Boolean searching*, will be explained and illustrated in the remainder of this chapter.

Let's assume that you've decided to write about *Lawrence of Arabia*. T. E. Lawrence was a key figure in the Middle East campaigns of World War I, a British scholar fascinated by the desert, whose guerrilla tactics against the Turks succeeded partly because he chose to live like and with the Bedouin tribes that fought with him. You've enjoyed the 1962 award-winning movie about Lawrence, but you'd like to find out whether it accurately represents his experience. Here are some issues and questions about Lawrence's life that might intrigue you. Acclaimed as a hero after the war, Lawrence chose to enlist in the Royal Air Force at the lowest rank, under an assumed name. Why? He died at the age of 46 in a mysterious motorcycle crash. Was this an accident? He contributed to the development of a new kind of military tactics. Why was his kind of guerrilla warfare so effective? He hoped to gain political independence for the Bedouin tribes. What prevented him?

One place to start your search about Lawrence of Arabia is an *encyclopedia*, which will provide you with a brief overview of his life and so help you to narrow down your topic. (See Appendix A.) *Britannica, New Columbia*, or *Encarta* are all good choices. If you consult www.encarta.msn.com on the Internet, you'll be prompted to type in a question or keyword. So, you type "Lawrence of Arabia." Why use quotation marks? They identify your keyword as a single *phrase*, so your results will be restricted to information about the Lawrence you're looking for. The database's computer has only a literal understanding of your purpose. Without quotation marks, Lawrence of Arabia will be interpreted as a request for information about anyone or anything named Lawrence and any material about Arabia. Throughout your searching, you should submit the request as a phrase in quotation marks.

In its response, *Encarta* offers you a choice: an article about Lawrence of Arabia (adventurer) or an article about *Lawrence of Arabia* (motion picture). At this stage, you'll probably want to click on and read both; you're interested in comparing the movie version with Lawrence's actual experiences. In fact, clicking on the entry for Lawrence of Arabia (adventurer) gives you more choices. There are subheadings for references to Lawrence in other articles:

Assistance to Faisal I
Guerrilla tactics
Role in the Arab revolt against Turkey during World War I

Choosing and reading any of these articles can help you decide what aspect of Lawrence's life you want to write about.

Carrying out research is all about choices. You type in a request in a database, and you receive a list of topics or sources to choose from. You read an article about your subject, and at the end you find a list of additional articles headed "Bibliography" or "Further Reading." You look at a Web site, and throughout the text you see *hyperlinks*—underlined words, phrases, or Web addresses—that will lead you to related Web pages. Finding sources is not difficult; the real challenge is learning which ones to choose first.

What Is Boolean Searching?

Boolean searching, named after George Boole, a nineteenth-century mathematician, is a method of focusing your topic to get the best possible results from your computer search. If you are too broad in your wording, you'll get an exceedingly long list of sources, which will be unmanageable; if you're too specific in your wording, you'll get a very short list, which can bring your research to a dead halt.

To carry out a Boolean (or advanced) search, you refine your topic by *combining words*, using *phrases* to express complex subjects, and inserting "operators"—AND, OR, NOT—between keywords. (Sometimes, the operators are symbols, such as +, rather than words.) In effect, you must ask yourself what you do and what you don't want to know about your topic. Let's apply these guidelines to a database search for information about Lawrence of Arabia.

"Lawrence of Arabia" is your subject expressed as a phrase: the search will include only those sources in which the entire phrase is found and omit all those in which both "Lawrence" and "Arabia" appear only separately.

"Lawrence of Arabia" AND "guerrilla warfare" limits the search to those sources that contain *both* phrases. A book that mentions Lawrence but not guerrilla warfare won't appear in the results list, and vice versa.

"Lawrence of Arabia" OR "T. E. Lawrence" expands the search by expressing the topic two ways and potentially multiplying the number of sources found.

"Lawrence of Arabia" NOT "motion picture" limits the search by excluding sources that focus on the film rather than the man.

Using Computer Searches to Locate Books

Databases that contain books are usually place-specific. In other words, a particular library produces a computerized database that lists all the books housed in its building or group of buildings. The library in the next town will have a different database for its holdings. Your own college library almost certainly has such a database listing all the books on its shelves, organized and searchable by author, by title, and by subject. Your library can also provide you with comparable databases for other libraries in the area or major libraries across the globe. If you want to examine a full range of the books in existence on a particular topic, you can look up that topic in the database of the Library of Congress or the New York Public Library, both of which make their vast holdings available through the Internet. If you locate a book that seems important for your research and your own library does not have it, your librarian can probably arrange for an *interlibrary loan* from a library that does.

Let's search the Library of Congress Online Catalog (http://catalog.loc.gov/) for books about Lawrence of Arabia. On the catalog home page, click "Guided Search." Figure 5-1 shows you the interactive screen on which you begin your search. Next to "Search," you type in *Lawrence of Arabia.* For this search, you don't have to use quotation marks to indicate that your keyword is a phrase; further along the line, there's a drop-down menu (you click on the arrow and the choices drop down) that lets you choose among "any of these," "all of these," or "as a phrase." (This means that you can choose to search for items categorized under either *Lawrence* or *Arabia,* those categorized under both *Lawrence* and *Arabia,* or those categorized under the specific phrase *Lawrence of Arabia.*) So you highlight and click "as a phrase." Another drop-down menu allows you to choose in which part of the library's holdings the search will take place. Since you want the widest possible base for your search, you highlight and click "Keyword Anywhere." And, in the final menu, you're given the option to do a Boolean search by choosing to pair *Lawrence of Arabia* with an operator (AND, OR, or NOT) and another word or phrase. You decide not to exercise this option yet, and just click "Begin Search."

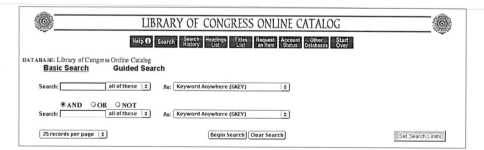

Figure 5-1. Library of Congress Online Catalog Search Form

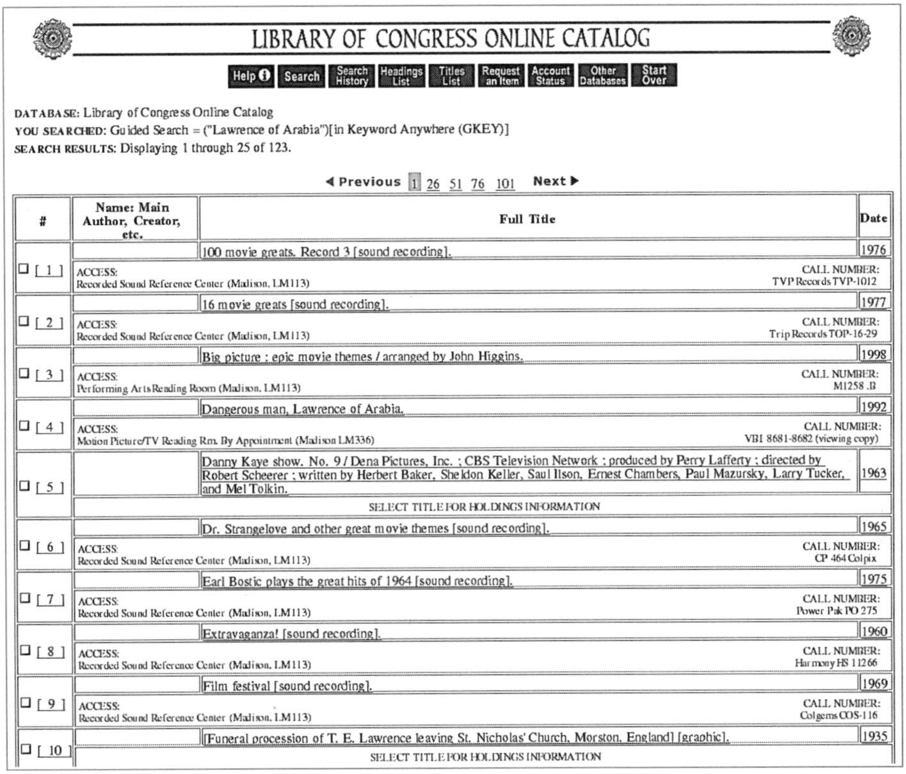

LIBRARY OF CONGRESS ONLINE CATALOG

Help | Search | Search History | Headings List | Titles List | Request an Item | Account Status | Other Databases | Start Over

DATABASE: Library of Congress Online Catalog
YOU SEARCHED: Guided Search = ("Lawrence of Arabia")[in Keyword Anywhere (GKEY)]
SEARCH RESULTS: Displaying 1 through 25 of 123.

◀ Previous 1 26 51 76 101 Next ▶

#	Name: Main Author, Creator, etc.	Full Title	Date
[1]		100 movie greats. Record 3 [sound recording].	1976
	ACCESS: Recorded Sound Reference Center (Madison, LM113)	CALL NUMBER: TVP Records TVP-1012	
[2]		16 movie greats [sound recording].	1977
	ACCESS: Recorded Sound Reference Center (Madison, LM113)	CALL NUMBER: Trip Records TOP-16-29	
[3]		Big picture : epic movie themes / arranged by John Higgins.	1998
	ACCESS: Performing Arts Reading Room (Madison, LM113)	CALL NUMBER: M1258 .B	
[4]		Dangerous man, Lawrence of Arabia.	1992
	ACCESS: Motion Picture/TV Reading Rm. By Appointment (Madison LM336)	CALL NUMBER: VBI 8681-8682 (viewing copy)	
[5]		Danny Kaye show. No. 9 / Dena Pictures, Inc. ; CBS Television Network ; produced by Perry Lafferty ; directed by Robert Scheerer ; written by Herbert Baker, Sheldon Keller, Saul Ilson, Ernest Chambers, Paul Mazursky, Larry Tucker, and Mel Tolkin.	1963
	SELECT TITLE FOR HOLDINGS INFORMATION		
[6]		Dr. Strangelove and other great movie themes [sound recording].	1965
	ACCESS: Recorded Sound Reference Center (Madison, LM113)	CALL NUMBER: CP 464 Colpix	
[7]		Earl Bostic plays the great hits of 1964 [sound recording].	1975
	ACCESS: Recorded Sound Reference Center (Madison, LM113)	CALL NUMBER: Power Pak PO 275	
[8]		Extravaganza! [sound recording].	1960
	ACCESS: Recorded Sound Reference Center (Madison, LM113)	CALL NUMBER: Harmony HS 11266	
[9]		Film festival [sound recording].	1969
	ACCESS: Recorded Sound Reference Center (Madison, LM113)	CALL NUMBER: Colgems COS-116	
[10]		[Funeral procession of T. E. Lawrence leaving St. Nicholas' Church, Morston, England] [graphic].	1935
	SELECT TITLE FOR HOLDINGS INFORMATION		

Figure 5-2. Library of Congress Online Catalog: Search Results

As Figure 5-2 indicates, even though your search for Lawrence of Arabia has produced 123 titles, the results aren't very helpful. The Library of Congress has media other than print in its collections, and none of the first ten items listed are books; most are material related to the movie. Since the first search took less than a minute, though, you can easily try again. To focus on historical information about the man rather than the movie, this time you try "Lawrence of Arabia" NOT "motion picture." Once you've been more explicit about what you want, the results are more rewarding. This Titles List contains fewer items (92), but most of them are actually about T. E. Lawrence. Now you must decide which are worth looking at.

Figure 5-3 shows a sequence of twenty-four books from the middle of the list. Looking carefully at the titles and dates of publication enables you to exclude quite a few. Some are fiction (Eden's *Murder of Lawrence of Arabia*); some deal with very narrow topics (Allen's *Medievalism of Lawrence of Arabia*); one is about "the female Lawrence of Arabia" (Gertrude Bell's *Desert and the Sown*); and some are duplicates. Repetition is a recurring problem in computerized searches. The same book can appear as a reprint (with the same contents, but a new cover, possibly paperback) or in a new edition (with revisions or with new

☐ [19]	Allen, M. D. (Malcolm Dennis), 1951-	Medievalism of Lawrence of Arabia / M.D. Allen.		1991
	ACCESS: Jefferson or Adams Bldg General or Area Studies Reading Rms		CALL NUMBER: D568.4.L45 A64 1991	
☐ [20]	Armitage, Flora.	Desert and the stars; a biography of Lawrence of Arabia. Illustrated with photos.		1955
	ACCESS: Jefferson or Adams Bldg General or Area Studies Reading Rms		CALL NUMBER: D568.4.L45 A68	
☐ [21]	Arnold, Julian Biddulph, 1863-	Lawrence of Arabia [by] Julian Biddulph Arnold.		1935
	ACCESS: Rare Book/Special Collections Reading Room (Jefferson LJ239)		CALL NUMBER: D568.4.L45 A7	
☐ [22]	Baxter, Frank C. (Frank Condie), 1896-1982.	Annotated check-list of a collection of writings by and about T. E. Lawrence, Lawrence of Arabia, with many other things collateral to the story of his military, literary, and personal life and to the history of the Arab revolt and the Palestine campaign		1968
	ACCESS: Jefferson or Adams Bldg General or Area Studies Reading Rms		CALL NUMBER: Z8491.5 .B3	
☐ [23]	Bell, Elise. [from old catalog]	Fall of Constantinople. [Sound recording]		
	LIBRARY OF CONGRESS HOLDINGS INFORMATION NOT AVAILABLE			
☐ [24]	Bell, Elise. [from old catalog]	Lawrence of Arabia. [Phonodisc]		
	LIBRARY OF CONGRESS HOLDINGS INFORMATION NOT AVAILABLE			
☐ [25]	Bell, Gertrude Lowthian, 1868-1926.	Desert and the sown : the Syrian adventures of the female Lawrence of Arabia / by Gertrude Bell ; new introduction by Rosemary O'Brien ; with frontispiece by John Sargent.		2001
	SELECT TITLE FOR HOLDINGS INFORMATION			
☐ [26]	Blackmore, Charles.	In the footsteps of Lawrence of Arabia / Charles Blackmore.		1986
	ACCESS: Jefferson or Adams Bldg General or Area Studies Reading Rms		CALL NUMBER: D568.4.L45 B54 1986	
☐ [27]	Broughton, Harry.	Lawrence of Arabia and Dorset; compiled by Harry Broughton.		1966
	ACCESS: Jefferson or Adams Bldg General or Area Studies Reading Rms		CALL NUMBER: DA670.D7 B75 1966	
☐ [28]	Browne, Maurice, 1884-1961.	[Notebook on T.E. Lawrence].		1900
	ACCESS: Jefferson or Adams Bldg General or Area Studies Reading Rms		CALL NUMBER: D568.4.L45 B75 1900z Rosenwald Coll	
☐ [29]	Burbidge, William Frank.	Mysterious A.C. 2, a biographical sketch of Lawrence of Arabia, by Wm. F. Burbidge ...		1943
	ACCESS: Jefferson or Adams Bldg General or Area Studies Reading Rms		CALL NUMBER: D568.4.L45 B8	
☐ [30]	Carrington, Charles Edmund, 1897-	T. E. Lawrence (of Arabia) by Charles Edmonds [pseud.]		1936
	ACCESS: Jefferson or Adams Bldg General or Area Studies Reading Rms		CALL NUMBER: D568.4.L45 C3 1936	
☐ [31]	Churchill, Winston, Sir, 1874-1965.	Great contemporaries.		1973
	ACCESS: Jefferson or Adams Bldg General or Area Studies Reading Rms		CALL NUMBER: D412.6 .C5 1973	
☐ [32]	Churchill, Winston, Sir, 1874-1965.	Great contemporaries.		1971
	ACCESS: Jefferson or Adams Bldg General or Area Studies Reading Rms		CALL NUMBER: D412.6 .C5 1971	
☐ [33]	Churchill, Winston, Sir, 1874-1965	Great contemporaries, by the Rt. Hon. Winston S. Churchill, C.H., M.P. With 21 portraits.		1937
	ACCESS: Jefferson or Adams Bldg General or Area Studies Reading Rms		CALL NUMBER: D412.6 .C5 1937a	
☐ [34]	Crawford, Fred D.	Richard Aldington and Lawrence of Arabia : a cautionary tale / Fred D. Crawford.		1998
	ACCESS: Jefferson or Adams Bldg General or Area Studies Reading Rms		CALL NUMBER: D568.4.L45 A633 1998	
☐ [35]	Disbury, David George William.	T. E. Lawrence (of Arabia) -- a collectors booklist; compiled by David G. Disbury.		1972
	ACCESS: Jefferson or Adams Bldg General or Area Studies Reading Rms		CALL NUMBER: Z8491.5 .D57	
☐ [36]	Ebert, Richard.	Lawrence of Arabia / by Richard Ebert ; ill. by Roy Schofield.		1979
	LIBRARY OF CONGRESS HOLDINGS INFORMATION NOT AVAILABLE			
☐ [37]	Eden, Matthew.	Murder of Lawrence of Arabia : a novel / by Matthew Eden.		1979
	SELECT TITLE FOR HOLDINGS INFORMATION			
☐ [38]	Glen, Douglas.	In the steps of Lawrence of Arabia, by Douglas Glen.		1940
	ACCESS: Jefferson or Adams Bldg General or Area Studies Reading Rms		CALL NUMBER: DS207 .G6 1940	
☐ [39]	Graves, Richard Perceval.	Lawrence of Arabia and his world / Richard Perceval Graves.		1976
	ACCESS: Jefferson or Adams Bldg General or Area Studies Reading Rms		CALL NUMBER: D568.4.L45 G68 1976b	
☐ [40]	Graves, Richard Perceval.	Lawrence of Arabia and his world / Richard Perceval Graves.		1976
	ACCESS: Jefferson or Adams Bldg General or Area Studies Reading Rms		CALL NUMBER: D568.4.L45 G68 1976	
☐ [41]	Hyde, H. Montgomery (Harford Montgomery), 1907-	Solitary in the ranks : Lawrence of Arabia as airman and private soldier / by H. Montgomery Hyde.		1978
	LIBRARY OF CONGRESS HOLDINGS INFORMATION NOT AVAILABLE			
☐ [42]	Hyde, H. Montgomery (Harford Montgomery), 1907-	Solitary in the ranks : Lawrence of Arabia as airman and private soldier / [by] H. Montgomery Hyde.		1977
	ACCESS: Jefferson or Adams Bldg General or Area Studies Reading Rms		CALL NUMBER: D568.4.L45 H92 1977	

Figure 5-3. Library of Congress Online Catalog: Links to Additional Sources

material, such as a preface). As the entries for Winston Churchill indicate, each version receives a separate line in the catalog.

Another way to narrow down this list is to choose the most recent books since those authors probably have had access to the widest range of material about Lawrence. Winston Churchill was a very great prime minister of England and a prolific writer, but the chapter on Lawrence in his 1937 collection (reprinted in 1971 and 1973) is not likely to be the most comprehensive or objective among these titles. In fact, items 19 to 42 really contain only two titles immediately worth pursuing: books by Richard Perceval Graves and H. Montgomery Hyde. And since they're both over twenty years old, it's worth checking through the rest of the 92-item list to locate an even better possibility: an authorized biography by Jeremy Wilson.

As the underlining of each item on the list indicates, the Library of Congress Online Catalog provides hyperlinks to bibliographical information about each of its holdings. (See p. 254 for a discussion of hyperlinks.) Figures 5-4, 5-5, and 5-6 show the full records of the books by Graves, Hyde, and Wilson. Each computer screen specifies the length of the book, whether it has an index (so you can look up topics easily), whether it has a bibliography (so you can locate additional sources), and both the LC and Dewey classification numbers (so you can locate the book easily in your own library). Most important, it includes a list of "subjects" as a clue to the specific contents of each book. How would you decide which book to examine first?

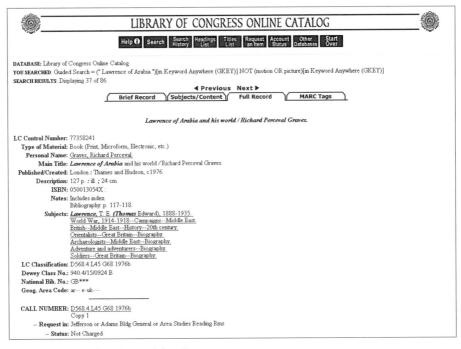

Figure 5-4. Catalog Record for Graves

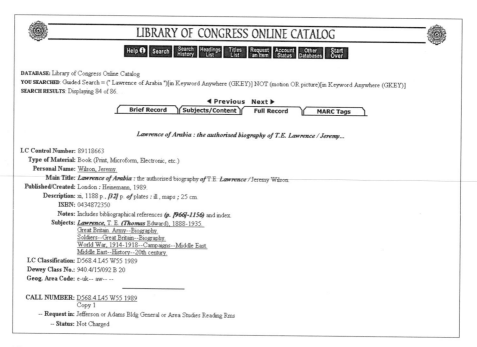

Figure 5-5. Catalog Record for Hyde

Figure 5-6. Catalog Record for Wilson

Lawrence of Arabia and His World is brief, with a brief bibliography. In addition to the basic subject that all the books have in common—T. E. Lawrence—Graves emphasizes World War I (and, specifically, the Middle East campaign) as well as Lawrence's experiences as an orientalist, archaeologist, and soldier. That's a lot of coverage for a hundred or so pages of text. If the book were more recent than 1976, you might want to read it as a supplementary overview to the *Encarta* article, but you have no special reason for making it a priority.

Solitary in the Ranks is longer, with a longer bibliography, and has a more specific focus: Lawrence's career as a private soldier in the RAF after the war. If you want to explore the enigma of Lawrence's reenlistment, this would obviously be a crucial source. But if you want to make comparisons with the motion picture, Hyde would be of peripheral interest.

Lawrence of Arabia: The Authorised Biography of T. E. Lawrence is over a thousand pages long in the original 1989 edition, with almost a hundred pages of notes and references. "Authorised" (or, in American spelling, "authorized") usually means that the subject, or his heirs, or his estate, has had enough confidence in this biographer to provide access to material not otherwise available. Wilson's work will undoubtedly be an important resource, although you may prefer to use the 1992 abridged edition (also listed in the Library of Congress Titles list), which is half as long and limits its focus to Lawrence's character and experiences.

Cross-referencing in the Library of Congress Online Catalog provides you with one more set of choices. As you can see in Figure 5-6, each of the subjects listed in the "Full Record" of a work is an underlined hyperlink, which means an opportunity to click on it for more information. If you choose the first and most basic subject, "Lawrence, T. E.," your screen will display 44 subtopics related to Lawrence, ranging from his death and burial to his psychology. Figure 5-7 shows some of the listings. If, for example, you click on "Military leader[s]hip," you're referred to Oliver Butler's *The Guerrilla Strategies of Lawrence and Mao*, which compares the military exploits of Lawrence—especially in guerrilla warfare—with those of Mao Zedong, the Chinese Communist leader. And this screen also contains another hyperlinked subject list, including guerrilla warfare, that would allow you to continue your search.

[1]	2	Lawrence, T. E. (Thomas Edward), 1888-1935 Manuscripts.	LC subject headings
[2]	1	Lawrence, T. E. (Thomas Edward), 1888-1935 Military leaderhip.	LC subject headings
[3]	1	Lawrence, T. E. (Thomas Edward), 1888-1935 Monuments.	LC subject headings
[4]	1	Lawrence, T. E. (Thomas Edward), 1888-1935. Oriental assembly.	LC subject headings
[5]	3	Lawrence, T. E. (Thomas Edward), 1888-1935 Poetry.	LC subject headings
[6]	2	Lawrence, T. E. (Thomas Edward), 1888-1935 Portraits.	LC subject headings
[7]	1	Lawrence, T. E. (Thomas Edward), 1888-1935 Psychology.	not applicable
[8]	3	Lawrence, T. E. (Thomas Edward), 1888-1935. Revolt in the desert Bibliography.	LC subject headings
[9]	6	Lawrence, T. E. (Thomas Edward), 1888-1935 Seven pillars of wisdom.	LC subject headings
[10]	3	Lawrence, T. E. (Thomas Edward), 1888-1935. Seven pillars of wisdom Bibliography.	LC subject headings
[11]	1	Lawrence, T. E. (Thomas Edward), 1888-1935. Seven pillars of wisdom Illustrations Exhibitions.	LC subject headings

Figure 5-7. Library of Congress Online Catalog: Browsing Results

In carrying out your computerized search for books on Lawrence, don't neglect a more traditional way of identifying sources: looking in the *bibliographies* of standard works on the subject, like Wilson's. This allows you to add to your own bibliography some of the titles that the authors of these works used in their research. The books on Lawrence will probably be shelved together in your library stacks, and you'll want to examine the table of contents, index, and bibliography of several before deciding which ones merit your time.

Using Computer Searches to Locate Periodical Articles

Finding appropriate periodical articles is more complicated than looking for books. Each issue of a periodical contains a dozen or so articles; each year, thousands of periodicals appear in English alone; many of the best ones have been publishing for decades, a few for centuries. There are huge numbers of items to catalog, and, as a result, there is no single database that includes every possible newspaper, magazine, and journal article on a specific topic.

Moreover, most computerized databases limit their coverage to periodicals published within the last ten years. The online version of the *New York Times Index*, for example, goes back only to 1996. If you're working on a historical topic or you simply want to find a wide range of information, you'll need to move back and forth from online systems to print indexes that list the contents of periodicals year by year. Academic databases are still in the process of transferring their print listings for earlier years to an electronic format.

The best approach is to search in more than one database. First, check the periodical database in your campus library, which should list all the articles in all the newspapers, magazines, and journals that the library owns. It will probably be cross-referenced so you can search using your keyword phrase, "Lawrence of Arabia." Your library will also have a listing of the other periodical databases available to you online and on CD-ROM. For example, under the heading "Humanities and History," Columbia University lists 94 online databases, ranging from the broadly useful (the *Oxford English Dictionary* or the *Dictionary of National Biography*) to the discipline-based (*Humanities Abstracts* or *Handbook of Latin American Studies*), to the highly specialized (*Koryosa*—which deals with the history of the Koryo dynasty in China). The *Social Sciences Index* and the *Humanities Index* are often good starting points for topics within those broad disciplinary areas. Appendix A has a selected listing of databases and other key reference works. Be aware, though, that many databases have restricted access and require a fee for use—which means you may have to do your searching at a computer in your college library's reference room.

Some databases provide only bibliographical listings of articles (sometimes called *citations*) and leave you to find the periodical and look up the article. Others provide *abstracts* of the articles that they list. An abstract is a brief summary of an article—a sentence or two—that helps you to decide whether you want to locate and read the entire article. There are databases that include *extracts*—samples from the articles—and a few will produce the *full text*, sometimes for a fee.

Like databases for books, electronic databases for periodicals often allow you to choose between a *basic search* and an *advanced search*. The advanced search provides more options for limiting the range of sources (only history? or the social sciences? or all available journals?); it allows you to refine your search with Boolean connectives; and it gives you the option of restricting your search to articles that have been *peer reviewed*. That means that a journal requires each of its articles to be read and approved by authorities in the field before it's accepted for publication. Peer review is, in effect, a guarantee of reasonable quality. Many databases also provide you with a choice between *browse* and *search*. Browsing enables you to review what's available on your specific topic by clicking through the subject categories that exist within the database. It's useful to browse before searching since it may help you to define what you're looking for and devise more precise keywords.

Some databases focus on popular periodicals rather than scholarly journals. The *Readers' Guide to Periodical Literature* can be useful for research on current issues, but it should not be the *only* database that you consult in preparing an academic essay. *Pro Quest* is a comprehensive database of more than 33,000 popular periodicals and professional journals, unfortunately limited to the last few years. A search for "Lawrence of Arabia" in *Pro Quest*'s Periodical Abstracts Research database resulted in eighteen listings, mostly reviews of recently published books on Lawrence. One of these books (which did not turn up in the Library of Congress search) was *Lawrence of Arabia and American Culture: The Making of a Transatlantic Legend*; judging from the reviews (which appear in full text), obtaining a copy would be particularly useful for an essay on the motion picture as a reflection of Lawrence's life.

Another excellent source of information on events and issues, both historical and contemporary, is the *New York Times Index*, which contains a century and a half's worth of listings from the *Times*. If you read a few articles in the *Times* starting in 1915, when Lawrence's exploits began to be widely known, you will be able to include in your essay a contemporary view of Lawrence's successes and failures. Like the *Readers' Guide*, *Pro Quest*, and most other databases, the *New York Times Index* makes extensive use of cross-referencing and hyperlinks, which will enable you to extend your search.

There are also a growing number of online databases, established by universities or commercial companies, that provide listings of scholarly articles across the disciplines, with abstracts of their contents. Some, like *JSTOR*, allow access only through university-sponsored computer systems (which have paid for their use); others, like *Ingenta*, allow anyone to review their listings and abstracts and, for a fee, obtain the text of entire articles. *Ingenta* has a search base index of more than half a million article summaries from two thousand academic publications. An *Ingenta* search for "Lawrence of Arabia," limited to 1995–2001, resulted in twenty-one listings; an expanded search, back to 1989, increased the number to thirty-seven (largely because a new print of the movie was released in 1989, generating a new wave of film reviews).

Figure 5-8 shows the beginning of the listings from the latter search. Notice that some of the articles are far too specific to be useful—focusing on Lawrence's

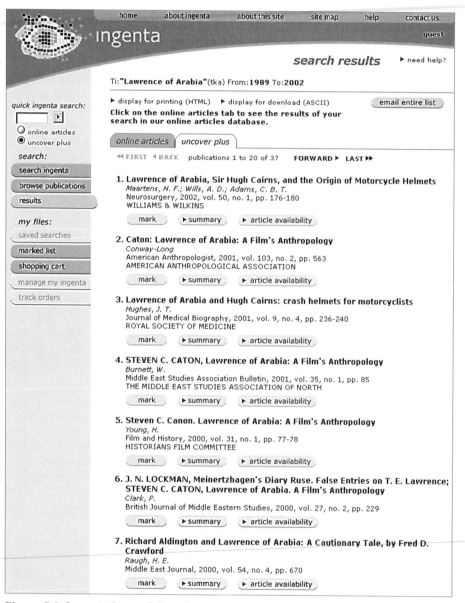

Figure 5-8. Ingenta Journal Search

Brough motorcycle, for example (8). But if you click on the summary of *First Person a Desert Engagement* (11), the abstract tells you that Michael Asher "retraces the steps of Lawrence of Arabia and discovers his greatness owes as much to his many weaknesses as his strengths," which makes this an article worth reviewing as background for any of the Lawrence essay topics under consideration. Similarly, Don Belt's article in *National Geographic* (12) discusses how and why Lawrence became involved in the Arab Revolt against

8. **Enigma Machine: Lawrence of Arabia's ultimate Brough.**
Cycle world, 2000, vol. 39, no. 8, pp. 80

(mark) (▸summary) (▸ article availability)

9. **Lawrence of Arabia: A Film's Anthropology, by Steven C. Caton**
Hanson, E.
Biography, 2000, vol. 23, no. 3, pp. 560-562
THE UNIVERSITY OF HAWAII PRESS

(mark) (▸summary) (▸ article availability)

10. **Standing in the light.**
Peachment, Chris
New statesman, 1999, vol. 12, no. 546, pp. 35

(mark) (▸summary) (▸ article availability)

11. **First Person a Desert Engagement.**
Asher, Michael
Geographical, 1999, vol. 71, no. 2, pp. 20

(mark) (▸summary) (▸ article availability)

12. **Lawrence of Arabia.**
Belt, Don
National geographic, 1999, vol. 195, no. 1, pp. 38

(mark) (▸summary) (▸ article availability)

13. **Kit Carson, John C. Fremont, Manifest Destiny, and the Indians; Or, Oliver North Abets Lawrence of Arabia.**
Canfield, J. Douglas
American indian culture and research journal, 1998, vol. 22, no. 1, pp. 137

(mark) (▸summary) (▸ article availability)

14. **On Films: Cinema Scope: A restored Lawrence of Arabia is fresher than two new films, The Myth of fingerprints and Going All The Way.**
Kauffmann, Stanley
The new republic, 1997, vol. 217, no. 14, pp. 28

(mark) (▸summary) (▸ article availability)

15. **Lawrence of Arabia as Archaeologist.**
Tabachnick, Stephen E.
The Biblical archaeology review, 1997, vol. 23, no. 5, pp. 40

(mark) (▸summary) (▸ article availability)

16. **Casualties of Amour.**
Glass, Charles
Premiere, 1996, vol. 10, no. 4, pp. 96

(mark) (▸summary) (▸ article availability)

17. **Lawrence of Arabia, Designer and Printer.**
Graalfs, Gregory T.
Print, 1996, vol. 50, no. 6, pp. 56

(mark) (▸summary) (▸ article availability)

Figure 5-8. *(continued)*

the Ottoman empire, useful material for essays with an emphasis on politics. One rule of database searching is never to assume that the first few listings are the most important and so ignore the rest. A *Cineaste* article, listed as number 19, in which Michael Wilson describes how he wrote the screenplay for *Lawrence of Arabia,* is essential reading for an essay about the film's authenticity. In fact, although the *Ingenta* database doesn't include it, the very next article in that issue of *Cineaste* is an account by Robert Bolt, Wilson's coauthor, of *his* approach to the film. Another rule of database searching is that no single database contains all the material you'll need. It always pays to look a little further.

Using Computer Searches to Locate Web Sites

Once you have an Internet account through your college or with a local server, you will have access to the millions of sites available on the *World Wide Web*. (In 2000, there were roughly eight hundred million sites.) A Web site can vary from a text-only page on a single screen to a complex, interconnected collection of pages combined with graphics, sound, and animation.

A central concept of the Web is *hypertext*, a system of codes that allows you to navigate by clicking on links and moving—or, rather, jumping—in a nonlinear way. If you choose, you can read through a Web-based document from beginning to end. If what you're reading isn't useful to you, at any point you can follow hypertext links to another part of the document, to a different document, or to another Web site. As you've seen, the databases used for computerized searches use underlined *hyperlinks* to allow you to move from search request to results page, from title listing to abstract, from related topics to new sources and new searches.

Web sites can be created by anyone who wants to set one up: governmental agencies, schools, businesses, nonprofit organizations, and individuals. Because they are ideal for distributing up-to-date information to a worldwide audience cheaply and easily, many Web sites are maintained by corporations for advertising purposes. That's one reason why you need to make doubly sure that information for research obtained through the Web is accurate and objective. As you'll learn in Chapter 6, not all Web sites are reliable or worth citing in your essay. Before you take notes or print out material, get some sense of the author's credentials and the material's validity.

The distinctive qualities of the Web—the speed with which it can be updated and searched, and the huge amount of information it contains—are both its strength and its weakness. It is fast, but fleeting. Web sites change and disappear without any notice, and the information that you thought you had on Monday may be unavailable by Friday. It is current, but not historical. The Web contains lots of material about today's issues, but there's very little that goes back more than a few years. It is huge, but indiscriminate. You can search for anything, but often find nothing useful for your purpose. Unless you're very focused in your search requirements, you're likely to receive a list of sites that seem randomly chosen and ranked. As Danny O'Brien wrote in "The Fine Art of Googling," search engines "may know the contents of all Web pages, but they know the meaning of none." Good research does not start and end with point and click.

To help you navigate the Internet and view Web sites, you must first access a *Web browser,* most commonly Netscape Navigator or Microsoft Internet Explorer. Then, to find the information that you want, you choose a *search engine:* a huge database containing indexes of keywords and phrases gathered from millions of Web sites. Search engines trawl the Web for new sites, organizing their contents into categories or cross-referenced indexes. You can tap into that information by visiting the engine's home page and starting a keyword search. Once you make your keyword request, the computer searches through its index, locates the addresses of Web sites that include those words, presents you with a list of results, and allows you to visit the sites by clicking on a link. Alternatively, if the search engine features a directory of subject categories, you can browse through the list of sites and click on those related to your topic.

Search engines are divided into two broad groups. *Web crawlers* use computers ("spiders") to compile, collate, and rank information mechanically, according to a formula or algorithm. *Hierarchical indexes* (also known as *Web directories*) employ staff to scan and categorize individual Web sites. In theory, human intelligence should do a better job of sorting, ranking, and avoiding duplication than a set formula does; but, in fact, practically all search engines—crawlers or indexes—can produce a hodgepodge of results, irrelevant to the topic you're searching for. One disadvantage of all search engines, whether humanly or mechanically generated, is that the descriptions come directly from the sites' owners and may or may not be accurate summaries of the contents.

Crawlers, like AltaVista, have very large databases and provide long lists of results, but do very little rational sorting. The sheer numbers of Web sites listed can be overwhelming if you search too broadly; but if you know precisely what you're looking for, you'll get a fast answer. One highly regarded crawler is *Google*, which does rank sites—according to their relative popularity—by calculating the number of hyperlinks that lead to them. Figure 5-9 shows Google's Advanced Search page set for a search for the phrase "Lawrence of Arabia." Notice that the operators (AND, OR, and NOT) are replaced by self-explanatory

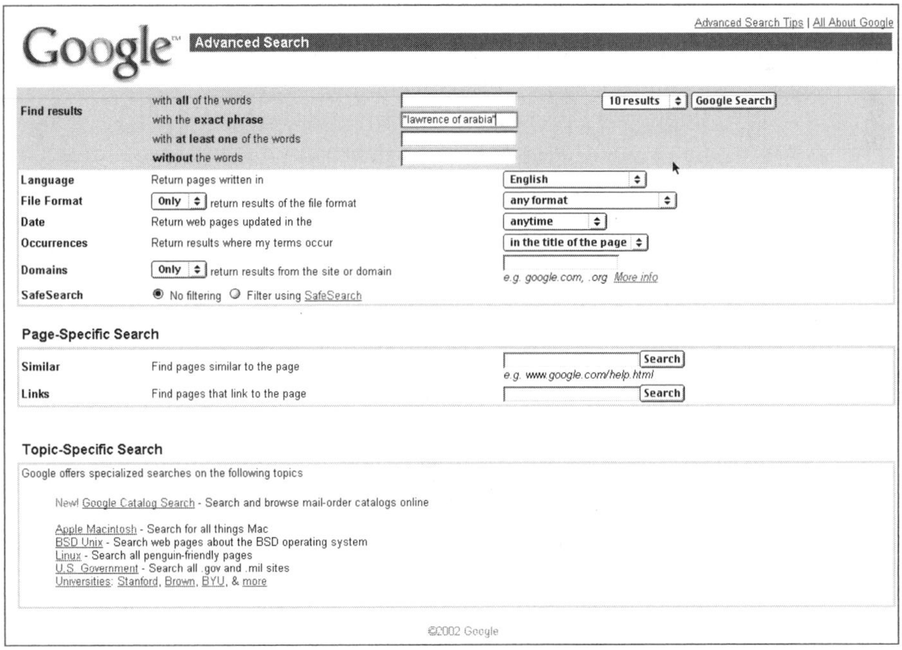

Figure 5-9. Google Advanced Search

phrases ("with *all* of the words," "with the *exact phrase*," "with *at least one* of the words," "*without* the words"). You can also choose between limiting your search to sites that explicitly focus on Lawrence and therefore mention him in the title, or accepting those that refer to him anywhere in the site. Even specifying that limitation, this search produced a list of 1,890 sites (known as "hits"). And, to illustrate the aberrations of Web searching, exactly the same Google search three weeks later increased the number of hits to 2,570.

The most popular of the hierarchical indexes, Yahoo has been in business since 1994 and so has reasonably well-developed listings. If your search topic is a broad one, Yahoo is a useful place to start since you're less likely to get an unmanageably long list of Web sites. On the other hand, you may end up with too few or none. One feature of a Yahoo search is the use of categories to organize the results. An advanced search for "Lawrence of Arabia" (restricted to sites added in the last four years) produced only nine hits, each one identified by its category: "Entertainment>movies and film" or "arts>authors" or "society and culture>personal home pages." These categories are intended for easy personal and commercial searching, not for academic research. It's not surprising that none of the nine sites deals with the life and character of T. E. Lawrence.

It's often said that search engines have catalogued less than 1 percent of what's really available on the Web. For this reason, no single search engine can achieve a truly exhaustive search. You usually have to carry out several searches before receiving a plausible results list. In fact, if your first few searches have been unsuccessful, you may want to cover as much ground as you can by using a *meta search engine:* a super-crawler that covers large tracts of Web material by scanning the contents of several other search engines. But to achieve such wide coverage, you have to provide a broad, unrefined topic, so meta engines don't always work well with complex searches.

One exception is Copernic, which relies on a relatively small number of other search engines and does some useful sorting of results. The results of a Copernic search for "Lawrence of Arabia" are quite promising. Of the forty-one Web documents listed, twelve focus on the motion picture and fourteen involve shopping offers, but fifteen actually appear to be about Lawrence himself. Excluding several repetitions and one or two questionable home pages, you'll end up with ten Web sites that have a reasonable chance of advancing your research.

Finally, there is also a growing number of "academic" search engines, usually sited at a university, that serve the same function for Web sites as databases do for periodicals and books. Database/search engines like Alphasearch, Bubl, and Argus have only a modest number of sites in their indexes, numbering in the thousands, not the millions. But the sites are read and selected by librarians or faculty (a form of peer review); they are objectively described and rationally ranked; and they are often accompanied by helpful hyperlinks or even bibliographies. Before starting a search, you're encouraged to browse through their list of their categories to see what topics are covered and whether yours is likely to be among them. Other useful search engines are those intended for special interests in areas such as finance, science, or law.

Managing Web Searches

- Choose a *search engine* that's appropriate for your topic: a *Web directory* when you want a few well-focused sites for a broad topic; a *Web crawler* when you want the maximum number of links for a concrete topic; a *meta search engine* when you want the widest possible range of information.

- Take time to read the "Help" section of the search engine that you choose. The more precise your search instructions, the greater the number of meaningful responses.

- Use more than one search engine, as necessary. Any two search engines are likely to produce disparate results. If one turns up little of interest, try another.

- Don't waste more than ten minutes on any search engine if the results seem unpromising. Try other engines, or use a database, or go to the library.

- If your search yields a list of a thousand sites, don't try to wade through them all. Look at the first twenty. If there's nothing at all worthwhile, refine your search with more operators, or try another search engine.

- Avoid commercial sites selling products. They rarely contain material appropriate for academic research, but sometimes pay to receive high rankings in searches.

- Don't settle for the first sites you find that seem remotely connected to your topic. Keep on searching until the information is solid.

- Watch out for dead links: Web sites that were indexed months or even years ago and are no longer being maintained by their owners. They can waste your time.

- Don't just add interesting possibilities to your "Favorites" or "Bookmarks" for later reading. The material will pile up, and you won't be able to absorb it easily. If you read (or, at least, skim) as you go along, you'll learn enough about your topic to give some direction to your search.

- Don't be tempted to open every link you come to and pursue stray pieces of information just because they're there. Before you click on a link, consider whether this information is likely to be useful to your present project. Surfing isn't research.

- Maintain concrete and reasonable expectations for your search. Decide what you want to get out of each session on the Internet, and concentrate on that goal. Search with a purpose.

Finding Other Sources on the Internet

E-mail enables people to communicate with each other, develop their own computer networks, and exchange information electronically, all over the world, in minutes. E-mail can also be used to get assistance in exploring a research topic. If you know the e-mail address of an expert in that field, you can send a message, asking questions or requesting specific information. Keep in mind, though, that academic and professional authorities have little time to answer unsolicited e-mail and, as the number of e-mail inquiries has increased, many are less willing to participate in students' research. If the person you plan to e-mail has already written a book or article on the subject, try consulting that instead. If you do send an e-mail, make sure that you are courteous in making your request. At the very least, you should be sufficiently familiar with the expert's work so that your inquiry will seem serious and warrant a response. (Review the suggestions for approaching an interview subject in Appendix D.) Remember that any information obtained through e-mail that is subsequently used in an essay must have its source cited. (See Appendix B for the appropriate format.)

Listserv subscriptions are another way to gain information through e-mail. These are, basically, e-mail exchanges between people interested in a particular subject. When your address is added to the mailing list, you receive e-mail from members of the group and can send e-mail in return. Large mailing lists are usually automated, with a computer (called a listserv) receiving and distributing e-mail to and from you and the other group members. You may also have access to previous "discussions" and messages through the archives. Not all listservs are open to the public, and some are moderated: volunteers screen all messages to ensure that they are appropriate for distribution. One disadvantage of listserv membership is that your e-mail inbox is likely to get overloaded. (You may want to establish a second e-mail address just for listserv.) Remember, too, that material obtained through e-mail or, indeed, from the Internet in general, has not been validated for accuracy to the same extent as works that have gone through the selection processes used by publishers of books and periodicals. You can search for listservs at www.topica.com or www.cyberfiber.com.

Usenet newsgroups provide a similar means of access to information, through a worldwide network of electronic bulletin boards, each devoted to a particular subject. Using your Web browser or specialized software called newsreaders, you can post messages to one or more newsgroups, read messages other people have posted, and reply to those messages. Unlike postings to listservs, those to newsgroups do not come to your own e-mail; you need to go to the bulletin board to see them and to respond or to post messages of your own. Older postings are removed from the bulletin board periodically, although many newsgroups now archive their old messages for a certain time. You can find archived Usenet messages in searchable engines such as Google, AltaVista, or Yahoo. Be aware that the same concerns about reliability and accuracy of Internet information apply to Usenet groups.

One limitation of both listservs and Usenet groups is that they are mostly limited to current issues and popular culture; you're not likely to find many historical topics, like Lawrence of Arabia. But there are exceptions: if your research topic were the Civil War, you could read the postings to the newsgroup soc.history.war.us-civil war, or you could obtain information from participants in that or other listservs or newsgroups interested in the Civil War simply by posting your questions. Here's what such a question might look like:

> I know that in the North, men born between 1818 and 1843 had to register for
>
> the draft. What about aliens? Did they have to register? If not, did they have to
>
> prove that they were not citizens? Where would I obtain records?

Before posting such a request for information, you might check to see if the question has already been answered on the listserv's or newsgroup's FAQ: a document, posted by volunteers, that answers Frequently Asked Questions about the procedure for participants or the subject of discussion.

SAVING AND RECORDING INFORMATION FOR YOUR BIBLIOGRAPHY

Finding sources of information is only the first step in research. As you scan the sources that you find, you have to decide which ones are worth including in your essay as well as the best way to save them. Before the computer and the copying machine were invented, a researcher had to make immediate and firm choices, *taking notes* from useful material and rejecting everything else. Later on, those notes would become the basis for the essay. There are definite advantages in taking and working from notes. You gain a firm grasp of the topic; you will develop ideas of your own as you summarize and paraphrase what you read; and you can more easily estimate the progress of your research, deciding whether your sources are numerous and thorough enough to support your essay.

But the twenty-first century does provide some convenient alternatives. Even if you take notes, it makes sense to copy key pages from books and articles so that, as you write, you can check your version of the material against the actual text. Having that text discourages inadvertent plagiarism since it will be very clear which ideas and language are the source's and which are yours. Copies also make it possible to write comments in the margin and circle or highlight key points. If it becomes necessary as you organize your essay, you can always cut-and-paste text or interleave copied pages from different sources in a sequence corresponding to your outline.

Once you have located and briefly examined a book or periodical article or a Web site and decided that it is worth saving, you should not only copy pages, but also write a few preliminary notes about the source's probable usefulness. Jot down your opinion of the work's scope and contents, strong or weak points, and relevance to your topic, as well as any impressions about the author's reliability as a source. Often, you can make these tentative judgments just by examining the table of contents and leafing or scrolling through the pages. If you forget to note down your reactions, you'll find it more difficult to prioritize your reading when you're pressed for time at a later stage of your research.

Notes are also useful in preparing your bibliography and essential if you're asked to submit an annotated bibliography. A bibliography is a complete list of all the works that you use in preparing your essay. What's included in a bibliography can differ at various stages of your work:

- A *preliminary* or *working* bibliography consists of all the sources that you find worth recording and saving as you do your research.

- A *final* bibliography (sometimes called "Works Cited" or "References") consists of the material that you have actually used in writing your essay.

- An *annotated* bibliography includes a brief comment after each item, describing the work's scope and specific focus and suggesting its relevance and usefulness to the development of your topic.

The annotations in a bibliography are usually no more than a sentence or two, just enough to help your reader understand the relative importance of each source. An example of an annotated bibliography is below, on pp. 263–264.

Copying and Recording Print Material

If you copy pages from books or periodicals, keep in mind that you may not always remember how that extract fit into the author's sequence of ideas. Provide yourself with a brief explanation of context at the top of the first copied page: the focus of the chapter, the author's previous point. Otherwise, you may have to go back to the library while writing your essay and find the original source. It's also helpful to copy some or all of the bibliography in the back of a key text.

Place the book carefully in the copier to avoid cutting off material at the top, bottom, or sides of the page; days or weeks later, if you want to quote, it may be difficult to reconstruct missing language. You should make especially sure that the page numbers show on the copies since those numbers are crucial in the citation of your sources. Even the most experienced researchers make such mistakes standing at the copying machine with a long line of people waiting their turn.

If you think that you might want to use a specific book or article in your essay, you should record some basic publication information for your bibliography. For a book, one way to keep the details legible and accurate is to copy the title page and the copyright page (the back of the title page) at the same time that you copy extracts. For a periodical article, copy the cover and the table of contents. Of course, if you used a database to identify books and periodical articles, most of the information that you need will be included in the results list. (That's one reason why it's useful to download or print the results pages of your database searches.) But even if you have those lists saved on your computer, the information that you'll need will be scattered over a number of downloaded files. At some point, you'll have to put it all together in a single file.

Start the file for your bibliography early in the research process, and every time you find a source you're likely (but not necessarily certain) to use, add it to the file. Transcribe the information from the databases that you've downloaded and the stack of title pages that you've copied. Or, if you use a word processing program (like Nota Bene) that automatically prepares a bibliography in any of the standard formats, enter the data about each new source into the fields of the database. It's important to be accurate and consistent in recording each entry. Check the spelling of the author's name. Don't abbreviate unless you're sure you'll remember the significance of each symbol. Make it clear whether the place of publication was Cambridge, Massachusetts or Cambridge, England. Leave blank spaces if, for example, you've forgotten to include the publisher's name or the journal's volume number.

The majority of college research essays use MLA (Modern Language Association) style for documentation. To prepare a final bibliography in MLA style (or, indeed, in most other styles), you should include the following facts in your preliminary list:

For Print Books

- the full name of the author(s)
- the exact title, underlined or italicized
- the name of the editor(s) (for an anthology) or the name of the translator (for a work first written in a foreign language)
- the date and place of publication and the name of the publisher
- the original date of publication and the date of the new edition or reprint, if the book has been reissued
- the inclusive page numbers and any other information for a specific chapter or other section (such as the author and title of an introduction or of a selection within an anthology)
- the volume number, if the book is part of a multivolume work
- the call number, so that you will not need to return to the catalog if you decide to locate the book again

For Print Articles

- the full name of the author(s)
- the title of the article, in quotation marks
- the exact title of the periodical, underlined or italicized

- the volume and issue numbers (if any) and the date of the issue
- the inclusive page numbers of the article
- the call number of the periodical, so that you will not need to return to the database if you decide to locate the article again

Copying and Recording Web Material

Downloading material from the Web is the equivalent of copying print texts. If you click on a document and can't make up your mind whether it's worth saving, you can "bookmark" it, or include it among the "favorites" on your browser. Once you're sure it's a solid source, click "Save As" on the File menu, choosing a name that will be easily recognizable and (if you want to save space on your hard drive) selecting a "text only" option rather than saving the complete document, graphics and all. If the document is large, you may want to highlight extracts and then copy-and-paste them to a file in your word processing program. (Since the content of a Web site can change from day to day—or the site itself can disappear—it's a good idea to download if you have any inclination at all to use the source.) Early on in your research, create a new folder named for your paper topic and, after that, save all Web material to that folder, so it won't be scattered all over your hard drive. Downloading enables you to read the text at your leisure without online charges.

Printing out a Web document is also helpful. Web graphics can be distracting; computer screens are hard on the eyes. In addition, having a print copy allows you to put comments in the margins and highlight important points. Actually, once you've downloaded a document, you can always add your own notes on the screen, without printing it, either between paragraphs or (if you're careful) within the text. Just use brackets or some other identifying mark to indicate where your words start and stop.

It's particularly important to keep a running record of *URLs*—the numbers, letters, and symbols that identify each Web page—so that if you want to go back to a page you can do so easily. (Be careful with the spelling of Web addresses.) Don't assume that you'll remember a URL. If you've downloaded Web material, saving it under a convenient name, you may have to search hard to reconstruct its address. A Web page that you've bookmarked will have the correct URL clearly indicated in the "favorites" list. Often, by checking the "history" list on your browser you can locate the Web page you used a few days or weeks ago. On the whole, though, it's safest to have a single file that records all your sources, with complete bibliographic information. And save it! And copy it to a floppy disk!

To compile your working bibliography, you need to add information about Web sources to the file where you're storing data about print sources. Many Web documents were previously or simultaneously published in print; in those cases, you may have to provide both the print and the electronic data. On many sites, however, the kind of bibliographic information shown in print sources is not provided or is difficult to find. Look for and record any of the following items that you can identify:

For Web Material

- the name of the author(s) of the article or other document or of the person(s) who created the site
- the title of the article or other document, in quotation marks
- the title of the book or periodical or of the site, underlined or italicized, or a description, such as *Home page*
- any volume number, issue number, or other identifying number
- any print publication information, including the date
- the date of publication on the Web, or of the most recent update
- the range or total number of pages, paragraphs, or other sections, if they are numbered on the site
- the name of any sponsoring organization (such as an academic department)
- the date of access: when you downloaded the site or took notes from it
- the Web address (URL)

Obviously, this information can vary depending on the kind of document you're intending to use. An individual's home page, for example, would require nothing more than the author's name, the indication that it is a home page, the date of access, and the URL. But serious research is much more likely to depend on Web sites that come from academic or professional (or even commercial) sponsorship, and it's necessary to indicate all those details in the bibliography. Examples of bibliographical entries for citing Web sources can be found in Appendix B.

Here's how you put together some of the information you've recorded about Lawrence of Arabia and turn it into an *annotated bibliography* (following MLA style):

The Myth of Lawrence of Arabia in the Movies:

An Annotated List of Sources Consulted

Butler, Oliver J. The Guerrilla Strategies of Lawrence and Mao:
    An Examination. Houston: Butler, 1974. Useful background for
    understanding the success of Lawrence's campaigns against the
    Turks and evaluating the movie's accuracy, particularly the bombing
    of the train.

Hodson, Joel C. Lawrence of Arabia and American Culture: The Making
    of a Transatlantic Legend. Westport: Greenwood, 1995. This book

focuses on the impact the Lawrence myth had on American culture. The last part is particularly useful in analyzing the movie's presentation of Lawrence, especially his alleged homosexuality.

Kauffmann, Stanley. "On Films: The Return of El Aurans. Lawrence of Arabia Reissued, Restored to Its Original Length." New Republic 20 Feb. 1989: 26–28. One of the most eminent film critics reassesses the significance of the film.

Lawrence, T. E. The Letters of T. E. Lawrence of Arabia. Ed. David Garnett. 1938; London: Spring, 1964. This is a comprehensive collection of Lawrence's correspondence, which provides an especially detailed and moving picture of his later years in the RAF.

---. The Seven Pillars of Wisdom. London: Pike, 1926. Lawrence's own interpretation of what happened in the campaign against the Turks is written in a flowery and sometimes opaque style. Nevertheless, it's essential reading.

Waters, Irene. "The Lawrence Trail." Contemporary Review 272 (Apr. 1998). 10 Aug. 2001 <http://firstsearch.oclc.org/WebZ/FSPage? . . . essionid=sp03sw11-54325-cq6mvlsy~u80zsh>. This is little more than a personal narrative following Lawrence's path through the desert in the 1917 campaign. Useful only for local color.

Williams, Sian. Home page. 2 July 2001 < http://www.ouphrontis .co.uk/>. Although rather dramatic in style, this site is very useful, especially for its links to other Web pages about Lawrence (man and film) which don't appear on any search results lists.

Wilson, Jeremy. Lawrence of Arabia: The Authorised Biography of T. E. Lawrence. London: Heinemann, 1989. Although not the most recent, this is the most comprehensive of the biographies of Lawrence and covers every aspect of his life. The bibliography could be more helpful.

---. The Lawrence of Arabia Factfile. March 2001. Castle Hill Press. 4 May 2001 <http://www.castle-hill-press.com/teweb/index.htm>. This is a superb, searchable Web site containing information about Lawrence, maps and chronology, bibliography, and a link to the journal T. E. Lawrence Studies.

Wilson, Michael. "Lawrence of Arabia: Elements and Facets of the Theme." Cineaste 21 (4) 1995: 30. This article, though brief, provides interesting insights into how the screenwriter thought he was representing Lawrence's life.

How Much Research Is Enough?

Research is open-ended. You can't know in advance how many sources will provide adequate support for your topic. Your instructor may stipulate that you consult at least five authorities, or ten, or fifteen; but that is probably intended to make sure that everyone in your class does a roughly equal amount of research. Quantity is not the crucial issue. There's little point in compiling the required number of source materials if the works on your list are minor, or trivial, or peripheral to the topic. Your bibliography could contain hundreds of sources—whole sections of a database or whole pages of an index—but would that be the basis for a well-documented essay? At various stages of your research, you may think that you have located enough sources. When that happens, try asking yourself these questions:

- Do my sources include a few of the "standard" books on my topic by well-known authorities? The most recent books? Contemporary accounts (if the topic is historical)?

- Have I checked databases and indexes to find the most authoritative periodical articles, whether in print or on the Web? Have I included the best ones among my sources?

- Does Web material supplement my research, rather than dominate it?

- Have I discussed any questions about my research with my instructor or with a librarian?

- Have I taken notes of my own ideas and thoughts about the topic?

- Without consulting sources, can I talk about the subject convincingly and fluently? Have I succeeded in doing this with a friend?

- Is a point of view or thesis emerging from my research?

- Have I gathered a critical mass of information, copied excerpts, and downloaded material so that my essay has the prospect of substantial support?

- Do I feel ready to start writing an essay?

EXERCISE 18: COMPILING A WORKING BIBLIOGRAPHY

The following is a list of four different topics for a research essay dealing with the broad subject of *advertising,* followed by a bibliography of twenty articles, arranged in order of their publication dates. Each item in the bibliography is followed by a note giving a brief description of its contents.

Examine the bibliography carefully and choose a set of appropriate sources for each of the four essay topics. You are not expected to locate and read these articles; use the notes to help you make your decisions.

The bibliography is numbered to make the distribution process easier. List the numbers of the articles that you select underneath each topic. You will notice that many of the articles can be used for more than one topic.

Topics

A. What is an appropriate role for advertising in our society? What are the advertiser's responsibilities?

B. Feminists have argued that the image of women created by the advertising industry remains a false and objectionable one. Is that claim valid?

C. How do advertising agencies go about manipulating the reactions of consumers?

D. To what extent does advertising serve the public? harm the public?

1. Signorielli, Nancy. "Gender Stereotypes in MTV Commercials: The Beat Goes On." *Journal of Broadcasting & Electronic Media* Winter 1994: 91–101. This long article examines the presentation of gender roles through commercials to the typically adolescent viewer of MTV. The depiction of women as linked primarily to sexuality is also discussed.

2. Sengupta, Subir. "The Influence of Culture on Portrayals of Women in Television Commercials." *International Journal of Advertising* 1995: 314–333. This technical study compares Japanese and American television commercials and the way in which cultural influences affect the depiction of women in advertising.

3. Hitchon, Jacqueline C., and Chingching Chang. "Effects of Gender Schematic Processing on the Reception of Political Commercials for Men and Women Candidates." *Communication Research* Aug. 1995: 430–458. Another scholarly survey focusing on the appeal to gender in the marketing of commercials for political candidates.

4. Tauchi, Teresa. "Truth in Advertising." *HaasWeek Home* 30 Oct. 1995. Online. Internet. http://haas.berkeley.edu/~haasweek/issues/XXII_10/index.html. 13 Oct. 1997. A chatty little story about tasteless ads, often offensive to women, and the need for more responsible behavior on the part of advertising executives.

5. Elliott, Dorinda. "Objects of Desire." *Newsweek* 12 Feb. 1996: 41. This news story concerns the potentially big market for exotic underwear in Asia, and the ways in which advertising can sell more push-up bras to Asian women.

6. Lafky, Sue, Margaret Duffy, Mary Steinmaus, and Dan Berkowitz. "Looking through Gendered Lenses." *Journalism & Mass Communication Quarterly* Summer 1996: 379–388. Full of jargon, this article describes a study of gender-role stereotyping. High school students were given magazine ads to show how quickly they are influenced by stereotypes of gender.

7. Miller, Molly. "The Color of Money." *Mother Earth News* Feb. 1996: 78–89. The subject is environmental protection, and the false claims about their environmental policies that some companies have made in their advertisements.

8. LaTour, Michael S., Robin L. Snipes, and Sara J. Bliss. "Don't Be Afraid to Use Fear Appeals." *Journal of Advertising Research* Mar. 1996: 59–67. A video based on an appeal to the viewers' fears raised some ethical concerns; this article shows how potential criticism was avoided by trying out the video on a focus group.

9. Pratt, Charlotte A., and Cornelius B. Pratt. "Nutrition Advertisements in Consumer Magazines." *Journal of Black Studies* Mar. 1996: 504–523. The authors focus on claims made about potential benefits to health in advertisements for various foods.

10. McFadden, Daniel L., and Kenneth E. Train. "Consumers' Evaluation of New Products." *Journal of Political Economy* Aug. 1996: 683–703. This is a technical article about how people accept new products through their own or other people's experiences, and how that process can be word-of-mouth information; the authors map out a step-by-step process for evaluation that might be helpful to advertisers.

11. Attas, Daniel. "What's Wrong with 'Deceptive' Advertising?" *Journal of Business Ethics* Aug. 1999: 49–59. This is essentially a defense of deceptive advertising, examining the responsibility of the advertiser and the responsibility of the consumer. It is written in sociological jargon.

12. McNamara, Tracy. "Defining the Blurry Line between Commerce and Content." *Columbia Journalism Review* Jul./Aug. 2000: 31, 35. This is a comparison between buying in stores and buying on the Internet, showing how much easier it is to click on a purchase than to shop in person for an item. Essentially, it is comparing the ethics of print journalism with the ethics of Web commerce.

13. Nordlinger, Pia. "Taste: Anything Goes." *Wall Street Journal* 15 Sept. 2000: W17. This focuses on the proliferation of semi-pornographic ads in magazines, and the questionable standards set by the editors. The author is clearly disapproving of the "prurient" images.

14. White, Candace, and Katherine N. Kimmick. "One Click Forward and Two Clicks Back: Portrayal of Women Using Computers in Television Commercials." *Women's Studies in Communication* Fall 2000: 392–412. Based on a survey of 351 TV commercials, this article shows that the image of women in computer ads is definitely more menial than that of men, confirming the usual stereotypes.

15. Smith, April. "In TV Ads, the Laugh's on Men . . . Isn't It?" *Los Angeles Times* 24 Oct. 2000: E1. This describes images of men in commercials, concluding that they are just as stereotyped as those of women—except the image is that of beer-drinking, dopey sports fans. The point is that male viewers don't get offended by such ads.

16. Harker, Debra, and Michael Harker. "The Role of Codes of Conduct in the Advertising Self-Regulatory Framework." *Journal of Macromarketing* Dec. 2000: 155–166. This article discusses whether or not the advertising industry is capable of self-regulation in dealing with offensive or misleading advertising. Its findings are based on an Australian survey.

17. Martinson, David L. "Using Commercial Advertising to Build an Understanding of Ethical Behavior." *Clearing House* Jan./Feb. 2001: 131–135. The general purpose of the article is to discuss how schools can teach students ethics. The author suggests that the ethical issues surrounding commercial advertising are a good vehicle for teaching moral decision making.

18. Gardner, Marilyn. "Slim But Curvy—the Pursuit of Ideal Beauty." *Christian Science Monitor* 24 Jan. 2001: 16. The author writes about idealized images of women in advertisements, exploring the connection between extreme thinness on the page and increasing obesity among the readers. According to the author, these ideals of beauty are unrealistic.

19. Teinowitz, Ira. "Senators Seek Bill to Protect Privacy of Kids." *Advertising Age* 19 Feb. 2001: 35. This describes the position of congressional groups for and against regulation of the advertising industry's efforts to market directly to children when they are "captive audiences" in school.

20. McKay, Betsy. "New Diet Coke Campaign Plays Up Sex." *Wall Street Journal* 23 Mar. 2001: B7. The author reports on the new commercials for Diet Coke, analyzing their appeal to consumers and citing the market analysis Coke used to appeal to a wide audience.

EXERCISE 19: FINDING AND SELECTING SOURCES

Each of the historical figures on the following list has been the subject of a motion picture. (The dates and, where necessary, titles of the films are in parentheses.) Choose one figure and then compile a preliminary bibliography for an essay that sets out to determine to what extent the film is authentic. (Since this is a *preliminary* bibliography and you're not being asked to write the essay, you need not have seen the film in order to start the research process.)

Using databases and search engines, search for sources that are clearly linked to your topic. Print out a list of the first twenty or thirty items from each search, eliminate those that are obviously commercial or trivial, and choose those that might appropriately be included in a preliminary bibliography. You do not have to examine the books, articles, or Web sites in order to make your selection; base your choices on the descriptions, summaries, or abstracts provided by the database or search engine. If you don't find sufficient material in your first search, keep trying.

Your preliminary bibliography should contain at least ten items, with a balance of one-third books, one-third print periodical articles, and one-third Web material. Hand in the results lists from your searches with the appropriate choices marked. If your instructor requests it, also prepare a formal bibliography using MLA format.

Benito Juarez (*Juarez* 1939)

Charles Gordon (*Khartoum* 1966)

Charles Lindbergh (*Spirit of St. Louis* 1957)

Cleopatra (1963)

Cole Porter (*Night and Day* 1946)

Dian Fossey (*Gorillas in the Mist* 1988)

El Cid (1961)

Eleanor of Aquitaine (*The Lion in Winter* 1968)

Emma Hamilton (*That Hamilton Woman* 1941)

Erwin Rommel (*The Desert Fox* 1951)

Gandhi (1982)

George Patton (*Patton* 1970)

George III (*The Madness of King George* 1994)

Hans Christian Andersen (1952)

Isadora Duncan (*Isadora* 1968)

Lillian Hellman (*Julia* 1977)

Marie Antoinette (1938)

Marie Curie (*Madame Curie* 1943)

Michael Collins (1996)

Mikhail Kutuzov (*War and Peace* 1956)

Oscar Wilde (1998)

Queen Victoria (*Mrs. Brown* 1997)

T. S. Eliot (*Tom and Viv* 1994)

Thomas Jefferson (*Jefferson in Paris* 1995)

William Gilbert or Arthur Sullivan (*Topsy Turvy* 1999)

William Randolph Hearst (*Citizen Kane* 1941)

William Wallace (*Braveheart* 1995)

Wyatt Earp (*My Darling Clementine* 1946)

ASSIGNMENT 12: PREPARING A TOPIC PROPOSAL
FOR A RESEARCH ESSAY

A. Choose a broad topic that, for the next few weeks, you will research and develop into an extended essay of eight or more pages.

- If you have a *person or an event* in mind, but do not have sufficiently detailed knowledge to decide on a focus and target date, wait until you have done some preliminary reading. Start with an encyclopedia article or an entry in a biographical dictionary; then use the online databases and search engines, as well as any bibliographies that you find along the way.

- If you select a *contemporary subject or issue for argument,* search for books, journal and newspaper articles, and Web sites that will help you to formulate a few questions to be explored in your essay.

B. Compile a preliminary bibliography, based on your search results. At this point, you need not examine all the sources, take notes, or plan the organization of your essay. Your purpose is to assess the *amount* and, as much as possible, the *quality* of the material that is available. Whether or not your instructor asks you to hand in your preliminary bibliography, make sure that the publication information that you record is accurate and legible. Indicate which sources your library has available and which may be difficult to obtain.

C. Submit a topic proposal to your instructor, describing the probable scope and focus of your essay. (If you are considering more than one topic, suggest a few possibilities.) Be prepared to change the specifics of your proposal as you learn more about the number and availability of your sources.

▪ 6 ▪

Evaluating Sources

Locating sources comes before *choosing* sources. In the first step, you look for possible material, promising material, from print sources and from the Web. That becomes your preliminary bibliography. In the second step, you decide which of the possibilities are worth including in your essay. Those will be the contents of your final bibliography. In this chapter, you'll learn more about the process of choosing sources.

LEARNING MORE ABOUT YOUR SOURCES

Your sources provide the *evidence* to support the thesis of your essay. Few of us know enough about most subjects to write about them from our own knowledge and experience. We have to rely on the evidence of others, usually in written form, published in print or on the Web. If the evidence isn't valid, then the work that depends on it will lose its credibility. For this reason, it's essential that—before you start writing—you evaluate each potential source to determine whether it's solid enough to support your essay or so shoddy as to discredit it.

Evaluating sources doesn't have to take a great deal of time. You do have to read enough of each text to make some judgments about its *substance* and its *tone*. You have to understand what kind of work it is—whether it's *plausible,* whether it's *appropriate* for the essay that you're writing. You need to be sure it's *relevant* to your topic. And since a good source should be *authoritative,* you must explore the author's claims to your serious consideration.

EVALUATING PRINT SOURCES

Let's assume that you've begun research for an essay on *animal rights.* You've often wondered about the motivations of vegetarians. As a meat-eater yourself, you're curious about the arguments used by animal rights advocates to discourage the slaughter of living creatures for the table. You are also aware of an ongoing controversy about the use of animals in medical experiments.

Your library holds many of the books and periodicals that have turned up in your database searches. How do you determine which ones to read seriously? How do you weigh one source of evidence against another and decide which ideas should be emphasized in your essay? Since all the books and articles have been chosen for publication, each one has presumably undergone some form of selection and review. Would it have been published if its author's authority was questionable? Why is it necessary to inquire further? How can information about these sources help you in the writing of your essay?

Credentials

At the most basic level, you want to find out whether the author of a book or article about animal rights can be trusted to know what he or she is writing about. Here's where the person's education and professional experience become relevant. Is the writer an academic? If so, what's the field of specialization? A *psychologist* might provide insights into the personal beliefs motivating vegetarians, but would probably be less concerned with the ideology of the animal rights movement. A *philosopher* will present theoretical arguments, but the analysis may be too abstract to provide you with concrete examples for developing your thesis. An *economist* might seem to be an unlikely source to support this topic, but the movement toward vegetarianism has had serious consequences for the agricultural economy as well as the retail world of the supermarket. What about *home economists?* Any database search on "'animal rights' AND vegetarianism" will include a number of cookbooks and helpful guides for good nutrition, but the authors of such books are much less likely to possess academic qualifications. Does that matter? More important, do you want to include that kind of material in your essay? What kind of essay are you writing, anyway? One that stresses the theoretical arguments behind the animal rights movements? The practical motivation? The economic consequences? Evaluating sources can give your essay focus and direction.

How can you find out about an author's background?

- Check a book's *preface* (including acknowledgments), which will often contain biographical information.

- Read the "blurb" on the jacket cover—often laudatory—which should include some basic facts among the hype.

- Look for *thumbnail biographies* at the beginning or end of periodical articles, or grouped together somewhere in the issue. Be aware that such brief biographies (often written by the authors themselves) can be vague or even misleading. "A freelance writer who frequently writes about this topic" can describe a recognized authority or an inexperienced amateur.

- Do a *Web search* using the author's name. See what other books and articles the author has published.

- Consult one of the many *biographical dictionaries and encyclopedias* available on the Web.

- Check the *Book Review Index* on the Web. If the book is a recent one, there will probably be many reviews available.

- Routinely check the level and extent of the *documentation* that the author provides. Footnotes or parenthetical notes and a comprehensive bibliography usually indicate a serious commitment to the subject.

Peter Singer is the author of *Animal Liberation: A New Ethics for Our Treatment of Animals.* After a database search turns up this title, you find the book on the library shelves, note that it was published in 1975 (but revised in 1990), and wonder whether it's worth delving into a book that's more than twenty-five years old. So you search for his name in the *Encarta* encyclopedia and find the following:

Singer, Peter (1946–), Australian philosopher and bioethicist. Born in Melbourne, Australia, Singer studied at the University of Melbourne and at the University of Oxford, in England. He began his career lecturing ethics [sic] at Oxford from 1971 to 1973. He subsequently worked at various universities in North America and Australia. In 1977, he became a professor of philosophy at Monash University in Melbourne. Singer also became closely associated with the university's Centre for Human Bioethics, which is dedicated to the study of the moral implications of biomedical discoveries. . . . In 1999 he became a professor at Princeton University's Center for Human Values.

The article goes on to describe Singer as a *rationalist,* who views ethical issues from a utilitarian point of view and so advocates actions that result in the greatest good for the greatest number of people. He has written, cowritten, or edited twenty-two books, the most recent in 2000, some in areas of pure philosophy (*Hegel; Marx*) but most dealing with matters of ethical choice.

What do you learn from this information? Singer holds impeccable academic credentials and has had a long and estimable academic career. As a philosopher, he is likely to root his work on animal rights in abstract arguments. As an ethicist, he is likely to provide plenty of concrete examples to illustrate his arguments.

So far, *Animal Liberation* seems like a certain choice for your preliminary bibliography and, quite probably, your final bibliography. Is there anything more that you need to know about it?

Impartiality

Sometimes you have to make allowances for an author's individual approach to a subject, especially if the topic is a contentious one like animal rights. In the simplest terms, a declared vegetarian is likely to have a vested interest in the arguments against using animals for food and may present those arguments in a way that's less than impartial. There's nothing intrinsically wrong with having one's own point of view. Few people—however learned or knowledgeable—succeed in being totally detached or objective, whether about their beliefs or their areas of professional expertise. But there's a big difference between an acknowledged personal interest and an underlying prejudice.

The issue here is *bias:* the special concern or personal angle that might affect an author's opinion or treatment of a subject. The existence of bias isn't necessarily wrong or bad, and it needn't prevent you from using and citing a source. It's simply one factor that can affect your understanding of an author's ideas. A dogmatic writer will probably want to convert you at all costs. A narrow-minded writer will ignore or downplay opposing points of view. You may conclude that either is too biased to be credible. But a third author, who also cares passionately about a subject, may advocate a set of ideas in the strongest terms and yet remain credible. Such writers are usually aware of and acknowledge their bias—and seek to persuade or convince rather than bludgeon their readers into submission. Don't reject an interesting source just because you believe that the writer may have a special interest in the subject. Once you have identified a possible bias, you can disregard it as harmless, or adjust your judgment to allow for its influence, or—if the bias is really prejudice in disguise—reject the source as not worth your time.

Looking further at the *Encarta* profile, you notice that Peter Singer's books tend to have strong titles, urging action: *Animal Liberation, In Defence of Animals, Ethics into Action, Democracy and Disobedience.* Clearly, he's not an ivory tower philosopher, and so, curious to learn more about his activities, you do a Copernic search. You don't have to click on any of the thirty-three items on the results lists to learn that Singer has been called the world's "most controversial ethicist" and that a petition was started to protest his appointment to a named chair at Princeton. There are references to his "infanticide excesses" and "utilitarian horrors" as well as comparisons with Hitler's Nazism. On the other hand, there are other Web sites that appear to support his views and praise his reasoned defense of his ethical beliefs. Since the *Encarta* and Copernic searches have taken only a few minutes, you try one more, and find a four-page article in *Current Biography* that provides an analysis of reactions by reviewers to many of Singer's works. Focusing on those that deal with *Animal Liberation,* you find praise for his documentation and for his "unhysterical and engaging" style. He is referred to as a propagandist, and he is apparently a successful one, since *Animal Libera-tion* is described by one reviewer as "one of the most thoughtful and persuasive books that I have read in a long time."

What can you conclude now? That the present controversy over Singer may or may not concern his 1975 work, which is the one that's most relevant to your research. That he has his detractors and his supporters, which is understandable given his contentious subject. That you should judge for yourself by reading *Animal Liberation,* while being alert for the possibility of a biased presentation.

Style and Tone

Writers aim their work at particular audiences and adjust the content and style accordingly. A children's book about kindness to animals would be an un-likely candidate for inclusion in a research paper; both style and content would be overly simplified and lack credibility. At the other extreme, technical papers in the sciences and social sciences are often written in a dense style, with a vo-cabulary incomprehensible to someone outside the discipline; essentially, one academic is writing for an audience of peers. You would probably want to avoid reading—and citing—a journal article that focuses on the methodology for a survey of animal rights activists or analyzes the chemical basis of nutrients needed in a vegetarian diet.

Nonfiction books are often categorized as:

Popular: intended to attract the widest possible audience and, therefore, be accessible to people with a wide range of educational backgrounds. A pop-ular treatment of a serious subject is likely to emphasize colorful detail rather than abstractions and complexities.

General interest: intended for an audience that is interested in but has no spe-cial grounding in a subject. General interest books provide a thorough in-troduction, with some level of complexity, but without a lot of technical description.

Academic: intended for a limited audience in the field. An academic book is usually published by a university press and contains a level of scholarship and depth of analysis that might well be beyond the comprehension of the general public.

Periodicals also serve a wide range of readers. Most have a marketing "niche," appealing to a specific audience with well-defined interests and read-ing habits. Since readership varies so greatly, articles on the same subject in two different periodicals are likely to differ widely in their content, point of view, and presentation. A newsmagazine like *Time* or *Newsweek* might provide factual information on an animal rights demonstration; the article would be short and lively, filled with concrete illustrations and quotations. It would not have the same purpose, nor cite the same kinds of evidence, nor use the same vocab-ulary as a longer article on the animal rights movement in a general interest periodical like *Psychology Today*. And that, in turn, would have little in common with an essay in a scholarly journal on the moral basis of the contractarian argument supporting the rights of animals. Researchers must allow for this wide variation in style and tone when they select and use their sources.

Journals in the social sciences frequently include articles intended for a narrow audience, using a conventional structure and professional terminology that can sometimes seem like jargon. At the beginning of such articles, you're likely to find a "review of the literature": a summary of the contributions that other sociologists or psychologists have made to an understanding of the topic. Here's a typical paragraph taken from "Social Work and Speciesism," an article by David B. Wolf in the journal *Social Work:*

> There are many connections between our treatment of animals and environmental integrity; these touch on issues such as hunger, poverty, and war. Toffler (1975) suggested that the most practical hope for resolving the world's food crisis is a restriction of beef eating that will save billions of tons of grain. Ehrlich and Ehrlich (1972) reported that production of a pound of meat requires 40 to 100 times as much water as the production of a pound of wheat. Altschul (1964) noted that in terms of calorie units per acre, a diet of grains, vegetables, and beans will support 20 times as many people as a diet of meat. . . .

In effect, Wolf is summarizing the evidence of his sources in the topic sentence and then citing them, one by one. This pattern of presentation should not be imitated in an essay written for a basic writing course, nor is it usually a good idea to include such a "review of the literature" as a source within your essay. You would be quoting or paraphrasing Wolf, who is paraphrasing Toffler or Altschul. Better to eliminate the middleman (Wolf) and go directly to the source (Altschul or Toffler).

You can often decide to dismiss or pursue an article just by considering the title of the periodical. In an *Ingenta* search for articles on "animal rights," the results list (152) included periodicals ranging from *Chemical and Engineering News* to *Broiler Industry* to *Restaurant Business* to *Vegetarian Times*. It's highly unlikely that articles in any of those four periodicals would be suitable for a research essay on "animal rights." What about *Gender and Society*? If you're especially interested in gender issues and wonder whether activism on behalf of animals may be gender specific, that might be an excellent article to include in your preliminary bibliography. *Animal Law?* That depends on the technical level of the article. You'd have to see it to decide whether the issues are presented in accessible language or in professional "legalese." *Audubon?* Here, again, the issue is audience. Is the article intended to appeal to a limited group of nature lovers, or will its content interest a broader audience?

The style and tone of a book or article should be appropriate for your level of research. If you find a source too erudite, then you'll have difficulty understanding it and presenting it to your readers. If you find that a source is written in a superficial, frivolous, or overly dramatic style, then it's not serious or authoritative enough to include in your essay. In the case of Peter Singer's *Animal Liberation*, you've already found out from the *Current Biography* summary that his style is regarded as accessible; according to one reviewer, it was "intended for the mass market." Something can also be learned about the style and tone of a book just by considering the publisher. Most of Singer's books come from Oxford University Press or Cambridge University Press, but *Animal Liberation* was published by Random House, a "general interest" house eager to sell books to the general public. Finally, you open the book to a chapter that particularly interests you and glance at a few sentences:

> Becoming a vegetarian is not merely a symbolic gesture. Nor is it an attempt to isolate oneself from the ugly realities of the world, to keep oneself pure and so without responsibility for the cruelty and carnage all around. Becoming a vegetarian is the most practical and effective step one can take toward ending both the killing of nonhuman animals and the infliction of suffering upon them.

The language is clear; the sentences compelling. You hope that Singer will at some point present the arguments of the nonvegetarian and realize that, if he does not, it will be your job to find the appropriate sources and do so.

Currency

One indication of a work's usefulness for your purpose is its *date*. Only in the last few years has animal rights emerged as an issue of international importance. As a rule, in the sciences and social sciences, the most recent sources usually replace earlier ones. Unless you're interested in providing a historical review of attitudes toward animals, your research would probably focus on representative works published over the last ten or twenty years. An article about vegetarianism as practiced in the 1930s would probably be of little value to you. On the other hand, Singer's 1975 *Animal Liberation* is now regarded as a seminal work—a key influence on later writers about animal rights—and would therefore not lose currency.

For research on historical and biographical topics, you need to know the difference between *primary* and *secondary* sources.

> *A primary source is a work that is itself the subject of your essay or (if you are writing a historical research essay) a work written during the period that you are writing about that gives you direct or primary knowledge of that period.*

"Primary source" is frequently used to describe an original document—such as the Constitution—or memoirs and diaries of historical interest, or a work of literature that, over the years, has been the subject of much written commentary.

> *A secondary source can be any commentary written both after and about the primary source.*

A history textbook is usually a secondary source. So are most biographies. While you generally study a primary source for its own sake, the secondary source is important—often, it only exists—because of its primary source.

- If you are asked to write an essay about *Huckleberry Finn*, and your instructor tells you not to use any secondary sources, you are to read only Mark Twain's novel and not consult any commentaries.

- T. E. Lawrence's *Seven Pillars of Wisdom* is a secondary source if you are interested in guerrilla warfare, but a primary source if you are studying Lawrence.

- If you read the *New York Times* to acquire information about Lawrence's desert campaign in World War I, you are using the newspaper as a primary source since it was written during the period you are studying. But when you look up a *Times* movie review of *Lawrence of Arabia*, then you are locating a secondary source in order to learn more about your primary subject.

Currency is not always essential for research about historical and biographical subjects, which usually includes primary sources. Even out-of-date secondary sources can be useful. Lowell Thomas's 1924 biography of T. E. Lawrence is still of moderate interest in part because Thomas was present during the desert campaigns and could provide firsthand (although not necessarily unbiased) information. Nevertheless, because research is always unearthing new facts about people's lives, Thomas's work has long been superseded by new biographies that feature a broader range of information. For a biographical or historical essay, you should consult some primary sources, one or two secondary sources written at the time of the event or during the subject's lifetime, and the most recent and reliable secondary sources. It is the sources in the middle—written a few years after your target date, without the perspective of distance—that often lack authenticity or objectivity.

Internet searches can make the evaluation of books and periodical articles quick and easy. But obtaining this kind of information shouldn't dominate your research process. If you're building a lengthy preliminary bibliography—ten or more sources—and you're writing an essay in which you anticipate that no single source will be emphasized, don't waste time looking up every author. On the other hand, if you're likely to be working with only a few key sources and if you are ignorant of their authors' qualifications, invest some time in finding out about these authors and their writings.

EVALUATING WEB SOURCES

Finding out about *print sources*—books, journals, and periodical articles—can help you understand your subject and strengthen your research. It is useful to do so, but not always essential. Finding out about *Web sources* can be crucial to the credibility of your essay. It should become a routine part of your research practice.

You need to evaluate Web sources for two reasons:

- *An overabundance of information.* The profusion of material on the Web far exceeds the number of available print articles and books. What do you do when the keyword "animal rights" in a Yahoo search produces 137,000 Web sites? First, you narrow down your search; next, you evaluate what's left and decide which sites to access and examine.

- *An absence of editorial or peer review.* When a book or article is submitted for print publication, editors or specialist reviewers judge its quality, accuracy, and timeliness, based on their knowledge of comparable material. If the work is published, the reader can assume that it meets a reasonably high standard. There is no comparable process for reviewing most material appearing on the Web. No one at Google or Yahoo is qualified to make choices or is in charge of maintaining standards. Each of the 137,000 Web sites on animal rights is presented as equal to the rest. Even search engines that claim to rank responses do not actually do so in a meaningful way. The basis for ranking—if any—tends to be commercial, not intellectual.

One way to avoid the quagmire of endless results lists is to start your search with *academic databases that include Web material.* When a college library compiles a database, the contents are likely to be reliable. That is by no means true of databases that are compiled randomly or those that accept payment from sites in return for inclusion in search engine lists. If, initially, you don't know which databases are academic or if your access is limited to general search engines, that's all the more reason to narrow down your topic with an advanced Boolean search. Then, scan the search engine's results list looking for *Web sites sponsored by academic institutions or governmental agencies* and accessing them first. One or two reliable, comprehensive sites can lead you, via hyperlinks, to the best material about your subject on the Web. For example, one of the links in the 137,000-hit Yahoo search on animal rights led to a Google Directory that, in turn, listed four sites, all sponsored by governmental or academic institutes, which serve as clearinghouses for Web sites about animal rights. One, from the University of British Columbia, provides thirty-four links to relevant and credible sites. Some are appropriate for a college-level essay; some are not. But they're all worth examining.

Since the Web is a new medium and there are very few rules or standard procedures, evaluating Web sites can be a hit-or-miss process. But the categories are the same as those for evaluating works in print: credentials, impartiality, style and tone, and currency.

Credentials

As with print sources, the material's credibility greatly depends on the author's *qualifications.* If the name of the author (or *"owner"*) appears on the site, then you must try to find out about that person's background and credentials and determine his or her relevance to the topic. What else has the owner published?

Does he appear in other writers' bibliographies? Has she any professional experience in a discipline appropriate to this subject? Does the site contain a link to the owner's home page, or is there a section of the site specifically about the owner (often called "About Me")?

Much of the time, you'll find no single author taking responsibility for the site. Instead, there will be a *sponsoring organization,* which will probably include an "About Us" section, describing the group's collective purpose or "mission." If there's no "About" link, then it may be possible to do a Web search for more information about the sponsor. Is the organization commercial or nonprofit? (The "com" and "org" in the URL used to distinguish between the two, but that's no longer the rule.) What's the reason for creating a site about this topic? Is there a political or cultural agenda? If the sponsor is commercial, what's the motive for expending resources on this Web site?

A second element to look for is *documentation.* Appropriate documentation tells you that the author or sponsor understands the basic requirements for presenting academic scholarship; seeing bibliographical references or endnotes gives you some assurance that the information contained in the site is reliable. It's probable that documentation found in Web pages will consist of hyperlinks to other Web sources; you will want to click on some of these, to evaluate the quality of the linked sources and perhaps add them to your bibliography.

Impartiality

You should keep in mind that people and organizations usually create Web sites not to provide a fair, well-balanced account of an issue, but to sell something: a product, a cause, a point of view, a life style. Bias isn't to be avoided on the Web; it's considered a legitimate basis for self-presentation. So you do have to scrutinize what you find, searching for the larger context behind narrow reasoning and imagining rebuttals for one-sided arguments.

As you begin to read a Web page, consider the *nature of the content.* Is it personal opinion? Is it self-serving? Is it advocacy? commercial? ideological? academic? Does the owner apparently have an ax to grind? Does the site present fact or opinion? Or does it present opinion as fact? Are you the target of propaganda for a cause or advertising for a product? Can you tell the difference between the site of a pet food company with a feature on animal welfare, that of an advocacy group organizing a rally against cruelty to animals, and that of a university veterinary department publishing a report on the use of animals in experiments?

Whatever the degree of bias, worthwhile Web material should provide a convincing presentation and reasonable support for its assertions. As you begin to read, consider whether the site has a discernible thesis or point, or whether it was put on the Web purely to indulge the owner's desire for self-revelation. Is there a clear context established for the material? Does the author make an initial statement of intention, purpose, and scope? Many sites are the spatial equivalent of a soundbite. Their authors don't engage in complex analysis and argument. Is there supporting evidence? A logical sequence of ideas or just a series of claims? A convincing level of fact and detail? Does the author anticipate and deal with potential objections to opinions? Is the evidence mostly anecdotal, depending on stories ("It happened to me")? Are examples and anecdotes relevant to the topic?

Don't assume that you should automatically or arbitrarily exclude poorly supported or one-sided Web material (or print sources) from your bibliography. Rather, you should make yourself aware of the flaws in your sources and, if you choose to include them in your essay, compensate for their deficiencies by finding stronger or complementary sources so that your essay will become well balanced and well supported.

Style and Tone

In a free-wheeling medium like the Web, there are few rules about *style* or *tone*. Many sites, particularly home pages developed by individual owners, will be presented informally, as if the writer were delivering a monologue or holding a one-sided conversation. The lack of rigor or purpose suggested by this kind of presentation should raise some doubts as soon as you click on and start reading the site. Is the material clearly *focused* and *coherent*? Is the *tone* dispassionate, or conversational, or hysterical? Is the *language* inflammatory? Overly enthusiastic? Frivolous? Is it full of superlatives? Is the argument presented in neutral language, or are there slurs or innuendoes about those holding opposing views? Does the writer follow the basic rules of grammar? Can the material be summarized or paraphrased?

As with print material, it is helpful to consider the intended *audience*. Web sites frequently target niche audiences. What sort of user does a specific Web page hope to attract? The general public? Then the content may be worth your consideration. Or is it aimed at juveniles? If so, the approach and style are probably too simplistic to be useful for an academic essay. Does the author assume that the reader shares a common religious background or political assumptions? A reader unfamiliar with these beliefs or causes may find the contents hard to understand or accept. Is the sponsor a local group that's appealing to a grassroots audience? The site's purpose and level of detail may be so narrow that it is likely to interest only those who live in that area.

The *appearance of the site* itself can help you to evaluate the content. Is there any logic to its construction? Is it well designed? Easy to use? Or is it sprawling and hard to follow? Does it have a plan or method of organization? If it's a large site, are there links—on the home page and elsewhere—that enable you to go directly to pages that interest you? Are additions and updates integrated into existing material, or left dangling at the end? Are there graphics? Do they help your understanding of the site, or do they distract you?

Currency

In print sources, currency is estimated in decades; in Web sources, it's often a matter of months or even days. If you don't download or print material quickly, you may not have access to that information when you actually need it. The site may have disappeared from the Web. Other sites, however, will linger on even when they have lost their currency. The owners are no longer taking responsibility for regular maintenance and updating. If the subject of your essay is a current issue and you need to find and use up-to-the-minute sources, you should be very careful about checking the date at the end of each Web site. And, whatever the subject, you should note the date of the site's last update and any revisions or modifications, to compare its currency with that of your other sources and, eventually, to include a complete reference to the site in your bibliography.

EVALUATING WEB SOURCES ABOUT ANIMAL RIGHTS

To demonstrate some of these evaluative criteria, let's look at a few of the sixty-three Web sites found in a Copernic search using the keywords "animal rights." As is usually the case, the results list includes several commercial sites selling products totally unrelated to the subject of the search. Most of the others are sponsored by organizations or individuals actively advocating the cause of equal rights for animals and urging the public to join in protesting various instances of "speciesism." Such sites are typically crammed with news stories about animal exploitation, links to like-minded organizations, offers for products and services (often supporting vegetarianism), and invitations to participate in online discussions, attend rallies and events, and register for membership—often requiring fees or contributions—in the common cause. The range of links found in one site includes "Recent Petitions," "The Joy of Adopting an Older Animal," "Featured Shelter of the Month," "Ways to Help Animals without Leaving Your Computer," "Dogs in Heaven," and "Tiny Tim—a Kitten's Story."

The home page of AnimalConcerns.org (Figure 6-1) is typical. Crowded with lists and choices, the site is busy and difficult to navigate. The links and options are all intended to educate the reader about the plight of animals and encourage participation in their defense. One set of links grouped together as "News Headlines" features stories about smuggled exotic animals and Paul McCartney's recent engagement—not especially appropriate for research into the issues surrounding animal rights. A separate group of "in-depth" articles are neither deep nor complex. "Birdie Treats" from *Mothering* magazine and "Milk: Does It Do a Body Good?" appear to be aimed at an intellectually unsophisticated audience. Several of the articles are written by Teresa D'Amico, whose qualifications in this area are nowhere cited. Indeed, although there's a list of "About" links, it's hard to find anything more specific than a generalized

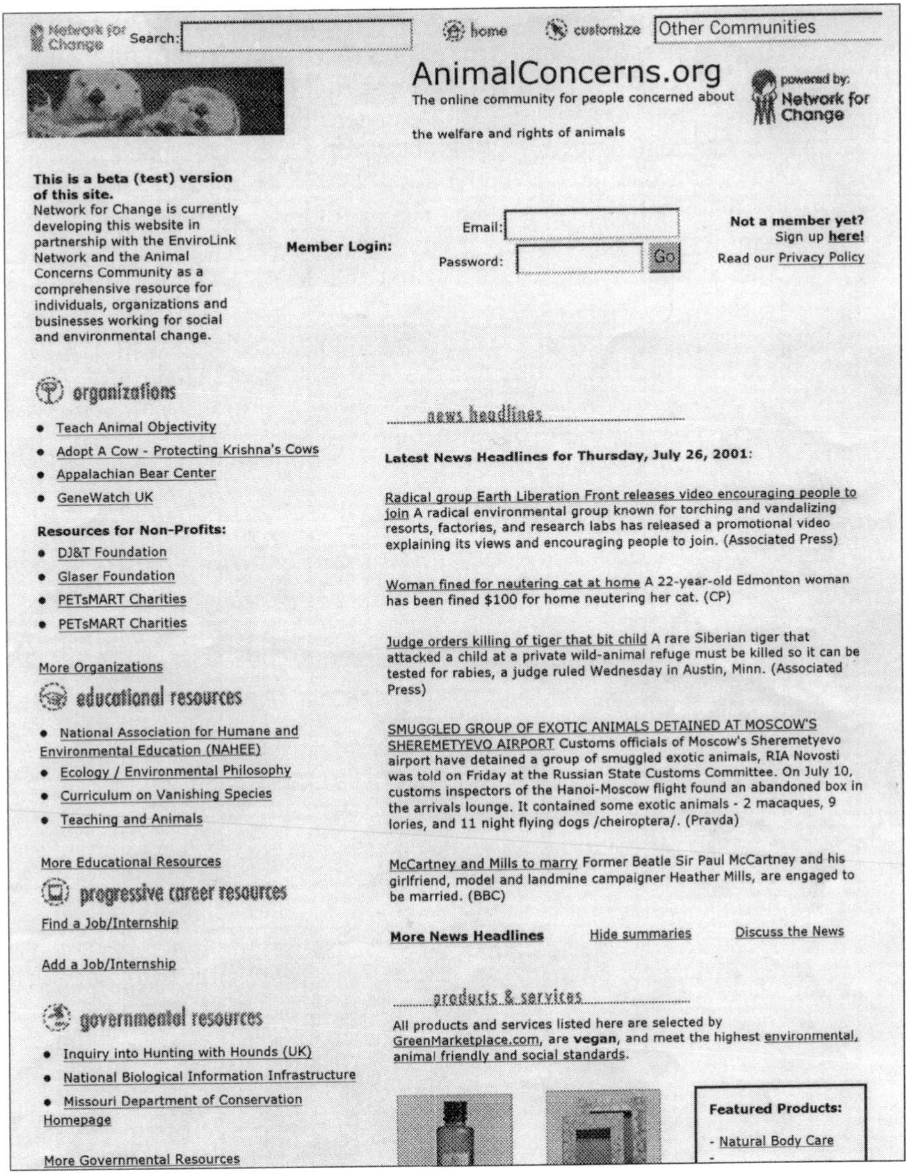

Figure 6-1. AnimalConcerns Community Web Site

manifesto relating to the campaign for animal rights. Such a site may be effective as propaganda but it has little value for the serious researcher.

One of the strengths of AnimalConcerns.org is its emphasis on *local interests*. You're invited to learn about neighborhood polluters and provided with lists of nearby organic farms. As a medium of communication, the Web is particularly suited to this kind of amateur, grassroots appeal. It provides an international pulpit for anyone with a cause, even if the cause itself affects a relatively small number of people. In effect, the Web is serving as a community bulletin board. That's why the "animal rights" search result includes so many sites devoted to the activities of local groups. Students for Ethical Animal Treatment, for example, is the home page for a student group at Truman State University; it provides details of fund-raising bake sales and vegan potluck suppers. Sites like these, while admirable as grassroots operations, are little more than a distraction for researchers looking for more broadly based information.

Animal rights is a provocative topic that lends itself to a hard sell and offers no amnesty to opposing views. In fact, there are very few sites dealing with this issue that take a neutral stance. What can vary is the tone in which the propaganda is presented. Contrast, for example, the presentation of Americans for Medical Progress (AMP) (Figure 6-2) and the Stop Animal Abuse site (Figure 6-3). The first is a stark page featuring a relatively brief salvo condemning the

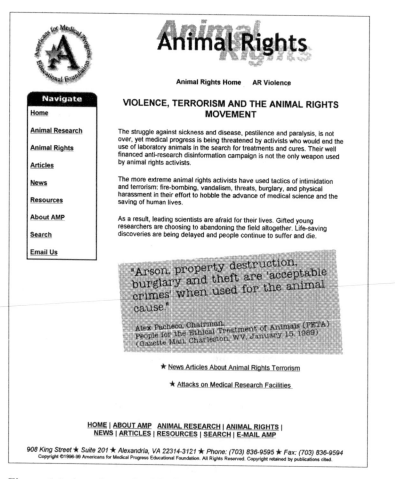

Figure 6-2. Americans for Medical Progress Web Site

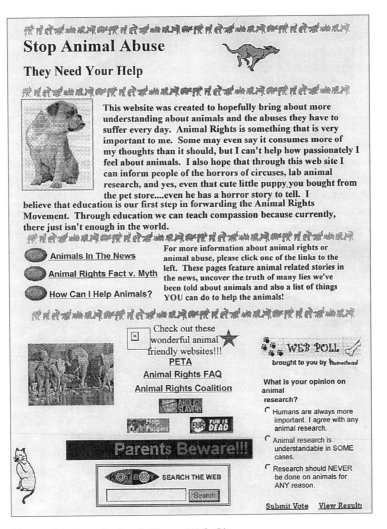

Figure 6-3. Stop Animal Abuse Web Site

animal rights movement for resorting to violent tactics in its efforts to halt the use of animals in medical research. The language is strong and effective. The centerpiece is an inflammatory quotation from the leader of an animal rights organization that is left to speak for itself. Are violent actions appropriate in defense of a good cause? In defense of *this* cause? If you intend to make this issue the focus of your research, you might gain some helpful material by clicking on the links provided on this page—as long as you remain aware of the underlying bias and make an effort to balance your presentation.

Before going further, you should also click on the link About AMP to find out more about the sponsoring organization. It's reassuring that the sponsors provide an address and phone number at the bottom of the home page (many sites do not) and disquieting that they have apparently not updated the site in some time (the copyright is limited to 1996–99). The site's credibility is enhanced by a listing of the Board of Directors and National Advisory Council that includes several eminent names in the health professions; but there are also several representatives of the pharmaceutical industry, which stands to benefit a great deal from continuing to use animals in developing new drugs. On balance, this is a site that merits some cautious exploration.

No information at all is provided about the owner of the Stop Animal Abuse site. The search feature is managed by HotBot; the Web poll is sponsored by Homestead; but the writer remains anonymous. The site contains a very personal, heartfelt account of one person's commitment to the cause. Both tone and language are gushing; the structure—paragraph and Web site—is rambling; the content is trivial. There is nothing here that is worth quoting, or paraphrasing, or summarizing—nothing here that is suitable for inclusion in a research essay.

Some Web sites fail to identify the author; others do so unconvincingly. Brian Carnell at Animalrights.net tells us that his site "is simply my daily web log chronicling things that amaze, annoy and/or puzzle me." Stephen Ronan's credentials for establishing a list of animal rights links on the site of the WWW Virtual Library are presented as follows: "Stephen Ronan lives in the USA. His companions of other species are, for the most part, rabbits."

In contrast, Chris MacDonald, who prepared a comparable list of links for the Center for Applied Ethics, provides a two-page biography (plus picture) that includes his academic qualifications, professional experience, research, and Web sites. Whose links are likely to inspire more confidence, Ronan's or MacDonald's? It's significant that the Center for Applied Ethics is affiliated with the University of British Columbia, while the WWW Virtual Library is described as "the oldest catalog of the web . . . run by a loose confederation of volunteers" who develop Web sites in their particular areas of expertise. The description includes an offer to anyone who's interested to prepare a site for the Virtual Library—no credentials requested or apparently required. It's this casual approach to competency that makes research on the Web so risky.

Without a doubt, it takes time and patience to evaluate Web sources. You have to inspect each site to make sure it's reliable before downloading it. Is it authoritative? Is it at an appropriate level? Will it make a contribution to your essay? And however scrupulous you may be about selecting Web sources, your research can't stop there.

> *If you want your essay to be successful and receive a commensurate grade, don't get all or even most of your sources from the Internet.*

Many important authors still publish their work only in traditional print forms. If you don't include these sources in your research, your essay will lack balance and completeness.

How will your instructor realize that your research is exclusively from the Web? In "How the Web Destroys the Quality of Students' Research Papers," Professor David Rothenberg says that "it's easy to spot a research paper that is based primarily on information collected from the Web," partly because no books are included in the bibliography. Most disturbing to Professor Rothenberg is the mindlessness of the Web research process:

> You toss a query to the machine, wait a few minutes, and suddenly a lot of possible sources of information appear on your screen. Instead of books that you have to check out of the library, read carefully, understand, synthesize and then tactfully excerpt, these sources are quips, blips, pictures, and short summaries that may be downloaded magically to the dorm-room computer screen. Fabulous! How simple! The only problem is that a paper consisting of summaries of summaries is bound to be fragmented and superficial, and to demonstrate more of a random montage than an ability to sustain an argument through 10 to 15 double-spaced pages.

There are no shortcuts to thorough research. Use the Internet as you would use any tool available to you, but try to resist its facile charms.

INTEGRATING SOURCES

So far, we've been looking at ways to evaluate sources one by one, making sure that each is worth including in your research. But sources won't appear in your essay one at a time, each in splendid isolation. They must work well together. They must be *compatible*.

Authors write for different audiences. Their work varies in tone, in style, in level of detail. As we've seen, the sources that you find on the Web or in the library may have nothing at all in common but their subject. Before you can decide which ones belong together in your essay, you need to be able to describe them. As you glance through a book, or an article, or Web material, ask yourself:

- Does the content seem primarily theoretical or practical?
- How often does the author offer concrete evidence to support conclusions? What kind of evidence? Facts? Examples? Anecdotes? Documentation?
- Does the author's thesis depend on a series of broad propositions or arguments, linked together into an argument?
- What is the scope of the work? Does it include many aspects of your broad subject, or does it focus on one?
- How abstract or technical is the language? Do you have difficulty understanding the sentences or following the argument?

In the end, the sources that you include in your essay should be at roughly the same *level of difficulty*. This does not mean that they should be identical: the same range of ideas, the same length, the same style and depth of evidence. But it does mean you should be able to move from one to the other easily as you write about them; you should be able to integrate them into your own approach to the subject.

Let's look at three different sources—all books—dealing with the subject of animal rights:

1. The first is an extended consideration of the arguments for and against strict enforcement of animal rights that relies heavily on philosophical abstractions to make its points; the author supports the use of animals in medical experiments.

2. The second recounts the history of the animal rights movement, taking a neutral stance. The authors rely on concrete evidence to demonstrate that animal rights campaigners are often the products of their culture.

3. The third is a sociological study of animal rights activists and their motivations. The text relies heavily on interview transcripts.

Here are excerpts from these three sources:

1. A number of authors [have] contributed to an image of humans as the great despoilers, the beings who are always out of place and can do nothing right in the natural world. Some paint an idyllic and completely unrealistic picture of pristine, peaceful nature, beyond our blundering rapacious hands. Others exclaim despairingly that the world would be a better place without humans. . . . What these ideas have in common is a nostalgia for simpler times and a veiled lament for a lost Edenic paradise. In fact, guilt and the need for repentance through self-punishment pervade much contemporary writing on the environment and our relationship to animals. The fable of the Fall of Man has now acquired a secular guise, and a group of righteous pop environmental philosophers and animal liberationists are the new self-appointed apostles of redemption.

MICHAEL ALLEN FOX, from *The Case for Animal Experimentation: An Evolutionary and Ethical Perspective*

2. The meat and food industry has inadvertently contributed to the anthropomorphic intuitions that drive animal protection demands. At least since Charlie the Tuna, food commercials have thoroughly personified their own products. In one commercial, two anthropomorphic cows shoot at a Lea and Perrins bottle, "the steak sauce only a cow could hate." The only speaking parts in an ad for Roy Rogers' chicken club sandwich belong to two fast-talking goldfish. Talking chickens, fish, and other animals seem clever, but they also remind sensitive viewers of the origins of their food.

JAMES M. JASPER and DOROTHY NELKIN, from *The Animal Rights Crusade: The Growth of a Moral Protest*

3. A quietly spoken public servant, Rhett decided some years ago to take the step to animal rights activism. He claims it was the inconsistency in our treatment of animals that was the catalyst for his activism and the cause of some tension in his personal relationships:

> But I can tell you that when I was a child, I was presented with an inconsistency which always stuck in my mind. And that was that my father would never eat fowl, and at Christmas time he would always have a chop or something like that. And the reason was that when he was a child, his father brought home some chickens. The kids had made pets of them, and then they were served up for Christmas dinner. He was so upset that he refused to participate in the killing of chooks [young birds]. . . . This was when I was quite young, and I could see that he was being inconsistent, but I'm grateful for the inconsistency because if I hadn't had that example of someone who was sensitive, I mean, who knows? It might have taken me ten more years or something. I don't know.
>
> LYLE MUNRO, from *Compassionate Beasts:*
> *The Quest for Animal Rights*

Can these three sources be integrated into the same essay? They aren't equivalent; in many ways, they aren't even similar. But each is relevant and interesting in its own way. What you *don't* want to do is to plunk down excerpts from these three sources side by side, in adjoining sentences. Remember that your sources are your evidence. You use them to illustrate *your* ideas, your understanding of the issues involved in the animal rights movement.

The excerpt from Fox is notably abstract. He hardly touches on the issues of animal exploitation, but rather tries to interpret the significance of this growing impulse to identify with the more natural environment represented by animals. Jasper and Nelkin are more concerned with practical cause-and-effect: advertising strategies portraying animals as if they were human have encouraged people to identify with the animal rights movement. It's easy to follow the examples of Charlie the Tuna and the Roy Rogers goldfish. Rhett's personal experiences are of a very different order. He doesn't have a thesis to prove; he doesn't provide you with a topic sentence that shows you where this excerpt might be placed in your essay. It's up to you to interpret his musings and determine how—or whether—they fit in with the other sources.

How you use these three sources depends on the kind of essay you intend to write. Will your thesis be *abstract*? If you intend to emphasize the political and philosophical premises underlying this issue—do animals have the same rights that humans do?—then you'll focus your attention on Fox's book, summarizing his arguments and, in the process, figuring out what you really believe. In this way, you determine your research priorities. As you develop your thesis, you'll go on to read other books like Fox's and find many of the same ideas with new arguments and new conclusions. You'll notice that authors writing on this abstract level tend to be familiar with each other's theories and argue with each other on paper. The same names will appear again and again. Your essay will become one more voice in an ongoing dialogue.

Or are you planning a more *practical* thesis? You might be more interested in the relatively rapid emergence of this movement. Why has animal rights become such a hot issue? Is it our affluence that enables us to express concern about the plight of animals? Is it our increasing urbanization? Or is it the absence of other compelling causes? This thesis would be more "popular" in its approach to the subject and would require less rigorous sources. That doesn't diminish its value for your essay. A popularization is no more than a simplification of a difficult subject. In a sense, a college research essay has to be "popular" since it serves as evidence of a student's understanding of the subject, not as a contribution to scholarly knowledge. Your thesis would be supported by secondary sources like Jasper and Nelkin or by primary sources like the evidence of activists like Rhett.

As you develop your thesis and decide whether or not to take the popular approach, remember to consider the level of your course. In an introductory course, you are expected only to grasp the broad concepts that are basic to the discipline; so your instructor will probably not want you to go out of your depth in hunting scholarly sources for your essay. On the other hand, in an advanced course, you are preparing to do your own research; so you need to demonstrate your understanding of the work of others as well as the methods that are commonly used in that field. In an advanced course, the popular approach can be regarded as superficial.

What's crucial is that you *include in your bibliography only sources that you yourself understand*. If you come across a difficult source that seems too important to leave out, do consult your instructor, or a librarian, or the staff of the writing center on your campus. But never cite sources whose writing makes no sense to you, no matter how eminent and qualified these authorities may be.

Another consideration is the assigned length of your essay. If you're writing fewer than ten pages, you would be wise to limit your sources to those that blend well together because they are of the same order of difficulty. The writers don't have to agree with each other, but their scope and approach should be roughly equivalent. But in a longer essay of ten pages or more, you'll have an opportunity for leisurely development, and you can position different kinds of sources in different parts of the essay, each where it is most appropriate and where it will have the most convincing effect.

There is actually a common theme that runs through the three excerpts on animal rights. Fox writes about our generalized feelings of guilt for having plundered our natural heritage; Jasper and Nelkin imply that our anthropomorphic identification with cartoon animals has made us into guilty vegetarians; and Munro's Rhett describes his father's ambivalence about eating chicken, which brings him close to guilt by association. All three excerpts support the following paragraph, which analyzes one of the more complex motivations underlying the animal rights movement. (Note that, within a formal research essay, this paragraph would necessarily contain a citation for each source; the process of documentation will be explained in Chapter 8.)

> Animal rights activists pursue their cause with great passion and intensity, as if the fate of the Earth depended on the success of their mission. They seem to be trying to compensate for or even undo all the harm that man has done to the natural environment and particularly to its living creatures. In Fox's view, their yearning to return to the Garden of Eden is linked to a sense of guilt and a compulsion to atone for our culture's crimes against nature. He refers, somewhat contemptuously, to a "nostalgia for simpler times" that seems unrealistic and sentimental. Fox seems to be saying that we wallow too easily in a kind of Disneyland view of animals. Jasper and Nelkin support that view when they describe the anthropomorphic world of commercials in which Charlie the Tuna and the Roy Rogers goldfish become our friends. It's easy to read that kind of sentimentality into the personal experience of Rhett, the animal rights activist, whose father never got over the guilt of eating the chickens that had been his pets.

You will have noticed that this paragraph is essentially negative about the animal rights movement, reflecting Fox's bias. (Indeed, the paragraph relies heavily on Fox's ideas, which makes sense since he offers more of them than the other authors do.) Depending on your chosen thesis, you could build on the implication that animal rights is little more than sentimental claptrap, supplying further evidence, or you could rebut Fox's point, arguing that Rhett and his father are displaying an admirable sensitivity to the needs of living creatures. Where you take these ideas is up to you; it's your essay.

Guidelines for Choosing Sources

As you choose sources for your essay, consider the following:

- the author's background and qualifications to write on that subject;
- the date of the work, whether it is a primary or secondary source, and (if secondary) whether its information is still timely;
- the scope of the work and the extent to which it deals with your topic;
- the depth of detail, the amount and kind of evidence presented, the documentation of sources, and the level of analysis and theory;
- the degree to which you understand and feel comfortable with the author's language and style; and
- the way in which possible sources could be used together in your essay.

EXERCISE 20: EVALUATING INTERNET SOURCES

The following passages have been excerpted from the first few frames of Web sites found in an advanced Google search using the keywords "Battle of Wounded Knee" NOT "1973." (The search was focused on the 1890 battle, rather than the demonstration that took place at the same site in 1973.) The purpose of the search was to compile a preliminary bibliography for an essay examining the extent to which the U.S. government carried out an aggressive policy of extermination against Native Americans in the nineteenth century. The Web material in this exercise was not chosen at random but represents some of the typical noncommercial sites found in the search. The excerpts have not been edited.

Read through the eight passages. Making allowances for repetition, examine the way in which each writer presents information about the Battle of Wounded Knee, paying special attention to tone and style. Consider the probable audience for which each site was intended. Then decide which sites you would read through to the end and which ones, if any, you would be likely to include in a preliminary bibliography for a 10- to 12-page essay assigned in an introductory level course.

1. After Sitting Bull's death, Big Foot feared for the safety of his band, which consisted in large part of widows of the Plains wars and their children. Big Foot himself had been placed on the list of "fomenters of disturbances," and his arrest had been ordered. He led his band toward Pine Ridge, hoping for the protection of Red Cloud. However, he fell ill from pneumonia on the trip and was forced to travel in the back of a wagon. As they neared Porcupine Creek on December 28, the band saw 4 troops of cavalry approaching. A white flag was immediately run up over Big Foot's wagon. When the two groups met, Big Foot raised up from his bed of blankets to greet Major Samuel Whitside of the Seventh Cavalry. His blankets were stained with blood and blood dripped from his nose as he spoke.

   Whitside informed him of his orders to take the band to their camp on Wounded Knee Creek. Big Foot replied that they were going that way, to Pine Ridge. The major wanted to disarm the Indians right then but was dissuaded by his scout John Shangreau, in order to avoid a fight on the spot. They agreed to wait to undertake this until they reached camp. Then, in a moment of sympathy, the major ordered his army ambulance brought forward to accept the ill Minneconjou chief, providing a warmer and more comfortable ride. They then proceeded toward the camp at Wounded Knee Creek, led by two cavalry troops with the other two troops bringing up the rear with their Hotchkiss guns. They reached the camp at twilight.

2. The events at Wounded Knee (South Dakota) on December 29, 1890, cannot be understood unless the previous 400 years of European occupation of the *New World* are taken into consideration. As Dee Brown has pointed out in *Bury My Heart at Wounded Knee* (pp. 1–2):

"'So tractable, so peaceable, are these people,' Columbus wrote to the King and Queen of Spain [referring to the Tainos on the island of San Salvador, so was named by Columbus], 'that I swear to your Majesties there is not in the world a better nation. They love their neighbors as themselves, and their discourse is ever sweet and gentle, and accompanied with a smile; and though it is true that they are naked, yet their manners are decorous and praiseworthy.'

"All this, of course, was taken as a sign of weakness, if not heathenism, and Columbus being a righteous European was convinced the people should be 'made to work, sow and do all that is necessary and to *adopt our ways.*' Over the next four centuries (1492–1890) several million Europeans and their descendants undertook to enforce their ways upon the people of the New World."

Many accounts (from both sides: US Army and Lakota) of this shameful episode exist, and many of those can be found on the Internet. The following is a brief, edited description (from *The Great Chiefs* volume of Time-Life's *The Old West* series) of events. Links to further resources and descriptions follow.

3. Wounded Knee, A Wound That Won't Heal Did the Army Attempt To Coverup the Massacre of Prisoners of War?

Historical reference material from:
The Official Bulletin National Indian War Veterans U.S.A. Section One, Section Two, Section Three and Section Four.

The Medals of Wounded Knee

Medals of dis-Honor

. . . more Medals of dis-Honor

Medals of dis-Honor Campaign
An email campaign has been initiated so as to force the U.S. Government to rescind the twenty medals of dis-Honor awarded participants in the Massacre at Wounded Knee. Your help is solicited . . . an input form is provided for your convenience

Lieutenant Bascom Gets His Due..

Rescindment Petition Comments

Senator McCain Responds to the Rescindment Petition

My Response to McCain

Wokiksuye Canpe Opi . . . a site dedicated to rescindment of the "medals of dis-Honor."

4. Eyewitness to a Massacre

Philip Wells was a mixed-blood Sioux who served as an interpreter for the Army. He later recounted what he saw that Monday morning:

"I was interpreting for General Forsyth *(Forsyth was actually a colonel)* just before the battle of Wounded Knee, December 29, 1890. The captured Indians had been ordered to give up their arms, but Big Foot replied that his people had no arms. Forsyth said to me, 'Tell Big Foot he says the Indians have no arms, yet yesterday they were well armed when they surrendered. He is deceiving me. Tell him he need have no fear in giving up his arms, as I wish to treat him kindly.' Big Foot replied, 'They have no guns, except such as you have found.' Forsyth declared, 'You are lying to me in return for my kindness.'"

5. The round up of the Lakota was in response to the growing fear and ignorance on the part of the US Govt. The white people did not know about the culture, beliefs, or lives of the Lakota and saw them as a threat to the society they were trying to preserve: the white society. The Lakota were seen as outsiders; the "other" in a world where a person's looks and background determined who belonged here. Through much of American history, where a person was born also determined if they belonged. Ironically, the Native Americans were here on this land first, but were treated as though they were visitors. Their assumption was that because they look different or act different, they are not the same; they are not Americans. The white people refused to recognize the Lakota's right to the land and did everything in their power to remove them. This ignorance led to violence in an obvious act of proving power and control.

Col. James W. Forsyth ordered the Sioux people to be disarmed. A shot was fired and the fighting ensued. The federal troops fired on the Lakota with rifles and powerful, rapid-shooting Hotchkiss guns. Sioux casualties totaled 153 dead and 44 wounded, half of whom were unarmed women and children. Survivors were pursued and butchered by US troops. Cavalry losses totaled 25 dead and 39 wounded. Charges were brought against Col. Forsyth for his part in the bloodshed, but a court of inquiry exonerated him.

At the time, and continually after, people regarded the confrontation as a massacre. This terrible blow to the Lakota people proved to break down their strength in fighting back. To subsequent generations of Indians, it "symbolized the injustices and degradations inflicted on them by the US government" (Robert Utley). It later served as an inspiration for the 1973 occupation at Wounded Knee.

We must never forget this moment in US history of the horrific destruction of human life and liberty. For many, the picture of US history is filled with tales of brave rebels, fighting for a belief in equality, such as the ideals which started and founded the nation. However, not many recognize the hypocritical actions of the nation which went against this idea of equality. This is just another example where the question of "Who belongs?" and "Who has a right to 'American' liberties?" is tested. The Lakota were never allowed a place in the nation, forced to give up their land and suffered immensely in loss of lives and rights. The Wounded Knee massacre serves as a reminder to a time when those people seen as "foreigners" were exterminated and refused their rights as Americans.

6. No one knows what caused the disturbance, no one claims the first shot, the Wounded Knee Massacre began fiercely with the Hotchkiss guns raining fragmentation shells into the village at a combined rate of 200 or more rounds a minute. The 500 well armed Cavalry Troopers were well positioned using crossing fire to methodically carry out what is known as the Wounded Knee Massacre.

   Almost immediately most of the Sioux Indian men were killed. A few Sioux Indians mustered enough strength barehanded to kill 29 soldiers and wound 39 more. The bravery of these people was to no avail for as long as an Indian moved, the guns kept firing. Unarmed Sioux Indian Women and children were Mercilessly Massacred. A few ran as far as three miles only to be chased by the long knives of the Cavalry and put to death.

   Of the original 350 Indians one estimate stated that only 50 survived. Almost all historical statistics report over 200 Indians being killed on that day but government figures only reported the Indian dead as 64 men, 44 women and girls, and 18 babies. All of the bodies were buried in one communal grave.

   If the Battle of the Little Big Horn had been the beginning of the end, Wounded Knee was the finale for the Sioux Indians. This was the last major engagement in American history between the Plains Indians and the U. S. Army. Gone was the Indian dream, pride and spirit.

7. The James W. Forsyth Papers document the career of a nineteenth-century military officer in the American West and, in particular, his service in the Wounded Knee campaign. The collection spans the dates 1865–1932, but the bulk of the material falls in the period 1870–98.

   The collection is arranged in six series with oversize material housed at the end. Series I, Correspondence, contains letters to and from Forsyth arranged chronologically with two letterpress copybooks of similar material. Series II, Wounded Knee Papers, consists of printed papers and manuscripts documenting the actions taken on December 29 and 30, 1891. Series III, Military Papers, contains documents by and about James W. Forsyth, his son-in-law, son, and other military officers. Carte-de-visites and cabinet photographs collected by Forsyth can be found in Series IV, Photographs. Series V, Forsyth Family Papers, consists of a few items belonging to Forsyth's two daughters as well as personal papers of James W. Forsyth. Series VI, Dennison Family Papers, contains financial receipts of Governor William Dennison's family (James W. Forsyth's in-laws) and a book belonging to the governor.

8. "Sometimes dreams are wiser than waking," says Black Elk, Oglala Sioux Indian who took part in the Ghost Dance Religion during the late 19th century. The Wounded Knee epidemic took place in December 29, 1890 between the U.S. government and the Sioux Indians in South Dakota. Primarily, the outbreak occurred at Wounded Knee in part result of the growing support of the Ghost Dance Religion. Army leaders feared the religion would lead to an Indian uprising and called for troops to be sent to keep things under control. Thus, the hostilities that drug out between the U.S. government and the Sioux Indians in South Dakota are an important historical event that unfolded in U.S. western history. When reviewing the Wounded Knee battle, it is of utmost importance for various teachers who want to gain more knowledge of this epidemic that took place to fully understand insights about when, where, what, and why this battle occurred in 1890 in South Dakota. Furthermore, the Sioux Ghost Dance Religion played a crucial role in "triggering" the hostilities and events that lead up to the Wounded Knee battle.

First, before going into depth about the history of Wounded Knee Creek battle, it is important to understand the need for history. Why do we study and need to know history? Well, David E. Kyvig and Myron A. Marty believe history is an essential part of human development: We all need to know who we are, how we have become what we are, and how to cope with a variety of situations in order to conduct our own lives successfully. We also need to know what to expect from people and institutions around us. Organizations and communities require the same self understanding in order to function satisfactorily. For individuals and groups alike, experience produces a self-image and a basis for deciding how to behave, manage problems, and plan ahead. We remember sometimes accurately, sometimes not-what occurred, the causes of certain responses or changes, and learn reactions to different circumstances. These memories, positive and negative, help determine our actions.

EXERCISE 21: CHOOSING INTERNET SOURCES

The following list of twenty-six Web sites has been compiled from searches on Google and Copernic using the keywords "TV Violence." Assume that you are preparing a preliminary bibliography for an essay examining the links between violence on television and violent crimes in American schools. Review the list of Web sites and choose those sites that you would definitely want to explore. Be prepared to give your reasons for including or excluding each site.

Your instructor may ask you to click on some or all of the sites before you do your ranking. If many of the sites are no longer being maintained, you may be asked to do a new search on the same topic, choosing twenty-six sites (preferably noncommercial) and indicating those that, in your opinion, seem relevant and reliable.

1. Violence as a Public Health Problem
   http://www.hula.net/~hulaboy/3_stv.htm
   Argues forcefully that the children most at risk for the aggressive behavioral effects of media violence are also very possibly those that are at the greatest risk for delinquency due to parental behavior.

2. Sociology and Philosophy Essays: TV & Violence
   http://www.magicdragon.com/EmeraldCity/Nonfiction/socphil.html
   Essays by Jonathan Vos Post, on various topics, including one on the correlation between television and violence.

3. APA HelpCenter: Warning Signs of TV Violence
   http://helping.apa.org/warningsigns
   The American Psychological Association and MTV team up to get important information to the nation's youth about warning signs of violent behavior, including violence in schools.

4. Parents Should 'Tune Out' TV Violence
   http://www.newstimes.com/archive96/nov1396/rge.htm
   Attorney General Richard Blumenthal in Hartford Conn joined his counterparts across the country in asking parents to monitor the amount of television their children watch and tune out violent ones.

5. Welcome to the Lion & Lamb Project!
   http://www.lionlamb.org/
   The Lion & Lamb Project is engaged in the most basic type of prevention work: helping parents teach their young children that violence is not an option.

6. Children and television violence
   http://www. abelard.org/tv/tv.htm
   Abelard's front page. Violence on television affects children negatively, according to psychological research.

7. National Television Violence Study
   http://www.ccsp.ucsb.edu/ntvs.htm
   The National Television Violence Study is the largest ongoing scientific study of television violence ever undertaken. Sponsored by the University of California at Santa Barbara.

8. Television Violence: A Review of the Effects on Children of Different Ages
   www.media-awareness.ca/eng/med/home/resource/tvviorp.htm
   This 70-page report was prepared by Wendy L. Josephson, Ph.D. for the Department of Canadian Heritage, February 1995.

9. Effects of Television Violence on Memory for Commercials
   www.apa.org/journals/xap/xap44291.html
   Brad J. Bushman Department of Psychology Iowa State University
   An article from the *Journal of Experimental Psychology* describing a controlled experiment.

10. The UCLA Television Violence Report 1996
    http://ccp.ucla.edu/Webreport95/history.htm

Congressional interest in television violence began in 1954 with the creation of a Senate Subcommittee to Investigate Juvenile Delinquency

11. FCC Debate On Kids TV
    http://www.cep.org/
    What are the key issues surround [sic] the FCC's debate on kids TV? Stop here for review and analysis of key issues, quotations, events, and ideas in the battle for education on the airways. Source: Center for Educational Priorities.

12. National Coalition on TV Violence
    http://www.nctvv.org/
    Links and information resources on a variety of topics including community action, countermeasures, background information on rating systems and censorship issues.

13. UNESCO International Clearing House on Children and Violence on the Screen
    http://www.nordicom.gu.se/unesco.html
    The Clearinghouse is to contribute to and effectivize knowledge on children, young people and media violence, seen in the perspective of the UN Convention on the Rights of the Child. Our prime task is to make new knowledge and data known to prospective users all over the world.

14. Information Packet: Violence and the Media
    http://interact.uoregon.edu/MediaLit/JCP/violence.html
    Includes: Video Resources, Media Violence and Media Literacy, Bibliography: Children and Media, and Bibliography: Violence and Media. Source: Jesuit Communication Project, Toronto.

15. Impact of Television Violence
    http://www.ksu.edu/humec/impact.htm
    Questions about the effects of television violence have existed since the earliest days of this medium. Source: John P. Murray, Kansas State University.

16. Violence on Television
    http://www.sofcom.com.au/TV/violence.html
    Violent programs on television lead to aggressive behavior by children and teenagers who watch those programs. This article on Australia's #1 online television guide explores what students and parents can do. Source: American Psychological Association.

17. Stand Up for Buffy
    http://www.scoobygang.com/Standup/stframe.html
    Fans of "Buffy the Vampire Slayer" band together to protest the postponement of the season finale due to supposed concerns about its violent content.

18. Children and TV Violence
    http://www.parenthoodweb.com/articles/phw247.htm
    Children and TV Violence article from ParenthoodWeb.

19. Does TV Kill?
http://www.pbs.org/wgbh/pages/frontline/teach/tvkillguide.html
PBS Study guide to the Frontline production of "Does TV Kill?"

20. The Effects of Electronic Media On A Developing Brain
http://interact.uoregon.edu/MediaLit/FA/MLArticleFolder/effects. html
Screenagers emotionally understand electronic media in ways that adults
don't—as a viral [sic] replicating cultural reality, instead of as a mere com-
municator of events. Source: Robert Sylwester, University of Oregon.
Linked to the Media Literacy Online Project at the University of Oregon.

21. Children and Television Violence
http://www.allsands.com/Kids/childtelevision_twd_gn.htm
An essay on television violence and children. Copyright by Pagewise.

22. TV Violence and Young People
http://www.vicnet.net.au:80/vicnet/health/TVViolencefactsheet.html
Young people in Australia watch an average of three to four hours of television daily. Television can be a powerful influence in developing value
systems and shaping behavior. Unfortunately, much of today's television
programming is violent. Source: Centre for Adolescent Health.

23. Does TV Violence Harm Youth?
http://wildcat.arizona.edu/~wildcat/papers/old-wildcats/fall94/
September/September1,1994/02_2_m.html
The disruptive viewings, of violence and carnage on television, can eventually take a toll on a person and the way they view life someday.

24. Telecommunications Act of 1996
ftp://ftp.loc.gov/pub/thomas/c104/s652.enr.txt
Full text of the Telecommunications Law is available via FTP. Source: Pub
Docs US Congress.

25. Violence In The Media
http://www.duke.edu/~cars/vmedia.html
A personal media violence page, dedicated to bringing together various resources which can be used to study media violence. Linked to the Institute
on Media Violence at Duke University.

26. Violent Media is Good for Kids
http://www.motherjones.com/reality_check/violent_media.html
Author Gerard Jones argues that violence in videogames and other media
give [sic] children a tool to master their rage.

EXERCISE 22: EVALUATING SOURCES

Each of the following passages has been extracted from an article, Web site, or
book on the general subject of *fast food*. Most of these excerpts deal with the experience of eating at restaurants like McDonald's.

A. Carefully examine the distinctive way in which each passage presents its information, noting especially:

- the amount and kind of evidence that is cited
- the expectations of the reader's knowledge and understanding
- the relative emphasis on generalizations and abstract thinking
- the characteristic tone and vocabulary
- the date of publication

B. Take into consideration what you may already know about some of these periodicals, books, or Web sites and the audience for each. Then decide how—or whether—you would use these sources together in a single research essay exploring fast food as a reflection of American culture.

C. Write a thesis for such an essay, and then decide which sources you would definitely use in writing your essay. Be prepared to justify your choice.

1. The cafeteria, an American contribution to the restaurant's development, originated in San Francisco during the 1849 gold rush. Featuring self-service, it offers a wide variety of foods displayed on counters. The customer makes his selections, paying for each item as he chooses it or paying for the entire meal at the end of the line. Other types of quick-eating places originating in the United States are the drugstore counter, serving sandwiches or other snacks; the lunch counter, where the diner is served a limited quick-order menu at the counter; and the drive-in, "drive-thru," or drive-up restaurant, where patrons are served in their automobiles. So-called *fast-food restaurants,* usually operated in chains or as franchises and heavily advertised, offer limited menus—typically comprising hamburgers, hot dogs, fried chicken, or pizza and their complements—and also offer speed, convenience, and familiarity to diners who may eat in the restaurant or take their food home. Among fast-food names that have become widely known are White Castle (one of the first, originating in Wichita, Kan., in 1921), McDonald's (which grew from one establishment in Des Plaines, Ill., in 1955 to more than 15,000 internationally within 40 years), Kentucky Fried Chicken (founded in 1956), and Pizza Hut (1958). Many school, work, and institutional facilities provide space for coin-operated vending machines that offer snacks and beverages. . . .

In many modern restaurants, customers now prefer informal but pleasant atmosphere and fast service. The number of dishes available, and the elaborateness of their preparation, has been increasingly curtailed as labor costs have risen and the availability of skilled labor decreased. The trend is toward such efficient operations as fast-food restaurants, snack bars, and coffee shops. The trend in elegant and expensive restaurants is toward smaller rooms and intimate atmosphere, with authentic, highly specialized and limited menus.

from "American Contributions to Restaurant Development,"
Encyclopedia Britannica, britannica.com

2. Of course, fast-food and national restaurant chains like Krispy Kreme that serve
   it have long been the object of criticism by nutritionists and dietitians. Despite
   the attention, however, fast-food companies, most of them publicly owned and
   sprinkled into the stock portfolios of many striving Americans (including mine
   and perhaps yours), have grown more aggressive in their targeting of poor inner-city communities. One of every four hamburgers sold by the good folks at
   McDonald's, for example, is now purchased by inner-city consumers who, disproportionately, are young black men.

      In fact, it was the poor, and their increasing need for cheap meals consumed
   outside the home, that fueled the development of what may well be the most
   important fast-food innovation of the past twenty years, the sales gimmick known
   as "supersizing." At my local McDonald's, located in a lower-middle-income area
   of Pasadena, California, the supersize bacchanal goes into high gear at about five
   P.M., when the various urban caballeros, drywalleros, and jardineros get off work
   and head for a quick bite. Mixed in is a sizable element of young black kids traveling between school and home, their economic status apparent by the fact that
   they've walked instead of driven. Customers are cheerfully encouraged to "supersize your meal!" by signs saying, "If we don't recommend a supersize, the
   supersize is free!" For an extra seventy-nine cents, a kid ordering a cheeseburger,
   small fries, and a small Coke will get said cheeseburger plus a supersize Coke
   (42 fluid ounces versus 16, with free refills) and a supersize order of french fries
   (more than double the weight of a regular order). Suffice it to say that zconsump-
   tion of said meals is fast and, in almost every instance I observed, very complete.

      But what, metabolically speaking, has taken place? The total caloric content
   of the meal has been jacked up from 680 calories to more than 1,340 calories.
   According to the very generous U.S. dietary guidelines, 1,340 calories represent more than half of a teenager's recommended daily caloric consumption,
   and the added calories themselves are protein-poor but fat- and carbohydrate-
   rich. Completing this jumbo dietetic horror is the fact that the easy availability
   of such huge meals arrives in the same years in which physical activity among
   teenage boys and girls drops by about half.

                                        GREG CRITSER, from "Let Them Eat Fat,"
                                                   Harper's Magazine (3/1/00)

3. An international coalition of Greek Communists, animal rightsers, farmers,
   unions, affluent anarchists, left-wing intellectuals, right-wing nationalists, Luddites, Chinese Communists, radical Pakistani Muslims, parochial separatists, and
   malcontents of a thousand other varieties have all declared one restaurant chain
   to be the locus of evil in the modem world. And yet that same chain is so popular it manages to open a new store somewhere in the world every 17 hours.
   Clearly, there is a conflict of visions here.

      To be sure, a big part of it is that "anti-McDonald's" equals "anti-American"
   in many places, and America's unquestioned dominance puts a bee under some

people's berets. This is especially the case in France, where McDonald's is the only thing short of pedophilia or boxed wine that is safe for everyone to hate. . . .

But anti-Americanism only partly accounts for the phenomenon. For exam-   3
ple, protesters will often attack a Mickey D's even if the U.S. embassy is more convenient. When Breton separatists wanted to send a signal to Paris last month, they blew up a McDonald's, killing a 28-year-old breakfast-shift leader. (It was a mixed signal, to be sure, because McDonald's is even less popular in Paris than in Brittany.)

McDonald's-ism represents more than Americanism: The company long ago   4
surpassed Coca-Cola and Nike as the true force of globalization. Political scien-tists constantly use McDonald's as a metaphor; *The Economist,* the worldwide tip sheet on global prosperity, uses a "Big Mac Index" to measure disparities in purchasing power around the globe; environmentalists spin conspiracy theories about the company's plot to create a "McWorld"; and anarchists just want to open a fresh can of whupass on the Hamburglar. Tom Friedman of the *New York Times* formulated his "Golden Arches Theory of Conflict Prevention": No two na-tions with a McDonald's ever went to war with each other. (This was true for mil-lennia, until the U.S.-led air war with Yugoslavia. Another first for Bill Clinton.)

But what does McDonald's-ism stand for, really? Well—to borrow a phrase   5
from Burger King—it stands for "having it your way." McDonald's is perceived by its enemies as a plague-carrier, imposing the pestilence of Western consumer culture and low standards on every hamlet. The reality is exactly the opposite: McDonald's sprouts up naturally wherever there is enough economic oxygen to sustain it.

As historian David Halberstam points out in *The Fifties,* McDonald's was a   6
natural product of postwar American prosperity. Young families flocking to the suburbs—often with both parents working—wanted a fast, clean place where they could feed the kids affordable, high-quality meals, on the parents' own sched-ule. Anyone who has needed a quick coffee and one-handed meal, on the way to a 9 A.M. business meeting or parent-teacher conference, understands the vi-tal role McDonald's plays for the typical worker. Indeed, for all the silliness about the company's exploiting women, the chain was an unsung hero in women's lib-eration—allowing overworked women an opportunity for a convenient meal. One of the company's first slogans was "Give mom a night off." This eventually became "You deserve a break today."

That model hasn't changed. In the current issue of *Foreign Affairs,* Harvard   7
China scholar James L. Watson makes a persuasive case that the success of McDonald's in China is dependent on similar economic changes: "As in other parts of East Asia, the startup date for McDonald's corresponds to the emergence of a new class of consumers with money to spend on family entertainment."

When Golden Arches go up, it's not the hoisting of an American flag, but   8
rather a sign that a country is raising its own standards. McDonald's is the ca-nary in the coal mine of economic success. Despite the fact that French farm-

ers are the company's chief antagonists, France's 800 McDonald's buy 80 percent of their ingredients in France, sustaining 45,000 French beef producers. The same pattern obtains throughout most of the world.

JONAH GOLDBERG, from "The Specter of McDonald's,"
National Review (6/5/00)

4. With today's hectic lifestyles, time-saving products are increasingly in demand. Perhaps one of the most obvious examples is fast food. The rate of growth in consumer expenditures on fast food has led most other segments of the food-away-from-home market for much of the last two decades. Since 1982, the amount consumers spent at fast food outlets grew at an annual rate of 6.8 percent (through 1997), compared with 4.7 percent growth in table service restaurant expenditures. The proportion of away-from-home food expenditures on fast food increased from 29.3 to 34.2 percent between 1982 and 1997, while the restaurant proportion decreased from 41 to 35.7 percent (Clauson). |1|

At roughly $109.5 billion in 1997, fast food sales are approaching the amount spent at table service restaurants ($114.3 billion in 1997, including tips), despite fast food's much lower average cost per meal. Between 1990 and 1997, fast food prices rose only an average of about 2 percent per year, according to the Consumer Reports on Eating Share Trends (CREST) data, implying increased consumption caused the majority of expenditure growth. |2|

People want quick and convenient meals; they do not want to spend a lot of time preparing meals, traveling to pick up meals, or waiting for meals in restaurants. As a result, consumers rely on fast food. Knowing this, fast food providers are coming up with new ways to market their products that save time for consumers. For example, McDonald's currently has outlets inside nearly 700 (out of 2,374) Wal-Mart stores across the United States, and almost 200 outlets in Chevron and Amoco service stations. These arrangements are becoming more common in the fast food industry. Consumers can combine mealtime with time engaged in other activities, such as shopping, work, or travel. |3|

MARK D. JEKANOWSKI, from "Causes and Consequences
of Fast Food Sales Growth," *Food Review* (1/1/99)

5. . . . McDonald's sales reached $1.3 billion in 1972, propelling it past Kentucky Fried Chicken as the world's largest fast-food chain. It has kept this position ever since. Annual sales now exceed $3 billion. McDonald's is the nation's leading buyer of processed potatoes and fish. Three hundred thousand cattle die each year as McDonald's customers down another three billion burgers. A 1974 advertising budget of $60 million easily made the chain one of the country's top advertisers. Ronald McDonald, our best-known purveyor of hamburgers, French fries, and milkshakes, rivals Santa Claus and Mickey Mouse as our children's most familiar fantasy character. |1|

How does an anthropologist, accustomed to explaining the life styles of diverse cultures, interpret these peculiar developments and attractions that influence the daily life of so many Americans? Have factors other than low cost, taste, fast service, and cleanliness—all of which are approximated by other chains—contributed to McDonald's success? Could it be that in consuming McDonald's products and propaganda, Americans are not just eating and watching television but are experiencing something comparable in some respects to a religious ritual? A brief consideration of the nature of ritual may answer the latter question.   2

Several key features distinguish ritual from other behavior, according to anthropologist Roy Rappaport. Foremost, are formal ritual events—stylized, repetitive, and stereotyped. They occur in special places, at regular times, and include liturgical orders—set sequences of words and actions laid down by someone other than the current performer.   3

Rituals also convey information about participants and their cultural traditions. Performed year after year, generation after generation, they translate enduring messages, values, and sentiments into observable action. Although some participants may be more strongly committed than others to the beliefs on which rituals are based, all people who take part in joint public acts signal their acceptance of an order that transcends their status as individuals.   4

In the view of some anthropologists, including Rappaport himself, such secular institutions as McDonald's are not comparable to rituals. They argue that rituals involve special emotions, nonutilitarian intentions, and supernatural entities that are not characteristic of Americans' participation in McDonald's. But other anthropologists define ritual more broadly. Writing about football in contemporary America, William Arens (see "The Great American Football Ritual," Natural History, October 1975) points out that behavior can simultaneously have sacred as well as secular aspects. Thus, on one level, football can be interpreted simply as a sport, while on another, it can be viewed as a public ritual.   5

While McDonald's is definitely a mundane, secular institution—just a place to eat—it also assumes some of the attributes of a sacred place. And in the context of comparative religion, why should this be surprising? The French sociologist Emile Durkheim long ago pointed out that some societies worship the ridiculous as well as the sublime. The distinction between the two does not depend on the intrinsic qualities of the sacred symbol. Durkheim found that Australian aborigines often worshiped such humble and nonimposing creatures as ducks, frogs, rabbits, and grubs—animals whose inherent qualities hardly could have been the origin of the religious sentiment they inspired. If frogs and grubs can be elevated to a sacred level, why not McDonald's?   6

I frequently eat lunch—and occasionally, breakfast and dinner—at McDonald's. More than a year I ago, I began to notice (and have subsequently observed more carefully) certain ritual behavior at these fast-food restaurants. Although for natives, McDonald's seems to be just a place to eat, careful observation of   7 what goes on in any outlet in this country reveals an astonishing degree of formality and behavioral uniformity on the part of both staff and customers. Particularly impressive is the relative invariance in act and utterance that has developed in the absence of a distinct theological doctrine. Rather, the ritual aspect of McDonald's rests on twentieth-century technology—particularly automobiles, television, work locales, and the one-hour lunch.

CONRAD P. KOTTAK, from "Rituals at McDonald's," reprinted in Ronald Revisited: The World of Ronald McDonald (1983)

6. Workers were not the only ones constrained by McDonald's routines, of course. The cooperation of service-recipients was crucial to the smooth functioning of the operation. In many kinds of interactive service work . . . constructing the compliance of service-recipients is an important part of the service worker's job. The routines such workers use may be designed to maximize the control each worker has over customers. McDonald's window workers' routines were not intended to give them much leverage over customers' behavior, however. The window workers interacted only with people who had already decided to do business with McDonald's and who therefore did not need to be persuaded to take part in the service interaction. Furthermore, almost all customers were familiar enough with McDonald's routines to know how they were expected to behave. For instance, I never saw a customer who did not know that she or he was supposed to come up to the counter rather than sit down and wait to be served. This customer training was accomplished through advertising, spatial design, customer experience, and the example of other customers, making it unnecessary for the window crew to put much effort into getting customers to fit into their work routines.

McDonald's ubiquitous advertising trains consumers at the same time that it tries to attract them to McDonald's. Television commercials demonstrate how the service system is supposed to work and familiarize customers with new products. Additional cues about expected customer behavior are provided by the design of the restaurants. For example, the entrances usually lead to the service counter, not to the dining area, making it unlikely that customers will fail to realize that they should get in line, and the placement of waste cans makes clear that customers are expected to throw out their own trash. Most important, the majority of customers have had years of experience with McDonald's, as well as with other fast-food restaurants that have similar arrangements. The company estimates that the average customer visits a McDonald's twenty times a year . . . and it is not uncommon for a customer to come in several times per week. For many customers, then, ordering at McDonald's is as routine an interaction as it is for the window worker. Indeed, because employee turnover is so high, steady customers may be more familiar with the work routines than the workers serving them are. Customers who are new to McDonald's can take their cue from more experienced customers.

Not surprisingly, then, most customers at the McDonald's I studied knew   3
what was expected of them and tried to play their part well. They sorted themselves into lines and gazed up at the menu boards while waiting to be served. They usually gave their orders in the conventional sequence: burgers or other entrees, french fries or other side orders, drinks, and desserts. Hurried customers with savvy might order an item "only if it's in the bin," that is, ready to be served. Many customers prepared carefully so that they could give their orders promptly when they got to the counter. This preparation sometimes became apparent when a worker interrupted to ask, "What kind of dressing?" or "Cream and sugar?," flustering customers who could not deliver their orders as planned.

McDonald's routines, like those of other interactive service businesses, depend   4
on the predictability of customers, but these businesses must not grind to a halt if customers are not completely cooperative. Some types of deviations from standard customer behavior are so common that they become routine themselves, and these can be handled through subroutines. . . . McDonald's routines work most efficiently when all customers accept their products exactly as they are usually prepared; indeed, the whole business is based on this premise. Since, however, some people give special instructions for customized products, such as "no onions," the routine allows for these exceptions. At the franchise I studied, workers could key the special requests into their cash registers, which automatically printed out "grill slips" with the instructions for the grill workers to follow. Under this system, the customer making the special order had to wait for it to be prepared, but the smooth flow of service for other customers was not interrupted.

ROBIN LEIDNER, from *Fast Food, Fast Talk: Service Work*
and the Routinization of Everyday Life (1993)

7. Getting a lot of food for little cost in a fast-food restaurant is often more illu-   1
sion than reality. For example, the big, fluffy (and inexpensive) bun that surrounds the burger makes it seem bigger than it is. To further the illusion, the burger and various fixings are sized to stick out of the bun, as if the bun, as large as it is, cannot contain the "tremendous" portion within. Similarly, special scoops arrange fries in such a way that a portion looks enormous. The bags and boxes seem to bulge at the top, overflowing with french fries. The insides of the boxes for McDonald's large fries are striped to further the illusion. In fact, there are, given the price, relatively few fries in each package, a few pennies worth of potato. Indeed, there is a huge profit margin in the fries. Reiter reports that at Burger King, fries are sold at 400 percent of their cost! Drinks at Burger King involve a 600 percent markup. (This is due, in part, to all the ice used to create the im-

pression that people get more of a drink than they actually do.) Indeed, given the enormous rush of people into this business, and the huge growth in fast-food outlets, it is clear that there are great profits to be made. Thus, in fact, the consumers' calculus is wrong—they are *not* getting a lot for a little.

To be fair, fast-food restaurants probably give more food for less money than is the case in a traditional restaurant. However, fast-food restaurants make up for this by doing much more business than a traditional restaurant. They may earn less profit on each meal, but they sell many more meals. 2

The emphasis on the number of sales made and the size of the products of-fered are not the only manifestations of calculability in fast-food restaurants. Another example is the great emphasis on the speed with which a meal can be served. In fact, Ray Kroc's first outlet was named *McDonald's Speedee Service Drive-In*. At one time, McDonald's sought to serve a hamburger, shake, and french fries in 50 seconds. The restaurant made a great breakthrough in 1959 when it served a record 36 hamburgers in 110 seconds. Today, Burger King seeks to serve a customer within three minutes of entering the restaurant. The drive-through window drastically reduces the time required to process a customer through the fast-food restaurant. Speed is obviously a quantifiable factor of mon-umental importance in a *fast*-food restaurant. 3

Speed is even more important to the pizza-delivery business. Not only does the number sold depend on how quickly the pizzas can be delivered, but also, a hot, fresh pizza must be transported quickly to arrive so, even though special insulated containers keep the pizzas hot longer. However, this emphasis on rapid delivery has caused several scandals. Pressure to make fast deliveries has led young delivery people to become involved in serious and sometimes fatal auto-mobile accidents. 4

Still another aspect of the emphasis on quantity lies in the precision with which every element in the production of fast food is measured. For example, great care is taken to be sure that each raw McDonald's hamburger weighs 1.6 ounces, no more, no less; there are ten hamburgers to a pound of meat. The precooked hamburger measures precisely 3.875 inches in diameter, the bun, exactly 3.5 inches. McDonald's invented the "fatilyzer" to ensure that its regular ham-burger meat had no more than 19% fat. This is important because greater fat content would lead to greater shrinkage during cooking and prevent the ham-burger from appearing too large for the bun. Besides giving the illusion that there are a lot of fries in each package, the french-fry scoop helps make sure that each package has about the same number of fries. The new automatic drink dispensers ensure that each cup gets the correct amount of soft drink with nothing lost to spillage. 5

GEORGE RITZER, from *The McDonaldization of Society:
An Investigation into the Changing Character
of Contemporary Social Life* (1996)

8.

About Us

The **International Movement for the Defense of and the Right to Pleasure** officially came into being on November 9, 1989 at the Opera Comique in Paris. [1]

Its Manifesto was endorsed by delegates from Argentina, Austria, Brazil, Denmark, France, Germany, Holland, Hungary, Italy, Japan, Spain, Sweden, Switzerland, United States and Venezuela. [2]

The Official Manifesto

Our century, which began and has developed under the insignia of industrial civilization, first invented the machine and then took it as its life model. [3]

We are enslaved by speed and have all succumbed to the same insidious virus: *Fast Life,* which disrupts our habits, pervades the privacy of our homes and forces us to eat *Fast Foods.* [4]

To be worthy of the name, Homo Sapiens should rid himself of speed before it reduces him to a species in danger of extinction. [5]

A firm defense of quiet material pleasure is the only way to oppose the universal folly of *Fast Life.* [6]

May suitable doses of guaranteed sensual pleasure and slow, long-lasting enjoyment preserve us from the contagion of the multitude who mistake frenzy for efficiency. [7]

Our defense should begin at the table with *Slow Food.* Let us rediscover the flavors and savors of regional cooking and banish the degrading effects of *Fast Food.* [8]

In the name of productivity, *Fast Life* has changed our way of being and threatens our environment and our landscapes. So *Slow Food* is now the only truly progressive answer. [9]

That is what real culture is all about: developing taste rather than demeaning it. And what better way to set about this than an international exchange of experiences, knowledge, projects? [10]

Slow Food guarantees a better future. [11]

Slow Food is an idea that needs plenty of qualified supporters who can help turn this (slow) motion into an international movement, with the little snail as its symbol. [12]

SLOW FOOD, *http://www.slowfood.com/cgi-bin/ slowfood.all/slowfood-com/scripts/chiasmo/manifesto*

EVALUATING ELEVEN SOURCES ABOUT ERNEST HEMINGWAY

Assume that you are gathering information for an essay about *Ernest Hemingway's life in Paris in 1924 and 1925.* From your introductory reading, you have already become familiar with some of the basic facts. You know that the novelist Hemingway and his wife, Hadley, traveled to Paris with their infant son, Bumby; that the Hemingways had very little money; that they associated with many of the literary figures who lived in Paris at the time; that they took occasional trips to Spain for the bull running and to Austria for the skiing; and that Hemingway was working on a novel called *The Sun Also Rises*. Now, through research, you intend to fill in the details that will enable you to construct a portrait of Hemingway and his Paris experiences. You have selected a preliminary bibliography of eleven sources. Here is the *annotated preliminary bibliography*; the comments are based on a rapid examination of each source and are intended for your own use in completing research and organizing the essay.

Baker, Carlos. *Hemingway: A Life Story*. New York: Scribner's, 1969. 563 pages of biography, with 100 pages of footnotes. Everything seems to be here, presented in great detail.

Donaldson, Scott. *Hemingway: By Force of Will*. New York: Viking, 1977. The material isn't organized chronologically; instead, the chapters are thematic, with titles like "Money," "Sex," and "War." Episodes from Hemingway's life are presented within each chapter. The introduction calls this "a mosaic of [Hemingway's] mind and personality." Lots of footnotes.

Griffin, Peter. *Less Than a Treason: Hemingway in Paris*. New York: Oxford UP, 1990. Part of a multivolume biography. Covers Hemingway's life from 1921–1927, exclusively. Griffin says in the preface that his goal is not to "analyze this well examined life" but "to recreate it." Reads like a novel. A little bit choppy and anecdotal, and documentation format is unwieldy. Should probably be cautious about Griffin's preoccupation with EH's stories as autobiographical/psychological documents, but could be useful for speculations on connections between personal life and work.

Gurko, Leo. *Ernest Hemingway and the Pursuit of Heroism*. New York: Crowell, 1968. This book is part of a series called "Twentieth-Century American Writers": a brief introduction to the man and his work. After fifty pages of straight biography, Gurko discusses Hemingway's writing, novel by novel. There's an index and a short bibliography, but no notes. The biographical part is clear and easy to read, but it sounds too much like a summary.

Hemingway, Ernest. *A Moveable Feast*. New York: Scribner's, 1964. This is Hemingway's own version of his life in Paris. It sounds authentic, but there's also a very strongly nostalgic tone, so I'm not sure how trustworthy it is.

Hemingway in Paris. Home page. 13 Oct. 1997 <http://204.122.127.50/WSHS/ Paris/htm/>. Three photos of the Hemingways' apartment, with brief comments.

Hemingway, Leicester. *My Brother, Ernest Hemingway.* Cleveland: World, 1962. It doesn't sound as if the family was very close. For 1924–1925, he's using information from Ernest's letters (as well as commonly known facts). The book reads like a thirdhand report, very remote; but L. H. sounds honest, not as if he were making up things that he doesn't know about.

Hotchner, A. E. *Papa Hemingway.* New York: Random House, 1955. This book is called a "personal memoir." Hotchner met Hemingway in 1948, and evidently hero-worshiped him. Hemingway rambled on about his past, and Hotchner tape-recorded much of it. The book is their dialogue (mostly Hemingway's monologue). No index or bibliography. Hotchner's adoring tone is annoying, and the material resembles that of *A Moveable Feast,* which is better written.

Meyers, Jeffrey. *Hemingway: A Biography.* New York: Harper, 1985. 572 pages of bio. Includes several maps, and two chronologies: illnesses and accidents, and travel. Book organized chronologically, with every year accounted for, according to table of contents. Well documented, and seems less gossipy than Griffin.

Reynolds, Michael. *Hemingway: The Paris Years.* Cambridge, Mass.: Blackwell, 1989. Second of three-volume biography. Includes a chronology covering December 1921–February 1926, five very basic outline maps ("Hemingway's Europe 1922–26," "France," "Switzerland," "Italy," and "Key points for Hemingway's several trips through France and Spain"). Chapters grouped into sections by single years, from "Part One: 1922," to "Part Four: 1925."

Sokoloff, Alice Hunt. *Hadley, the First Mrs. Hemingway.* New York: Dodd, 1973. This is the Paris experience from Hadley's point of view, most of it taken from her recollections and from the standard biographies. (Baker is acknowledged.) It's a very slight book—102 pages—but there's an index and footnotes, citing letters and interviews that some of the other biographers might not have been able to use.

Examining the Sources

The preliminary notes describing these eleven sources seem to be the outgrowth of two separate processes. In the first place, the student is noting basic facts about each biography—the *length* of the book, the amount of *documentation*, the potential *bias* of the writer (if it is easily recognized), and the *organization* of the material. But there are also several comments on tone, impressions of the way in which the information is being presented: "sounds like . . ." or "reads like. . . ." How were these impressions formed?

Let's begin with the biography, which, according to the annotations, may be the most thorough and complete of the eleven (although one of the oldest). Here is Carlos Baker's account of Ernest and Hadley Hemingway immediately after their arrival in Paris:

The first problem in Paris was to find an apartment. Ezra's pavillon in the rue Notre Dame des Champs was too cold and damp for the baby, but there was another available flat on the second floor of a building farther up the hill. It was a pleasant street sloping down from the corner of the Avenue de l'Observatoire and the Boulevard du Montparnasse, an easy stroll from the Luxembourg Gardens, where Hadley could air the baby, a stone's throw from an unspoiled café called La Closerie des Lilas, and much closer to Gertrude Stein's than the former walk-up apartment in the rue du Cardinal Lemoine. The whole neighborhood was a good deal prettier and more polite than that of the Montagne Ste.-Geneviève, though not much quieter. The Hemingways' windows at Number 113 looked down upon a sawmill and lumberyard. It was owned and operated by Pierre Chautard, who lived with his wife and a small dog on the ground floor. The whine of the circular saw, the chuff of the donkey-engine that drove it, the hollow boom of newly sawn planks being laid in piles, and the clatter of the ancient camions that carried the lumber away made such a medley that Ernest was often driven to the haven of the Closerie des Lilas to do his writing.

In the apartment itself, a dark tunnel of a hall led to a kitchen with a stone sink and a two-ring gas burner for cooking. There was a dining room, mostly filled by a large table, and a small bedroom where Ernest sometimes worked. The master bedroom held a stove and double bed, with a small dressing room large enough for the baby's crib. Hadley quickly rehired the *femme de ménage,* Madame Henri Rohrback, who had worked for her off and on before. Marie was a sturdy peasant from Mur-de-Bretagne. She and her husband, who was called Ton-Ton, lived at 10 bis, Avenue des Gobelins. Her own nickname was Marie Cocotte, from her method of calling the chickens at home on the farm in Brittany. She took at once to the child and often bore him away in a carriage lent by the Straters to see Ton-Ton, who was a retired soldier with time on his hands. Madame Chautard, the wife of the owner of the sawmill, was a plump and childless woman with brassy hair and a voice so harsh that it made the baby cry. She seemed to be envious of Hadley's motherhood. Watching the child drink his daily ration of orange juice she could only say scornfully, "*Il sera un poivrot comme sa mère.*"* Of the baby's many nicknames— Gallito, Matt, and Joe—the one that stuck was Bumby, which Hadley invented to signify his warm, plump, teddy-bearish, arm-filling solidity which both parents admired and enjoyed.

*"He'll become a lush like his mother."

CARLOS BAKER

What makes Baker's description so effective is the *impressive amount of detail*. You cannot help believing a biographer who offers so much specific information about everyone and everything with even the remotest connection to his subject. You expect to be told what Hemingway ate for dinner and, indeed, in reporting the novelist's skiing trip to Schruns, Baker writes that the cook prepared "great roasts of beef, with potatoes browned in gravy, jugged hare with wine sauce, venison chops, a special omelette soufflé, and homemade plum pudding." On the other hand, you are sometimes told more than you want to know. There's a house-that-Jack-built effect in the sentences about the Hemingways' nursemaid who was a "sturdy peasant from Mur-de-Bretagne," who had a husband named Ton-Ton, who lived in the Avenue des Gobelins, whose nickname was the result of . . . and so on. Nevertheless, Baker tells a good story and his description of the apartment is effective: notice the description of the sounds that Hemingway must have heard from his windows.

Next, in sharp contrast to all this detail, we have a comparable passage from the biography by Leo Gurko (which the bibliography described as "a summary"). *Gurko* is dealing with the same material as *Baker,* in less than one-tenth the space, and naturally offers much less detail.

> Paris in the 1920s was everyone's catalyst. It was the experimental and ferment-   1
> ing center of every art. It was highly sophisticated, yet broke up naturally into small
> intimate quartiers. Its cafés were hotbeds of intellectual and social energy, pent up
> during the war and now released. Young people from all over the world flocked
> to Paris, drawn not only by the city's intrinsic attractions but by the devaluation of
> the franc.
>
> The young Hemingways settled on the Left Bank, and since they were short of   2
> money, rented modest rooms in an ancient walkup. They moved several times, tak-
> ing flats that were usually on the top floor, five or six flights up, commanding good
> views of the roofs of Paris. This was somehow in tune with a passion to absorb
> the city. Hemingway did much of his writing in cafés, where he would sit for hours
> over a beer or *Pernod* with paper spread before him. He took long walks through
> the streets and gardens, lingered over the Cézannes in the Luxembourg Museum,
> and let the great city permeate his senses.
>
> LEO GURKO

Baker was trying as much as possible to draw the reader into the scene and to share the Hemingways' own experience of Paris. In contrast, *Gurko* is outside the scene, describing what he, the observer, has seen over the distance of time. He does not hesitate to tell his reader what to think—about Paris, about its expatriate population, and about the Hemingways. Notice in this short passage how *Gurko* moves from verifiable facts to his own hypothesis:

> The Hemingways put themselves on short rations, ate, drank, and entertained
> as little as possible, pounced eagerly on the small checks that arrived in the mail
> as payment for accepted stories, and were intensely conscious of being poor. The

sensation was not altogether unpleasant. Their extreme youth, the excitement of living abroad, the sense of making a fresh start, even the unexpected joy of parenthood, gave their poverty a romantic flavor.

LEO GURKO

Gurko's book does not document his sources; the reader is asked to accept Gurko's assertion that being poor in Paris was "not altogether unpleasant" for Hemingway, because of its romantic connotations. Other biographers, however, may not agree with this statement. Remember that Gurko's hypothesis is one person's opinion and is not to be confused with fact or presented as such in a research essay. Acceptance of his opinion depends on Gurko's credentials as an authority on Hemingway and on what other established authorities have to say.

Here's a final excerpt from Gurko's biography, as a starting point for a second group of comparisons. Notice his tendency to generalize and summarize and, especially, to speak for Hemingway. Then contrast *Gurko's* approach with that of *Alice Sokoloff:*

He was becoming increasingly devoted to imaginative writing, to the point where his newspaper assignments and the need to grind out journalistic pieces were growing more and more irksome. Another threat to his work was the "arty" atmosphere of Paris. The cafés of the city, he soon recognized, were filled with aesthetes of one kind or another who wanted to be artists, talked incessantly and even knowledgeably about art, but never really produced anything. There were a hundred of these clever loafers and dilettantes for every real writer. Hemingway developed a contempt and even fear of them, perhaps because there was in him, as in most genuine artists, a feeling of uncertainty about his own talent. He drove himself to hard work and avoided the café crowd as much as he could.

LEO GURKO

It was a worldly crowd, full of intellectual and artistic ferment, some of it real, some of it bogus, some of them obsessed with their own egos, a few of them deeply and sincerely interested in Ernest's talent. The Hemingways' finances were as restricted as ever, but these people "could offer them all the amenities, could take them anywhere for gorgeous meals," could produce any kind of entertainment and diversion. Although Ernest accepted it all, Hadley thought that he resented it and always kept "a very stiff upper front to satisfy himself." He did not want "simply to sink back and take all this," but the success and admiration was heady stuff and he could not help but enjoy it.[1] Hadley used to be wryly amused when Ernest and Gertrude Stein would talk about worldly success and how it did not mean anything to them.[2] The fact that this was true for a part of him, and that he despised anything false or pretentious, was a source of inner conflict which sometimes expressed itself in malice.

[1] John Dos Passos. *The Best Times* (New York: New American Library, 1966), p. 143.
[2] Interview with Hadley Richardson Hemingway Mowrer, January 18, 1972.

ALICE SOKOLOFF

Sokoloff's conclusions differ from *Gurko's*: she points to a conflict in Hemingway's reaction to his Paris acquaintances, and offers footnotes to support her suggestion. In another sense, Sokoloff's commentary is limited: because the subject of her biography is Hadley Hemingway, she is describing events from Hadley's point of view. On the other hand, Sokoloff's presentation makes it fairly easy to figure out where Hadley's version leaves off and the biographer's account begins, and the story is told coherently.

Leicester Hemingway's account of his brother's life is far more confusing; most of his information comes from letters, and he makes little attempt to sort out the contents into a form that the average reader can follow easily:

> Things were going very well for Ernest, with his home life as well as with his writing. Bumby was beginning to talk and Ernest was learning that a child could be more fun than fret. With wife and son he took off for Schruns in the Vorarlberg when good skiing weather set in. For months they were deep in the snow up there, working and enjoying the sports, before returning to Paris in mid-March. [1]
>
> Ernest wrote the family that when they camped in the mountains, up above 2,000 meters, there had been lots of ptarmigan and foxes, too. The deer and chamois were lower down. [2]
>
> He said Bumby weighed twenty-nine pounds, played in a sand pile with shovel and pail, and was always jolly. His own writing was going very well. *In Our Time* was out of print and bringing high prices, he said, while his stories were being translated into Russian and German. . . . [3]
>
> Hadley added other details, thanking the family for the Christmas box which had been delayed more than two months in customs, but had arrived without damage to the fruit cake—Mother's one culinary triumph besides meat loaf. She wrote that Bumby had a wonderful nurse who had taken care of him while she and Ernest spent days at a stretch in mountain huts to be near good snow. [4]
>
> LEICESTER HEMINGWAY

Ernest's writing is mixed up with Bumby's pail and shovel and fruitcakes for Christmas. This is certainly raw material. The biography offers no interpretation at all for the reader to discount or accept. The material is stitched together so crudely that one has to spend time sorting out important details from trivia. Certainly, this biography would be a poor choice for the student who was beginning research on this topic; but the details might provide interesting background once the events of 1924–1925 were made more familiar by other biographies.

Next, here are three more recent biographies of Hemingway. How do they describe the apartment near the lumberyard?

> "Hemingway had then and has always a very good instinct for finding apartments in strange but pleasant localities," wrote Gertrude Stein, "and good femmes de menage and good food." They arrived in France on January 29, 1924, and soon found [1]

a flat above a noisy sawmill, near Pound's old studio, at 113 rue Notre Dame des Champs, where the street curves parallel to the Boulevard Montparnasse.

But the flat had more character than comfort. American friends, who were used to living well in France, were shocked by the squalor. Kitty Cannell said: "The Hemingways lived in a cold-water apartment that gave on[to] a lumber yard in the Montparnasse quarter. It had neither gas nor electric light." And the journalist Burton Rascoe wrote: "They lived, at the time, in an incredibly bare hovel, without toilet or running water, and with a mattress spread on the floor for a bed; it was in the court of a lumber yard, on the second floor, to which one climbed by a flight of rickety steps."

JEFFREY MEYERS

Meyers attempts to give some idea of what the Hemingways themselves were experiencing, not by piling on physical details, but by providing a kaleidoscope of eyewitness impressions, rather like interviews in a documentary film or the accumulation of evidence at a trial. An explicit interrogation of the testimony here and the speakers might be helpful, and reminiscences aren't always reliable (the other biographers mention the lack of electricity, but no one else says there was no running water), but this passage does alert us to some of the issues of class that colored Hemingway's experience of Paris, and words like "squalor" and "hovel" offer a contrast to the romantic picture drawn by Baker.

Just before he'd left New York, Ernest had heard from Ford Madox Ford. Ford had written that, since the Pounds were traveling, the Hemingways could spend a few weeks in the Pounds' flat at 70 Rue Notre Dames des Champs. But Ford had made a mistake. When Ernest arrived at Pound's apartment, he learned that, although Ezra was, as Ford said, traveling, he had left no key. Ernest, exhausted and desperate, trudged through the wet snow toward the noise of a band saw, a few buildings down the street. In a small square of black, dripping trees and narrow old wooden houses, he found Pierre Chautard, a carpenter.

When Ernest asked if the carpenter knew of a place to stay, Chautard showed him a five-room flat over the sawmill. The kitchen had a slimy slate sink and a gas stove, with piles of burnt matches beneath the two burners. The place was furnished, Chautard said. But Ernest saw little more than a big bed in one room and a big table in another. Still, there was the pleasant smell of fresh-cut lumber, and windows all around. Madame Chautard, a foulmouthed, henna-haired harridan, sneered at the young couple and suggested she was doing them a favor—especially with the baby. Though he wanted to, Ernest did not haggle over the rent. For himself, his wife, and his son, nothing mattered more than a good night's sleep.

PETER GRIFFIN

Griffin's entire book is devoted to Hemingway's experiences in Paris, so we should expect a level of detail to at least rival that of Baker. Griffin acknowledges in his preface his indebtedness to Baker, and we recognize here some of the same details we learned in Baker: the slate sink, the gas stove, the big table. Baker passed over why, specifically, the Hemingways were in the Montparnasse district; Griffin gives us some sense of how professional and personal lives were entangled, with messages from Pound being relayed by another literary luminary, Ford Madox Ford. Is this additional information useful?

On February 8, after much shopping, Ernest leased a second-floor apartment at 113 rue Notre-Dame-des-Champs, a stone's throw from Ezra's studio and directly behind Montparnasse. A month's rent was 650 francs, almost three times their Cardinal Lemoine rent, but the space was better, the location closer to their friends, and with the franc fluctuating at twenty-one to the dollar, the real cost was about $30 monthly. The apartment had no electricity, and the lumberyard buzz saw in the courtyard below whined steadily during working hours, but their old *femme de menage*, Marie Rohrbach, returned to help with the baby. As February rain mixed with snow, Hadley, sick and physically worn out, watched her furniture move once more into new quarters. "We have the whole second story," she told mother-in-law Grace, "tiny kitchen, small dining room, toilet, small bedroom, medium size sitting room with stove, dining room where John Hadley sleeps and the linen and his and our bath things are kept and a very comfortable bedroom . . . you're conscious all the time from 7 A.M. to 5 P.M. of a very gentle buzzing noise. They make door and window frames and picture frames. The yard is full of dogs and workmen[,] and rammed right up against the funny front door covered with tarpaulin is the baby's buggy."

Despite the lumberyard's noise, the new apartment was an improvement over their first Paris home. Here they were only a few minutes walk from the Notre-Dame-des-Champs Metro station, the Luxembourg Gardens, Sylvia's bookshop and Gertrude Stein's place on the rue de Fleurus. The neighborhood was less working class, less down at the heels. At one end of the street stood the Clinique d'Accouchement, for which both Ernest and Hadley hoped they would have no use. (In his 1924 day book, mostly blank, Ernest was keeping careful track of Hadley's monthly periods.) Nearby, on the Boulevard Montparnasse, in good weather and bad, their American friends gathered to drink and talk at the Select, the Rotonde and the Dome where one could gossip, leave messages, borrow money, repay debts and keep generally abreast of local news.

MICHAEL REYNOLDS

Here is another full-length work devoted to the Paris years. Like *Griffin*, *Reynolds* professes his debt to Carlos Baker, and he sees the significance of the new flat in much the same light as did Baker: better, more convenient location, with the disadvantages of the apartment minimized. Like *Meyers*, Reynolds relies on eyewitness reports, in this case a letter written by Hadley, giving her own impressions of the new apartment and directly contradicting Burton Rascoe's assertion that there was no toilet (although in writing to her mother-in-law she might have minimized the "squalor").

In fact, an Internet source confirms the lack of a toilet. "Hemingway in Paris" provides three photographs: the circular stairway leading into the apartment, the window of Hemingway's room (with a plaque honoring him), and the out- side of the building, including a café. The prose commentary is brief, indicating that there was no hot water and no toilet, "only a chamber pot located in a niche on each floor of the winding staircase."

Finally, here are five descriptions of Hemingway as a baby sitter, odd-job man, and scavenger, all dealing with similar experiences:

> Ernest was working fairly hard. He awoke early in the spring mornings, "boiled the rubber nipples and the bottles, made the formula, finished the bottling, gave Mr. Bumby a bottle," and wrote for a time at the dining-room table before Hadley got up. Chautard had not begun his sawing at that hour, the street was quiet, and Ernest's only companions were Mr. Bumby and Mr. Feather Puss, a large cat given them by Kitty Cannell and named with one of Hadley's nicknames. But Ernest was truly domestic only in the early mornings. He took the freedom of Paris as his per- sonal prerogative, roving as widely as he chose. There was a gymnasium in the rue Pontoise where he often went to earn ten francs a round by sparring with profes- sional heavyweights. The job called for a nice blend of skill and forbearance, since hirelings must be polite while fighting back just enough to engage, without enrag- ing, the emotions of the fighters. Ernest had befriended a waiter at the Closerie des Lilas and sometimes helped him weed a small vegetable garden near the Porte d'Orléans. The waiter knew that he was a writer and warned him that the boxing might jar his brains. But Ernest was glad enough to earn the extra money. He had al- ready begun to save up to buy pesetas for another trip to Spain in July.
>
> CARLOS BAKER

> When there were the three of us instead of just the two, it was the cold and the weather that finally drove us out of Paris in the winter time. Alone there was no prob- lem when you got used to it. I could always go to a café to write and could work all morning over a café crème while the waiters cleaned and swept out the café and it gradually grew warmer. My wife could go to work at the piano in a cold place and with enough sweaters keep warm playing and come home to nurse Bumby. It was wrong to take a baby to a café in the winter though; even a baby that never cried and watched everything that happened and was never bored. There were no baby-sitters then and Bumby would stay happy in his tall cage bed with his big, loving cat named F. Puss. There were people who said that it was dangerous to leave a cat with a baby. The most ignorant and prejudiced said that a cat would suck a baby's breath and kill him. Others said that a cat would lie on a baby and the cat's weight would smother him. F. Puss lay beside Bumby in the tall cage bed and watched the door with his big yellow eyes, and would let no one come near him when we were out and Marie, the *femme de ménage*, had to be away. There was no need for baby-sitters. F. Puss was the baby-sitter.
>
> ERNEST HEMINGWAY

Ernest wanted me to see the neighborhood where he had first lived; we started on Rue Notre-Dame-des-Champs, where he had lived over a sawmill, and slowly worked our way past familiar restaurants, bars and stores, to the Jardin du Luxembourg and its museum, where, Ernest said, he fell in love with certain paintings that taught him how to write. "Am also fond of the Jardin," Ernest said, "because it kept us from starvation. On days when the dinner pot was absolutely devoid of content, I would put Bumby, then about a year old, into the baby carriage and wheel him over here to the Jardin. There was always a *gendarme* on duty, but I knew that around four o'clock he would go to a bar across from the park to have a glass of wine. That's when I would appear with Mr. Bumby—and a pocketful of corn for the pigeons. I would sit on a bench, in my guise of buggy-pushing pigeon-lover, casing the flock for clarity of eye and plumpness. The Luxembourg was well known for the classiness of its pigeons. Once my selection was made, it was a simple matter to entice my victim with the corn, snatch him, wring his neck, and flip his carcass under Mr. Bumby's blanket. We got a little tired of pigeon that winter, but they filled many a void. What a kid that Bumby was—played it straight—and never once put the finger on me."

A. E. HOTCHNER

. . . As he grew older (and *A Moveable Feast* was the last book he finished), Hemingway laid increasing stress on the poverty he suffered in Paris. Without question, Ernest and Hadley Hemingway lived on a relatively scant income during those years, but they were never so badly off as the writer, in retrospect, liked to believe.

In any case, poverty is virtually apotheosized in *A Moveable Feast*. As the title hints, a gnawing hunger for food and drink symbolizes Hemingway's indigence. According to the legend constructed in this book, Hemingway worked all day in his unheated garret, too poor to buy firewood or afford lunch. At least he does not tell here the unlikely yarn that appears in A. E. Hotchner's biography: the one about Hemingway catching pigeons in the Luxembourg Gardens in order to satisfy a rumbling stomach. But poverty, and its symbolic hunger, are nonetheless celebrated. "You got very hungry when you did not eat enough in Paris," Hemingway writes, because of the good things on display in the *pâtisseries* and at the outdoor restaurants. Mostly he and Hadley survived on leeks (*poireaux*), but at least so frugal a diet enabled one to savor, truly, the joys of eating well when an unexpected windfall made it possible for them to dine out.

SCOTT DONALDSON

In the late spring of 1925, when the cold rains that ended the winter had come and gone and the warmth of the sun increased each day, Ernest loved to take his son in the stroller, "a cheap, very light, folding carriage, down the streets to the Closerie des Lilas." They would each have brioche and café au lait, Ernest pouring some of the hot coffee into the saucer to cool it, and to let Bumby dip his brioche before eating. Ernest would read the papers, now and then looking up to see his son attentive to everything that passed on the boulevard. After breakfast, Ernest would wheel Bumby across the street from the cafe and past the Place de l'Observatoire. Bumby loved to see the bronze horses rearing in the fountain spray that made the June air smell so clean.

PETER GRIFFIN

Characteristically, *Baker* describes exactly how the father tended his son, pausing to explain the full name and the origins of their cat. *Griffin* pays the same attention to detail, without being so exhaustive. *Hemingway* himself, years after the event, describes much the same relationship, but with a completely different emphasis and set of details. These three passages are not in conflict; but they are not at all the same kind of writing and, in fact, they provide an excellent illustration of the difficulties of combining sources written in different modes for different kinds of audience. The Hemingway who reminisced for *A. E. Hotchner* offers a somewhat different version of the same experience, a version criticized in *Donaldson*'s extract, which tries to distinguish between nostalgia and truth. Unlike *Gurko*'s, *Donaldson*'s presentation is detailed; unlike *Baker* and *Griffin*, he has an outsider's perspective, and the combination, backed up by documentation, is quite convincing.

In what order, then, would you consult these ten books for full-scale research? You might begin with Gurko's brief account, to establish the sequence of events, and then fill in the details by reading Baker's longer version or the more recent, comprehensive biographies by Meyers or Reynolds, which depend so much on Baker's earlier work. Donaldson gets pushed down the list to third or fourth, primarily because his biography is not chronological; gathering the scattered references to 1924 will be easier once the overall chronology has been made clear by Gurko, Baker, Meyers, or Reynolds. Now, you can also draw on the details to be found in the works by "interested" parties: wife, brother, friend, and the author himself. And, at intervals, you should stop reading and note-taking to compare these various versions of one life and determine which of the sources was in a position to know the truth—the man himself thirty years later? his correspondence at the time? records left by his wife (whom, in fact, he divorced in 1929)? his biographers, whose information is presented secondhand? a combination of all the sources?

EXERCISE 23: COMPARING SOURCES

In the middle of the night of November 29, 1942, a Boston nightclub called the Cocoanut Grove burned down, resulting in the deaths of at least 300 people. Read the following three accounts of this disaster, and be prepared to discuss the differences in content, organization, tone, purpose, and point of view. What is the thesis of each article? Consider how you would use the three articles in a single research essay dealing with the Cocoanut Grove disaster. Are these three variations interchangeable?

NEW YORK TIMES, 30 NOVEMBER 1942

300 KILLED BY FIRE, SMOKE AND PANIC IN BOSTON RESORT—DEAD CLOG EXITS—Terror Piles Up Victims as Flames Suddenly Engulf Nightclub—Service Men to Rescue—Many of Them Perish—Girls of Chorus Leap to Safety—150 Are Injured

BOSTON, Sunday, Nov. 29—More than 300 persons had perished early this morning in flames, smoke and panic in the Cocoanut Grove Night Club in the midtown theatre district. 1

The estimate of the dead came at 2 A.M. from William Arthur Reilly, Fire Commissioner, as firemen and riggers searched the ruins for additional bodies. It was a disaster unprecedented in this city. 2

The chief loss of life resulted from the screaming, clawing crowds that were wedged in the entrance of the club. Smoke took a terrific toll of life and scores were burned to death. 3

At the Boston City Hospital officials said there were so many bodies lined up in corridors that they would attempt no identifications before daybreak. 4

Commissioner Reilly stated that an eyewitness inside the club said the fire started when an artificial palm near the main entrance was set afire. 5

Martial law was clamped on the entire fire area at 1:35 A.M. Sailors, Coast Guardsmen, shore patrolmen and naval officers dared death time and again trying to get at bodies that were heaped six feet high by one of the entrances. 6

Firemen said that many bodies were believed to have fallen into the basement after the main floor collapsed. 7

A chorus boy, Marshall Cook, aged 19, of South Boston, led three co-workers, eight chorus girls and other floor show performers totaling thirty-five to an adjoining roof from the second-floor dressing rooms and from there they dropped to the ground from a ladder. 8

Scores of ambulances from nearby cities, the Charlestown Navy Yard and the Chelsea Naval Hospital poured into the area, but the need for ambulances became so great that even railway express trucks were pressed into service to carry away victims. At one time victims, many of them dead, lay two deep in an adjoining garage. 9

Many of the victims were soldiers, sailors, marines and Coast Guardsmen, some of them junior officers, visiting Boston for a weekend of merrymaking. In the throng were persons who had attended the Holy Cross–Boston College football game. 10

Scores of dead were piled up in the lobbies of the various hospitals as the doctors and nurses gave all their attention to the 150 injured. 11

A "flash" fire, believed to have started in the basement, spread like lightning through the dance floor area, and the panic was on. All available nurses and priests were being called into the disaster area. 12

Among the dead were a marine and one who appeared to be a fireman. Casualties were arriving at hospitals so rapidly that they were being placed in the corridors wherever a suitable place could be found. 13

It appeared probable that the greatest loss of life was in the newly opened lounge of the night club in Broadway. Here, one policeman said, burned and suffocated persons were heaped to the top of the doors, wedged in death. 14

The night club was a one-and-a-half story building with a stucco exterior. The blaze was said to have broken out in the basement kitchen at 10:17 P.M. just as the floor show performers were preparing for their next performance. Performers on the second floor were met by terrific smoke and flame as they started downstairs. Their stories were the only ones available, as those who had escaped the dance floor and tables were too hysterical to talk. 15

A temporary morgue and hospital were set up in the garage of the Film Exchange Transfer Company at the rear of the club in Shawmut Street. At least fourteen persons, suffocated and lying in grotesque positions, were lying on the garage floor at one time, while scores of injuries were cared for by garage workers and others. 16

The city's Civilian Defense Workers were called to the scene to maintain order and to give first aid to those suffering from burns and smoke inhalation. Every hospital in the area soon was loaded with the victims. 17

At least thirty-five performers and their friends were rescued by the quick actions of Marshall Cook, a South Boston boy. He was met by a blast of flame as he started down stairs, went back to the dressing room and organized those caught there. 18

He then smashed his way through a window, carrying away the casing. Through this opening he led a group to an adjoining room, where a small ladder was found. The ladder was not long enough to reach the street, but Cook and several other male performers held the top end over the roof's edge and guided the women over the side. They had to jump about 6 feet to reach the ground. 19

At the City Hospital bodies were piled on the floors, many so burned that there was no attempt to identify them immediately. Many service men were among the victims, many of whom were partly identified through their uniforms. 20

Buck Jones, the film star, was believed to be one of the victims. 21

Among the first at the scene was the Rev. Joseph A. Marcus of Cranwell School, Lenox, who administered the last rites for at least fifty persons. In the meantime, thirty or forty ambulances rushed to the fire, these coming from Lynn, Newton, and Brookline. Despite the hindrances caused by automobiles parked in the streets, some of the dead and injured were taken from nearby buildings, where they had been left covered only by newspapers. 22

Abraham Levy, a cashier at the Cocoanut Grove, said there were about 400 in the place, including many sailors. 23

Sailors saved many lives, pulling people through the doors and out of danger. A fireman said that he saw at least thirty bodies lying on the floor, and that he believed some of them were firemen. 24

Among the spectacular escapes were those of two of the eight chorus girls, who   25
leaped from the second floor and were caught by two of the male dancers. They
were Lottie Christie of Park Drive, Boston, and Claudia Boyle. They jumped into the
arms of Andrew Louzan and Robert Gilbert. Louzan and Gilbert had climbed out of
a window of their dressing room to an adjoining roof and then descended by ladder.

TIME, 7 DECEMBER 1942
CATASTROPHE: BOSTON'S WORST

Holy Cross had just beaten Boston College: downtown Boston was full of men &   1
women eager to celebrate or console. Many of them wound up at Cocoanut Grove:
they stood crowded around the dimly lighted downstairs bar, filled the tables around
the dance floor upstairs. With them mingled the usual Saturday night crowd: soldiers & sailors, a wedding party, a few boys being sent off to Army camps.

At 10 o'clock Bridegroom John O'Neil, who had planned to take his bride to   2
their new apartment at the stroke of the hour, lingered on a little longer. The floor
show was about to start. Through the big revolving door, couples moved in & out.

At the downstairs bar, a 16-year-old busboy stood on a bench to replace a light   3
bulb that a prankish customer had removed. He lit a match. It touched one of the
artificial palm trees that gave the Cocoanut Grove its atmosphere; a few flames shot
up. A girl named Joyce Spector sauntered toward the checkroom because she was
worried about her new fur coat.

Panic's Start

Before Joyce Spector reached the cloakroom, the Cocoanut Grove was a scream-   4
ing shambles. The fire quickly ate away the palm tree, raced along silk draperies, was
sucked upstairs through the stairway, leaped along ceiling and wall. The silk hang-
ings, turned to balloons of flame, fell on table and floor.

Men & women fought their way toward the revolving door; the push of bodies   5
jammed it. Nearby was another door; it was locked tight. There were other exits,
but few Cocoanut Grove patrons knew about them. The lights went out. There
was nothing to see now except flame, smoke and weird moving torches that were
men & women with clothing and hair afire.

The 800 Cocoanut Grove patrons pushed and shoved, fell and were trampled.   6
Joyce Spector was knocked under a table, crawled on hands & knees, somehow was
pushed through an open doorway into the street. A chorus boy herded a dozen
people downstairs into a refrigerator. A few men & women crawled out windows;
a few escaped by knocking out a glass brick wall. But most of them, including Bridegroom John O'Neil, were trapped.

Panic's Sequel

Firemen broke down the revolving door, found it blocked by bodies of the dead,   7
six deep. They tried to pull a man out through a side window; his legs were held tight

by the mass of struggling people behind him. In an hour the fire was out and firemen began untangling the piles of bodies. One hard bitten fireman went into hysterics when he picked up a body and a foot came off in his hand. They found a girl dead in a telephone booth, a bartender still standing behind his bar.

At hospitals and improvised morgues which were turned into charnel houses for the night, 484 dead were counted; it was the most disastrous U.S. fire since 571 people were killed in Chicago's Iroquois Theater holocaust in 1903. One Boston newspaper ran a two-word banner line: BUSBOY BLAMED. But the busboy had not put up the Cocoanut Grove's tinderbox decorations, nor was he responsible for the fact that Boston's laws do not require nightclubs to have fireproof fixtures, sprinkler systems or exit markers.

BERNARD DEVOTO, *HARPER'S,* FEBRUARY 1943
THE EASY CHAIR

On the last Sunday morning of November, 1942, most inhabitants of greater Boston learned from their newspapers that at about the time they had gone to bed the night before the most terrible fire in the history of their city had occurred. The decorations of a crowded night club had got ignited, the crowd had stampeded, the exits had jammed, and in a few minutes hundreds of people had died of burns or suffocation. Two weeks later the list of dead had reached almost exactly five hundred, and the war news was only beginning to come back to Boston front pages. While the Allied invasion of North Africa stalled, while news was released that several transports engaged in it had been sunk, while the Russians and the Germans fought monstrously west of Stalingrad and Moscow, while the Americans bombed Naples and the RAF obliterated Turin and conducted the war's most widespread raids over western Europe, while the Japs tried again in the Solomons and mowed down their attackers in New Guinea, while a grave conflict of civilian opinion over the use of Admiral Darlan developed in America and Great Britain, while the anniversary of Pearl Harbor passed almost unnoticed—while all this was going on the Boston papers reported it in stickfuls in order to devote hundreds of columns to the fire at the Cocoanut Grove. And the papers did right, for the community has experienced an angry horror surpassing anything that it can remember. For weeks few Bostonians were able to feel strongly about anything but their civic disaster.

There is irony in such preoccupation with a minute carnage. In the same fortnight thousands of men were killed in battle. Every day, doubtless, more than five hundred were burned to death, seared by powder or gasoline from bombed dumps, in buildings fired from the sky, or in blazing airplanes and sinking ships. If these are thought of as combatants meeting death in the line of duty, far more than five hundred civilians were killed by military action in Germany, Italy, France, Great Britain, Russia, China, Australia, and the islands of the Pacific. Meanwhile in two-thirds of the world civilians died of torture and disease and starvation, in prison camps and wire stockades and the rubble of their homes—they simply came to their last breath and died, by the thousand. At a moment when violent death is commonplace, when it is inevitable for hundreds of thousands, there is something grotesque in being shocked by a mere five hundred deaths which are distinguished from the day's routine only by the fact that they were not inevitable. When hundreds of towns are bombed repeatedly, when cities the size of Boston are overrun by invading armies, when many hundreds of Boston's own citizens will surely be killed in battle in the next few weeks, why should a solitary fire, a truly inconsiderable slaughter, so oppress the spirit?

That oppression provides perspective on our era. We have been so conditioned to horror that horror must explode in our own backyard before we can genuinely feel it. At the start of the decade our nerves responded to Hitler's murdering the German Jews with the outrage properly felt in the presence of cruelty and pain. Seven years later our nerves had been so overloaded that they felt no such outrage at the beginning of a systematic effort to exterminate an entire nation, such as Poland. By progressive steps we had come to strike a truce with the intolerable, precisely as the body develops immunity to poisons and bacteria. Since then three years of war have made the intolerable our daily bread, and every one of us has comfortably adapted to things which fifteen years ago would have driven him insane. The extinction of a nation now seems merely an integral part of the job in hand. But the needless death of five hundred people in our home town strikes through the immunity and horrifies us.

The fire at the Cocoanut Grove was a single, limited disaster, but it exhausted Boston's capacity to deal with an emergency. Hospital facilities were strained to the limit and somewhat beyond it. If a second emergency had had to be dealt with at the same time its victims would have had to wait some hours for transportation and a good many hours for treatment. If there had been three such fires at once, two-thirds of the victims would have got no treatment whatever in time to do them any good. Boston is an inflammable city and it has now had instruction in what to expect if a dozen hostile planes should come over and succeed in dropping incendiary bombs. The civilian defense agencies which were called on justified themselves and vindicated their training. The Nurses' Aid in particular did a memorable job; within a few hours there was a trained person at the bed of every victim, many other Aids worked to exhaustion helping hospital staffs do their jobs, and in fact more were available than could be put to use. Nevertheless it was clearly demonstrated that the civilian agencies are nowhere near large enough to take care of bombings if bombings should come. There were simply not enough ambulances; Railway Express Company trucks had to be called on to take the injured to hospitals and the dead to morgues. The dead had to be stacked like cord wood in garages because the morgues could take no more; the dying had to be laid in rows in the corridors of hospitals because the emergency wards were full. The drainage of doctors into the military service had left Boston just about enough to care for as many victims as this single fire supplied. Six months from now there will be too few to handle an

3

4

equal emergency; there are far too few now for one twice as serious. One plane-load of incendiaries would start more fires than the fire department and its civilian assistants could put out. There would be more injured than there are even the most casually trained first-aiders to care for. Hundreds would be abandoned to the igno-rant assistance of untrained persons, in streets so blocked by rubble and so jammed with military vehicles that trained crews could not reach them even when trained crews should be free. Boston has learned that it is not prepared to take care of it-self. One doubts if any community in the United States is.

Deeper implications of the disaster have no direct connection with the war. An 5 outraged city has been confronting certain matters which it ordinarily disregards. As a place of entertainment the Cocoanut Grove was garish but innocuous and on the whole useful. It has been called "the poor man's Ritz"; for years people had been going there to have a good time and had got what they were looking for. With the naive shock customary in such cases, the city has now discovered that these people were not receiving the minimum protection in their pleasures to which they were entitled and which they supposed they were receiving.

The name of the night club suggests the kind of decorations that cluttered it; the 6 public supposed that the law required them to be fireproof; actually they burned like so much celluloid. The laws relating to them were ambiguous and full of loopholes; such as they were, they were not enforced. The public supposed that an adequate number of exits were required and that periodic inspections were made; they were not. There were too few exits for the customary crowds, one was concealed, an-other could not be opened, and panic-stricken people piled up before the rest and died there by the score. The public supposed that laws forbidding overcrowding were applied to night clubs and were enforced; on the night of the fire the place was packed so full that movement was almost impossible, and it had been just as crowded at least once a week throughout the years of its existence. The public supposed that laws requiring safe practice in electric wiring and machinery were enforced; the official investigations have shown that the wiring was installed by unlicensed electri-cians, that a number of people had suspected it was faulty, and that in fact officials had notified the club that it was violating the law and had threatened to take ac-tion—but had not carried out the threat. Above all, the public supposed that an ad-equate building code taking into account the realities of modern architecture and modern metropolitan life established certain basic measures of protection. It has now learned that the Boston building code is a patched makeshift based on the con-ditions of 1907, and that though a revision which would modernize it was made in 1937, various reasons have held up the adoption of that revision for five years.

These facts have been established by five official investigations, one of them made 7 by the Commonwealth of Massachusetts in an obvious expectation that the munic-ipal authorities of Boston would find convincing reasons to deal gently with them-selves. They have turned up other suggestive facts. The Cocoanut Grove was once owned by a local racketeer, who was murdered in the routine of business. The present owners were so expertly concealed behind a facade of legal figureheads that for twenty-four hours after the fire the authorities were not sure that they knew who even one of them was and two weeks later were not sure that they knew them all. An intimation that financial responsibility was avoided by a technically contrived bankruptcy has not yet been followed up as I write this, and other financial details are still lost in a maze of subterfuges. It is supposed that some of the club's employees had their wagescale established by terrorism. Investigators have encountered, but so far have not published, the customary free-list and lists of those entitled to discounts. Presumably such lists contemplated the usual returns in publicity and business favors; presumably also they found a use in the amenities of regulation. Names and business practices of the underworld have kept cropping up in all the investigations, and it is whispered that the reason why the national government has been conducting one of them is the presence at the club of a large amount of liquor on which the latest increase in revenue taxes ought to have been paid but somehow had not been.

In short, Boston has been reminded, hardly for the first time, that laxity in municipal responsibility can be made to pay a profit and that there can be a remunerative partnership between the amusement business and the underworld. A great many Bostonians, now writing passionate letters to their newspapers and urging on their legislators innumerable measures of reform, have gone farther than that. They conclude that one of the reasons why the modernized building code has not been adopted is the fact that there are ways of making money from the looser provisions of the old code. They suppose that one reason why gaps and loopholes in safety regulations are maintained is that they are profitable. They suppose that one reason why laws and regulations can be disregarded with impunity is that some of those charged with the duty of enforcing them make a living from not enforcing them. They suppose that some proprietors of night clubs find that buying immunity is cheaper than obeying safety regulations and that they are able to find enforcement agents who will sell it. They suppose that civil irresponsibility in Boston can be related to the fact that a lot of people make money from it.

But the responsibility cannot be shouldered off on a few small grafters and a few underworld characters who have established business relations with them, and it would be civic fatuousness to seek expiation for the murder of five hundred citizens in the passage of some more laws. The trouble is not lack of laws but public acquiescence; the damaging alliance is not with the underworld but with a communal reverence of what is probably good for business. Five hundred deaths in a single hour seem intolerable, but the city has never dissented at all to a working alliance between its financial interests and its political governors—a partnership which daily endangers not five hundred but many thousand citizens. Through Boston, as through every other metropolis, run many chains of interests which might suffer loss if regulations for the protection of the public's health and life were rigorously enforced. They are sound and enlightened regulations, but if they should be enforced then re-

8

9

tail sales, bank clearings, and investment balances might possibly fall off. The corner grocery and the downtown department store, the banks and the business houses, the labor unions and the suburban housewife are all consenting partners in a closely calculated disregard of public safety.

Since the system is closely calculated it usually works, it kills only a few at a time, 10 mostly it kills gradually over a period of years. Sometimes however it runs into another mathematical certainty and then it has to be paid for in blocks of five hundred lives. At such times the community experiences just such an excess of guilt as Boston is feeling now, uncomfortably realizing that the community itself is the perpetrator of wanton murder. For the responsibility is the public's all along and the certain safeguard—a small amount of alertness, civic courage, and willingness to lose some money—is always in the public's hands. That means not the mayor's hands, but yours and mine.

It is an interesting thing to hold up to the light at a moment when millions of 11 Americans are fighting to preserve, among other things, the civic responsibility of a self-governing people. It suggests that civilians who are not engaged in the war effort, and who feel intolerably abased because they are not, could find serviceable ways to employ their energies. They can get to work chipping rust and rot from the mechanisms of local government. The rust and rot are increasing because people who can profit from their increase count on our looking toward the war, not toward them. Your town may have a police force of no more than four and its amusement business may be confined to half a dozen juke joints, but some percentage of both may have formed a partnership against your interests under cover of the war.

Certainly the town has a sewage system, a garbage dump, fire traps, a rudimen- 12 tary public health code, ordinances designed to protect life, and a number of Joe Doakes who can make money by juggling the relationship among them. Meanwhile the ordinary hazards of peace are multiplied by the conditions of war, carelessness and preoccupation increase, and the inevitable war pestilence is gathering to spring. The end-products do not look pleasant when they are seen clearly, especially when a community realizes that it has killed five hundred people who did not need to die.

▪7▪

Writing the Research Essay

In Chapter 7, you take the evidence and information that you have been collecting from your sources and transform them into an essay. At this stage of the writing process, you begin to make the sources your own—by taking notes; by developing a thesis; by deciding which information is relevant and important to that thesis; by organizing the material into a sequence of paragraphs in support of the thesis; and, finally, by expressing your ideas and explaining your evidence to the reader, as far as possible in your own words.

SAVING INFORMATION

You should start to plan your research essay in much the same way that you would work on any other essay. Whatever the topic, you will probably accumulate a large quantity of written notes that serve as the raw materials for your synthesis. Here, the term "notes" refers to any of the products of your research: your own summaries and paraphrases, quotations, photocopies of book pages and articles, printouts and downloaded copies of Web material, class lecture notes, stories clipped from newspapers and magazines, and jottings of your own ideas about the topic.

More specifically, when you engage in research, you often "take notes": you read through a text, sometimes quickly and sometimes slowly, deciding as you go which information you want to use in your essay and writing it down as summary, paraphrase, and quotation. Before the days of computers, notes were usually handwritten on index cards or lined pads, ready to be organized into a sequence that would become the outline of an essay. The text of books and articles was pared down to handwritten notes that, in turn, were rewritten into the sentences of an essay. Many students still prefer this slow but thorough way of absorbing ideas and information.

Now, technology offers an alternative. More often than not, text from a book goes through a copying machine and becomes a photocopied page; the words of the text remain the same. Online articles or Web sites get downloaded and appear in a file on your computer screen; the words of the text remain the same. Certainly, copying the original text can be useful: for example, you may want to include a small portion in your essay verbatim, as quotation. But, at some point, most of it will have to be rewritten in your own words, in your own voice. Otherwise, you will not be writing an essay; you will be compiling an anthology of quotations.

Downloading presents a particular temptation. The information is available right there, on your screen, and by clicking a few keys you can transfer it directly into the file you've created for your research essay. You can keep on cut-and-pasting from other Web sites and database articles, and type in some extracts from photocopies; and you'll end up with something that contains sentences and paragraphs and meets the minimum number of assigned pages. It may look like an essay—but will it read like an essay?

The cut-and-paste method of writing an essay involves no writing. Technically, you are presenting the results of your research by assembling an electronic scrapbook. Your instructor will easily observe that the writing component of the assignment hasn't been fulfilled and will grade the "essay" accordingly. Cut-and-paste may be easy to do, but it doesn't achieve its purpose.

Learning to write essays means learning to speak for yourself. Learning to write research essays means using the skills of summary and paraphrase to present your sources. And you can't delay doing that until you're at the point of writing the essay. If you were dealing with only one or two authors, you might be able to move back and forth from the source file to the essay file (or have them both on a split screen) and write directly from your sources. But juggling a dozen or more authors, each on a different screen, you'll find it hard to achieve any kind of coherent structure for your essay. What's the solution? Take notes!

TAKING NOTES

If it's your preference or if your access to a computer is limited, by all means use the traditional method of taking handwritten notes on index cards or a pad of paper. There can be no more thorough or reliable bridge between your research and your essay. But if you opt for convenience, establish a new computer file at the onset of your research. This file will not be the one used for the writing of your essay; it will be exclusively for notes. As you start working with a new source, open that file, put the bibliographical information about that source clearly at the start of a new section, and type in your version of the material that you may want to use. Don't copy-type (except for the occasional quotation). Use your own words.

When you've finished your notes, you'll have one long file ready to be printed out and reorganized, or simply reorganized on the screen. Once you've worked out your sequence of ideas, you can transfer your notes into your essay file. The difference is that, this way, you will be cut-and-pasting your own work.

Here are some other guidelines for note-taking:

1. Don't start taking notes until you have compiled most of your preliminary bibliography. Choosing materials to copy and to download will help you gradually to understand the possibilities of your subject and decide on a potential thesis. But if you start taking notes from the first few texts that you find, you may be wasting time pursuing an idea that will turn out to be impractical or that the evidence ultimately won't support. You may discover, for example, that there's very little documented information about the gunfight at the OK Corral, and so shift your focus to Billy the Kid.

2. Unless it's prohibitively expensive, try to take notes from photocopies of books and articles, rather than the texts themselves; that way, you'll always have the copies to refer to if there's a confusion in your notes. (The copies will also be useful if your instructor asks you to submit some of your sources.) Print out downloaded material and work from the printed copy so that you don't have to keep shifting from file to file. It's hard to take good notes if you don't have the text in front of you as you write.

3. Use paraphrase and summary. As you learned in Chapter 2, quotation should be the exception, not the rule. Copying the author's language will make it more difficult for you to shift to your own writing style later on. You want to avoid producing an anthology of cannibalized quotations. The effort of paraphrasing and summarizing also helps you to understand each new idea. In your notes, always try to explain the author's exact meaning.

4. Include evidence to support the broader ideas that you're writing about. If you're writing about corruption in the Olympic games, don't simply allude to issues like the use of performance-enhancing drugs or the influence of network television in the scheduling of events. Cite facts to illustrate your point. You won't remember the range of evidence as you're writing the paper unless you include examples in your notes.

5. Differentiate your own ideas from those that you are paraphrasing. When you take notes, you're working slowly and concentrating on what you're reading. It's at that time that you're most likely to develop your own comments and ideas, spinning them off from the text. Be careful to indicate in

your notes what's yours and what's the source's. Later on, you'll need to know which material to document. Using square brackets [like these] around your own ideas is a good way of making this distinction.

6. Keep a running record of page references. You'll need to cite the exact page number for each reference, not an approximate guess. It isn't enough to write "pp. 285–91" after a few paragraphs of notes. Three weeks or three hours later, how will you remember on which page you found the point that you're about to cite in your essay? If you're quoting or paraphrasing a source in some detail, make a slash and insert a new page number to indicate exactly where you turned the page. Put quotation marks around all quotations *immediately*.

7. Always include complete bibliographical information for each source. If you don't have a clear record of details like place of publication, volume number, or URL, you won't be able to hand in a finished bibliography. It's convenient to have all that information in one place. Either start a new file just for bibliography or include that information at the beginning of each section of your notes.

Guidelines for Taking Good Notes

1. Don't start taking notes until you have compiled most of your preliminary bibliography.
2. Try to take notes from photocopies of books and articles and printouts of sources, rather than the texts themselves.
3. Use paraphrase and summary, rather than quotation.
4. Include evidence to support the broader ideas that you're writing about.
5. Differentiate your own ideas from those that you are paraphrasing.
6. Keep a running record of page references.
7. Always include complete bibliographical information for each source.

Organizationally, you can take notes in either of two ways: *by source* or *by topic*. Taking notes by source is the more obvious way. You start your computer file (or your cards or pad) with the first source, presenting information in the order of its appearance. Then you go on to the second, the third, and so on. Figure 7-1 on p. 332 shows notes for an essay, organized by source, describing the 1871 fire that devastated Chicago. The source (described in detail earlier in the file) is the *New York Times* for October 15, 1871. Notice that each item in the list is assigned a number; this will be useful later on, when you are organizing your notes to write your essay. The source has also been assigned an identifying

NY Times, 10/15/71, p. 1   Source J

1. city normal again
2. still martial rule; Gen. Sheridan in charge
3. citizens working at night to watch for new outbreak of fire
4. newspapers moved to other locations
5. estimate 1,000 dead
6. earlier reports of looting and loss of life not exaggerated
7. waterworks won't open until next day
8. two-thirds of the city still using candlelight
9. suffering mostly among "humbler classes"
10. businessmen are "buoyant"
11. bread is 8 cents
12. saloons are closed at 9:00 P.M. for one week

Figure 7-1. Notes Grouped by Source

letter; if you have two sources with the same name (for example, the *Times* for two different dates), you'll be able to distinguish between them.

There's nothing wrong with taking notes by source. It's easy, and it clarifies which information belongs to which source. The disadvantage is that your notes remain raw material, with no organizational pattern imposed on them.

Taking notes by topic is a more sophisticated system. Once you've decided the basic events or issues that your essay will cover, each of those topics gets assigned a separate section of your notes file. For example, early in the note-taking process, one student decided that she would definitely write about the aftermath of the Chicago fire; one section of her notes would be devoted to efforts to contain and put out the blaze. After that, every time she came across a new point about *fire fighting*—no matter what the source—she scrolled through (or searched) her file, looking for the topic name and then adding that information. Similar sections were established to deal with *food supplies* and *looting*. Figure 7-2 shows a sample of her notes.

All the searching and scrolling takes time, but, ultimately, organizing notes by topic makes it much easier to organize your essay. In fact, because your information is already categorized, you can often skip a whole stage in the process and begin to write your essay from your notes without much additional organization. But taking notes by topic does require you to make a list, either written or mental, of possible categories or note topics while you're still doing your research. And you may not be completely sure about your thesis and structure that early in the process. When you take notes by topic, it's also vital to make sure that *each* point is followed by its source and the relevant page number.

Fire Fighting

All engines and hose carts in city come (NYT 10/8, p. 5)
Water station on fire, with no water to put out small fires
     (Hall, p. 228)
all engines out there; fire too big to stop (NYT 10/8, p. 5)
fire department "demoralized"; bad fire previous night; men
were drinking afterwards; fire marshal "habitually drunk"
     (NYT 10/23, p. 2)

Figure 7-2. Notes Grouped by Topic

EXERCISE 24: TAKING NOTES ON TWO TOPICS

Reread the three articles dealing with the Cocoanut Grove fire of 1942 at the end of Chapter 6. Head one file "Causes of the Fire" and take a set of notes on that topic. Head another file "The Fire's Intensity and Speed" and take a second set of notes on the second topic. Each set of notes should make use of all three sources.

EXERCISE 25: TAKING NOTES ON THREE TOPICS

Assume that you are doing research on Native Americans and that you have come across the following source in the library. After doing a preliminary evaluation of the passage, take a set of notes for an essay entitled "The Decline of Indian Culture," a second set of notes for an essay entitled "Indian Social Attitudes," and a third set of notes for an essay entitled "The Influence of Indians on Early European Settlements."

Like many comfortable stories, the story of the Indians' destruction hides other stories that are less so. For starters, it leaves out that the destruction was and is actually worse than can be easily described. A well-informed person probably knows of the bigger and more famous massacres, but big and small massacres took place in many states over the years. Killing Indians was once the official policy of the state of California, which spent a million dollars reimbursing Indian-hunters for the ammunition they used. Helen Hunt Jackson's history of Indian-white relations, *A Century of Dishonor*, published in 1881, recounted episodes of killing and mistreatment which have long faded into the past. Its modern reader can weep at descriptions of massacres he has never heard of—does anyone besides those who live in the town of Gnadenhutten, Ohio, know of the slaughter in 1780 of the peaceful Indians at the Moravian mission there? Jackson's book could be revised and reissued today, with another hundred years added to the title. After the frontier gunfire died down, violence and untimely death found other means. The Indian was supposed to be heading off to join his ancestors in the Happy Hunting Ground, and the path he might take to get there (alcoholism? pneumonia? car wreck? the flu epidemic of 1918?) apparently did not need to be too closely explained. The violence continued, and continues today. Among the Navajo, the largest tribe in the United States, car accidents are the leading cause of death. Especially in Western towns that border big reservations, stabbings and fights and car wrecks are a depressingly regular part of life.

Also, the destruction story gives the flattering and wrong impression that European culture showed up in the Americas and simply mowed down whatever was in its way. In fact, the European arrivals were often hungry and stunned in their new settlements, and what they did to Indian culture was more than matched for years by what encounters with Indians did to theirs. Via the settlers, Indian crops previously unknown outside the Americas crossed the Atlantic and changed Europe. Indian farmers were the first to domesticate corn, peanuts, tomatoes, pumpkins, and many kinds of beans. Russia and Ireland grew no potatoes before travelers found the plant in Indian gardens in South America; throughout Europe, the introduction of the potato caused a rise in the standard of living and a population boom. Before Indians, no one in the world had ever smoked tobacco. No one in the Bible (or in any other pre-Columbian text, for that matter) ever has a cigarette, dips snuff, or smokes a pipe. The novelty of breathing in tobacco smoke or chewing the dried leaves caught on so fast in Europe that early colonists made fortunes growing tobacco; it was America's first cash crop. That the United States should now be so determined to stamp out all smoking seems historically revisionist and strange.

Surrounded as we are today by pavement, we assume that Indians have had to adapt to us. But for a long time much of the adapting went the other way. In the land of the free, Indians were the original "free"; early America was European culture reset in an Indian frame. Europeans who survived here became a mixture of identities in which the Indian part was what made them American and different than they had been before. Influence is harder to document than corn and beans, but as real. We know that Iroquois Indians attended meetings of the colonists in the years before the American Revolution and advised them to unite in a scheme for self-government based on the confederacy that ruled the six Iroquois nations; and that Benjamin Franklin said, at a gathering of delegates from the colonies in Albany in 1754, "It would be a strange thing if six nations of ignorant savages should be capable of forming a scheme for such a union and be able to execute it in such a manner as that it has subsisted for ages and appears indissoluble, and yet that a like union should be impracticable for ten or a dozen English colonies." His use of the term "ignorant savages" is thought to have been ironical; he admired the Iroquois plan, and it formed one of the models for the U.S.

Constitution. We know, too, that Thomas Jefferson thought that American government should follow what he imagined to be the Indian way. He wrote: ". . . were it made a question, whether no law, as among the savage Americans, or too much law, as among the civilized Europeans, submits man to the greatest evil, one who has seen both conditions of existence would pronounce it to be the last . . . It will be said, that great societies cannot exist without government. The savages, therefore, break them into small ones."

Indian people today sometimes talk about the need to guard their culture carefully, so that it won't be stolen from them. But what is best (and worst) about any culture can be as contagious as a cold germ; the least contact passes it on. In colonial times, Indians were known for their disregard of titles and for a deep egalitarianism that made them not necessarily defer even to the leading men of their tribes. The route this trait took as it passed from Indian to white was invisible. Probably, contagion occurred during official gatherings, as when an exalted person arrived at a frontier place from the governor's palace or across the sea. The Indians spoke to the exalted person directly, equals addressing an equal, with no bowing or scraping or bending of the knee. Then, when their white neighbors got up to speak, perhaps ordinary self-consciousness made it hard to act any differently—to do the full routine of obeisance customary back in England—with the Indians looking on. Or maybe it was even simpler, a demonstration of the principle that informal behavior tends to drive out formal, given time. However the transfer happened, in a few generations it was complete; the American character had become thoroughly Indian in its outspokenness and all-around skepticism on the subject of who was and was not great.

IAN FRAZIER, from *On the Rez*

DEVELOPING A LIST OF TOPICS

Once you have all your notes in a computer file or on cards or a pad, you need to organize them into a plan for your essay. (If you've already organized your notes by topic, you can skip this stage.) The first step is to *take inventory:* you search for ideas worth developing in your essay by (1) reviewing your notes and (2) identifying and writing down all the major topics that you have learned and thought about during your research.

Here's a list of topics taken from a set of notes about the Chicago fire of 1871:

Mrs. O'Leary's cow kicks over the lantern: did that start the fire?
Extent of the damage
Preventing panic
Feeding the homeless
Dealing with those trapped within buildings
Drought conditions the previous summer

Preventing looting
Beginning to rebuild the city
Mobilizing manpower to fight the fire
Improvising hospital conditions
Providing shelter
How the fire spread
Crowd control
Fighting the fire
Organizing the firefighters and police
Sounding the alarm

Since the subject of this essay is an event, the items on the list are factual and brief. An essay that deals with ideas rather than events is likely to have a preliminary list of topics with longer, more abstract entries. Notice that, at this point, the sequence of the entries doesn't matter; the points are in random order, just as they were found in the notes. Nor do you have to include supporting evidence at this stage. That's why the list is so skinny. You are extracting what's important from the mass of your notes; you are looking for the bones of your essay.

Guidelines for Taking Inventory of Your Notes and Forming Paragraph Topics

- *Do write down in any order the important ideas* that you find in your notes. At this point, the items don't have to be related to each other in sequence.

- *Don't try to summarize* all your notes or even summarize each of your notes. At this point, you are working on organizing your topics, not summarizing your research.

- *Don't try to link the ideas that you write down to specific sources.* At this point, there is no special reason to place the names of the sources next to your new list of ideas; not every statement in your new list will necessarily be included in your essay. Later, you will decide which source to use in support of which topic sentence.

- *Do think about your own reactions* to the information that you have collected. At this point, the many strands of your research begin to become the product of your own thinking. Now, you are deciding what is worth writing about.

- *Do use your own words.* At this point, even if you only jot down a phrase, it should be your own version of the source's idea. Even if the information has appeared in ten different articles and you've included it ten different times in your notes, you are now, in some sense, making it your own.

PLANNING A STRATEGY

Essays about events or people tend to have a straightforward organization based on a time sequence, with a beginning, middle, and end. You certainly will have a general conclusion to support—"The rescue and rehabilitation efforts after the Chicago fire were competently carried out"—but the bulk of the essay will analyze what happened during and after the fire in sequential order.

Abstract topics require a more complex structure. Your organizational strategy will be linked to your *thesis* or central idea—the basis of your essay's development. Essays about abstract ideas and issues are often *arguments*. The thesis is likely to be a general proposition that you intend to prove, citing your research as evidence.

In Chapter 1, you learned that most arguments are based on a combination of two kinds of logical reasoning:

- *Deductive reasoning:* You provide a series of linked premises, based on assumptions that you and your reader share, that leads to a logical conclusion.

- *Inductive reasoning:* You provide a range of evidence from which you construct a logical conclusion.

In practice, these two basic logical tools—the use of linked premises, and the use of evidence—are used together to develop the most common patterns of argument: cause-and-effect and problem-and-solution.

The *cause-and-effect* essay establishes a causal link between two circumstances. The thesis usually answers the question, "Why?" Let's assume that your general subject is *high school dropouts*. Why is the high school dropout rate as high as it is today? Here are a few typical answers:

Because class sizes are too large

Because students are poorly prepared to handle the work

Because many students are foreign born and can't speak English well

Because local governments are not providing sufficient funding

Because family life is breaking down, leaving students without support and discipline

Clearly, this inventory list suggests many possible causes. You may initially be inclined to write about all of them, giving each one equal weight. If you do, your essay may be long and unmanageable, with a thesis that pulls the reader in many contradictory directions. But if you focus on only one cause, you run the risk of oversimplifying your argument. You need to consider which of these causes is *most responsible* for its effect—the high dropout rate—and which ones have a *contributing influence*.

Analyzing your list should also help you to determine which causes work together. For example, the problem of class size is probably linked to—caused by—the problem of inadequate funding. Here you have a smaller cause-and-effect embedded within the larger one: inadequate funding results in overly large classes which, in turn, contribute to the drop-out rate.

The links between causes—like funding and class size—form the *deductive* part of your argument. But the causes in the list above also lend themselves to *inductive* support. By the time you finish your research, you should be able to determine whether your inductive evidence supports your deductive argument about the reasons why students drop out. Assuming that it does, your essay will present factual evidence, including statistics, about class sizes, student preparedness, language difficulties, and diminished local budgets for education. The last point on your list—family breakdown—is the most abstract and so the most difficult to support. You would need to develop a series of deductive premises, along with evidence, to make a strong causal link between the decline of family life and the incidence of high school dropouts.

Let's assume that you decide on the following thesis: *The poor educational environment, resulting from inadequate funding, makes it hard for students to learn, so they drop out.* What kinds of counterarguments would you have to anticipate and rebut? While your research supports your thesis, you have also found authorities who argue that students from strong family backgrounds perform well and stay in school even in overcrowded, poorly funded districts. You can continue to defend your preferred thesis, but you must also acknowledge your opponents' views, while pointing out their limitations.

The *problem-and-solution* essay often incorporates the cause-and-effect essay, using five stages:

1. *Establish that a problem exists.* Explain why it is a problem, and anticipate the negative consequences if nothing is done.

2. *Analyze the causes of the problem.* Here, you can include a modified version of the cause-and-effect strategy: emphasize the major causes, but remind your reader that this is a complex issue, with a number of contributory influences working together. Provide some evidence, but not necessarily the full range of your research.

3. *Assert the best solution.* Using the evidence of your research, demonstrate why the preferred solution will work and indicate how you would go about implementing it.

4. *Anticipate counterarguments and answer them.* Your research has turned up authorities who have recommended different solutions. What are the advantages and disadvantages of those solutions? Is your solution better? Why?

5. *Conclude in a spirit of accommodation.* Assert your solution once again, but also consider acknowledging the complexity of the problem and making room for some of your opponents' ideas. Sometimes the arguments on either side of an issue are too evenly balanced for certainty, and you need to find a solution within common ground.

ARRANGING THE ORDER OF TOPICS

At some point in the process of organizing your essay, your skinny list of ideas becomes an outline. An *outline* is a list of the major and minor points supporting an essay's thesis, presented in a pattern that reflects their relative importance. The major points will probably all be *parallel* or of the same kind: the *reasons* why x is true, or the *ways* in which y happens, or the *differences* between x and y, or the chief *characteristics* of z. These major points—the items on your inventory—are given the most prominent place in the outline, usually at the left-hand margin. Secondary material—the ideas, information, or examples being used as supporting evidence—appears directly under each major point and slightly to the right. If there are different kinds of evidence to support a point or a group of examples, each is listed on a separate line. Traditionally, outlines are written in a standard format, with major and minor points assigned numbers and letters of the alphabet to keep them in order.

There is absolutely no need to create a formal outline, with its letters and numbers, unless your instructor requires it or you find it useful for organizing your information. You can indicate the relationships between ideas simply by the way you place them on the page.

What is important is that you revise and expand your inventory of major topics, making new lists out of old ones, adding and deleting ideas, changing the order to correspond to your strategy. When that inventory list is as good as you can make it, you have a sequence that will roughly correspond to the sequence of paragraphs in your essay. (In a formal outline, that list would correspond to the items preceded by Roman numerals and capital letters.)

How do you decide on the best order for your topic list? Outlining is all about priorities and relationships. How are ideas linked together? Which is more important? What does your reader need to know first? What information does your reader need in order to understand a second, more complex point? How does one idea lead into another?

Look for an *organizing principle*. In a historical essay, the ordering principle is frequently time: the deployment of troops has to be described before the actual battle. In a personality profile, dominant qualities will take precedence over minor quirks. Problems get described before solutions; causes are analyzed in order to understand their effects. One rationale for your sequence might be "most compelling" to "least compelling" reason. But an even stronger rationale is "most fundamental" to "most complex": you start with your most basic point and demonstrate how everything else rests on that central idea.

In addition to rearranging the order of your topics, you also have to expand your inventory by adding supporting evidence for each major topic. (In effect, you are filling in the secondary tiers of your outline.) Under headings like fire fighting and medical care, you insert factual information demonstrating that the authorities in Chicago reacted to the fire as efficiently as circumstances allowed. Similarly, having established a linked set of the causes and subcauses that encourage a higher dropout rate, you distribute the material gathered in your research—statistics, surveys, anecdotes, theories—under the appropriate topics.

Guidelines for Arranging Your Order of Topics

■ *Evaluate your inventory list of important ideas.*

✓ Notice which ideas are in the mainstream of your research, discussed by several of your sources, and which ones appear only in one or two sources.

✓ Consider whether you have enough evidence to support all of your topics.

✓ Think about eliminating topics that seem minor or remote from your subject and your thesis.

✓ Look for and combine topics that restate the same point.

✓ If you are developing an argument essay, make sure that each of the key points supporting your side, as well as your counterarguments to the opposition, is supported by your research.

■ *Think about the sequence of ideas on your final list and the possible strategies for organizing your essay.*

✓ How does your list of ideas help to establish a thesis?

✓ Are you working with a collection of reasons? Consequences? Problems? Dangers?

✓ What kind of essay are you writing? Cause-and-effect? Problem-and-solution? Explanation of a procedure? Evaluation of reasons for an argument?

If you are developing a historical or biographical topic:

✓ Did the event fall into distinct narrative stages?

✓ What aspects of the scene would an observer have noticed?

✓ Which of your subject's activities best reveals his or her personality?

If you are developing an argument:

✓ Does your issue lend itself to a cause-and-effect or a problem-and-solution essay?

✓ Do your main reasons require deductive or inductive support?

✓ Which are your most compelling arguments?

■ *Arrange your list of topics in a sequence that has meaning for you, carries out your strategy, and develops your thesis in a clear direction.*

COMPLETING YOUR OUTLINE

Your final organizing task is to organize your notes in accordance with your outline. This can be done either *directly on the computer,* working from your outline, or by *cross-referencing.* You may need to use a combination of both methods.

Using the Computer to Organize Your Essay: Let's assume that most of your notes are contained in a file on your computer. If you originally organized your notes *by topic,* you simply rearrange your notes on the screen, section by section, so that the topics correspond to the sequence of those in your outline. This is one time when cutting-and-pasting is a quick and acceptable method of getting your work done. (Alternatively, you can split the screen between your notes file and your essay file, establish your outline topics in your essay file, and drag portions of your notes from one file to the appropriate place in the other. But dragging can be a messy business, and it's possible to lose or misplace material in the process.) Be sure to safeguard your notes. Instead of cutting-and-pasting, try copying-and-pasting so that your original file of notes remains intact. Keep a backup version of both your note file and your essay file on a separate disk. Above all, *save your work at regular and frequent intervals.*

If you originally organized your notes *by source,* organizing your essay now becomes a more complex process. If your topic is straightforward and your essay is under ten pages, you can probably rearrange your notes directly on the computer, as described in the previous paragraph. You place your outline in your essay file, with wide gaps between the topics, and start to move items (cutting or copying-and-pasting) from one file to the other. Instead of transferring whole sections as you would if you had organized your notes by topic, you'll be pulling out a quotation or a paragraph or an example from your notes and finding the right place for it in your outline sequence. This can be tedious and painstaking work. You have to be extremely careful to *make sure that the source of each piece of information is indicated next to it before you move it.* Otherwise, as you write your essay, you won't be able to document your sources. Without documentation of sources, your research efforts have no validity. This is why it saves time and effort to organize your notes by topic when you originally write them.

Using Cross-Referencing to Organize Your Essay: If you're working on a lengthy and complicated essay with a set of notes organized by source, or if a large portion of your notes is on paper rather than in a computer file, your best option is to use cross-referencing to complete your outline and organize your essay. Cross-referencing is used before physically moving material from file to file. Once again, you're working from two sets of material:

- *Your completed outline of topics.* The topics are listed either on the screen or on a long pad. Make sure to leave wide gaps between each item. Assign a number (preferably a Roman numeral), in sequence, to each topic in your outline.

- *Your notes.* It's easiest to have everything on paper, including printouts of any computer notes. Assign an identifying letter to each source (placing it at the top of each page of notes devoted to material from that source). If you have twelve sources, you'll be using A–L. Assign an Arabic numeral to each separate piece of information within the notes from a specific source.

Now, once again, slowly read through all your research notes, this time keeping your outline of topics in front of you. Every time you come across a point in your notes that should be cited in support of a topic on your outline, immediately:

1. Place the number of the outline topic (III) next to the reference in your notes.

2. Place the source's identifying letter (F) and the identifying number of the item in your notes (9) under the relevant topic in your outline.

For the system to work, you must complete both stages: notes must be keyed to the outline, and the outline must be keyed to each item in your research notes. The notes and the outline criss-cross each other; hence the term *cross-referencing*.

To illustrate cross-referencing, here is an example taken from the notes and outline for an essay on the Chicago fire. The outline was divided into three main sections: the *causes* of the fire, the *panic* during the fire, and *restoring order* after the fire. Figure 7–3 shows an excerpt from the notes, with roman numerals written in the margins to indicate cross-references to three specific paragraph

Source G

Times, October 11, "The Ruined City," p. 1

1. The fire has stopped and there has been some "blessed rain."
2. 20-30 people have died in their homes.
XI 3. Plundering everywhere – like a scene of war
   A. A thief suffocated while trying to steal jewelry from a store.
   B. People who were caught pilfering had to be released because the jail burned down.
X 4. Lake used for drinking water.
5. People dying of exposure.
XI 6. Little food: people searching the ruins
IX 7. Difficulties of transporting supplies
XI 8. Meeting of citizens at church to help protect what was left, to help homeless, and to provide water if further fires broke out

Figure 7-3. Cross-referencing

topics.

Here are the topics, which come from the last section of the outline:

IX. Feeding the homeless *G6 / G7*

X. Providing basic services *G4*

XI. Protecting life and property *G3 / G8*

When you have finished cross-referencing:

- Your outline will have a precise list of sources to be cited for each major point, and
- Your research notes will have code numbers in most (but not necessarily all) of the margins.

Cross-referencing helps you to avoid time-consuming searches for references while you are writing the essay. When you start to work on the paragraph dealing with feeding the homeless, you consult your outline and immediately go to Source G, Items 6 and 7. (References to other sources will also have been placed next to Item IX on your outline.) The accumulated information will become the basis for writing that paragraph.

A few of the items in the notes for Source G have no cross-references next to them. Some will be cross-referenced to other topics in this outline, and haven't yet been given their reference numbers. Items 2 and 5, for example, would probably come under the heading of Casualties, in the section on panic during the fire. On the other hand, not all the notes will necessarily be used in the essay. Some items simply won't fit into the topics chosen for the outline and will be discarded.

When you are developing a complex research topic, it is helpful to print out your outline and your notes, to identify outline topics and sections of your notes through numbers and letters, and to match up your notes with your outline by cross-referencing, using numbers and letters in the margins. Only when you are satisfied with your organization, and when the topics in your outline are fully supported by information from your notes, should you turn to the computer and copy-and-paste on the screen.

Guidelines for Organizing Your Essay

1. Read through your list of notes, thinking about your thesis and the appropriate strategy for your essay.
2. Write down a list of potential paragraph topics.
3. Revise the list, adding and deleting items, and indicating possible supporting evidence.
4. Rearrange the order of the items on the list until the topics are in logical sequence.
5. If necessary, cross-reference your notes and your outline.
6. Integrate your notes into your outline by transferring them to your essay file.

EXERCISE 26: WRITING AN OUTLINE WITH CROSS-REFERENCING

Read the following set of notes, organized by source, for an essay on immigration.

1. Write an outline of topics for an essay to be called "The Economic and Social Consequences of Immigration in the United States Today."
2. Cross-reference the notes with your outline.

As you consider the information in these notes, remember that, if this exercise were preparation for an assigned essay, you could return to any of the sources, if you wished, and add details or examples to develop a topic that does not have enough supporting information.

Source A

Borjas, George J. "Tired, Poor, On Welfare." *National Review* 13 (Dec. 1993): 40–42.

1. It's true that immigrants contribute more in taxes to the nation's economy than they consume in welfare payments.

2. But the cost of living in this country and of using services and facilities adds an enormous amount to the cost of their support. That isn't being considered in most pro-immigration arguments. In this regard, immigrants do potentially take more than they give.

3. In 1990, a greater percentage of immigrants than natives received welfare. Immigrants comprise 8% of the population; they receive 13% of the cash benefits distributed.

4. Recent immigrants are less skilled than their counterparts 100 years ago. (B. says he's not saying that immigrants come to this country expressly to live on welfare.)

5. Whether immigrants want to work or not isn't the point; they don't have the skills, so they go on welfare.

6. B. fears creation of a new underclass of the unskilled. "A welfare state cannot afford the large-scale immigration of less-skilled persons." (42)

Source B

Brimelow, Peter. "Time to Rethink Immigration?" *National Review* 22 (June 1992): 30–46.

1. Cites large numbers of recent immigrants. Between 1951 and 1990, about one-fifth of the population of Jamaica had immigrated to the U.S.

2. 85% of legal immigrants between 1971 and 1990 were from the Third World.

3. Consequence: "The American ethnic mix has been upset." (31) White population of U.S. fell by 13% from 1960–90. The projection: by 2020, whites would only be 61% of population.

4. U.S. birthrate has declined since big waves of immigration at turn of century; therefore, new immigrants now have greater opportunity to dominate.

5. Major historical influence on U.S. culture has been British and German.

6. Proponents of present immigration policy are urging "Americans to abandon the bonds of a common ethnicity and instead to trust entirely to ideology to hold together their state." (35) Historically, this bond of ideology hasn't been successful (e.g., USSR).

7. Melting pot tradition: "cultural synthesis . . . a pattern of swallowing and digestion" of immigrant groups (e.g., Irish immigrants eventually abandoned antisocial tendencies like dysfunctional families, alcoholism, disease). (36)

8. Economic argument: immigrants needed to perform jobs no one else will do. Instead, why not force unemployed Americans to work for their welfare? Or encourage a higher birth rate?

9. Cultural characteristics of each immigrant group predict whether that group will thrive or fail in new country. Cultural qualities of current major immigrant groups include unfortunate antisocial tendencies (like violence); this will have "economic consequences" for U.S.

10. Cites Borjas: welfare benefits to immigrants cost $1 billion more than they pay in taxes.

11. Hispanics in particular aren't being urged to assimilate; their tendency to support bilingualism and multiculturalism is deplorable.

Source C
Custred, Glynn. "Country Time." *National Review* 16 (June 1997): 39–40.

1. To maintain an orderly society, our country needs common cultural values, including "shared meanings, myths, and values conveyed in a common language, realized in national symbols, and supported by formal institutions, especially public education." (39)

2. Immigration can easily disturb this sense of community.

3. Earlier waves of immigration weren't a threat to national stability because those immigrants assimilated easily and willingly.

4. Immigrants in the last three decades aren't content to assimilate. They demand multiculturalism, which "drives [the nation] apart." (39) Multiculturalists attack the very concept of linguistic and cultural unity, which they regard as simply a way of oppressing ethnic and racial minorities. Custred depicts multiculturalists as whining for their rights.

5. The nation is becoming increasingly divided without any effort by our business and government leaders to prevent it.

6. The more immigrants allowed in, the more likely the newcomers will remain in their "ethnic enclaves" and this divisive multicultural attitude will grow.

7. Example: 86 languages spoken in California schools.

8. Disregard the argument that U.S. needs new workers. The danger of social tension resulting from immigration would be just as serious an economic threat.

Source D
Fukuyama, Francis. "Immigrants and Family Values." *Commentary* May 1993: 26–32.

1. "The symptoms of cultural decay are all around us, but the last people in the world we should be blaming are recent immigrants." (26)

2. Rejects Brimelow's argument that culture determines economic success for immigrants.

3. American identity doesn't derive from a specific culture; it's rooted in (a) ideals of democracy that transcend ethnicity, and (b) a consumer culture. Both are available to any immigrant group.

4. Do non-European immigrant groups threaten basic American values (e.g., nuclear family, success through hard work)? Decline of family structure and work ethic results from our declining postindustrialist society, not from values of new immigrants, who tend to have strong family loyalties (e.g., Asian immigrants: large families, economically successful).

5. Fear of immigration really directed at Hispanics: some Hispanics have had social problems, and many Americans lump together Hispanics with blacks as "a vast threatening underclass." (29)

6. F. cites diversity of Hispanics: some good, some bad. Problems really arise from poverty.

7. Reason for cultural disruption in U.S. has to do with economic and social change. Newly arrived immigrants didn't create sexual revolution, feminism, alienating workplace, single-parent households.

8. Clamor for multiculturalism comes more from leaders than from the average immigrant, for whom preserving ethnicity is not a primary goal.

9. Real issue: do we believe so strongly in our cultural heritage that we insist that all immigrants assimilate, or do we "carry respect for other cultures to the point that Americans no longer have a common voice with which to speak to one another?" (31)

Source E
Glazer, Nathan. "The Closing Door." *The New Republic* 27 Dec. 1993. Rpt. in *Arguing Immigration.* Ed. Nicolaus Mills. New York: Simon and Schuster, 1994. 37–47.

1. Some immigrants (mostly Asians) come with better education and work skills than most Americans have. Some are less qualified than Americans (mostly Hispanics and Caribbean blacks).

2. Even within these groups, ability to work and support themselves varies.

3. The economic argument isn't the crucial one. Whether we import cheap labor or not isn't the point (Japan thrives on a low immigration rate).

4. Those who use the economic argument to propose restrictions are really responding to the perceived threat of a more diverse nation. But they shouldn't be called bigots or racists. The preference for people of one's own culture is natural. "There is a difference between recognizing those who are in some sense one's own, with links to a people and a culture, and a policy based on dislike, hostility, or racial antagonism." (44)

5. Why doesn't U.S. assimilate immigrants the way it used to? "It is a different country: less self-confident, less willing to impose European and American customs and loyalty as simply the best in the world." (44)

6. G. is very tolerant of the movement to restrict immigration. "They ask why the stream of immigration should be so unrepresentative of the nation that already exists." (45)

Source F

McCarthy, Kevin. "Immigration by the Numbers." *New York Times* 15 Oct. 1997: 28.

1. McC. is a demographer who produces studies of the impact of immigrants on the California economy. Such statistics are used and sometimes distorted by proponents and opponents of present immigration policy. The issue is: does immigration have a positive effect on the national economy?

2. "No matter what ideologues on both sides say, immigration is neither absolutely good or evil."

3. On balance, California has gained more than it has lost from the availability of a low-wage immigrant work force.

4. But low-skilled workers (immigrant and native) are earning less and less.

5. Immigrants without skills aren't thriving.

6. The state is burdened by providing services to immigrants.

7. McC. suggests "modest" changes in policy: (a) scale back the number of immigrants admitted to halfway between present number and the number in the 1960s; and (b) try for a formula that favors immigrants with education and skills, rather than low-skilled immigrants who are being admitted to join family members already here.

Source G

Krikorian, Mark. "Will Americanization Work in America?" *Freedom Review* Fall 1997: <www.cis.org/articles/1997/freedom_review.html>. 22 Aug. 2001.

1. We've been experiencing the largest influx of immigrants in American history, with no end in sight. 900,000 green cards given to potential citizens in 1996.

2. Why has immigration become such a hot issue? Those who favor an open access policy say that opposition to immigration results from a fear of multiculturalism, which is likely to "weaken America's national identity." Krikorian questions this "romanticized and sanitized" myth.

3. There are other difficult issues. For example, the National Research Council has issued a report expressing fears that the increased rate of immigration is turning the U.S. into a nation of haves and have-nots. Some immigrants have

skills that feed into our present economic needs; they are likely to benefit from emigrating to America. Unskilled workers—like those who didn't finish high school in their own country—will have little chance of managing on their own, let alone thriving economically.

4. Most of the newest wave of immigrants are likely to be uneducated. Far from contributing to the tax base, they will become a drain on our public services. [This is Krikorian's analysis of the arguments, not his opinion.]

5. The very fact that the number of immigrants is the largest in our history makes it unlikely that they will assimilate quickly (e.g., learn English). These groups are large enough to support their own cultural institutions, so they need not mingle with native-born Americans or other immigrant groups. (Example: Spanish-speaking radio and television stations. Univision (Los Angeles) is the fifth-largest TV network.)

6. This cultural "clustering" prevents true diversity. It also discourages intermarriage since few immigrants have the opportunity to meet people (except employers) outside their culture. Still, Krikorian asserts that most immigrant populations are, in fact, willing to marry outside their cultures, suggesting the "potential amalgamation of the immigrant stock."

7. Krikorian's major point is that America is finding it extremely difficult to encourage assimilation among immigrants because it can't itself decide on its own national identity. There are too many different versions of history. Who should be our hero—George Washington or Malcolm X? Which holiday should we celebrate—Lincoln's birthday or Cinco de Mayo?

8. A study of immigrant children in 1992 and again in 1995 showed a significant decline in identification with American heritage and values.

9. Our view that our society ought to be multicultural too deep to be easily modified or reversed. Our present immigration population only encourages the breakup of our society into smaller, self-sustaining groups. It's unlikely that we will soon be able to return to a "common civic culture." [Note: Krikorian himself seems neutral on these issues.]

WRITING INTEGRATED PARAGRAPHS

Writing a research essay resembles putting together a *mosaic*. Each paragraph has a basic design, determined by its topic sentence. To carry out the design, a paragraph might contain a group of reasons or examples to illustrate its main

> ## Guidelines for Constructing Paragraphs in a Research Essay
>
> 1. *Each paragraph should possess a single main idea, usually expressed in the topic sentence, that supports the development of your essay's thesis.* That topic controls the arrangement of all the information in the paragraph. Everything that is included should develop and support that single idea, without digressions.
> 2. *The body of the paragraph should contain information taken from a variety of sources.* The number of different sources that you include in any one paragraph depends partly on the number of authors in your notes who have touched on its main idea and partly on the contribution each can make to the development of your topic.

idea, *or* an extended explanation to develop that idea in greater detail, or a comparison between two elements introduced in the first sentence. These are the same paragraphing patterns that you use in all your writing. What makes the research essay different is the fact that the materials are assembled from many sources.

Imagine that the notes that you have taken from several different sources are boxes of tiles, each box containing a different color. You may find it easier to avoid mixing the colors and to work *only* with red tiles or *only* with blue, or to devote one corner of the mosaic to a red pattern and another to a blue. In the same way, you may find it both convenient and natural to work with only one source at a time and to avoid the decisions and the adjustments that must be made when you are combining different styles and ideas. But, of course, it is the design and only the design that dictates which colors should be used in creating the pattern of the mosaic, and it is the design or outline of your essay that dictates which evidence should be included in each paragraph.

When you present a topic in a given paragraph, you must work with all the relevant information that you have gathered about that topic, whether it comes from one source or from many. Of course, you may have too much material; you may find it impossible to fit everything into the paragraph without overloading it with repetition. These rejected pieces may not fit into another part of the essay; instead, they will go back into their boxes as a backup or reserve fund of information.

The criteria for judging the quality of a paragraph remain the same—*clarity*, *coherence*, and *unity*.

- Do integrate your material so that your reader will not be distracted by the differing sources or made aware of breaks between the various points.

- Don't integrate your material so completely that you forget to provide appropriate acknowledgment of your sources.

Here is a paragraph from an essay about the novelist F. Scott Fitzgerald, in which four different explanations of an incident are presented, each at suitable length. Formal documentation of the sources has been omitted; but, to emphasize the variety and complexity of the research, the names of the sources and the attributing verbs and phrases have been underlined. The writer is describing an affair between Fitzgerald's wife, Zelda, and Edouard Jozan, a young Frenchman.

> There is a lack of agreement about the details of the affair as well as its significance for the Fitzgeralds' marriage. According to one of Fitzgerald's biographers, Jozan and Zelda afterwards regarded it as "nothing more than a summer flirtation." But Ernest Hemingway, in his memoirs, wrote much later that Scott had told him "a truly sad story" about the affair, which he repeated many times in the course of their friendship. Gerald and Sara Murphy, who were present that summer and remembered the incident very well, told of being awakened by Scott in the middle of a September night in order to help him revive Zelda from an overdose of sleeping pills. The Murphys were sure that this incident was related to her affair with Jozan. Nancy Milford, Zelda's biographer, believes that the affair affected Zelda more than Scott, who, at that time, was very engrossed in his work. Indeed, Milford's account of the affair is the only one that suggests that Zelda was so deeply in love with Jozan that she asked Scott for a divorce. According to an interview with Jozan, the members of this triangle never engaged in a three-way confrontation; Jozan told Milford that the Fitzgeralds were "the victims of their own unsettled and a little unhealthy imagination."

This paragraph gives a brief but adequate account of what is known about the events of that summer of 1924. The writer does not try to rush through the four accounts of the affair, nor does he reduce each one to a phrase, as if he expected the reader to have prior knowledge of these people and their activities. In the context of the whole essay, the paragraph provides enough information for the reader to judge whose interpretation of the affair is closest to the truth.

ACCOMMODATING ARGUMENT IN YOUR PARAGRAPHS

When you write a paragraph based on *induction,* the topic sentence should clearly summarize the range of evidence being cited. Here is an example from Edward Tenner's *Why Things Bite Back,* a book about the dangers of technological progress:

> The startling wartime successes of penicillin created the dangerous myth of an antibiotic panacea. Even after the U.S. Food and Drug Administration began to

require prescriptions in the mid-1950s, an antibiotic injection or prescription re-mained for many people the payoff of a medical encounter. They resisted the med-ical fact that antibiotics can do nothing against colds and other viral diseases. In many other countries, antibiotics are still sold legally over the counter to patients who may never get proper instructions about dosage or the importance of com-pleting a course of treatment. Dr. Stuart B. Levy of Boston cites an Argentinian busi-nessman who was cured of leukemia but died of an infection by the common bacterium *E. coli.* Ten years of self-medication had produced plasmids in his body that were resistant to every antibiotic used. Governments, too, have unintentionally pro-moted resurgence. Indonesian authorities have literally ladled out preventive doses of tetracycline to 100,000 Muslim pilgrims for a week at a time. Since the Mecca pilgrimage has historically been one of the great mixing bowls of microorganisms, it is especially disturbing to learn that half of all cholera bacilli in Africa are now resistant to tetracycline.

Paragraphs presenting inductive evidence tend to be long. Tenner makes his point about the "dangerous myth" of penicillin in the topic sentence, but he doesn't immediately cite evidence. He first explains the "danger" in the second sentence, and the "myth" in the third. Only then does he introduce his first sup-porting point—self-medication in countries without drug regulation—with Dr. Levy's example of the antibiotic-resistant Argentinian businessman. Signaled by the transitional word "too," Tenner's second example—the Mecca pilgrim-age—increases the scale of potential danger.

In contrast to the specific examples of induction, an article on "Methods of Media Manipulation" starts in a *deductive* mode, with a series of premises:

> We are told by people in the media industry that news bias is unavoidable. What-ever distortions and inaccuracies found in the news are caused by deadline pres-sures, human misjudgment, budgetary restraints, and the difficulty of reducing a complex story into a concise report. Furthermore—the argument goes—no com-munication system can hope to report everything, selectivity is needed.
>
> I would argue that the media's misrepresentations are not at all the result of in-nocent error and everyday production problems, though such problems certainly do exist. True, the press has to be selective, but what principle of selectivity is involved?
>
> Media bias usually does not occur in random fashion; rather, it moves in the same overall direction again and again, favoring management over labor, corpo-rations over corporate critics, affluent whites over low-income minorities, offi-cialdom over protesters. . . . The built-in biases of the corporate mainstream media faithfully reflect the dominant ideology, seldom straying into territory that might cause discomfort to those who hold political and economic power, including those who own the media or advertise in it.

The initial presentation of Michael Parenti's argument is based on a dichotomy—contrast—between the media's view of news bias and his own.

There is a disputed primary premise (bias is or is not avoidable) and a disputed secondary premise (one can't print everything vs. one prints what pleases one's corporate masters). Parenti's premises are developed in more detail, and the article goes on to support those premises through induction, by citing evidence of such manipulative tactics as "suppression by omission" and "framing."

While the opening of Parenti's article presents the opposition's argument as well as his own, the tone is grudging, even hostile. He leaves no room for accommodation between the two points of view. Yet, whenever possible, it is useful to acknowledge some merit in your opponents or in their argument. Here are excerpts from two essays supporting opposite sides of the "wilderness preservation" issue. In the first, John Daniel is arguing that the advancement of science, if uncontrolled, can do harm to unspoiled land. He is careful, however, to distinguish between his allies and his enemies:

> I don't mean to indict science in general. Many of the foremost champions of wild nature are scientists, and their work has done much to warn us of the environmental limits we are transgressing. I am arguing only against interventionist science that wants to splice genes, split atoms, or otherwise manipulate the wild—science aimed more at control than understanding, science that assumes ownership of the natural mysteries. When technological specialists come to believe that nature is answerable to their own prerogatives, they are not serving but endangering the greater community.

In William Tucker's view, society has more compelling interests, to which the wilderness movement must sometimes defer. But, before stating his argument, he pays his dues to nature:

> I am not arguing against wild things, scenic beauty, pristine landscapes, and scenic preservation. What I am questioning is the argument that wilderness is a value against which every other human activity must be judged and that human beings are somehow unworthy of the landscape. The wilderness has been equated with freedom, but there are many different ideas about what constitutes freedom. . . .

Interestingly enough, Tucker then proceeds to move from his impeccably fair presentation to an argument that approaches *ad hominem*—a personal attack:

> It may seem unfair to itemize the personal idiosyncrasies of people who feel comfortable only in wilderness, but it must be remembered that the environmental movement has been shaped by many people who literally spent years of their lives living in isolation.

Citing John Muir, David Brower, and Gary Snyder, leaders of the Sierra Club who spent much time alone in the mountains, Tucker continues:

There is nothing reprehensible in this, and the literature and philosophy that emerge from such experiences are often admirable. But it seems questionable to me that the ethic that comes out of this wilderness isolation—and the sense of ownership of natural landscapes that inevitably follows—can serve as the basis for a useful national philosophy.

Whatever his disclaimers, Tucker is rooting one of his key arguments against the wilderness movement in the personal preferences of three men. He does not, however, resort to using slanted, exaggerated, or dismissive language about his opponents. In contrast, here is Robert W. McChesney's attack on commercialism in the media:

> The commercial blitzkrieg into every nook and cranny of U.S. culture, from schools to sport to museums to movie theaters to the Internet, has lessened traditional distinctions of public service from commercialism.

The word "blitzkrieg"—literally, lightning battle—originally referred to the German army in World War II. It immediately conjures up an image of a mechanized, pitiless army rolling over everything in its path, a reference reinforced by the domestic, vulnerable image of "nook and cranny," used to describe U.S. culture, the victim. Without even articulating his point, McChesney has created a lingering association between corporations and Nazis. This is a clever use of language, but is it a fair argument? In the next example, Leslie Savan also uses emotionally charged language to attack a similar target:

> Advertising now infects just about every organ of society, and wherever advertising gains a foothold it tends to slowly take over, like a vampire or a virus.

The brutal swiftness of the blitzkrieg has been replaced by the slow insinuation of an infection, but both images are deadly and unyielding. (The allusion to a vampire must have been tempting—advertising leaves viewers bloodless and brainwashed—but it should not be placed in tandem with the insidious, slowly creeping image of infection.) Interestingly enough, McChesney and Savan are both adopting the tactics of the commercial media that they condemn: using powerful images in an attempt to force their readers into agreement.

PRESENTING ARGUMENTS FAIRLY

Perhaps the greatest disservice that you can do your sources is to distort them so that your reader is left with a false impression of what they have said or written. Such distortion is most likely to happen when you are writing an argumentative essay.

Mistakes to Avoid When Summarizing an Argument

1. Don't be one-sided; present *both* sides of an argument.

2. Don't omit crucial parts of the source's reasoning; provide a complete account of the argument.

3. Don't quote ideas out of context: make sure that you—and your reader—understand whether the source really supports the idea that you are citing.

4. Don't twist the source's ideas to fit your own purpose; provide a fair presentation.

---

1. **Present both sides of the argument.**

One way of shading an argument to suit your own ends is to *misrepresent the strength of the opposition*. Let us assume that you are working with a number of articles, all of which are effectively presented and worth citing. Some clearly support your point of view; others are openly opposed; and a few avoid taking sides, emphasizing related but less controversial topics. If your essay cites only the favorable and neutral articles, and avoids any reference to the views of the opposition, you have presented the issue falsely. Using ostrich tactics will not convince your reader that your opinions are right; on the contrary, your unwillingness to admit the existence of opposing views suggests that your point of view has some basic flaw. A one-sided presentation will make you appear to be either biased or sloppy in your research. If the sources are available and if their views are pertinent, they should be represented and, if you wish, refuted in your essay.

2. **Provide a complete account of the argument.**

Sometimes, distortions occur accidentally, because you have presented only a *partial* account of a source's views. In the course of an article or a book, authors sometimes examine and then reject or accept a variety of views before making it clear which are their own conclusions. Or an author may have mixed opinions about the issue and see merit in more than one point of view. If you choose to quote or paraphrase material from only one section of such a work, then you must find a way to inform your reader that these statements are not entirely representative of the writer's overall views.

3. **Make sure that you—and your reader—understand whether the source really supports the idea that you are citing.**

Ideas can get distorted because of the researcher's misunderstanding, careless note taking, or hasty reading. Remember to check the entire section of the article or all your notes before you attribute an opinion to your source, to make sure that you are not taking a sentence out of context or ignoring a statement in the next paragraph or on the next page that may be more typical of the writer's thinking. Writers often use an argumentative strategy that sets up a point with which they basically disagree in order to shoot it down shortly thereafter. Don't confuse a statement made for the sake of argument with a writer's real beliefs.

4. Provide a fair presentation.

Occasionally, you may be so eager to uphold your point of view that you will cite any bit of material that looks like supporting evidence. To do so, however, you may have to twist the words of the source to fit your ideas. This is one of the worst kinds of intellectual dishonesty—and one of the easiest for a suspicious reader to detect: one has only to look up the source. If you cannot find sufficient arguments and if your sources' evidence does not clearly and directly support your side, then you should seriously consider switching sides or switching topics.

Here is a fairly clear instance of such distortion. In an essay on the need for prison reform, Garry Wills is focusing on the *deficiencies of our society's penal system;* he is not directly concerned with the arguments for or against the death penalty. But the student citing Wills in a research essay is writing specifically in support of capital punishment. To make Wills's argument fit into the scheme of this essay, the student must make some suspiciously selective references. Here is a paragraph from the research essay (on the left), side by side with the source.

Although the death penalty may seem very harsh and inhuman, is this not fair and just punishment for one who was able to administer death to another human being? A murderer's victim always receives the death penalty. Therefore, the death penalty for the murderer evens the score, or, as stated in the Bible, "an eye for an eye, and a tooth for a tooth." According to Garry Wills, "take a life, lose your life." Throughout the ages, society has demanded that man be allowed to right his wrongs. Revenge is our culture's oldest way of making sure that no one "gets away with" any crime. As Wills points out, accord-	The oldest of our culture's views on punishment is the *lex talionis,* an eye for an eye. Take a life, lose your life. It is a very basic cry—people must "pay" for their crimes, yield exact and measured recompense. No one should "get away with" any crime, like a shoplifter taking something un-paid for. The desire to make an offender suffer equivalent pain (if not compensatory excess of pain) is very deep in human nature, and rises quickly to the surface. What is lynching but an impatience with even the slightest delay in exacting this revenge? It serves our social myth to say that this impatience, if denied immediate gratification, is replaced by

ing to this line of reasoning, the taking of the murderer's life can be seen as his payment to society for his misdeed.

something entirely different—by an impersonal dedication to justice. Only lynchers want revenge, not those who wait for a verdict. That is not very likely. Look at the disappointed outcry if the verdict does not yield even delayed satisfaction of the grudge.

In the essay, the writer is citing only *part* of Wills's argument and thus makes him appear to support capital punishment. Wills is being misrepresented because (unlike the writer) he considers it fair to examine the views of the opposing side before presenting his own arguments. The ideas that the student cites are not Wills's, but Wills's presentations of commonly accepted assumptions about punishment. It is not entirely clear whether the writer of the research essay has merely been careless, failing to read past the first few sentences, or whether the misrepresentation is intentional.

INTEGRATING YOUR SOURCES: AN EXAMPLE

To illustrate the need for careful analysis of sources before you write your paragraphs, here is a group of passages, all direct quotations, which have been gathered for a research essay on college athletics. The paragraph developed from these sources must support the writer's *thesis:*

> Colleges should, in the interests of both players and academic standards, outlaw the high-pressure tactics used by coaches when they recruit high school players for college teams.

The first three statements come from college coaches describing recruiting methods that they have observed and carried out; the last four are taken from books that discuss corruption in athletics.

I think in the long run, every coach must recognize this basic principle, or face the alumni firing squad. Recruiting is the crux of building a championship football team.

STEVE SLOAN, Texas Tech

Athletics is creating a monster. Recruiting is getting to be cancerous.

DALE BROWN, Louisiana State University

You don't out-coach people, you out-recruit them.

PAUL "BEAR" BRYANT, University of Alabama

It is an athletic maxim that a man with no special coaching skills can win games if he recruits well and that a tactician without talented players is a man soon without a job.

KENNETH DENLINGER

There is recruiting in various degrees in every intercollegiate sport, from crew to girls' basketball and from the Houston golf dynasty that began in the mid-50's to Southern California importing sprinters and jumpers from Jamaica.

J. ROBERT EVANS

The fundamental causes of the defects in American college athletics are too much commercialism and a negligent attitude towards the educational opportunity for which the college exists.

CARNEGIE FOUNDATION, 1929

[Collier's magazine, in 1905, reported that] Walter Eckersall, All-American quarterback, enrolled at Chicago three credits short of the entrance requirement and his teammate, Leo Detray, entered the school before he even graduated high school. In addition the University of Minnesota paid two players outright to play in a single game (Nebraska: 1902). A quarterback and an end also from Minnesota admitted shaving points during the 1903 Beloit game.

JOSEPH DURSO

Examining the Sources

Your paragraph will focus on *recruiting high school stars,* as opposed to developing students who enter college by the ordinary admissions procedure. Which of these ideas and observations might help to develop this paragraph? In other words, which statements should be represented by *paraphrase* or perhaps by *direct quotation?*

I think in the long run every coach must recognize this basic principle, or face the alumni firing squad. Recruiting is the crux of building a championship football team.

STEVE SLOAN

This very broad generalization seems quotable at first, largely because it sums up the topic so well; but, in fact, because it does no more than sum up the topic, it does not advance your argument any further. Therefore, you need not include it if your topic sentence makes the same point. (In general, you should write your own topic sentences rather than letting your sources write them for you.) The phrase "alumni firing squad" might be useful to quote in a later paragraph, in a discussion of the specific influence of alumni on recruiting.

Athletics is creating a monster. Recruiting is getting to be cancerous.

DALE BROWN

Coach Brown's choice of images—"cancerous" and "monster"—is certainly vivid; but the sentence as a whole is no more than a *generalized opinion about recruiting*, not an explanation of why the situation is so monstrous. Quoting Brown for the sake of two words would be a mistake.

You don't out-coach people, you out-recruit them.

PAUL "BEAR" BRYANT

This is the first statement that has advanced a specific idea: the coach may have a *choice* between building a winning team through recruiting and building a winning team through good coaching; but recruiting, not coaching, wins games. Coach Bryant, then, is not just making a rhetorical point, as the first two coaches seem to be. His seven-word sentence is succinct, if not elaborately developed, and would make a good introduction to or summation of a point that deserves full discussion.

The remaining four statements suggest a wider range of approach and style.

Walter Eckersall, All-American quarterback, enrolled at Chicago three credits short of the entrance requirement and his teammate, Leo Detray, entered the school before he even graduated high school. In addition, the University of Minnesota paid two players outright to play in a single game (Nebraska: 1902). A quarterback and an end also from Minnesota admitted shaving points during the 1903 Beloit game.

JOSEPH DURSO

This passage is as much concerned with corruption as recruiting and indicates that commercialism is nothing new in college athletics. Although the information is interesting, it is presented as a list of facts, and the language is not worth quoting. You may, however, want to summarize the example in your own words.

The fundamental causes of the defects in American college athletics are too much commercialism and a negligent attitude towards the educational opportunity for which the college exists.

CARNEGIE FOUNDATION

This extract from the 1929 Carnegie Foundation study is phrased in abstract language that is characteristic of foundation reports and academic writing in general. This style can be found in most textbooks (including this one) and in many of the sources that you use in college. The foundation presents its point clearly enough and raises an important idea: an athlete recruited to win games (and earn fame and fortune) is likely to ignore the primary reason for going to college—to acquire an education. Nevertheless, there is no compelling reason to quote this statement. Remember that you include quotations in your essay to enhance your presentation; the quotation marks automatically prepare the reader for special words and phrasing. But the prose here is too colorless and abstract to give the reader anything to focus on; a paraphrase is preferable.

> There is recruiting in varying degrees in every intercollegiate sport, from crew to girls' basketball and from the Houston golf dynasty that began in the mid-50's to Southern California importing sprinters and jumpers from Jamaica.
>
> J. ROBERT EVANS

This statement presents a quite different, more detailed level of information; it lists several sports, including some not known for their cutthroat recruiting practices. But details do not necessarily deserve quotation. Will these references be at all meaningful to the reader who is not familiar with the "Houston golf dynasty" or Jamaican track stars? To know that recruitment is not limited to cash sports, such as football, is interesting, but such specifics date quickly: in a few years, they may no longer be a useful frame of reference for most readers.

> It is an athletic maxim that a man with no special coaching skills can win games if he recruits well and that a tactician without talented players is a man soon without a job.
>
> KENNETH DENLINGER

Largely because of parallel construction, the last comment sounds both sharp and solid. In much the same way as Coach Bryant's seven words, but at greater length, Kenneth Denlinger sums up the contrast between coaching and recruiting, and suggests which one has the edge. Because the statement gives the reader something substantial to think about and because it is well phrased, Denlinger is probably worth quoting.

Should the writer include the statements by Bryant and by Denlinger, both of which say essentially the same thing? While Bryant's firsthand comment is commendably terse and certainly authoritative, Denlinger's is more complete and self-explanatory. A solution might be to include both, at different points in the paragraph, with Bryant cited at the end to sum up the idea that has been developed. Of course, the other five sources need not be excluded from the paragraph. Rather, if you wish, all five may be referred to, by paraphrase or brief reference, with their authors' names cited.

Here is one way of integrating this set of statements into a paragraph. (Note that, in this version, there is no documentation: none of the sources—except those quoted—is cited.)

In college athletics, what is the best way for a school to win games? Should a strong team be gradually built up by training ordinary students from scratch, or should the process be shortened and success be assured by actively recruiting players who already know how to win? The first method may be more consistent with the traditional amateurism of college athletics, but as early as 1929, the Carnegie Foundation complained that the focus of college sports had shifted from education to the material advantages of winning. Even earlier, in 1903, there were several instances of players without academic qualifications who were "hired" to guarantee victory. And in recent years excellence of recruiting has become the most important skill for a coach to possess. Kenneth Denlinger has observed, "It is an athletic maxim that a man with no special coaching skills can win games if he recruits well and that a tactician without talented players is a man soon without a job." It follows, then, that a coach who wants to keep his job is likely to concentrate on spotting and collecting talent for his team. Coaches from LSU, Alabama, and Texas Tech all testify that good recruiting has first priority throughout college athletics. According to Bear Bryant of Alabama: "You don't out-coach people, you out-recruit them."

One problem that can arise as you are crafting your paragraph is what to do with material that casts doubt on or flatly contradicts the point you're making. (Frequently, you come across that material *after* you have worked out your thesis and structure.) Here, for example, is an excerpt from *College Sports Inc.* by Murray Sperber. How does it fit with the paragraph on recruiting to win?

Coaches who cheat do so for the same reasons that some gamblers try for an illegal advantage. They are extremely competitive, obsessed with winning, and will bend or break the rules to obtain the winning edge. They subscribe to the dictum that "winning is the only thing," that losing is not merely defeat but also a loss of self-worth. When gamblers or coaches cheat and succeed, they consider themselves "smart" and they show no remorse or inclination to stop. Only when caught do recriminations and blame—"Pressure from the school made me do it"—appear.

The coaches referred to in the earlier student paragraph about recruiting assume that winning is the point of college athletics. The author of the paragraph is focusing on the best way to win—recruiting—and the only criticism of the primacy of winning is a slight complaint by the Carnegie Foundation about the materialism of college athletics. Now, not only does Sperber denigrate the "win at all costs" philosophy, but he suggests that the impetus to win and cheat (and, presumably, recruit at the expense of good sportsmanship) comes from the egoism of the coaches themselves, rather than the pressure from college officials and alumni.

What do you do with this excerpt from Sperber? Should you rewrite your paragraph on recruiting to include Sperber's opinions and attempt to reconcile them with the material provided by your other sources? In this situation, do two things:

1. **Examine the new source more completely to see if the author provides a broader context for these contradictory opinions.**

   In fact, Sperber also has a good deal to say about the commercialism of college sports, pointing out that athletic departments resemble business enterprises, with program directors who are in the "entertainment business." His book indicates that the "winning is everything" philosophy derives as much from institutional (and media) expectations as from the competitive obsessions of individual coaches.

2. **If the point made by the new source is worth developing, it may be preferable to do so in a separate paragraph.**

   The "recruiting" paragraph focuses on *what* coaches do to win, not why they do it. Sperber, however, is more concerned with motivation—quite a different topic and an equally interesting one. Your essay may benefit from an exploration of this point, but to develop and support it properly, you will probably have to find more sources that deal with the pressures to compete to win. The more you read, the more new directions you are likely to find for the development of your essay.

SELECTING QUOTATIONS

Now that you are working with a great variety of sources, you may find it difficult to limit the number of quotations in your essay and to choose quotable material. If you are doubtful about when and what to quote, review the sections on quotation in Chapter 2 and Chapter 4, starting on pp. 65 and 168. As a rule, the more eminent and authoritative the source, the more reason to consider quoting it.

Are the quoted phrases in the following excerpt worth quoting? Charles Dickens is describing the house that he has rented, the Chateau des Moulineux:

Dickens rattled off a list of phrases in his attempt to describe this idyllic place. It was to become his "best doll's house," "our French watering place," and "this abode of bliss." More than anything else it would become a "happy, happy place."

Such a list of separately quoted phrases creates an awkward, disconnected effect, which, if used too often, becomes tedious to read.

Descriptions are often more difficult to paraphrase than ideas; as a result, they tend to be presented in such a sequence of quoted phrases. If your source states that the walls of the room were painted sea-green and the furniture was made out of horsehair and covered with light-brown velvet, you may find it next to impossible to find appropriate synonyms to paraphrase these descriptive terms. "Crin de cheval" covered with fuzzy beige fabric? Mediterranean colors decorating the walls? The result is hardly worth the effort. If the man's

> ## *Guidelines for Quoting*
>
> 1. *Never quote something just because it sounds impressive.* The style of the quotation—the level of difficulty, the choice of vocabulary, and the degree of abstraction—should be compatible with your own style. Don't force your reader to make a mental jump from your own characteristic voice and wording to a far more abstract, flowery, or colloquial style.
>
> 2. *Never quote something that you find very difficult to understand.* When the time comes to decide whether and what to quote, stop and observe your own reactions. Rapidly read the quotation. If you find it difficult to understand on the first try, then either attempt to paraphrase the point or leave it out entirely. If you become distracted or confused, your reader will be, too.
>
> 3. *Quote primary sources—if they are clear and understandable.* When you are working on a biographical or historical research essay, you may encounter special problems in deciding whether or not to quote. Primary sources often have a special claim to be quoted. For example, you would be more likely to quote one of Hemingway's own descriptions of Paris in 1925 than a comparable sentence by one of his biographers. A person who witnessed the Chicago Fire has a better claim to have his original account presented verbatim than does a historian decades later.
>
> 4. *Use single and double quotation marks to differentiate between primary and secondary sources.* When quoting primary sources, it is essential to make the exact source of the quotation clear to your reader.

eyes are described as dark blue, don't alter the phrase to "piercing blue" or "deep azure" or "ocean pools." If you place "dark blue" in a sentence that is otherwise your own writing, you may omit the quotation marks.

EXERCISE 27: INCORPORATING SOURCES INTO A PARAGRAPH

The following unfinished student paragraph is followed by brief excerpts from sources.

1. Decide which excerpt contains the most appropriate sentence for quotation. (It is not necessary to quote the entire excerpt.) For the purposes of this exercise, assume that all the sources are qualified authorities.

2. Paraphrase the other excerpts.

3. Complete the paragraph by using both paraphrase and quotation, citing two or three sources. Maintain a consistent tone and (except for the quotation) a single voice. Do not digress too far from the topic sentence.

Student Paragraph

From childhood on, the instinct to fight is basic to our culture's concept of masculinity. With few exceptions, aggression is a dominant force in the heroes that young boys admire. . . .

Sources

The particularly brutal and angry aggression that is a virtually integral part of some forms of competitive athletics increases the likelihood of imitative violence among crowds dominated by young adult males. One theory holds, for example, that anonymity and excitement allow fans to put aside more readily the inhibitions that would keep them from being openly aggressive in other situations. Violence on the playing field then holds out to them an example they are more likely to follow.

DANIEL GOLEMAN

Superman . . . support[s] a fantasy world with Superman acting as a vigilante, solving problems with violence, while maintaining the status quo. A reading of the character of Superman reveals not the simple battles of good versus evil, but rather a vigilante operating without legitimate authority. Answerable to nothing except his own code of ethics, Superman utilizes violence and physical strength as his primary method of operation.

NORMA PECORA

In life, as in a foot-ball game, the principle to follow is: Hit the line hard, don't foul and don't shirk but hit the line hard.

THEODORE ROOSEVELT

Aggression is part of man's very nature, rooted deep in the unconscious, in the history of the race, and in the early experiences of the child. It is always and inevitably expressed; mankind is fortunate in having found ways for releasing it without much injury to anyone.

PAUL WEISS

ASSIGNMENT 13: ORGANIZING AND
WRITING THE RESEARCH ESSAY

1. Read through all the essays in Appendix E. (In a full-scale research project, these readings would form a substantial part, but not all, of your sources.

Check with your instructor about whether you may use additional sources.) Develop a topic for a research essay using most or all of these sources.

2. Write down a tentative list of main ideas, based on these sources, that should be discussed in an essay dealing with your subject. Also include your own ideas on the subject.

3. Develop an outline based on your list of ideas, and consider possible theses for the essay and the strategy that will best fit your thesis and sources.

4. After you have compiled a substantial list of topics and developed a tentative thesis, reread the passages, cross-referencing the topics on your list with the relevant material from the essays. While you do not have to use up everything in all of the readings, you should include all relevant points.

5. Develop this outline into an eight- or ten-page essay.

▪ 8 ▪

Acknowledging Sources

When you engage in research, you continually come into contact with the ideas and the words of other writers; as a result, the opportunities to plagiarize—by accident or by intention—increase tremendously. You must therefore understand exactly what constitutes plagiarism.

Plagiarism is the unacknowledged use of another person's work, in the form of original ideas, strategies, and research, or another person's writing, in the form of sentences, phrases, and innovative terminology.

- Plagiarism is the equivalent of *theft*, but the stolen goods are intellectual rather than material.
- Like other acts of theft, plagiarism is against the law. The copyright law governing publications requires that authorship be acknowledged and (if the borrowed material is long enough) that payment be offered to the writer.
- Plagiarism violates the moral law that people should take pride in, as well as profit from, the fruits of their labor. Put yourself in the victim's place. Think about the best idea that you ever had, or the paragraph that you worked hardest on in your last paper. Now, imagine yourself finding exactly the same idea or exactly the same sentences in someone else's essay, with no mention of your name, with no quotation marks. Would you accept the theft of your property without protest?

366

- Plagiarists are not only robbers, but also cheats. People who bend or break the rules of authorship, who do not do their own work, will be rightly distrusted by their classmates, teachers, or future employers, who may equate a history of plagiarism with laziness, incompetence, or dishonesty. One's future rarely depends on getting a better grade on a single assignment; on the other hand, one's lifelong reputation may be damaged if one resorts to plagiarism in order to get that grade.

But plagiarism is a bad risk for a more immediate and practical reason. As you observed in Exercise 9, an experienced teacher can usually detect plagiarized work quite easily. If you can't write your own essay, you are unlikely to do a good enough job of adapting someone else's work to your needs. Anyone can learn to write well enough to make plagiarism an unnecessary risk.

Finally, you will not receive greater glory by plagiarizing. On the contrary, most instructors believe that students who understand the ideas of their sources, apply them to the topic, and put them in their own words deserve the highest grades for their mastery of the basic skills of academic writing. There are, however, occasions when your instructor may ask you not to use secondary sources. In such cases, you would be wise to do no background reading at all, so that the temptation to borrow will not arise.

DOCUMENTING INFORMATION

Acknowledging your sources—or *documentation*—means telling your reader that someone other than yourself is the source of ideas and words in your essay. Acknowledgment can take the form of *quotation marks* and *citation of the author's name*—techniques that are by now familiar to you—or more elaborate ways to indicate the source, which will be explained later in this chapter. There are guidelines to help you decide what can and what cannot safely be used without acknowledgment, and these guidelines mostly favor complete documentation.

By conservative standards, *you should cite a source for all facts and evidence in your essay that you did not know before you started your research*. Knowing when to acknowledge the source of your knowledge or information largely depends on common sense. For example, it is not necessary to document the fact that there are fifty states in the United States or that Shakespeare wrote *Hamlet* since these facts are common knowledge. On the other hand, you may be presenting more obscure information, like facts about electric railroads, which you have known since you were a child, but which may be unfamiliar to your readers. Technically, you are not obliged to document that information; but your audience will trust you more and will be better informed if you do so. In general, if the facts are not unusual, if they can be found in a number of standard sources, and if they do not vary from source to source or year to year, then they can be considered common knowledge, and the source need not be acknowledged.

Let's assume that you are preparing to document your essay about *Lawrence of Arabia*. The basic facts about the film—the year of release, the cast, the director, the technicians, the Academy Awards won by the film—might be regarded as common knowledge and not require documentation. But the cost of the film, the amount grossed in its first year, the location of the premiere, and the circumstances of production are relatively unfamiliar facts that you would almost certainly have to look up in a reference book. An authority on film who includes such facts in a study of epic films is expected to be familiar with this information and, in most cases, would not be expected to provide documentation. But a student writing on the same subject would be well advised to do so.

Similarly, if you are writing about the most recent World Cup and know who won a specific match because you witnessed the victory on television, then it would probably not be necessary to cite a source. Issues surrounding the World Cup—such as the use of steroids—are less clearly in the realm of common knowledge. You may remember news broadcasts about which athletes may or may not have taken steroids before a match, but the circumstances are hardly so memorable in their details that you would be justified in writing about them from memory. The articles that you consult to jog your memory would have to be documented.

DOCUMENTING IDEAS FOUND IN YOUR SOURCE

Your objective is both to acknowledge the source and to provide your reader with the fullest possible background. Let us assume that one of the ideas that you are writing about was firmly in your mind—the product of your own intellect—long before you started to work on your topic. Nevertheless, if you come across a version of that idea during your research, you should cite the source, even though the idea was as much your own as the author's. Of course, in your acknowledgment, you might state that this source is confirming *your* theories and indicate that you had thought of the point independently.

Perhaps, while working on an essay, you develop a new idea of your own, stimulated by one of your readings. You should make a point of acknowledging the source of inspiration and, perhaps, describing how and why it affected you. (For example: "My idea for shared assignments is an extension of McKeachie's discussion of peer tutoring.") The reader should be made aware of your debt to your source as well as your independent effort.

PLAGIARISM: STEALING IDEAS

If you present another person's ideas as your own, you are plagiarizing *even if you use your own words*. To illustrate, the paragraph on the left, by Leo Gurko, is taken from a book, *Ernest Hemingway and the Pursuit of Heroism;* the paragraph on the right comes from a student essay on Hemingway. Gurko is listed in the student's bibliography and is cited as the source of several quotations elsewhere in the essay. But the student does not mention Gurko anywhere in *this* paragraph.

Source	Student Essay
The Hemingways put themselves on short rations, ate, drank, and entertained as little as possible, pounced eagerly on the small checks that arrived in the mail as payment for accepted stories, and were intensely conscious of being poor. The sensation was not altogether unpleasant. Their extreme youth, the excitement of living abroad, the sense of making a fresh start, even the unexpected joy of parenthood, gave their poverty a romantic flavor.	Despite all the economies that they had to make and all the pleasures that they had to do without, the Hemingways rather enjoyed the experience of being poor. They knew that this was a more romantic kind of life, unlike anything they'd known before, and the feeling that everything in Paris was fresh and new, even their new baby, made them sharply aware of the glamorous aspects of being poor.

The *language* of the student paragraph does not require quotation marks, but unless Gurko is acknowledged, the student will be guilty of plagiarism. These impressions of the Hemingways, these insights into their motivation, would not have been possible without Gurko's biography—and Gurko deserves the credit for having done the research and for having formulated the interpretations. After reading extensively about Hemingway, the student may have absorbed these biographical details so thoroughly that he feels as if he had always known them. But the knowledge is still secondhand, and the source must be acknowledged.

PLAGIARISM: STEALING WORDS

When you quote a source, remember that the quoted material will require two kinds of documentation:

1. *The acknowledgment of the source of the information or ideas* (through a system of documentation that provides complete publication information about the source and possibly through the citation of the author's name in your sentence), and

2. *The acknowledgment of the source of the exact wording* (through quotation marks).

It is not enough to supply the author's name in parentheses (or in a footnote) and then mix up your own language and that of your sources. The author's name tells your reader nothing at all about who is responsible for the choice of words. Equally important, borrowing language carelessly, perhaps in an effort to use paraphrase, often garbles the author's meaning.

Here is an excerpt from a student essay about Henrik Ibsen, together with the relevant passage from its source:

Source	*Student Essay*
When writing [Ibsen] was sometimes under the influence of hallucinations, and was unable to distinguish between reality and the creatures of his imagination. While working on *A Doll's House* he was nervous and retiring and lived in a world alone, which gradually became peopled with his own imaginary characters. Once he suddenly remarked to his wife: "Now I have seen Nora. She came right up to me and put her hand on my shoulder." "How was she dressed?" asked his wife. "She had a simple blue cotton dress," he replied without hesitation. . . . So intimate had Ibsen become with Nora while at work on *A Doll's House* that when John Paulsen asked him why she was called Nora, Ibsen replied in a matter-of-fact tone: "She was really called Leonora, you know, but everyone called her Nora since she was the spoilt child of the family."	While Ibsen was still writing *A Doll's House*, his involvement with the characters led to his experiencing hallucinations that at times completely incapacitated his ability to distinguish between reality and the creations of his imagination. He was nervous, distant, and lived in a secluded world. Gradually this world became populated with his creations. One day he had the following exchange with his wife:
	Ibsen: Now I have seen Nora. She came right up to me and put her hand on my shoulder.
P. F. D. TENNANT, *Ibsen's Dramatic Technique*	Wife: How was she dressed?
	Ibsen: (without hesitation) She had a simple blue dress.
	Ibsen's involvement with his characters was so deep that when John Paulsen asked Ibsen why the heroine was named Nora, Ibsen replied in a very nonchalant tone of voice that originally she was called Leonora, but that everyone called her Nora, the way one would address the favorite child in the family (Tennant 26).

The documentation at the end of the student's passage may refer the reader to Tennant's book, but it fails to indicate the debt that the student owes to Tennant's *phrasing* and *vocabulary*. Phrases like "distinguish between reality and the creatures of his imagination" must be placed in quotation marks, and so should the exchange between Ibsen and his wife. Arranging these sentences as dialogue is not adequate acknowledgment.

In fact, the problem here is too complex to be solved by inserting a few quotation marks. The student, who probably intended a paraphrase, has substituted some of her own words for Tennant's; however, because she keeps the original sentence structure and many of the original words, she has only succeeded in obscuring some of her source's ideas.

At times, the phrasing distorts the original idea: the student's assertion that Ibsen's hallucinations "incapacitated his ability to distinguish between reality and the creations of his imagination" is very different from "[Ibsen] was sometimes under the influence of hallucinations and was unable to distinguish between reality and the creatures of his imagination." Many of the substituted words change Tennant's meaning: "distant" does not mean "retiring"; "a secluded world" is not "a world alone"; "nonchalant" is a very different quality from "matter-of-fact." Prose like this is neither quotation nor successful paraphrase; it is doubly bad, for it both *plagiarizes* the source and *misinterprets* it.

EXERCISE 28: UNDERSTANDING WHEN TO DOCUMENT INFORMATION

Here are some facts about the explosion of the space shuttle *Challenger*. Consider which of these facts would require documentation in a research essay—and why.

1. On January 28, 1986, the space shuttle *Challenger* exploded shortly after takeoff from Cape Canaveral.
2. It was unusually cold in Florida on the day of the launch.
3. One of the *Challenger's* booster rockets experienced a sudden and unforeseen drop in pressure 10 seconds before the explosion.
4. The explosion was later attributed to the failure of an O-ring seal.
5. On board the *Challenger* was a $100 million communications satellite.
6. Christa McAuliffe, a high school social studies teacher in Concord, New Hampshire, was a member of the crew.
7. McAuliffe's mission duties included conducting two classroom lessons taught from the shuttle.
8. After the explosion, classes at the high school were canceled.
9. Another crew member, Judith Resnick, had a Ph.D. in electrical engineering.
10. At the time of the explosion, President Ronald Reagan was preparing to meet with network TV news correspondents to brief them on the upcoming State of the Union address.
11. The State of the Union address was postponed for a week.

EXERCISE 29: ACKNOWLEDGING SOURCES

Here are two excerpts from two books about the Industrial Revolution in England. Each excerpt is followed by a passage from a student essay that makes use of the ideas and the words of the source without any acknowledgment at all.

1. Compare the original with the plagiarized passage.
2. Insert the appropriate quotation marks.
3. Underline the paraphrases.

Source A

Materially the new factory proletariat was likely to be somewhat better off [than domestic workers who did light manufacturing work in their own homes]. On the other hand it was unfree, under the strict control and the even stricter discipline imposed by the master or his supervisors, against whom they had virtually no legal recourse and only the very beginnings of public protection. They had to work his hours or shifts, to accept his punishments and the fines with which he imposed his rules or increased his profits. In isolated areas or industries they had to buy in his shop, as often as not receiving their wages in truck (thus allowing the unscrupulous employer to swell his profits yet further), or live in the houses the master provided. No doubt the village boy might find such a life no more dependent and less impoverished than his parents'; and in Continental industries with a strong paternalist tradition, the despotism of the master was at least partly balanced by the security, education, and welfare services which he sometimes provided. But for the free man entry into the factory as a mere "hand" was entry into something little better than slavery, and all but the most famished tended to avoid it, and even when in it to resist the draconic discipline much more persistently than the women and children, whom factory owners therefore tended to prefer.

E. J. HOBSBAWM, *The Age of Revolution 1789–1848*

Student Essay

The new factory proletariat was likely to be better off materially than those who did light manufacturing in their homes, but it was unfree. There was strict control and discipline imposed by the owner and his supervisors. They had no legal recourse and only the very start of public protection. The despotism of the master was at least a little bit set off by the security, education, and welfare services that he sometimes provided. But entry into the factory as a hand wasn't much better than slavery.

Source B

Most of the work in the factories was monotonously dreary, but that was also true of much of the work done in the homes. The division of labor which caused a workman to perform over and over only one of the several processes needful for the production of any article was intensified by the mechanical inventions, but it had already gone so far in the homes that few workers experienced any longer the joy of creation. It was, indeed, more of a physical strain to tend a hand loom than a power loom. The employment of women and children in the factories finally evoked an outcry from the humanitarians, but the situation was inherited from the domestic system. In the homes, however, most of the children worked under the friendly eyes of their parents and not under the direction of an overseer. That to which the laborers themselves most objected was "the tyranny of the factory bell." For the long hours during which the power kept the machines in motion, the workers had to tend them without intermission, under the discipline established by the employer and enforced by his foreman. Many domestic laborers had to maintain equally long hours in order to earn a bare subsistence, but they were free to begin, stop and rest when they pleased. The operatives in the factories felt keenly a loss of personal independence.

W. E. LUNT, History of England

Student Essay

Factory work was monotonous and dreary, but that was also true of work at home. Humanitarians cried out against the employment of women and children, but that was inherited from the domestic system. What annoyed the laborers the most was the dictatorship of the factory bell. The workers had to stay at the machines without intermission, maintaining long hours to earn a bare subsistence. Those who worked in their homes were free to begin, stop, and rest whenever they felt like it. Factory workers keenly felt a loss of personal freedom.

EXERCISE 30: IDENTIFYING PLAGIARISM

A. In 1995, the *Chronicle of Higher Education* reported that Stanley N. Ingber, a professor of law at Drake University, had recently been accused of plagiarizing the content and language of portions of three works by Michael J. Perry, a professor of law at Northwestern University. Professor Ingber had used ten passages without attribution in two articles. Other evidence suggested that Professor Ingber might have previously plagiarized passages from an article written by Mark G. Yudof, of the University of Texas at Austin.

Here, side by side, as published in the *Chronicle*, are parallel excerpts from Perry's 1982 *The Constitution, the Courts, and Human Rights* (on the left) and Ingber's 1994 "Judging Without Judgment: Constitutional Irrelevancies and the Demise of Dialogue." Examine them and determine whether, in your opinion, Ingber has plagiarized Perry's work.

I want to emphasize that I am *not* claiming that the Court always gives right answers. Of course it does not. . . . My basic point is simply this: In the constitutional dialogue between the Court and the other agencies of government—a subtle, dialectical interplay between Court and polity—what emerges is a far more self-critical political morality than would otherwise appear. . . .	I want to emphasize that I am *not* claiming that the Court always gives right answers, because of course it does not. My basic point is simply that from the constitutional dialogue between the Court and the other agencies of government—a subtle, dialectical interplay between Court and polity—a far more self-critical political morality emerges than would otherwise appear.

B. In 1999, the *New York Times* reported that the publishers of a new biography of John Paul Jones by James Mackay had decided to halt production of the book while investigating allegations that Mackay had plagiarized much of its contents. (In 1997, after similar charges, an earlier book by Mackay was withdrawn by a different publisher, and the copies were destroyed at the author's expense.)

Here, side by side, as published in the *Times,* are parallel excerpts from Samuel Eliot Morison's 1959 *John Paul Jones: A Sailor's Biography* (on the left) and James Mackay's *I Have Not Yet Begun to Fight: A Life of John Paul Jones* (on the right). Examine them and determine whether, in your opinion, Mackay has plagiarized Morison's work.

During his career, he visited some of the most beautiful parts of the world—Cape Breton, the Windward Islands, Jamaica, Galicia, Brittany, the Hebrides, the Baltic and the Black Sea; yet not once in his voluminous correspondence does he indicate any appreciation of them; and in only one letter, about the great gale of October 1780, does he mention the majesty of the sea.	In the course of his career he visited some of the most beautiful parts of the world—the Caribbean Islands, Nova Scotia, Galicia, the Baltic and the Black Sea as well as the eastern seaboard of America and the coasts of Britain—yet nowhere in his vast correspondence does he betray any appreciation of them. In only one letter, written in October 1780, in the aftermath of a great storm, does he allude to the majesty of the sea.
His characteristic features were a sharp, wedge-shaped nose, high cheekbones and a strong, cleft chin. His expression showed pride, eagerness, sagacity and intellectual alertness.	His outstanding features were a sharp, wedge-shaped nose, high cheekbones, and a strong, cleft chin. His expression showed pride, eagerness, sagacity and intellectual alertness.

USING DOCUMENTATION

In addition to using quotation marks and citing the author's name in your text, you also need to provide your reader with more detailed information about your sources. This documentation is important for two reasons:

1. By showing where you found your information, you are providing proof that you did your research. Including the source's *publication history* and the *specific page* on which you found the information assures your reader that you have not made up fictitious sources and quotations. The systems of documentation that are described in this chapter and in Appendix B enable your reader to distinguish your ideas from those of your sources, to know who was responsible for what, by observing the parenthetical notes or numbered notes.

2. Documentation also enables your readers to learn more about the subject of your essay. Methods of documentation originally developed as a way for serious scholars to share their findings with their colleagues—while making it entirely clear who had done the original research. The reader of your research essay should be given the option of going back to the library and locating the materials that you used in writing about the topic. Of course, the essay's *bibliography* can serve this purpose, but not even the most carefully annotated bibliography guides readers to the book and the precise page that will provide the information that they need. Documentation, then, provides a direct link between an interesting sentence in the paper and the source in the library that will satisfy your readers' interest.

Using Parenthetical Notes

The most widely accepted system of documentation is based on the insertion directly into your essay of the author's name and the page on which the information can be found, placed in parentheses. This style of documentation is called the Modern Language Association (MLA) style. It has replaced footnotes and endnotes as the most common form of documentation, and it will probably be the style you use in writing general research essays, especially those in the humanities. Documenting through parenthetical notes is much less cumbersome than preparing an additional page of endnotes or placing footnotes at the bottom of the page. MLA style also allows your reader to see the source's name while reading the essay, instead of having to turn to a separate page at the back. Readers who want to know more about a particular source than the author's name and the number of the page containing the information can turn to the "Works Cited" page, which provides all the necessary details of publication.

Another frequently used kind of parenthetical documentation is the one recommended by the American Psychological Association (APA) for research in the social and behavioral sciences. APA style is described on pp. 469–476 of Appendix B.

For those writing essays on a computer, many software packages (especially those, like Nota Bene, specializing in academic writing) provide documentation automatically, in a choice of styles—provided that basic information about each work cited has been entered into the computer.

Here is what an excerpt from a biographical essay about Ernest Hemingway would look like using MLA style. Notice that the parenthetical notes are meaningless unless the reader can refer to an accurate and complete bibliography placed at the end of the essay on a page titled "Works Cited."

Hemingway's zest for life extended to women also. His wandering heart seemed only to be exceeded by an even more appreciative eye (Hemingway 102).

Hadley was aware of her husband's flirtations and of his facility with women

(Sokoloff 84). Yet, she had no idea that something was going on between Hemingway and Pauline Pfeiffer, a fashion editor for Vogue magazine (Baker 159). She was also unaware that Hemingway delayed his return to Schruns from a business trip in New York, in February 1926, so that he might spend more time with this "new and strange girl" (Hemingway 210; also Baker 165).

Works Cited

Baker, Carlos. Ernest Hemingway: A Life Story. New York: Scribner's, 1969.
Hemingway, Ernest. A Moveable Feast. New York: Scribner's, 1964.
Sokoloff, Alice Hunt. Hadley: The First Mrs. Hemingway. New York: Dodd, 1973.

Many of the basic rules for using MLA style are demonstrated in the previous example. Here are some points to observe.

1. **Format and Punctuation.**

   The placement of the parenthetical note within your sentence is governed by a set of very precise rules, established by conventional agreement. Like rules for quotation, these must be followed without any deviation.

   a. *The parenthetical note is intended to be a part of your sentence, which should not end until the source has been cited.* For this reason, terminal punctuation (period or question mark) should be placed *after* the parenthetical note.

   Incorrect

   Unlike most American writers of his day, Hemingway rarely came to New York; instead, he spent most of his time on his farm near Havana. (Ross 17).

   Correct

   Unlike most American writers of his day, Hemingway rarely came to New York; instead, he spent most of his time on his farm near Havana (Ross 17).

   b. *If the parenthetical note follows a quotation, the quotation should be closed before you open the parentheses.* Remember that the note is not part of the quotation and therefore has no reason to be inside the quotation.

   Incorrect

   Hemingway's farm consisted of "a domestic staff of nine, fifty-two cats, sixteen dogs, a couple of hundred pigeons, and three cows (Ross 17)."

   Correct

   Hemingway's farm consisted of "a domestic staff of nine, fifty-two cats, sixteen dogs, a couple of hundred pigeons, and three cows" (Ross 17).

c. *Any terminal punctuation that is part of the quotation* (like a question mark or an exclamation point) *remains inside the quotation marks.* Remember also to include a period at the end of the sentence, *after* the parenthetical note.

Incorrect

One critic reports that Hemingway said of The Old Man and the Sea, "Don't you think it is a strange damn story that it should affect all of us (me especially) the way it does" (Halliday 52)?

Correct

One critic reports that Hemingway said of The Old Man and the Sea, "Don't you think it is a strange damn story that it should affect all of us (me especially) the way it does?" (Halliday 52).

d. *When you insert the parenthetical note, leave one space before it and one space after it*—unless you are ending the sentence with terminal punctuation (period, question mark), in which case you leave no space between the closing parenthesis and the punctuation, and you leave the customary one space between the end of that sentence and the beginning of the next one.

Incorrect

Given Hemingway's intense awareness of literary tradition, style, and theory, it is strange that many critics and readers have found his work primitive(Cowley 47).

Correct

Given Hemingway's intense awareness of literary tradition, style, and theory, it is strange that many critics and readers have found his work primitive (Cowley 47).

2. Placement.

The parenthetical note comes at the end of the material being documented, whether that material is quoted, paraphrased, summarized, or briefly mentioned. By convention, your reader will assume that the *parenthetical note signals the end of the material from that source.* Anything that follows is either your own idea, independently developed, or taken from a new source that will be documented by the next parenthetical note later in the text.

One critic has remarked that it has been fashionable to deride Hemingway over the past few years (Cowley 50). However, though we may criticize him, as we can criticize most authors when we subject them to close scrutiny, we should never forget his brilliance in depicting characters having grace under the pressure of a sterile, valueless, painful world (Anderson 1036).

3. Frequency.

Each new point in your essay that requires documentation should have its own parenthetical note. Under no circumstances should you accumulate references to several different sources for several sentences and place them in a single note at the end of the paragraph. All the sources in the Hemingway paragraph cannot be covered by one parenthetical note at the end.

Incorrect

> The sources of Hemingway's fiction have been variously named. One critic has said he is driven by "personal demons." Another believes that he is occupied by a desire to truly portray reality, with all its ironies and symbols. Finally, still another has stated that Hemingway is interested only in presenting "fragments of truth" (Cowley 51; Halliday 71; Levin 85).

Correct

> The sources of Hemingway's fiction have been variously named. One critic has said he is driven by "personal demons" (Cowley 51). Another believes that he is occupied by a desire to truly portray reality, with all its ironies and symbols (Halliday 71). Finally, still another has stated that Hemingway is interested only in presenting "fragments of truth" (Levin 85).

4. Multiple Notes in a Single Sentence.

If you are using a large number of sources and documenting your essay very thoroughly, you may need to cite two or more sources at separate points in the same sentence.

> Even at this early stage of his career, Hemingway seemed to have developed a basic philosophy of writing. His ability to perceive situations clearly and to capture the exact essence of the subject (Lawrence 93–94; O'Faolain 113) might have stemmed from a disciplined belief that each sentence had to be "true" (Hemingway 12) and that a story had to be written "as straight as you can" (Hemingway 183).

The placement of notes tells you where the writer found which information. The reference to Lawrence and O'Faolain must be inserted in midsentence because they are responsible only for the information about Hemingway's capacity to focus on his subject and capture its essence; Lawrence and O'Faolain are not responsible for the quoted material at the end of the sentence. The inclusion of each of the next two parenthetical notes tells you that a reference to "true" sentences can be found on page 12 of the Hemingway book and a reference to "straight" writing can be found on page 183.

5. **Multiple Sources for the Same Point.**

If you have two sources to document the same point, you can demonstrate the completeness of your research by placing both in the same parenthetical note. The inclusion of Lawrence and O'Faolain in the same note—(Lawrence 93–94; O'Faolain 113)—tells you that much the same information can be found in both sources. Should you want to cite two sources but emphasize only one, you can indicate your preference by using "also."

> Hemingway's ability to perceive situations clearly and to capture the exact essence of the subject (Lawrence 93–94; also O'Faolain 113) may be his greatest asset as a writer.

There is, of course, a limit to how many sources you can cram into a single pair of parentheses; common sense will tell you what is practical and what is distracting to the reader. Usually, one or two sources will have more complete or better documented information; those are the ones to cite. If you wish to discuss the quality of information in your various sources, then you can use an explanatory endnote to do so (see p. 388 on explanatory notes).

6. **Referring to the Source in the Text.**

In the previous examples, the writer of the Hemingway essay has chosen not to cite any sources in the text itself. That is why each parenthetical note contains a name as well as a page number. *If, however, you do refer to your source as part of your own presentation of the material, then there is no need to use the name twice; simply insert the page number in the parenthetical note.*

> During the time in Paris, Hemingway became friends with the poet Ezra Pound, who told Hemingway he would teach him how to write if the younger novelist would teach him to box. Noel Stock reports what Wyndham Lewis saw when he walked in on one of their boxing sessions:
>
> > A splendidly built young man [Hemingway] stript to the waist, and with a torso of dazzling white, was standing not far from me. He was tall, handsome, and serene, and was repelling with his boxing gloves—I thought without undue exertion—a hectic assault of Ezra's. (88)

Because Stock's name is cited in the text, it need not be placed in parentheses; the page number is enough. Stock's book would, of course, be included in the list of "Works Cited." Also notice that the parenthetical note works just as well at the end of a lengthy, *indented* quotation; but that, because the quotation is indented, and there are no quotation marks to signify its end, it terminates with a period placed *before* the parenthetical note, which follows separated by *two* spaces.

7. **Including the Source's Title.**

Occasionally, your bibliography will include more than one source by the same author or sources by different authors with the same last name. To avoid confusion and to specify your exact source, use an abbreviated title inside the parenthetical note. Had the author of the Hemingway essay included more than one work by Carlos Baker in the bibliography, the parenthetical note would look like this:

> Yet, she had no idea that something was going on between Hemingway
> and Pauline Pfeiffer, a fashion editor for Vogue magazine (Baker, Life Story
> 159).

If you are working from a newspaper or periodical article that does not cite an author, use an abbreviation of the article's title in your parenthetical note (unless you have referred to the title in your text, in which case you need only include the page number in your note).

8. **Referring to a Whole Work.**

Occasionally, you may refer to the overall theme of an entire work, citing the title and the author, but no specific quotation, idea, or page. If you refer to a work as a whole, no page numbers in parentheses are required.

> Hemingway's The Sun Also Rises focuses on the sterility and despair pervading modern culture.

9. **Referring to a Source by More Than One Author.**

Occasionally, you will need to refer to a book that is by two, or three, or even more authors. If you refer to a text by two or three authors, cite their last names, joined by "and." (If you have mentioned the authors' names in your text, just include a page reference in parentheses.) If you refer to a text by more than three authors and you have not mentioned them in your text, it is acceptable (and saves space) to cite the name of the first author followed by et al., unitalicized, and then the page number, all within parentheses. *Et al.* is Latin for "and others."

Two Authors

> We may finally say of the writer Hemingway that he was able to depict the
> turbulent, often contradictory, emotions of modern man in a style as
> starkly realistic as that of the sixteenth century painter Caravaggio, who,

art historians tell us, seems to say, "Here is actuality [. . .] without decep-tion or pretence. [. . .]" (Janson and Cauman 221).

More than Three Authors

Hemingway did what no other writer of his time did: he captured the plight and total disenchantment of his age in vivid intensity (Spiller et al. 1300).

10. Referring to One of Several Volumes.

You may use a single volume from a set of several volumes. If so, refer to the spe-cific volume by using an arabic numeral followed by a colon and a space if a page number follows. In your "Works Cited," be sure to list all the volumes. (See Appendix B for proper bibliographic entry of a set of volumes.)

Perhaps Hemingway's work can be best summed up by Frederick Cop-pleston's comment concerning Camus: both writers prove that human greatness is not shown in escaping the absurdity of modern existence, but "in living in the consciousness of the absurd and yet revolting against it by . . . committing [. . .] [one]self and living in the fullest manner possible" (3: 393).

11. Referring to a Work of Literature.

If you refer to specific passages from a well-known play, poem, or novel, then you need not cite the author; the text's name is sufficient recognition. Use ara-bic numerals separated by periods for divisions such as act, scene, and line in plays and for divisions like books and lines in poems. For novels, cite the page number followed by a semicolon, "ch.," and the chapter number.

Play

Hemingway wished to show reality as truly as he could, even if he found man, as did King Lear, nothing but "a poor, bare, fork'd animal [. . .]" (3.4.106–7).

Poem

Throughout his career as a writer, Hemingway struggled to make sense of the human condition so powerfully and metaphorically presented in The Waste Land: "Son of man/ . . . you know only/ A heap of broken images" (2.21–23).

Novel

In The Sun Also Rises, toughness is an essential for living in the modern age, but even toughness has its limits in the novel; as Jake says, "It is aw-fully easy to be hard-boiled about everything in the daytime, but at night it is another thing" (34; ch. iv).

12. Referring to a Quotation from an Indirect Source.

When you quote a writer's words that you have found in a work written by someone else, you begin the citation with the abbreviation "qtd. in." This form shows the reader that you are quoting from a secondhand source, not the original.

In "Big Two-Hearted River," Hemingway metaphorically captures the pervasive atmosphere of his time in the tersest of descriptions: "There is no town, nothing [. . .] but the burned over country" (qtd. in Anderson 1027).

13. Referring to Sources That Do Not Appear in Print.

Sometimes you may cite information from nonprint sources such as interviews, films, or radio or television programs. If you do, be sure that the text mentions (for an interview) the name of the interviewer and/or the person being interviewed or (for a film) the name of the producer, director, and/or scriptwriter; these names should also appear in your list of "Works Cited." (For proper bibliographic form of nonprint sources, including the Internet, see Appendix B.)

Interview

In an unpublished interview conducted by the writer of this essay, the poet Phil Arnold said that a lean style like Hemingway's may be just as artificial as an elaborate one.

Preparing to Document Your Essay

- Whether you take notes or use photocopies of your sources, remember always to write down the information that you will need for your notes and bibliography.

- Look at the front of each book or periodical and jot down or photocopy the publication information.

- When you move notes from one file to another on your computer, make sure that the source's name goes with the relevant material.

- As you work on the first draft of your essay, include the author's name and the relevant page number in parentheses after every reference to one of your sources, to serve as a guide when you document your essay. Even in this early version, your essay will resemble the finished product, with MLA documentation.

- Finally, when the essay is ready for final typing, read through it again, just to make sure that each reference to a source is covered by a parenthetical note.

MLA Style: A Sample Page

Reference to an article with no author

Reference to an author with two or more works listed in the bibliography

"Passive euthanasia" can be described as helping someone to die by doing nothing and, according to *The Economist*, "happens in hospitals all the time" ("Euthanasia War" 22). It usually involves deliberate withholding of life-prolonging measures (Keown, "Value" 6). Failing to resuscitate a patient who has suffered a massive heart attack is one example of passive euthanasia. Another is deciding not to feed terminally ill patients who are unable to feed themselves. By contrast, removing the feeding tube from a patient who is being fed that way would be considered active euthanasia.

The distinction between active and passive euthanasia is really about responsibility. In passive euthanasia, the doctor or relative has done nothing directly to end the patient's life and so has less moral responsibility. An intermediate form of euthanasia—assisted suicide—is more controversial. In assisted suicide, a doctor or other person provides a terminally ill person with the means—pills, for example—and the medical knowledge necessary to commit suicide.

Orentlicher reference contains page number only; author mentioned in text

In the *Journal of the American Medical Association*, Dr. David Orentlicher categorizes assisted suicide as a form of passive euthanasia (1844). Derek Humphrey's *Final Exit*, which describes ways to commit suicide painlessly, and the

Reference to an entire work; no page citation needed

organization Compassion in Dying, which helps terminally ill patients to end their lives, are both sources of instruction in assisted suicide (Belkin 50; also Elliott 27).

Reference to two sources containing similar information; emphasis on Belkin

The professional people who care for the sick and the dying think that there is a great difference between active euthanasia and passive euthanasia or assisted suicide. One panel of distinguished physicians declared themselves in favor, by a margin of 10 to 2, of doctor-assisted suicide for hopelessly ill patients who request it (Orentlicher 1844).

Standard reference; author mentioned in the note

Constructing a "Works Cited" Page

None of the parenthetical notes explained above would make complete sense without a "Works Cited" page. The technical forms for bibliographic entries according to MLA style are described in Appendix B on pp. 458–469. Following is a sample "Works Cited" page for all of the parenthetical notes about Hemingway found earlier in this chapter.

Works Cited

Anderson, Charles W. Introduction. "Ernest Hemingway." American Literary
Masters. Ed. Charles W. Anderson. New York: Holt, 1965. 1023–114.

Arnold, Philip. Telephone interview. 3 Nov. 1993.

Baker, Carlos. Ernest Hemingway: A Life Story. New York: Scribner's, 1969.

Coppleston, Frederick. Maine de Biran to Sartre. New York: Doubleday, 1974.
Vol. 9 of A History of Philosophy. 9 vols. 1946–74.

Cowley, Malcolm. "Nightmare and Ritual in Hemingway." Hemingway: Twentieth
Century Perspectives. Ed. Robert P. Weeks. Englewood Cliffs: Prentice,
1962. 40–51.

Halliday, E. M. "Hemingway's Ambiguity: Symbolism and Irony." Hemingway:
Twentieth Century Perspectives. Ed. Robert P. Weeks. Englewood Cliffs:
Prentice, 1962. 52–71.

Hemingway, Ernest. A Moveable Feast. New York: Scribner's, 1964.

---. The Sun Also Rises. 1926. New York: Scribner's, 1964.

Janson, H. W., and Samuel Cauman. A Basic History of Art. New York: Abrams,
1971.

Lawrence, D. H. "In Our Time: A Review." Hemingway: Twentieth Century
Perspectives. Ed. Robert P. Weeks. Englewood Cliffs: Prentice, 1962. 93–94.

Levin, Harry. "Observations on the Style of Ernest Hemingway." Hemingway:
Twentieth Century Perspectives. Ed. Robert P. Weeks. Englewood Cliffs:
Prentice, 1962. 72–85.

Ross, Lillian. "How Do You Like It Now, Gentlemen?" Hemingway: Twentieth Century
Perspectives. Ed. Robert P. Weeks. Englewood Cliffs: Prentice, 1962. 17–39.

Shakespeare, William. King Lear. The Riverside Shakespeare. Ed. Frank Kermode.
Boston: Houghton, 1974. 1249–305.

Spiller, Robert E., et al. Literary History of the United States. 3rd ed., rev.
London: Macmillan, 1963.

Stock, Noel. The Life of Ezra Pound. New York: Pantheon, 1970.

SIGNALING THE TRANSITIONS BETWEEN SOURCES

If you go to considerable trouble to find and select the right materials to support your ideas, you will want to use paraphrase and, where appropriate, include your sources' names in your sentences as a way of keeping them before your reader's eye.

In general, the citation of an author's name signals to your reader that you are starting to use **new** *source material; the parenthetical note signals the* point of termination *for that source.*

If the name is not cited at the beginning, readers may not be aware that a new source has been introduced until they reach the parenthetical note. Here is a brief passage from an essay that illustrates this kind of confusion:

The year 1946 marked the beginning of the postwar era. This meant the demobilization of the military, creating a higher unemployment rate because of the large number of returning soldiers. This also meant a slowdown in industry, so that layoffs also added to the rising rate of unemployment. As Cabell Phillips put it: "Motivation [for the Employment Act of 1946] came naturally from the searing experience of the Great Depression, and fresh impetus was provided by the dread prospect of a massive new wave of unemployment following demobilization" (292–93).

Here, the placement of the citation—"As Cabell Phillips put it"—creates a problem. The way in which the name is introduced into the paragraph firmly suggests that Cabell Phillips is responsible for the quotation and only the quotation. (The fact that the quotation is nothing more than a repetition of the first three sentences, and therefore need not have been included in the essay, may also have occurred to you.) Anyone reading the essay will assume that the reference to Phillips covers only the material that starts with the name and ends with the page number. The coverage is not expected to go back any farther than the beginning of the sentence. Thus, in this passage, *the first three sentences are not documented.* Although the writer probably took all the information from Phillips, his book is not being acknowledged as the source. "Probably" is not an adequate substitute for clear documentation. Phillips's name should be cited somewhere at the beginning of the paragraph (the second sentence would be a good place); alternatively, an "umbrella" note could be used (see pp. 390–391).

You may need to insert a parenthetical note in midsentence if that single sentence contains references to *two* different sources. For example, you might want to place a note in midsentence to indicate exactly where the source's opinion leaves off and your own begins:

These examples of hiring athletes to play in college games, cited by Joseph Durso (6), suggest that recruiting tactics in 1903 were not as subtle as they are today.

If the page number were put at the end of the sentence, the reader would assume that Durso was responsible for the comparison between 1903 and the present; but he is not. Only the examples must be documented, not the conclusion drawn from these examples. In this case, the *absence* of a parenthetical note at the end of the sentence signals to the reader that this conclusion is the writer's own.

Here is a passage in which the techniques of documentation have been used to their fullest extent and the transitions between sources are clearly indicated. This example is taken from Jessie Bernard's "The Paradox of the Happy Marriage," an examination of the woman's role in American marriage. At this point, Bernard has just established that more wives than husbands acknowledge that their marriages are unhappy:

> These findings on the wife's marriage are especially poignant because marriage in our society is more important for women's happiness than for men's. "For almost all measures, the relation between marriage, happiness and overall well-being was stronger for women than for men," one study reports (Bradburn 150). In fact, the strength of the relationship between marital and overall happiness was so strong for women that the author wondered if "most women are equating their marital happiness with their overall happiness" (Bradburn 159). Another study based on a more intensive examination of the data on marriage from the same sample notes that "on each of the marriage adjustment measures . . . the association with overall happiness is considerably stronger for women than it is for men" (Orden and Bradburn 731). Karen Renne also found the same strong relationship between feelings of general well-being and marital happiness: those who were happy tended not to report marital dissatisfaction; those who were not, did. "In all probability the respondent's view of his marriage influences his general feeling of well-being or morale" (64); this relationship was stronger among wives than among husbands (Renne 63).[2] A strong association between reports of general happiness and reports of marital happiness was also found a generation ago (Watson).
>
> [2]Among white couples, 71 percent of the wives and 52 percent of the husbands who were "not too happy" expressed marital dissatisfaction; 22 percent of the wives and 18 percent of the husbands who were "pretty happy" expressed marital dissatisfaction; and 4 percent of the wives and 2 percent of the husbands who were "very happy" expressed marital dissatisfaction.

This paragraph contains *six* parenthetical *notes* to document the contents of seven sentences. Four different works are cited, and, where the same work is cited twice consecutively (Bradburn and Renne), the reference is to a different page. The material taken from page 64 of Renne covers a sentence and a half, from the name "Karen Renne" to the parenthetical note; the remainder of the sentence comes from page 63. Finally, there is no page reference in the note citing Watson, since Bernard is referring the reader to the entire article, not to a single part of it. Notice also that:

- Bernard quotes frequently, but she never places quotations from two different sources together in the same sentence.
- She is careful to use her own voice to provide continuity between the quotations.
- The reader is never in doubt as to the source of information.

Although Bernard does not always cite the name of the author, we are immediately told in each case that there is a source—"one study reports"; "the author wondered"; "another study based on a more intensive examination of the data on marriage from the same sample"; "Karen Renne also found." These phrases not only acknowledge the source but also provide vital transitions between these loosely related points.

EXERCISE 31: USING PARENTHETICAL NOTES

The following paragraph, taken from a research essay about the Industrial Revolution, is based on the source materials in Exercise 29. Compare the paragraph with its sources, and then decide where the parenthetical notes should be placed. Insert the notes, making sure that you distinguish the source material from the writer's own contributions to the paragraph.

The Industrial Revolution caused a major change in the working environment of most people in England. Historians have described the painful transition from working in the home and on the farm to working in the factory. E. J. Hobsbawm points out that most factory employees were at the mercy of the master and his foremen, who controlled their working hours with "draconic discipline." According to W. E. Lunt, those who previously did spinning and weaving in their homes had worked as long and as hard as the workers in the new textile factories, but they had been able to maintain more control over when and how they performed their tasks. It was the male workers who especially resented their loss of freedom and tended to be more resistant to discipline, and so manufacturers found it desirable to hire women and children, who were more passive and obedient. The long hours and bleak and unhealthy environment of the factories must have been particularly hard on the women and children who worked in them. Indeed, Lunt observes that it was their plight that "finally evoked an outcry from the humanitarians." Ultimately, then, an improvement in working conditions came about because of respect for the frailty of women and children, not because of respect for the rights of all workers.

USING EXPLANATORY NOTES

You will have noticed that, in the excerpt from Bernard on p. 386, following the second parenthetical reference to Renne, there is a number. This calls the reader's attention to a separate note appearing at the bottom of the paragraph. (In the actual essay, the note would appear either at the bottom of the page or, together with other notes, on a separate sheet at the end of the essay.) Jessie Bernard is using an *explanatory note* as a way of including information that does not quite fit into the text of her essay.

If your research has been thorough, you may find yourself with more material than you know what to do with. It can be tempting to use up every single point on your note cards and cram all the available information into your essay. But if you include too many extraneous points, your reader will find it hard to concentrate on the real topic of your paragraph. To illustrate this point, here are two paragraphs dealing with the domestic life of Charles Dickens: one is bulging; the other is streamlined. The first contains an analysis of Dickens's relationship with his sister-in-law; in the second, he decides to take a holiday in France.

Paragraph 1

Another good friend to Charles Dickens was his sister-in-law. Georgina had lived with the family ever since they had returned from an American tour in June 1842. She had grown attached to the children while the couple was away (Pope-Hennessy 179–80). She now functioned as an occasional secretary to Dickens, specifically when he was writing A Child's History of England, which Pope-Hennessy terms a "rather deplorable production." Dickens treated the history of his country in a very unorthodox manner (311). Dickens must have felt close to Georgina since he chose to dictate the History to her; with all his other work, Dickens always worked alone, writing and correcting it by himself (Butt and Tillotson 20–21). Perhaps a different woman would have questioned the relationship of her younger sister to her husband; yet Kate Dickens accepted this friendship for what it was. Pope-Hennessy describes the way in which Georgina used to take over the running of the household whenever Kate was indisposed. Kate was regularly too pregnant to go anywhere. She had ten children and four miscarriages in a period of fifteen years (391). Kate probably found another woman to be quite a help around the house. Pope-Hennessy suggests that Kate and her sister shared Charles Dickens between them (287).

Paragraph 2

In 1853, three of Dickens's closest friends had died (Forster 124),[5] and the writer himself, having become even more popular and busy since the publication of David Copperfield (Maurois 70), began to complain of "hypochondriacal whisperings" and also of "too many invitations to too many parties" (Forster 125). In May of that year, a kidney ailment that had plagued Dickens since his youth grew worse (Dickens, Letters 350), and, against the advice of his wife, he decided to take a holiday in Boulogne (Johnson 757).[6]

[5]The friends were Mr. Watson, Count d'Orsay, and Mrs. Macready.

[6]Tillotson, Dickens's doctor, who had been in Boulogne the previous October, was the one to encourage him to go there.

The first paragraph obviously contains too much information, most of which is unrelated to this topic. Pope-Hennessy's opinion of the history of England and the history of Kate's pregnancies are topics that may be worth discussing, but not in this paragraph. This extraneous material could be shifted to other paragraphs of the essay, placed in explanatory notes, or simply omitted.

The second, much shorter paragraph suggests that related but less important detail can usefully be put into explanatory notes where, if wanted, it is always available. Readers of the second paragraph are being given a choice: they can absorb the essential information from the paragraph alone, or they can examine the topic in greater depth by referring also to the explanatory notes.

Explanatory notes should be reserved for information that, in your view, is useful and to some degree relevant to the topic; if it is uninteresting and way off the point, simply omit it. If you indulge too often in explanatory notes, your notes may be longer than your essay. Also remember to find out whether including explanatory notes is acceptable to your instructor.

AVOIDING EXCESSIVE NOTES

Complex research was needed to gather the numerous details found in the biographical essays about Ernest Hemingway and Charles Dickens, and the writers of these essays use numerous parenthetical notes to document their sources. Here is a brief example:

Dickens's regular work habits involved writing at his desk from about nine in the morning to two in the afternoon (Butt and Tillotson 19; Pope-Hennessy 248), which left a good deal of time for other activities. Some of his leisure each day was regularly spent in letter-writing, some in walking and riding in the open air (Pope-Hennessy 305, quoting Nathaniel Sharswell). Besides this regular routine, on some days he would devote time to reading manuscripts which Wills, his sub-editor on Household Words, would send to him for revision and comment (Forster 65; Johnson 702).

In this passage, three parenthetical notes are needed for three sentences because a different biographer is the source for each piece of information. To combine all the sources in a single note would confuse, rather than simplify, the acknowledgments. In addition, the writer of this essay is not only making it clear where the information came from, but is also providing the reader with a *choice of references*. The writer has come across the same information in more than one biography, has indicated the duplication of material in her notes, and has decided to demonstrate the thoroughness of her research by citing more than one reference. Since the sources are given equal status in the notes (by being placed in alphabetical order and separated by a semicolon), the reader can assume that they are equally reliable. Had the writer thought that one was more thorough or more convincing than another, she would either have omitted the secondary one or indicated its status by placing it after "also" (Johnson 702; also Forster 65).

But an abundance of parenthetical notes does not always indicate sound research. As the following example demonstrates, excessive documentation only creates clutter.

> In contrast to the Dickenses' house in London, this setting was idyllic: the house stood in the center of a large garden complete with woods, waterfall, roses (Forster 145), and "no end of flowers" (Forster 146). For a fee, the Dickenses fed on the produce of the estate and obtained their milk fresh from the landlord's cow (Forster 146). What an asset to one's peace of mind to have such a cooperative landlord as they had (Pope-Hennessy 310; Johnson 758; Forster 147) in the portly, jolly Monsieur Beaucourt (Forster 147)!

Clearly, this entire passage is taken from three pages in Forster's biography of Dickens, and a single note could document the entire paragraph. What information is contained in the sentence leading up to the triple parenthetical note that justifies citing three sources? And what does the last note document? Is it only Forster who is aware that Monsieur Beaucourt is portly and jolly? To avoid tiring and irritating his readers, the writer here would have been well advised to ignore the supporting evidence in Pope-Hennessy and Johnson, and use a single reference to Forster. The writer was undoubtedly proud of his extensive research, but he seems more eager to show off his hours in the library than to provide a readable text for his audience.

USING UMBRELLA NOTES

As in the previous example, sometimes the logical sequence of your ideas or information requires you to cite the same source for several sentences or even for several paragraphs at a stretch. Instead of repeating "Forster 146" again and again, you can use a single note to cover the entire sequence. These notes are sometimes called *umbrella notes*, because they cover a sequence of sentences as an umbrella might cover more than one person. Umbrella notes are generally used in essays where the sources' names are not often cited in the text, and so the reader cannot easily figure out the coverage by assuming that the name and the parenthetical note mark the beginning and ending points. An umbrella simply means that you are leaving the reader in no doubt as to how much material the note is covering.

An umbrella note consists of an explanation of how much material is being covered by a source. Such a note is too long to be put in parentheses within the text and generally takes the form of *an explanatory note placed outside the body of your essay.* Here is an example:

> [2]The information in this and the previous paragraph dealing with Dickens's relationship with Wilkie Collins is entirely derived from Hutton, Dickens-Collins Letters 41–49.

Inside your essay, the superscript number 2 referring the reader to this note would follow right after the *last* sentence that uses material from Hutton to discuss Dickens and Wilkie Collins.

Of course, umbrella notes work only when you are using a single source for a reasonably long stretch. If you use two sources, you have to distinguish between them in parenthetical notes, and the whole point of the umbrella—to cut down on the number of notes—is lost.

Umbrella notes must also be used with caution when you are quoting. Because the umbrella provides the reference for a long stretch of material, the citation usually includes several pages; but how will the reader know on which page the quotation appears? Sometimes you can add this information to the note itself:

> [2]The information in this and the previous paragraph is entirely derived from Hutton, Dickens-Collins Letters 41–49. The two quotations from Dickens's letters are from pages 44 and 47, respectively.

However, if you use too many umbrella notes, or if you expect a single note to guide your reader through the intricacies of a long paragraph, you will have abused the device. Your essay will have turned into a series of summaries, with each group of paragraphs describing a single source. That is not what a research essay is supposed to be.

THE FINAL BIBLIOGRAPHY

While the bibliography is always an essential part of the research essay, it becomes especially important when you use MLA documentation, since it is the only place where your reader can find publication information about your sources. Which works you include in your final bibliography may depend on the wording and intention of your assignment. There is an important difference between a list of works that you have *consulted* or *examined* and a list of works that you have *cited* or actually used in writing your essay. Many instructors restrict the bibliography to "Works Cited," but you may be asked to submit a list of "Works Consulted." Remember that one purpose of a "Works Consulted" bibliography is to help your readers to find appropriate background information, not to overwhelm them with the magnitude of your efforts. Don't present a collection of thirty-five titles if you actually cite only five sources in your essay.

An appropriate final bibliography of "Works Cited" for an undergraduate essay consists of all the sources that you used and documented, through parenthetical notes, in your essay.

If you consulted a book in the hope that it contained some relevant information, and if it provided nothing useful, should you include it in your final bibliography? You might do so to prevent your readers from repeating your unnecessary research and attempting to consult works with misleading titles in the belief that they might be useful, but only if your bibliography is *annotated* so that the book's lack of usefulness can be pointed out. Finally, if you have been unable to locate a source and have thus never examined it yourself, you may not ordinarily include it in your final bibliography, however tempting the title may be.

PREPARING THE
ANNOTATED BIBLIOGRAPHY

Annotating your bibliography (described in Chapter 5, pp. 259–264) is an excellent way to demonstrate the quality of your research. But, to be of use, your brief annotations must be informative. The following phrases do not tell the reader very much: "an interesting piece"; "a good article"; "well-done"; "another source of well-documented information." What is well done? Why is it interesting? What is good about it? How much and what kind of information does it contain? A good annotated bibliography will answer some of these questions.

The bibliography on pp. 394–396 presents the basic facts about the author, title, and publication, as well as some *evaluative information*. If the annotations were omitted, these entries would still be perfectly correct, for they conform to the standard rules for bibliographical format. Without the annotation, one would simply have to change the heading to "Works Consulted" or "Works Cited."

Guidelines for Bibliographical Entries

(Additional models can be found in Appendix B, p. 458)

1. The bibliography is always listed on a *separate sheet* at the *end* of your research essay. The title should be centered, one inch from the top of the page.

2. Each entry is *double-spaced*, with double spacing between entries.

3. Each bibliographical entry starts with *the author's last name at the margin;* the second line of the entry (if there is one) is indented *five spaces*. This format enables the reader's eye to move quickly down the list of names at the left-hand margin.

4. The bibliography is in *alphabetical order,* according to the last name of the author.

   ■ If there are two authors, only the first has the last name placed first: "Woodward, Robert, and Carl Bernstein."

   ■ If an author has more than one work included on your list, do not repeat the name each time: alphabetize or arrange chronologically by publication date the works by that author; place the name at the margin preceding the first work; for the remaining titles, replace the name with three hyphens, followed by a period and one space.

   Freud, Sigmund. Civilization and Its Discontents. London: Hogarth, 1930.

   ---. Moses and Monotheism. New York: Knopf, 1939.

   ■ A work that has no author should be alphabetized within the bibliography according to the first letter of the title (excluding "The"); the title is placed at the margin as the author's name would be.

5. A bibliographical entry for a book is read as a list of three items—author, title (underlined), and publication information—with *periods between each piece of information.* Each period is followed by *one* space. All the information should always be presented in exactly the same order that you see in the model bibliography on pp. 394–396. Place of publication comes first; a colon separates place and name of publisher; a comma separates publisher and date.

6. A bibliographical entry for a *periodical* starts with the author's name and the article title (in quotation marks), each followed by a period and one space. Then comes the name of the periodical, underlined, followed by one space (and no punctuation at all). What comes next depends on the kind of periodical you are citing.

(continued)

(continued)

- For *quarterly and monthly journals,* include the volume number, followed by a space, and then the year in parentheses, followed by a colon.
- For *weekly or biweekly journals,* include only the full date—day, month, and year—followed by a colon.

All periodical entries end with the inclusive pages of the article, first page to last, followed by a period.

Tobias, Sheila, and Carol Weissbrod. "Anxiety and Mathematics: An Update." Harvard Educational Review 50 (1980): 61–67.

Winkler, Karen J. "Issues of Justice and Individual's Rights Spur Revolution in Political Philosophy." Chronicle of Higher Education 16 April 1986: 6–8.

7. Each entry of the bibliography ends with a period.

HEMINGWAY IN 1924: AN ANNOTATED BIBLIOGRAPHY

Baker, Carlos. Hemingway: A Life Story. New York: Scribner's, 1969. 563 pages of biography, with 100 pages of footnotes. Everything seems to be here, presented in great detail.

Donaldson, Scott. Hemingway: By Force of Will. New York: Viking, 1977. The material isn't organized chronologically; instead, the chapters are thematic, with titles like "Money," "Sex," and "War." Episodes from Hemingway's life are presented within each chapter. The introduction calls this "a mosaic of [Hemingway's] mind and personality."

Griffin, Peter. Less Than a Treason: Hemingway in Paris. New York: Oxford UP, 1990. Part of a multivolume biography. Covers Hemingway's life from 1921–1927, exclusively. Griffin says in the preface that his goal is not to "analyze this well examined life" but "to recreate it." Not surprisingly, it reads like a novel, with an omniscient narrator with access to Hemingway's emotions.

Gurko, Leo. Ernest Hemingway and the Pursuit of Heroism. New York: Crowell, 1968. This book is part of a series called "Twentieth-Century American Writers": a brief introduction to the man and his work. After fifty pages of straight biography, Gurko discusses Hemingway's writing, novel by novel.

There's an index and a short bibliography, but no notes. The biographical part is clear and easy to read, but it sounds too much like summary.

Hemingway, Ernest. A Moveable Feast. New York: Scribner's, 1964. This is Hemingway's own version of his life in Paris. It sounds authentic, but there's also a very strongly nostalgic tone, so it may not be trustworthy.

Hemingway in Paris. Home page. 13 Oct. 1997 <http://204.122.127.50/WSHS/Paris/HTM/>. Three photos of the Hemingways' apartment, with brief comments.

Hemingway, Leicester. My Brother, Ernest Hemingway. Cleveland: World, 1962. For 1924–1925, L.H. uses information from Ernest's letters (as well as commonly known facts). The book reads like a third-hand report, very remote; but L.H. sounds honest, not as if he were making up things that he doesn't know about.

Hotchner, A. E. Papa Hemingway. New York: Random, 1955. This book is called a "personal memoir." Hotchner met Hemingway in 1948, evidently hero-worshiped him, and tape-recorded his reminiscences. The book is their dialogue (mostly Hemingway's monologue). No index or bibliography. Hotchner's adoring tone is annoying, and the material resembles that of A Moveable Feast, which is better written.

Meyers, Jeffrey. Hemingway: A Biography. New York: Harper, 1985. Includes several maps, and two chronologies: illnesses and accidents, and travel. Book organized chronologically, with every year accounted for, according to table of contents. Well-documented critical biography, with personal anecdotes taking a back seat to literary. Less gossipy, more circumspect in claims than Griffin.

Reynolds, Michael. Hemingway: The Paris Years. Cambridge, Mass.: Blackwell, 1989. Second of three-volume biography. Includes a chronology covering December 1921–February 1926 and five maps ("Hemingway's Europe 1922–26," "France," "Switzerland," "Italy," and "Key points for Hemingway's several trips through France and Spain").

Sokoloff, Alice Hunt. Hadley, the First Mrs. Hemingway. New York: Dodd, 1973. This is the Paris experience from Hadley's point of view, most of it taken from her recollections and from the standard biographies. (Baker is acknowledged.) It's a very slight book—102 pages—but there's an index and footnotes, citing letters and interviews that some of the other biographers might not have been able to use.

Weeks, Robert P., ed. Hemingway: Twentieth Century Perspectives. Englewood
Cliffs: Prentice, 1965. Contains many important essays on Hemingway's
life and art. Offers a selected annotated bibliography.

Young, Philip. Ernest Hemingway. Minneapolis: U of Minnesota P, 1959. A short
psychobiography of Hemingway's life. Offers stimulating insights, but
suffers from the limitations of psychoanalysis.

EXERCISE 32: PREPARING THE BIBLIOGRAPHY

Correct the errors of form in the following bibliography:

Becker, Howard S, Geer, Blanche, and Everett C. Hughes. Making the Grade:
New York (1968) Wiley.

Dressel, Paul L.. College and University Curriculum, Berkeley (California):
McCutcheon, 1971

(same)----Handbook of Academic Evaluation. San Francisco (California): Jossey-
Bass: 1976.

J. F. Davidson, "Academic Interest Rates and Grade Inflation," Educational
Record.   56, 1975, pp. 122–5

(no author). "College Grades: A Rationale and Mild Defense." AAUP Bulletin,
October 1976, 320–1.

New York Times. "Job Plight of Young Blacks Tied to Despair, Skills Lack," April
19, 1983: Section A page 14.

Milton Ohmer, Howard R. Pollio and James A. Eison. GPA Tyranny, Education
Digest 54   (Dec 1988): 11–14.

Leo, John. "A for Effort". Or for Showing Up. U.S. News & World Report, 18 Oct,
1993: 22.

Kennedy, Donald. What Grade Inflation? The New York Times June 13, 1994:
All.

Bretz, Jr., Robert D. "College Grade Point Average as a Predictor of
Adult Success: a Meta-analytical Review and Some Additional Evidence" Public
Personnel Management 18   (Spring 1989): 11–22.

PRESENTING YOUR ESSAY

A well-presented research essay must conform to a few basic mechanical rules:

1. Type your essay on a computer. Make sure that you use a letter-quality printer.
2. Double-space throughout the essay.
3. Use 8½-by-11-inch paper; leave 1½-inch margins.
4. Use only one side of the page.
5. Number each page.
6. Proofread your essay, and print out the revised version.
7. Include graphics or illustrations only with your instructor's permission.
8. Include your name, the name of the course, the date, and the title of the essay, either on a separate title page or on the first page of the essay.

Check with your instructor for any other special rules that may apply to the assignment.

A Checklist for Revision

As you read and re-read your essay, keep the following questions in mind.

1. Does the essay have a single focus that is clearly established and maintained throughout?
2. Does the essay have a thesis or a consistent point of view about the events or issues being described?
3. If it is a narrative essay, does the narration have a beginning, middle, and end? If it is an argument essay, are all assumptions explained and defended, and are all obvious counterarguments accommodated or refuted?
4. Does the essay begin with an informative introduction?
5. Does the essay end on a conclusive note?
6. Does each paragraph have a clear topic sentence?
7. Does each paragraph contain one and only one topic? Should any paragraphs be merged or deleted?
8. Are the paragraphs long enough to be convincing? Is each point supported by facts and information?
9. Does the development of the essay depend entirely on a dry listing of facts and examples, or do you offer explanations and relevant commentary? Is there a good balance between generalization and detail?
10. Do you use transitions to signal the relationship between separate points?

(continued)

(continued)

11. Is there unnecessary repetition? Are there any sentences that lack content or add nothing to the essay?
12. Is the style appropriate for a formal essay? Do the sentences seem too conversational, as if you were sending an E-mail?
13. Does the reader get a sense of the relative importance of the sources being used?
14. Do you use one source for very long stretches at a time?
15. Is there an appropriate number of notes rather than too many or too few?
16. Is it clear how much material is covered by each note?
17. In essays containing endnotes, do notes provide important explanatory information?
18. Are the quotations well chosen?
19. Is paraphrase properly used? Is the style of the paraphrase consistent with your style?
20. Do you use enough citations? Does the text of the essay make it clear when you are using a specific source, and who that person is?
21. Is the essay convincing? Will your reader accept your analysis, interpretation, and arguments?

· 9 ·

Three Research Essays

The following three student research papers, on three very different subjects, use three different kinds of documentation.

The first writer is analyzing an issue and constructing an *argument*. In presenting some of the reasons why some people advocate and others condemn the practice of euthanasia, the writer hopes to persuade her readers that terminally ill people should have the right to choose the time of their deaths. The writer documents her sources with MLA documentation. She summarizes, paraphrases, or quotes her sources, using brief and unobtrusive parenthetical notes, generally at the ends of the sentences. Almost everything that the writer wants to say is said within the body of the essay, so there are only a few endnotes.

The second writer also explores a social issue, but here the *analysis* is supported by evidence presented in *narrative* form. To find out why cannibalism remains one of society's strongest taboos, the writer describes a series of real events, historical and recent, ordinary and exotic. She also reviews a number of the anthropological theories that attempt to explain these events. This essay will help you to understand the usefulness of the traditional footnote or endnote and bibliographic form of documentation. The writer is working with a great deal of precise detail, frequently referring to a group of sources to support specific points. She also presents a great deal of background information that cannot be included in the body of her paper. The separate endnotes provide enough room to cite all the sources and explain some of the points they are making.

The third writer also combines *narrative and analysis* by describing the aftermath of the strange event that happened in 1908 at Lake Tunguska, Siberia, and then analyzing some of the many theories that have been used to explain that event over the last ninety-five years. The bibliography for this essay contains relatively few sources, which are cited less frequently than the sources are in the first two essays. The writer's purpose is to help his readers understand what might have happened at Lake Tunguska and to clarify the scientific explanations. He is not using numerous sources to reconstruct the event in complete detail, or trying to convince his readers, by citing authorities, that his conclusions are the right ones. Like many essays in the sciences, this paper uses a variation of the author-year method of parenthetical note documentation. (This variation, often called APA after the American Psychological Association, is described in Appendix B, on pp. 469–476.) Having the date, as well as the author, included within the body of the essay is especially useful when you are reading about scientific theories developed over a span of ninety-five years.

Maria Catto

English 102

Spring 2001

Euthanasia: The Right to Die

Someone you love is suffering from terminal cancer. He asks you to hand him a bottle of lethal tablets so that he can die without prolonged agony. Would you do it? Should you? Incidents such as this one, in which one person asks another for help to die, raise the issue of euthanasia. At the center of this problem is the right of a person to die with the least suffering and the most dignity and comfort. In this essay, I will consider some of the reasons why euthanasia is so vigorously opposed, and why, in spite of that opposition, we must insist on our right to decide for ourselves when to end our own lives.

Euthanasia means the benign termination of a life before it has run its natural course (Keown, "Value" 6). A crucial distinction is made between active and passive euthanasia. According to Yale Kamisar, "active euthanasia" means directly causing the death of another person through an intended action. If that person has participated in and agreed to the decision to end his or her life, the appropriate term is "active voluntary euthanasia" (229). Administering a fatal drug to a dying person, injecting an air bubble into his bloodstream, or giving her some other means to shorten her life all exemplify active euthanasia. The most famous example of someone engaging in active euthanasia is Jack Kevorkian, the doctor from Michigan, who has helped patients to die using his "suicide machine," a tank of carbon monoxide and a mask (McHugh 15–21; Belkin 50; Elliott 27).

"Passive euthanasia" can be described as helping someone to die by doing nothing and, according to The Economist, "happens in hospitals all the time" ("Euthanasia War" 22). It usually involves deliberate withholding of life-prolonging measures (Keown, "Value" 6). Failing to resuscitate a patient who has suffered a massive heart attack is one example of passive euthanasia. Another is deciding not to feed terminally ill patients who are unable to feed themselves. By contrast, removing the feeding tube from a patient who is being fed that way would be considered active euthanasia.

The distinction between active and passive euthanasia is really about responsibility. In passive euthanasia, the doctor or relative has done nothing directly to end the patient's life and so has less moral responsibility. An intermediate form of euthanasia—assisted suicide—is more controversial. In assisted suicide, a doctor or other person provides a terminally ill person with the means—pills, for example—and the medical knowledge necessary to commit suicide. In the Journal of the American Medical Association, Dr. David Orentlicher categorizes assisted suicide as a form of passive euthanasia (1844). Derek Humphrey's Final Exit, which describes ways to commit suicide painlessly, and the organization Compassion in Dying, which helps terminally ill patients to end their lives, are both sources of instruction in assisted suicide (Belkin 50; also Elliott 27).

The professional people who care for the sick and the dying think that there is a great difference between active euthanasia and passive euthanasia or assisted suicide. One panel of distinguished physicians declared themselves in favor, by a margin of 10 to 2, of doctor-assisted suicide for hopelessly ill patients who request it (Orentlicher 1844). But most doctors are adamantly opposed to carrying out any form of active euthanasia. Sue Woodman finds that the general public makes a similar distinction, approving of euthanasia only if the terminology used allows them to evade the issue. In one survey, many more people were willing to endorse "death with dignity" than "voluntary euthanasia" (154).

In the past, euthanasia was not a topic for such public debate and criticism. In part, this was because death rarely occurred in a public place. People of all ages died at home, in a natural and familiar setting, with their loved ones around them;[1] therefore, no one except family members or a doctor was likely to know whether the patient was or wasn't helped to die. Also, doctors formerly lacked the knowledge and the means to try to prolong a dying person's life. Patient and relatives were sustained through their ordeal by their religious faith and by the ideal of a "good death."

Today, as a result of advances in medical science, it has become both possible and, many say, desirable to try to prolong a dying person's life. Indeed, it is often considered criminal not to try to do so. We all hope to live forever, and tend to regard every death as avoidable. This attitude is encouraged by the "high-tech atmosphere" existing in most hospitals today, especially in intensive care units, which supports the idea that science is stronger than death, and encourages doctors to think of death as "an unacceptable outcome of medical therapy" (Fackelmann 232). George J. Annas of the Boston University School of Medicine considers whether patients have the right to refuse to have their lives prolonged and concludes that "the proper role of medical technology" is at the center of the debate over euthanasia: "Is technology going to be our master or our servant? Is technology going to take on a life of its own such that we give it rights of its own? Or are we going to reassert our dominant role in controlling technology and using it for human ends?" ("Symposium"). Those concerned in answering these questions include the patient, the patient's family, and the doctor and nursing staff, all of whom may be affected by their differing conceptions of God or divinity or fate.

Those who are most fervently opposed to euthanasia tend to believe, for religious reasons, that no individual has the right to take his or her own life; that decision must be left to God (Koop 70). They insist that our lives are not our private possessions but are held in trust ("Last Rights"). In their view, "every life has intrinsic value, irrespective of the individual's mental state or physical condition" (Vallely 13). They argue that no human being—not even the dying person—can ever be certain when death is about to happen or whether euthanasia is really necessary. So, they want to turn the matter over to God, to whom they attribute perfect objectivity and omniscience.

Advocates of euthanasia think that this argument is a way of avoiding human responsibility. The ideals of our society include the belief that we are all individuals capable of self-determination. Having control over one's own life is part of being human; to be prevented from having control over one of the major decisions in one's life is "a form of tyranny, . . . an ultimate denial of respect for persons" (Keown, "Value" 20; also Brock 89). Before becoming ill, most patients were free to choose their style of life, to decide when to eat, when to sleep, and how to take care of themselves. Why, then, should they be deprived of the right to choose whether to live or to die? Having witnessed his father's lingering death, Dr. Charles McKhann expresses views that are atypical for a physician: "It seems unfair that people who manage their own affairs successfully in life should be required to turn over so much of their death and dying to others" (2). It is as if the ability to reason and make moral choices no longer matters when someone is dying.[2]

Staunch opponents of euthanasia also insist that society exists to nurture and protect human life, not to terminate it. Wesley Smith argues that it is wrong to kill except in war or for self-defense or public safety (6). But Joseph Fletcher takes Smith's point and turns it upside down. He finds it interesting that you are permitted to kill in your own defense but not to help someone in agony: "You may end your neighbor's life for your own sake, but you may not do it for his sake" (93). Similarly, it is acceptable for veterinarians to put extremely sick animals out of their misery, but the same privilege is not usually extended to human beings. Smith thinks this is an appropriate distinction: because humans are of a different order—a higher order—from animals, their lives must be preserved at any cost. To do otherwise would be murder (208). But calling euthanasia murder implies that the victim's life is being taken against her will. That is far from true if the person is suffering, near to death, and just wants it to happen sooner (McKhann 5).

The central issue is that, very often, the dying person is experiencing great suffering. There is nothing dignified about death from a disease like cancer. Aside from pain, many patients experience totally debilitating symptoms like nausea and the inability to swallow. In some cases, the death is not only agonizing but ugly and degrading.[3] Even hospices can't guarantee a "good" death (Stephany 112). Physicians are unavoidably and uncomfortably aware of these horrors, yet they insist that it is possible to provide an appropriate "medical environment" for dying and find a "level of care that optimizes comfort and dignity" (Wanzer 169). They argue that, if the patient receives sufficient medication, the pain will be alleviated and the person will no longer want to die (Smith 13). While it is true that doctors still tend to under-medicate the terminally ill (Woodman 163), the level of sedation needed to make such pain tolerable often deprives the patient of his remaining aware-ness and satisfaction with life (McKhann 30).

Indeed, for many patients, life is no longer worth living because they are deprived of all the activities and many of the experiences that made their lives worthwhile (Brock 96). They are too weak to talk, too weak to read (McKhann 30–31). According to a 2001 study, when dying people contem-plate the possibility of euthanasia, it's not the pain that motivates them; it's the social isolation and emotional suffering. They don't want to be helpless, dependent, and isolated from their friends and family. One patient admitted that he felt a "loss of self, of the dignity and wholeness of my body, as well as spirit" ("Exploring the Angst"). "One may reasonably ask," writes Charles McKhann, "is the function of medicine to preserve biological life or to preserve the person as he defines himself?" (35).

Another reason that terminally ill patients sometimes request euthanasia is to spare their families the emotional and financial burdens of a prolonged dying. Here is one man's view:

> Spending [money] to visit the children and grandchildren is one
> thing. Spending it to stare at four walls in a nursing home, unable
> to remember my name or address, is something else altogether. I
> have no intention of giving my money to a doctor who cannot help
> me, or a nursing home that I didn't choose and where I don't want
> to live. (McKhann 42)

Is this a sufficient reason for a physician to help the patient to an immediate death? Is the desire to spare one's family the equivalent of intolerable suffer-ing? This dilemma becomes more difficult when the third party to the prob-lem—the family—takes a strong stand for or against. If the family is horrified by the prospect of euthanasia, then the physician who obliges the patient will have to face the wrath of his relatives when he is no longer around to en-dorse the decision. If the family eagerly approves euthanasia, then the physi-cian has to worry about their ulterior motives. This is an even more sensitive issue if the patient is too sedated or demented to participate in the decision. Although Charles McKhann insists that this kind of familial abuse does not happen often (165), there are numerous horror stories about patients whose lives were terminated without their request or consent. Robert Twycross tells of an old man dying of cancer, whose symptoms were under control. When he asked to go home and die there, his children would not allow it.

> Instead, they pointed to their father's suffering and the need to fin-
> ish things quickly "in the name of humanity." When the doctor re-
> fused, they threatened to sue him. Because the patient insisted on
> going home, a social worker went to investigate. She discovered
> that the patient's house was empty and that every piece of furni-
> ture had been taken by the family. (161)

A patient in this situation would certainly feel that there was no point in prolonging an unwanted life.

Opponents of euthanasia argue that patients who insist that they want to die don't really mean it; it's the depression speaking. It is, they say, irrational to want to die, and so anyone who does must be in an extreme and unnatural emotional state. The person must be medicated with antidepressants into being more hopeful ("Last Rights"). Writing of his experience in a hospice, Robert Twycross insists that people who think they want to die change their minds as soon as their pain is alleviated and they regain their sense of hope. Of the 44 terminal cancer patients whom he studied, three-fourths never wished for death; the ones who did were mostly depressed to begin with and, he believes, would have benefited from medication (142–43; also Finnis 27). In contrast, Theresa Stephany, who is a nurse, has found that patients who knowingly choose death over a compromised life aren't usually depressed; rather, they are "realistic" (111–12). In John Keown's view, responsible doctors in countries where euthanasia is permitted must take care in deciding if a patient asking for euthanasia really has reason to believe that life isn't worth living ("Netherlands" 262).[4]

American doctors who are strongly opposed to all forms of euthanasia argue that the Hippocratic oath, which they must swear when they receive their medical degrees, pledges them to save lives, not to end them

(Gaylin et al. 26). In one of its many statements on this subject, the American Medical Association declares that "the power to assist in intentionally taking the life of a patient is antithetical to the central mission of healing that guides both medicine and nursing. It is a power that most physicians and nurses do not want and could not control" (Woodman 176). Similarly, the American Nursing Association has issued a statement that accepts the occasional necessity for "foregoing life-sustaining treatments," but rejects more aggressive forms of euthanasia as a "violat[ion of] the ethical traditions of the profession" ("ANA"). This defensive stance is partly attributable to the paternalism that surrounds the medical profession. Patients are encouraged to believe that the doctor knows best and, traditionally, have been reluctant to question a physician's decision. Acknowledging this authority, doctors say that it would be all too easy for them to abuse the privilege if they were given direct power over life and death (Woodman 73).[5]

Another strong professional objection to euthanasia is based on the special relationship that is supposed to exist between doctor and patient. Again, the American Medical Association gives the official view:

> To allow or force physicians to participate in activity ending the lives of patients would so dramatically and fundamentally change the entire patient/physician relationship that it would undermine the principles we, as a society, hold most dear. We must never lose sight of the caveat that physicians are healers [. . .]. (Smith 162)

This "essential bond of trust" is evidently so fragile that, in a survey of cancer patients, many said that they would change doctors if their physician made any mention of assisted suicide (Smith 5).[6] But that is a long way from explaining why a doctor should refuse any discussion with a patient who openly contemplates some form of euthanasia. Doctors are supposed to comfort if they cannot heal. Howard Brody points out that, far from being comforted, such a patient can only feel abandoned by his doctor (137).

Some doctors, of course, are genuinely concerned that they will make the wrong decision: "We are simply afraid that we'll prove to be human. . . . We'll make errors of judgment, bad calls—and they'll be irrevocable" (Woodman 183). Others cannot bring themselves to admit that they have failed to save a patient. Many find it difficult to break the news that an illness is terminal; because there is no positive way to help, they even tend to avoid visiting dying patients (McKhann 136–37). But while doctors may have moral and personal reservations about their own role in euthanasia, do they have a right to impose their objections on those colleagues who are willing to accept this responsibility (Brock 90–91; Brody 138)?

Understandably, doctors have reason to be concerned with their own welfare as well as that of their patients. One very real fear is that they will be sued for having failed to use every possible means to ensure that the dying live as long as possible. According to Charles McKhann, many also fear legal charges if they actually engage in a provable form of euthanasia (39): "It is clear, both legally and professionally, that doing less rather than more is safer for the physician" (144). Many instances of euthanasia remain a private matter for the doctor and the family. But if charges are brought against a physician, he or she can sometimes receive more than a token sentence. In Britain, Dr. Nigel Cox was found guilty of attempted murder because he had given a lethal injection to a 70-year-old woman who was dying a painful death. He had known her for thirteen years and had the support of the patient, her family, and (when the case became known) the public. He received a year's suspended sentence (Woodman 71–72) and, presumably, a great deal of bad publicity and a loss of reputation.

Euthanasia is a complex issue partly because it lends itself so well to the "slippery slope" argument: once you start, where will you stop? On a practical level, keeping a terminally ill patient alive is usually expensive. All the new technology requires maintaining costly machines and providing high-level nursing care. If the patient is comatose, sedated, or demented, costs can soar. Even if health insurance agencies pick up the tab, what is the point if the patient is going to die anyway? HMOs are fully aware that death costs less than treatment; so, ultimately, it's in their interests to encourage euthanasia to the extent that the medical profession and the public will allow ("Last Rights"). Opponents of euthanasia understandably suspect that hospitals, concerned with costs, might be tempted to practice euthanasia without patients' consent ("Euthanasia War" 22). This is the slippery slope:

once a society makes it legal or acceptable or convenient to kill one patient, then what's to stop it from killing many (Elliott 26)?

When making the slippery slope argument, critics of euthanasia also generally express concerns about its wider implications as a social policy. They point to the terrible precedent of Nazi Germany and the eugenics movement of the early twentieth century, which attempted to eliminate everyone who did not meet a certain standard of social excellence and desirability, such as the mentally and the chronically ill (Smith 76–77). If euthanasia is ever going to become acceptable social policy, it is important to recognize those fears as legitimate and to establish guidelines that safeguard the rights of patients and those who care for them.

The experience of the Netherlands, where rules permitting euthanasia have been in place since 1984, provides precedents to follow and to avoid. The Dutch Medical Association declared that the patient must be competent to initiate the request, which has to be voluntary; that the patient must be experiencing intolerable suffering (not necessarily physical); that euthanasia must be a last resort in cases where there is no likelihood of improvement; that the request must be "durable" over a fixed waiting period; and that, before consenting, the physician must first consult with an experienced colleague (Keown, "Netherlands" 264).

Whether or not you believe that these guidelines have proven to be safe, effective social policy for the Netherlands depends on whom you read. John Keown's analysis of the Remmelink Report, a 1990 survey of the practice of euthanasia in the Netherlands, concludes that half of all doctors whose practice included terminally ill patients had participated in euthanasia. (Only 12% of doctors said that they would never do so.) Of all the deaths that occurred in the Netherlands in 1990, about 1.8% resulted from euthanasia. The bad news was that in 0.8% (about a thousand patients), the patient's consent had not been obtained. The report evidently did not specify how many of those patients were competent to make the decision. In Keown's view, these figures give credence to the argument that, once you start to engage in euthanasia, the practice will be abused ("Netherlands" 268–69). Wesley Smith, an ardent proponent of the slippery slope argument, projects these figures on to the United States: if we adopted the Dutch guidelines, there would be 85,000 cases of involuntary euthanasia deaths per year (99). Smith concludes that "the Dutch have proved that once killing is accepted as a solution for one problem, tomorrow it will be seen as the solution of hundreds of problems" with the specter of the Nazis not far off (109).

Those who are sympathetic to the need for some form of euthanasia take a more tolerant view of the Dutch experience. Calling it a "flawed model," Charles McKhann acknowledges the wrongful deaths documented in the Remmelink Report; but he argues that no one should confuse the Dutch with the Nazis. They are doing the best they can to relieve suffering humanely (129–30).[7] A later study of the euthanasia statistics in the Netherlands shows that, from 1990 to 1995, there was no sharp increase in the number of deaths from euthanasia. Most patients who requested euthanasia did so, not because of pain, but because of the poor quality of their lives. Far from being the very old, who might have been disposed of as nuisances, they were mostly between 55 and 75 ("Last Rights").

The key component of the Dutch or any other socially sanctioned program of euthanasia has to be voluntary consent. Doctors and social workers have to be sure that the patient hasn't been swayed by excessive concern for family members or, indeed, by the family's coercion. For this reason, supporters of the right to euthanasia frequently recommend that each individual write a "living will" relatively early in life while still healthy and undeniably competent to make decisions (Humphrey). Such a legal document states that, should the person be incapable of making such a decision, he or she is establishing certain preferences among the options that might be available for his or her care. Typically such wills instruct doctors not to start or to stop any procedures intended to sustain life if the condition is terminal. They do not, however, authorize doctors to assist in suicide efforts or to engage in active euthanasia (Living Will).

Euthanasia is the Greek term for "good death." Today, for most of us, the dread of death is so great that we will go to any lengths to avoid it for those we love, as well as for ourselves. It may be that the right to choose euthanasia would never have become a significant social issue if death were

still a more integral part of our lives and if the circumstances in which it typically takes place were easier to bear. As Charles McKhann acknowledges, we
have become "a society that needs greater acceptance of death and dying, not
in violence but in peace" (188). At present, we are more concerned with keeping people alive than with the quality of the lives that are being prolonged.
Until we can have some assurance of a compassionate death—without un-
bearable cost to others and to society—we should not be intimidated by the
church, the law, or the medical profession. Just as we choose the way we
live, so should we be able to choose the way we die.

Notes

[1]According to a survey in Time, 70 years ago more than half the deaths that took place in the United States occurred at home (Tifft 68). A more recent survey shows that the trend is for Americans to die in hospitals, nursing homes, and other institutions ("The Right to Choose").

[2]Not everyone endorses this right to self-determination. Wesley Smith believes that this desire to dispose of our lives as we see fit is nothing more than "near-absolute individualism" that will result in the kind of "social anarchy that asphyxiates true freedom" (6).

[3]In 1971, the British Medical Association reported that most people, no matter how serious their illnesses are, do not die in agony, but, rather, peacefully and with dignity. Thirty years later, even the strongest opponents of euthanasia don't try to present such a rosy view; they simply evade the issue.

[4]A separate issue concerns patients who are incompetent: demented, or suffering from Alzheimer's disease, or in a coma. Their trust can be abused if euthanasia is performed when it's not possible for them to give their consent; on the other hand, they're also "victims of severe suffering and pointless prolongation of life" (McKhann 98).

[5]Woodman points out the concern of many doctors that, once they are given the power to make choices about life and death, the rationale will start to expand to include not just the terminally ill, but also the chronically ill (217–18).

[6]But Smith also observes that, these days, few people have longstanding relationships with their doctors, so that it becomes difficult for doctors to read their patients' true preferences and intentions (145). That comment takes some credibility away from his assertion of an "essential bond of trust."

[7]McKhann believes that, in the United States, we are not so inhumane that we would abuse the practice of euthanasia if it were to become legally accepted. Because we have invented this bogey, he says, we are forcing "these unfortunate people [to] live out their final days in agony, or sedated into oblivion, in order to save our children and their children from becoming social monsters" (188).

Catto 13

Works Cited

"ANA Praises Supreme Court Decision on Physician-Assisted Suicide." ANA
    Web Page. 26 June 1997. American Nurses Association. 23 Aug.
    2001 <http://www.ana.org/pressrel/1997/june26.htm>.

Belkin, Lisa. "There's No Simple Suicide." New York Times Magazine 14 Nov.
    1993: 48–55+.

Brock, Dan W. "Physician-Assisted Suicide Is Sometimes Morally Justified."
    Physician-Assisted Suicide. Ed. Robert Weir. Bloomington: Indiana
    UP, 1997. 86–106.

Brody, Howard. "Assisting in Patient Suicides Is an Acceptable Practice for
    Physicians." Physician-Assisted Suicide. Ed. Robert Weir.
    Bloomington: Indiana UP, 1997. 136–51.

Elliott, Carl. "Dying Rites: The Ethics of Euthanasia." New Scientist 20 June
    1992: 25–27.

"The Euthanasia War." Economist 21 June 1997: 21–24.

"Exploring the Angst of the Terminally Ill." New York Times 14 Aug. 2001: F6.

Fackelmann, Kathy. "A Question of Life or Death." Science News 9 Oct. 1982:
    232–33.

Finnis, John. "A Philosophical Case against Euthanasia." Euthanasia
    Examined: Ethical, Clinical and Legal Perspectives. Ed. John Keown.
    Cambridge: Cambridge UP, 1995. 23–36.

Fletcher, Joseph. "Sanctity of Life versus Quality of Life." Euthanasia: The
    Moral Issues. Ed. Robert M. Baird and Stuart E. Rosenbaum.
    Buffalo: Prometheus, 1989. 85–95.

Gaylin, Willard, et al. "Doctors Must Not Kill." Euthanasia: The Moral Issues.
    Ed. Robert M. Baird and Stuart E. Rosenbaum. Buffalo: Prometheus,
    1989. 25–28.

Humphrey, Derek. Final Exit: The Practicalities of Self-Deliverance and
    Assisted Suicide for the Dying. Eugene: Hemlock Society, 1991.

Kamisar, Yale. "Physician-Assisted Suicide: The Last Bridge to Active
    Voluntary Euthanasia." Euthanasia Examined: Ethical, Clinical
    and Legal Perspectives. Ed. John Keown. Cambridge: Cambridge UP,
    1995. 225–60.

Keown, John. "Euthanasia and the Value of Life." Euthanasia Examined:
     Ethical, Clinical and Legal Perspectives. Ed. John Keown. Cambridge:
     Cambridge UP, 1995. 6–23.

---. "Euthanasia in the Netherlands: Sliding Down the Slippery Slope?"
     Euthanasia Examined: Ethical, Legal and Clinical Perspectives. Ed.
     John Keown. Cambridge: Cambridge UP, 1995. 261–96.

Koop, C. Everett. "The Right to Die: The Moral Dilemmas." Euthanasia: The
     Moral Issues. Ed. Robert M. Baird and Stuart E. Rosenbaum.
     Buffalo: Prometheus, 1989. 69–83.

"Last Rights." Economist 21 June 1997. 19 July 2001 <http://
     www.britannica.com>.

The Living Will and Values History Project. Voluntary Euthanasia Society of
     Scotland. 16 Jan. 1996. 23 Aug. 2001 <http://www.euthanasia.org/
     lwvh.html>.

McHugh, Paul R. "The Kevorkian Epidemic." The American Scholar Winter
     1997: 15–27.

McKhann, Charles. A Time to Die. New Haven: Yale UP, 1999.

Orentlicher, David. "Physician Participation in Assisted Suicide." Journal of
     the American Medical Association 262 (1989): 1844–45.

"The Right to Choose." Economist 26 Mar. 1983: 223.

Smith, Wesley. Forced Exit: The Slippery Slope from Assisted Suicide to
     Legalized Murder. New York: Times Books, 1997.

Stephany, Theresa M. "Physician-Assisted Euthanasia Is Necessary."
     Euthanasia: Opposing Viewpoints. Ed. Carol Wekesser. San Diego:
     Greenhaven, 1995. 111–14.

"Symposium: When Sophisticated Medicine Does More Harm Than Good."
     New York Times 30 Mar. 1986: E6.

Tifft, Susan. "Debate on the Boundary of Life." Time 11 Apr. 1983: 68–70.

Twycross, Robert G. "Where There Is Hope, There Is Life: A View from the
     Hospice." Euthanasia Examined: Ethical, Clinical and Legal
     Perspectives. Ed. John Keown. Cambridge: Cambridge UP, 1995.

Vallely, Paul. "Uncomfortable Endings." Independent on Sunday 16 May
     1999: 13.

Wanzer, Sidney H., et al. "The Physician's Responsibility Towards Hopelessly Ill Patients." Euthanasia: The Moral Issues. Ed. Robert M. Baird and Stuart E. Rosenbaum. Buffalo: Prometheus, 1989. 163–77.

Woodman, Sue. Last Rites: The Struggle over the Right to Die. New York: Plenum, 1998.

Lee Myers

Anthropology 1

December 22, 2001

Why Is Eating People Wrong?

In a 1957 Broadway revue, the comic duo Flanders and Swann sang about a young cannibal boy who defies his family, insisting:

> I don't eat people
>
> I won't eat people
>
> Eating people is wrong.

His puzzled father reasons with him:

> People have always eaten people
>
> What else is there to eat?
>
> If the Juju had meant us not to eat people
>
> He wouldn't have made us of meat.[1]

Yet, despite accusations of cowardice ("You're afraid of ending up in the pot yourself"), the boy continues to resist the temptation of "roast leg of insurance salesman."

Part of the song's humor comes from its reversal of expectations: it assumes that cannibalism is normal, that the boy's high moral tone is just squeamishness, and that there's no good reason not to eat human flesh. In "The Reluctant Cannibal" Flanders and Swann are tapping into the audience's horror of and fascination with one of the last remaining social taboos. We are being encouraged to wonder whether eating people really is wrong.

Understanding the "why" of cannibalism depends on knowing the circumstances—the "when." Anthropologists tend to divide instances of cannibalism into broad categories based on motivation. "Survival cannibalism" caused by hunger is far more acceptable to Western morality than the various tribal customs known as "ritual cannibalism."[2] Anyone, even so-called civilized people, can be driven to cannibalism in extreme conditions. Petrinovich suggests that such behavior in times of crop failure or flood or war should not be regarded as pathological but as quite sensible, even natural, under the circumstances. During such disasters, normal moral constraints must be suspended: "It is as though the outer coverings of society have been peeled away to reveal the basic core of human nature."[3] Petrinovich describes the extreme consequences of starvation: everything within the body shrinks, including oxygen consumption, and strength and coordination weaken; but intellectual performance is not affected,[4] so presumably one can still make reasonable moral decisions.

Cannibalism would seem to be a reasonable choice in time of extreme famine. While the nutritional value of human flesh has been much debated, Garn and Block say that a man weighing fifty kilograms would provide sufficient protein for one day for sixty people, "skimpily." But if only one edible man was available in a week, the group wouldn't find the effort of killing him "nutritionally worthwhile."[5] During the Egyptian famine of 1201, when babies were sold "roasted or boiled," the Egyptians were horrified at first, but they grew used to it and some even "conceived such a taste for these detestable meats that they made them their ordinary provender, eating them for enjoyment and [thinking up] a variety of preparation methods."[6] In modern times, war has prompted outbreaks of cannibalism, particularly during sieges. In Paris, during the Franco-Prussian War, there was a butcher shop on the Ile St. Louis that was well known for supplying unusually fine meat.[7] During the siege of Leningrad in World War II, when one million people—one-third of the city's population—died, numerous "crimes-for-food" were committed.[8] According to Aleksandr Solzhenitsyn, in the prison camps of the Gulag Archipelago, hunger existed "to the point at which parents ate their own children."[9] As recently as the 1990s, extreme famine occurred in Russia and the Ukraine, which led to at least thirty documented murders in which bodies were sold for food.[10]

As these historical precedents suggest, anyone might engage in survival cannibalism if all sources of food disappeared. Perhaps the most well-publicized incident of this sort occurred in 1972, in the Andes, when the plane carrying a party of forty-five members of a Uruguayan rugby team with their families and friends crashed in bad weather. Injured and exposed to the bitter cold, the twenty-seven survivors existed on a daily ration of one square of chocolate, one teaspoon of jam, a bit of toothpaste, and a small mouthful

of wine in a deodorant cap.[11] When these supplies ran out and search
efforts had evidently been called off, the leader of the survivors, Roberto
Canessa, argued that the group had a moral duty to stay alive, that they had
been given the gift of life and were responsible for sustaining it. God wanted
them to live, they concluded. He had spared them from the crash and had
given them the dead bodies to eat. It would be wrong to reject this gift on the
grounds of squeamishness[12] for "refus[ing] to live would be a form of
suicide, a mortal sin."[13] Good Catholics, the survivors were very conscious
of the sacrament of Holy Communion as they prepared the bodies,[14] and
this theme was echoed by some of the Catholic priests who were sympathetic
to them when, after seventy-two days, they returned to civilization:

> The body must have a worthy purpose, and in [this] case, this pur-
> pose was to serve as food for the survivors. The living who still
> have strength must preserve themselves, and this the survivors
> tried faithfully to do. Of course, one must treat the dead with re-
> spect—and one symbol of the survivors' respect was to choose
> them for food.[15]

Treating the dead with respect is important in understanding acts of
cannibalism. The Andes party had certain advantages over most other survival groups: they all knew and cared for each other and could work together
to survive.[16] (Indeed, they were finally rescued by their own initiative: the
two strongest set out to walk out of the mountains and find help.) Throughout, they maintained a sense of charity and morality, made their decisions in
relative harmony, and went about the dreadful business of cannibalism with
some delicacy. For example, one group prepared each portion of meat and a
different group consumed it, and none of the dead women were regarded as
candidates for consumption. In addition, the Andes party, believing that they
had done nothing wrong, decided when rescue was imminent not to hide the
pieces of flesh that had been stockpiled. Of course, since so many had died
in the crash, they had not had to make the dreadful decision to kill in order
to survive.[17]

In 1846, when the Donner Party was stranded by blizzards in the
Rocky Mountains, they had none of these advantages. Starting from Illinois

Myers 4

and intending to settle in California, this group of eighty-seven farmers and townspeople (most of whom were women and children), eventually joined by two Indians, was trapped by the onset of an unusually early winter. They were not used to camping or fending for themselves, nor could they forage for food or read a trail. Still, they were highly organized, holding meetings to make decisions. First they gradually abandoned their goods and their twenty ox-drawn wagons as they pushed on through the waist-deep snow. But most eventually decided to wait out the winter in two camps: sixty people (about half children) in three cabins and twenty-one (again about half children) in a single cabin at a nearby site. Ironically, they had shelter, warmth, and clothing, and they were relatively safe; they just had no food. Once the oxen were slaughtered, they had nothing.[18]

A party of five women and twelve men went off on improvised snowshoes to see if they could get through a pass and bring back help. On Christmas day, they huddled together in a blizzard, with blankets over them for communal warmth, until they were completely covered by snow; after thirty hours under the blankets, they were safe, but they were beginning to be delirious and demented. After several more days without food, they discussed struggling on until one of them died, and then eating the corpse.[19] At this point, the all-important issue of a lottery also arose as they tried to find a way to decide "who should die to furnish food for the others."[20] After five days with no food at all, they did begin to eat the corpses of group members, roasting and drying the flesh so they could carry it further.[21] But a week later, this had been consumed, and they inevitably had to decide whether one of the women (who was slowing the party down) should be killed for food or whether, since she was a wife and mother, they should, instead, choose a widow. Fortuitously, at this point they stumbled across the two dying Indians, who had earlier left the party anticipating their probable fate, and it was decided to finish them off.[22] Stewart writes about the degeneration of the snowshoe group's moral sense:

> At first they had waited for a comrade who fell behind, and had
> flinched at drawing lots to see who should die, and had shrunk
> from cannibalism, even when it meant eating only a man already

> dead. Then they had eaten the food which centuries of civilization had forbidden them. Then as the mania of starvation worked upon them, they had plotted to kill men of another race, and then men or even women of their own race. . . . Now they were ready to sink to a still lower level.[23]

Of the seventeen in the snowshoe group, seven ultimately made it to California.

Later in the winter, relief parties began to come back through the pass, bringing food with them, often getting stuck themselves in the continuing blizzards and needing rescue. These relief parties would find a few demented people, a few mangled corpses, and one or two survivors in their right minds. Of the original Donner Party, forty-two died and forty-seven survived. Afterward, according to the television documentary Snowbound, newspaper accounts distorted the story, implying that the survivors had enjoyed practicing cannibalism. The sensational treatment of the experience ultimately stigmatized the survivors and even their descendants.

Three crucial issues, then, affect our understanding of survival cannibalism: eating human flesh, killing to obtain a supply of it, and choosing who will be killed. In general, society has accepted eating human flesh "as a reasonable solution to the problem of starvation" provided that no one is killed for the purpose.[24] As Thomas Hodgkinson points out, "the crime is in the murdering, not in the eating."[25] And the crime of killing for food can be mitigated if a formal procedure—like a lottery—is used to ensure fairness. Another kind of survival situation—the shipwreck—illustrates the perils of choosing who is to die by lottery.

By the nineteenth century, shipwrecks happened frequently enough for customary procedures to be developed for the conduct of cannibalism when those on board were cast away. Otherwise, as hunger grew intense, there would be a frenzy of wild killing and eating. In 1816, for example, the survivors of the shipwreck of the Medusa, after consuming those already dead, resorted to the worst excesses of cannibalism.[26] So, a customary order developed for selecting who was to be killed and eaten when the food ran out: dying people first, then slaves or other outsiders within the group, then male passengers, then single (male) crew members. This sequence was based on the belief that, for the good of the whole group, the strong deserved to survive (and the weak to be eaten).[27] Still, it often happened that the survivors, huddled in a small rowboat, would all be crew members, making the choice more difficult. Under those circumstances, a lottery was supposed to take place to legitimize the decision.[28]

But holding an orderly lottery among starving men in an open boat required strong leadership and deference to the captain's authority, which easily eroded under the pressure of hunger and fear. Even if it was held, the lottery was often rigged. In the eighteenth-century shipwrecks of the Peggy, the Dolphin, the Tyger, and the Zong, it was invariably a slave or a foreigner who lost the lottery.[28] Indeed, in 1874, when the crew of the Euxine was set adrift in an open boat, the one "dark-skinned Italian boy" lost the lottery three times running.[30] Sometimes the crew didn't go through the motions of holding a lottery, but the survivors would swear that they had done so. In 1826, after no food at all for ten days, the twenty-one survivors of the Francis Mary eventually ate nine of their number. The six who were eventually rescued did not specify whether any were killed for food, and, as was usually the custom, no one asked them.[31]

The 1884 wreck of the Mignonette was unusual for several reasons and led to a public debate about cannibalism at sea.[32] The four crew members, stranded in an open dinghy, had only a couple of tins of turnips and resorted to drinking their own urine. As in other shipwrecks of this era, even if they had met a boat, it was unlikely to stop since the captain would be reluctant to share its limited supplies with four more men. After fifteen days, three of the crew discussed killing the seventeen-year-old cabin boy, who was near death,[33] and, after some disagreement, they did so.[34] Once they were picked up, Captain Tom Dudley was honest enough to admit that they had killed Richard Parker and that lots had not been drawn. In fact, they hadn't even bothered to throw the remains of Parker overboard when they saw the rescue boat coming. The result of their candor was that Dudley and his first officer were arrested and tried for murder. Although the public sympathized with them—even Parker's mother said that she didn't blame these "poor, unfortunate men"[35]—the courts and the press took a high moral tone and found them guilty, sentencing them to hang. According to the Spectator, it was

> high time that the hideous tradition of the sea which authorizes starving sailors to kill and eat their comrades, should be exposed in a Court of Justice and sailors be taught once for all that the special dangers of their profession furnish no excuse for a practice as directly opposed to human as it is to divine law.[36]

What annoyed the Establishment was not that they had committed cannibalism but that they made no pretense about it and expressed no remorse.[37] Ultimately, they were pardoned, amid suggestions that exposure had made them mad and that they were not to be held to the normal standards of civilized behavior. In effect, the whole trial, sentence, and pardon were intended to make a point and set a precedent. Thereafter, when crews were cast away and had to resort to the "custom of the sea," they knew better than to confess as Dudley had.

Instances of survival cannibalism after shipwrecks still occur today. Recently, a survivor of the 1961 Bay of Pigs invasion of Cuba revealed that he and his comrades, stranded on a raft for sixteen days, had agreed, in extremity, to eat the bodies of those already dead.[38] In 1988, after twenty-eight days at sea in a leaky boat, a group of Vietnamese resorted to eating the dead and killing the dying. One man, Phung Quang Minh, took charge and made the decision to do this. Despite their gratitude at the time, the survivors later complained that Phung had taken advantage of their weakness and forced them into it, threatening that otherwise they'd be targeted next. Phung, however, insisted that he, too, thought cannibalism was wrong, but that there'd been no choice; now, he'd been scapegoated because the others didn't want to acknowledge their responsibility.

> I was only a member in a group of persons, so I didn't have the ability to force all of them to follow me. I was only a man who was thinking more clearly than the others. I had to do what I did to keep all the people living. We were at sea in huge waves. I had no other choice.[39]

And, in March 2001, sixty people, trying to cross the Caribbean from the Dominican Republic to Puerto Rico, had engine trouble and ran out of food and water. After twenty-two days, amid violent fights, they turned to cannibalism. One of the only two survivors insisted that he had not participated, but doctors say that he couldn't possibly have stayed alive without cannibalism.[40]

It is difficult to understand why people struggling for survival should be so severely stigmatized. Under less extreme situations, armies kill the enemy and police kill suspected criminals. Why is it so much worse to kill for food if one is starving? It is easy to share Stewart's compassionate view of the Donner Party's cannibalism: "Humanity may fall into many worse degradations."[41] So why did cannibalism become one of the most powerful cultural taboos in Western civilization? Probably because eating dead humans could so quickly degenerate into killing live humans, as it did among the Donner Party:

> Once the taboo against cannibalism was broken, it became easier to engage in, harvesting members of the expedition became more efficient, and there seemed to be little moral revulsion to the practice. This initial resistance against engaging in cannibalism, followed by an unquestioning acceptance by most, is to be found in almost all of the instances of survival cannibalism.[42]

Anthropologists have, therefore, concluded that the potential for cannibalism is in all of us, whether we practice it or not.[43]

Despite—or because of—the powerful taboo, our fascination with cannibalism remains as strong as ever.[44] This attraction is often expressed in folk tales and myth[45] and in the arts and popular culture.[46] With few exceptions (such as "Cannibalism in the Cars" or the movie based on the Andes survivors), these entertainments are not concerned with the hardships and difficult choices of survival cannibalism, but focus on the violence and the horror of sociopathic cannibalism. According to Harris, "it is part of human nature to pay rapt attention to unusual sights and sounds such as blood spurting from wounds and loud shrieking and howling."[47] For decades, American audiences have flocked to see horror movies featuring cannibalism, from The Night of the Living Dead, in which "a young girl is transformed into a ghoul and then begins to dine on her mother,"[48] to the extremely bloody and violent Hannibal, which took in $58 million in its opening weekend.[49] Even serious academics who write about cannibalism tend to use narrative techniques and language that sensationalize the subject. Accounts of cannibalism are often fictionalized into stories, with use of the present tense, exotic details, and imaginary conversations to make the events seem more immediate and real. Anthropologists are particularly apt to do this when describing acts of ritual cannibalism among "primitive" tribes.[50]

In survival cannibalism, abnormal circumstances cause people to behave abnormally. In ritual cannibalism, eating people is normal behavior.[51] The classic figure in ritual cannibalism is the tribal warrior, wearing a feathered skirt and waving a hatchet while dancing around the cooking pot containing the captured enemy or an aged matriarch of the tribe. Exocannibalism—eating those outside the tribe—was practiced for political reasons (to terrorize enemies[52] and assimilate their strength[53]) and for spiritual reasons (to propitiate the gods). There were also practical reasons: when a warring group of tribesmen brought back captives to the village, there was rarely a surplus of provisions available to feed them. It made economic sense to regard the prisoner as food and "absorb him into the group."[54] The chief of the Miranha tribe was very pragmatic about this: "When I have killed an enemy it is better to eat him than let him go to waste. . . . The bad thing is not being eaten, but death. . . . You whites are really too dainty."[55] Nor was ritual cannibalism always the wild orgy of revenge depicted in missionaries' tales. It was an organized activity, integrated into the culture according to traditional rules. "To cannibals," says MacClancy, "the idea of unregulated man-eating—consuming anyone, anywhere, any time, anyhow—is as horrific as it is to us. If one is going to indulge in human meat, one must do it in the ritually prescribed manner."[56]

The basis for endocannibalism—eating members of one's own tribe—was respect for one's family and tribal elders that was demonstrated by making their tomb one's own living body: "Far better to be inside a warm friend than under the cold ground."[57] In the nineteenth century, a Mayoruna

Myers 10

tribesman asked a European: "When you die, wouldn't you rather be eaten by your own kinsmen than by maggots?"[58] But children were not always eager to consume the flesh of their parents[59] and the motives for doing so were not always to the parents' advantage. Endocannibalism could be used as a form of population control, like infanticide, and the means of disposing of the aged were sometimes violent or vicious.[60]

Although anthropologists theorize that tribes have engaged in ritual cannibalism for at least two million years,[61] it has been very difficult to document specific instances. What information there is about prehistoric cannibalism comes from excavated bones that have been examined for intentional fractures and marks indicating where to cut, just as one would prepare an animal for eating.[62] There is evidence that Peking Man "roasted his victims and ate their brains" 500,000 years ago, that Cro-Magnon man "cracked leg bones and [broke] skulls 30,000 years ago,[63] and that Neanderthal man removed the meat and marrow from bones 100–120,000 years ago.[64] Still, anthropologists are now being extremely careful about attributing cannibalism to prehistoric tribes.[65]

The issue of whether and what sort of ritual cannibalism occurred— or still occurs—has become a sensitive one, in part because of controversy over the allegations in William Arens's 1979 work, The Man-Eating Myth. In effect, Arens declared that ritual cannibalism simply did not exist, that it consisted of rumors with no factual basis, that it lacked first-hand, eyewitness evidence.[66] According to Arens, hardly ever do anthropologists claim to have witnessed the act of cannibalism themselves; their accounts are based largely on hearsay.[67] He even asserts that there are instances of anthropologists badgering tribes for stories about cannibalism even when the poor villagers deny it.[68] Many anthropologists have understandably felt under attack by Arens,[69] and, in turn, have criticized his motives and methods. Petrinovich, for example, calls him "more of a sensation-hungry journalist than an exact historian" and Hodgkinson notes that most of the anthropological community regard him as a "sensationalist revisionist."[70]

But Arens's charges had a broader, more political purpose. He finds it significant that cannibalism tends to be attributed to primitive people, usually at a time before the white man has come to civilize them. The cannibals are regarded as distant versions of ourselves, "reflections of us as we once were" before we became civilized.[71] And so we have reason to feel superior to these people, a feeling that can lead, among extremists, to xeno-phobia.[72] Pickering also points out how well cannibalism feeds into Western-ers' conviction of the superiority of our culture. We believe that every society has a path of development, and some are more advanced than others. Canni-balism is assumed to be integral to a society at a primitive stage; therefore, any society that is aboriginal also had to be cannibalistic. Such views also justified colonialism: colonists could take over whole blocks of territory and subsume whole societies, convinced that "the dispossessed would benefit from the technological, political, social, religious, and moral superiority of the invader."[73] Tannahill points out that the tendency to demonize these tribes increased as Western Europe sought to colonize remote parts of the world and as government officials, traders, and missionaries competed for who could publish the most exotic and horrifying stories of these strange cul-tures for the pleasure of the reading public.[74] That political agenda is illus-trated by classic attributions of cannibalism to pre-Columbian Carib Indians and Aztecs.

When Columbus landed on Hispaniola, he saw no signs of cannibal-ism among the Caribs, but that did not stop him from telling everyone, when he returned to Europe, that the natives of the New World were cannibals. By his third journey to the Americas, he "had become so experienced in these matters that he was able to identify man-eaters by their looks."[75] In Arens's view, Columbus presented this savage picture to justify the slave trade, which was to be the outgrowth of his explorations. He wasn't able to bring back much in the way of spices and gold, but he was able to bring back an equally valuable commodity: slaves. Such barbarians deserved nothing better than slavery, so slavers could believe, in good conscience, that they were helping to save the souls of unspeakable people. In fact, although royal and papal policy at first banned any enslavement of the Caribbean islanders, an exception was made for any tribe thought to be cannibals. Thus, all sorts of tribes were labeled cannibals, whether they were or they weren't, whether they were warlike or whether they were peaceful,[76] and, ultimately, "the in-digenous cultures of the Caribbean were all but destroyed."[77]

The demonization of the Aztecs took a different form because, as almost everyone acknowledges, they did engage in violent, cruel sacrifices to the gods, with bodies bound and tortured, and hearts dripping with blood. The issue is whether they then ate their victims and, if so, whether it was ritual cannibalism (and thus a barbaric act) or survival cannibalism resulting from food shortages (and so marginally more acceptable). The more melodramatic of the anthropologists have no doubt that it was the former:

> To keep the mystical forces of the universe in balance and to uphold social equilibrium, the Aztec fed their gods human flesh. By the act of consecration the sacrificial victims were incarnated as gods. Through eating the victims' flesh, men entered into communion with their gods, and divine power was imparted to men.[78]

Harris is similarly certain that the Aztecs were cannibals and provides endless bloody details of torture and killing. But he believes that the motive was survival, that food, especially protein and fat, was in short supply, and that the sacrifices to the gods were a necessary part of the Aztec economy, with each dead prisoner given to a member of the community for consumption: "The Aztec priests can legitimately be described as ritual slaughterers in a state-sponsored system geared to the production and redistribution of substantial amounts of animal protein in the form of human flesh."[79] Thus, Harris suggests with irony, the introduction of domestic animals to the Aztecs was just as much a reason for the decline of cannibalism as the arrival of Christian missionaries.[80] He believes that Europeans could afford to be highly moral about cannibalism because their agricultural economy didn't require them to engage in it. Still, they had just as many bloody wars with just as high a proportion of the population killed—only they weren't eaten.[81]

Arens, as one might expect, doubts very much whether cannibalism ever took place in Mexico at all. He speculates that the rumors of the Aztecs' eating the enemy were a form of military propaganda on both sides,[82] and even questions whether ceremonial sacrifices—a "colorful barbaric scenario" —actually occurred, noting that even in the worst sieges by the conquistadors, the defenders starved rather than eat each other. Resentful of the existence of "such an advanced civilization in the New World," the Europeans were forced to demonize the Aztecs in order to justify the conquistadors' campaign of exploitation and expropriation.[83] But like the conquistadors and the missionaries, Arens, too, seems to be imposing his own political agenda. He is determined to uphold "'primitive' cultures as ecologically and morally exemplary," even if it requires the demonization of his anthropologist colleagues.[84] To suggest otherwise would be politically incorrect.[85]

Throughout all these theories and countertheories, the emphasis is on the evils of ritual cannibalism (if it existed at all), but rarely on the bloodshed and killing that must have accompanied it. Western society continues to tolerate violence, bloodshed, and even murder; but is horrified at the possibility that flesh could be consumed as an accepted rite of a culture:

> It is interesting that some anthropologists are willing to concede that human sacrifice of the most brutal sort took place, but are unwilling to accept the fact that ritual cannibalism took place. They can accept the proposition that these people horribly tortured and mutilated living captives, but not that they took a bite afterward. For some, the act of cannibalism appears to be justifiable if it was necessary for people to survive, but not if it was part of the theatre of life.[86]

What's really significant is not whether the reports of cannibalism are or aren't true, but why they have always fascinated so broad an audience, retained their status as a shocking taboo, and so evolved into a cultural myth for the West. Surely, our attitudes toward cannibalism say more about us, our desires, and our fears than they do about the man-eaters. In Petrinovich's paraphrase of Pogo, "we have found the cannibals, and they are us."[87]

Myers 14

Notes

[1]The Reluctant Cannibal, CD, Michael Flanders and Donald Swann, The Flanders and Swann Collection (HMV Easy, 1999).

[2]Typical motivational charts are found in Hans Askenasy, Cannibalism: From Sacrifice to Survival (Amherst: Prometheus, 1994) 224; Laurence R. Goldman, "From Pot to Polemic: Uses and Abuses of Cannibalism," The Psychology of Cannibalism, ed. Laurence R. Goldman (Westport: Bergin & Garvey, 1999) 14; Lewis Petrinovich, The Cannibal Within (New York: Aldine de Gruyter, 2000) 6. Few anthropologists include sociopathic cannibalism (e.g., Jeffrey Dahmer or Hannibal Lecter) in their charts.

[3]Petrinovich, 6.

[4]Petrinovich, 15–16.

[5]Stanley M. Garn and Walter D. Block, "The Limited Nutritional Value of Cannibalism," American Anthropologist 72 (1970): 106. MacClancy states that, for forty to have a decent meal each day for a month, they'd have to eat eight fat adults. Jeremy MacClancy, Consuming Culture (New York: Holt, 1993) 170.

[6]Askenasy, 64–65, quoting Reay Tannahill, Flesh and Blood: A History of the Cannibal Complex (Briarcliff Manor: Stein & Day, 1975).

[7]Askenasy, 69; Richard Cunningham, The Place Where the World Ends (New York: Sheed & Ward, 1973) 115.

[8]Dr. John Baker, commenting in Alexander Marengo, Cannibal (3BM TV Productions Channel 4 [UK], 2001).

[9]Quoted in Askenasy, 80. During recent Russian and Ukrainian famines, parents were known to eat their own children as an "act of Christian kindness" to put them out of their misery, and it has been traditional in China, as early as the famines of 594 BC, for families to swap children so that parents would not have to eat their own. Marengo.

[10]"You begin to crave meat of any sort—you act different to the way you act when there's a supermarket around the corner." Dr. Timothy Taylor, commenting in Marengo.

[11]Piers Paul Read, Alive: The Story of the Andean Survivors (Philadelphia and New York: Lippincott, 1974) 59.

[12]Read, 84–85.

[13]Cunningham, 87.

[14]One of the survivors said that they had specifically emulated the Last Supper and that the "intimate communion among us [was] what helped us to subsist." "Survivors of Andes Air Crash Admit Dead Saved Their Lives," New York Times 26 Dec. 1972: A9. See also Tannahill, 176.

[15]Cunningham, 199. Several of those commenting on the experience of the Andes survivors observe that the subsequent reactions from those in Uruguay, even the relatives of those eaten, were sympathetic. Askenasy asks whether this amnesty from reproach, public and private, would have occurred had the survivors not been members of Uruguay's elite. Askenasy, 105. Tannahill also wonders "whether they would have met with quite such general warmth and understanding if they had come from New York's Harlem. . . ." Tannahill, 175.

[16]Petrinovich cites another survival experience characterized by a sense of community that led to survival. After a week, three survivors of an air crash in Idaho determined to eat the father of one of them, justifying their decision by attributing to him the desire to help them survive. (He had covered his daughter with his coat just before he died.) They, too, gained the strength needed to walk down to civilization, and they, too, did not deny what they had done, citing the model of communion and their common religious belief. Subsequently, there was no criticism from relatives, clergy, or the law. Petrinovich, 76.

[17]Much of the material in this paragraph comes from Petrinovich, 69–71. Petrinovich also notes that the first person the Andes survivors contemplated eating was the dead pilot, the one person who had no ties to the group. Petrinovich, 73.

[18]The material in this and subsequent paragraphs about the Donner Party comes from George R. Stewart Jr., Ordeal by Hunger: The Story of the Donner Party (New York: Holt, 1936) and from Petrinovich, 22–28.

[19]Stewart, 130–33.

[20]Petrinovich, 24. It's unclear what actually happened. Did they fail to agree on a lottery, or did they have one but disregarded it since the person who lost was particularly well liked? There was also a suggestion that two of the men would shoot it out and the loser would be eaten.

[21]Like the Andes survivors, they showed some delicacy: "They observed only one last sad propriety; no member of a family touched his own dead." Stewart, 133. This did not last, however; later, when a man died, a woman began to butcher his body in the presence of his widow.

[22]A recent documentary about the fate of the Donner Party noted that, under these extreme conditions, the corpses no longer looked like dead bodies; they looked like food. Snowbound: Curse of the Sierras, Wrath of God (WNET, New York. The History Channel, 2001).

[23]Stewart, 145. Stewart's melodramatic language and high moral tone are typical of writings on cannibalism.

[24]Petrinovich, 73. Also Askenasy, 170.

[25]Thomas Hodgkinson, "Cannibalism: A Potted History," The Independent (London) 17 Mar. 2001: 27.

[26]Askenasy provides a dramatic account of maritime cannibalism in 1899: one of five men on a raft was about to die, but before he did, "the knife was plunged into his heart, and the blood trickled out to be drunk by the half-famished, half-thirsty mortals by his side. While the fearful feast was in progress, [another man died]. Like birds after fresh prey the man-eaters rushed to the second victim, stabbed him, and sucked the milk-warm blood as it oozed from the great slash about his heart." Askenasy, 87.

[27]Those who died and then were eaten or who lost the lottery were "almost invariably the weakest, most vulnerable, disliked or isolated individuals. Slaves were eaten first, black men before white, women before men, passengers before crew, unpopular members before the rest." Petrinovich, 49. Among the crew, cabin boys were first to go. Neil Hanson, The Custom of the Sea (New York: Wiley, 1999) 132.

[28]Petrinovich, 50.

[29]Petrinovich, 51–53.

[30]Petrinovich, 60. Apparently, the first two lotteries were disputed, but after the third the boy was killed.

[31]Askenasy, 2–10. One woman on the boat was very tough about claiming rights to the blood of her fiance as he died; she fended off all the others, saying later that she did it from pure hunger.

[32]The description of the Mignonette is taken from A. W. Brian Simpson, Cannibalism and the Common Law (Chicago: U of Chicago P, 1984) and Hanson.

[33]They didn't want to wait until he died, even though that was imminent, because blood was very life-sustaining, and it "would congeal in his veins" and be undrinkable once he was dead. Hanson, 116.

[34]The two mates said that they should all die together, but Captain Dudley was more pragmatic: "It be hard for four to die, when perhaps one might save the rest." Simpson, 61.

[35]Simpson, 84. Petrinovich confirms that the public is rarely determined to punish or censure those who resort to survival cannibalism. Petrinovich, 10–11.

[36]Hanson, 172.

[37]The court was all in favor of hypocrisy: "For humanity's sake, we must regret that such confessions as have fallen from these rescued men ever came to the light of day." Hanson, 200.

[38]Bay of Pigs Survivor Says He Turned to Cannibalism," Seattle Times 16 Apr. 1998: 14 Oct. 2000 <http://www.seattletimes.NWsource.com/new/nation_world/htm/198/pigs_041698_html>.

[39]Askenasy, 90.

[40]Molly Watson, "Refugees Ate Bodies as Boat Drifted at Sea," Evening Standard (London) 21 Mar. 2001: 5.

[41]Stewart, 295.

[42]Petrinovich, 25. Askenasy wonders whether our apparently built-in revulsion to cannibalism is a result of genetic programming because "cannibalism would be counterproductive to our species' survival." Askenasy, 225. On the other hand, Cunningham points out that one bite does not necessarily lead to future craving. Cunningham, 102.

[43]While there has been considerable disagreement about whether the potential for cannibalistic behavior is genetic or cultural, recent studies conclude that the tendency is innate. William Arens, The Man-Eating Myth (New York: Oxford UP, 1979) 130.

[44]"Most human beings appear to need a few taboos, and for the time being cannibalism seems to serve that purpose admirably." Askenasy, 231.

[45]There are references to cannibalism in Homer, Ovid, Herodotus, and Caesar (e.g., eat the old and women since they're useless for battle). Cunningham, 99. Fairy tales like Hansel and Gretel and Jack and the Beanstalk contain references that would lead outsiders to assume that Western Europe had a history of cannibalism. Arens, 148; Cunningham, 100.

[46]Sweeney Todd and Candide are very successful musicals with prominent references to cannibalism. In "Cannibalism in the Cars," Mark Twain makes a tongue-in-cheek point about the exotic and forbidden nature of cannibalism by having twenty-four respectable businessmen, stuck in a blizzard on a train, choose a selection of victims for dinner by using impeccable parliamentary procedure, debate (youth vs. size), and editorial comment about the succulence of the main dish: "I like Harris. He might have been better done, perhaps, but . . . no man ever agreed with me better than Harris. . . ." Mark Twain, "Cannibalism in the Cars," The Complete Short Stories of Mark Twain, ed. Charles Neider (New York: Bantam, 1983) 14.

[47]Marvin Harris, Cannibals and Kings: The Origins of Culture (New York: Random, 1977) 104. Cunningham calls Count Dracula "a cannibal with sadistic tendencies." Cunningham, 101.

[48]Arens, 147. Also George A. Romero, dir., Night of the Living Dead (1968).

[49]Ridley Scott, dir., Hannibal (MGM and Universal Studios, 2001). This popular fascination with cannibalism can be found in many of the home pages on the Internet. See, for example, Sam Schechner, "The New Cannibalism," The College Hill Independent 17 Apr. 1997: 29 Sept. 2000 <http://www.netspace.org/indy/issue/04-17-97/features3.html>. Another approach to this solemn taboo is spoof: one apparently authentic Web site offers a variety of human meats for sale, with recipes such as manburgers, "catering to the sophisticated human meat consumer." See the Web site www.manbeef.com.

[50]Gardner notes the temptation of people writing about cannibalism to insert juicy details. Don Gardner, "Anthropophagy: Myth and the Subtle Ways of Ethnocentrism," The Psychology of Cannibalism, ed. Laurence R. Goldman (Westport: Bergin & Garvey, 1999) 35.

[51]Diamond calls this "customary cannibalism": "the consumption of

human flesh . . . as a non-emergency custom." Jared Diamond, "Archae-ology: Talk of Cannibalism," Nature 7 Sept. 2000: 25.

[52]Lewis cites the Tupinamba of the Amazon, who treated their pris-oners like heros, wined and dined them, and then ritually killed and ate them. I. M. Lewis, Religion in Context: Cults and Charisma (Cambridge: Cambridge UP, 1986) 75. MacClancy describes the Big Nambas of northern Vanuatu, who ate only their enemies, and the Hurons of southern Canada, for whom ritual cannibalism was "a socially approved means of invigorating themselves, of securing peace, of demonstrating tribal strength, and of vent-ing otherwise dangerous feelings." MacClancy, 170; 171–72. During the Cru-sades, one source, William of Tyre, describes acts of ritual cannibalism among the crusaders, and there are contemporary accounts that attribute both survival and ritual motives, but Paul Crawford downplays the issue on his Web site, stating that the "significance [of cannibalism] to the First Cru-sade is probably not great." Paul Crawford, "Crusaders as Cannibals," Home Page 31 Aug. 2000: 4 May 2001 <http://www.ukans.edu/medieval/melcher/matthias/t68/0058/html>. As recently as the Cultural Revolution in China in the 1960s, followers of Mao engaged in cannibalism for the pur-pose of terrorism, killing teachers thought to be "class enemies," forcing other teachers to cut out the dead man's heart and liver, and then eating them: "The yard was full of the smell of students cooking their teachers." More than thirty years later, in interviews, these cannibals still express great pride in their actions. Marengo.

[53]Tribal cannibalism is an act of revenge, in which the captured en-emy is "tortured and reduced to food in the ultimate act of domination." Peggy Reeves Sanday, Divine Hunger: Cannibalism as a Cultural System (Cambridge: Cambridge UP, 1986) 6.

[54]Harris, 104.

[55]Quoted in Askenasy, 11–12.

[56]MacClancy, 169–70.

[57]Cunningham, 104. MacClancy cites the Hua, who ate their parents to replenish their vital essence. MacClancy, 170.

[58]Askenasy, 11.

Myers 20

[59]Malinowski observed some Trobriand Islanders eating the body of a deceased man as an act of "filial piety"; the sons were clearly revolted by what they had to do, but had no way of escaping it. Cited in Lewis, 71.

[60]For example, the old person could be bound up in a tree, surrounded by a ritual dance; on a signal, he or she would be shaken out of the tree and disposed of in a mass killing. Cunningham, 106.

[61]"Cannibalism," Microsoft Encarta Online Encyclopedia 2000: 5 Oct. 2001 <http://encarta.msn.com>.

[62]Diamond.

[63]Cunningham, 97–98.

[64]The evidence of six skeletons recently found in a cave site is regarded as "controversial" since the possible reasons for these incisions—including cannibalism—have yet to be convincingly determined. B. Bower, "Cave Finds Revive Neandertal [sic] Cannibalism," Science News 2 Oct. 1999: Science News Online. 5 Nov. 2000 <http://www.sciencenews.org/sn_arc99/10_2_99/fob4ref.htm>.

[65]Tim D. White, Prehistoric Cannibalism at Mancos (Princeton: Princeton UP, 1992) 348.

[66]Arens, 21. Arens refers to the anecdotal evidence and sensational tone found in many accounts of cannibalism and the dramatic reconstructions—"probably happened" or "one would imagine"—that lead the reader to believe that the vilest things occurred.

[67]Arens, 36. This view is supported by MacClancy: "There are relatively few authoritative accounts by trustworthy eyewitnesses of anthropophagites in action. The vast majority of accounts depend not on observed events but on stories told to Westerners." MacClancy, 168. See also Goldman, 14.

[68]Arens, 142–45.

[69]"What Arens essentially did was lay down a challenge: he required other anthropologists to produce proof of ritual anthropophagy," evoking an "emotional response" from the anthropological community. (They may also have resented Arens's popular success.) Hodgkinson, 27. Anthropologists who discover instances of cannibalism attract considerable attention, which

can enhance their scholarly reputations. In effect, Arens was accusing anthropologists like White of "fortune-hunting." Goldman, 15.

[70]Petrinovich, 13 and Hodgkinson. In discussing Arens's theories, Askenasy suggests that what Arens is doing is equivalent to Holocaust denial. Askenasy, 49–50.

[71]Arens, 19.

[72]Arens, 145. According to Arens, we feel free to attribute the vilest behavior to remote tribesmen; if we said similar things about minority groups within our own cultures, we would be heavily censured. Some of the more extreme writings on cannibalism bear out Arens's views. Maerth, for example, spins theories about humans being a mongrel race who originally gained their strength and aggressiveness from eating the superior specimens of hominoid ape. Oscar Maerth, The Beginning Was the End, trans. Judith Hayward (London: Michael Joseph, 1973).

[73]Michael Pickering, "Consuming Doubts: What Some People Ate? or What Some People Swallowed?" The Psychology of Cannibalism, ed. Laurence R. Goldman (Westport: Bergin & Garvey, 1999) 63. Gardner, too, acknowledges that we "attribut[e] cannibalism to alien others [as] an effective instrument of demonization." This is all part of the colonial degradation (and also scapegoating) of subject peoples. Gardner, 28.

[74]Tannahill, 150. MacClancy points out that cannibalism was good for business: "As astute missionaries knew, putting 'cannibal' in the title of their books widened their market and increased sales or donations from fervent Christians." MacClancy, 168.

[75]Arens, 44.

[76]Arens, 47–51. See also Petrinovich, 5. Askenasy alludes to the use of cannibalism by the church as a rationale for colonizing: "Since Christians, of course, did not devour one another, it became their duty to civilize the mindless savages." Askenasy, 231.

[77]Arens, 54.

[78]Sanday, 7. See also Tannahill, 86.

[79]Harris, 109. Harris calculates executioners would work for four days and nights, continuously, killing approximately 14,000 prisoners; this is an estimate based on two minutes per killing. Harris, 106.

[80]Harris, 110.

[81]Harris, 122–23. Harris cites another crucial distinction between Europe and the Americas: Europe tended toward a pattern of imperial expansion, and a successful empire doesn't kill and eat those it conquers; rather, it incorporates them into the empire, with safety exchanged for obedience. If you go in for cannibalism, you'll never be able to negotiate peace because no enemy will ever want to get into your clutches.

[82]In contemporary records, there is a report that the Aztecs ate roasted babies: "Cortes does not confirm or elaborate on this statement, but as a military man, it is likely that he realized the import this would have on the home front." Arens, 60.

[83]Arens, 77. See also Hodgkinson, 27.

[84]Petrinovich, 150 and Hodgkinson, 28. The quotation is from Hodgkinson.

[85]Petrinovich, 149.

[86]Petrinovich, 101.

[87]Petrinovich, 216.

Works Cited

Arens, William. The Man-Eating Myth. New York: Oxford UP, 1979.

Askenasy, Hans. Cannibalism: From Sacrifice to Survival. Amherst:
    Prometheus, 1994.

"Bay of Pigs Survivor Says He Turned to Cannibalism." Seattle Times 16 Apr.
    1998: 14 Oct. 2000. <http://www.seattletimes.NWsource.com/new/
    nation_world/htm/198/pigs.041698_html>.

Bower, B. "Cave Finds Revive Neandertal [sic] Cannibalism." Science News
    2 Oct. 1999: Science News Online. 5 Nov. 2000 <http://
    www.sciencenews.org/sn_arc99/10_2_99/fob4ref.htm>.

Cannibalism." Microsoft Encarta Online Encyclopedia 2000: 5 Oct. 2001
    <http://encarta.msn.com>.

Crawford, Paul. "Crusaders as Cannibals." Home Page 31 Aug. 2000: 4 May
    2001 <http://www.ukans.edu/medieval/melcher/matthias/t68/
    0058/html>.

Cunningham, Richard. The Place Where the World Ends. New York: Sheed &
    Ward, 1973.

Diamond, Jared. "Archaeology: Talk of Cannibalism." Nature 7 Sept. 2000:
    25–26.

Gardner, Don. "Anthropophagy: Myth and the Subtle Ways of Ethno-
    centrism." The Psychology of Cannibalism. Ed. Laurence R.
    Goldman. Westport: Bergin & Garvey, 1999.

Garn, Stanley M., and Walter D. Block. "The Limited Nutritional Value of
    Cannibalism." American Anthropologist 72 (1970): 106.

Goldman, Laurence R. "From Pot to Polemic: Uses and Abuses of
    Cannibalism." The Psychology of Cannibalism. Ed. Laurence R.
    Goldman. Westport: Bergin & Garvey, 1999.

Hanson, Neil. The Custom of the Sea. New York: Wiley, 1999.

Harris, Marvin. Cannibals and Kings: The Origins of Culture. New York:
    Random, 1977.

Hodgkinson, Thomas. "Cannibalism: A Potted History." The Independent
    (London) 17 Mar. 2001: 27–29.

Lewis, I. M. Religion in Context: Cults and Charisma. Cambridge: Cambridge
     UP, 1986.

MacClancy, Jeremy. Consuming Culture. New York: Holt, 1993.

Maerth, Oscar. The Beginning Was the End. Trans. Judith Hayward. London:
     Michael Joseph, 1973.

Marengo, Alexander. Cannibal. 3BM TV Productions Channel 4 (UK). 2001.

Petrinovich, Lewis. The Cannibal Within. New York: Aldine de Gruyter, 2000.

Pickering, Michael. "Consuming Doubts: What Some People Ate? or What
     Some People Swallowed?" The Psychology of Cannibalism. Ed.
     Laurence R. Goldman. Westport: Bergin & Garvey, 1999.

Read, Piers Paul. Alive: The Story of the Andean Survivors. Philadelphia and
     New York: Lippincott, 1974.

The Reluctant Cannibal. CD. Michael Flanders and Donald Swann. The
     Flanders and Swann Collection. HMV Easy, 1999.

Romero, George A., dir. Night of the Living Dead. 1968.

Sanday, Peggy Reeves. Divine Hunger: Cannibalism as a Cultural System.
     Cambridge: Cambridge UP, 1986.

Schechner, Sam. "The New Cannibalism." The College Hill Independent 17
     Apr. 1997. 29 Sept. 2000 <http://www.netspace.org/indy/issue/
     04-17-97/features3.html>.

Scott, Ridley, dir. Hannibal. MGM and Universal Studios. 2001.

Simpson, A. W. Brian. Cannibalism and the Common Law. Chicago: U of
     Chicago P, 1984.

Snowbound: Curse of the Sierras. Wrath of God. WNET, New York. The
     History Channel. 2001.

Stewart, George R., Jr., Ordeal by Hunger: The Story of the Donner Party.
     New York: Holt, 1936.

"Survivors of Andes Air Crash Admit Dead Saved Their Lives." New York
     Times 26 Dec. 1972: A9.

Tannahill, Reay. Flesh and Blood: A History of the Cannibal Complex.
     Briarcliff Manor: Stein & Day, 1975.

Twain, Mark. "Cannibalism in the Cars." The Complete Short Stories of Mark
     Twain. Ed. Charles Neider. New York: Bantam, 1983.

Watson, Molly. "Refugees Ate Bodies as Boat Drifted at Sea." Evening Standard (London) 21 Mar. 2001: 5.

White, Tim D. Prehistoric Cannibalism at Mancos. Princeton: Princeton UP, 1992.

David Morgan

Natural Science I

December 15, 2001

Explaining the Tunguskan Phenomenon

The Tunguska River Valley in Siberia has always been an area of swamps and bogs, forests and frozen tundra, sparsely populated, and remote and inaccessible to most travelers. It was at dawn on June 30, 1908, that witnesses in the Tungus observed a light glaring more brightly than anything they had ever seen. This cosmic phenomenon, they said, was bluish-white in color and gradually became cigarlike in shape. Just as terrifying to the few people inhabiting that part of Siberia was the tremendous noise that accompanied the light, a noise that was reported to have been heard 1,000 kilometers from the site (Parry, 1961). Some who were in the vicinity were deafened, while others farther away apparently became speechless and displayed other symptoms of severe trauma. The Tungus community refused to go near the site or speak of the occurrence, and some even denied that it had ever happened (Crowther, 1931). The event was so frightening to these simple peasants that many believed it had been an act of divine retribution, a punishment by a god demanding vengeance (Baxter & Atkins, 1976).

Since 1921, when the first perilous expedition to the Tungus region confirmed that a remarkable event had indeed taken place, scientists have attempted to explain what it was and why it happened. Almost 95 years later, the various theories developed to explain the explosion in the Tunguska Valley have become almost as interesting a phenomenon as the original occurrence. Like doctors trying to diagnose a disease by examining the symptoms, scientists have analyzed the fragmentary evidence and published theories that supposedly account for it. However, no theory has been entirely convincing. The purpose of this essay is to provide a brief description of some of the major interpretations of the Tunguska occurrence and to suggest that, in their efforts to substantiate their theories, scientists can be fallible.

At dawn on that day in June 1908, a huge object evidently came from space into the earth's atmosphere, breaking the sound barrier, and, at

7:17 a.m., slammed into the ground in the central Siberian plateau. Moments before the collision, a thrust of energy caused people and animals to be strewn about, structures destroyed, and trees toppled. Immediately afterward, a pillar or "tongue" of fire could be seen in the sky several hundred miles away; others called it a cylindrical pipe. A thermal air current of extremely high temperature caused forest fires to ignite and spread across 40 miles, melting metal objects scattered throughout the area. Several shock waves were felt for hundreds of miles around, breaking windows and tossing people, animals, and objects in the air. Finally, black rain fell from a menacing-looking cloud over a radius of 100 square miles. It is no wonder that the peasants of the Tunguska River Valley thought that this was the end of the world (Krinov, 1966; Baxter & Atkins, 1976).

For a variety of reasons, this devastating occurrence remained almost unknown outside Russia--and even outside central Siberia--for many years. The Tungus was extremely remote, even for Russia, which is such a vast country that transportation and communication between places can be slow and difficult. The few people living in the area who actually witnessed what happened were mostly peasants and nomadic tribesmen, and did not have much opportunity or inclination to talk about what they had seen. There was little publicity, and what there was was limited to local Siberian newspapers (Krinov, 1966). During that summer, there was a lot of discussion in the newspapers of the European capitals about peculiar lights and colors seen in the northern skies, unusually radiant sunsets, some magnetic disturbances, and strange dust clouds (Cowan, Atluri, & Libby, 1965). But, since news of the events at the Tungus River had hardly yet been heard even in Moscow, there was no way for scientists in other countries to see a connection between these happenings.

It was only in 1921, when Russia was relatively stable after years of war, revolution, and economic problems, that the first expedition to investigate the event at Tunguska actually took place (Crowther, 1931). That it occurred then at all was largely because an energetic Russian scientist, Leonid Kulik, had become fascinated by meteorites. He read in an old Siberian newspaper that, in 1908, a railway train had been forced to stop because a meteorite fell in its path—a story that was quite untrue. Kulik thought that he might become the discoverer of the greatest meteorite ever found on earth and determined to search for evidence that such a meteorite existed. Authorized by the Soviet Academy, Kulik led a series of expeditions to the Tungus River. In 1921, he did not even reach the site, for the route was almost impassable. In 1927, and annually for the next few years, Kulik did, indeed, explore the devastated area and was able to study the evidence of what had happened and listen to the oral accounts of the event provided by those inhabitants who were still alive and who were willing to talk to him. Finally, in 1938–39, Kulik traveled to the Tungus for the last time, for the purpose of taking aerial photographs that might confirm his meteorite theory (Baxter & Atkins, 1976).

Kulik and his fellow investigators believed that whatever had happened at the Tungus River had been caused by a meteorite. So, what they expected to find was a single, vast crater to mark the place where the meteorite had landed. Such a crater, however, was simply not there (Cowan, Atluri, & Libby, 1965). Instead, Kulik found a vast devastated and burned area, a forest of giant trees with their tops cut off and scattered around (Crowther, 1931). In 1928, without the benefit of an aerial view of the region, Kulik concluded from his various vantage points on the ground that, around the circumference of the area where the meteorite had landed, there was a belt of upright dead trees, which he named the "telegraph pole forest." Scattered around the perimeter of the frozen swamp, which he called the "cauldron," were groups of fallen trees, with their tops all pointing away from the direction of where the blast had occurred (Cowan, Atluri, & Libby, 1965). None of this was consistent with Kulik's meteorite theory, and he could only attribute the odd pattern of upright and fallen trees to a shock wave or "hot compressed-air pockets," which had missed some trees and affected others (Baxter & Atkins, 1976). The account of his discovery in the Literary Digest of 1929 states that "each of the falling meteoric fragments must have worked, the Russian scientists imagine, like a gigantic piston," with compressed air knocking trees down like toothpicks ("What a Meteor," 1929, p. 34). Kulik continued to insist that the fire and the resultant effect on the trees was the result of a meteorite explosion. But the Russian scientist V. G. Fesenkov estimated that such destruction could only have been caused by an object of at least several hundred meters, and that, if anything of this size or force had hit the ground, it would have left a crater (Baxter & Atkins, 1976).

Kulik found other evidence that could not easily be explained by the meteorite theory. Although there was no trace of a single large crater (Cowan, Atluri, & Libby, 1965), there were numerous shallow cavities scattered around the frozen bog (Olivier, 1928). For several years, Kulik attempted to bore into the ground, seeking evidence that these pits and ridges were formed by lateral pressure caused by gases exploding from the meteorite's impact. Kulik described the scene as "not unlike a giant duplicate of what happens when a brick from a tall chimney-top falls into a puddle of mud. Solid ground actually must have splashed outward in every direction." In this account, the supposed meteorite became "the great swarm of meteors" that "must have traversed" the atmosphere for several hundred miles, pushing ahead of it a "giant bubble of superheated atmosphere" that was "probably responsible" for the burned countryside ("What a Meteor," 1929, p. 33). All the "must have's" and "probably's" make a good narrative, but are not scientifically convincing.

Similarly, Kulik endeavored to explain eyewitness accounts of the huge fireball in the sky that burned one observer's shirt off his back and threw him off his porch (Cowan, Atluri, & Libby, 1965). Such extreme heat waves had never before been known to have accompanied the fall of a meteorite, but Kulik decided that this meteorite was much larger than those previously recorded and that therefore it would have released much more energy upon impact and that would account for such radiant heat (Baxter & Atkins, 1976). So obsessed was Kulik with the idea that somewhere buried in the Tungus swamp was a phenomenal meteorite that he focused the efforts of all the expeditions to the area during his lifetime on digging beneath the frozen tundra and to some extent neglected the examination of other evidence that might have further threatened the theory that he was determined to prove (Parry, 1961). Initially, he was successful in convincing the scientific community that his theory was correct. It is most interesting to read excerpts from The American Weekly of 1929 flatly asserting that a meteorite had fallen in Siberia and that Professor Kulik had brought back photographs of the giant crater that he found, as well as small samples of meteoric materials. The article is accompanied by a photograph of Professor Kulik measuring "the main crater, where the largest mass of this celestial visitor buried itself in the earth" (Quoted in "What a Meteor," p. 34).

While Kulik's expeditions were still searching for evidence of a meteorite, other scientists were hypothesizing that the Tunguska explosion might have been caused by a small comet, which would account for the absence of a crater. Comets are composed of ice, frozen gases, and dust, and as they travel around the sun, they develop a long tail. Upon impact, a comet might give off a trail of gases and dust, which would create a bright and colorful night sky similar to that observed after the explosion. This would not be true of a meteorite, which has no gaseous trail and thus leaves no trace in the atmosphere. It has also been suggested that the observed direction of the object's travel was more typical of a comet than a meteorite (Florensky, 1963). If the comet had blown up approximately two miles above the site, that would explain why some trees survived while others did not (Parry, 1961). On the other hand, there is no evidence that a comet had ever crashed on earth before, or caused a comparable change in magnetic and atmospheric phenomena, or even come so close without being sighted (Baxter & Atkins, 1976). Those scientists supporting the comet theory have suggested that, although it is unusual for any comet to come that close to earth without anyone sighting it, the one landing at Tunguska might have been small enough to go by unnoticed. But that idea is contradicted by Fesenkov's estimate that, to cause such destruction, the nucleus of the Tunguskan comet—if there was one—would have been only slightly smaller than those of well-documented comets that were visible at great distances (Cowan, Atluri, & Libby, 1965).

The next major explanation for the cosmic phenomenon at Tunguska could only have been formulated after World War II, when the scientific community had learned how to make atomic explosions and had become familiar with their aftermath. Aleksander Kazantsev, a Russian scientist and (equally important) science-fiction writer, had visited Hiroshima after the atom bomb explosion and had studied the data describing its impact and aftermath. Because of certain similarities in the blast effects—the burnt yet upright trees, the mushroom cloud, the black rain—Kazantsev and other scientists concluded that the blast of 1908 was an atomic explosion estimated at a minimum of ten times the strength of the one at Hiroshima (Parry, 1961). Witnesses had described the blinding flash and withering heat at Hiroshima in much the same way that the Siberian peasants described the frightening blast at Tunguska. The melting heat that Kulik found so inconsistent with his meteorite theory was more consistent with an atomic explosion (Baxter & Atkins, 1976). It is worth pointing out that scientists went on to develop the hypothesis that a nuclear explosion had occurred at Tunguska even though their theorizing was largely based on stories told by ignorant peasants, believers in devils and wrathful gods, who could quite easily have exaggerated what had actually happened to improve their stories. Even though these eyewitness accounts were gathered twenty or more years after the actual event, and had quite possibly entered the folklore of the countryside (Krinov, 1966), they were still regarded as the purest evidence.

To test whether a nuclear explosion might have occurred, scientists examined the trees for radioactivity and for any unusual increase in normal growth patterns, shown by greater spacing between the age lines, that might have been the result of radioactivity. What they found was that some trees at the site grew to be four times greater than what would normally have been expected. Similarly, scabs that appeared on the hides of local reindeer were explained as being the result of radioactive contamination (Baxter & Atkins, 1976). This evidence, by no means conclusive (Florensky, 1963), was cited as proof that such an atomic explosion had taken place, just as Kulik had cited the existence of shallow pits in the terrain as proof that a meteorite had exploded.

Assuming that what happened at Tunguska was the result of an atomic blast, and faced with the fact that nuclear fission was not within man's grasp before the 1940s, Kazantsev and his colleagues concluded that the phenomenon must have involved extraterrestrial beings and that the explosion was caused by a UFO, propelled by atomic energy, that crashed (Parry, 1961). The pattern of devastation on the ground, as seen from the air, suggested that the object took a zigzag path, changing its direction as it came closer and closer to earth. Advocates of the UFO theory argue such a change in direction would not have been possible with a natural object like a meteorite or comet, and that the object—a spacecraft—was driven by intelligent beings who were trying to land without hitting a more densely populated area. They hypothesize that the craft had some mechanical problem that made it necessary to land but that the initial angle of its trajectory was too shallow for landing and would only have bounced the craft back into space. So the navigators tried to maneuver and correct the angle, but swerved, came down too sharply, and exploded (Baxter & Atkins, 1976). On the other hand, it seems just as possible that a natural object swerved or that debris from a nonatomic explosion was thrown in zigzag directions than that navigators from outer space ran into mechanical troubles and crash-landed. If probability is going to be disregarded in order to support one theory, then the same suspension of the natural order of things can be used to confirm an equally unlikely theory.

In the late 1950s, an exploratory team examined the Tunguska site with an advanced magnetic detector and, in 1962, scientists magnified the soil and found an array of tiny, colored, magnetic, ball-shaped particles, made of cobalt, nickel, copper, and germanium (Baxter & Atkins, 1976). According to extraterrestrial-intelligence specialists, these could have been the elements used for electrical and technical instruments, with the copper used for communication services and the germanium used in semiconductors (Parry, 1961). However, controlled experiments would be necessary to make this atomic-extraterrestrial argument convincing.

Scientists who find the UFO and extraterrestrial explanations less than credible have turned to the most recent theories of physics and astronomy to explain what might have happened in the Tungus. Some (including Kazantsev) argue that such an explosion might have been caused by debris from space colliding with the earth (Morrison & Chapman, 1990), or by anti-matter, which exploded as it came in contact with the atmosphere (Parry, 1961). Alternatively, the explosion might have been caused by a "black hole" hitting the earth in Siberia and passing through to emerge on the other side. Those opposing these theories point, again, to the absence of a crater and to the numerous eyewitness accounts that describe the shape of the object and the sound of the blast, all of which would be inconsistent with antimatter or black-hole theories (Baxter & Atkins, 1976). However, a 1973 article in

Morgan 8

Nature asserts that a black hole would not, in fact, leave a crater, but would simply enter the earth at a great velocity and that a shock wave and blast might possibly accompany its entrance (Jackson & Ryan, 1973). Comparisons have also been made with a similar but smaller incident that happened in 1930, in a stretch of Brazilian jungle as remote as Tunguska. Eyewitnesses reported the appearance of three fireballs, resulting in a one-megaton explosion and massive destruction of the forest. Coincidentally or not, the explosion occurred at the same time as the yearly Perseids meteor shower. The investigation into this phenomenon has been hampered by the unavailability of the eyewitness accounts, contained in diaries that are held by the Vatican (Stacy, 1996).

Even with the trail getting colder, scientists have not given up on finding out what occurred on June 30,1908. In recent years, conferences have taken place almost annually, in Moscow and in Krasnoyarsk, Siberia, to exchange theories and examine on-site evidence. Andrei Ol'khovatov, an independent scientist with a Web site devoted to Tunguska, believes that the explosion was "a manifestation of tectonic energy" related to the release of atmospheric energy in several notable earthquakes that have demonstrated some of the same electrical and fiery phenomena (Ol'khovatov, 2001). In 1999, an expedition from the University of Bologna, headed by Dr. Luigi Foschini and focused on Lake Ceko, not far from Lake Tunguska, used sonar and underwater cameras before drilling for samples from the lake bed ("Return to Tunguska," 1999; Foschini, 1999). Most recently, Dr. Robert Foot of the University of Melbourne has claimed that the cause of the Tunguska explosion must have been "mirror matter": matter that exists in the universe to spin in the opposite direction from the normal spinning of subatomic material and so "maintain left-right symmetry in the Universe." Foot says that mirror matter is "very hard to detect," but "interaction between atoms in the air and mirror atoms" could happen and might have caused an explosion of Tunguskan dimensions ("What Lies Beneath," 2001).

What is most fascinating about the Tunguska Valley phenomenon is that, despite all the advances in science over the past 95 years, investigators cannot now be any more certain of the cause of the blast than they were in 1921, when Kulik first came near the site. None of the theories presented is wholly convincing, for all of them rely to some extent on human observers, whose accounts of events are notoriously unreliable, or hypotheses based on ambiguous evidence, without the support of controlled tests and experiments. Even the introduction of modern, high-tech equipment has not established a convincing explanation.

Examining these hypotheses about what did or did not land and explode in Siberia does teach us that scientific theories are sometimes based on the selective interpretation of evidence and that scientists, like everyone else, tend to believe their own theories and find the evidence that they want to find. Although the language that they use is very different, the accounts of what happened at Tunguska according to Kulik, Kazantsev, and their other scientific colleagues are not so very different from what the local peasants say that they saw. Both have a closer resemblance to science fiction than science fact.

References

Baxter, J., & Atkins, T. (1976). The fire came by: The riddle of the great Siberian explosion. Garden City, NY: Doubleday.

Cowan, C., Atluri, C. R., & Libby, W. F. (1965, May 29). Possible antimatter content of the Tunguska meteor of 1908. Nature (London), 861–865.

Crowther, J. G. (1931). More about the great Siberian meteorite. Scientific American, 144(5), 314–317.

Florensky, K. P. (1963, November). Did a comet collide with the earth in 1908? Sky and Telescope, 268–269.

Foschini, L. (1999, July 28). Last operations in Tunguska. Department of Physics University of Bologna Web Page. Retrieved August 19, 2001, from http://www.th.bo.infn.it/tunguska/press2807_en.htm

Jackson, A. A., & Ryan, M. P. (1973, September 14). Was the Tungus event due to a black hole? Nature (London), 88–89.

Krinov, E. L. (1966). Giant meteorites. London: Pergamon.

Morrison, D., & Chapman, C. R. (1990). Target earth: It will happen. Sky and Telescope, 261–265.

Olivier, C. P. (1928). The great Siberian meteorite. Scientific American, 139(1), 42–44.

Ol'khovatov, A. (2001, June 28). Home page. Retrieved August 19, 2001, from http://www.geocities.com/capecanaveral/cockpit/3240/tunguska.htm

Parry, A. (1961). The Tungus mystery: Was it a spaceship? In Russia's Rockets and Missiles (pp. 248–267). London: Macmillan.

Return to Tunguska. (1999, June 28). bbc News. Retrieved August 19, 2001, from http://www.BBC.co.uk/hi/english/sci/tech/newsid.380000/380060.htm

Stacy, D. (1996). Another Tunguska? The Anomalist. Retrieved August 20, 2001, from http://www.anomalist.com/reports/tunguska.html

What a meteor did to Siberia. (1929, March 16). Literary Digest, 33–34.

What lies beneath. (2001, July 28). New Scientist, 17.

Appendix A

Some Useful Reference Sources

GUIDELINES FOR USING REFERENCE WORKS

- With few exceptions, the reference works listed below are databases that can be found only on the Internet. Because most of them are available only by arrangement with fee-paying institutions, you will probably have to access them through computers in your college library or local public library (unless your college provides a network that includes dormitory computers). For that reason, URLs are not indicated here.

- Computerized databases generally include only the last five to ten years of source material. Some are beginning to make their archives available online, but for journal and periodical sources before the 1990s, you may have to consult the bound print indexes in your reference library.

- Some reference sources are entirely bibliographical. They consist of long lists of articles and (sometimes) books, each followed by the essential publication information. Each entry is called a *"citation."* These indexes are usually arranged by topic. You may have to try several keywords before you find the articles that you need. If, for example, you are doing research on educational television, you would look up "education," "television," and the names of some of the programs you intend to write about, as well as the obvious choice "educational television." Most indexes are cross-referenced.

451

- Some reference sources contain *abstracts,* or summaries of articles, as well as citations. Sources containing abstracts often cover a specific discipline, summarizing many (but not necessarily all) of the articles published each year in that discipline. Such sources, which are themselves often called abstracts, sometimes have two sections: the first contains a series of summaries of articles, chosen for their special interest or excellence and arranged by subject; the second contains a list of all the articles published in that field in that year. Although abstracts give you a convenient preview, you will find that many of the articles are highly technical and may therefore be difficult to read and write about.

- An increasing number of reference sources contain some *full-text* articles, which enable you to read or download the material without using microfilm or microfiche. In some cases, access to full-text articles requires an additional fee.

- Most journals have converted to microfilm or microfiche access for their back issues. Ask the reference librarian to help you if you are using this apparatus for the first time.

- Certain reference works (usually those containing tables or charts) may require special software—like Adobe Acrobat—for reading on a computer screen.

- If you can't find a specific reference work or if you are not sure which database to use, check with a librarian. As long as you can tell librarians the broad or (preferably) the narrow subject of your research, they will be willing and able to help you.

GENERAL ENCYCLOPEDIAS

- *Britannica Online.* An online version of the print *Encyclopaedia Britannica,* first published in 1929 and regularly revised.
- *Encyclopedia American Online.* Contains full-text articles.
- *Grolier Multimedia Encyclopedia Online.* Contains full-text articles and maps.
- *The World Factbook.* Contains information drawn from many government agencies about each country in the world.

SPECIALIZED ENCYCLOPEDIAS

- *The Grove Dictionary of Art Online.* Contains a full-text dictionary and a full-text encyclopedia.
- *The Johns Hopkins Guide to Literary Theory & Criticism.* Contains full-text encyclopedia of literary theory and criticism from Plato to modern times.
- *McGraw-Hill Encyclopedia of Science and Technology.* Contains full-text articles on modern science and technology.

- *Merck Index.* A chemistry handbook.
- *New Grove Dictionary of Music and Musicians,* 2nd ed. Contains full-text information about music.
- *Routledge Encyclopedia of Philosophy.* An international and interdisciplinary encyclopedia of philosophy.

BIOGRAPHIES

- *American National Biography.* Contains 175,000 biographies of men and women from American history.
- *Annual Obituary.* Collects profiles of prominent people who died during the year, arranged by month of death.
- *Biography Index.* Contains citations (not biographies) for biographical articles and books.
- *Contemporary Authors.* Covers more than 90,000 contemporary writers in various media (full text).
- *Current Biography.* Contains citations of articles about prominent contemporary people.
- *Dictionary of American Biography.* Contains biographical articles about noted Americans who died before December 31, 1980.
- *Dictionary of National Biography.* Contains biographical articles about noted Britons who died before 1985.
- *New York Times Obituary Index*: obituaries of prominent people.

GENERAL INDEXES

- *AlphaSearch.* Contains searchable databases (organized by topic) that provide links to a limited number of academic Web sites, including primary sources.
- *Argus Clearinghouse.* Contains a group of searchable databases for Web material, chosen and organized by librarians.
- *Article First.* Contains citations and abstracts for articles across the disciplines (including popular culture).
- *Book Review Digest.* Contains citations and abstracts for book reviews in various periodicals.
- *BUBL.* Contains a catalog of Internet resources, based on approximately 11,000 sites, that provides five relevant Web sources for each subject.
- *Catalog of United States Government Publications.* Contains citations for government-published documents.
- *ClariNews.* Contains current stories—3,500 added each day—from such sources as UPI, AFP, and Reuters.

- *Contents First.* Contains the table of contents from periodicals (mostly 1990–present) across the disciplines.
- *Editorials on File.* Contains selected editorials on subjects of contemporary interest, with each editorial preceded by a summary of the issue being discussed.
- *Essay and General Literature Index.* Contains citations for essays (1985–present) in most disciplines of the humanities and social sciences.
- *FactSearch.* Contains facts and statistics (1984–present) on social, environmental, and political issues from 300 publications (including the Congressional Record).
- *Facts on File.* Contains summaries of issues and events, with selected bibliographies.
- *Historical Newspapers Online.* Contains indexes to the *New York Times* (1851–1923) and the *Times* of London (1790–1900).
- *Ingenta* (includes *Uncover*). Contains citations and short summaries for a range of academic journals. (Full-text articles available for a fee.)
- *International Data Base.* Contains statistical data about topics like ethnicity, income, migration, and religion for the world's countries.
- *JSTOR.* Contains full-text articles from more than 120 scholarly journals in areas such as anthropology, economics, history, philosophy, literature, and the sciences.
- *Lexis-Nexis Academic Universe.* Contains the full texts of articles (mid-1980s–present) from sources in areas such as broadcast media, business, politics, and law.
- *Library of Congress Catalog.* Contains the most comprehensive listing of books, new and out of print.
- *National Newspaper Index.* Contains citations to five major newspapers (1990–present) including the *New York Times, Wall Street Journal,* and *Washington Post.*
- *News Index.* Includes the current issue and back issues of 300 news periodicals.
- *New York Times Index.* Contains citations to the newspaper from 1851 to the present.
- *PCI: Periodicals Contents Index.* Provides citations for selected articles across the disciplines published between 1770 and 1993.
- *Project Muse.* Contains full-text articles (1999–present) from over 100 scholarly journals across the disciplines.
- *Pro Quest.* Includes *News Collection* (some full-text articles) and *Periodical Abstracts* (citations, abstracts, and some full-text articles from general interest and trade periodicals).
- *Readers' Guide Abstracts.* Contains citations as well as abstracts (from 1984–present) for articles from popular and general-interest periodicals.

- *Statistical Abstract of the United States.* Contains the full text (1995–present) of tables and charts in areas such as commerce, health, law, trade, and criminal justice.
- *Vertical File Index.* Lists pamphlets on all subjects issued by commercial, not-for-profit, and governmental organizations.

INDEXES AND ABSTRACTS: HUMANITIES

- *American Film Institute Catalog.* Includes listings of American films from 1893–1970 (excluding 1951–1960).
- *Art Index.* Contains citations (1929–present) and abstracts (1984–present) for articles about art history, including architecture, archaeology, crafts, film and photography, and graphic arts.
- *Arts and Humanities Citation Index.* Contains citations for articles (1975–present) from over 1,000 arts and humanities journals.
- *Historical Abstracts.* Contains citations and abstracts for articles (1982–present) about world history (excluding the United States) from 2,000 journals.
- *Humanities Abstracts.* Contains citations (1984–present) and abstracts (1994–present) for articles in humanities journals.
- *International Index to Music Periodicals.* Contains citations and abstracts from 300 scholarly and popular periodicals about music.
- *International Index to the Performing Arts.* Contains full citations (1964–present) and abstracts (1998–present) for articles in areas such as dance and drama.
- *Internet Movie Database.* Compiles facts about films.
- *MLA International Bibliography.* Indexes articles from more than 3,000 journals, as well as other documents in the fields of language, literature, and linguistics.
- *Past Masters.* Contains a full-text selection of primary sources in the areas of philosophy and social and economic thought.
- *The Philosopher's Index.* Contains citations and abstracts for articles on philosophy and related areas.

INDEXES AND ABSTRACTS: SOCIAL SCIENCES AND PROFESSIONAL STUDIES

- *Business Periodicals Index.* Lists articles from more than 100 periodicals dealing with business management.
- *Crime in the United States.* Includes annual tables containing crime statistics (1995–present).

- *Education Full Text.* Lists citations and abstracts (1983–present) as well as some full texts (1994–present) from 500 periodicals.
- *Education Index.* Contains citations to periodicals.
- *ERIC.* Contains citations, abstracts, and some full-text articles (1966–present) for journals of education and other periodicals.
- *Handbook of International Economic Statistics.* Contains statistics from countries around the world.
- *Index Legal Periodicals.* Contains citations to articles as well as a table of cases and book reviews.
- *International Bibliography of the Social Sciences.* Contains citations for articles in social science journals.
- *International Political Science Abstracts.* Contains citations and abstracts (1989–present) for articles from 840 journals including international relations.
- *National Criminal Justice Reference Service Abstracts Database.* Contains citations and abstracts (1972–present) for periodical articles.
- *Nursing and Allied Health Database.* Includes citations to articles in the fields of health education and social services.
- *PAIS International.* Contains citations (1972–present) and abstracts (1985–present) for articles from 460,000 journals in areas such as environmental studies, government, and political science.
- *Political Science and Government Abstracts.* Contains articles and abstracts (1975–present) for articles and books.
- *Psychological Abstracts (PsychINFO).* Contains citations, with subject and author indexes, to periodicals.
- *Social Sciences Abstracts.* Contains citations (1983–present) and abstracts (1994–present) for periodicals.
- *Social Sciences Citation Index Expanded.* Contains citations (some full text) for articles in social science journals.
- *Social Work Abstracts.* Contains citations and abstracts (1977–present) for articles from journals dealing with social work and social welfare.
- *Sociological Abstracts.* Contains citations and abstracts (1963–present) for articles in periodicals.

INDEXES AND ABSTRACTS: SCIENCES

- *Annual Reviews.* Contains full-text reviews of topics in biomedical, physical, and social science journals.
- *Anthropological Literature.* Contains citations for articles in periodicals and collections.

- *Applied Science and Technology Abstracts.* Contains citations and abstracts for articles from periodicals and book reviews.
- *Biological Abstracts.* Contains citations and abstracts from journals.
- *Biological and Agricultural Index.* Contains citations from journals.
- *Bio One.* Contains full-text articles (2000–present) from 300 journals in the biological, ecological, and environmental sciences.
- *Chemical Abstracts.* Contains citations and some full-text articles for periodicals.
- *Engineering Village 2.* Contains databases and other material in all subdisciplines of engineering.
- *General Science Abstracts.* Contains citations and abstracts for articles from periodicals.
- *Science Citation Index Expanded.* Contains citations to articles in scientific and technical journals.
- *Science Direct.* Contains full-text articles from journals published by Elsevier (and key journals from other publishers).

Some Basic Forms for Documentation: MLA, APA, and Endnote

MLA STYLE

The following is a list of model bibliographical and parenthetical entries for MLA style. The proper bibliographical form that will appear in alphabetical order on your "Works Cited" page is followed by a sample parenthetical documentation that might appear in the text. The sample documentation in this list will usually contain the author's name; but remember that in your essay you will often mention the author's name in your text, thus making necessary only the parenthetical documentation of the page(s) of your source. You can find guidelines for preparing MLA documentation in Chapter 8, on pp. 375–384. See also the list of "Works Cited" in the student essay "Euthanasia: The Right to Die" in Chapter 9. For more details and examples, as well as guidelines for kinds of sources not listed below, see the fifth edition of the *MLA Handbook for Writers of Research Papers* (1999).

PRINT SOURCES

Book by a Single Author

Veysey, Laurence R. The Emergence of the American University. Chicago: U of
Chicago P, 1965.

(Veysey 23)

Book by Two Authors

Postman, Neil, and Charles Weingartner. Teaching as a Subversive Activity. New
York: Dell, 1969.

(Postman and Weingartner 34–36)

Book by More Than Three Authors

Spiller, Robert E., et al. Literary History of the United States. London: Macmillan,
1946.

(Spiller et al. 67)

Edited Collection Written by Different Authors

Wheelwright, Philip, ed. The Presocratics. New York: Odyssey, 1966.

(Wheelwright 89)

✓Essay from a Collection Written by Different Authors

Webb, R. K. "The Victorian Reading Public." From Dickens to Hardy. Ed. Boris
Ford. Baltimore: Penguin, 1958. 205–26.

(Webb 209)

Book Published in a Reprinted Edition

Orwell, George. Animal Farm. 1946. New York: Signet, 1959.

(Orwell 100)

✓Book Published in a New Edition

> Baugh, Albert C. A History of the English Language. 2nd ed. New York: Appleton,
>
>   1957.
>
> (Baugh 21)

Work in Translation

> Lorenz, Konrad. On Aggression. 1966. Trans. Marjorie Kerr Wilson. New York:
>
>   Bantam, 1969.
>
> (Lorenz 45)

Book Published in Several Volumes

> Tocqueville, Alexis de. Democracy in America. Ed. Phillips Bradley. 2 vols. New
>
>   York: Knopf, 1945.
>
> (Tocqueville 2: 78)

One Volume in a Set or Series

> Granville-Barker, Harley. Prefaces to Shakespeare. Vol. 2. London: Batsford,
>
>   1963.
>
> Gaff, Jerry G. Institutional Renewal through the Improvement of Teaching. New
>
>   Directions for Higher Ed. 24. San Francisco: Jossey-Bass, 1978.
>
> (Granville-Barker 193)
>
> (Gaff 45)

Book in an Edited Edition

> Kirstein, Lincoln. By With To & From. Ed. Nicholas Jenkins. New York: Farrar,
>
>   1991.
>
> Jenkins, Nicholas, ed. By With To & From. By Lincoln Kirstein. New York: Farrar,
>
>   1991.
>
> (Kirstein 190)
>
> (Jenkins xiii)

The second entry indicates that you are citing the work of the editor (not the author); therefore, you place the editor's name first.

Introduction, Preface, Foreword, or Afterword

> Spacks, Patricia Meyer. Afterword. Sense and Sensibility. By Jane Austen. New
> York: Bantam, 1983. 332–43.
>
> (Spacks 338)

Article in an Encyclopedia

> "American Architecture." Columbia Encyclopedia. 3rd ed. 1963.
>
> ("American Architecture")

Notice that no page numbers are needed for either the bibliographical entry or the parenthetical reference when the source is an encyclopedia. If the article is signed by an author, list the author's name at the beginning of the bibliographical entry and identify the source in your parenthetical documentation by using the author's name. If you are citing a little-known or specialized encyclopedia, provide full publication information, including the place of publication and the publisher.

Publication of a Corporation, Foundation, or Government Agency

> Carnegie Council on Policy Studies in Higher Education. Three Thousand
> Futures: The Next Twenty Years for Higher Education. San Francisco:
> Jossey-Bass, 1980.
>
> United States. Bureau of the Census. Abstract of the Census of Manufactures.
> Washington: GPO, 1919.
>
> Coleman, James S., et al. Equality of Educational Opportunity. U.S. Dept. of
> Health, Education, and Welfare. Washington: GPO, 1966.
>
> (Carnegie Council 34)
>
> (Bureau of the Census 56)
>
> (Coleman et al. 88)

Pamphlet or Brochure

The entry should resemble the entry for a book. If the author's name is missing, begin the entry with the title; if the date is missing, use the abbreviation *n.d.*

> More, Howard V. Costa de la Luz. Turespana: Secretaria General de Turismo,
> n.d.
>
> (More 6)

Classic Work

Job. The Jerusalem Bible. Reader's Edition. Ed. Alexander Jones. Garden City:
  Doubleday, 1968.

Homer. The Odyssey. Trans. Robert Fitzgerald. Garden City: Doubleday, 1963.

(Job 3:7)

(Odyssey 7.1–16)

Article in a Scholarly Journal with Continuous Pagination

Shepard, David. "Authenticating Films." The Quarterly Journal of the Library of
  Congress 37 (1980): 342–54.

(Shepard 350)

The four journals constituting Volume 37 are treated as a single continuous
work for purposes of pagination. The first journal in Volume 38 will start again
with page 1.

Article in a Scholarly Journal without Continuous Pagination

Burnham, Christopher C. "Expressive Writing: A Heretic's Confession." Focuses
  2.1 (1989): 5–18.

(Burnham 7–8)

Article in a Monthly Magazine

Loye, David. "TV's Impact on Adults." Psychology Today Apr. 1978: 87+.

(Loye 87)

The plus sign after the page number indicates that the article is not printed on
consecutive pages, but skips to later pages.

Article in a Weekly Magazine

Meyer, Karl E. "Television's Trying Times." Saturday Review 16 Sept. 1978:
  19–23.

(Meyer 21)

Article in a Newspaper

> Goldin, Davidson. "In a Change of Policy, and Heart, Colleges Join Fight Against
>
> Inflated Grades." New York Times 4 July 1995, late ed.: 8.
>
> (Goldin)

No page number is required in a parenthetical citation of a one-page article. If a page number is required and the newspaper is divided into separately numbered sections, include the section designation before the page number in both the bibliographical entry and the citation, e.g., *B6*.

Article without an Author

> "How to Get Quality Back into the Schools." US News & World Report 12 Sept.
>
> 1977: 31–34.
>
> ("How to Get Quality" 33)

Letter to the Editor

> Kropp, Arthur J. Letter. Village Voice 12 Oct. 1993: 5.
>
> (Kropp)

Editorial

> "Justice Berger's Contradictions." Editorial. New York Times 27 June 1995, late
>
> ed.: A16.
>
> ("Justice Berger's Contradictions")

Review

> Appiah, K. Anthony. "Giving Up the Perfect Diamond." Rev. of The Holder of the
>
> World, by Bharati Mukherjee. New York Times Book Review 10 Oct. 1993: 7.
>
> (Appiah)

Interview

> Berger, John. Interview with Nikos Papastergiadis. American Poetry Review.
>
> July–Aug. 1993: 9–12.
>
> (Berger 10)

Personal or Published Letter

Hans, James S. Letter to the author. 18 Aug. 1991.

Keats, John. "To Benjamin Bailey." 22 Nov. 1817. John Keats: Selected Poetry
and Letters. Ed. Richard Harter Fogle. New York: Rinehart, 1952.
300–303.

(Hans)

(Keats 302)

Unpublished Dissertation

Eastman, Elizabeth. "'Lectures on Jurisprudence': A Key to Understanding Adam
Smith's Thought." Diss. Claremont Grad. School, 1993.

(Eastman 34)

Map or Chart

Spain, Portugal, and North Africa. Map American Automobile Association,
1993–94.

(Spain)

Cartoon

Trudeau, Garry. "Doonesbury." Cartoon. Charlotte Observer 23 Dec. 1988: B12.

(Trudeau)

ELECTRONIC SOURCES

Using the sample below as a general guide, attempt to ascertain as many of the
elements of citation as are appropriate to your source. If you cannot find some
of the information, cite what is available. Remember that if you need to break a
URL at the end of a line, break it only after a slash.

Author's last name, First name, Middle initial. "Title of the Article or Other Document." Title of Book, Periodical, or Web Site. Name of editor or translator of
text. Original print publication information. Date of electronic publication
or most recent update. Range or total number of pages, paragraphs, or
other sections, if numbered in the text. Name of sponsoring institution or
organization. Date of access <URL>.

Scholarly Project

The Camelot Project. Ed. Alan Lupack and Barbara Tepa Lupack. 11 Dec. 2001.
U of Rochester. 4 Feb. 2002 <http://www.lib.rochester.edu/camelot/
cphome.stm>.

(Camelot)

Book within a Scholarly Project

Skene, Felicia. Penitentiaries and Reformatories. Edinburgh: Edmonston and
Douglas, 1865. Victorian Women Writers Project. Ed. Perry Willett. 10 Dec.
1996. Indiana U. 11 Mar. 1998 <http://www.indiana.edu/~letrs/vwwp/
skene/skene~reform.html>.

(Skene)

Information Database

Art History Research Centre. Ed. Leif Harmsen. Feb. 2000. Dept. of Art Hist., Con-
cordia U. 19 Nov. 2001 <http://arthistory.Concordia.ca/AHRC/index.htm>.

(Art History)

Article in an Information Database

Jarvis, Edward. "The Increase of Human Life. I." The American Memory
Collections. Lib. of Congress. 12 Feb. 2002 <http://memory.loc.gov/
cgibin/query/D?ncps:15:.temp/~ammem_Aeog::>.

(Jarvis)

Professional Web Site

UC Berkeley Ancient History and Mediterranean Archaeology Home Page. 3 Oct.
2001. Dept. of Ancient History and Mediterranean Archaeology, U of California, Berkeley. 2 Jan. 2002 <http://ls.berkeley.edu/dept.ahma>.

(UC Berkeley)

Personal Web Site

Wong, James. Home page. 12 May 1998 <http://logic.simplenet.com/
jameswong/>.

(Wong)

Article in a Scholarly Journal

Osborne, Lawrence. "A Pirate's Progress: How the Maritime Rogue Became a
Multicultural Hero." Linguafranca 8.2 (March 1998): 47 pars. 17 Mar. 1998
<http://www.linguafranca.com>.

(Osborne, par. 16)

Article in a Newspaper

Kelly, Michael, "Non-Judgment Day at Yale." Washington Post 18 Dec. 2001.
19 Dec. 2001 <http://www.washingtonpost.com/wp-dyn/articles/
A62924-2001Dec18.html>.

(Kelly)

Article in a Magazine

Horowitz, David. "Refuting Chomsky." Salon 8 Oct. 2001. 3 Dec. 2001 <http://
www.salon.com/news/col/horo/2001/10/08/chomsky/index_np.html?x>.

(Horowitz)

Newsgroup Posting

Watson, Hunter. "Soviet Collapse." Online posting. 31 Dec. 2001. 5 Jan 2002
<news:soc.history.moderated>.

(Hunter)

Article from a Database on CD-ROM

Burke, Marc. "Homosexuality as Deviance: The Case of the Gay Police Officer."
British Journal of Criminology 34.2 (1994): 192–203. PsycLit. CD-ROM.
SilverPlatter. Nov. 1994.

(Burke 195)

Article without a URL from an Online Service

"New Respect, Not Reproach." NEA Today Feb. 2002. ProQuest Direct. New York
U Lib. 12 Feb. 2002 <http://www.umi.com/proquest/>.

("New Respect")

This format is used for online services that you obtain through a library. Note that the URL given at the end of the entry is for the home page of the service, not for the article itself. If you are citing an article from a service that you subscribe to personally, after the name of the service add the word *Keyword* or *Path*, followed by a colon and the keyword or the sequence of headings you followed to obtain the article; use semicolons between the headings.

Work in an Indeterminate Medium

If you cannot determine the medium of a source (if you are accessing it through a library network, for example, and cannot tell whether it is from a CD-ROM or the Web), include the label *Electronic* and the name of the network, its sponsoring organization, or both.

Simpson, James B. Simpson's Contemporary Quotations. Boston: Houghton,

1988. New York, Bartleby.com, 2000. Electronic. Bobcat Plus, New York U.

12 Feb. 2002.

(Simpson)

E-mail

Wittreich, Joseph. E-mail to the author. 12 Dec. 2002.

(Wittreich)

Review

Staples, Brent. "Common Ground." Rev. of One Nation, After All, by Alan Wolfe.

New York Times on the Web 8 Mar. 1998. 12 Apr. 1998 <http://

www.nytimes.com/books/98/03/08/reviews/980308.08staple.html>.

(Staples)

OTHER KINDS OF SOURCES

Personal or Telephone Interview

Nussbaumer, Doris D. Personal interview. 30 July 1988.

Albert, John J. Telephone interview. 22 Dec. 1989.

(Nussbaumer)

(Albert)

Broadcast Interview

Kennedy, Joseph. Interview with Harry Smith. This Morning. CBS. WCBS, New
York. 14 Oct. 1993.

(Kennedy)

Lecture

Auchincloss, Louis, Erica Jong, and Gloria Steinem. "The 18th Century Woman."
Symposium: Metropolitan Museum of Art, New York. 29 Apr. 1982.

(Auchincloss, Jong, and Steinem)

Live Performance

Tommy. By Pete Townshend. Dir. Des McAnuff. St. James Theater, New York.
3 May 1993.

(Tommy)

Film

Dr. Strangelove. Dir. Stanley Kubrick. Columbia Pictures, 1963.

Kubrick, Stanley, dir. Dr. Strangelove. Columbia Pictures, 1963.

Put the film first if you wish to emphasize material from the film; however, if
you are emphasizing the work of the director, list that name first.

(Dr. Strangelove)

(Kubrick)

Television or Radio Program

Serge Pavlovitch Diaghilev 1872–1929: A Portrait. Prod. Peter Adam. BBC.
WNET, New York. 12 July 1982.

(Diaghilev)

Audio Recording

Tchaikovsky, Piotr. The Tchaikovsky Collection. Audiocassette. CBS Special
Products, 1989.

(Tchaikovsky)

Videocassette

Wuthering Heights. Dir. William Wyler. 1939. Videocassette. Embassy, 1987.

(Wuthering)

Work of Art

Brueghel, Pieter. The Beggars. Louvre, Paris.

(Brueghel)

APA STYLE

The format for documentation recommended by the American Psychological Association is used primarily in the social and behavioral sciences, especially sociology and psychology. It is also often employed in subjects like anthropology, astronomy, business, education, linguistics, and political science.

Like MLA style, APA documentation is based on parenthetical references to author and page. The chief difference is that, in the APA system, you include the work's *date of publication* after the author's name, both within parentheses.

MLA

Primitive religious rituals may have been a means for deterring collective violence (Girard 1).

Brain Theory suggests two extremes of writing style, the appositional and the propositional (Winterowd and Williams 4).

APA

Primitive religious rituals may have been a means for deterring collective violence (Girard, 1972, p. 1).

Brain Theory suggests two extremes of writing style, the appositional and the propositional (Winterowd & Williams, 1990, p. 4).

As with MLA style, if you cite the author's name or the date of publication in your sentence, it is not necessary to repeat it in the parentheses.

In 1972, Girard suggested that primitive religious rituals may have been a means for deterring collective violence (p. 1).

According to Winterowd and Williams (1990), Brain Theory suggests two extremes of writing style, the appositional and the propositional (p. 4).

Here is what the bibliography for these two entries would look like in MLA style and in the style recommended by APA for student papers.

MLA

WORKS CITED

Girard, René. Violence and the Sacred. Baltimore: Johns Hopkins UP, 1972.

Winterowd, W. Ross, and James D. Williams. "Cognitive Style and Written Discourse." Focuses 3 (1990): 3–23.

APA

REFERENCES

Girard, R. (1972). Violence and the sacred. Baltimore: Johns Hopkins University Press.

Winterowd, W. R., & Williams, J. D. (1990). Cognitive style and written discourse. Focuses, 3, 3–23.

These are some of the ways that APA bibliographical style for student papers differs from MLA style:

- Authors' first and middle names are designated by initials. When there are multiple authors, all are listed last name first, and an ampersand (&) is used instead of *and*.

- Two or more works by the same author are listed chronologically. Instead of using a dash for repeated names (as in MLA style), you start each entry with the author's full name.

- The date of publication (in parentheses) is placed immediately after the author's name.

- In the title of a book or article, only the first word, the first word of the subtitle, and proper nouns and adjectives are capitalized.

- The title of a section of a volume (e.g., an article in a periodical or a chapter of a book) is neither underlined nor surrounded by quotation marks.

- The volume number of a journal is underlined.

- The bibliography is titled *References* rather than *Works Cited*.

Since the identification of sources greatly depends on the dates that you cite, you must be careful to clarify the dating, especially when a single author has published two or more works in the same year. Here, for example, is an excerpt from a bibliography that distinguishes among three sources by the same author published in 1972:

Carnegie Commission on Higher Education. (1972a). The campus and the city: Maximizing assets and reducing liabilities. New York: McGraw-Hill.

Carnegie Commission on Higher Education. (1972b). The fourth revolution: Instructional technology in higher education. New York: McGraw-Hill.

Carnegie Commission on Higher Education. (1972c). The more effective use of resources: An imperative for higher education. New York: McGraw-Hill.

And here is how one of these sources would be documented in the essay:

In its report The More Effective Use of Resources, the Carnegie Commission on Higher Education recommended that "colleges and universities develop a 'self-renewal' fund of 1 to 3 percent each year taken from existing allocations" (1972c, p. 105).

The following is a brief list of model entries for APA style. Each bibliographical form that will appear in alphabetical order on the "References" page is followed by a sample parenthetical reference as it might appear in your text. Whenever there is an author, the sample parenthetical references in this list will contain the author's name; remember that in your essay, you will often mention the author's name (and the date) in your text, with only the page of the source needed in the parenthetical reference. For additional examples of the use of APA style, look at "Explaining the Tunguskan Phenomenon," the third research essay in Chapter 9.

PRINT AND AUDIOVISUAL SOURCES

Book by a Single Author

Veysey, L. R. (1965). The emergence of the American university. Chicago: University of Chicago Press.

(Veysey, 1965, p. 45)

Book by More Than One Author

Postman, N., & Weingartner, C. (1969). Teaching as a subversive activity. New York: Dell.

(Postman & Weingartner, 1969, p. 143)

When a source has three to five authors, name them all in the first text reference or parenthetical note; then, in all subsequent references or notes, list only the first author's name followed by "et al." For sources with six or more authors, use "et al." in the first reference or note as well. Always list all authors in bibliographical entries.

Edited Collection Written by Different Authors

> Wheelwright, P. (Ed.). (1966). The presocratics. New York: Odyssey.
> (Wheelwright, 1966, pp. 2–3)

Essay from a Collection Written by Different Authors

> Webb, R. K. (1958). The Victorian reading public. In B. Ford (Ed.), From Dickens
> to Hardy (pp. 205–226). Baltimore: Penguin.
> (Webb, 1958, pp. 210–212)

Work in Translation/Work Published in a Reprinted Edition

> Lorenz, K. (1969). On aggression (M. K. Wilson, Trans.). New York: Bantam.
> (Original work published 1966)
> (Lorenz, 1966/1969, p. 75)

Work Published in a New Edition

> Baugh, A. C. (1957). A history of the English language (2nd ed.). New York:
> Appleton-Century-Crofts.
> (Baugh, 1957, p. 288)

Book with No Author

> World atlas. (1984). New York: Simon and Schuster.
> (World Atlas, 1984)

Article in an Encyclopedia

> American architecture. (1963). In Columbia encyclopedia (3rd ed.). New York:
> Columbia University Press.
> ("American Architecture," 1963)

Publication of a Corporation, Foundation, or Government Agency

> Carnegie Council on Policy Studies in Higher Education. (1980). Three thousand
> futures: The next twenty years for higher education. San Francisco:
> Jossey-Bass.
> (Carnegie Council, 1980, p. 110)

Article in a Periodical Numbered Only by Volume

Plumb, J. H. (1976). Commercialization of childhood. Horizon, 18, 16–29.

(Plumb, 1976, p. 20)

Article in a Monthly Periodical

Bales, K. (2002, April). The social psychology of modern slavery. Scientific American, 286(4), 80–88.

(Bales, 2002, p. 83)

Article in a Weekly Periodical

Begley, S. (2002, March 11). The schizophrenic mind. Newsweek, 44–51.

(Begley, 2002, p. 48)

Include the volume number if the periodical has one.

Article without an Author

Cheap shot. (2002, March 18). The New Republic, 226, 9.

("Cheap Shot," 2002)

Article in a Newspaper

Goldin, D. (1995, July 4). In a change of policy, and heart, colleges join fight against inflated grades. The New York Times, late ed., p. 8.

(Goldin, 1995)

Unpublished Dissertation

Eastman, E. (1993). "Lectures on jurisprudence": A key to understanding Adam Smith's thought. Unpublished doctoral dissertation, Claremont Graduate School.

(Eastman, 1993)

Film

Kubrick, S. (Director). (1963). Dr. Strangelove [Motion picture]. United States: Columbia Pictures.

(Kubrick, 1963)

ELECTRONIC SOURCES

The APA *Publication Manual* advises that citations for information taken from the Internet should specify the location of the information as precisely as possible, citing specific documents rather than home pages, for example. The *Manual* also emphasizes the need to check URLs frequently to make sure they still work and to update them if necessary. If a document is no longer available, it suggests, you may want to replace it with another source or simply not use it in your paper. If a document has no page numbers, cite paragraph numbers if they are visible onscreen, using the paragraph symbol (¶) or the abbreviation *para*.

Internet Article Based on a Print Source

> Lang, J., & Smith, T. (2002). The medicinal uses of Yerba Mate [Electronic version]. Journal of Ethnobotany, 4, 19–24.
>
> (Lang & Smith, 2002, p. 22)

If you have reason to think that the electronic version of the article is not the same as the print version (for example, if it does not include page numbers) or if it includes additional data or commentaries, instead of *[Electronic version]* include the date you retrieved the article and the URL.

> Lang, J., & Smith, T. (2002). The medicinal uses of Yerba Mate. Journal of Ethnobotany, 4, 19–24. Retrieved February 13, 2002, from http://jeb.org/articles.html
>
> (Lang & Smith, 2002, p. 22)

Article in an Internet-Only Journal

> Biglan, A., & Smolkowski, K. (2002, January 15). The role of the community psychologist in the 21st century. Prevention & Treatment, 5, Article 2. Retrieved February 13, 2002, from http://www.journals.apa.org/prevention/volume5/pre0050002a.html
>
> (Biglan & Smolkowski, 2002)

Journal Article Retrieved from a Database

> Swingley, D., & Fernald, A. (2002). Recognition of words referring to present and absent objects by 24-month-olds. Journal of Memory and Language, 46, 39–56. Retrieved February 12, 2002, from PsycINFO database.
>
> (Swingley & Fernald, 2002, p. 46)

Article in an Internet-Only Magazine

Horowitz, D. (2001, October 8). Refuting Chomsky. Salon. Retrieved November
11, 2001, from http://www.salon.com/news/col/horo/2001/10/08/
chomsky/index_np.html?x

(Horowitz, 2001, ¶2)

Document from a University Web Site

Stimson, S. C., & Milgate, M. (2001). Mill, liberty and the facts of life. Retrieved
January 14, 2002, from University of California at Berkeley, Institute of
Governmental Studies Web site: http://www.igs.berkeley.edu/
publications/workingpapers/WP2001-2.pdf

(Stimson & Milgate, 2001, p. 12)

Document from a Private Organization's Web Site

American Civil Liberties Union. (1999). Worker's rights. Retrieved March 4, 2000,
from http://www.aclu.org/issues/immigrant/workerrights.html

(American Civil Liberties Union, 1999)

Paper Presented at a Conference or Symposium

Patrick, W. C., III. (2001, February 13). The threat of biological warfare. Paper
presented at the Marshall Institute's Washington Roundtable on Science
and Public Policy. Document retrieved January 2, 2002, from
http://www.marshall.org/PatrickRT.htm

(Patrick, 2001)

Newsgroup Posting

Watson, H. (2001, December 31). Soviet collapse. Message posted to
news://soc.history.moderated

(Watson, 2001)

If the posting has an identifying number, give it in brackets after the subject
line: *Soviet collapse [Msg 3].* If the newsgroup does not archive postings, do not
include the posting in the "References" list, but cite it in the text as follows:

(B. Spatt, personal communication, April 25, 2002)

NUMBERED BIBLIOGRAPHY

In this method, used primarily in the abstract and engineering sciences, you number each entry in your bibliography. Then, each citation in your essay consists of only the number of the work that you are referring to, placed in parentheses. Remember to include the page number if you quote from your source.

Theorem 2 of Joel, Shier, and Stein (2) is strengthened in the following theorem:

The following would be a consequence of the conjecture of McMullen and Shepher (3, p. 133):

Depending on your subject, you arrange your bibliography in alphabetical order (biology or mathematics) or in the order in which you cite the sources in your essay (chemistry, engineering, or physics). Consult your instructor or a style sheet that contains the specific rules for your discipline.

ENDNOTE/FOOTNOTE DOCUMENTATION

Until a few decades ago, documentation for most research essays was provided by *footnotes* or *endnotes*. In this system, a sequence of numbers in your essay is keyed to a series of separate notes containing publication information, which appear either at the bottom of the pages where the numbers appear (footnotes) or on a separate page at the end of the essay (endnotes). It also often includes a bibliography at the end of the essay. Many authors still use footnotes or endnotes, and some of your instructors may ask you to use this system of documentation.

This brief excerpt from a biographical essay about Ernest Hemingway shows you what the endnote/footnote system looks like.

Hemingway's zest for life extended to women also. His wandering heart seemed only to be exceeded by an even more appreciative eye.[6] Hadley was aware of her husband's flirtations and of his facility with women.[7] Yet, she had no idea that something was going on between Hemingway and Pauline Pfeiffer, a fashion editor for Vogue magazine.[8] She was also unaware that Hemingway delayed his return to Schruns from a business trip to New York, in February 1926, so that he might spend some more time with this "new and strange girl."[9]

[6]Ernest Hemingway, A Moveable Feast (New York: Scribner's, 1964) 102.

[7]Alice Hunt Sokoloff, Hadley: The First Mrs. Hemingway (New York: Dodd, Mead, 1973) 84.

[8]Carlos Baker, Ernest Hemingway: A Life Story (New York: Scribner's, 1969) 159.

[9]Hemingway 210. Also Baker 165.

If your instructor asks you to use endnotes or footnotes, do not put parenthetical source references, as in MLA or APA style, anywhere within the text of the essay. Instead, at each place where you would insert a parenthetical reference, put a number to indicate to your reader that there is a corresponding footnote or endnote.

When inserting the numbers, follow these rules:

- The note number is raised slightly above the line of your essay. Many word processing programs have provision for various styles of documentation, including inserting footnotes/endnotes. If yours does not, leave two spaces in the line and insert the number neatly by hand in the first space, slightly above the line, once the essay is finished.

- The notes are numbered consecutively: if you have twenty-six notes in your essay, the number of the last one should be 26. There is no such thing as "12a." If "12a" appears at the last moment, then it becomes "13," and the remainder of the notes should be renumbered.

- Every note should contain at least one separate piece of information. Never write a note that states only, "See footnote 3." The reader should be told enough to make it unnecessary to consult footnote 3.

- While a note may contain more than one piece of information (for example, the source reference as well as some additional explanation of the point that is being documented), the note should have only one number. Under no circumstances should two note numbers be placed together, like this: [6,7].

Unless your instructor specifies otherwise, use endnotes rather than footnotes and include a bibliography.

The *format of the bibliography* is the same as the "Works Cited" format for parenthetical documentation that was described in Chapter 5 and Chapter 8: the sources are alphabetized by last name, with the second and subsequent lines of each entry indented. The entries themselves are the same as the forms for MLA bibliographical entries listed at the beginning of this appendix. The bibliography starts on a new page following the list of endnotes, or following the essay if you are using footnotes.

The *format of the notes* resembles the bibliography entries in reverse: the first line of the note is indented five spaces, with the second and subsequent lines flush with the left margin. The note begins with a raised number, corresponding to the number in the text of the essay; the author's name is in first name/last name order; author and title are separated by commas, not periods; publication information is placed in parentheses; and the note ends with the page reference and a period.

Start the list of endnotes on a new page after the text of the essay, numbering it (and any subsequent pages) in sequence with the rest of the pages. Center the title *Notes* one inch from the top of the page, double space, and begin the first entry. Double space both within entries and between entries.

Here is a list of seven notes, illustrating some of the most common forms, followed by a bibliography consisting of the same seven sources:

NOTES

[1]Helen Block Lewis, Psychic War in Men and Women (New York: New York UP, 1976) 43.

[2]Gertrude Himmelfarb, "Observations on Humanism and History," in The Philosophy of the Curriculum, ed. Sidney Hook (Buffalo: Prometheus, 1975) 85.

[3]Harvey G. Cox, "Moral Reasoning and the Humanities," Liberal Education 71.3 (1985): 196.

[4]Lauro Martines, "Mastering the Matriarch," Times Literary Supplement 1 Feb. 1985: 113.

[5]Carolyn See, "Collaboration with a Daughter: The Rewards and Cost," New York Times 19 June 1986, late ed.: C2.

[6]Andrew R. Heinze, "Jews and American Popular Psychology: Reconsidering the Protestant Paradigm of Popular Thought," The Journal of American History 88.3 (2001), 14 Feb. 2002 <http://www.historycooperative.org/journals/jah/88.3/heinze.html>.

[7]Paul Crawford, "Crusaders as Cannibals," Home page, 31 Aug. 2000, 4 May 2001 <http://ukans.edu/medieval/melcher/matthias/t68/0058/html>.

WORKS CITED

Cox, Harvey G. "Moral Reasoning and the Humanities." Liberal Education 71.3 (1985): 195–204.

Crawford, Paul. "Crusaders as Cannibals." Home page. 31 Aug. 2000. 4 May 2001 <http://ukans.edu/medieval/melcher/matthias/t68/0058/html>.

Heinze, Andrew R., "Jews and American Popular Psychology: Reconsidering the Protestant Paradigm of Popular Thought." The Journal of American History 88.3 (2001): 57 pars. 14 Feb. 2002 <http://www.historycooperative.org/journals/jah/88.3/heinze.html>.

Himmelfarb, Gertrude. "Observations on Humanism and History." In The Philosophy of the Curriculum. Ed. Sidney Hook. Buffalo: Prometheus, 1975. 81–88.

Lewis, Helen Block. Psychic War in Men and Women. New York: New York UP, 1976.

Martines, Lauro. "Mastering the Matriarch." Times Literary Supplement 1 Feb. 1985: 113.

See, Carolyn. "Collaboration with a Daughter: The Rewards and Cost." New York Times 19 June 1986, late ed.: C2.

Another kind of endnote or footnote, known as the *short form*, should be used when you are citing the same source more than once in your essay. The first time you cite a new source, you use the long form, as illustrated above, which contains detailed information about publication history. The second time you cite the same source, and all subsequent times, you write a separate note, with a new number, but now you use a shorter form, consisting of the author's name and a page number:

⁶Lewis 74.

The short form can be used here because there is already a long-form entry for Lewis on record in a previous note. If your bibliography contained two works by Lewis, then you would have to include an abbreviated title in the short form of the note:

⁶Lewis, Psychic War 74.

The short form makes it unnecessary to use any Latin abbreviations, like *ibid.* or *op. cit.*, in your notes.

For an example of the use of endnote documentation in a full-length essay, see "Why Is Eating People Wrong?" in Chapter 9. For advice about using footnotes rather than endnotes, and for more examples and guidelines for kinds of sources not illustrated above, see the fifth edition of the *MLA Handbook for Writers of Research Papers* (1999).

NOTES PLUS PAGE NUMBERS IN THE TEXT

If you are using only one or two sources in your essay, it is a good idea to include one footnote at the first reference and, thereafter, cite the page number of the source in the text of your essay.

For example, if your essay is exclusively about Sigmund Freud's *Civilization and Its Discontents*, document your first reference to the work with a complete note, citing the edition that you are using:

*Sigmund Freud, Civilization and Its Discontents (Garden City:

Doubleday, 1958) 72. All further citations refer to this edition.

This single note explains to your reader that you are intending to use the same edition whenever you cite this source. All subsequent references to this book will be followed by the page reference, in parentheses, usually at the end of your sentence.

Freud has asserted that "the greatest obstacle to civilization [is] the

constitutional tendency in men to aggression against one another . . . " (101).

This method is most useful in essays on literary topics when you are focusing on a single author, without citing secondary sources.

Interviewing and Field Research

As well as the books, articles, films, videos, and other research materials available at your library, personal interviews and field research can provide worthwhile information for your research essay. A well-conducted interview with an expert in the field, if it is carefully focused on your topic, can give you information unavailable from any other source. A personal interview can also enrich your essay with details, based on actual experience, that will capture and hold your audience's interest. Similarly, your own observation of an event or environment can be a source of valuable information. Through close observation of the river flowing past a sewage treatment plant or of the behavior of people during a political demonstration, you can collect data to support your thesis, to supplement the texts you have read, and to suggest alternative interpretations of the issues and ideas developed in your essay.

As you progress through your college's general education curriculum, you will probably find that some professional fields and academic disciplines, such as literature or history, depend most on library research, while others, such as sociology or science, often call for direct observation and interviewing by the researcher. For many of the topics that you explore across the curriculum, your essays will benefit from a combination of both library and personal investigation.

INTERVIEWING

Sources for Interviews

You will want to interview experts or authorities who are both knowledgeable and appropriate sources of information about your specific topic. First, consider the faculty on your campus, not only as direct sources of information but as sources of referrals to other experts in the field at nearby colleges and universities. If your general topic is the Holocaust, for example, you may want to interview a faculty member with that specialization in your college's history, sociology, or Judaic studies department. You may, in fact, come across the names of appropriate faculty at your college in the course of your library research.

An entirely different source of direct information is a person who has had personal experience with some aspect of your essay topic. As you talk about your research on the Holocaust, one of your friends might tell you about an aunt living nearby, someone who, for example, survived the concentration camps at Auschwitz. That woman's recollections can be just as appropriate and important an addition to your essay as a professor's more theoretical comments, lending it human drama or highlighting a particular issue that interests you.

Some essays can be enhanced by interviewing several sources. For example, if you were preparing a report on an environmental issue in your town—let's say, the purity of its water supply—you would want to learn about the impact of the new sewage treatment plant on the local environment. Of course, you would want to talk to the plant's manager; but you might also consult the managers of local businesses to determine some of the economic implications, and to some public health officials to learn about the kinds of health hazards the plant is intended to avoid. In this case, a single source would not cover the possible spectrum of responses.

Interviews can be time-consuming, and direct information derived from interviews will probably have to be combined with notes taken from your reading. You need to know in advance what kinds of interview will be most useful and appropriate—if any—and, thus, not waste your time and that of your source.

Planning an Interview

Whether in person or on the telephone, interviews require careful planning and preparation. First, you have to establish a courteous and professional relationship with your subject (that is what the person you are interviewing is generally called). Most potential interview subjects will be pleased to participate in your research. Your interest enhances the value of their knowledge and experience, and they are likely to enjoy being cited as authorities and having their ideas quoted and read.

You are more likely to get someone to consent to an interview if you write or phone first to make an appointment. Arrange your appointments as soon as possible once you have focused your topic and identified candidates for interviews. Since your potential subjects are likely to have busy schedules, allow enough time to make initial contact and then to wait a week or two, if necessary, until the person has enough time to speak with you at length. This way you can avoid having your initial conversation turn into an interview before you are quite prepared for it—which can be awkward if you don't have your questions ready.

When you call or write to those whom you hope to interview, politely identify yourself; then briefly describe your topic and the special focus of your essay. Ask for an interview of 20 to 30 minutes at a later time convenient for the subject. If appropriate, mention the name of the person who suggested this source, or refer to the publication in which you saw the subject's name. Your objective is to convey your own serious interest in the topic and in your subject's knowledge of the topic. Be friendly, but professional. If someone is reluctant to be interviewed, you should retreat gracefully. At the same time, don't hesitate to ask for a referral to someone else who might be in a better position to provide helpful information.

Preparing for an Interview

Because your interview, whether in person or on the phone, will probably be brief, you need to plan in advance what you intend to say and ask so that you can use the time effectively. Careful preparation is also a compliment to your interview subjects and shows respect for their expertise.

Reviewing your research notes, make a focused list of questions in writing beforehand, tailoring them to your specific paper topic and to your source's area of knowledge. If, for example, you are going to interview the manager of a sewage treatment plant on the Hudson River about the effective removal of PCBs from the water, you don't want to use up ten minutes asking about plant management. It can be helpful to prepare a questionnaire, leaving space between the questions for you to take notes. You can use the same questionnaire, with variations, for a whole series of personal interviews.

Recording Information during an Interview

During the actual interview, you will be listening intently to your subject's responses and thinking about your next question. But as a researcher, you have another challenge. You need to take away with you a comprehensive record of the interview so that you can quote your expert accurately and cite information authoritatively. Most successful interviewers use one of two techniques to record the interview, or a combination of both: tape recording and note taking.

Tape Recording

If you plan to use a tape recorder, make sure you ask your subject's permission in advance; test the equipment beforehand (especially if it's borrowed for the occasion); and know how to operate it smoothly. Bring it to the interview with the tape already loaded in the machine, and be sure the batteries are fresh. (Bring along a second tape in case the first one jams or breaks, and carry extra batteries.) When the interview is about to begin, check again to see if your subject has any objection to your recording the conversation. Then, to avoid making your subject self-conscious, put the tape recorder in an unobtrusive place. After that, don't create a distraction by fiddling with the machine.

Note Taking

Even if you plan to tape-record the interview, come prepared to take careful notes; bring notebook and pens, as well as your list of questions or questionnaire. One way of preparing for detailed note taking—the kind that will provide you with accurate direct quotations to use in your essay—is to rehearse. Pair off with a classmate who is also preparing for an interview, and practice interviewing and note taking (including handling the tape recorder). Also review the instructions for Assignment 7 and Assignment 8 in Chapter 4 (pp. 180–181, 188–189). If your subject presents a point so well that you know you'll want to quote it, write it down rapidly but carefully, and—then and there—read it back to make sure that you have transcribed the statement correctly.

Conducting the Interview

Arrive on time (not late and not early)! Once you've been invited to sit down and your equipment is set up, *briefly* remind your subject of the essay topic and your reason for requesting the interview. Then get right down to your "script": ask each question clearly, without hurrying; be alert to recognize when the question has been fully answered (there is usually a pause); and move briskly on to the next question. Otherwise, let your subject talk freely, with minimum interruption. Remember that you are the receiver, not the provider, of information, and let your subject do almost all the talking.

Sometimes, a particular question will capture your subject's interest, and you will get a more detailed answer than you expected. Be aware of the time limit for the interview; but if you see a promising line of questioning that you didn't anticipate, and your subject seems relaxed and willing to prolong the conversation, take advantage of the opportunity and ask follow-up questions. What if your subject digresses far away from the topic of your essay? At the first opportunity, ask whether there is a time constraint. If there is, politely indicate that you have three or four more questions to ask and you hope that there will be enough time to include them.

No matter how careful your preparations, a good interview won't go exactly as you planned. You should aim to participate in a conversation, not direct an interrogation. At the end, your subject should feel that the time has passed too quickly and, ideally, offer to speak with you again, if necessary, to fill up any gaps. To maintain that good impression, be sure to send a brief note of thanks to your subject no longer than a day or two after the interview. Later on, you may want to send a copy of the completed essay.

Using Interview Sources in Your Essay

Since the purpose of the interview is to gather information (and to provide yourself with a few apt quotations), you need to have clear notes to work from as you organize your essay. If you used a tape recorder, you should transcribe the interview as soon as you can; if you took notes, you should go over them carefully, clarify confusing words, and then type a definitive version. Otherwise, you may find yourself deciphering your almost-illegible notes at a later time or searching through the entire tape to find a specific sentence that you want to quote. Transcribe the interview accurately, without embroidering or revising what your subject actually said. Keep the original notes and tapes; your instructor may want to review them along with your essay.

Working with notes from an interview is almost exactly the same as working with notes from library research. As you organize your essay (following the process described in Chapter 7), you cross-reference your notes with a list of the topics for your essay, choosing information from the interview that might be cited to support the major points in your outline. When you begin to choose quotations, you may want to review the section on "Selecting Quotations," pp. 362–363. Remember that it is the well-chosen and carefully placed source that carries authority, not the number of words quoted. Finally, document each use of material taken from your interview, whether it is ideas or words, with a parenthetical reference. (See Appendix B for the appropriate bibliographical entry.)

FIELD RESEARCH

Like interviewing, field research is a way of supplementing the material you take from texts and triggering new ideas about your topic. When you engage in field research, you are gathering information directly, acting as an observer, investigator, and evaluator within the context of an academic or professional discipline. If you are asked by your anthropology instructor to describe and analyze a family celebration as an ethnographer would, your observations of Thanksgiving dinner at home would be regarded as field research.

In many of your college courses, you will be expected to engage in field research. When, for example, the nursing program sends students to a nearby hospital for their clinical practice and asks for a weekly report on their work with patients, these students are doing field research. Other students may participate in a cooperative education program involving professional internships in preparation for potential careers; the reports these interns prepare on their work experiences are based on field research. Whatever the course, your instructor will show you how to connect your field research activities to the theories, procedures, and format characteristic of that discipline. Still, there are certain practices common to most kinds of field research that you need to know from the beginning. Let's follow that process from assignment to essay as you develop a simple topic based on field research.

Your sociology professor has suggested that, although college students like to think of themselves as unique individuals, certain patterns clearly underlie their characteristic behavior. As an example, he asserts that both male and female students prefer to work and relax with members of the opposite sex. He is asking each of you to test this hypothesis by choosing a place on campus to observe students as they go about their daily routine, keeping in mind two questions: Are there patterns one can observe in these students' behavior? What might be the significance of these patterns? If you were assigned this project, your work would fall into three stages: gathering the information, analyzing that information, and writing the essay.

Gathering Information

According to your instructor's guidelines for this essay based on field research, you will need to perform at least six separate observations for 20 to 30 minutes each at a site of your choice and, later, be prepared to hand in copies of your accumulated observation notes along with your essay. So your first important decision concerns the location for gathering information about students' behavior: the cafeteria? the library? a particular class? the student union? the college bookstore? a classroom or another place on campus where students congregate? You decide to observe students gathered at the row of benches outside Johnson Hall, the busiest classroom building, extending from the bookstore on the right to the student union building on the left; these benches also face a field where gym classes meet and the baseball team practices. Since this area is an important junction on the campus, you can assume that enough students will appear to provide basic information for your field research.

Planning the Observations

To conform to your instructor's requirements and obtain all the information you need for your essay, you should prepare for your observation sessions quickly and carefully. First, establish a schedule that will fulfill the guidelines for the assignment. Since your first class in Johnson Hall is at 11 A.M., and you are free before that, you decide to schedule your observations for the half hour before class, that is, from 10:30 to 11:00 A.M. on Monday, Wednesday, and Friday, for the next two weeks.

You will need to set aside a separate notebook for recording your observations. For each session, start a fresh page, and indicate the date and the times when you begin and end your sessions. Such specific information is what establishes your authority as a field researcher. Before your first session, consider making a diagram of the site, roughly sketching in the location of the buildings, placing the seven benches correctly, and assigning each a number.

As with interviewing, a list of prepared questions will help you to spend your time profitably. This time, however, your object is not to ask for information, but to set up a framework for your observations and, possibly, a potential structure for your essay. For this assignment, you are basically trying to find out:

- How many students are spending time at this site?
- Where are they and what are they doing?
- Do they stay for the whole observation period, or do they come and go?

Engaging in Observation

Your work consists of careful observing and precise note taking. You are not trying to write a narrative or, at this point, understand the significance of what you are seeing; you are only trying to record your subjects' activities accurately to provide notes for future reflection.

Some people may feel self-conscious to have an observer watching them closely and writing down everything they do. To avoid potential questions or confrontations, try to do your observing and note taking unobtrusively, without staring too hard at any one person. If someone asks what you are doing, be prepared to say that you are working on an assignment for a college class, that you aren't going to identify anyone by name, and that you would be grateful for the person's cooperation. As with interview subjects, you will find that most subjects of field research are sympathetic and helpful. If someone speaks to you, take advantage of the opportunity to combine observations with a little formal interviewing, and possibly gain a useful quotation for your essay. If someone objects to being included in your study, however, you should immediately turn your attention elsewhere, or move on and try again at another time.

A portion of your notes for one session might look like that shown in Figure C-1.

After a couple of sessions, you may feel that you have a general idea of the range of students' behavior at the site, so you can begin to look specifically for repeated instances of certain activities: studying together or individually, eating, relaxing. But you will need to keep an open mind and eye about what you might observe. Again as with interviewing, your subjects' behavior may not absolutely conform to your planned questions, so you may need to add new questions as the sessions progress. For example, you may not have realized until your third session that students sitting on the benches closest to the playing field are focusing on the sports activities there; from then on, you will be looking for that behavior.

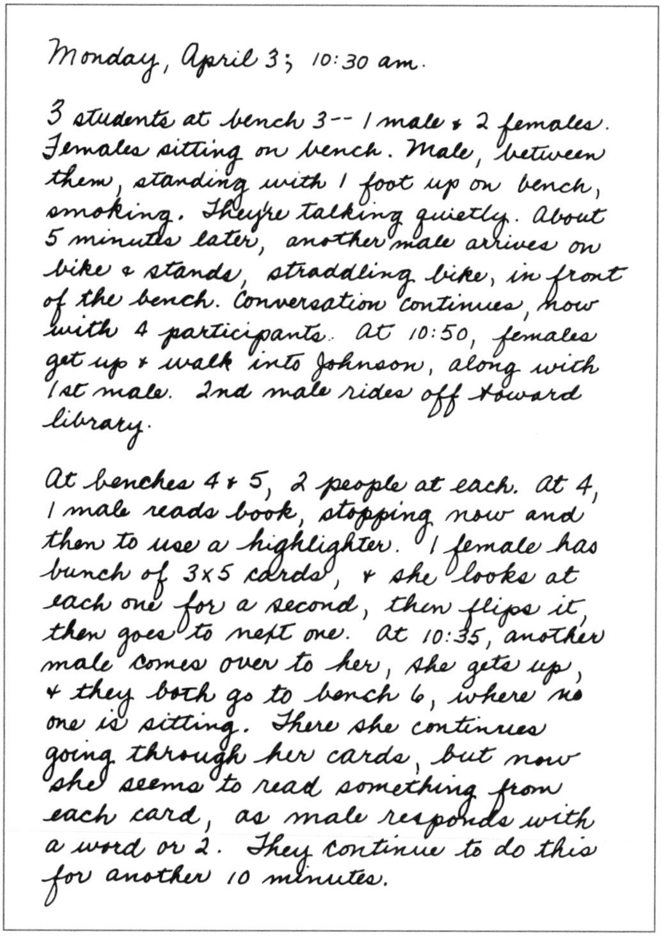

> Monday, April 3; 10:30 am.
>
> 3 students at bench 3 -- 1 male & 2 females. Females sitting on bench. Male, between them, standing with 1 foot up on bench, smoking. They're talking quietly. About 5 minutes later, another male arrives on bike & stands, straddling bike, in front of the bench. Conversation continues, now with 4 participants. At 10:50, females get up & walk into Johnson, along with 1st male. 2nd male rides off toward library.
>
> At benches 4 & 5, 2 people at each. At 4, 1 male reads book, stopping now and then to use a highlighter. 1 female has bunch of 3×5 cards, & she looks at each one for a second, then flips it, then goes to next one. At 10:35, another male comes over to her, she gets up, & they both go to bench 6, where no one is sitting. There she continues going through her cards, but now she seems to read something from each card, as male responds with a word or 2. They continue to do this for another 10 minutes.

Figure C-1

For this assignment, you would continue observing until you complete the number of observations specified; but for your own field research in a project for a course in your major field, you might conduct observations for most of a semester. As a professional researcher (like Margaret Mead when she was observing Pacific Island adolescents for her classic book *Coming of Age in Samoa*), you might even live with a tribe, studying their culture for a year or more.

Analyzing Your Information

When you have all your observations recorded, you are ready to move on to the next stage: reviewing your notes to understand what you have seen, and analyzing what you have learned. You have probably noticed that this overlaps with the previous observation stage; as you watched students in front of Johnson Hall, you were already beginning to group their activities into several categories: studying, casual conversations, watching sports, eating, sleeping.

Once you establish these categories, you pull out of your notes the specific references that match the category, noting the date and time of each instance. So now you have several new pages that look like those shown in Figure C-2.

Studying

girl and guy with flash cards 4/6 10:35
group of 5 with science notes 4/8 10:30 – 10:58
(they told me about their 11 am quiz --
all in same class)
guy with book and highlighter 4/6
10:30 – 10:45

Sports watching

observations 2, 4, 5, 6: groups of 2 – 5 guys at
benches 1, 2, 3 (facing sports field).
Groups generally talked, pointed,
laughed, while gym classes did
aerobics.

observations 4, 5: during baseball team
practice, guys in small groups
cheered, pointed; several stood up
and walked over to edge of path
that overlooks field.

female pairs watching sports
during 4, 5, but no groups.

observations 1, 2: no sports scheduled
then; few people on benches 1, 2,
and 3.

Figure C-2

You may want to chart your observations to represent at a glance such variables as these: How many students studied, or watched sports, or socialized? Which activities were associated with males or with females? If your sessions took place during different times of the day, the hour would be another variable to record on your chart.

As you identify categories, you need to ask yourself some questions to help you characterize each one and define the differences among some of your subjects' behaviors. For example: Are these differences determined by gender, as with the sports watchers, or by preferred methods of learning, like solitary or group study? As you think through the possible conclusions to be drawn from your observations, record them in your notebook, for these preliminary analyses will later become part of your essay.

Writing the Essay

An essay based on field research generally follows a format appropriate to the particular discipline. Your instructor will provide detailed guidelines and, perhaps, refer you to an article in a professional journal to use as a model. For the essay analyzing student behavior, you might present your findings according to the following outline:

Purpose: In the first section, you state the problem—the purpose of your field research—clearly indicating the question(s) you set out to investigate.

Method: Here, you explain your choice of site, the times and number of your observation sessions, and the general procedure for observation that you followed, including any exceptions to or deviations from your plan.

Observations: Next, you record the information you gathered from your observations, not as a list of random facts, but as categories or groupings that make the facts coherent to the reader. In many disciplines, this kind of information can be presented through charts, graphs, or tables.

Analysis: The heart of your essay, here is where you explain to your readers the significance of your observations. If, for example, you decided that certain activities were gender related, you would describe the basis for that distinction. Or you could discuss your conclusion that students use the benches primarily as a meeting place to socialize. Or you might make the connection between studying as the most prevalent student activity outside Johnson Hall and the scheduling of midterms during the time of your observations.

Conclusions: At the end of your essay, you remind your readers—and the instructor who is evaluating your work—that your purpose throughout has been to answer the questions and clarify the problems posed in the first paragraph. What did you discover that can illuminate your response to your professor's assertions about students' behavior?

Using Field Research

There are several important points to remember about using field research:

1. In actual practice across the curriculum, field research is usually combined with library research. As part of your investigation, you will often be asked to include in an early section of your essay a "literature search," that is, a summary of some key articles on your topic. This summary shows that you are familiar with an appropriate range of information and, especially, the major work in the field.

2. Whether you emphasize library or field research depends on the purpose and nature of your essay. If field research is integral to your topic, you will be acting as the principal investigator and interpreter of new data, and the library research will serve only as a supplement to your field research. Otherwise, you should integrate your field research into your essay as you would any other source of information.

3. For field research, careful documentation is especially important since you are asking your reader to trust the data that you yourself have gathered and upon which your speculations and conclusions are based. You can create this trust by making careful and repeated observations, recording them in detail and accurately, and presenting them in a clear and logical manner.

4. The methods of analyzing data obtained through field research are, in most cases, specific to particular disciplines. So you should indicate to your readers, by reference to authorities or models, that you are observing the conventions of the field you are working in. It is especially important that, after consultation with your instructor, you use the appropriate method of documenting both your field research and your library research, so that a reader can clearly distinguish the work of the previous investigators who are your secondary sources from your own primary contributions.

Appendix D

Writing Essay Examinations

Instructors give essay examinations for three reasons:

- To make sure that you have read and understood the assigned reading;
- To test your analytical skills;
- To find out if you can integrate what you have read with the ideas and information that you have learned in lectures and class discussion.

Since your instructor is usually not trying to test your memory, essay examinations are often open-book, allowing you to refer freely to the source. But in any exam, even a take-home assignment, there is likely to be some time pressure. To prepare, you should have read all the material carefully in advance and outlined, underlined, or annotated the text.

READING THE QUESTION

You determine your strategy by carefully examining the wording of the question before you begin to plan and write your essay. First, you must accept that someone else is providing the topic for your essay. The person who wrote the question wants to pinpoint a single area to be explored, and so you may have very little scope. However restrictive it may seem, you must stay within the boundaries of the question. If you are instructed to focus on only a small section of the text, summarizing the entire work from beginning to end is inappropriate. If you are asked to discuss an issue that is raised frequently throughout the work, paraphrasing a single paragraph or page is pointless. Do not include extraneous information just to demonstrate how much you know. Most teachers are more impressed with aptness and conciseness than with length.

The controlling verb of the question will usually provide you with a key. Different verbs will require different approaches. You are already familiar with the most common terms:

summarize; state; list; outline; condense; cite reasons

What is sometimes forgotten under pressure is that you are expected to carry out the instructions literally. *Summarize* means condense: the reader expects a short but complete account of the specified subject. On the other hand, *list* should result in a sequence of short entries, somewhat disconnected, but not a fully developed series of paragraphs.

Other directions may be far broader:

describe; discuss; review; explain; show; explore; determine

Verbs like these give you a wide scope. Since they do not demand a specific strategy, be careful to stay within the set topic, so that you do not explain or review more than the readers want to know about.

Still other verbs indicate a more exact method of development, perhaps one of the strategies that you have already worked with in Assignment 5 in Chapter 3:

compare and contrast; illustrate; define; show the reasons; trace the causes; trace the effects; suggest solutions; analyze

Notice that none of the verbs so far has provided an opportunity for personal comment. You have been asked to examine the text, to demonstrate your understanding of its meaning and its implications, but you have not been asked for your opinion. However, several verbs do request commentary:

evaluate; interpret; criticize; justify; prove; disagree

Although these verbs invite a personal response, they do not give you freedom to write about whatever you choose. You are still confined to the boundaries of the set subject, and you should devote as much of your essay as possible to demonstrating your understanding of what you have read. *A brilliant essay that ignores the topic rarely earns the highest grade.* If you have worked hard to prepare for the essay, you would be foolish to ignore the question. Don't reinterpret the directions in order to write about what is easiest or what would display your abilities to best advantage or what you figured out earlier would be asked. Just answer the question.

PLANNING AND DEVELOPING THE ESSAY

Even when you have worked out what you are expected to write about, you are still not ready to start writing. Your reader will also judge the way in which your essay is constructed, so organize your thoughts before you begin to write. No elaborate outline is necessary.

Guidelines for Planning and Developing Your Essay

1. *List some of the main points that come into your head, reduce the list to a manageable number, and renumber the sequence.* This process does not take very long and it can prevent unnecessary repetition, unintentional omissions, mixed-up sequences, and overemphasis.
2. *Develop each point separately.* Don't try to say everything at the same time. Consult your list, say what is necessary about each item, and then move on to the next.
3. *Develop each point adequately.* Each reason or cause or criticism deserves convincing presentation. Unless you are asked for a list, don't just write down one sentence and rush away to the next item. You will write a more effective essay by including some support for each of your points. Do not make brief, incomplete references to ideas because you assume that the reader will know all about them. It is your responsibility to explain each one so that it makes sense by itself.
4. *Refer back to the text.* Whenever possible, demonstrate that you can cite evidence or information from the assigned reading. If you think of two possible examples or facts, one from the source and one from your own experience or knowledge, and if you haven't enough time to include both, the safe choice will come from the source. However, you must always mark the transition between your own presentation of ideas and your reference to the source by citing its title, or the name of its author, or both.

ANALYZING AN ESSAY
AND AN ESSAY QUESTION

Carefully read through George Stade's "Football—The Game of Aggression." Assume that you have previously read this essay and that you have between forty-five minutes and an hour to answer the following question:

Although he acknowledges that it can be violent, George Stade suggests that football may serve a constructive social function. Considering some of his descriptive comments about the sport, explain why football may not be as healthy for society as Stade implies.

FOOTBALL—THE GAME OF AGGRESSION
George Stade

There are many ways in which professional football is unique among sports, and as many others in which it is the fullest expression of what is at the heart of all sports. There is no other major sport so dependent upon raw force, nor any so dependent on a complex and delicate strategy; none so wide in the range of specialized functions demanded from its players; none so dependent upon the undifferentiated athletic *sine qua non,* a quickwitted body; none so primitive; none so futuristic; none so American.

Football is first of all a form of play, something one engages in instinctively and only for the sake of performing the activity in question. Among forms of play, football is a game, which means that it is built on communal needs, rather than on private evasions, like mountain climbing. Among games it is a sport; it requires athletic ability, unlike croquet. And among sports, it is one whose mode is violence and whose violence is its special glory.

In some sports—basketball, baseball, soccer—violence is occasional (and usually illegal); in others, like hockey, it is incidental; in others still, car racing, for example, it is accidental. Definitive violence football shares alone with boxing and bullfighting, among major sports. But in bullfighting a man is pitted not against another man, but against an animal, and boxing is a competition between individuals, not teams, and that makes a great difference. If shame is the proper and usual penalty for failures in sporting competitions between individuals, guilt is the consequence of failing not only oneself and one's fans, but also one's teammates. Failure in football, moreover, seems more related to a failure of courage, seems more unmanning than in any other sport outside of bullfighting. In other sports one loses a knack, is outsmarted, or is merely inferior in ability, but in football, on top of these, a player fails because he "lacks desire," or "can't take it anymore," or "hears footsteps," as his teammates will put it.

Many sports, especially those in which there is a goal to be defended, seem enactments of the games animals play under the stimulus of what ethologists, students of animal behavior, call *territory*—"the drive to gain, maintain, and defend the exclusive right to a piece of property," as Robert Ardrey puts it. The most striking symptom of this drive is aggressiveness, but among social animals, such as primates, it leads to "amity for the social partner, hostility for the territorial neighbor." The territorial instinct is closely related to whatever makes animals establish pecking orders; the tangible sign of one's status within the orders is the size and value of the territory one is able to command. Individuals fight over status, groups over *lebensraum*[1] and a bit more. These instincts, some ethologists have claimed, are behind patriotism and private property, and also, I would add, codes of honor, as among

[1] Literally, living space. The word is often most associated with the territory thought by the Nazis to be essential to Germany's political and economic security.

ancient Greeks, modern Sicilians, primitive hunters, teen-age gangs, soldiers, aristocrats, and athletes, especially football players.

The territorial basis of certain kinds of sports is closest to the surface in football, whose plays are all attempts to gain and defend property through aggression. Does this not make football *par excellence* the game of instinctual satisfactions, especially among Americans, who are notorious as violent patriots and instinctive defenders of private property? . . . Even the unusual amity, if that is the word, that exists among football players has been remarked upon. . . . And what is it that corresponds in football to the various feathers, furs, fins, gorgeous colors by means of which animals puff themselves into exaggerated gestures of masculine potency? The football player's equipment, of course. His cleats raise him an inch off the ground. Knee and thigh pads thrust the force lines of his legs forward. His pants are tight against his rump and the back of his thighs, portions of the body which the requirements of the game stuff with muscle. . . . Even the tubby guard looks slim by comparison with his shoulders, extended half a foot on each side by padding. Finally, the helmet, which from the esthetic point of view most clearly expresses the genius of the sport. Not only does the helmet make the player inches taller and give his head a size proportionate to the rest of him; it makes him anonymous, inscrutable, more serviceable as a symbol. The football player in uniform strikes the eye in a succession of gestalt[2] shifts; first a hooded phantom out of the paleolithic past of the species; then a premonition of a future of spacemen.

In sum, and I am almost serious about this, football players are to America what tragic actors were to ancient Athens and gladiators to Rome: models of perennially heroic, aggressive, violent humanity, but adapted to the social realities of the times and places that formed them.

[2]I.e., perceptual.

ANSWERING THE QUESTION

At first, you may have some difficulty determining the focus of your essay since the question includes more than one key word to help you work out your strategy. The main verb in this question is *explain*. You are being asked to account for something, to help your reader understand what may not be entirely clear. *Explain* also implies persuasion: your reader must be convinced that your explanation is valid.

- If the question asked you to explain *something that is confusing* in Stade's essay, your task would be to provide an interpretive summary of some part of the text. For example, you might have been asked to explain the differences, with illustrations, between violence that is occasional, incidental, and accidental, discussing the implications of these distinctions for sports in general.

- If the question asked you to explain *some related point that Stade omits* from his discussion, your task would be to extend his reasoning, perhaps to discuss causes or effects, or to contrast and compare. For example, you might have to explain why football lends itself to a greater degree of violence than other sports, or explain the parallel between the way football players and animals defend their territory.

- If the question asked you—as it does—to *evaluate the author's reasoning* in forming his conclusions, you would then examine Stade's "almost serious" conclusions and demonstrate—explain—the limitations of his arguments and examples; in other words, argue against his position.

The essay question raises the point that Stade may have underestimated the harmful effects of football, a sport so violent that it could undermine the social benefits that it otherwise provides. To answer the question, then, you must accept the assumption that Stade may be overenthusiastic about football, *whether or not you agree,* and proceed to point out the implications and the shortcomings of his analysis. In a sense, writing a good essay depends on your willingness to allow your views to be shaped by the examiner's, at least for the duration of the exam.

The question defines the *limits* as well as the strategy of your essay. It does not permit you to dispute Stade on grounds that are entirely of your choosing. You are firmly instructed to focus your attention on the conflict between violence and social benefit. It would be foolish to ignore these instructions and write only about the glories of football or to condemn the sport for reasons unrelated to the violence of its play.

What should you be evaluating in your essay, and how many comments are "some"? Stade makes the following points in support of his view that football can be a useful social ritual:

- It fosters individual strength and determination.

- It develops cooperation and teamwork.

- It teaches players how to acquire and defend territory and thus encourages nationalism and the patriotic defense of one's country.

- It provides players and spectators with the opportunity to act out their aggressions in a controlled and relatively harmless way.

These points should certainly be on the list of paragraph topics that you jot down as you plan your essay. Since these ideas are embedded within the paragraphs of Stade's essay, you should use your own ordering principle—least violent to most (potentially) violent might be a good choice. Each of your paragraphs should begin with a description of one characteristic of the sport as Stade presents it, followed by your own explanation of the social disadvantages or benefits that might result.

Resist the temptation to devote too much space to a single aspect of the sport. For example, if you spend too much time discussing Stade's comments about uniforms and the extent to which the football player is magnified and dehumanized by his padding and his helmet, you may not be able to develop your discussion of whether football encourages patriotism or a more divisive and dangerous nationalism. Stade's essay is based on his belief that people participate in sports as a way of expressing passions and impulses that have no place in our normal daily occupations. He implies that, if this outlet is eliminated, our instincts for violence may spill over into activities where they would be far more dangerous. This argument has often been used to justify violence as depicted on television and in the movies. While you are not expected to analyze the issue with the expertise of a trained psychologist or sociologist, your essay should reflect your awareness of and your views on Stade's conception of football as a way of controlling our aggressive instincts.

INTRODUCING YOUR TOPIC

Examination essays, like all essays, require an introduction. Before beginning to explore some of the issues inherent in George Stade's analysis, you should provide a short introduction that defines the author's topic and your own. Your later references to his ideas will need a well-established context; therefore, try to define Stade's conception of football (which might differ from someone else's) right at the outset of your essay. Although the introduction need not be longer than two or three sentences, *cite your source*—the name of the author and the name of the essay, both properly spelled—and state exactly what it is that you and your author are concerned about. To demonstrate the frustration of reading an introduction that is shrouded in mystery, look at the first paragraph from a student essay answering the question that has just been analyzed:

> The attitude of the author of this essay is highly supportive of a sport that may be the most violent in the world. It is true that players acquire a lot of skills and learn about teamwork, as well as receiving huge sums of money and becoming public idols. However, there are also risks and dangers that result, for spectators and those watching on television, as well as for those on the field wearing team uniforms, which he fails to point out in this brief essay.

"He," of course, is George Stade, and the sport under discussion is football. The student had read and understood the source essay, but is so eager to begin commenting on Stade's ideas that she fails to establish a context for her arguments. Here is a more informative introduction:

> In "Football--The Game of Aggression," George Stade presents the game of football as a necessary evil and a useful social ritual. He does not deny that the game, more than most sports, is based on a potentially lethal kind of aggression. But, contrasting football with other sports, he finds that it also encourages a sense of teamwork and an instinct for patriotism, which can be valuable both to

the individual and to society. Left unclear is whether ritualizing violence through sports does, in fact, result in a less violent society, or whether watching football players maul each other in weekly combat only encourages spectators to imitate their heroes.

PRESENTING YOUR ESSAY TO THE READER

Students often choose to divide their time into three parts. For example, if you have forty minutes during which to write an essay, try the following timetable:

- ten minutes to analyze the question and plan a strategy
- twenty minutes to write the essay
- ten minutes to proofread and correct it

During in-class examinations, students often waste vital minutes by painstakingly transcribing a new copy from their rough drafts. While *your handwriting must be legible,* it is not necessary to hand in a clean copy. Teachers expect an exam essay to have sentences crossed out and words inserted. They are used to seeing arrows used to reverse sentences and numbers used to change the sequence of paragraphs. It makes no sense to write the last word of your first draft and then, without checking what you have written, immediately take a clean sheet of paper and start transcribing a copy to hand in. Because transcription is such a mechanical task, the mind tends to wander and the pen makes errors that were not in the original draft. Take time to proofread your essay, to locate grammatical errors, and to fill in gaps in continuity. As long as your corrections and changes are fairly neat and clear, your instructor will not mind reading the first draft and will probably be pleased by your efforts to improve your writing.

Readings for a Research Essay

The essays in this appendix are sources for you to work with if your instructor asks you to write a research essay based on Assignment 13 (pp. 364–365). These ten readings could form the entire bibliography for your research essay. Or (with your instructor's permission) you may wish to supplement these essays with additional sources of your own choosing.

Caplan, Arthur L. "What's Wrong with Eugenics?" *Am I My Brother's Keeper?* Bloomington: Indiana UP, 1997.

Dreger, Alice. "When Medicine Goes Too Far in the Pursuit of Normality." *New York Times*, 28 July 1998.

Gosden, Roger. "Well-born." *Designing Babies*. New York: Freeman, 1999.

Harris, John. "Clones, Genes, and Human Rights." *The Genetic Revolution and Human Rights*. Ed. Justine Burley and Richard Dawkins. New York: Oxford UP, 1999.

Kitcher, Philip. "Inescapable Eugenics." *The Lives to Come*. New York: Touchstone Books, 1996.

Lewin, Tamar. "Boom in Gene Testing Raises Questions on Sharing Results." *New York Times* 21 July 2000.

Rifkin, Jeremy. "A Eugenic Civilization." *The Biotech Century*. New York: Penguin Putnam, 1998.

Rothman, Barbara Katz. "On Order." *Clones and Cloning.* Ed. Martha C. Nussbaum and Cass R. Sunstein. New York: Norton, 1998.

Silver, Lee M. "The Virtual Child." *Remaking Eden.* New York: Avon, 1997.

Wilson, James Q. "The Paradox of Cloning." *Ethics of Human Cloning.* New York: HarperCollins/AEI Press, 1998.

WELL-BORN
from *Designing Babies*
Roger Gosden

Victorian Britain boasted an Empire on which the sun never set and that depended on vigorous administration and military firmness. It was a country that had been used to winning, but, toward the end of the century, it began to suffer a number of humiliating setbacks with nationalist struggles in the Indian subcontinent and the African colonies. In the Sudan, the Mahdi had boxed in General Gordon and taken Khartoum; in South Africa, the Zulu nation, armed under Cetshwayo only with spears, inflicted several humiliating defeats on British troops. When the Boer Wars began, the nation was lamenting the fact that as many as one in three of the men who were screened for military service had to be rejected as medically unfit. The decimation of Britain's youth in World War I compounded the national pessimism, and it was feared that with only the unfit left for the girls back home to marry, the next generation would be even feebler than the last.   1

These anxieties were given a gloss of scientific respectability by reference to Darwinian theory. Forty years after the death of the great biologist, evolution by natural selection was widely accepted and carried intellectual gravitas. Charles Darwin had shown in *On the Origin of Species* that each generation of animals produces more offspring than needed to maintain the population so that competition for food and breeding partners caused a "struggle for existence." Only individuals that were best fitted to the conditions would survive. Darwin realized that our species had shrugged off natural selection but hesitated to apply any conclusions from nature to human society, voicing his apprehensions only occasionally: "We civilized men . . . do our utmost to check the process of elimination; we institute poor-laws; and our medical men exert their utmost skill to save the life of every one to the last moment. . . . Thus the weak members of civilized societies propagate their kind. No one who has attended to the breeding of domestic animals will doubt that this must be highly injurious to the race of man." He mainly kept his head below the parapet on these matters, but his younger cousin, Sir Francis Galton, had no misgivings about standing up and airing his opinions.   2

Galton was a polymath who took in his stride pioneering research on weather maps, fingerprint identification, twinning, and quantitative biology. Today, he is mainly remembered for studying human inheritance and for coining a word that would   3 haunt the next century—"eugenics," from the Greek meaning "well-born." Galton regarded eugenics as a corollary to evolutionary theory, for "natural selection rests upon excessive production and wholesale destruction; eugenics on bringing no more individuals into the world than can properly be cared for, *and those only of the best stock.*" Rooted in evolutionary theory, eugenics sounded intellectually respectable and, with its goal of improving the well-being of the population, seemed socially responsible, too. But the eugenics movement, which started in biology, ended up— to its lasting shame—as ideology.

Believing that cream should be permitted to rise to the top, Galton encouraged families to enter competitions for the prettiest and brightest-looking baby. He also studied the pedigrees of famous men to discover the secret of high achievers and, in his book *Hereditary Genius* reached the conclusion that "if a twentieth part of the cost and pains were spent in measures for the improvement of the human race that is spent on the improvement of the breed of horses and cattle, what a galaxy of genius might we not create." On a darker and more practical note, he advocated "the hindrance of marriages and the production of offspring by the exceptionally unfit"—what we now call "negative eugenics." He urged people to act responsibly in matters of reproduction, as in everything else. but it was not long before others were suggesting compulsory sterilization and abortion for people too feckless or ignorant to care about the public interest. Had Galton been able to envision the future course of science, he would have applauded the genetic screening of parents and fetuses and the creation of sperm banks for superintelligent donors. The repair of genetic faults and "enhancement" of babies—"positive eugenics"—were undreamed of in his day, but they became the ultimate goal for his successors, who urged that technology should seek to effect a destiny that evolutionary selection was always too blind and slow to reach.

In the 1600s—long before eugenics and Darwinism—the Reverend Robert Burton of Oxford expressed similar thoughts: "It is the greatest part of our felicity to be well born, and it were happy for humankind if only such parents as are sound of body and mind should be suffered to marry." Making babies was never regarded as just a private matter; it was held to be a function of the social organism. Burton went on in a pessimistic vein to say that "in giving way for all to marry that will, too much liberty and indulgence in tolerating all sorts, there is a vast confusion of hereditary diseases, no family secure, no man free from some grievous infirmity." Blame for the ills of society has often been laid at the door of vulnerable or minority groups, and long before the advent of "scientific" eugenics it was tempting to suggest that relieving them of their reproductive liberty was the remedy. Historical precedents seemed to point to the selection of the fittest as a formula for a successful society. I remember being taught at school that asceticism and social responsibility were responsible for the military glory of Sparta: parents were forced to abandon weak boys at birth, and when the survivors reached a certain age, they were thrown into a pit full of water to let nature decide who was fit enough to become a citizen of that supposedly virtuous state. Galton and his successors, who received plenty of instruction in the classics, no doubt impressed by the achievements of ancient societies, were full of hope for what science could do for theirs.

After Galton died in 1911 and World War I was over, others carried forward the eugenics banner, and in England none with greater passion than Marie Stopes, the redoubtable family planning crusader. She traveled up and down the country setting up women's health clinics, appealing to working women for reproductive restraint, and berating the dysgenic effects of war. She declared that it was in women's interests to have no more than two or three children and worried that those who demonstrated most enthusiasm for birth control were the educated elite and gentry.

6

Concerns about being overwhelmed by inferior stock soon spread from Britain to continental Europe and America, where eugenics was vigorously taken up and introduced into the academic curriculum of many universities. Fears were fanned that the "original" American stock was being diluted by mass immigration of aliens from southern European countries. Bowing to trade union pressure and pandering to public prejudice, President Coolidge enacted legislation in 1924 to restrict the numbers entering the country. In referring to people with learning difficulties and physical disabilities, the National Conference on Race Betterment had menacingly warned a few years previously that "in prolonging lives of defectives we are tampering with the functioning of the social kidneys." The climate was emerging for eugenic laws in many states to authorize compulsory sterilization and abortion, and thousands of U.S. citizens went under the knife over the two decades after World War I. People who were judged ill-equipped mentally or physically to produce children were the targets; they were more often females than males. No matter how convincingly the opponents argued against social Darwinism—and some came from the nation's top universities—rhetoric won the day.

7

In Britain, a national review committee was established in the 1930s, and although eugenic legislation failed to make it into the statute books, poor and illegitimate children were still being sent into isolation and virtual servitude in Australia right up to the 1950s, signaling their low value in the eyes of the nation that bore them. There has recently been publicity about the sterilization laws in liberal democracies. Some of the laws established before World War II in Scandinavian countries and Switzerland were not repealed until the early 1970s. In one of the Swiss cases of the 1940s, and typical of many, a young woman was forced to have an abortion at two months of pregnancy and then to be sterilized because she was deemed by the investigators to be "feeble-minded, morally weak, idiotic, and promiscuous." It is discreditable that so many years after eugenics had been relegated to the scrap heap by biologists such laws were still being used to exercise prejudice. Unsurprisingly, some of the victims still alive today are now seeking compensation.

8

In Germany, however, events took an even more ugly turn. The Swiss law of 1928 in the canton of Vaud was fashioned into the law for Prevention of Hereditary Disease in Posterity in July 1933, when the Nazi Party came to power. A campaign for

9

racial hygiene began with the purpose of eliminating birth defects. Doctors who were members of the Nazi Party presided over genetic health courts, and although few had much, if any, formal training in genetics, they pronounced over cases of deformity, schizophrenia, and mental retardation; men and women who were deemed unworthy to contribute their genes to the next generation were sterilized or euthanized.

INESCAPABLE EUGENICS
from *The Lives to Come*
Philip Kitcher

For over two centuries, first British colonial officials and later the Indian government have struggled to stamp out the practice of female infanticide in rural villages of Northern India. Bound by the caste system, families view daughters as an economic burden and until recently have resorted to crude methods of freeing themselves from such expensive chattels. Baby girls have been killed at birth, usually through asphyxiation or drowning, and even those who are permitted to survive suffer abuse, neglect, and markedly higher mortality rates than their brothers. The arrival of more advanced medical techniques, including amniocentesis, has brought a more humane option. Pregnant women can discover the sex of the fetus and choose to terminate the pregnancy if they find they are carrying a female; in some regions of Northern India, dramatically skewed sex ratios at birth reveal that this has become a popular strategy.

It couldn't happen here, of course—or so you might suppose. Western societies are not governed by prejudices masquerading as religious doctrine, and though progress toward the acceptance of women as equals in the affluent world has been unsteady, imperfect, and incomplete, widespread prenatal testing would probably not issue in *dramatically* unbalanced sex ratios. (Whether it would lead to a preponderance of two-child families, with elder brother and younger sister, is a further question.) But we should not congratulate ourselves too quickly, for we have preferences aplenty. Unlike Caesar, many people do not want to surround themselves with those who are fat. Even people who think it barbaric to persecute homosexuals are often disappointed to discover that a child is gay or lesbian, a fact reflected in the difficulty homosexuals frequently find in telling parents of their sexual orientation. And in many socioeconomic strata in meritocracies, where brains are taken to be key to at least modest levels of security and success, fathers and mothers hope fervently that their children will obtain an average score (or better) on the tests that are supposed to measure intelligence. Genes indicating low IQ or same-sex preference will be very hard to find—and may not exist—but researchers already claim to have found genetic causes of obesity. Although sex selection may be improbable in Western societies, ten years hence prospective parents sharing the attitudes now common may terminate pregnancies because tests disclose the

1

2

presence of fetal genes indicating obesity, or perhaps genes that are suspected (quite possibly incorrectly) of causing homosexuality or low intelligence.

We have traveled roads like this before. The history of eugenics in Western societies offers a succession of prospects, some whimsical, most dismal, many tragic. Little harm was done by the eugenic exhibits at American state and county fairs, in which proud examples of prize human stock paraded before their neighbors, adorned with ribbons though presumably not decorated with rings through their noses or bells on their toes. Some of the work done at the former Eugenics Record Office at Cold Spring Harbor on Long Island, now transformed into one of the world's major centers in molecular genetics, bears a similar aura of dizziness. Convinced that the large number of naval officers in some families pointed to a hereditary yen for the sea, Charles Davenport, founding director of the Record Office, earnestly sought the allele for what he called "thalassophilia" (literally "love of the sea"), which he took to be a sex-linked recessive expressed only in males.

Most early-twentieth-century eugenic projects had far darker effects. Davenport's office also amassed studies to show the genetic inferiority and undesirability of the peoples from Eastern and Southern Europe. Congress responded by trumpeting the need for racial purity, and quickly transformed rhetoric into action. In 1924 a new Immigration Act greatly restricted the number of people who could enter the United States from the "undesirable" parts of Europe. Combining official immigration policy with the use of intelligence tests, tests whose cultural biases appear dumbfounding in retrospect, Henry Goddard, who pioneered the idea of screening for intelligence at Ellis Island, succeeded in returning to Europe thousands who would be destroyed by totalitarian regimes.

American obsessions with genetic purity were not simply directed at resisting corruption from without. It was also considered important to extirpate the putrescence of homegrown genetic infections spread by the shiftless and degenerate members of the population who often bred in far greater numbers than their respectable (middle-class, white, Protestant) counterparts. In the 1920s eugenicists publicly lamented the relatively low birthrates of graduates from elite universities. Determined to prevent America from being overrun with "the feebleminded," they campaigned for compulsory sterilization laws and won partial victories through legislation to "treat" the inmates of institutions in many states. Even during the 1940s and 1950s, sterilization was sometimes made a condition of discharge from mental hospitals and prisons.

By then, of course, knowledge of Nazi eugenic practices had caused changes in attitude, not only in those countries (such as Britain) in which eugenic pronouncements had not issued in social policy, but also in America. Beginning in 1933, Hitler had introduced compulsory sterilization on a far grander scale than anything enacted elsewhere, using it as the first instrument in the promotion of "race biology." Other tools followed, and by 1939 the Nazis were using more direct means to eliminate those they judged biologically inferior—people diagnosed as suffering from mental disorders, homosexuals, Gypsies, and Jews. Both the brutality of the methods and the patent attempt to portray social prejudice as objective biology appalled the world. "Eugenics" became a term tightly associated with Hitler's profoundly evil practices, a word with so powerful a stigma that it can instantly stop debate.

So when it is suggested that contemporary molecular biology will inevitably contribute to a revival of eugenics, the implications seem clear: We should have none of it. Genetic testing appears benign when it focuses on reducing the incidence of those rare but terrible diseases that afflict children with massive disruptions of development and early death. . . . Children born with Hurler syndrome show decelerated development toward the end of their first year. They typically deteriorate, growing abnormally and losing cognitive functions, and virtually all die before they are ten years old. Children with Sanfilippo syndrome may survive longer, but they are severely retarded, and their aggressive behavior is frequently difficult to manage. Unlike Hurler children, who are usually "placid and lovable," Sanfilippo patients may be wild and unreachable even when in the most tender and informed care. Many surely find the ability to predict these syndromes liberating, enabling prospective parents to prevent the inexorable decay of the Hurler child or the incomprehensible ferocity of children with Sanfilippo syndrome. Yet for at least some readers of the history of eugenics, these are the first steps on the road to a dreadful destination. In this view, once we begin thinking in terms of "innate defects," social pressures will expand the category of genetic deficiencies, and we shall end by cloaking injustice and prejudice in professions of biology, less monstrously than Hitler, or even than Davenport, but nonetheless harmfully enough.

Others harbor different fears. They are moved by fictional portrayals of individuals and societies who meddle with life and who try to shape people according to some distorted vision of the good. They see contemporary molecular biology as moving towards Baron Frankenstein's laboratory or the Central London Hatchery of *Brave New World.* Today we undertake timid ventures in prenatal testing and gene replacement; tomorrow we shall dispassionately design children and "decant" them into a ruthlessly planned world that has lost its humanity.

Because fine-grained genetic engineering is still remote and may be impossible, fear of Frankenstein is easier to dismiss than anxieties about repeating the errors of our eugenic past. At present, indeed for the foreseeable future, we cannot select *for* the human traits we deem desirable, shaping people according to our ideals, but we can select *against,* terminating those pregnancies in which fetuses bear unwanted alleles. Northern Indians already do it in a very particular way. Members of affluent societies will soon have the opportunity on a large scale. No doubt, initially, they will be moved by concern for the misery associated with the most devastating diseases—but where will they stop?

Eugenics was officially born in the writings of Charles Darwin's cousin, Francis   10
Galton, who campaigned for applying knowledge of heredity to shape the characteristics of future generations. In retrospect, we can recognize the new theoretical
science as a mixture of a study of heredity and some doctrines about the value of
human lives. Galton's approach to studying inheritance, by looking for statistical
features of the transmission of phenotypes, was original and was discarded by the
growing number of his eugenic descendants who embraced Mendelian genetics.
With characteristic Victorian confidence, however, Galton did not offer a critical discussion of the values underlying his judgments about proper and defective births.
Assuming that his readers would agree about the characteristics that should be
promoted, he set about the business of promoting them.

Separated from Galton by over a century, we can see how eugenic judgments have   11
mixed science with the values of dominant groups and also how the prejudices
have been so powerful as to distort scientific conclusions: Men with a mania for
eradicating "feeblemindedness" convinced themselves that there must be genes to
be found and duly "found" them. A fundamental objection to eugenics challenges
the presupposition that there is *any* system of values that can properly be brought
to bear on decisions about genetic worth. Galton's Olympian confidence that he
could decide which lives would best be avoided easily provokes the reaction that we
should abandon the pretense of being able to judge for others. People with severe
disabilities who have attended workshops for human geneticists sometimes pose the
question forcefully in words, sometimes even more vividly in their presence and
determination: Who are you to decide if I should live?

Yet even as we admire those who have overcome extraordinary adversity to   12
make rewarding lives for themselves, we should remember the dreadful clarity of
some examples of genetic disease. Those who watch the inevitable decay of children
born with Hurler syndrome or Canavan's disease, those who see the anguish of parents as they care for children whose genes prevent development beyond the abilities of an infant have no difficulty in deciding that similar sufferings should be
avoided. In the spring of 1994, at a public discussion of the impact of the Human
Genome Project in Washington, D.C., a man in late middle age protested the tendency to see only the problems of the Project, relating how his daughter had given
birth to two children with neurofibromatosis. His tone, not his words, conveyed the
grief of his family as well as his conviction that abstract fears of eugenic consequences should not block attempts to spare others similar agonies.

As a theoretical discipline, eugenics responds to our convictions that it is irre-   13
sponsible not to do what can be done to prevent deep human suffering, yet it must
face the challenge of showing that its claims about the values of lives are not the
arrogant judgments of an elite group. Of course, if eugenics were *simply* a theoretical discipline, pursued by Galton's successors in their studies, there would be little
fuss. Precisely because some are concerned about a revival of eugenic *practices,*
while others fear that the label "eugenics" will be misapplied to humane and re-

sponsible attempts to eliminate pain and grief, questions about the eugenic implications of contemporary molecular biology have more than academic interest. Unless we look past the swastika and achieve a clearer picture of eugenics in action,
these important questions will prove irresolvable.

Exactly when are people practicing eugenics? The Nazi doctors, the Americans   14
worried about "racial degeneracy," would-be social reformers like Sidney Webb and
George Bernard Shaw, and peasant families in Northern India, do not agree on very
much, but all of them hope to modify the frequency with which various character-
isitics are present in future populations. Eugenic practice begins with an intention to
affect the kinds of people who will be born.

Translating that intention into social action requires four types of important de-   15
cision. First, eugenic engineers must select a group of people whose reproductive
activities are to make the difference to future generations. Next, they have to determine whether these people will make their own reproductive decisions or
whether they will be compelled to follow some centrally imposed policy. Third, they
need to pick out certain characteristics whose frequency is to be increased or diminished. Finally, they must draw on some body of scientific information that is to be
used in achieving their ends. Practical eugenics is not a single thing. Human history already shows a variety of social actions involving four quite separate components, each of which demands separate evaluation.

Introducing contemporary molecular biology into prenatal testing will lead us   16
to engage in *some* form of eugenics, but that consequence, by itself, does not settle
very much. For it is overwhelmingly obvious that some varieties are far worse than
others. Greater evils seem to be introduced if we move in particular directions with
respect to the four components: More discrimination in the first, more coercion
in the second, focusing on traits bound up with social prejudices in the third, using
inaccurate scientific information in the fourth. Unsurprisingly, Nazi eugenics was just
as bad as we can imagine with respect to each component. The Nazis discriminated among particular populations for their reproductive efforts, selecting the
"purest Aryans" for positive programs, using "special treatment" on groups of "un-
desirables." Starting with compulsory sterilization, they proceeded to the ultimate
form of coercion in the gas chambers. The repeated comparison between Jews
and vermin and the absurd—but monstrous—warnings about the threats to Nordic
"racial health" display the extent to which prejudice pervaded their division of human characteristics. Minor, by comparison, is the fact that much of their genetics was
mistaken.

Scientific inaccuracies infect other past eugenic practices in ways that appear   17
more crucial. Henry Goddard's efforts to keep America pure led him to administer intelligence tests to newly arriving immigrants; even the staunchest contemporary advocate of IQ would have difficulty defending Goddard's assumption that his
tests measured "innate hereditary tendencies." Those cast up at the foot of the

Statue of Liberty found that their inability to produce facts about the recent history of baseball indicated their lack of native wit. Likewise, decisions to sterilize the inmates of state institutions often rested on abysmally poor evidence. Carrie Buck and her sister Doris were victims of the zeal to dam up the feebleminded flood, and it was Carrie's case that provoked one of the most chilling lines in the history of Supreme Court decisions. In 1927, finding in favor of the lower court decision in *Buck* v. *Bell*, Justice Oliver Wendell Holmes pronounced that "three generations of imbeciles are enough."

The three generations of imbeciles were three members of the Buck family. Carrie Buck's mother had been diagnosed as "feebleminded," Carrie herself had been placed in the Virginia Colony for Epileptics and Feebleminded; on the basis of a Stanford-Binet intelligence test, she was assigned a mental age of nine. The third generation consisted of her illegitimate daughter, Vivian, seven months old at the time that the original decision for sterilization was made. Because a Red Cross worker thought that she had "a look" about her and a member of the Eugenics Record Office claimed, on the basis of a test for infants, that she had below-average intelligence, Vivian too was classified as feebleminded. Three generations of feeblemindedness demonstrated that the defect was hereditary.   18

At least the classifications of Carrie Buck and Vivian were quite erroneous. Vivian died while still a young child, but she had completed second grade and had impressed her teachers. In 1980, when she was in her seventies, Carrie Buck was rediscovered and was visited by doctors and scholars concerned with the history of sterilization laws. They found an ordinary woman who read the newspaper daily and who tackled crossword puzzles. The central figure in the tragic story was no "imbecile," not even according to the technical criterion which eugenic enthusiasts employed to grade the feebleminded (imbeciles were adults with a mental age between six and nine).   19

Failure to distinguish the components of eugenic practice blurs our vision of the injustices that have been done. What is the real moral of the case of Carrie Buck? Not simply that the judgment was mistaken, that Carrie and her sister Doris, both of whom were sterilized, did not carry genes for "feeblemindedness." Besides the scientific error, the practice of compulsory sterilization also destroyed something fundamental to people's lives. Even if Carrie, Doris, and Vivian had borne genes that set limits to their mental development, should they have been forced to give up all hopes of bearing children? Like the Nazis, albeit on a far smaller scale. American eugenicists carried out a coercive practice: They compelled some individuals to follow a social policy that was divorced from any aspirations that those who were treated may have had. Doris lived outside the asylum, married, and tried to have children. Only much later did she understand what had been done to her.   20

The brutal compulsion of the Nazi eugenics program prompted an important change in postwar efforts to apply genetic knowledge. Everyone is now to be her   21 (or his) own eugenicist, taking advantage of the available genetic tests to make the reproductive decisions she (he) thinks correct. If genetic counseling, practiced either on the limited scale of recent decades or in the much more wide-ranging fashion that we can anticipate in the decades to come, is a form of eugenics, then it is surely *laissez-faire* eugenics. In principle, if not in actuality, prenatal testing is equally available to all members of the societies that invest resources in genetic counseling. Ideally, citizens are not coerced but make up their own minds, evaluating objective scientific information in light of their own values and goals. Moreover, the extensive successes of molecular genetics inspire confidence that our information about the facts of heredity is far more accurate than that applied by the early eugenicists. As for the traits that people attempt to promote or avoid, that is surely their own business, and within the limits of available knowledge, individuals may do as they see fit. Laissez-faire eugenics, the "eugenics" already in place and likely to become ever more prominent in years to come, is a very different form of eugenics from the endeavors of Davenport, Goddard, and Hitler's medical minions.

22   Identifying the gulf between laissez-faire eugenics and the horrors that underlie the stereotype makes room for discussing the important questions surrounding applications of molecular genetics but does not resolve them. Banning prenatal tests by tagging them with the ugly name "eugenics" should not substitute for careful thought about their proper scope and limits. Everything depends on the *kind* of eugenics we practice.

23   We know that some genetic conditions cause their bearers to lead painful or truncated lives in all the environments that we know how to arrange for them. We know also how to identify, before a fetus is sentient, whether or not the fetus carries one of those conditions. Naively, we might try to avoid the smear of eugenics by insisting that nobody should use this information for selective abortions—we shall not interfere with the genetic composition of future populations. But once we have the option of intervening, this allegedly "noneugenic" decision shares important features with eugenic practices. Tacitly, it makes a value judgment to the effect that *unplanned* populations are preferable to *planned* populations. More overtly, it imposes a bar on decisions that individuals might have wished to make, depriving them of the chance to avoid great future suffering by terminating pregnancies in which fetuses are found to carry genes for Sanfilippo syndrome, neurofibromatosis, or any of a host of similarly devastating disorders. When we know how to shape future generations, the character of our descendants will reflect our decisions and the values that those decisions embody. For even if we compel one another to do nothing, that is to judge it preferable not to intervene in the procreation of human life, even to subordinate individual freedom to the goal of "letting what will be, be."

24   Molecular knowledge pitches us into some form of eugenic practice, and laissez-faire eugenics looks initially like an acceptable species. Yet its character deserves a closer look.

The most attractive feature of laissez-faire eugenics is its attempt to honor indi-   25
vidual reproductive freedom. Does it succeed? Are the resources of prenatal testing in affluent societies equally open to all members of the population? Do they help
people to make reproductive decisions that are genuinely their own? And is that
really a proper goal? Since individual reproductive decisions have aggregate consequences for the composition of the population, should there not be restrictions
to avoid potentially disastrous effects? Finally, because individual decisions may
be morally misguided—as with those who would select on the basis of sex—will
laissez-faire eugenics foster evil on a grand scale?

WHAT'S WRONG WITH EUGENICS?
from *Am I My Brother's Keeper?*
Arthur Caplan

Arguments that are commonly made against the morality of trying to design per-   1
fect children fall roughly into three categories. One set of arguments is that coercion or a lack of choice on the part of parents in the choice of the traits of their
children or in any area of reproductive choice is unacceptable. Thus the Nazi dream
of perfecting a super race of perfect Aryans by eliminating the unfit, the handi-
capped, and those seen as genetically inferior is ethically repugnant because the government forcibly imposes its vision of perfection by force, sterilization, or murder.
In the case of the Nazis their desire to increase the health of future generations was
tied to the killing of those identified as less than perfect, along with coercive marriage and breeding for those believed to have desirable traits.

Some who find the pursuit of perfection objectionable on moral grounds are   2
worried about more than coercion. They note that it is simply not clear which traits
or attributes are properly perceived as perfect or optimal. The decision about
what trait or behavior is good or healthy depends upon the environment and circumstances that a child will face. To pick traits, features, or attributes in the abstract
is to simply reify prejudice into a strategy for the creation of optimality.

These arguments, while of grave concern in light of the history of abuse and geno-   3
cide tragically manifest throughout this century, are not ultimately persuasive as
the basis for prohibiting reproduction in the service of perfection. For the objections focus not on the desirability of perfection but on the means used to achieve
this goal or uncertainty about what traits fulfill it.

Certainly it is morally objectionable to allow governments or institutions to com-   4
pel or coerce persons into having children. The right to reproduce without interference from third parties is one of the fundamental freedoms recognized by
international law and moral theories from a host of ethical traditions. It is also
morally wrong to allow the state to impose its vision of the future by force. However, the goal of obtaining perfection or pursuing health with respect to reproduc-

tion is not made objectionable by these arguments. What is morally wrong is coercion or compulsion or arbitrariness with respect to reproductive decisions. . . .

As for the objection that decisions about perfection are more a matter of taste   5
and prejudice than they are value judgments rooted in solid empirical evidence,
that is, in many instances, true. Decisions to produce tall children or those who have
blue eyes are merely reflections of cultural or social preferences rather than objective properties having anything to do with disease or health. But there are certain
traits, such as physical stamina, strength, speed, mathematical ability, dexterity, and
acuity of vision, which are related to health in ways that command universal assent
in almost any cultural or social setting imaginable. It would be hard to argue that a
parent who wanted a child with better memory or greater physical dexterity was
simply indulging his or her biases or prejudices. As long as no coercion or force is
used to compel persons to make choices about their children that are in conformity with particular visions of what is good or bad, healthy or unhealthy, there would
seem to be enough consensus about the relationship between certain physical and
mental attributes and health to permit parents to choose certain traits, features,
and capacities for their unborn children in the name of their health.

Moreover, it is not even necessary to achieve consensus about what is objec-   6
tively good in order to allow parents to pursue a goal of genetic enhancement to
improve the lot of their offspring. Parents might concede that their vision of perfection is to some degree subjective but still insist upon the right to pursue their
own values. Since we accept this point of view with respect to child rearing, allowing parents to teach their children religious values, hobbies, and customs as they
see fit, it would be difficult to reject it as overly subjective when matters turn to
the selection of a genetic endowment for one's child.

Some maintain that efforts to genetically design children by picking embryos, by   7
genetic engineering, or by controlling the use of gametes are morally wrong because
they limit what the child can become. Imposing a parent's wishes on a child when
a parent picks the height, aptitudes or appearance of the child is not something
the child can do anything about.

To object to efforts to perfect kids on the basis of diminished malleability is not   8
persuasive. Kids have no choice in their parents as it is, and it is hard to believe
that it is more just to ask a child to accept the random luck of reproduction rather
than sincere efforts to improve their lot. Given the latitude that parents have to
shape and mold their children, restrictions on parental choice of biological makeup
would ease doubt on the morality of the entire practice of parenting as it is now
known in all contemporary societies.

A second set of objections commonly raised against trying to achieve perfec-   9
tion hinges on concerns about slippery slopes of various types. . . . Some observers
worry that any opening of the door to permit parents to pick the traits of their children will lead inevitably to the government's forcing its vision of perfection upon
anyone who wants to have children. But this argument has problems as well. It

flies in the face of a number of facts about the pursuit of perfection in other areas of health care.

For many years, cosmetic surgeons, psychoanalysts, and sports medicine special- 10 ists have been plying their trades without any slope having developed in society to the effect that those with big noses or poor posture must visit specialists and have these traits altered. Some choose to avail themselves of these specialists in the pursuit of perfection. Most do not. If there is a slope from permitting individual choice of one's child's traits to limiting the choices available to parents, it is a slope that does not start with individual choice. And if there is a problem of a slope, then it must be shown why it is morally permissible to seek perfection after one is born but why such efforts would also be wrong if engaged in prenatally.

It is certainly true that twentieth-century history is full of instances of genocide, 11 mass murder, and ethnic cleansing. These are, nevertheless, problems of politics, government, and ideology. There is nothing inherent in the decision to indulge one's preferences about the traits of one's child that is morally wrong as long as those preferences do nothing to hurt or impair the child. If there are slippery slope problems that confound the morality of eugenics, they lie in the flaws of politics, not in the desire to have a "better" baby.

A third set of objections to allowing eugenic desires to influence parenting is 12 that it will lead to fundamental social inequalities. Allowing parental choice about the genetic makeup of their children may lead to the creation of a genetic "over-class" that has unfair advantages over those whose parents did not or could not afford to endow them with the right biological dispositions and traits. Or it may lead to too much homogenization in society where diversity and difference disappear in a rush to produce only perfect people, leaving anyone with the slightest disabil-ity or deficiency at a distinct disadvantage.

Equity and fairness are certainly important concepts in societies that are com- 13 mitted to the equality of opportunity for all citizens. However, a belief that everyone deserves a fair chance may mean that society must do what it can to ensure that the means to implementing eugenic choices are available to all who desire them. It may also mean that a strong obligation exists to compensate for any differences in biological endowment with special programs and educational opportunities. In a world that tolerates so much inequity in the circumstances under which children are brought into being, it would be hard to argue that there was something more of-fensive or more morally problematic about biological advantages as opposed to social and economic advantages. And in a world that gives large numbers of privi-leged persons the right to pursue the best education for their children in situa-tions and contexts that may well produce homogeneity in the end results, it would also be difficult to argue that the pursuit of perfection or enhancement at the cost of homogeneity should be allowed when the intervention is environmental but not when it is biological. . . .

While force and coercion, compulsion and threat, have no place in procreative 14
choice, it is not so clear that it is any less ethical to allow parents to pick the eye
color of their child or to create a fetus with a propensity for mathematics than it
is to permit them to teach their child the values of a particular religion, to incul-
cate a love of sports by taking the child to games and exhibitions, or to require
the child to play the piano.

If there is an argument to be made against eugenics, it would seem to be most 15
persuasive against group or population eugenics. Efforts to shift the composition
of the gene pool would seem to require or be more prone to slip toward the imposition of a vision by government or other powerful institutions. Insofar as coercion and force are absent and individual choice is allowed to hold sway, then,
presuming fairness in access to the means of enhancing our offspring, it is hard to
see what is wrong with trying to create better babies.

THE VIRTUAL CHILD
from *Remaking Eden*
Lee Silver

In its original connotation, eugenics referred to the idea that a society might be 1
able to improve its gene pool by exerting control over the breeding practices of
its citizens. In America, early twentieth-century attempts to put this idea into practice brought about the forced sterilization of people deemed genetically inferior
because of (supposed) reduced intelligence, minor physical disabilities, or possession
of a (supposed) criminal character. And further "protection of the American gene
pool" was endeavored by congressional enactment of harsh immigration policies
aimed at restricting the influx of people from Eastern and Southern Europe—
regions seen as harboring populations (which included all four grandparents of
the author of this book) with undesirable genes. Two decades later, Nazi Germany
used an even more drastic approach in its attempt to eliminate—in a single generation—those who carried undesirable genes. In the aftermath of World War II,
all of these misguided attempts to practice eugenics were rightly repudiated as discriminatory, murderous, and infringing upon the natural right of human beings to
reproductive liberty. *Eugenics* was now clearly a dirty word.

While eugenics was defined originally in terms of a lofty *outcome*—the improve- 2
ment of a society's gene pool—its contemporary usage has fallen to the level of a
process. In its new meaning, eugenics is the notion of human beings exerting control over the genes that are transmitted from one generation to the next—irrespective of whether the action itself could have any effect on the gene pool, and
irrespective of whether it's society as a whole or an individual family that exerts
the control. According to this definition, the practice of embryo screening is clearly

eugenics. Since eugenics is horrible, it follows logically that embryo screening is horrible.

Although the fallacy in this logic is transparent, it is remarkable how often it is used by contemporary commentators to criticize reprogenetic technologies. A recent book entitled *The Quest for Perfection: The Drive to Breed Better Human Beings* uses this theme over and over again to castigate one reproductive practice after another. But simply placing a eugenics label on something does not make it wrong. The Nazi eugenics program was wrong not only because it was mass murder, but also because it was an attempt at genocide. The forced sterilizations in America were wrong because they restricted the reproductive liberties of innocent people. And restrictive immigration policies directed against particular regions of the world are still wrong because they are designed to discriminate directly against particular ethnic groups. Clearly, none of these wrongs can be applied to the voluntary practice of embryo screening by a pair of potential parents. . . .

When embryo selection is equated with choosing children, there is a palpable sense of revulsion. It is not hard to understand this feeling. Often in the past, and in some places still, genetic choice is exercised through infanticide. The particular choice made most often in some Third World countries is boy babies over girl babies, who are suffocated or drowned soon after birth. In other societies, it is infants with physical disabilities that are most often killed.

But the analogy of embryo screening to infanticide is a false one. What embryo screening provides is the ability to select genotypes, not children. Today, parents can use the technology to make sure that their *one* child—whom they had always planned on bringing into the world—is not afflicted with Tay-Sachs.

Even in the future, when it becomes possible to draw computer images based on genetic profiles, embryos will still not be *real* children. Virtual children exist only in one's mind, and the consummation of an actual fertilization event is not even a prerequisite for their creation. Once genetic profiles have been obtained for any man and any woman, it becomes possible to determine the virtual gametes that each might produce. Each combination of a virtual male gamete and a virtual female gamete will produce a virtual child. . . .

[That it is wrong to tamper with the natural order is a concern] expressed by many who are not particularly religious in the traditional sense. Still, they feel that there is some predetermined goal for the evolution of humankind, and that this goal can only be achieved by the current *random* process through which our genes are transmitted to our children. However, unfettered evolution is never predetermined, and not necessarily associated with progress—it is simply a response to unpredictable environmental changes. If the asteroid that hit our planet 60 million years ago had flown past instead, there would never have been any human beings at all. And whatever the natural order might be, it is not necessarily good. The smallpox virus was part of the natural order until it was forced into extinction by human intervention. I doubt that anyone mourns its demise.

The purpose of medicine is to prevent suffering and heal those with disease. Based on this definition, it is clear that embryo selection could be put to uses that lie far outside this scope. But medical doctors have used their knowledge and skills to work in other nonmedical areas such as nontherapeutic cosmetic surgery. If we accept the right of medical doctors to enter into nonmedical business practices, we have to accept their right to develop private programs of embryo selection as well.

One could argue that since the embryo screening technology was developed with the use of government funds, it should only be used for societally approved purposes. But government funds have been used in the development of nearly all forms of modern technology, both medical and nonmedical. This association has never been viewed as a reason for restricting the use of any other technology in private profit-making ventures.

Many prospective parents choose not to learn the sex of their child before birth, even when it is known to their physician through prenatal testing. There is the feeling that this choice allows the moment of birth to be one of parental discovery. If a child's characteristics were pre-determined in many more ways than just sex, many fear that the sense of awe associated with birth would disappear. For some, this may be true. But this is a personal concern that could play a role in whether an individual couple chooses embryo selection for themselves. It can't be used as a rationale to stop others whose feelings are different.

If embryo selection were available to all people in the world and there was general acceptance of its use, then the gene pool might indeed be affected very quickly. The first result would be the almost-complete elimination of a whole host of common alleles with lethal consequences such as Tay-Sachs, sickle cell anemia, and cystic fibrosis.

There are some who argue that it would be wrong to eliminate these alleles, or others, because they might provide *a hidden advantage to the gene pool*. This is another version of the "natural order" argument, based here on the idea that even alleles with deleterious effects in isolated individuals exist because they provide some benefit to the species as a whole. Those who make this argument believe that all members of a species somehow function together in genetic terms.

This point of view has no basis in reality. It results from a misunderstanding of what the gene pool is, and why we should, or should not, care about it. The concept of the gene pool was invented as a tool for developing mathematical models by biologists who study populations of animals or plants. It is calculated as the frequencies with which particular alleles at particular genes occur across all of the members of a population that interbreed with each other.

Most healthy individuals are not carriers of the Tay-Sachs or cystic fibrosis   14 alleles, and if given the choice, I doubt if anyone would want to have his or her genome changed to become a carrier. So on what basis can we insist that others receive a genotype that we've rejected? There is none. Genes do not function in human populations (except in a virtual sense imagined by biologists), they function within individuals. And there is no species-wide knowledge or storage of particular alleles for use in future generations.

In fact, there is not even a tendency or rationale for a species to preserve itself   15 at all. At each stage throughout the evolution of our ancestors—from rodentlike mammals to apelike primates to *Australopithecus* to *Homo habilis* to *Homo erectus* and, finally, *Homo sapiens*—small groups of individuals gained genetic advantages that allowed them to survive even as they participated in the death of the species from which they arose! Survival and evolution operate at the level of the individual, not the species.

There are some who are not concerned about abstract concepts like the gene   16 pool and evolution so much as they are worried that the genetic elimination of mental illness (an unlikely possibility) would prevent the birth of future Ernest Hemingways and Edgar Allan Poes. This worry is based on the demonstrated association between manic depression (also known as bipolar affective disorder) and creative genius.

This could indeed be a future loss for society. But once again, how can we insist   17 that others be inflicted with a predisposition to mental disease (one we wouldn't want ourselves) on the chance that a brilliant work of art would emerge? And if particular aberrant mental states are deemed beneficial to society, the use of hallucinogenic or other types of psychoactive drugs that could achieve the same effect—in timed doses—would seem preferable to mutant genes. It is also important to point out that the perceived loss of mad genius from future society is virtual, not real. If the manic depressive Edgar Allan Poe were never born, we wouldn't miss *The Raven*. Likewise, we don't miss all of the additional piano concertos that Mozart would have composed if he hadn't died at the age of thirty-four.

With the use of embryo selection, prospective parents will be able to ensure   18 that their children are born without a variety of non-life-threatening disabilities. These will include a wide range of physical impediments, as well as physiological disabilities (such as deafness or blindness) and learning disabilities.

Many people with hereditary disabilities have overcome adversity to live long   19 and fruitful lives. These people are concerned that the widespread acceptance of embryo selection against their disabilities could reinforce the attitude that they are not full-fledged members of society.

Of course, disabilities can result from either genetic or environmental factors. And one common environmental cause of disability in the past was the polio virus, which resulted in paralysis, muscular atrophy, and often physical deformity. Inoculation of children with the polio vaccine was not generally seen as discriminatory against those who were already disabled. Why should genetic inoculation against disability be viewed any differently? 20

One difference could be in the access of society's members to the inoculation. The polio vaccine was provided to all children, regardless of class or socioeconomic status, while embryo selection may only be available to those families who can afford it. The philosopher Philip Kilcher suggests that as a consequence, "the genetic conditions the affluent are concerned to avoid will be far more common among the poor—they will become 'lower-class' diseases, other people's problems. Interest in finding methods of treatment or for providing supportive environments for those born with the diseases may well wane." 21

This is a serious concern. But it is important to point out that the privileged class already reduces the likelihood of childhood disabilities through their superior ability to control the environment within which a fetus and child develops. People who argue that embryo selection should *not* be used to prevent serious childhood disabilities because it's unfair to those families who are unable to afford the technology should logically want to ban access of the privileged class to environmental advantages provided to their children as well. Political systems based on this premise have not fared well at the end of the twentieth century. 22

The alternative method for preventing inequality is referred to as "utopian eugenics" by Kitcher and is based on the vision of George Bernard Shaw of a society in which all citizens have free and equal access to the same disease-preventing technologies (and environments). Although discrimination would not be based on class differences in this utopian society, it could still be aggravated by the overall reduction in the number of disabled persons. 23

It's important to understand the nature of the relationship that might exist between embryo selection and discrimination against the disabled. Embryo selection will not itself be the cause of discrimination, just as the polio vaccine could not be blamed for discrimination against those afflicted with polio. All it could do, perhaps, is change people's attitudes toward those less fortunate than themselves. An enlightened society would not allow this to happen. Is it proper to blame a technology in advance for the projected moral shortcomings of an unenlightened, future society? 24

I distinguished embryo selection from abhorrent eugenic policies of the past with the claim that embryo selection would be freely employed in Western society by prospective parents who were not beholden to the will of the state. As a consequence, the use of the technology would not be associated with any restrictions on reproductive liberty. 25

There are social science critics who say that this claim is naive. They fear that   26
societal acceptance of embryo selection will lead inevitably to its use in a coercive
manner. Coercion can be both subtle and direct. Subtle pressures will exist in the
form of societal norms that discourage the birth of children deemed unfit in some
way. More direct pressures will come from insurance companies or state regulations
that limit health coverage only to children who were embryonically screened for the
absence of particular disease and predisposition genotypes.

How coercion of this type is viewed depends on the political sensibilities of the   27
viewer. Civil libertarians tend to see any type of coercion as an infringement on
reproductive rights. And liberal libertarians would be strongly opposed to policies
that discriminated against those born with avoidable medical conditions.

Communitarians, however, may view the refusal to preselect against such med-   28
ical conditions as inherently selfish. According to this point of view, such refusal
would—by necessity—force society to help the unfortunate children through the
expenditure of large amounts of resources and money that would otherwise be
available to promote the welfare of many more people.

The communitarian viewpoint is considered shocking to many in America today   29
because, as Diane Paul says, "the notion that individual desires should sometimes
be subordinated to a larger social good has itself gone out of fashion, to be replaced by an ethic of radical individualism." Embryo selection is currently used by
a tiny fraction of prospective parents to screen for a tiny number of disease genotypes. For the moment, its influence on society is nonexistent. In fact, there are many
critics who think that far too much attention is devoted to a biomedical "novelty
item" with no relevance as a solution to any of the problems faced by the world. But
with each coming year, the power of the technology will expand, and its application will become more efficient. Slowly but surely, embryo selection will be incorporated into American culture, just as other reproductive technologies have been in
the past. And sooner or later, people will be forced to consider its impact on the society within which they live.

The nature of that impact will depend as much on the political *status quo* and   30
social norms of the future as they do on the power of the technology itself. In a
utopian society of the kind imagined by George Bernard Shaw, all citizens would
have access to the technology, all would have the chance to benefit from it, but
none would be forced to use it. In this vision of utopia, embryo selection would take
an entire society down the same path, wherever it might lead. Unfortunately, if future protocols of embryo selection remain in any way similar to those used now, the
technology will remain prohibitively expensive, and utopian access would bankrupt
a country.

A different scenario emerges if Americans hold fast to the overriding impor-   31
tance of personal liberty and personal fortune in guiding what individuals are allowed and able to do. The first effects on society will be small. Affluent parents
will have children who are less prone to disease, and even more likely to succeed (on

average) than they might have been otherwise as a simple consequence of the affluent environment within which they are raised. But with each generation, the fruits of selection will accumulate. . . .

It is impossible to predict the cumulative outcome of generation upon generation of embryo selection, but some things seem likely. The already-wide gap between the rich and the poor could grow even larger as well-off parents provide their children not only with the best education that money can buy, and the best overall environment that money can buy, but the "best cumulative set of genes" as well. Emotional stability, long-term happiness, inborn talents, increased creativity, and healthy bodies—these could be the starting points chosen for the children of the rich. Obesity, heart disease, hypertension, alcoholism, mental illness, and predispositions to cancer—these will be the diseases left to drift randomly among the families of the underclass.

But before we rush to ban the use of embryo selection by the privileged, we must carefully consider the grounds on which such a ban would be based. Is this future scenario different—in more than degree—from a present in which embryo selection plays no role at all? If it is within the rights of parents to spend $100,000 for an exclusive private school education, why is it not also within their rights to spend the same amount of money to make sure that a child inherits a particular set of their genes? Environment and genes stand side by side. Both contribute to a child's chances for achievement and success in life, although neither guarantees it. If we allow money to buy an advantage in one, the claim for stopping the other is hard to make, especially in a society that gives women the right to abort for any reason at all.

These logical arguments have been tossed aside in some countries like Germany, Norway, Austria, and Switzerland, as well as states like Louisiana, Maine, Minnesota, New Hampshire, and Pennsylvania, where recently passed laws seem to prohibit the use of embryo selection for any purpose whatsoever. In these countries and states, no distinction is made between the prevention of Tay-Sachs disease and selection in favor of so-called positive traits.

But if the short history of surrogacy is any guide, all such attempts to limit this technology will be doomed to failure. Many Tay-Sachs–carrying parents will surely feel that it is their "God-given" right to have access to a technology that allowed earlier couples to have nonafflicted children and just as surely, there will always be a clinic in some open state or country that will accommodate their wishes. And if the technology is available for this one purpose, it will also be available for others.

It certainly does seem that embryo selection will be with us forever—whether we like it or not—as a powerful tool to be used by more and more parents to choose which of their genes to give to their children. But as we shall now see, the power of this tool pales in comparison to what becomes possible when people gain the ability to choose not only from among their own genes, but from any gene that one can imagine, whether or not it already exists.

A EUGENIC CIVILIZATION
from *The Biotech Century*
Jeremy Rifkin

In the coming decades, scientists will learn more about how genes function. They will become increasingly adept at turning genes "on" and "off." They will become more sophisticated in the techniques of recombining genes and altering genetic codes. At every step of the way, conscious decisions will have to be made as to which kinds of permanent changes in the biological codes of life are worth pursuing and which are not. A society and civilization steeped in "engineering" the gene pool of the planet cannot possibly hope to escape the kind of ongoing eugenics decisions that go hand in hand with each new advance in biotechnology. There will be enormous social pressure to conform with the underlying logic of genetic engineering, especially when it comes to its human applications.

Parents in the Biotech Century will be increasingly forced to decide whether to take their chances with the traditional genetic lottery and use their own unaltered eggs and sperm knowing their children may inherit some "undesirable" traits, or undergo corrective gene changes on their sperm, eggs, embryos, or fetus, or substitute egg or sperm from a donor through *in vitro* fertilization and surrogacy arrangements. If they choose to go with the traditional approach and let genetic fate determine their child's biological destiny, they could find themselves culpable if something goes dreadfully wrong in the developing fetus, something they could have avoided had they availed themselves of corrective genetic intervention at the sex cell or embryo stage.

Consider the following scenario. Two parents decide not to genetically "program" their fetus. The child is born with a deadly genetic disease and dies prematurely and needlessly. The genetic trait responsible for the disease could have been deleted from the fertilized egg by simple gene surgery. In the Biotech Century, parents' failure to correct genetic defects *in utero* may well be regarded as a heinous crime. Society could conclude that every parent has a responsibility to provide as safe and secure an environment as humanly possible for their unborn child. Not to do so might be considered a breach of parental duty for which the parents could be held morally, if not legally, liable. Mothers have already been held liable for having given birth to crack cocaine–addicted babies and babies with fetal alcohol syndrome. Prosecutors have argued that mothers passing on these painful addictions to their unborn children are culpable under existing child abuse statutes, and ought to be held liable for the effect of their lifestyle on their babies.

Even more ominously, "wrongful life" and "wrongful birth" lawsuits have begun to appear in the United States. More than three hundred such cases have made their way through the courts. In the case of "wrongful birth" lawsuits, parents of a seriously ill or disabled child sue their physician or hospital claiming the child should never have been born. The lawsuits charge negligence on the part of the health provider for not advising parents of a potential health problem with their unborn, and of not making available information on screening procedures which could have been performed and whose results could have been used to make an informed decision on whether or not to abort the fetus. In "wrongful life" lawsuits, the claim is brought on behalf of the child or by the child, claiming that he or she should never have been born. While the current spate of lawsuits are aimed at attending physicians, it's not unlikely that in the case of "wrongful life" lawsuits, children, in the future, might similarly charge their parents with negligence for not performing the appropriate screening tests or for ignoring the results of the screens and bringing the baby to term.

One of the most interesting of these suits was brought in 1975 by Paul and Shirley   5
Berman against two New Jersey doctors. The Bermans' daughter, Sharon, was born with Down syndrome. The Bermans argued that the doctors were negligent in not advising them of the desirability of undergoing amniocentesis, despite the fact that Mrs. Berman was thirty-eight years old at the time of her pregnancy, and therefore at risk of having a Down syndrome child.

The Bermans contended that had they known that they were carrying a child with   6
Down syndrome, they would have had an abortion. They filed a claim of "wrongful life," seeking compensation for the suffering the child would experience during her lifetime, as well as a claim for "wrongful birth" to compensate for their own "emotional anguish."

The New Jersey Supreme Court denied the Bermans' claim of "wrongful life,"   7
arguing that the claim was "metaphysical" in nature, and that the court could not be put in a position of judging "the difference in value between life in an impaired condition and the utter void of nonexistence." In his opinion, Justice Morris Pashman wrote, "Ultimately the infant's complaint is that she would be better off not to have been born. Man, who knows nothing of death or nothingness, cannot possibly know whether that is so." (The New Jersey Supreme Court did award the Bermans "emotional damages," however, for their "wrongful birth" claim for the "mental and emotional anguish" caused by having a child with Down syndrome.) While six states have passed laws limiting or forbidding compensation for "wrongful life" claims, several courts have recognized a child's right to bring such cases.

It is likely that as new screening technologies become more universally available,   8
and genetic surgery at the embryonic and fetal stages becomes more widely acceptable, the issue of parental responsibility will be hotly debated, both in the courts and in the legislatures. The very fact that parents will increasingly be able to intervene to ensure the health of their child before birth is likely to raise the concomitant issue of the responsibilities and obligations to their unborn children. Why shouldn't parents be held responsible for taking proper care of their unborn child? For that matter, why shouldn't parents be held liable for neglecting their child's welfare in the womb in cases where they failed to or refused to screen for and correct genetic defects that could prove harmful to their offspring?

Proponents of human genetic engineering argue that it would be cruel and irresponsible not to use this powerful new technology to eliminate serious "genetic disorders." The problem with this argument, says *The New York Times* in an editorial entitled "Whether to Make Perfect Humans," is that "there is no discernible line to be drawn between making inheritable repair of genetic defects and improving the species." The *Times* rightly points out that once scientists are able to repair genetic defects, "it will become much harder to argue against additional genes that confer desired qualities, like better health, looks or brains."

If diabetes, sickle-cell anemia, and cancer are to be prevented by altering the genetic makeup of individuals, why not proceed to other less serious "disorders": myopia, color blindness, dyslexia, obesity, left-handedness? Indeed, what is to preclude a society from deciding that a certain skin color is a disorder? In the end, why would we ever say no to any alteration of the genetic code that might enhance the well-being of our offspring? It is difficult to imagine parents rejecting genetic modifications that promised to improve, in some way, the opportunities for their progeny.

Prospective parents are already using genetic screening tests of their unborn children for purposes other than identifying debilitating diseases, suggesting that generic intervention in the womb will likely be used in the future as much for whim and enhancement as for prevention or cure of illness. In 1955, researchers announced a successful procedure for determining the sex of a child by observing cells in the amniotic fluid. The test was first used in the 1960s for pregnant women with a history of hemophilia in their family. As males are the ones generally afflicted with the disease, pregnant women could elect to abort a male fetus. With the widespread use of amniocentesis in the 1970s, screening for sex became routine and doctors began reporting women selectively aborting normal male and female fetuses as a means of ensuring sibling gender balance in their families.

Recent surveys have found increasing support for non-therapeutic "value preference" abortions. In one study, researchers reported that 11 percent of couples would abort a fetus that was predisposed to obesity. The adoption of germ line therapy in the coming years is likely to shift emphasis from abortion to enhancement as increasing numbers of parents choose to "correct" cosmetic defects in the egg, sperm, or embryonic cells to ensure the birth of the best baby that medical science can produce.

We already have a strong inkling of how far parents might be willing to go to genetically enhance their children. The introduction of genetically engineered human growth hormone (hGH) has transformed the enhancement issue from an abstract intellectual concern to a hotly debated issue over public policy. In the 1980s both the Genentech and Eli Lilly companies were awarded patents to market a new genetically engineered growth hormone to the few thousand children suffering from dwarfism in the United States. The perceived market for the hormone was considered so small that both companies were awarded "orphan" drug status. This special designation allows the drug companies a number of compensations, including a monopoly over the sale of their product for seven years, as a reward for their willingness to invest so heavily in a drug designed to have such a limited market potential. By 1991, however, genetically engineered growth hormone had far eclipsed its original market expectations, becoming one of the best-selling pharmaceutical drugs in the country. Eli Lilly and Genentech now share a market of nearly $500 million in sales, making human growth hormone one of the greatest commercial success stories in the history of the pharmaceutical industry.

Since there are so few children in the United States suffering from dwarfism, it is obvious that doctors across the country have been prescribing the hormone for normal children, who, while they may be shorter than their peers, do not suffer from a growth hormone deficit. Where parents have been reluctant to ask for the hormone, the children have begun to on their own. Many young men have found the hormone helpful in building and sustaining muscle development and have been purchasing it illegally on the black market. One survey carried out in a suburb of Chicago reported that more than 5 percent of suburban tenth-grade boys were illegally taking the drug.

Mindful that tall people generally do better in life—command higher salaries, attract more desirable mates, and enjoy other similar perks—many parents are anxious to add an additional few inches onto their children and are willing to pay the exorbitant price for the weekly injections if it will give their children a leg up on the competition.

To ensure an ever-expanding market for the genetically engineered hormone, both Genentech and Eli Lilly have mounted an aggressive public relations and marketing campaign—with the help of local physicians—to redefine normal shortness as an "illness." With the encouragement and financial support of the two drug companies, a number of researchers and pediatricians are arguing that children in the bottom 3 percent of height in their age group might be defined as abnormal and in need of growth hormone to catch up with their peers. If their assumptions become the orthodoxy among pediatricians and family physicians, genetically engineered growth hormone could be used by up to ninety thousand children born each year in the United States, with a potential market of eight to ten billion dollars in sales.

Surprisingly, the NIH has weighed in on the side of the drug companies and is currently conducting a twelve-year research project—partially funded by Eli Lilly—to assess the effect of genetically engineered human growth hormone on short-statured children who do not suffer from growth hormone deficiency but were merely born into families with shortness in their family trees. It should be pointed out that, by law, the NIH is prevented from experimenting on healthy children and exposing them to unnecessary health risks. The Foundation on Economic Trends petitioned the agency in a series of formal legal challenges designed to ferret out the Institutes' rationale for what appeared to be purely cosmetic or enhancement experiments on healthy children. Determined to find a legal justification for these precedent-setting non-therapeutic experiments, NIH argued, in the words of NIH spokesperson Micheala Richardson, "These kids are not normal. They are short in a society that looks at that unfavorably."

Even *The Journal of the American Medical Association* was forced to concede the obvious. In an editorial, the *Journal* said, "We do not usually call prejudice-induced conditions, which confer cultural disadvantages but have no intrinsic negative health effects, diseases."   18

Redefining short-statured children—who are not suffering from growth hormone deficiency—as abnormal simply because society looks unfavorably on short people punishes the victim of prejudice for not measuring up to the norms imposed by the majority. That the NIH could be party to such a flagrant and egregious violation of ethical standards speaks forcefully to the new eugenics wind blowing over the land—a eugenics motivated by the push of the marketplace and the pull of consumer desire for better, more perfect children.   19

Dr. John D. Lantos, of the Center for Clinical Medical Ethics at the University of Chicago, summed up the importance of the hGH marketing campaign in furthering a new commercially driven eugenics era. He observes,   20

> Until growth hormone came along, no one called normal shortness a disease. It's become a disease only because a manipulation [hGH] has become available and because doctors and insurance companies, in order to rationalize their actions, have had to perceive it as one. What we are seeing is two things—the commodization of drugs that are well-being enhancers and the creeping redefinition of what it means to be healthy.

The robust market for hGH as an enhancement therapy is indicative of the vast commercial potential of genetic therapies for purposes that will likely transcend strictly medical uses. According to a 1992 Harris poll, 43 percent of Americans "would approve using gene therapy to improve babies' physical characteristics." With Americans already spending billions of dollars on cosmetic surgery to improve their looks and psychotropic drugs to alter their mood and behavior, the use of generic therapies to enhance their unborn children seems a likely prospect.

Many advocates of germ line intervention are already arguing for enhancement therapy. They contend that the current debate over corrective measures to address serious illnesses is too limited and urge a more expansive discussion to include the advantage of enhancement therapy as well. As to the oft-heard criticism that genetic enhancement will favor children of the rich at the expense of children of the poor—as the rich will be the only ones capable of paying for generic enhancement of their offspring—proponents argue that the children of well-off parents have always enjoyed the advantages that wealth and inheritance confer. Is it such a leap, they ask, to want to pass along genetic gifts to their children along with material riches? Advocates ask us to consider the positive side of germ line enhancement,   21 even if it gives an advantage to the children of those who can afford the technology. "What about . . . increasing the number of talented people. Wouldn't society be better off in the long run?" asks Dr. Burke Zimmerman.

The Economist suggested in an editorial that society should move beyond old-fashioned hand-wringing moralism on the subject and openly embrace the new commercial eugenics opportunities that will soon become available in the marketplace. The editors asked,

> What of genes that might make a good body better, rather than make a bad one good? Should people be able to retrofit themselves with extra neurotransmitters, to enhance various mental powers? Or to change the color of their skin? Or to help them run faster, or lift heavier weights?

The Economist editorial board made clear that its own biases lay firmly with the marketplace. The new commercial eugenics, its editors argue, is about ensuring greater consumer freedom so that individuals can make of themselves and their heirs whatever they choose. The editorial concluded with a ringing endorsement of the new eugenics.

> The proper goal is to allow people as much choice as possible about what they do. To this end, making genes instruments of such freedom, rather than limits upon it, is a great step forward.

Dr. Robert Sinsheimer, a long-standing leader and driving force in the field of molecular biology, laid out his eugenics vision of the new man and woman of the Biotech Century:

> The old dreams of the cultural perfection of man were always sharply constrained by his inherited imperfections and limitations. . . . To foster his better traits and to curb his worse by cultural means alone has always been, while clearly not impossible, in many instances most difficult. . . . We now glimpse another route—the chance to ease the internal strains and heal the internal flaws directly, to carry on and consciously perfect far beyond our present vision this remarkable product of two billion years of evolution. . . . The old eugenics would have required a continual selection for breeding of the fit, and a culling of the unfit. . . . The horizons of the new eugenics are in principle boundless—for we should have the potential to create new genes and new qualities yet undreamed. . . . Indeed, this concept marks a turning point in the whole evolution of life. For the first time in all time, a living creature understands its origin and can undertake to design its future. Even in the ancient myths man was constrained by essence. He could not rise above his nature to chart his destiny. Today we can envision that chance—and its dark companion of awesome choice and responsibility.

While the notion of consumer choice would appear benign, the very idea of eliminating so-called genetic defects raises the troubling question of what is meant

22

23

by the term "defective." Ethicist Daniel Callahan of the Hastings Center penetrates to the core of the problem when he observes, "Behind the human horror at genetic defectiveness lurks . . . an image of the perfect human being. The very language of 'defect,' 'abnormality,' 'disease,' and 'risk' presupposes such an image, a kind of proto-type of perfection."

The all-consuming preoccupation with "defects" or "errors" among medical researchers and molecular biologists puts them very much at odds with most evolutionary biologists. When evolutionary biologists talk of "mutations," they have in mind the idea of "different 'readings' or 'versions' of a relatively stable archetype. James Watson and Francis Crick's discovery of the DNA double helix in the 1950s, however, brought with it a new set of metaphors and a new language for describing biological processes which changed the way molecular biologists perceive genetic mutations. The primary building block of life was described as a code, a set of instructions, a program, to be unraveled and read. The early molecular biologists, many of whom had been trained first as physicists, were enamored with what they regarded as the universal explanatory power of the information sciences. Norbert Wiener's cybernetic model and modern communications and information theory provided a compelling new linguistic paradigm for redefining how we talk about both physical and biological phenomena. . . . It is within the context of this new language that molecular biologists first began to talk of genetic variation as "errors" in the code rather than "mutations." The shift from the notion of genetic mutations in nature to genetic errors in codes represents a sea change in the way biologists approach their discipline, with profound implications for how we structure both our relationship to the natural world and our own human nature in the coming Biotech Century.

The significance of this shift in language became apparent to this author more than a decade ago during a debate on the future of biotechnology with the late Dr. Bernard Davis who was, at that time, chairman of the Department of Microbiology and Molecular Genetics at Harvard University. The debate took place at the annual conference of the American Association for the Advancement of Science. At one point during the discussion, the subject turned to the issue of human germ line therapy. I asked Dr. Davis if he supported the idea of using germ line therapy to eliminate the nearly four thousand or so monogenic diseases from the gene pool of the human race. His answer was an unqualified yes.

In his enthusiasm to correct the genetic programs, Davis had lost touch with the most elemental assumptions of evolutionary biology. What he perceived as errors to be fixed, more traditional biologists would view as variations on a theme— a rich reservoir of genetic diversity that is essential to maintaining the viability of a species against ever-changing environments and novel external challenges. We have learned, long ago, that recessive traits and mutations are essential players in the evolutionary schema. They are not mistakes, but rather options, some of which become opportunities. Eliminating so-called "bad" genes risks depleting the genetic pool and limiting future evolutionary options. Recessive gene traits are far too complex and mercurial to condemn as simple errors in the code. We are, in fact, just beginning to learn of the many subtle and varied roles recessive genes play, some of which have been critically important, in insuring the survival of different ethnic and racial groups. For example, the sickle-cell recessive trait protects against malaria. The cystic fibrosis recessive gene may play a role in protecting against cholera. To think of recessive traits and single gene disorders, then, as merely errors in the code, in need of reprogramming, is to lose sight of how things really work in the biological kingdom.

Treating genetic disorders by eliminating them at the germ line level, in the sex cells, is far different from treating genetic disorders by way of somatic gene surgery after birth. In the former instance, the genetic deletions will result, in the long run, in a dangerous narrowing of the human gene pool upon which future generations rely for making evolutionary adaptations to changing environments. Somatic gene surgery, on the other hand, if it proves to be a safe, therapeutic way to treat serious diseases that cannot be effectively treated by more conventional approaches, would appear to have potential value.   27

The idea of engineering the human species—by making changes at the germ line level—is not too dissimilar from the idea of engineering a piece of machinery. An engineer is constantly in search of new ways to improve the performance of a machine. As soon as one set of defects is eliminated, the engineer immediately turns his attention to the next set of defects, always with the idea in mind of creating a more efficient machine. The very idea of setting arbitrary limits to how much "improvement" is acceptable is alien to the entire engineering conception.   28

The new language of the information sciences has transformed many molecular biologists from scientists to engineers, although they are, no doubt, little aware of the metamorphosis. When molecular biologists speak of mutations and genetic diseases as errors in the code, the implicit, if not explicit, assumption is that they should never have existed in the first place, that they are "bugs," or mistakes that need to be deprogrammed or corrected. The molecular biologist, in turn, becomes the computing engineer, the writer of codes, continually eliminating errors and reprogramming instructions to upgrade both the program and the performance. This is a dubious and dangerous role when we stop to consider that every human being brings with him or her a number of lethal recessive genes. Do we then come to see ourselves as miswired from the get-go, riddled with errors in our code? If that be the case, against what ideal norm of perfection are we to be measured? If every human being is made up of varying degrees of error, then we search in vain for the norm, the ideal. What makes the new language of molecular biology so subtly chilling is that it risks creating an unattainable new archetype, a flawless, errorless, perfect being to which to aspire—a new man and woman, like us, but without the warts and wrinkles, vulnerabilities and frailties, that have defined our essence from the very beginning of our existence.   29

No wonder so many in the disability rights community are becoming increasingly frightened of the new biology. They wonder if, in the Biotech Century, people like themselves will be seen as errors in the code, mistakes to be eliminated, lives to be prevented from coming into being. Then again, how tolerant are the rest of us likely to be when we come to see others around us as defective, as mistakes and errors in the code?   30

The question, then, is whether or not humanity should begin the process of engineering future generations of human beings by technological design in the laboratory. What are the potential consequences of embarking on a course whose final goal is the "perfection" of the human species?   31

THE PARADOX OF CLONING
from *Ethics of Human Cloning*
James Q. Wilson

There are both philosophical and utilitarian objections to cloning. Two philosophical objections exist. The first is that cloning violates God's will by creating an infant in a way that does not depend on human sexual congress or make possible the divine inculcation of a soul. That is true, but so does in vitro fertilization. An egg and a sperm are united outside the human body in a glass container. The fertilized egg is then put into the body of either the woman who produced it or another woman hired to bear the infant. When first proposed, in vitro fertilization was ethically suspect. Today, it is generally accepted—and for good reason. Science supplies what one or both human bodies lack, namely, a reasonable chance to produce an infant. Surely God can endow that infant with a soul. Cloning, of course, removes one of the conjugal partners, but it is hard to imagine that God's desire to bestow a unique soul can be blocked by the fact that the infant does not result from an egg and sperm's joining but instead arises from an embryonic egg's reproducing itself.   1

The other philosophical objection is that cloning is contrary to nature. That is often asserted by critics of cloning who do not believe in an active God. I sympathize with that reaction, but few critics have yet made clear to me what compelling aspect of nature cloning violates. To the extent that such an objection has meaning, I think it must arise from the danger that the cloned child will be put to various harmful uses. If so, the objection cannot easily be distinguished from the more practical problems.   2

One set of those problems requires us to imagine scientists' cloning children to harvest organs and body parts or to produce for later use many Adolf Hitlers or Saddam Husseins. I have no doubt that there will arise mad scientists willing to do those things. After all, they have already created poison gas and conducted grisly experiments on prisoners of war and concentration-camp inmates.   3

But under what circumstances will such abuses occur? Largely, I think, when the cloned child has no parents. Parents, whether they acquire a child by normal birth, artificial insemination, or adoption, will, in the overwhelming majority of cases, become deeply attached to the infant and care for it without regard to its origin. The parental tie is not infallible—infanticide occurs, and some neonates are abandoned in trash bins—but it is powerful and largely independent of the origin of the child. If cloning is to occur, the central problem is to ensure that it be done only for two-parent families who want a child for their own benefit. We should remember that a clone must be borne by a female; it cannot be given birth in a laboratory. A human mother will carry a human clone; she and her husband will determine its fate. Hardly any parents, I think, would allow their child to be used as an organ bank for defective adults or as the next-generation proxy for a malevolent dictator. If the cloned child is born in the same way as a child resulting from marital congress, can it matter to the parents how it was conceived? And if it does not matter to the parents, should it matter to us?

We already have a kind of clone: identical twins. They are genetically identical humans. I have not heard of any twin's being used against its will as an unwitting organ bank for its brother or sister. Some may surrender a kidney or bone marrow to their sibling; many may give blood; but none, I think, has been "harvested." The idea that a cloned infant, born to its mother, would be treated differently is, I think, quite far-fetched.

At some time in the future, science may discover a way to produce a clone entirely in the laboratory. That we should ban. Without human birth, the parents' attitude toward the infant will be deeply compromised. Getting a clone from a laboratory would be like getting a puppy from a pet store: Both creatures might be charming, but neither would belong in any meaningful emotional sense to the owner. And unclaimed clones would be disposed of the same way as unclaimed puppies—killed.

There may be parents who, out of fear or ideology, can be persuaded to accept a clone of a Hussein in hopes that they can help produce an unending chain of vicious leaders. That is less far-fetched. We already know from the study of identical twins reared in different families that they are remarkably similar. A cloned Hussein would have an IQ close to that of his father and a personality that (insofar as we can measure such things) would have roughly a 50 percent chance of being like his. Each clone would be like an identical twin: nearly the same in appearance, very similar in intelligence and manner, and alike (but not a duplicate) in personality. We know that the environment will have some effect on each twin's personality, but it is easy to overestimate that. I am struck by how many scientists interested in cloning have reflexively adopted the view that the environment will have a powerful effect on a cloned child. (Cloning seems to have given a large boost to environmentalists.) But that reaction is exaggerated. From the work of Dr. Thomas Bouchard at the University of Minnesota, we know that

giving identical twins different environments produces only slightly greater differences in character.

Our best hope for guarding against the duplication of a Saddam Hussein is   8
a practical one. Any cloned offspring would reach maturity forty or so years after his
father was born, and by then so much would have changed—Hussein, Sr., would
probably not even be in power, and his country's political system might have
been profoundly altered—that it is unlikely that Hussein, Jr., could do what his
father did.

We do not know how many parents will request cloning, but some will. Suppose   9
that the father cannot provide sperm or the mother is unable to produce a fertil-
izable egg. Such a family now has only three choices—remain childless, adopt, or
arrange some form of assisted reproduction involving the sperm, egg, or even womb
of a third party (artificial insemination, in vitro fertilization, or surrogate motherhood). Cloning would create a fourth choice: duplicate the father or the mother.
Some parents who do not want to remain childless will find the last choice more
attractive than adoption, which introduces a wholly new and largely unknown genetic factor into their family tree. Cloning guarantees that the child's genetic makeup
will be identical to that of whichever parent is cloned.

There is, of course, a risk that cloning may increase the number of surrogate   10
mothers, with all the heartbreak and legal complexities that that entails, but I suspect
that surrogates would be no more common for clones than they are for babies
conceived in vitro. . . .

There is one important practical objection to the widespread use of cloning. As   11
every evolutionary scientist knows, the survival of a species depends on two
forces—environmental change that rewards some creatures and penalizes others
and sufficient diversity among the species that, no matter what the environment,
some members of the species will benefit.

Cloning creates the opportunity for people to maximize a valued trait. Suppose   12
we wish to have children with a high IQ, an athletic physique, easily tanned skin, or
freedom from a particular genetic disease. By cloning persons who have the desired trait, we can guarantee that the trait will appear in the infant.

That may make good sense to parents, but it is bad news for the species. We have   13
no way of knowing what environmental challenges will confront us in the future.
Traits that today are desirable may become irrelevant or harmful in the future;
traits that now are unappealing may become essential for human survival in the
centuries ahead.

That problem is one for which there is no obvious individual solution. People max-   14
imizing the welfare of their infant can inhibit the welfare of the species. One way to
constrain a couple's efforts to secure the "perfect" child would be to restrict their
choice of genes to either the father or the mother. They could secure a specific genetic product, but they could not obtain what they might think is the ideal product.

But the real constraint on the misuse of cloning comes from a simple human tendency. Many parents do not want a child with particular traits. Conception is a lottery. It produces an offspring that gets roughly half its genes from its father and half from its mother, but the mixture occurs in unpredictable and fascinating combinations. All parents spend countless delightful hours wondering whether the child has its mother's eyes or its father's smile or its grandfather's nose or its grandmother's personality. And they watch in wonder as the infant becomes an adult with its own unique personality and mannerisms.

15

I think that most people prefer the lottery to certainty. (I know they prefer sex to cloning.) Lured by the lottery, they help meet the species' need for biological diversity. Moreover, if parents are tempted by certainty but limited to cells taken from either the father or the mother, they will have to ask themselves hard questions.

16

Do I want another man like the father, who is smart and earns a lot—but whose hair is receding, who has diabetes, and who is so obsessed with work that he is not much fun on weekends? Or do I want another woman like the mother, who is bright and sweet—but who has bad teeth, a family risk of breast cancer, and sleeps too late in the morning?

17

Not many of us know perfect people, least of all our own parents. If we want to clone a person, most of us will think twice about cloning somebody we already know well. And if we can clone only from among our own family, our desire to do it at all will be much weakened. Perhaps parents' love of entering the reproductive lottery is itself a revelation of evolution at work, one designed to help maintain biological diversity.

18

In one special case we may want to clone a creature well known to us. My friend Heather Higgins has said that cloning our pets—or at least some pets—may make sense. I would love to have another Labrador retriever just like Winston and another pair of cats exactly like Sarah and Clementine.

19

The central question facing those who approach cloning with an open mind is whether the gains from human cloning—a remedy for infertility and substitute for adoption—are worth the risks of farming organs, propagating dictators, and impeding evolution. I think that, provided certain conditions are met, the gains will turn out to exceed the risks.

20

The conditions are those to which I have already referred. Cloning should be permitted only on behalf of two married partners, and the mother should—absent some special medical condition that doctors must certify—carry the fertile tissue to birth. Then the offspring would belong to the parents. That parental constraint would prevent organ farming and the indiscriminate or political misuse of cloning technology.

21

The major threat cloning produces is a further weakening of the two-parent family. Cloning humans, if it can occur at all, cannot be prevented, but cloning unmarried

22

persons will expand the greatest cultural problem our country now faces. A cloned child, so far as we now know, cannot be produced in a laboratory. A mother must give it birth. Dolly had a mother, and if humans are produced the same way, they will have mothers, also. But not, I hope, unmarried mothers. Indeed, given the likely expense and difficulty of cloning, and the absence from it of any sexual pleasure, we are unlikely to see many unmarried teenage girls choosing that method. If unmarried cloning occurs, it is likely to be among affluent persons who think that they are entitled to act without the restraints and burdens of family life. They are wrong.

Of course, an unmarried or unscrupulous person eager for a cloned offspring may travel from the United States to a place where there are no restrictions of the sort I suggest. There is no way to prevent that. We can try to curtail it by telling anyone who returns to this country with a child born abroad to an American citizen that one of two conditions must be met before the child will be regarded as an American citizen. The parent bringing it back must show by competent medical evidence either that the child is the product of a normal (noncloned) birth or adoption or that the child, though the product of cloning, belongs to a married couple who will be responsible for it. Failing that, the child could not become an American citizen. But, of course, some people would evade any restrictions. There is, in short, no way that American law can produce a fail-safe restraint on undesirable cloning.   23

My view—that cloning presents no special ethical risks if society does all in its power to establish that the child is born to a married woman and is the joint responsibility of the married couple—will not satisfy those whose objections to cloning are chiefly religious. If man is made in the image of God, can man make himself (by cloning) and still be in God's image? I would suggest that producing a fertilized egg by sexual contact does not uniquely determine that image and therefore that nonsexual, in vitro fertilization is acceptable. And if that is so, then nonsexually transplanting cell nuclei into enucleated eggs might also be acceptable.   24

That is not a view that will commend itself to many devout Christians or Jews. I would ask of them only that they explain what it is about sexual fertilization that so affects God's judgment about the child that results.   25

ON ORDER
from *Clones and Cloning*
Barbara Katz Rothman

Cloning is about control. It's about introducing predictability and order into the wildly unpredictable crapshoot that is life. If normal procreation is the roll of a hundred thousand dice, a random dip in the gene pool, cloning is a carefully placed order. And that's where it gets interesting: It is *order* both in the sense of pre-   1 dictability and control, and in the sense of the market, an order placed, a human being on order.

In a perfect world, we could think about the value of the first form of order, the value of predictability and control in procreation, without thinking about the second form of order, the power of the market. In our world, the two are hopelessly, endlessly entangled. I personally am not convinced that predictability and control are really achievable in human procreation, nor am I convinced that they would be good things to achieve. But those points are at least open for debate, for discussion. I am completely convinced that market forces are an evil in human procreation.

That leaves me in the funny kind of place I often am with the new technologies of procreation: Thank goodness they don't work terribly well. The only thing that could make them worse would be if they got better.

Predictability has its limits in procreation. Think for a moment about identical twins, "nature's own clone" as it were. Identical is a funny word. It means they're the same. And so they are, strikingly so, which is why people noticed that they are a particular kind of twin. Identical twins arise from the same fertilized egg. One zygote becomes two people. Or even more rarely, three. At the moment of zygotic zero, when the egg and the sperm join, the twins are not only identical, they are one and the same. Very soon after that they split and go their separate ways.

If the splitting occurs within the first three days, they each develop their own placentas. If splitting occurs a bit later, between the fourth and the eighth day, they, each within its own amniotic sac, share a placenta. If the splitting is later still, they will share a single sac too. And later than that, the twins themselves may be joined, "Siamese" twins, two people in a more-or-less shared body.

How identical are identical twins? Right there, in the very same woman, nestled in the very same womb, they go their separate ways, experiencing life differently. Genetic changes take place as the eternal splitting and building of cells occur. Mutations can occur differently in each. One could be born a boy, with the full X, Y chromosomes; the other, missing the Y chromosome in many of its cells, a girl. A girl, with one X and no second sex chromosome, a condition known as Turner's syndrome, can be the "identical" twin of her brother, grown of the same fertilized egg.

And even without dramatic mutations occurring, twins are not the same baby twice. At birth they do not weigh the same: Their rates of growth can be very different. Placed here or there, in the same womb in the same woman in the same environment, they're not having the same experience. *Here* isn't *there,* and nothing is ever the same.

They don't even have the same "genetic" diseases. Type I diabetes, for example, has been traced to a gene located on the small arm of the sixth chromosome. One variation of that gene, one allele, "causes" autoimmune diabetes. In one twin. In one identical twin the gene causes diabetes and in the other the same gene does not cause diabetes. If one twin has type I diabetes, the chances of an identical twin having it are only 30 percent. More than two-thirds of the time the identical twin will not have this "genetic" disease. Some genes are more powerful, in which case the odds of a shared disease or trait go up; some are less powerful, and the odds go down. Diseases, traits, characteristics—two people, two individuals from one fertilized egg. You can't predict which will be which, how it will play itself out over time.

You can't get away from the idea of chance. Start with the same egg and the same sperm forming the same zygote in the same woman, and one twin gets sick and asks "Why me?" Clone the same cell and each person produced will be different from the source of the cell, and different from each other. No matter how much we want to control, to predict, to answer that question of "Why?" the answer sometimes really is just *because,* luck, chance.

That is *not* what we used to think science was about. Physicists have had to come to terms with that uncertainty, raising it to a principle. Classic physics thought that you could know it all, "that our cosmos is governed by mathematically precise laws at all scales, from inside of an atom to the totality of the universe." And then chance raised its head, and "the positions and movement of the invisible atoms that make up all objects were now lost in a probabilistic blur. While the universe remained determinate, the revised mathematical constructs of physics—more accurately reflecting the way atoms behave—could no longer promise completely predictable events and objective, universal knowledge." You can't, it seems, know it all.

Predictability and control are forever slipping out of our hands, crumbling as we touch them. When you're working with small herds of sheep, say, cloned to produce some expensive, exotic protein in their milk for medicinal purposes, a certain percentage of error is to be expected, accounted for. It is accounted for in two senses: It is part of the "account" or narrative of what might happen. (Shit happens!) And it is accounted for in the ledger books, an anticipated expense. Most of the errors that can be expected will not matter: Only a few will affect the single and sole purpose for which the sheep were cloned: the production of that protein in their milk.

With people, the accounting gets a lot more complicated, in both senses. Errors are not to be written off, and our expectations are rarely so narrowly confined.

We—those of us who have been around the track a few times—know how this latest "advance" in human procreative technology is going to be brought to us, marketed to us. It is going to be the solution to some heartrending problem. There's going to be a very good reason to do it the first time: some irreplaceable bone marrow donation, or some man who is the very, very, very last of his family, preferably made so by some cataclysmic political tragedy like the Holocaust. The guy will have absolutely, totally, no sperm whatsoever. Or maybe it will be . . . But I don't want to do this, don't want to give anybody any ideas.

For that first time, any success will probably be success enough. Later though, if we begin to make cloning routine, offer it as a service at the growing number of fertility clinics, the expectations will be more specific and at the same time more generalized. People will want to predict and control the kinds of children they are creating, or why bother using the technology?

And the "kinds of children" they might create are understood to be products 15
of the nucleus of the cell from which they are created. Genetics—not just as a science or a set of technologies, but genetics as an ideology, as the way we are more
and more thinking about life—is the descendent of classical patriarchal thinking. In
a patriarchy, a father-based kinship system, men are the source of life; women the
vessels. Life on earth is the product of the many and varied seeds of the earth; human life is the product of the seeds of man. The earth itself, in this thinking, is only
the place, the location, where seeds are planted. The very words we use for earth—
dirt, soil—indicate the disdain in which location is held relative to the glorious, powerful life-giving seed. In our more enlightened, modified patriarchy, women are also
recognized as having seeds, but the primacy of the seed remains. Seeds count.

The idea of cloning suggests that the essence, the true essential quality, the very 16
thing that makes a being itself—what once might have been called the soul—lies
in the nucleus of its cells. Everything else is reduced to environment, background,
ground, earth, dirt.

To hear the talk of the geneticists, one would think that the contents of that cell 17
nucleus, the hundred thousand or so segments of DNA that constitute the "genes,"
are themselves the miracle of life. All life-forms begin in DNA; all life then is DNA;
and maybe all life is, is DNA. They—the geneticists who have pushed to translate the
full length of DNA into the letters GCAT so that it can be "read" and "mapped"—
sound religious, awestruck, overwhelmed by the power and the majesty of the DNA:
It's the Bible, the Holy Grail, the Book of Man. Those are their very words. Our fate,
James Watson tells us, lies not in our stars but in our genes.

On a more mundane, work-a-day level, the DNA is called a code, an encyclopedia, 18
an instruction kit, a program, and most often, a blueprint. Well, sure. I started out
as a little cell with a nucleus of DNA and here I am. Those must have been plans
in there.

But it took about fifty years to get where I am now, and I think that's worth 19
thinking about. When you have the code or the plans for a person, you don't have
the person. If you take my very DNA and clone it, make copies, and let those copies
grow into people, it will take fifty years for them to get where I am now. And a lot
happens in those fifty years.

If I want to build a cabin, and I have a blueprint, I could gather a bunch of peo- 20
ple and machines and do it in a few days, or I could work with hand tools by myself on weekends for the next ten years. A blueprint doesn't have time or growth
built into it and so a blueprint isn't really a good analogy for DNA.

A recipe might make more sense if we want analogies. Baking bread, for in- 21
stance, combines making something with growth, the growth of the yeast that gives
bread its rise. I've baked a lot of bread in my time, and I've learned that the same
recipe under different circumstances results in different breads. Use a flour from
a wheat grown in one part of the country and you have a different mineral composition and a slightly different taste than if you use flour from a wheat grown

somewhere else. Bake on a humid day and you get a heavier bread from the same recipe than on a dry day. Bake on a hot day and the bread rises faster and has bigger air holes. Bake the same bread every day for a week, and no two loaves will be exactly the same: The web, that distinctive pattern of holes, will vary from loaf to loaf. Bake it in different pans or in different ovens, and you'll have differently textured crusts.

I've also made a couple of babies in my life. And while I understand about the DNA and the plans and the blueprints and all that, I also remember the rituals of avoidance. I read the ingredients on every food package before I used it, hesitating to put things I couldn't pronounce into the growing body of my baby. I avoided coffee, and cat litter dust, and, by the time of the second pregnancy when the rules had changed, alcohol. I read books about fetal development until I decided it was to-tally incapacitating: How could I possibly walk down the subway steps, cross a street and breathe exhaust fumes, even get out of bed, on arm-bud development day? All that blueprint following wasn't happening somewhere else. It was happening in my belly, day after day after day after day.

Its that element of time that seems so strangely absent in the discussion of cloning and DNA, in the thinking of genetic determinists. One of the Nobel laureates in genetics likes to hold up a compact disk at his lectures and say "This is you." As if the genes that were there at the moment of zygotic zero when I began fifty years ago, and the me that stands here now, were one and the same.

BOOM IN GENE TESTING RAISES QUESTIONS ON SHARING RESULTS

Tamar Lewin

As genetic testing becomes increasingly common, those who choose to learn their genetic risks, and the health professionals who treat them, are facing difficult decisions about how—and whether—to share the results with family members who share their genes.

And the new genetic information is creating new kinds of rifts, when one family member finds out what another family member does not want to know, or when family members react differently to the same knowledge.

"One woman who'd had ovarian cancer was tested for the breast cancer gene mutations mostly for the sake of her two adult daughters," said Katherine Schneider, senior genetics counselor at the Dana Farber Cancer Institute in Boston. "But when she told them she had it, they were so devastated that they didn't talk with her for two years. They didn't want to know.

"I tell that story a lot.

"There's nothing easy about any of this. But before testing, it's important to talk not only about what the information will mean for you, but what it might mean to your sisters, your children, your cousins."

Genetic tests are now commonplace, what with prenatal tests diagnosing   6
hundreds of syndromes, midlife tests for mutations linked to breast and ovarian
cancer, and—with the human genome newly mapped—more and more familial
disorders.

The scientific advances have created debate about public policy on genetic dis-   7
crimination. But the private effects on family dynamics are just as complex, as patients and health professionals adjust to thinking about family not just as flesh and
blood, but flesh and blood and genes.

Usually, patients are happy to share health information with family members for   8
whom it may be important, often asking the doctor or genetic counselor for a written explanation to pass along.

But when patients want to keep the information to themselves, health profes-   9
sionals may encounter situations that mix social problem and soap opera, and be
ethically and legally pulled into uncharted waters.

A young man in Washington State called his genetics counselor to confess a   10
guilty conscience: Several months earlier, he told her, he had made a sperm donation. And while he knew his test results had shown that he had an inheritable syndrome that causes heart trouble and, often, early death, he did not mention it to the
sperm bank. Troubled, the counselor called the sperm bank and found that there
had, indeed, been successful pregnancies with the man's sperm. She offered to
counsel those families but does not know whether the sperm bank even passed
on the information.

In a New York family with three adult daughters, the two married daughters know   11
that their mother, who had breast cancer as a young woman, has been tested and
found to carry a gene mutation associated with a high risk of breast and ovarian cancer. The mother has forbidden them to tell their unmarried sister, who has always
felt herself to be the least attractive, for fear that it might make her less marriage-
able. They have obeyed, but want the family doctor to make sure she has frequent
mammograms and screenings.

Two sisters who know their mother had genetic testing before she died of ovar-   12
ian cancer want to find out her test results. But the Pennsylvania medical center
that did the testing will not release the results to the young women without the
consent of their stepfather, who has a dismal relationship with them.

The sisters could, of course, have had their own genetic tests, but they had hoped   13
by learning more about their family's history to avoid the process.

The center's ethics committee is now revising its consent forms to require all   14
patients tested to specify which family members should have access to the results after their death.

One California genetics counselor tells of her confusion when a couple who had   15
a child with cystic fibrosis came to discuss their risks for future pregnancies, and
in providing a family history, the wife mentioned that her estranged half-sister had
a baby who died from a serious congenital defect. It was nothing genetic, she assured

the counselor. But the counselor knew otherwise: The sister had been an earlier client.

"It just rang a bell in my head," the counselor said.   16

"I remembered the name, and I remembered telling her it was genetic, and she   17
should tell her relatives. I didn't know what to do. But I didn't want to breach confidentiality for either one of them."

Eventually, she called the previous client on the pretext of a routine records   18
check. "I played dumb, saying I just happened to have her file on my desk," the
counselor said, "and I'd noticed we'd talked about telling her family the results, and
I was just following up for the records, wondering if that conversation had taken
place, and she said, why, no, it hadn't."

"So I reminded her why it was important. And a few days later, I had a call   19
from the current client, who said the funniest thing had happened, she'd had a call
from her half-sister, and there was a genetic problem."

Often, the decision to pass on information is a delicate one, depending not only   20
on such factors as the relatives' closeness, ages and emotional health, but also the
nature of the disease and the severity of the risk. Where there is no treatment,
or the risk is small, the case for sharing painful knowledge becomes less compelling.
And the need to share information may be temporary, experts say, as the era approaches when complete genetic profiles become a routine part of individual health
records. Meanwhile, the cost of testing even a single gene can run from several
hundred to several thousand dollars.

Still, Josephine Wagner Costalas, a genetic counselor at Fox Chase Cancer Cen-   21
ter in Philadelphia, has an unspoken worry whenever she counsels a patient who
has tested positive for the breast cancer gene mutations.

"My worst nightmare is the scenario where I might have a patient who tests   22
positive and doesn't tell her relatives," Ms. Costalas said, "and a few years later
her sister will discover she has metastatic cancer, with a bad prognosis, and she'll find
out that there was this information showing she was at risk. And maybe she'll sue
me, saying I should have picked up the phone and told her, 'Your sister's positive,
you should get tested.' This is all so new, and there are no clear guidelines, so I
worry."

Still, Ms. Costalas does not pressure her patients to share their results. "If peo-   23
ple aren't sure about sharing the information, I ask them to think about what it
would be like if the situation were reversed," she said. "Would they want to know?
But I do believe patients need to decide for themselves what they want to do."

And when several family members come in together, there are other issues.   24
"What if they have different results?" Ms. Costalas said.

"Who do you tell first? What if they have different reactions?"   25

Andrea Shumsky, whom Ms. Costalas counseled recently, never had any doubt   26
about sharing her results. There has been a lot of cancer in Ms. Shumsky's family:
Her father had early-onset colon cancer, his sister had breast cancer, three of his

other siblings had colon cancer, and her grandfather had melanoma. Ms. Shumsky herself learned she had melanoma last year, on her 40th birthday, and the breast cancer gene mutations she was being tested for carry a higher risk of melanoma.

She listened as Ms. Costalas told her that the test was negative, that there was no sign that the melanoma was genetic, but that it might be worth pursuing further genetic testing for colon cancer. Then Ms. Costalas asked about Ms. Shumsky's plans to share her results.   27

"My sister knows I'm here, and I'm going to tell her the results as soon as I get home," Ms. Shumsky said. "And I'm going to tell her about the colon cancer. After walking around with a mole for years, and then finding out it was melanoma, I want everyone in my family to watch out for cancer.   28

"After I got my diagnosis, I called her doctor myself, and told him she needed melanoma screening. I know it's butting into her life, but if she never talks to me again, and I save her life, it's worth the risk."   29

Two years ago, the American Society of Human Genetics adopted a position recognizing the conflict between the health professions' duty to maintain confidentiality and the duty to warn about serious health risks. Health professionals should tell patients about potential genetic risks to their relatives, the statement said, and in some cases, they may be allowed to breach confidentiality to warn relatives at risk if the harm is "serious, imminent and likely" and prevention or treatment is available.   30

But there is little consensus on where to draw those lines. Generally, genetic counselors are more concerned about confidentiality and not pressuring patients, while physicians specializing in genetics are more concerned about the duty to warn, according to research by Dorothy C. Wertz, senior scientist at the Shriver Center in Waltham, Mass.   31

As a practical matter, though, most health professionals cannot warn relatives.   32

"In the end it's up to the patient, because in real life, we don't have relatives' names and phone numbers," said Helen Hixon, a genetic counselor in cardiology at Cedars Sinai hospital in Los Angeles. "We do tell people pretty strongly that they should warn their relatives, that they have a legal duty to do so."   33

Bioethics lawyers say that while patients may have some moral obligation, they have no legal duty to warn relatives. There have been at least two legal rulings, one in a 1995 Florida case and the other in a 1996 New Jersey case, giving conflicting signals on whether doctors can be held liable for not warning a patient's relatives about their risks of a hereditary form of cancer.   34

Although the tensions involving family disclosure of genetic risks are not new, the issue has become more complicated as genetic tests proliferate, and it becomes possible to identify a person's predisposition to common diseases.   35

"It used to be that most of these issues came up around rare disorders, where there was a recessive gene that became a problem only when it met up with another carrier," said Vivian Weinblatt, president elect of the National Society of Genetic Counselors.   36

"Now we're talking about areas where it's all gray, where it's a gene that predis-   37
poses you to some disease you might get anyway in late middle age."

The breast cancer gene mutations are the latest case in point and the fastest   38
growing area of testing. While most cases of breast and ovarian cancer are not
hereditary, women with specific mutations in the BRCA 1 or BRCA 2 genes have
a lifetime risk of breast or ovarian cancer over 50 percent, odds so high that many
women who test positive choose to have their breasts and ovaries removed.

"My mother died of breast cancer when I was 15, and my older sister got it   39
when she was 41," said a 43-year-old New York woman who had the preventive surgery but told only three people.

"I knew as soon as I tested positive that I would do anything I could to get my   40
odds down.

"But it's been awkward with my sister, who's against prophylactic surgery. I think   41
she's crazy, she thinks I'm crazy and we don't talk about it anymore. Instead of
it being a shared family thing, it's made us less close."

In some families, particularly Ashkenazi Jewish families, which are more likely to   42
carry the mutations, the testing is a pressure point.

"In one of our early research families, with a serious history of cancer, there   43
was a push from the family matriarch that anyone found to have the mutation
should get a mastectomy," said Jill Stopfer at the University of Pennsylvania Cancer Center. "The push was so strong that some of the younger women decided
they wouldn't get tested, not because they couldn't handle the results, but because
they were worried about the family pressure to have surgery."

WHEN MEDICINE GOES TOO FAR IN THE PURSUIT
OF NORMALITY
Alice Dreger

I realized recently that I suffer from a genetic condition. Although I have not ac-   1
tually had my genome screened, all the anatomical signs of Double-X Syndrome
are there. And while I could probably handle the myriad physiological disorders
associated with my condition—bouts of pain and bleeding coming and going for
decades, hair growth patterns that obviously differ from "normal" people's—the social downsides associated with it are troubling.

Even since the passage of the Americans With Disabilities Act, people with   2
Double-X remain more likely than others to live below the poverty line, more
likely to be sexually assaulted, and are legally prohibited from marrying people with
the same condition. Some potential parents have even screened fetuses and aborted
those with Double-X in an effort to avert the tragic life the syndrome brings. Perhaps you know Double-X by its more common name: womanhood.

This fact of my "genetic condition" came to me one evening as I sat in a confer-   3
ence room of our local hospital participating in a community dialogue sponsored

by the Human Genome Project. Our group had just finished reading a rather bleak description of the anatomy and life of the "average" woman with Turner's syndrome: "webbed neck, short stature, no chance for bearing children" and so on. Turner's syndrome, which affects roughly one in 2,500 girls born each year, arises when a person is born with a single X chromosome and no Y. It is, essentially, a "single-X syndrome."

Our group was discussing the genetic screening of pre-implantation embryos, and given the depressing description of Turner's provided to us, no wonder most everyone in the room, pro-choicers and pro-lifers alike, saw Turner's as a sad genetic disease.   4

But I had by then been studying human intersexuality—anatomical sexual varia-   5 tions, including Turner's—for several years, and had talked with and read the biographies and autobiographies of many people born intersexed. I knew that women with Turner's would describe their lives with more balance. So I began to think about how a woman with single-X and a sense of humor could describe the life of those of us women with double-X, and came up with the above portrayal.

My point is not that people with unusual genetic conditions do not suffer more   6 than those without them; clearly, many do. But I am troubled that I see ever more cases in which psychosocial problems caused by stereotypes about anatomy are being "fixed" by "normalizing" the anatomy. There are serious downsides to this, both for the person being "normalized" and for those around her.

Take for example the "treatment" of short stature. Some pharmaceutical   7 companies and physicians have advocated giving human growth hormone injections to very short children in an attempt to help them grow taller than they otherwise would. Profound short (and tall) stature may lead to disorders like back problems because our culture structures the physical world for average-height adults. But no one advocates using the hormone to prevent back problems.

Hormone treatments are used because of the presumption that an adult of short   8 stature will not fare as well socially as one of average size. Indeed, statistically, taller men are more likely than shorter men to be hired, given a raise or elected President.

Average-sized people see short people and tend to feel sorry for them. Getting   9 short children to grow more seems pretty beneficent.

The same kind of intended beneficence drives the medical management of chil-   10 dren born intersexed. Many physicians assume that intersexed children, with their unusual genitalia, will be rejected by family and peers. So they recommend early cosmetic surgery to try to erase the signs.

What's wrong with these "normalization" technologies? First, it isn't clear   11 that they work. It seems that if an unusual anatomy leads to a psychosocial problem, "normalizing" the anatomy should solve the problem. But of the few follow-up studies that have been done on intersex surgeries, none examine the psychological well-being of the subjects in any real depth. Most simply report on the status of the postsurgical anatomy, while a very few report on whether the subjects are married (psychological health is presumed from this).

Psychological follow-up on the growth hormone treatments is similarly lacking. 12
A study published in the March 28 *Lancet* reported that a randomized trial of the hormone in "short normal girls" resulted in the treated girls' averaging a final height of almost three inches more than the control group, but added that "no significant psychosocial benefits have yet been shown."

Perhaps we should not expect measurable psychological benefits from a gain of 13
about three inches. Yet recall that the entire "normalization" treatment for "short stature was designed to produce psychological benefits.

More worrisome than the loss of focus in these studies is the fact that these treat- 14
ments often backfire. Children subjected to these kinds of treatments often report feelings of inadequacy and freakishness as a direct result of their parents' and doctors' attempts at normalization. And the treatments are not without physical risks. For example, intersex surgeries all too frequently leave scarred, insensate, painful and infection-prone genitalia.

So anatomy-focused have we become that children with unusual conditions are 15
often not provided any professional psychological counseling.

Nor are their parents, who are dealing with their own feelings of confusion, 16
shame, grief and worry. The result is the message that the problem is primarily anatomical and, by consequence, a "fault" of the child and perhaps also the parents.

By extension, a dictate then kicks in: If you can fix it, you should. A friend of 17
mine recalls the time a plastic surgeon came up to him at a party, looked at his nose and said, "You know, I can fix that." When my friend said, "No thanks," the plastic surgeon appeared to think my friend a little crazy. As normalizing technologies become more accessible, people are expected to be bothered by their "unusual" features and expected to want to fix them.

Some surgeons say they normalize intersexed children because it is too hard 18
to be different. One points out that we still live in a nation where dark-skinned people have a harder time than light-skinned people do. But would he suggest we work on technologies to "fix" dark skin? Would we call people who refuse to lighten their children cruel Luddites?

The funny thing is, when I ask people with dark skin if they would change their 19
color, they tell me no, and when I ask women if they would rather be men, they tell me no, and I get the same response when I ask people with unusual anatomies if they would take a magic pill to erase their unusual features.

They tell me, instead, that they would support an end to social stereotypes and 20
oppression, but that they would not trade themselves in for a "better" model. This sentiment even comes from conjoined twins. Chang and Eng Bunker, the conjoined brothers born early in the nineteenth century and dubbed the Siamese twins, confessed that they preferred their state because it enabled them to bring a "double strength and a double will" to each purpose.

Similarly, women born with big clitorises confess to liking their unusual anatomy. 21
But this is the absolutely forbidden narrative—not only rejecting normalization
but actively preferring the "abnormal."

What do I suggest? First, a few basic realizations. In spite of medical advances, 22
unusual anatomies generally cannot be fixed in any significant way without significant risk, and that risk, when medically unnecessary, should be approved
by the person at risk.

We also need to remember that just because it makes sense that you ought to 23
be able to fix anatomically based psychosocial problems anatomically, that doesn't
mean it is so. Working to eliminate social stereotypes would be more effective
and better for everyone in the long run. I do not wish to see options entirely
withdrawn from mature patients; I am suggesting we slow down the normalization
of children, many of whom are likely to gain much more from acceptance and psychological support than injections and scalpels.

But how do we fix the social problems? When I talk about intersex, people 24
ask me, "But what about the locker room?" Yes, what about the locker room? If
so many people feel trepidation around it, why don't we fix the locker room? There
are ways to signal to children that they are not the problem, and normalization technologies are not the way.

Instead of constantly enhancing the norm—forever upping the ante of the 25
"normal" with new technologies—we should work on enhancing the concept
of normal by broadening appreciation of anatomical variation. Show potential parents, medical students and genetic counselors images of unusual anatomies other
than the deeply pathologized ones they are typically given. Allow those with the
unusual anatomies to describe their own lives in full and rich detail. Even let them
tell the forbidden narrative of enjoying their Double-X Syndromes.

CLONES, GENES, AND HUMAN RIGHTS
from *The Genetic Revolution and Human Rights*
John Harris

[In an article supporting human cloning, Harris cites eight hypothetical cases.]

1. A couple in which the male partner is infertile. They want a child genetically re- 1
lated to them both. Rather than opt for donated sperm they prefer to clone the
male partner knowing that from him they will get 46 chromosomes, and that from
the female partner, who supplies the egg, there will be mitochondrial DNA.
Although in this case the male genetic contribution will be much the greater,
both will feel, justifiably, that they have made a genetic contribution to their child.
They argue that for them, this is the only acceptable way of having children of
"their own." In what way is their preference unethical or contrary to human rights
or dignity?

2. A couple in which neither partner has usable gametes, although the woman could gestate. For the woman to bear the child she desires they would have to use either embryo donation or an egg cloned with the DNA of one of them. Again they argue that they want a child genetically related to one of them and that it's that or nothing. The mother in this case will have the satisfaction of knowing she has contributed not only her uterine environment but also nourishment, and will contribute subsequent nurture, and the father will have contributed his genes. In what way is their preference unethical or contrary to human rights or dignity?

3. A single woman wants a child. She prefers the idea of using all her own DNA to the idea of accepting 50 per cent from a stranger. What are the weighty ethical considerations that require her to be forced to accept DNA from a stranger and mother "his child" rather than her own?

4. A couple have only one child and have been told they are unable to have further children. Their baby is dying. They want to de-nucleate one of her cells so that they can have another child of their own. In what way is their preference unethical or contrary to human rights or dignity?

5. One partner has a severe genetic disease. The couple want their own child and wish to use the other partner's genome. In what way is their preference unethical or contrary to human rights or dignity?

6. An adult seems to have genetic immunity to AIDS. Researchers wish to create multiple cloned embryos to isolate the gene to see if it can be created artificially to permit a gene therapy for AIDS. In what way is their proposed course of action unethical or contrary to human rights or dignity?

7. As Michel Revel has pointed out, cloning may help overcome present hazards of graft procedures. Embryonic cells could be taken from cloned embryos prior to implantation into the uterus, and cultured to form tissues of pancreatic cells to treat diabetes, or brain nerve cells could be genetically engineered to treat Parkinson's or other neurodegenerative diseases. In what way would this be unethical or contrary to human rights or dignity?

8. Jonathan Slack has recently pioneered headless frog embryos. This methodology could use cloned embryos to provide histocompatible formed organs for transplant into the nucleus donor. In what way would this be unethical or contrary to human rights or dignity?

Acknowledgments

William Leach. Specified excerpt from pages 131–132 in *Land of Desire: Merchants, Power, and the Rise of a New American Culture*. Copyright © 1993 by William Leach. Used by permission of Pantheon Books, a division of Random House, Inc.

Blanche D. Blank. "A Question of Degree." Excerpt from "Degrees: Who Needs Them?" From *AAUP Bulletin*, Autumn 1972, a publication of the American Association of University Professors. Reprinted by permission.

Suzanne Winckler. "A Savage Life." From *The New York Times*, February 7, 1999. Copyright © 1999 by Suzanne Winckler. Reprinted by permission of the author.

Edwidge Danticat. "Westbury Court." Reprinted by permission of Edwidge Danticat and the Watkins/Loomis Agency.

Eric Nagourney. "Study Finds Families Bypassing Marriage." From *The New York Times*, February 15, 2000. Copyright © 2000 by The New York Times Company. Reprinted by permission.

Selwyn Raab. "Holdup Man Tells Detectives How to Do It." From *The New York Times*, March 5, 1975, p.A1+. Copyright © 1975 by The New York Times Company. Reprinted by permission.

Walter Kirn. "Summertime Dues." From *The New York Times* magazine, July 9, 2000. Copyright © 2000 by The New York Times Company. Reprinted by permission.

Bertrand Russell. "The Social Responsibility of Scientists." Extracts from *Fact and Fiction* by Bertrand Russell. Reprinted by permission of Taylor and Francis.

Timothy Ferris. "Interstellar Spaceflight: Can We Travel to Other Stars?" Copyright © 2000 by Timothy Ferris. Reprinted by permission.

Neal Gabler. "Molding Our Lives in the Images of the Movies." From *The New York Times* Arts & Leisure section, October 25, 1998. Copyright © 1998 by The New York Times Company. Reprinted by permission.

Louis Menand. "The Downside of the Upside of the Downside." Originally published in *The New York Times* magazine, January 9, 2000. Copyright © 2000 by Louis Menand. Reprinted by permission of the author.

Conor Cruise O'Brien. "Violence—and Two Schools of Thought." Reprinted by permission of The Observer News Service.

Ana Marie Cox. "In the Wake of the Scandal over Joseph Ellis, Scholars Ask 'Why?' and 'What Now?' " From *The Chronicle of Higher Education*, July 13, 2001. © 2001 by The Chronicle of Higher Education. Reprinted by permission.

Roger Sipher. "So That Nobody Has to Go to School If They Don't Want To." From *The New York Times*, September 21, 1967. Copyright © 1967 by The New York Times Company. Reprinted by permission.

Carl Singleton. "What Our Education System Needs Is More F's." From *The Chronicle of Higher Education*, 1954. Reprinted by permission of the author.

Steven M. Wise. "Why Animals Deserve Legal Rights." From *The Chronicle of Higher Education*. Reprinted by permission.

Leon Botstein. "Let Teenagers Try Adulthood." Originally published in *The New York Times*, May 17, 1999, Op-ed page. Copyright © 1999 by The New York Times Company. Reprinted by permission.

Roger Gosden. "Well-born." From *Designing Babies* by Roger Gosden. © 1999 by Roger Gosden. Reprinted by permission of Henry Holt and Company, LLC.

Philip Kitcher. "Inescapable Eugenics." From *The Lives to Come: The Genetic Revolution and Human Possibilities* by Philip Kitcher. Copyright © by Andrew Philip Kitcher. Reprinted with the permission of Simon & Schuster.

Arthur L. Caplan. "What's Wrong with Eugenics?" From *Am I My Brother's Keeper?* By Arthur L. Caplan. Copyright © 1998 by Indiana University Press. Reprinted with permission.

Lee M. Silver. "The Virtual Child." From *Remaking Eden* by Lee M. Silver. Copyright © 1998 by Lee M. Silver. Reprinted by permission of HarperCollins Publishers, Inc.

Jeremy Rifkin. "A Eugenic Civilization." From *The Biotech Century* by Jeremy Rifkin. Copyright © 1998 by Jeremy Rifkin. Used by permission of Jeremy P. Tarcher, a division of Penguin Putnam, Inc.

James Q. Wilson. "The Paradox of Cloning." From *Ethics of Human Cloning* by James Q. Wilson. Copyright © 1998 by James Q. Wilson. Reprinted by permission of HarperCollins/AEI Press, Inc.

Barbara Katz Rothman. "On Order." From *Clones and Cloning: Facts and Fantasies about Human Cloning* by Martha C. Nussbaum and Cass R. Sunstein, eds. Copyright © 1998 by Martha C. Nussbaum and Cass R. Sunstein. Used by permission of W.W. Norton & Company, Inc.

Tamar Lewin. "Boom in Gene Testing Raises Questions on Sharing Results." From *The New York Times*, July 21, 2000. Copyright © 2000 by The New York Times Company. Reprinted by permission.

Alice Dreger. "When Medicine Goes Too Far in the Pursuit of Normality." From *The New York Times*, July 28, 1998. Copyright © 1998 by The New York Times Company. Reprinted by permission.

John Harris. "Clones, Genes, and Human Rights." From *The Genetic Revolution and Human Rights*, edited by Justine Burley and Richard Dawkins. Copyright © 1999 by Oxford University Press. Reprinted by permission.

"American Contributions to Restaurant Development." Britannica.com 2000. © 2002 by Encyclopedia Britannica, Inc. Reprinted with permission from *Britannica.com*.

Index